# Solaris™ 8

# System Administrator Certification

## TRAINING GUIDE

QUE® CERTIFICATION

Bill Calkins

# Solaris™ 8 Training Guide (310-011 and 310-012): System Administrator Certification



International Standard Book Number: 1-57870-259-3

Library of Congress Catalog Card Number: 00-110874

Printed in the United States of America

First Printing: October, 2001
Second Printing with corrections: July, 2002

06 05 04 03 7 6 5 4 3 2

Interpretation of the printing code: The rightmost double-digit number is the year of the book's printing; the rightmost single-digit number is the number of the book's printing. For example, the printing code 02-1 shows that the first printing of the book occurred in 2002.

## Trademarks

All terms mentioned in this book that are known to be trademarks or service marks have been appropriately capitalized. Que Publishing cannot attest to the accuracy of this information. Use of a term in this book should not be regarded as affecting the validity of any trademark or service mark. Solaris is a trademark of Sun Microsystems, Inc.

## Warning and Disclaimer

Every effort has been made to make this book as complete and as accurate as possible, but no warranty of fitness is implied. The information provided is on an "as is" basis. The authors and the publisher shall have neither liability nor responsibility to any person or entity with respect to any loss or damages arising from the use of the information contained in this book or from the use of the CD or programs accompanying it.

**PUBLISHER**
David Dwyer

**ASSOCIATE PUBLISHER**
Stephanie Wall

**PRODUCT MARKETING MANAGER**
Stephanie Layton

**PUBLICITY MANAGER**
Susan Nixon

**MANAGING EDITOR**
Kristy Knoop

**ACQUISITIONS EDITOR**
Jeff Riley

**DEVELOPMENT EDITOR**
Ginny Munroe

**PROJECT EDITOR**
Suzanne Pettypiece

**COPY EDITOR**
Karen A. Gill
Linda Seifert

**TECHNICAL EDITORS**
Grant Cartensen
John Philcox

**COVER DESIGNER**
Aren Howell

**COMPOSITOR**
Amy Parker

**PROOFREADER**
Debbie Williams

**INDEXER**
Larry Sweazy

**MEDIA DEVELOPER**
Jay Payne

# Contents at a Glance

## Section III: Final Review



## Section IV: Appendixes

# Table of Contents

## Section 1: Part 1

## 6 Introduction to File Systems 185

## Section 2: Part II

## Section 3: Part III

## Section 4 Part IV

# About the Author

**Bill Calkins** is owner and president of Pyramid Consulting, a computer training and consulting firm located near Grand Rapids, Michigan, specializing in the implementation and administration of Open Systems. He also is the owner of `www.UnixEd.com`, a web site that provides online UNIX training materials. He has more than 18 years of experience in UNIX system administration, consulting, and training at more than 100 different companies. Bill has authored several UNIX textbooks, which are currently best sellers and used by universities and training organizations worldwide:

- *Solaris 2.6 Administrator Certification Training Guide, Part I,* (Publisher: New Riders Publishing, ISBN: 157870085X)
- *Solaris 2.6 Administrator Certification Training Guide, Part II,* (Publisher: New Riders Publishing, ISBN: 1578700868)
- *Solaris 7 Administrator Certification Training Guide, Part I and II,* (Publisher: New Riders Publishing, ISBN: 1578702496)

In addition, he has worked with Sun Press as a technical editor and was a major contributor to the following recently published technical manuals:

- *Solaris 7 Reference* (Author: Janice Winsor; Publisher: Prentice Hall PTR, ISBN: 0130200484)
- *Solaris 8 System Administrator's Reference Guide* (Author: Janice Winsor; Publisher: Prentice Hall PTR, ISBN: 0130277010)

Bill's professional interests include consulting, writing, teaching, and developing web-based training materials.

Bill has worked as an instructor in both corporate and university settings, and has helped thousands of administrators get their certification. His experience covers all varieties of UNIX, including Solaris, HP-UX, AIX, IRIX, Linux, and SCO. When he's not working in the field, he writes UNIX books and conducts training and educational seminars on various system administration topics. He draws on his many years of experience in system administration and training to provide a unique approach to UNIX training.

# About the Technical Editors

**Grant Carstensen** provided technical insight from an end-user's perspective as someone who is preparing for the Solaris 8 System Administration Certification exams. He is a Senior Systems Administrator with Computer Sciences Corporation (CSC), a major provider of information technology services based in El Segundo, California. He has more than 17 years of experience in IT—eight of those with different flavors of UNIX. For the past five years, he has focused on systems and network administration of predominantly SunOS and Solaris environments. Recently, he was the technical team lead and assistant project manager on a project for a new facility that implemented a mix of Solaris 8-based Sun servers, Windows NT 4.0-based Compaq servers, and Windows 2000 Professional-based Dell Precision workstations, using 18 separate TCP/IP local area networks (LANs) running on fiber-optic and copper-based Ethernet and Gigabit Ethernet. Grant has a bachelor of science degree in Business Administra-tion/Information Systems, and finds great amusement in his 16 year-old correspondence-course certifications in Microcomputer Repair and Computer Programming (COBOL).

**John Philcox** is owner and director of Mobile Ventures Limited, a computer consultancy based in Cheltenham, Gloucestershire in the United Kingdom, specializing in UNIX systems and networks. He has more than 20 years of experience in IT, 14 of those with the SunOS and Solaris environments. John is a Certified Solaris System Administrator, as well as a member of the Institution of Analysts and Programmers and the Institute of Management of Information Systems. He has worked in a number of large multivendor networks in both the public and private sectors of business. John is the author of *Solaris System Management,* and technical editor for *Solaris 2.6 Administrator Certification Guide, Part II*; *Solaris 7 Administrator Certification Guide, Part I and II*; and *Solaris 8 Security,* all published by New Riders..

# Dedication

*I want to thank my family once again for their support during this project. With this book, as with the past versions, it seems vacations always get delayed, and family time gets lost while trying to meet deadlines.*

*Glenda, (my wife), thanks for being my personal secretary while working on this book. If I relied on my own typing skills, this book would not have made the deadlines. I promise I'll try to learn how to type before the next version comes out. Thanks to Will (my oldest son) for watching the kids so Mom could type.*

# Acknowledgments

Again, I'd like to thank the technical editors who have stayed with me for the past couple of years. John Philcox and Grant Cartenson, I value your input greatly. It's been a great team effort, and the book would not be as complete without your help.

Ginny Munroe, my development editor, thanks for going easy on me with your red ink, your hard work, and long hours helping me meet the deadlines.

Thanks also to Jeff Riley, my acquisitions editor. You've gone to bat for me whenever I've asked you to. Furthermore, you've laughed at my warped sense of humor, which has helped keep me going during the final stages of this project. One of these days, we'll actually golf together and quit talking about it. Stay in touch.

To you, the reader. For buying my books and providing comments to improve the content with each new release. This book would not be what it is if it were not for your valuable input over the years. May the material in this book help you better your skills, enhance your career, and achieve your goal to become certified. Best of luck!

A lot of people behind the scenes make a book like this happen. I don't have a clue how it all works, but it must be a great team effort. A big thanks to everyone who edits the text, sets the type, prints the pages, and ships the book. My efforts would be lost in a closet somewhere if it weren't for your hard work.

# A Message from Que

As the reader of this book, you are our most important critic and commentator. We value your opinion and want to know what we're doing right, what we could do better, in what areas you would like to see us publish, and any other words of wisdom you're willing to pass our way.

As an Acquisitions Editor at Que, I welcome your comments. You can fax, email, or write me directly to let me know what you did or didn't like about this book—as well as what we can do to make our books better. When you write, please be sure to include this book's title, ISBN, and author, as well as your name and phone or fax number. I will carefully review your comments and share them with the authors and editors who worked on the book.

*Please note that I cannot help you with technical problems related to the topic of this book, and that due to the high volume of email I receive, I might not be able to reply to every message.*

Fax: 317-581-4666

Email: jeff.riley@quepublishing.com

Mail: Jeff Riley
Que Publishing
201 West 103rd Street
Indianapolis, IN 46290 USA

# Visit Our Web Site

`www.quepublishing.com`

On our web site, you'll find information about our other books, the authors with whom we partner, book updates and file downloads, promotions, and with technology experts, and a calendar of trade shows and other professional events with which we'll be involved. We hope to see you around.

Go to `www.quepublishing.com` and click the Contact link if you:

- Have comments or questions about this book.
- Want to report errors that you have found in this book.
- Have a book proposal or are interested in writing for Que.
- Would like us to send you one of our author kits.
- Are an expert in a computer topic or technology and are interested in being a reviewer or technical editor.
- Want to find a distributor for our titles in your area.
- Are an educator/instructor who wants to preview Que books for classroom use. In the body/comments area, include your name, school, department, address, phone number, office days/hours, text currently in use, and enrollment in your department, along with your request for either desk/examination copies or additional information.

# Call Us or Fax Us

You can reach us toll-free at 1-800-571-5840 + 9 + 3500 (ask for Que). If outside the U.S., please call 1-317-581-3500 and ask for Que. If you prefer, you can fax us at 1-317-581-4666, Attention: Que.

NOTE

**Technical Support for This Book** Although we encourage entry-level users to get as much as they can out of our books, keep in mind that our books are written assuming a non-beginner level of user knowledge of the technology. This assumption is reflected in the brevity and shorthand nature of some of the tutorials.

Que will continually work to create clearly written, thoroughly tested, and reviewed technology books of the highest educational caliber and creative design. We value our customers more than anything—that's why we're in this business—but we cannot guarantee to each of the thousands of you who buy and use our books that we will be able to work individually with you through tutorials or content with which you might have questions. We urge readers who need help in working through exercises or other material in our books—and who need this assistance immediately—to use as many of the resources that our technology and technical communities can provide, especially the many online user groups and list servers available.

# How to Use This Book

**New Riders has made an effort in its *Training Guide* series to make the information as accessible as possible for the purposes of learning the certification material. Here, you have an opportunity to view the many instructional features that have been incorporated into the books to achieve that goal.**

## Chapter Opener

Each chapter begins with a set of features designed to allow you to maximize study time for that material.

**List of Objectives:** Each chapter begins with a list of the objectives.

**Objective Explanations:** Immediately following each objective is an explanation of it, providing context that defines it more meaningfully in relation to the exam. Because the objectives list can sometimes be vague, the objective explanations are designed to clarify any vagueness by relying on the author's test-taking experience.

**Objectives**

The following objectives for the System Administrator Exam are covered in this chapter.

**Understand the boot process**

- A system administrator must understand the entire boot process, beginning from the proper power-on sequence to the steps that are performed when bringing the system into multiuser mode.

**Perform kernel initialization**

- Several steps are involved in initializing the kernel. Understanding how the Solaris kernel is configured, located, and loaded into memory is critical to system administration.

**Understand and control run levels**

- System run levels define which processes and services are started at various stages of the boot process. You'll need to understand all of the run levels available in Solaris.

**Use the run control scripts to stop or start services**

- The system administrator adds and modifies run control scripts to customize the startup of processes and services on Solaris systems. A detailed understanding of the programs and configuration files involved at the various run levels is required.

**Perform a system shutdown**

- Proper system shutdown is critical. Understanding proper system shutdown techniques ensures the integrity of the data on your system. There are several ways to shut down the system; the system administrator needs to understand the pros and cons of each method.

**Know the actions required to interrupt a nonresponsive system.**

- Occasionally, conventional shutdown methods might not work on an unresponsive system or on a system that has crashed. This chapter introduces when and how to use these alternative shutdown methods to bring the system down safely.

CHAPTER 1

**System Startup and Shutdown**

## Outline



**Chapter Outline:** Learning always gets a boost when you can see both the forest and the trees. To give you a visual image of how the topics in a chapter fit together, you will find a chapter outline at the beginning of each chapter. You will also be able to use this for easy reference when looking for a particular topic.

## Study Strategies

The following study strategies will help you prepare for the exam:

- ▶ As with every chapter of this book, you'll need a Solaris 8 system on which to practice. Practice every step-by-step example that is presented until you can perform the steps from memory. Also, as you practice creating file systems, you'll need some unused disk space with which to practice. I recommend an empty, secondary disk drive for this purpose.
- ▶ Become familiar with all the terms presented at the end of this chapter. You'll see them used throughout the exams. In addition, familiarize yourself with the various types of file systems described in this chapter, but specifically, pay close attention to the UFS file system type and UFS file system parameters. Most questions on the exam revolve around the UFS file system. In addition, make sure you understand the Logical Volume Manager. You don't need to know how to use it—just understand what it does and why you would use it.
- ▶ Make sure that you practice disk slicing. Understand how to create and delete disk slices, and pay close attention to the limitations inherent with standard disk slices. Practice partitioning a disk using the `format` utility until you have the process memorized.
- ▶ Finally, understand how to mount and unmount a file system as well as how to configure the /etc/vfstab file. Make sure that you understand all of the commands described in this chapter that are used to manage and display information about file systems, such as `df`, `fsck`, and `prtvtoc`.

**Study Strategies:** Each topic presents its own learning challenge. To support you through this, New Riders has included strategies for how to best approach studying in order to retain the material in the chapter, particularly as it is addressed on the exam.

# INSTRUCTIONAL FEATURES WITHIN THE CHAPTER

These books include a large amount and different kinds of information. The many different elements are designed to help you identify information by its purpose and importance to the exam and also to provide you with varied ways to learn the material. You will be able to determine how much attention to devote to certain elements, depending on what your goals are. By becoming familiar with the different presentations of information, you will know what information will be important to you as a test-taker and which information will be important to you as a practitioner.

TIP

Use the `probe-scsi` command to obtain a free open SCSI target ID number before adding a tape unit, CD-ROM drive, disk drive, or any other SCSI peripheral. Only devices that are powered on will be located, so make sure that everything is turned on. Use this command after installing a SCSI device to ensure that it has been connected properly and that the system can see it. Also, use this command if you suspect a faulty cable or connection. If you have more than one SCSI bus, use the `probe-scsi-all` command.

**Tip:** Tips appear in the margins to provide specific exam-related advice. Such tips may address what material is covered (or not covered) on the exam, how it is covered, mnemonic devices, or particular quirks of that exam.

**Note:** Notes contain various kinds of useful information, such as tips on the technology or administrative practices, historical background on terms and technologies, or side commentary on industry issues.

6 **Section I Part I**

NOTE

Solaris 8 introduced a new feature, which gives the ability to force a hanging system to halt. The new sequence to stop the system is Enter+~+Ctrl+B, which is equivalent to the Stop+A. There must be an interval of more than 0.5 seconds between characters, and the entire string must be entered in less than five seconds. This is true only with serial devices acting as consoles, and not for systems with keyboards of their own. If your console is connected to the serial port via a modem, you can send a break (Stop+A or L1+A) through the tip window by typing ~# (tilde+poun sign).

CAUTION

Forcing the system into the OpenBoot PROM using STOP+A or BREAK abruptly breaks execution of the operating system. It should be used only as a last effort to restart the system.

- When the system is initially powered on. If your system is not configured to start up automatically, it will stop at the user interface. If automatic startup is configured, you can make the system stop at the user interface by pressing the Stop+A keys after the display console banner is displayed, but before the system begins starting the operating system.
- If the system hardware detects an error from which it cannot recover. (This is known as a Watchdog Reset.)

## OpenBoot Firmware Tasks

The primary tasks of the OpenBoot firmware are as follows:

- Test and initialize the system hardware.
- Determine the hardware configuration.
- Start the operating system from either a mass storage device or a network.
- Provide interactive debugging facilities for testing hardware and software.
- Allow modification and management of system startup configuration, such as NVRAM parameters.

Specifically, OpenBoot will perform the following tasks necessary to initialize the operating system kernel:

1. Display system identification information and then run self-test diagnostics to verify the system's hardware and memory. These checks are known as POST (Power-On Self-Test).
2. Load the primary startup program, `bootblk`, from the default startup device.
3. The `bootblk` program finds and executes the secondary startup program, `ufsboot`, and loads it into memory.

   The `ufsboot` program loads the operating system kernel.

**Caution:** In using sophisticated information technology, there is always potential for mistakes or even catastrophes that can occur through improper application of the technology. Cautions appear in the margins to alert you to such potential problems.

**STEP BY STEP**

**1.4 Breaking Out of a Hung System**

1. Use the abort key sequence for your system (Stop+A or L1+A).

   The monitor displays the `ok` PROM prompt.

2. Type the `sync` command to synchronize the disks:
   ```
   ok sync
   ```
3. When you see the `syncing file systems` message, press the abort key sequence for your system again.

4. Type the appropriate `reset` command to reset the hardware and start the boot process:
   ```
   ok reset
   ```
5. After you receive the `login:` message, log in and type the following to verify that the system is booted to the specified run level:
   ```
   # who -r
   ```
6. The system responds with the following:
   ```
   run-level 3  Jun 9 09:19  3   0  S
   ```

**Step by Step:** Step by Steps are hands-on tutorial instructions that walk you through a particular task or function relevant to the exam objectives.

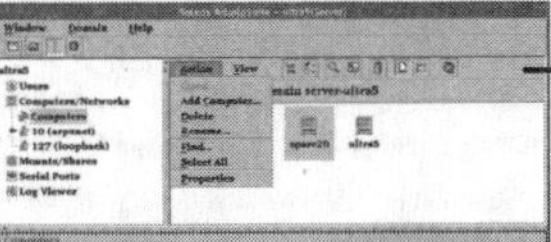

**FIGURE 19.22**
Computers/Networks window.

As shown in the pop-up menu on Figure 19.22, you can add a computer to the network.

Double-click the Computers icon, and all of the computers in your domain are displayed, as shown in Figure 19.23.

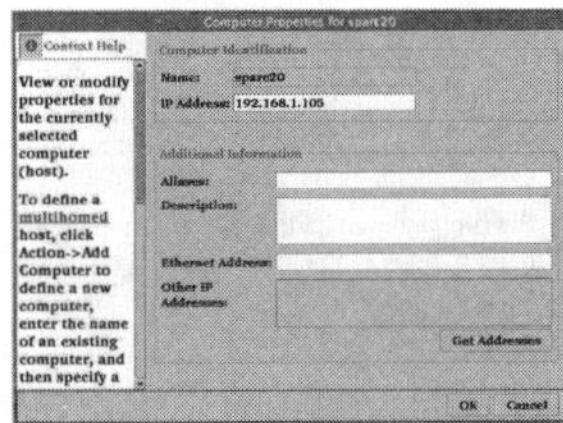

**FIGURE 19.23**
Computers in your domain.

Double-click the specific computer's icon, and the Computers Properties window appears, as shown in Figure 19.24.

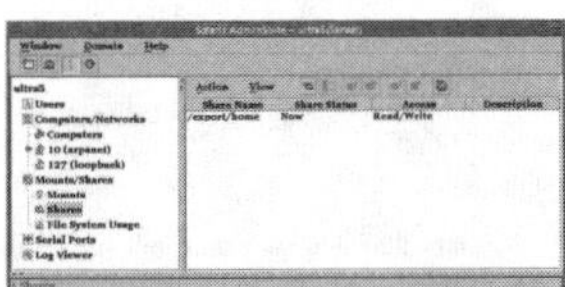

**FIGURE 19.24**
Computers Properties window.

**Figures:** Detailed figures help clarigy your understanding of the text.

# EXTENSIVE REVIEW AND SELF-TEST OPTIONS

At the end of each chapter, along with some summary elements, you will find a section called "Apply Your Knowledge" that gives you several different methods with which to test your understanding of the material and review what you have learned.

## CHAPTER SUMMARY

**KEY TERMS**

- OpenBoot
- Bootblock
- ufsboot
- OBP
- NVRAM
- PROM
- POST
- Device Tree
- Full Device Name
- Device Alias

This chapter provided a complete description of the OpenBoot environment; the PROM, the NVRAM, and the kernel.

In this chapter, I described how to access OpenBoot and the various commands available to test and provide information about the hardware.

I described the OpenBoot architecture. I explained how OpenBoot controls many of the hardware devices. Using the programmable user interface available in OpenBoot, the system administrator can set several parameters that control system hardware and peripherals.

Device names were also explained in this chapter. Throughout this book, I will be referring to various device names used in Solaris. It's important that you understand each one of them. I'll revisit this topic in Chapter 16, where devices and device drivers are covered in depth. Along with device names, I explained how to set temporary and permanent device aliases.

**Key Terms:** A list of key terms appears at the end of each chapter. These are terms that you should be sure to know and are comfortable defining and understanding when you go in to take the exam.

**Chapter Summary:** Before the "Apply Your Knowledge" section, you will find a chapter summary that wraps up the chapter and reviews what you should have learned.

**Exercises:** These activities provide an opportunity for you to master specific hands-on tasks. Our goal is to increase your proficiency with the product or technology. You must be able to conduct these tasks in order to pass the exam.

**Review Questions:** These short-answer questions allow you to quickly assess your comprehension of what you just read in the chapter.

154 **Section I Part I**

## APPLY YOUR KNOWLEDGE

### Exercises

#### 4.1 Software Package Administration

This exercise takes you through the task of installing, verifying, and removing software on a Solaris system using the command line.

**Estimated Time**: 20 minutes

1. List the software packages that are currently installed on your system by typing the following:

   ```
   pkginfo
   ```

2. Display a long-format listing of information for the SUNWman package installed on your system.

   ```
   pkginfo -l SUNWman
   ```

   What is listed for the status, install date, number of files, and number of blocks used by this package?

3. Remove the SUNWdoc package from your system with the following:

   ```
   pkgrm SUNWdoc
   ```

   Verify that the software package has been removed by repeating step 1.

   Now, we'll reinstall the software package. Log in as root, and insert the Solaris 8 Installation CD into the CD-ROM drive. Use `pkgadd` to spool the SUNWdoc package into the default spool area as follows:

   ```
   pkgadd -d
   //cdrom/sol_8_u3_sparc/s0/Solaris_8/Product \
   -s /var/spool/pkg SUNWdoc
   ```

4. Use the following commands to verify the presence of SUNWdoc in the default spool area:

5. Observe the messages displayed, and verify that the package is installed in /var/spool/pkg.

6. Reinstall the SUNWdoc package from the spool area as follows:

   ```
   pkgadd
   ```

7. Select the SUNWdoc package when you are prompted, and the package will be reinstalled.

8. To remove the SUNWdoc package from the spool area, type the following:

   ```
   pkgrm -s /var/spool/pkg
   ```

   Select the SUNWdoc package, and it will be removed from the spool directory.

9. You can now use the `pkgchk` command to check the completeness, pathname, file contents, and file attributes of the SUNWdoc package:

   ```
   pkgchk SUNdoc
   ```

### Review Questions

1. Which of the following commands is used to show software package information?

   A. `pkgadd`

   B. `pkgchk`

   C. `pkgparam`

   D. `pkginfo`

2. Which of the following commands verifies the accuracy of a software package installation?

   A. `pkgadd`

   B. `pkgchk`

APPLY YOUR KNOWLEDGE

## Answers to Review Questions

1. **D.** On a standard Solaris file system, a file system cannot span multiple disks or slices. It's only possible when using virtual file systems (that is, DiskSuite).
2. **A.** Disk configuration information is stored on the disk label.
3. **A.** The boot block stores the procedures used in booting the system. Without a boot block, the system does not boot.
4. **A.** The slice information for a particular disk can be viewed by using the `prtvtoc` command.
5. **A.** The following are virtual file systems: swapfs, procfs, lofs, cachefs, tmpfs, /var/run, and mntfs.
6. **D.** The format utility is used to retrieve corrupted disk labels, repair defective sectors, format and analyze disks, partition disks, and label disks.
7. **D.** Here are a few of the more important things contained in a superblock:
   - Size and status of the file system
   - Label (file system name and volume name)
   - Size of the file system's logical block
   - Date and time of the last update
   - Cylinder group size
   - Number of data blocks in a cylinder group
   - Summary data block
   - File system state (clean, stable, or active)
   - Pathname of the last mount point
8. **A., C.** An inode contains all of the information about a file except its name, which is kept in a directory. The inode information is kept in the cylinder information block and contains the following:
   - The type of the file (regular, directory, block special, character special, link, and so on)
   - The mode of the file (the set of read/write/execute permissions)
   - The number of hard links to the file
   - The user-id of the file's owner
   - The group-id to which the file belongs
   - The number of bytes in the file
   - An array of 15 disk-block addresses
   - The date and time the file was last accessed
   - The date and time the file was last modified
   - The date and time the file was created
9. **B.** `newfs` is the recommended command to create file systems.
10. **D.** As a general rule, a larger logical block size increases efficiency for file systems in which most of the files are large. Use a smaller logical block size for file systems in which most of the files are small.
11. **A.** The default number of bytes per inode is 2048 (2KB), which assumes that the average size of each file is 2KB or greater.
12. **A.**The file system fragment size is the smallest allocable unit of disk space, which is 1,024 bytes.

**Answers and Explanations:** For each Review and Exam question, you will find thorough explanations located at the end of the section.

# Introduction

I have been training Solaris System Administrators for more than 12 years. This book contains the training material that I use in my basic and advanced Solaris administration courses that, over the years, have helped thousands of Solaris administrators become certified. This is our third edition of the *Solaris Training Guide: System Administrator Certification*. It began with Solaris 2.6, then version 7, and now 8. Administrators from around the world have used this book when instruction from a Sun training center is either not available or not within their budget. Many of you have written to me with your success stories, suggestions, and comments. Your suggestions are what keep making this guide more valuable.

This book provides training materials for anyone interested in becoming a Sun Certified System Administrator for Solaris 8. When used as a study guide, this book will save you a great deal of time and effort searching for information you will need to know when taking the exam. This book covers the exam objectives in enough detail for the inexperienced administrator to learn the objectives and apply the knowledge to real-life scenarios. Experienced readers will find the material in this book to be complete and concise, making it a valuable study guide. This book is not a cheat sheet or cram session for the exam; it is a training manual. In other words, it does not merely give answers to the questions you will be asked on the exam. I have made certain that this book addresses the exam objectives in detail, from start to finish. If you are unsure about the objectives on the exam, this book will teach you what you need to know. After reading each chapter, assess your knowledge on the material covered using the review questions at the end of each chapter. When you have completed reading a section, use the ExamGear CD-ROM to assess your knowledge of the objectives covered on each exam. This CD-ROM contains sample questions that you are likely to see on the real exams. More sample questions are available at `www.unixed.com`, so make sure you visit this site to find additional training and study materials.

## How This Book Helps You

This book teaches you how to administer the Solaris 8 operating system. It offers you a self-guided training course of all the areas covered on the certification exams by installing, configuring, and administering the Solaris 8 operating environment. You will learn all of the specific skills to administer a system and specifically to become a Sun Certified System Administrator for Solaris 8.

Throughout the book, I provide helpful tips and real-world examples that I have encountered as a system administrator. In addition, I provide useful, real-world exercises to help you practice the material you have learned. The setup of this book is discussed in the following sections.

- **Organization**: This book is organized according to individual exam objectives. Every objective you need to know for installing, configuring, and administering a Solaris 8 system is in this book. I have attempted to present the objectives in an order that is as close as possible to that listed by Sun. However, I have not hesitated to reorganize them as needed to make the material as easy as possible for you to learn. I have also attempted to make the information accessible in the following ways:

- This introduction includes the full list of exam topics and objectives.
- Each chapter begins with a list of the objectives to be covered.
- Each chapter also begins with an outline that provides you with an overview of the material and the page numbers where particular topics can be found.

◆ **Instructional Features.** This book is designed to provide you with multiple ways to learn and reinforce the exam material. The following are some of the helpful methods:

- *Objective Explanations.* As mentioned previously, each chapter begins with a list of the objectives covered in the chapter. In addition, immediately following each objective is an explanation in a context that defines it more meaningfully.
- *Study Strategies.* The beginning of each chapter also includes strategies for studying and retaining the material in the chapter, particularly as it is addressed on the exam.
- *Review Breaks and Summaries.* Crucial information is summarized at various points in the book in lists or tables. Each chapter ends with a summary as well.
- *Key Terms.* A list of key terms appears near the end of each chapter.
- *Notes.* These appear in the margin and contain various types of useful information such as tips on technology or administrative practices, historical background on terms and technologies, or side commentary on industry issues.
- *Cautions.* When using sophisticated information technology, mistakes or even catastrophes are always possible because of improper application of the technology. Cautions appear in the margins to alert you to such potential problems.
- *Tips.* These appear in the margin and contain various kinds of useful information such as tips on technology or administrative practices, historical background on terms and technologies, or side commentary on industry issues.
- *Step by Steps.* These are hands-on, tutorial instructions that walk you through a particular task or function relevant to the exam objectives.
- *Exercises.* Found at the end of the chapters in the "Apply Your Knowledge" section, exercises are performance-based opportunities for you to learn and assess your knowledge.

◆ **Extensive Practice Test Options.** The book provides numerous opportunities for you to assess your knowledge and practice for the exam. The practice options include the following:

- *Review Questions.* These questions appear in the "Apply Your Knowledge" section at the end of each chapter. They allow you to quickly assess your comprehension of what you just read in the chapter. Answers to the questions are provided later in a separate section entitled "Answers to Review Questions."
- *Practice Exam.* A practice exam is included in the "Final Review" section for each exam (as discussed later.
- *ExamGear.* The special *Training Guide* version of the *ExamGear* software included on the CD-ROM provides even more practice questions that you are likely to encounter on the real exams. These questions are already on the CD that accompanies this book and just need to be "unlocked" so that you can access them.

NOTE: For a description of the New Riders *ExamGear*, Training Guide software, please see Appendix F, "Using the *ExamGear*, Training Guide Edition Software."

- **Final Review.** This part of the book provides you with three valuable tools for preparing for the exam, as follows:
    - *Fast Facts.* This condensed version of the information contained in the book will prove extremely useful for last-minute review.
    - *Study and Exam Prep Tips.* Read this section early on to help you develop study strategies. This section provides you with valuable exam-day tips and information on exam/question formats such as adaptive tests and case study-based questions.
    - *Practice Exam.* A full practice exam is included with questions written in styles similar to those used on the actual exam. Use the practice exam to assess your readiness for the real exam.
- **Appendixes.** The book includes valuable appendixes as well, including the history of Solaris (Appendix C), an overview of the Solaris certification process (Appendix D) a description of what is on the CD-ROM (Appendix E), and instructions for using the *ExamGear* (Appendix F).

These and all the other book features mentioned previously will enable you to thoroughly prepare for the exam.

## Conventions Used in This Book

- **Commands.** In the steps and examples, the commands you type are displayed in a special `monospaced` font.
- **Arguments and Options.** In command syntax, command options and arguments are enclosed in < >. (The italicized words within the < > symbols stand for what you will actually type. You don't type the < >.)

```
lp -d<printer name> <filename> <return>
```

- **Using the Mouse.** When using menus and windows, you will select items with the mouse. Here is the default mapping for a three-button mouse:

| | |
|---|---|
| Left button | Select |
| Middle button | Transfer/Adjust |
| Right button | Menu |

The Select button is used to select objects and activate controls. The middle mouse button is configured for either Transfer or Adjust. By default, it is set up for Transfer, which means this button is used to drag or drop list or text items. You use the left mouse button to highlight text, and then you use the middle button to move the text to another window or to reissue a command. The middle button can also be used to move windows around on the screen. The right mouse button, the Menu button, is used to display and choose options from pop-up menus.

- **Menu Options.** The names of menus and the options that appear on them are separated by a comma. For example, "Select File, Open" means to pull down the File menu and choose the Open option.
- **Code Continuation Character.** When a line of code is too long to fit on one line of a page, it is broken and continued to the next line. The continuation is preceded by a back slash.

## AUDIENCE

This book is designed for anyone who has a basic understanding of UNIX and wants to learn more about Solaris system administration. Whether you plan to become certified or not, this book is the starting point to becoming a Solaris System Administrator. It's the same training material that I use in my Solaris System Administration classes. This book covers the basic as well as the advanced system administration topics you need to know before you begin administering the Solaris operating system. My goal was to present the material in an easy-to-follow format, with text that is easy to read and understand. The only prerequisite is that you have used UNIX, you have attended a basic UNIX class for users, or you have studied equivalent material so that you understand basic UNIX commands and syntax. Before you begin administering Solaris, it's important that you have actually used UNIX.

This book is also intended for experienced system administrators who want to become certified. To pass the certification exams, you need to have a solid understanding of the fundamentals of administering Solaris. This book will help you review the fundamentals required to pass the certification exams.

## THE SUN CERTIFIED SYSTEM ADMINISTRATOR EXAMS

To become a Sun Certified System Administrator, you need to pass two exams: 310-011 (Part I) and 310-012 (Part II). Part I is a prerequisite for Part II. You will not receive a certificate until you have passed both examinations. Also, if you are already certified in Solaris 2.6 or 7, you must still pass exams 310-011 and 310-012 to be certified on Solaris 8.

Beware of fakes. I have seen some web sites promoting their own certification programs, so be sure to evaluate them carefully. Certification programs promoted by these sites are not the same as the Sun certification program, and you will not receive a certificate from Sun until you pass Sun's exams from a certified Sun testing center. Go to my web site (`www.unixed.com`) for links to the real exams and information on Sun's certification program if you are in doubt.

## EXAM 310-011

Exam 310-311 objectives are covered in the following sections.

### System Concepts

Match selected system administration terms to their respective definitions. You will also need to recognize various man page command options.

### The Boot PROM

Understand how to interrupt a non-responsive system. Understand methods used to manipulate custom device aliases.

## Installation

Describe the sequence of steps required to perform the Solaris 8 operating environment software installation on a networked, stand-alone system. Identify the function of the package administration commands. Understand how to install, verify, and remove operating system patches.

## Initialization and Shutdown

Match the Solaris run levels to their intended functions. Understand the function of the files or directories accessed during the boot process. Understand the commands used to change the run level of a system to a specified state.

## User Administration

Understand all aspects of administering users and groups.

## Security

Understand how to set and verify file and directory permissions. You also need to understand the commands used to create, modify, and delete access control lists (ACLs) on files.

## Process Control

Understand the commands that display information for all active processes on the system. Understand the effect of sending a specified signal to a process. Understand the various methods used to terminate an active process.

## File Systems

List the different types of file systems in the Solaris operating environment. Understand the configuration files associated with mounting and accessing file systems on all types of media.

## Files and Directories

Understand the methods and commands used to manage files and directories. Understand the various types of files, directories, links, and device files.

## The Boot Process

Understand the entire boot process with knowledge of the various configuration files and startup scripts.

## Disk Configuration

Understand how to add disk devices to a system. You also need to understand the device files associated with disk drives.

## Format

Understand how to use the `format` utility.

## Backup and Recovery

Understand the functional capabilities of the various backup, archive, and restore utilities in Solaris 8. Identify the commands and steps required to back up and restore a file system.

## Basic Command Syntax

Understand how to navigate through the Solaris 8 directory structure.

Understand the various metacharacters and how they can be use to access files and directories within the directory tree. Understand the commands needed to list the contents of directories and determine the file types within a directory. Understand the commands used to manipulate files and directories.

## Editor

Understand how to use the vi editor. You need to know the three modes of operation, how to position and move the cursor, create and delete text, and copy or move text. You also need to know how to use the search and replace functions in the vi editor.

## Remote Connection

Understand how to perform remote system operations and remote shell commands. Understand the subcommands that are used by the `ftp` utility to transfer files between a local system and a remote system.

# Exam 310-012

Exam 310-312 objectives are covered in the following sections.

## Client Server Relationship

Understand all of the types of servers and clients used in the Solaris 8 network environment.

## Solaris Network Environment

Define the function of each layer within the seven-layer OSI model and TCP/IP model. List the features and functions of the Ethernet. Describe the characteristics of RARP and ARP. Identify the commands that display information about the local network interface. Describe the relationship between the RPC service and the `rpcbind` process and how to list registered RPC services. Identify the steps necessary to start and stop network services via the command line.

## Solaris Syslog

Understand syslog and how to configure it. Understand the syntax of the syslog configuration file and its effect on syslod behavior.

## Disk Management

Understand the utilities used to create, check, and mount file systems. Understand the differences between physical disks and virtual disks. List the advantages of a virtual disk management application. Identify the characteristics and functions of Solstice DiskSuite and the Sun StorEdge Volume Manager.

## Solaris Pseudo File Systems and Swap Space

Understand the Solaris pseudo file systems. Understand swap and all of the steps required to create and add swap to the system.

## NFS

Understand the functions of an NFS server and an NFS client. Understand how to make resources available and unavailable for mounting as a shared resource. Understand how to enable automatic mounting of resources on an NFS client.

## AutoFS

Understand the benefits of using the `automount` utility and each of the types of automount maps. Understand how to configure, start, and stop the automounter.

## CacheFS

Understand how to configure the cache file system. Understand the commands used to monitor and manage the cache file system.

## Naming Services

Understand the purpose of each type of name service available in Solaris 8, and be able to compare and contrast their functionality. Understand how to configure the name service switch file for each type of name service.

## NIS

Understand the processes and components of the NIS master server, NIS slave server, and NIS client. Know the steps required to configure an NIS master, slave, and client. Understand the steps required to add, update, and propagate an NIS map.

## Role-Based Access Control (RBAC)

Understand the Role-Based Access Control (RBAC) facility in Solaris 8.

## Solaris Management Console and Solstice AdminSuite

Understand the features of the Solaris Management Console and the Solaris AdminSuite.

## JumpStart Automatic Installation

Understand the purpose of the three JumpStart servers. You need to know all of the commands used to set up and modify a JumpStart session between a server and its clients. In a nutshell, you need to know everything about configuring a Solaris JumpStart session. It's not uncommon for exam objectives to change or be shifted around. I highly recommend that before you start this book, you visit my web site at `www.unixed.com` to get the most up-to-date list of exam objectives, the errata for this book, up-to-date sample exam questions, and any other last-minute notes about these exams. I will provide all of the information you need to pass the exam—all you need to do is devote the time. Learning the objectives is the first step; the next step is to practice. You need to have access to a system running Solaris 8 so you can practice what you have learned. Unless you have a supernatural memory, it's going to be difficult to pass the exams without practice. Although it's best to have a Sun Sparc or Ultra system, downloading a free copy of Solaris 8 for your

Intel-based PC works great for practicing. I'll have up-to-date links for getting this software at www.unixed.com.

The fourth section of this book contains the appendixes. They provide some additional reading that I will refer to throughout the book. Although the material in the appendixes will not be on the exam, these sections provide useful background and supplementary information about the topics you will encounter.

In the back of this book is the ExamGear test CD that will prepare you for the questions you might see on the exam. It will thoroughly test your knowledge on all the exam objectives. If you are weak in any area, the sample questions will help you identify that area so that you can go back to the appropriate chapter and study the topic.

## WHAT'S NEW IN SOLARIS 8

This section covers some of the new features found in Solaris 8 that were not available in Solaris 7. Although most changes are minor, it's important to note the differences that apply to system administration. The name of the core operating system is SunOS 5.8. Enhancements in this release include the following:

- The Solaris Product Registry, which is a tool used to manage software installed using Solaris Web Start 3.0 or the Solaris management commands, such as `pkgadd`.
- `devfsadm` provides an improved mechanism for managing the special device files in the /dev and /devices directories. The `devfsadm` command replaces the `drvconfig`, `devlinks`, `disks`, `tapes`, `ports`, and `audlink` commands.
- CDE Common Desktop Environment version 1.4 provides the following:
  - A hot key editor to allow users to automate repetitive tasks
  - A `sdtimage` tool for capturing screen shots
  - Tooltips to provide a short description of an icon simply by placing the cursor over the icon
  - An extended Control Panel for desktop customization
  - Personal Desktop Assistant (PDA) sync software for synchronizing data from the Desktop calendar, mail, memo, and address to a PDA such as a Palm Pilot
  - An Audio Mixer
- PERL 5 is now included with the Solaris 8 operating environment.
- Universal Serial Bus (USB) support on Intel systems.
- A CD full of Freeware tools and libraries, such as the following:
  - bash. Shell-compatible command language interpreter
  - `gzip`. GNU zip compression utility
  - `zip`. Compression and file packaging utility
  - Many more utilities and programs
- Forcible `umount`, which allows the `umount` command to forcibly unmount a file system regardless of whether it is in use.
- Universal Disk Format (UDF) file system for exchanging data on CD-ROM and DVD-ROM.

- Deferred access time updates on UFS file systems.
- Apache Web Server and modules now bundled with Solaris 8.
- sendmail 8.9.3.
- Ipv6 next-generation Internet protocol.
- NFS server logging.
- DHCP manager GUI, which provides a Java-based graphical interface for configuring and managing the Solaris DHCP server and DHCP database.
- Remote console, which provides improved console features for troubleshooting remote systems.
- New commands to manage multiple CPUs and monitor processes such as `cpustat`, `cputrack`, and `prstat`.
- Role-Based Access Control (RBAC) so that administrators can assign limited administrative capabilities to normal, non-root users.
- Solaris Management Console 2.0 (SMC), which is a collection of GUI tools to make administering your servers easier.
- The Web Start Flash installation feature, which enables you to create a single reference installation of the Solaris operating environment on a machine and then replicate that installation on several machines.

These are the major enhancements that pertain to system administration. For a complete listing of changes and enhancements in Solaris 8, refer to the "What's New" collection of documents at `http://docs.sun.com`.

## Advice on Taking the Exam

More extensive tips are found in the Study and Exam Prep Tips and throughout the book, but keep in mind the following advice as you study for the exam:

- **Read all the material.** This book includes information not reflected in the exam objectives to better prepare you for the exam and for real-world experiences. Read all of the material to benefit from this.
- **Do the step-by-step exercises and complete the exercises in each chapter.** This will help you gain experience.
- **Use the questions to assess your knowledge.** Each chapter contains review questions and exam questions. Use these to asses your knowledge and determine where you need to re-review material.
- **Review the exam objectives.** Develop your own questions and examples for each topic listed. If you can develop and answer several questions for each topic, you should not find it difficult to pass the exam.
- **Relax and sleep before taking the exam.** Time for taking the examination is limited. However, if you have prepared and you know Solaris network administration, you will find plenty of time to answer all of the questions. Be sure to rest well for the stress that time limitations put on you as you take the exam.
- **If you don't know an answer to a question, just skip it and don't waste much time.** Don't be lazy during the examination, and answer all the questions as quickly as possible.

- Visit my web site, `www.unixed.com`. It contains the following:
  - Late-breaking changes that Sun might make to the exam or the objectives. You can expect Sun to change the exams frequently. Make sure you check here before taking the exam.
  - A FAQs page with frequently asked questions and errata regarding this book or the exams.
  - Links to other informative web sites.
  - Additional practice questions and sample exams.
  - An online forum where you can discuss certification-related issues with other system administrators.
  - Additional study materials, training programs, and seminars related to Solaris certification.
  - You can also email me directly from this web site with questions or comments about this book. I always try to answer each one personally.

When you feel confident, take the real exams and become certified. Don't forget to drop me an email and let me know how you did: `wcalkins@unixed.com`.

SECTION I

# PART 1

# CHAPTER 1

# System Startup and Shutdown

## OBJECTIVES

The following objectives for the System Administrator Exam are covered in this chapter.

**Understand the boot process**

▶ A system administrator must understand the entire boot process, beginning from the proper power-on sequence to the steps that are performed when bringing the system into multiuser mode.

**Perform kernel initialization**

▶ Several steps are involved in initializing the kernel. Understanding how the Solaris kernel is configured, located, and loaded into memory is critical to system administration.

**Understand and control run levels**

▶ System run levels define which processes and services are started at various stages of the boot process. You'll need to understand all of the run levels available in Solaris.

**Use the run control scripts to stop or start services**

▶ The system administrator adds and modifies run control scripts to customize the startup of processes and services on Solaris systems. A detailed understanding of the programs and configuration files involved at the various run levels is required.

**Perform a system shutdown**

▶ Proper system shutdown is critical. Understanding proper system shutdown techniques ensures the integrity of the data on your system. There are several ways to shut down the system; the system administrator needs to understand the pros and cons of each method.

**Know the actions required to interrupt a non-responsive system.**

▶ Occasionally, conventional shutdown methods might not work on an unresponsive system or on a system that has crashed. This chapter introduces when and how to use these alternative shutdown methods to bring the system down safely.

## Outline



## Study Strategies

The following strategies will help you study for the exam:

- When studying this chapter, I suggest that you practice each step-by-step process that I've outlined on a Sun system. Unfortunately, an Intel-based system running Solaris 8 does not provide the OpenBoot environment necessary to practice every topic that is described in this chapter. In addition to practicing the processes, practice the various options I describe for booting the system.
- During the boot process, watch the system messages, and familiarize yourself with every stage of the boot process. Watch the system messages that are displayed at bootup. You should understand each message displayed during the boot process from system power on to bringing the system into multiuser mode.
- Make sure that you thoroughly understand all the system run states, including when and where to use each of them. In addition, you must understand run control scripts and how they affect the system services. Practice adding your own run control scripts.
- Finally, practice shutting down the system. Make sure that you understand the advantages and disadvantages of each method presented.

# INTRODUCTION

System startup requires an understanding of the hardware and the operating system functions required to bring the system to a running state. This chapter discusses the operations that the system must perform from the time you power on the system until you receive a system logon prompt. In addition, it covers the steps required to properly shut down your system. After reading this chapter, you'll understand how to boot the system from the OpenBoot PROM (Programmable Read-Only Memory), and what operations must take place to start up the kernel and UNIX system processes.

# BOOTING THE SYSTEM

Bootstrapping is the process a computer follows to load and execute the bootable operating system. The name is coined from the phrase "pulling yourself up by your bootstraps." The instructions for the bootstrap procedure are stored in the boot PROM.

The boot process goes through the following phases:

1. Boot PROM phase. After you turn on power to the system, the PROM displays system identification information and runs self-test diagnostics to verify the system's hardware and memory. It then loads the primary boot program, called `bootblk`.
2. Boot program phase. The `bootblk` program finds and executes the secondary boot program (called `ufsboot`) from the ufs file system and loads it into memory. After the `ufsboot` program is loaded, it loads the kernel.
3. Kernel initialization phase. The kernel initializes itself and begins loading modules, using `ufsboot` to read the files. When the kernel has loaded enough modules to mount the root file system, it unmaps the `ufsboot` program and continues, using its own resources. The kernel starts the UNIX operating system, mounts the necessary file systems, and runs `/sbin/init` to bring the system to the "initdefault" state specified in /etc/inittab.

4. Init phase. The kernel creates a user process and starts the `/sbin/init` process, which starts other processes by reading the /etc/inittab file.

   The `/sbin/init` process starts the run control (rc) scripts, which execute a series of other scripts. These scripts (/sbin/rc*) check and mount file systems, start various processes, and perform system maintenance tasks.

## Power On

> **CAUTION**
>
> Always connect your cables before turning on the hardware, or you could damage your system.

Before powering on the system, make sure that all your connections are secure. Check the SCSI cables that connect your external disk drives, tape drives, and CD-ROM to the system to make sure they are properly connected. Check your network connection. Also, make sure that the keyboard and monitor are connected properly. Loose cables can cause your system to fail the startup process.

The correct sequence for powering on your equipment is to first turn on any peripherals (that is, external disk drives or tape drives); then turn on power to the system.

## Boot PROM and Program Phases

The bootstrap process begins after power-up when information located in the hardware's PROM chip is accessed. Sun calls this the OpenBoot firmware, and it is executed immediately after you turn on the system. I cover OpenBoot in detail in Chapter 2, "OpenBoot," but because it is part of the boot process, I'll also cover it briefly here.

The primary task of the OpenBoot firmware is to boot the operating system either from a mass storage device or from the network. OpenBoot contains a program called the monitor, which controls the operation of the system before the kernel is available. When a system is turned on, the monitor runs a Power-on self-test (POST) that checks such things as the hardware and memory on the system. If no errors are found, the automatic boot process begins. OpenBoot contains a set of instructions that locate and start up the system's boot program, and eventually start up the UNIX operating system.

The boot program is stored in a predictable area (sectors 1–15) on the system hard drive, CD-ROM, or other bootable device, and is referred to as the bootblock (`bootblk`). The bootblock is responsible for loading the secondary boot program (`ufsboot`) into memory, which is located in the ufs file system on the boot device. The path to `ufsboot` is recorded in the bootblock, which is installed by the Solaris installboot utility.

`ufsboot` locates and loads the two-part kernel. The kernel consists of a two-piece static core called `genunix` and `unix`. `genunix` is the platform-independent, generic kernel file; and `unix` is the platform-specific kernel file. When the system boots, `ufsboot` combines these two files into memory to form the running kernel.

The kernel (covered in detail later in this chapter) is the part of the operating system that remains running at all times until the system is shut down.

## Kernel Initialization Phase

The OpenBoot PROM automatically issues the `boot` command if the OpenBoot parameter `auto-boot` is set to true (default) and the OpenBoot PROM is not in fully secure mode. (See Chapter 2 for details on how this is set.) The system automatically starts the boot process after power has been turned on, and you do not see the `ok` prompt. To interrupt the auto-boot process, click Stop+A. The `ok` prompt appears. Table 1.1 lists the `boot` command options.

**TABLE 1.1**

**BOOT COMMAND OPTIONS**

| *Option* | *Description* |
|---|---|
| `-a` | An interactive boot |
| `-r` | A reconfiguration boot |
| `-s` | Boots into a single-user state |
| `-v` | Boots in verbose mode |

`ok boot -v`, for example, boots the system in verbose mode, which displays a full listing of system messages during the boot phase. The `-v` option can be used with other boot options to get verbose output.

The boot program is responsible for loading the UNIX kernel into memory and passing control of the system to it. The `boot` command must access the OpenBoot parameter `boot-device`. The alias assigned to the boot device (disk or disk#) tells the boot device where to find the kernel and how to start it up. For example, the alias disk provides the boot path /sbus@1,f8000000/esp@0,40000/sd@3,0:a.

## The *boot* Command

A noninteractive boot (`boot`) automatically boots the system using default values for the boot path. Initiate a noninteractive boot by typing the following command from the OpenBoot prompt:

```
ok boot
```

The system will boot without requiring more interaction.

An interactive boot (`boot -a`) stops and asks for input during the boot process. The system provides a dialog box, in which it displays the default boot values and gives you the option of changing them. You might want to boot interactively to make a temporary change to the system file or kernel. Booting interactively allows you to test your changes and recover easily if you have problems.

---

## STEP BY STEP

### 1.1 The Interactive Boot Process

1. At the `ok` prompt, type `boot -a` and press Enter. The boot program prompts you interactively.
2. Press Enter to use the default kernel (/kernel/unix) as prompted, or type the name of the kernel to use for booting and press Enter.
3. Press Enter to use the default modules directory path as prompted, or type the path for the modules directory and press Enter.

4. Press Enter to use the default /etc/system file as prompted, or type the name of the system file and press Enter.

5. Press Enter to use the default root file system type as prompted (ufs for local disk booting, or nfs for diskless clients).

6. Press Enter to use the default physical name of the root device as prompted, or type the device name.

The following output shows an example of an interactive boot session:

```
ok
ok boot -a
Boot device: /pci@1f,0/pci@1,1/ide@3/disk@0,0:a  File and args: -a
Enter filename [kernel/sparcv9/unix]:
Enter default directory for modules [/platform/SUNW,Ultra-5_10/kernel
/platform/sun4u/kernel /kernel /usr/kernel]:
Name of system file [etc/system]:

SunOS Release 5.8 Version Generic_108621-04 64-bit
Copyright 1983-2000 Sun Microsystems, Inc.  All rights reserved.
root filesystem type [ufs]:
Enter physical name of root device
[/pci@1f,0/pci@1,1/ide@3/disk@0,0:a]:
configuring IPv4 interfaces: hme0.
configuring IPv6 interfaces: hme0.
Hostname: unknown
metainit: unknown: there are no existing databases

The system is coming up.  Please wait.
checking ufs filesystems
/dev/rdsk/c0t0d0s5: is clean.
/dev/rdsk/c0t0d0s7: is clean.
/dev/rdsk/c0t0d0s6: is clean.
Starting IPv6 neighbor discovery.
Setting default IPv6 interface for multicast: add net ff00::/8: gateway
fe80::a00:20ff:fea2:6382
starting rpc services: rpcbind done.
Setting default IPv4 interface for multicast: add net 224.0/4:
syslog service starting.
syslogd: line 24: WARNING: loghost could not be resolved
Print services started.
volume management starting.
Mar 13 09:21:48
The system is ready.
ultra5 console login:
```

To view more detailed information during the boot process, use the -v option:

```
ok boot -v
```

The system responds with more detailed information:

```
ok boot -v
Resetting ...

Sun Ultra 5/10 UPA/PCI (UltraSPARC-IIi 270MHz), No Keyboard
OpenBoot 3.15, 128 MB memory installed, Serial #10642306.
Ethernet address 8:0:20:a2:63:82, Host ID: 80a26382.

Initializing Memory

Rebooting with command: boot -v
Boot device: /pci@1f,0/pci@1,1/ide@3/disk@0,0:a  File and args: -v

SunOS Release 5.8 Version Generic_108621-04 64-bit
Copyright 1983-2000 Sun Microsystems, Inc.  All rights reserved.
Ethernet address = 8:0:20:a2:63:82
mem = 131072K (0x8000000)
avail mem = 122306560
root nexus = Sun Ultra 5/10 UPA/PCI (UltraSPARC-IIi 270MHz)
pcipsy0 at root: UPA 0x1f 0x0
pcipsy0 is /pci@1f,0
PCI-device: pci@1,1, simba0
simba0 is /pci@1f,0/pci@1,1
PCI-device: pci@1, simba1
simba1 is /pci@1f,0/pci@1
PCI-device: ide@3, uata0
uata0 is /pci@1f,0/pci@1,1/ide@3
dad0 at pci1095,6460 target 0 lun 0
dad0 is /pci@1f,0/pci@1,1/ide@3/dad@0,0
      <ST34321A cyl 8892 alt 2 hd 15 sec 63>
root on /pci@1f,0/pci@1,1/ide@3/disk@0,0:a fstype ufs
PCI-device: ebus@1, ebus0
power0 at ebus0: offset 14,724000
power0 is /pci@1f,0/pci@1,1/ebus@1/power@14,724000
su0 at ebus0: offset 14,3083f8
su0 is /pci@1f,0/pci@1,1/ebus@1/su@14,3083f8
su1 at ebus0: offset 14,3062f8
su1 is /pci@1f,0/pci@1,1/ebus@1/su@14,3062f8
```

```
se0 at ebus0: offset 14,400000
se0 is /pci@1f,0/pci@1,1/ebus@1/se@14,400000
cpu0: SUNW,UltraSPARC-IIi (upaid 0 impl 0x12 ver 0x13 clock 270 MHz)
configuring IPv4 interfaces:SUNW,hme0 : PCI IO 2.0 (Rev Id = c1) Found
PCI-device: network@1,1, hme0
hme0 is /pci@1f,0/pci@1,1/network@1,1
 hme0.
configuring IPv6 interfaces: hme0.
Hostname: unknown
metainit: unknown: there are no existing databases

dump on /dev/dsk/c0t0d0s1 size 420 MB
SUNW,hme0 : Internal Transceiver Selected.
SUNW,hme0 : Auto-Negotiated  100 Mbps Half-Duplex Link Up
The system is coming up.  Please wait.
checking ufs filesystems
/dev/rdsk/c0t0d0s5: is clean.
/dev/rdsk/c0t0d0s7: is clean.
/dev/rdsk/c0t0d0s6: is clean.
Starting IPv6 neighbor discovery.
Setting default IPv6 interface for multicast: add net ff00::/8: gateway
fe80::a00:20ff:fea2:6382
starting rpc services: rpcbind done.
Setting default IPv4 interface for multicast: add net 224.0/4:
syslog service starting.
syslogd: line 24: WARNING: loghost could not be resolved
Print services started.
Mar 13 11:04:03 unknown pseudo: pseudo-device: tod0
Mar 13 11:04:03 unknown genunix: tod0 is /pseudo/tod@0
Mar 13 11:04:03 unknown pseudo: pseudo-device: pm0Mar 13 11:04:03 unknown genunix: pm0 is\
/pseudo/pm@0
Mar 13 11:04:04 unknown simba: PCI-device: SUNW,m64B@2, m640
Mar 13 11:04:04 unknown genunix: m640 is /pci@1f,0/pci@1,1/SUNW,m64B@2
Mar 13 11:04:04 unknown m64: m64#0: 1152x900, 4M mappable, rev 4750.7cvolume management starting.
Mar 13 11:04:06 unknown pseudo: pseudo-device: vol0
Mar 13 11:04:06 unknown genunix: vol0 is /pseudo/vol@0
Mar 13 11:04:07 unknown scsi: sd0 at uata0: target 2 lun 0
Mar 13 11:04:07 unknown genunix: sd0 is /pci@1f,0/pci@1,1/ide@3/sd@2,0
Mar 13 11:04:09 unknown ebus: fd0 at ebus0: offset 14,3023f0
Mar 13 11:04:09 unknown genunix: fd0 is /pci@1f,0/pci@1,1/ebus@1/fdthree@14,3023f0

Mar 13 11:04:15 unknown snmpdx:
The system is ready.

ultra5 console login:
```

NOTE

Several pages of information will be displayed, so I recommend that you pipe the `dmesg` command to `more`, as shown here: `/usr/sbin/dmesg|more`.

If you are not at the system console to watch the boot information, you can use the UNIX `dmesg` command to redisplay information that was displayed during the boot process, or view the information in the /var/adm/messages file.

To view messages displayed during the boot process, use one of the following methods:

- At a UNIX prompt, type `/usr/sbin/dmesg` and press Enter. The boot messages are displayed.
- At a UNIX prompt, type `more /var/adm/messages` and press Enter.

CAUTION

Do not modify the /etc/system file unless you are certain of the results. A good practice is always to make a backup copy of any system file you modify in case the original needs to be restored. Incorrect entries could prevent your system from booting. If a boot process fails because of an unusable /etc/system file, boot the system using the interactive option `boot -a`. When requested to enter the name of the system file, enter the name of the backup filename.

## System Run States

After the `boot` command initiates the kernel, it begins several phases of the startup process. The first task is for OpenBoot to load the kernel. As stated, by default, the kernel is named /kernel/unix and is located in the root (/) partition on the disk, with its path defined in an OpenBoot PROM alias named disk.

The kernel consists of a small static core and many dynamically loadable kernel modules. Many kernel modules are loaded automatically at boot time, but for efficiency, others—such as device drivers—are loaded from the disk as needed by the kernel. When the kernel loads, the system reads a file named /etc/system. Parameters in this file control which modules and parameters are to be loaded by the kernel at boot time. Occasionally, kernel parameters in this file need to be adjusted for performance tuning.

After control of the system is passed to the kernel, the system begins initialization and enters one of eight run states—also called init states—as described in Table 1.2. Because run state 4 is currently not used, only seven usable run states exist.

**TABLE 1.2**

**THE EIGHT SYSTEM RUN STATES**

| *Run State* | *Description* |
|---|---|
| 0 | Stops system services and daemons. Terminates all running processes. Unmounts all file systems. |

| *Run State* | *Description* |
|---|---|
| S,s | Single-user (system administrator) state. Only root is allowed to log in at the console, and any users logged in are logged out when entering this run level. All file systems previously mounted remain mounted and accessible. All services except the most basic operating system services are shut down in an orderly manner. |
| 1 | Single-user (system administrator) state. All file systems are still available. All services except the most basic OS services are shut down in an orderly manner. |
| 2 | Normal multiuser operation without NFS file systems shared. Sets the time zone variable. Mounts the /usr file system. Cleans up the /tmp and /var/tmp directories. Loads the network interfaces and starts processes. Starts the `cron` daemon. Cleans up the uucp tmp files. Starts the lp system. Starts the `sendmail` daemon. |
| 3 | Normal multiuser operation of a file server with NFS systems shared. Completes all the tasks in run level 2. Starts the NFS system daemons. |
| 4 | Alternative multiuser state (currently not used). |
| 5 | Power-down state. Shuts down the system so that it is safe to turn off power to the system. If possible, automatically turns off system power on systems that support this feature. |
| 6 | Reboots. |

**NOTE**

The difference between run level 1 and run level S,s is that in run level 1, users can still be logged in. If you issue an `init S`, user sessions are terminated. If you issue an `init 1`, users currently logged in will not be logged off. Run level 1 allows the system administrator to perform system maintenance while having users logged in. All services except the most basic operating system services are stopped, however. Run level S allows system maintenance such as system backups, in which all users must be off the system.

The init state in which the system is running defines the services and resources available to users. When preparing to perform a system administration task, you need to determine which init state is appropriate for the task. Use Table 1.3 to determine what init state to use for a particular task. A system can run in only one init state at a time.

**TABLE 1.3**

**THE EIGHT SYSTEM RUN STATES DEFINED**

| *Init State* | *When to Use It* |
|---|---|
| 0 | To shut down the system so that it is safe to turn off the power (system administrator state). |
| S,s | Single-user (system administrator) state. This run level is used when the system administrator is performing administrative tasks that require all users to be logged out of the system, such as when performing level 0 backups or repairing file systems. Any function that requires the system administrator to be in single-user mode should be run at this run level. |

*continues*

**TABLE 1.3** *continued*

**THE EIGHT SYSTEM RUN STATES DEFINED**

| *Init State* | *When to Use It* |
|---|---|
| 1 | Single-user (system administrator) state. This run level is used when the system administrator is performing administrative tasks and does not want additional users to log into the system, such as when performing backups and file system checks on file systems currently not in use by logged-in users. |
| 2 | For normal operations, when sharing of local file systems is not required. Multiple users can access the system and the entire file system. All daemons are running except NFS server and syslog. Use this run level when you want to ensure that remote hosts cannot mount local file systems (read more about NFS in Chapter 17, "The NFS Environment") or when you want the `syslogd` daemon inactive. |
| 3 | For normal operations, with NFS resource sharing available. This is the normal run level on most systems. |
| 4 | Alternative multiuser state (currently not used). |
| 5 | Power-down state. To shut down the operating system so that it is safe to turn off power to the system. All users are logged off the system, and the operating system services are stopped in an orderly manner. When complete, it's safe to turn off power to the system and all peripherals. If supported by the system hardware, the power to the system is automatically turned off. |
| 6 | To shut down the system to run level 0 and then reboot to multiuser level (or whatever level is the default in the inittab file). |

**NOTE** In previous versions of Solaris, this process was called *swapper* and had been renamed to *sched* in Solaris 8.

## Swapper

The first task for the kernel is to start the swapper process. The swapper process is the part of the kernel that schedules all other processes. The swapper has a process ID of 0 and is named sched. Its first job is to start up the init process.

# INIT Phase

The `/sbin/init` command generates processes to set up the system based on the directions in /etc/inittab. The `init` process is the parent of all other processes. It examines the contents of the /etc/inittab file to determine the order for starting up other processes and what to do when one of these processes ends. Each entry in the /etc/inittab file has the following fields:

```
id:runlevel:action:process
```

Table 1.4 provides a more detailed description of each field.

**TABLE 1.4**

**FIELDS IN THE INITTAB FILE**

| *Field* | *Description* |
|---|---|
| `id` | A unique identifier |
| `runlevel` | The run level |
| `action` | How the process is to be run |
| `process` | The name of the command to execute |

The following example shows a default /etc/inittab file:

```
ap::sysinit:/sbin/autopush -f /etc/iu.ap
ap::sysinit:/sbin/soconfig -f /etc/sock2path
fs::sysinit:/sbin/rcS sysinit       >/dev/msglog 2<>/dev/msglog </dev/console
is:3:initdefault:
p3:s1234:powerfail:/usr/sbin/shutdown -y -i5 -g0 >/dev/msglog 2<>/dev/msglog
sS:s:wait:/sbin/rcS                 >/dev/msglog 2<>/dev/msglog </dev/console
s0:0:wait:/sbin/rc0                 >/dev/msglog 2<>/dev/msglog </dev/console
s1:1:respawn:/sbin/rc1              >/dev/msglog 2<>/dev/msglog </dev/console
s2:23:wait:/sbin/rc2                >/dev/msglog 2<>/dev/msglog </dev/console
s3:3:wait:/sbin/rc3                 >/dev/msglog 2<>/dev/msglog </dev/console
s5:5:wait:/sbin/rc5                 >/dev/msglog 2<>/dev/msglog </dev/console
s6:6:wait:/sbin/rc6                 >/dev/msglog 2<>/dev/msglog </dev/console
fw:0:wait:/sbin/uadmin 2 0          >/dev/msglog 2<>/dev/msglog </dev/console
of:5:wait:/sbin/uadmin 2 6          >/dev/msglog 2<>/dev/msglog </dev/console
rb:6:wait:/sbin/uadmin 2 1          >/dev/msglog 2<>/dev/msglog </dev/console
sc:234:respawn:/usr/lib/saf/sac -t 300
co:234:respawn:/usr/lib/saf/ttymon -g -h -p "`uname -n` console login: " -T
sun -d /dev/console -l console -m ldterm,ttcompat
```

When the system is first booted, init starts all processes labeled sysinit in the inittab file. The initdefault entry in /etc/inittab identifies the default run level. In this example, the default is run level 3 (multiuser mode with network file sharing). The init daemon runs each process associated with this run level (that is, each entry that has a 3 in its run-level field). Each process is run using the entry from the action field. The action field can have one of the values listed in Table 1.5.

**TABLE 1.5**

**INITTAB ACTION FIELDS**

| *Field* | *Description* |
|---|---|
| sysinit | This field executes the process before init tries to access the console via the console prompt. init waits for its completion before it continues to read the inittab file. |
| powerfail | The system has received a powerfail signal. |
| wait | This field waits for the command to be completed before moving to the next entry containing the same run level. |
| respawn | init will restart the process if it dies. |

**NOTE** Many of the Solaris startup scripts can be identified by their "rc" prefix or suffix, which means "run control."

## rc Scripts

Each init state has a corresponding series of run control scripts, referred to as rc scripts and located in the /sbin directory, to control each init state. These rc scripts are as follows:

rc0

rc1

rc2

rc3

rc5

rc6

rcS

The `init` process executes the /sbin/rc<*n*> scripts, which in turn execute a series of other scripts located in the /etc directory. For each rc script in the /sbin directory, a corresponding directory named /etc/rc<*n*>.d contains scripts to perform various actions for that run level. For example, /etc/rc2.d contains files used to start and stop processes for run level 2. At bootup, rc scripts are run in numerical order until the default run level is reached; for example, to get to run level 3, /sbin/rc1, /sbin/rc2, and /sbin/rc3 are run.

All run control scripts are also located in the /etc/init.d directory. These files are linked to corresponding run control scripts in the /etc/rc<n>.d directories.

The following is a list of the default scripts located in /etc/rc2.d, which were put there when the operating system was installed. As described later, the system administrator will add customized scripts to this directory:

```
ls /etc/rc2.d
K06mipagent
K07dmi
K07snmpdx
K16apache
K28nfs.server
README
S01MOUNTFSYS
S05RMTMPFILES
S10lu
S20sysetup
S21perf
S30sysid.net
S40llc2
S47asppp
S69inet
S70uucp
S71ldap.client
S71rpc
S71sysid.sys
S72autoinstall
S72inetsvc
S72slpd
S73cachefs.daemon
S73nfs.client
S74autofs
S74syslog
```

**NOTE**

Although the scripts appear as files in each directory, the rc<n>.d directories contain hard links to the /etc/init.d directory. On other UNIX systems, startup scripts are sometimes found in /sbin/rc<n>.d and in /etc/rc<n>.d directories. Links were put into Solaris so that users who were accustomed to other flavors of UNIX (HP-UX, SunOS, and so on) could locate the startup files easily. In addition, any scripts they might have ported over that reference these startup files are compatible without modification. Also, by putting all the scripts in one location, /etc/init.d, it's convenient to find the script needed to start or stop a particular function without searching through all the /etc/rc<n>.d directories.

```
S74xntpd
S75cron
S75savecore
S76nscd
S80lp
S80PRESERVE
S80spc
S85power
S88sendmail
S88utmpd
S89bdconfig
S90wbem
S92volmgt
S93cacheos.finish
S94ncalogd
S95lvm.sync
S96ab2mgr
S99audit
S99dtlogin
```

The /etc/rc<n>.d scripts are always run in ASCII sort order. The number following the first letter (S or K) designates the order in which the scripts are run, and can be any numeric value. The name following the number does not relate to the order in which they are run. The scripts have names of this form:

```
[K,S][#][A-Z]
```

Files beginning with *K* are run to terminate (kill) a system process. Files beginning with *S* are run to start a system process. The actions of each run-control-level script are summarized in the following lists.

The /sbin/rc0 script runs the /etc/rc0.d scripts, which perform the following:

- Stop system services and daemons
- Terminate all running processes
- Unmount all file systems

The /sbin/rcS script runs the /etc/rcS.d scripts to bring the system up to single-user mode and to do the following:

- Establish a minimal network
- Mount /usr, if necessary

- Set the system name
- Check the / and /usr file systems
- Mount pseudo file systems (/proc and /dev/fd)
- Rebuild the device entries (for reconfiguration boots)
- Check and mount other file systems to be mounted in single-user mode

Run level init S is similar to run level 1, except that all file systems get mounted and are accessible.

The /sbin/rc1 script runs the /etc/rc1.d scripts and does the following:

- Stops system services and daemons except for the most basic OS services
- Enables all file systems to be available, and allows any logged-in users to remain logged in
- Brings the system up in single-user mode

> **TIP** Use the init S run level to perform system administration tasks when you want to ensure that other users cannot log in and access the system.

The /sbin/rc2 script sets the TIMEZONE variable, runs the /etc/rc2.d scripts, and does the following:

- Mounts all file systems
- Enables disk quotas if at least one file system was mounted with the quota option
- Saves editor temporary files in /usr/preserve
- Removes any files in the /tmp directory
- Configures system accounting
- Configures the default router
- Sets the NIS domain
- Sets the `ifconfig` netmask
- Reboots the system from the installation media or a boot server if either /.PREINSTALL or /AUTOINSTALL exists
- Starts `inetd`, `rpcbind`, and `named`, if appropriate
- Starts the Kerberos client-side daemon (`kerbd`)

- Starts NIS daemons (`ypbind`) and NIS+ daemons (`rpc.nisd`), if appropriate
- Starts `keyserv`
- Starts `statd`, `lockd`, `xntpd`, `vold`, and `utmpd`
- Mounts all NFS entries
- Starts `automount`
- Starts `cron`
- Starts the `lp` daemons
- Starts the `sendmail` daemon

The /sbin/rc3 script runs the /etc/rc3.d scripts and does the following:

- Cleans up sharetab
- Starts `nfsd`
- Starts `mountd`
- If boot server, starts `rarpd`, `rpld`, and `rpc.bootparamd`

The /sbin/rc5 and /sbin/rc6 scripts run the /etc/rc0.d scripts and do the following:

- Kill all active processes
- Unmount all file systems

## Using the Run Control Scripts to Stop or Start Services

The advantage of having individual scripts for each run level is that you can run these scripts individually to turn off processes in Solaris without rebooting or changing init states.

For example, you can turn off NFS server functionality by typing `/etc/init.d/nfs.server stop` and pressing Enter. After you have changed the system configuration, you can restart the functionality by typing `/etc/init.d/nfs.server start` and pressing Enter.

Use the pgrep command to verify whether the service has been stopped or started:

```
pgrep -f <service>
```

The pgrep utility examines the active processes on the system and reports the process IDs of the processes. See Chapter 9, "Process Control," for details on this command.

## Adding Scripts to the Run Control Directories

If you add a script, put the script in the /etc/init.d directory, and create a link to the appropriate rc<n>.d directory. Assign appropriate numbers and names to the new scripts so that they will be run in the proper sequence.

---

### STEP BY STEP

#### 1.2 Adding a Run Control Script

1. Become superuser.
2. Add the script to the /etc/init.d directory:

```
# cp <filename> /etc/init.d
# chmod 0744 /etc/init.d/<filename>
# chown root:sys /etc/init.d/<filename>
```

3. Create links to the appropriate rc<n>.d directory:

```
# cd /etc/init.d
# ln  <filename> /etc/rc2.d/S<nnfilename>
# ln  <filename> /etc/rc<n>.d/K<nnfilename>
```

4. Use the ls command to verify that the script has links in the specified directories:

```
# ls -l /etc/init.d/ /etc/rc2.d/ /etc/rc<n>.d/
```

The following example creates an rc script named "program" that will start up at run level 2 and stop at run level 0:

```
# cp program  /etc/init.d
# cd /etc/init.d
# ln  /etc/init.d/program  /etc/rc2.d/S100program
# ln  /etc/init.d/program  /etc/rc0.d/K100program
# ls -l /etc/init.d /etc/rc2.d /etc/rc0.d
```

*continues*

*continued*

The system will display the following:

```
/etc/init.d:
total 250
-rwxr--r-- 3 root sys     171 Jan  5  2000 ANNOUNCE
-rwxr--r-- 3 root sys    1881 Jan  5  2000 MOUNTFSYS
-rwxr--r-- 2 root sys     256 Jan  5  2000 PRESERVE
-rw-r--r-- 1 root sys     681 Jan  5  2000 README
-rwxr--r-- 2 root sys    2004 Jan  5  2000 RMTMPFILES
-rwxr--r-- 1 root sys     833 Jan  5  2000 acct
-rwxr--r-- 1 root sys     392 Mar 16  2000 acctadm
-rwxr--r-- 6 root sys     572 Dec 14  2000 apache
-rwxr--r-- 5 root sys     365 Jan  5  2000 asppp
-rwxr--r-- 5 root sys     447 Jan  5  2000 audit
-rwxr--r-- 5 root sys     364 Jan  5  2000 autofs
-rwxr-xr-x 2 root other 1558 Dec 16  1999 autoinstall
-rwxr--r-- 2 root        1153 Jan  5  2000 buildmnttab
-rwxr--r-- 1 root         271 Dec  7  1999 buttons_n_dials-setup
-rwxr--r-- 2 root sys    1101 Jan  5  2000 cachefs.daemon
-rwxr--r-- 2 root sys   392   Jan  5  2000 cachefs.root
-rwxr--r-- 2 root sys  5705   Jan  5  2000 cacheos
-rwxr--r-- 2 root sys     364 Jan  5  2000 cacheos.finish
-rwxr--r-- 2 root sys     517 Jan  5  2000 coreadm
-rwxr--r-- 5 root sys     504 Jan  5  2000 cron
-rwxr--r-- 3 root sys    1426 Feb 26 09:40 devfsadm
-rwxr--r-- 1 root sys     904 Jan  5  2000 devlinks
-rwxr--r-- 1 root sys     413 Jan  5  2000 dhcp
-rwxr--r-- 2 root sys     494 Jan  5  2000 dhcpagent
-rwxr--r-- 1 root sys     469 Jan  5  2000 drvconfig
-rwxr--r-- 5 root sys    2804 Dec  2  1999 dtlogin
-rwxr--r-- 5 root sys    1201 Jan  5  2000 inetinit
-rwxr--r-- 5 root sys    7134 Jan  5  2000 inetsvc
-rwxr--r-- 6 root sys     861 Jan  5  2000 init.dmi
-rwxr--r-- 6 root sys     404 Jan  5  2000 init.snmpdx
-rwxr--r-- 5 root sys    1131 Feb 23 09:29 init.wbem
-rwxr--r-- 2 root sys     382 Feb 26 09:40 initpcihpc
-rwxr--r-- 2 root sys     441 Jan  5  2000 initpcmcia
-rwxr--r-- 2 root sys     761 Jan  5  2000 keymap
-rwxr--r-- 5 root sys     413 Jan  5  2000 ldap.client
-rwxr--r-- 5 root sys     359 Jan  5  2000 llc2
-rwxr--r-- 5 root sys     460 Jan  5  2000 lp
-rwxr--r-- 6 root sys     344 Mar 20  2000 mipagent
-rwxr--r-- 1 root sys     491 Jan  5  2000 mkdtab
-rwxr--r-- 5 root sys     522 Dec 14  2000 ncad
```

```
-rwxr--r-- 2 root sys   2445 Jan  5  2000 ncakmod
-rwxr--r-- 5 root sys   1181 Jan  5  2000 ncalogd
-rwxr--r-- 2 root sys   8972 Jul 10  2000 network
-rwxr--r-- 3 root sys    836 Jan  5  2000 nfs.client
-rwxr--r-- 6 root sys    080 Jan  5  2000 nfs.server
-rwxr--r-- 5 root sys    514 Jan  5  2000 nscd
-rwxr--r-- 1 root sys    398 Jan  5  2000 pcmcia
-rwxr--r-- 2 root sys    989 Jan  5  2000 perf
-rwxr--r-- 5 root sys   1787 Jan  5  2000 power
-rw-r--r-- 3 root other    0 Jul 19 08:59 program
-rwxr--r-- 2 root sys   3193 Jan  5  2000 rootusr
-rwxr--r-- 5 root sys   2839 Jan  5  2000 rpc
-rwxr--r-- 2 root sys   2519 Jan  5  2000 savecore
-rwxr--r-- 5 root sys   1471 Jan  5  2000 sendmail
-rwxr--r-- 5 root sys    525 Jan  5  2000 slpd
-rwxr--r-- 5 root sys    610 Jan  5  2000 spc
-rwxr--r-- 2 root sys   2405 Jan  5  2000 standardmounts
-rwxr--r-- 2 root sys    611 Jan  5  2000 sysetup
-rwxr-xr-x 2 root other 1995 Dec 16  1999 sysid.net
-rwxr-xr-x 2 root other 1498 Dec 16  1999 sysid.sys
-rwxr--r-- 5 root sys    911 Jan  5  2000 syslog
-rwxr--r-- 1 root sys    304 Jan  5  2000 ufs_quota
-rwxr--r-- 5 root sys    597 Jan  5  2000 utmpd
-rwxr--r-- 2 root sys    327 Jan  5  2000 uucp
-rwxr--r-- 5 root sys    391 Jan  5  2000 volmgt
-rwxr--r-- 5 root sys    945 Jan  5  2000 xntpd

/etc/rc0.d:
total 122
-rwxr--r-- 3 root sys    171 Jan  5  2000 K00ANNOUNCE
-rwxr--r-- 6 root sys    344 Mar 20  2000 K06mipagent
-rwxr--r-- 6 root sys    861 Jan  5  2000 K07dmi
-rwxr--r-- 6 root sys    404 Jan  5  2000 K07snmpdx
-rw-r--r-- 3 root other    0 Jul 19 08:59 K100program
-rwxr--r-- 5 root sys   2804 Dec  2  1999 K10dtlogin
-rwxr--r-- 6 root sys    572 Dec 14  2000 K16apache
-rwxr--r-- 6 root sys   3080 Jan  5  2000 K28nfs.server
-rwxr--r-- 5 root sys    447 Jan  5  2000 K33audit
-rwxr--r-- 5 root sys    522 Dec 14  2000 K34ncad
-rwxr--r-- 5 root sys   1181 Jan  5  2000 K34ncalogd
-rwxr--r-- 5 root sys    391 Jan  5  2000 K35volmgt
-rwxr--r-- 5 root sys   1471 Jan  5  2000 K36sendmail
-rwxr--r-- 5 root sys    597 Jan  5  2000 K36utmpd
-rwxr--r-- 5 root sys   1131 Feb 23 09:29 K36wbem
-rwxr--r-- 5 root sys   1787 Jan  5  2000 K37power
```

*continues*

*continued*

```
-rwxr--r-- 5 root sys    460 Jan  5  2000 K39lp
-rwxr--r-- 5 root sys    610 Jan  5  2000 K39spc
-rwxr--r-- 5 root sys    504 Jan  5  2000 K40cron
-rwxr--r-- 5 root sys    514 Jan  5  2000 K40nscd
-rwxr--r-- 5 root sys    911 Jan  5  2000 K40syslog
-rwxr--r-- 5 root sys    945 Jan  5  2000 K40xntpd
-rwxr--r-- 5 root sys    364 Jan  5  2000 K41autofs
-rwxr--r-- 5 root sys    413 Jan  5  2000 K41ldap.client
-rwxr--r-- 3 root sys    836 Jan  5  2000 K41nfs.client
-rwxr--r-- 5 root sys   2839 Jan  5  2000 K41rpc
-rwxr--r-- 5 root sys    525 Jan  5  2000 K41slpd
-rwxr--r-- 5 root sys   7134 Jan  5  2000 K42inetsvc
-rwxr--r-- 5 root sys  11201 Jan  5  2000 K43inet
-rwxr--r-- 5 root sys   1365 Jan  5  2000 K50asppp
-rwxr--r-- 5 root sys    359 Jan  5  2000 K52llc2
-rwxr--r-- 3 root sys   1426 Feb 26 09:40 K83devfsadm
-rwxr--r-- 2 root sys    494 Jan  5  2000 K90dhcpagent

/etc/rc2.d:
total 160
-rwxr--r-- 6 root sys    344 Mar 20  2000 K06mipagent
-rwxr--r-- 6 root sys    861 Jan  5  2000 K07dmi
-rwxr--r-- 6 root sys    404 Jan  5  2000 K07snmpdx
-rwxr--r-- 6 root sys    572 Dec 14  2000 K16apache
-rwxr--r-- 6 root sys   3080 Jan  5  2000 K28nfs.server
-rw-r--r-- 1 root sys   1369 Jan  5  2000 README
-rwxr--r-- 3 root sys   1881 Jan  5  2000 S01MOUNTFSYS
-rwxr--r-- 2 root sys   2004 Jan  5  2000 S05RMTMPFILES
-rw-r--r-- 3 root other    0 Jul 19 08:59 S100program
-rwxr--r-- 2 root sys    611 Jan  5  2000 S20sysetup
-rwxr--r-- 2 root sys    989 Jan  5  2000 S21perf
-rwxr-xr-x 2 root other 1995 Dec 16  1999 S30sysid.net
-rwxr--r-- 5 root sys    359 Jan  5  2000 S40llc2
-rwxr--r-- 5 root sys   1365 Jan  5  2000 S47asppp
-rwxr--r-- 5 root sys  11201 Jan  5  2000 S69inet
-rwxr--r-- 2 root sys    327 Jan  5  2000 S70uucp
-rwxr--r-- 5 root sys    413 Jan  5  2000 S71ldap.client
-rwxr--r-- 5 root sys   2839 Jan  5  2000 S71rpc
-rwxr-xr-x 2 root other 1498 Dec 16  1999 S71sysid.sys
-rwxr-xr-x 2 root other 1558 Dec 16  1999 S72autoinstall
-rwxr--r-- 5 root sys   7134 Jan  5  2000 S72inetsvc
-rwxr--r-- 5 root sys    525 Jan  5  2000 S72slpd
-rwxr--r-- 2 root sys   1101 Jan  5  2000 S73cachefs.daemon
-rwxr--r-- 3 root sys    836 Jan  5  2000 S73nfs.client
```

```
-rwxr--r-- 5 root sys    364 Jan  5  2000 S74autofs
-rwxr--r-- 5 root sys    911 Jan  5  2000 S74syslog
-rwxr--r-- 5 root sys    945 Jan  5  2000 S74xntpd
-rwxr--r-- 5 root sys    504 Jan  5  2000 S75cron
-rwxr--r-- 2 root sys   2519 Jan  5  2000 S75savecore
-rwxr--r-- 5 root sys    514 Jan  5  2000 S76nscd
-rwxr--r-- 2 root sys    256 Jan  5  2000 S80PRESERVE
-rwxr--r-- 5 root sys    460 Jan  5  2000 S80lp
-rwxr--r-- 5 root sys    610 Jan  5  2000 S80spc
-rwxr--r-- 5 root sys   1787 Jan  5  2000 S85power
-rwxr--r-- 5 root sys   1471 Jan  5  2000 S88sendmail
-rwxr--r-- 5 root sys    597 Jan  5  2000 S88utmpd
lrwxrwxrwx 1 root other   31 Jun 25 15:57 S89bdconfig ->\
../init.d/buttons_n_dials-setup
-rwxr--r-- 5 root sys   1131 Feb 23 09:29 S90wbem
-rwxr--r-- 5 root sys    391 Jan  5  2000 S92volmgt
-rwxr--r-- 2 root sys    364 Jan  5  2000\
S93cacheos.finish
-rwxr--r-- 5 root sys   1181 Jan  5  2000 S94ncalogd
-rwxr--r-- 5 root sys    522 Dec 14  2000 S95ncad
-rwxr--r-- 5 root sys    447 Jan  5  2000 S99audit
-rwxr--5 root sys    28 04 Dec 2 1995 S99dtlogin
```

**TIP**

If you do not want a particular script to run when entering a corresponding init state, change the uppercase prefix (S or K) to some other character; I prefer lowercase (s or k). Only files with an uppercase prefix of S or K are run. For example, change S99mount to s99mount to disable the script.

## System Shutdown

Solaris has been designed to run continuously, seven days a week, 24 hours a day. Occasionally, however, you need to shut down the system to carry out administrative tasks. At other times, an application might cause the system to go awry, and the operating system must be stopped to kill off runaway processes and then be restarted.

**CAUTION**

Shutting down the system improperly can result in loss of data and the risk of corrupting the file systems.

You can shut down the system in a number of ways, using various UNIX commands. With Solaris, taking down the operating system in an orderly fashion is important. When the system boots, several processes are started. These must be shut down before you power off the system. In addition, information has been cached in memory and has not yet been written to disk. The process of shutting down Solaris involves shutting down processes, flushing data from memory to the disk, and unmounting file systems.

**TIP**

To avoid having your system shut down improperly during a power failure, use a UPS (uninterruptible power supply) capable of shutting down the system cleanly before the power is shut off.

## Commands to Shut Down the System

When preparing to shut down a system, you need to determine which of the following commands is appropriate for the system and the task at hand:

```
/usr/sbin/shutdown
/sbin/init
/usr/sbin/halt
/usr/sbin/reboot
/usr/sbin/poweroff
```

Stop+A or L1+A (to be used as a last resort; see the following Caution)

**CAUTION**

Using the Stop+A key sequence (or L1+A) abruptly breaks execution of the operating system, and should be used only as a last resort to restart the system.

The first three commands initiate shutdown procedures, kill all running processes, write data to disk, and shut down the system software to the appropriate run level. The `/usr/sbin/reboot` command does all of these tasks, but it then boots the system back to the state defined as initdefault in `/etc/inittab`. The `/usr/sbin/poweroff` command is equivalent to `init 5`. The last command, which is really a series of keystrokes, stops the system unconditionally.

### /usr/sbin/shutdown

Use the `shutdown` command when shutting down a system that has multiple users. The `shutdown` command sends a warning message to all users who are logged in, waits for 60 seconds (the default), and then shuts down the system to single-user state. A command option (`-g`) lets you choose a different default wait time. The `-i` option lets you define the init state that the system will be shut down to. The default is run level S.

The `shutdown` command performs a clean system shutdown, which means that all system processes and services are terminated normally and file systems are synchronized. You need superuser privileges to use the `shutdown` command.

When the `shutdown` command is initiated, all logged in users and all systems mounting resources receive a warning about the impending shutdown, and then they get a final message. For this reason, the `shutdown` command is recommended over the `init` command on a server with multiple users.

## STEP BY STEP

### 1.3 Shutting Down the System

1. As superuser, type the following to find out if users are logged in to the system:

```
# who
```

2. A list of all logged-in users is displayed. You might want to send mail or broadcast a message to let users know the system is being shut down.

3. Shut down the system by using the shutdown command:

```
# shutdown -i<init-state> -g<grace-period> -y
```

**TIP** When using either `shutdown` or `init`, you might want to give users more advance notice by sending an email message about any scheduled system shutdown.

The following describes the options for the `shutdown` command:

| | |
|---|---|
| `-i<init-state>` | Brings the system to an `init` state different from the default of S. The choices are 0, 1, 2, 5, and 6. |
| `-g<grace-period>` | Indicates a time (in seconds) before the system is shut down. The default is 60 seconds. |
| `-y` | Continues to shut down the system without intervention; otherwise, you are prompted to continue the shutdown process after 60 seconds. If you used the shutdown `-y` command, you are not prompted to continue; otherwise, you are asked, `Do you want to continue? (y or n)`. |

## /sbin/init

Use the `init` command to shut down a single-user system or to change its run level. The syntax is as follows:

```
init <run level>
```

`<run level>` is any run level described in Table 1.2. In addition, `<run level>` can be `a`, `b`, or `c`, which tells the system to process only /etc/inittab entries that have the a, b, or c run level set. These are pseudo-states, which can be defined to run certain commands, but which do not cause the current run level to change. `<run level>` can also be the keyword `Q` or `q`, which tells the system to re-examine the /etc/inittab file.

You can use `init` to place the system in power-down state (`init 0`) or in single-user state (`init 1`). For example, to bring the system down to run level 1 from the current run level, type the following:

```
init 1
```

The system responds with this:

```
INIT: New run level: 1
Changing to state 1.
Unmounting remote filesystems: /vol nfs done.
System services are now being stopped.
Mar 14 13:13:22 unknown /usr/sbin/vold[475]: problem unmounting /vol;
Interrupted system call
Mar 14 13:13:22 unknown pseudo: pseudo-device: tod0
Mar 14 13:13:22 unknown genunix: tod0 is /pseudo/tod@0
Mar 14 13:13:22 unknown pseudo: pseudo-device: pm0
Mar 14 13:13:22 unknown genunix: pm0 is /pseudo/pm@0
Print services stopped.
Mar 14 13:13:22 unknown syslogd: going down on signal 15
Killing user processes: done.
Change to state 1 has been completed.
Type control-d to proceed with normal startup,
(or give root password for system maintenance):
```

> **NOTE** The `telinit` command is available for compatibility. It is simply a link to the `/usr/sbin/init` command.

As another example, maybe you made a change to the /etc/inittab file and you want to have the system reread inittab and implement the change. Type the following:

```
init q
```

No system messages will be displayed, and the inittab file will be re-examined.

## /usr/sbin/halt

Use the `halt` command when the system must be stopped immediately, and it is acceptable not to warn current users. The `halt` command shuts down the system without delay, and does not warn other users on the system of the shutdown.

## /usr/sbin/reboot

Use the `reboot` command to shut down a single-user system and bring it into multiuser state. `reboot` does not warn other users on the system of the shutdown.

The Solaris `reboot` and `halt` commands perform an unconditional shutdown of system processes. These commands shut down the system much more quickly than the `shutdown` command, but not as gracefully, because they do not run the kill scripts located in /etc/rc<n>.d. No messages are sent to users. `reboot` and `halt` do not notify all logged-in users and systems mounting resources of the impending shutdown, but they do synchronize file systems.

In some cases, the quickness of such a reboot is useful in certain circumstances, such as when rebooting from the single user run state. Also, the capability to pass arguments to OpenBoot via the `reboot` command is also useful; for example:

```
reboot -- -rs
```

will reboot the system into run level s.

## /usr/sbin/poweroff

The `poweroff` command is equivalent to the `init 5` command.

> **NOTE** `init` and `shutdown` are the most reliable ways to shut down a system because they use rc scripts to kill running processes and shut down the system with minimal data loss. The `halt` and `reboot` commands do not run the rc scripts properly and are not the preferred method of shutting down the system.

# Stopping the System for Recovery Purposes

Occasionally, the system might not respond to the `init` commands specified earlier. A system that doesn't respond to anything, including `reboot` or `halt`, is called a "crashed" or "hung" system. If you try the commands just discussed but get no response, you can press Stop+A or L1+A to get back to the boot PROM (the specific Stop key sequence depends on your keyboard type). On terminals connected to the serial port, press the Break key.

> **NOTE** Solaris 8 introduced a new feature that has the capability to force a hanging system to halt. The new sequence to stop the system is <RETURN> <TILDE> <CONTROL B>, and is equivalent to Stop+A. An interval of more than 0.5 seconds must exist between characters, and the entire string must be entered in less than five seconds. This is true only with serial devices acting as consoles, and not for systems with keyboards of their own. If your console is connected to the serial port via a modem, you can send a break (Stop+A or L1+A) through the tip window by typing ~# (tilde pound sign).

The following is an example of how to break out of a hung system:

## STEP BY STEP

### 1.4 Breaking Out of a Hung System

1. Use the abort key sequence for your system (Stop+A or L1+A).

   The monitor displays the `ok` PROM prompt.

2. Type the `sync` command to synchronize the disks:

   ```
   ok sync
   ```

3. When you see the `syncing file systems` message, press the abort key sequence for your system again.

4. Type the appropriate `reset` command to reset the hardware and start the boot process:

   ```
   ok reset
   ```

5. After you receive the `login:` message, log in and type the following to verify that the system is booted to the specified run level:

   ```
   # who -r
   ```

6. The system responds with the following:

   ```
   run-level 3  Jun 9 09:19  3   0  S
   ```

## Turning Off the Power

Only after shutting down the file systems should you turn off the power to the hardware. Turn off power to all devices after the system is shut down. If necessary, also unplug the power cables. When power can be restored, use the following steps to turn on the system and devices.

## STEP BY STEP

### 1.5 Turning Off the Power

1. Plug in the power cables.
2. Turn on all peripheral devices such as disk drives, tape drives, and printers.
3. Turn on the CPU and monitor.

## CHAPTER SUMMARY

This chapter reviewed the Solaris startup and shutdown procedures. Powering up the system in the proper sequence, entering the OpenBoot PROM, booting the system, and loading the kernel were discussed.

Next, the various system init states were described, detailing how Solaris processes and services are started beginning from bootup and continuing to multiuser mode. The system administrator can further control these services by adding and removing run control scripts.

Finally, I described how important it is to shut down the system properly because the integrity of the data can be compromised if the proper shutdown steps are not performed. All the various commands used to shut down the system in an orderly manner were outlined.

In the next chapter, I'll describe OpenBoot in more detail. In the upcoming chapters, you'll learn more about the Solaris operating environment and—just as important—the computer hardware. Thorough knowledge of these two system components is essential before you can adequately troubleshoot system startup problems.

**KEY TERMS**

- Bootstrapping
- Bootblock
- Run state
- Init state
- Single-user mode
- Multiuser mode
- Run control script
- Interactive boot
- Reconfiguration boot

## APPLY YOUR KNOWLEDGE

# Exercises

Warning: Because some of the steps involved in the following exercises could render a system unbootable if not performed properly, do not perform these exercises on a production system.

### 1.1 Booting the System

This exercise takes you through the steps of powering on and booting the system.

**Estimated Time**: 5 minutes

1. Turn on power to all the peripheral devices, if any exist.
2. If the OpenBoot parameter `auto-boot` is set to false, you'll see the `ok` prompt shortly after powering on the system. If the system is set to `auto-boot`, you'll see a message similar to the following displayed on the screen:

```
SunOS Release 5.8 Version Generic_108621-04 64-bit

Copyright 1983-2000 Sun Microsystems, Inc. All
rights reserved.
```

   You'll see the system beginning the boot process. Interrupt the boot process by pressing the Stop+A keys. The `ok` prompt will appear.

3. At the `ok` prompt, type `boot` to boot the system.

### 1.2 Booting an Alternate Kernel

In this exercise, you'll practice booting from a backup copy /etc/system file. Use this process if your /etc/system file ever becomes corrupt or unbootable.

**Estimated Time:** 15 mintues

1. Log in as root.
2. Create a backup copy of the /etc/system file by typing:

```
cp /etc/system /etc/system.orig
```

3. Now remove the /etc/system file by typing:

```
rm /etc/system
```

4. Halt the system by typing:

```
/usr/sbin/shutdown -y -g0 -i0
```

5. At the `ok` prompt, boot the system using the interactive option to supply the backup name of the /etc/system file. This is done by typing:

```
boot -a
```

6. You'll be prompted to enter a filename for the kernel and a default directory for modules. Enter a `<return>` for each of these questions. When prompted to use the default `/etc/system` file:

```
Name of system file [etc/system]:
```

   enter the following:

```
/etc/system.orig
```

7. Later you'll be asked to enter the root file system type and the physical name of the root device. Enter a `<return>` for both questions.
8. When the system is ready, log in as root, and put the original `/etc/system` file back in place.

```
cp /etc/system.orig /etc/system
```

### 1.3 Using Run Control Scripts

In this exercise, practice creating run control scripts and shutting down the system.

**Estimated Time**: 10 minutes

1. Log in as root, and change to the /etc/init.d directory. Copy the file named `lp` to `test`.

```
cd /etc/init.d
cp lp test
```

## APPLY YOUR KNOWLEDGE

2. Use the vi editor to edit the file named test. Replace line 16 that reads

```
[ -f /usr/lib/lpsched ] && /usr/lib/lpsched
```

with a line that reads

```
echo ""; /usr/bin/banner "Ready"; echo ""
```

Now replace line 20 that currently reads

```
[ -f /usr/lib/lpshut ] && /usr/lib/lpshut
```

with the following line:

```
echo ""; /usr/bin/banner "System going
down"; echo ""
```

3. Verify that the test script runs properly with the start and stop arguments.

```
./test start
./test stop
```

4. Change to the /etc/rc2.d directory, and create a hard link to the test script that you just created.

```
cd /etc/rc2.d
ln /etc/init.d/test S22test
```

5. Change to the /etc/rcS.d directory, and create another link to the test script that will run when the system goes into run level S.

```
cd /etc/rcS.d
ln /etc/init.d/test K99test
```

6. Shut down the system to single user mode, and watch the output on the console. Does the shutdown message from the K99test script appear?

```
init S
```

7. Now halt the system.

```
/usr/sbin/shutdown -y -g0 -i0
```

8. At the ok prompt, boot up the system again, and watch the system messages on the console. Does the startup message from the S22test script appear?

```
boot
```

## Review Questions

1. Select the sequence of events that best describes the boot process.

   A. Boot PROM phase, boot program phase, kernel initialization phase, init phase

   B. Boot program phase, boot PROM phase, kernel initialization phase, init phase

   C. Boot program phase, boot PROM phase, init phase, kernel initialization phase

   D. Boot PROM phase, boot program phase, init phase, kernel initialization phase

2. What consists of a small static core and many dynamically loadable modules?

   A. kernel

   B. ufsboot

   C. shell

   D. bootblock

3. By default, how many usable system run states does Solaris 8 have?

   A. 3

   B. 7

   C. 6

   D. 8

## APPLY YOUR KNOWLEDGE

4. At this run state, all file systems are still available, and any logged-in users can remain logged in. All services except the most basic operating system services are shut down in an orderly manner.

   A. S

   B. 1

   C. 2

   D. 0

5. What is the first task for the kernel to start up?

   A. `sched`

   B. `init`

   C. `ufsboot`

   D. `load loadable modules`

6. How can system messages displayed at bootup be viewed later?

   A. By issuing the `dmesg` command

   B. By viewing the /var/messages file

   C. By issuing the `sysdef` command

   D. By viewing the /etc/boot.log file

7. To boot a system into single user state, what command is entered at the `ok` prompt?

   A. `boot`

   B. `boot -s`

   C. `boot -a`

   D. `boot -n`

8. Which command, typed at the `ok` prompt, stops and asks for input during the boot process?

   A. `boot -i`

   B. `boot -a`

   C. `boot -v`

   D. `boot -s`

9. Which of the following programs examines the contents of the /etc/inittab file to determine the order for starting up other processes and what to do when one of these processes ends?

   A. init

   B. boot

   C. kernel

   D. swapper

10. On a hung system, what is the proper sequence of operations if your system will not respond?

    A. Stop+A, sync, reset

    B. Stop+A, boot

    C. Stop+A, reset

    D. Stop+A, reset, sync, boot

11. Which of the following commands is equivalent to the init 5 command?

    A. `poweroff`

    B. `halt`

    C. `reboot`

    D. `boot -s`

## APPLY YOUR KNOWLEDGE

12. Which of the following programs is responsible for executing ufsboot?

    A. bootblock

    B. Kernel

    C. init

    D. boot

13. What command is used to change run levels?

    A. `run`

    B. `init`

    C. `kill`

    D. `su`

14. The respawn action in the /etc/inittab file does the following:

    A. Restarts the command

    B. Reboots the system

    C. Restarts all system processes

    D. Waits for a command to be completed

15. Where are the startup scripts for run state 3 located?

    A. /etc/rc.boot

    B. /etc/rc3

    C. /etc/rc3.d

    D. /sbin/rc3

16. What is the best method to add a run control script for run state 3?

    A. Add the script to /usr/local/bin

    B. Add the script to /etc/init.d, and link it to the /etc/rc3.d directory

    C. Add the script to /etc/rc3.d, and make a link to /etc/init.d

    D. Add the script to /sbin/rc3

## Answers to Review Questions

1. **A.** The boot process goes through the following four phases: Boot PROM phase, boot program phase, kernel initialization phase, and init phase.

2. **A.** The kernel consists of a two-piece static core called `genunix` and `unix.` `genunix` is the platform-independent generic kernel file, and `unix` is the platform-specific kernel file. When the system boots, `ufsboot` combines these two files and many dynamically loadable modules into memory to form the running kernel.

3. **B.** Solaris 8 has eight run states, but because run state 4 is currently not used, it only has seven usable run states.

4. **B.** Run level 1 is a single-user (system administrator) state in which all file systems are still available, and any logged-in users can remain logged in. All services except the most basic operating system services are shut down in an orderly manner.

## APPLY YOUR KNOWLEDGE

5. **A.** The first task for the kernel is to start the swapper process. The swapper process is the part of the kernel that schedules all other processes. The swapper has a process ID of 0, and is named sched. Its first job is to start up the init process.

6. **A.** Use the `dmesg` command to view system messages that were displayed during the boot process.

7. **B.** Issue the `boot -s` command at the OpenBoot `ok` prompt to boot the system into single user mode.

8. **B.** The `boot -a` command performs an interactive boot. With this option, you'll be prompted to enter the name of the kernel, the default modules directory, the name of the system file, the root file system type, and the device name for the root device.

9. **A.** The `/sbin/init` command generates processes to set up the system based on the directions in /etc/inittab. The init process is the parent of all other processes. It examines the contents of the /etc/inittab file to determine the order for starting up other processes and what to do when one of these processes ends.

10. **A.** Stop the operating system using the Stop+A abort key sequence. Type the `sync` command to synchronize the disks. At the `ok` prompt, type the `reset` command to reset the hardware and start the boot process.

11. **A.** The `poweroff` command is equivalent to the `init 5` command, which takes the system into run state 5, the Power-down state.

12. **A.** The `bootblk` program finds and executes the secondary boot program, called `ufsboot`, from the ufs file system and loads it into memory.

13. **B.** Use the `init` command to change run levels.

14. **A.** In the /etc/inittab file, the respawn statement will restart the process if it dies.

15. **C.** A corresponding directory named /etc/rc<n>.d contains scripts to perform various actions for that run level. For example, startup scripts for run level 3 are located in the /etc/rc3.d directory.

16. **B.** To add a run control script for run state 3, add the script to the /etc/init.d directory and link it, via a hard link, to the /etc/rc3.d directory.

## OBJECTIVES

The following test objectives are covered in this chapter:

**Understand the OpenBoot environment, architecture, and interface**

- The system administrator must be familiar with the following OpenBoot topics:

**Get help in OpenBoot**

- You should understand all of the commands available in OpenBoot. In addition, its helpful to understand the help facility in OpenBoot to obtain additional information on commands and parameters.

**Use OpenBoot PROM commands to view system configuration information**

- The system administrator needs to understand how to identify hardware components via the OpenBoot PROM. You'll need a complete understanding of how to use OpenBoot commands to set and modify configuration parameters that control system boot up and hardware behavior.

**Set and display PROM full device names**

- Devices have unique names, representing both the type of the device and location of that device in the system-addressing structure called the device tree. It's important that you understand the components of device names, the commands used to examine the device tree, and device aliases.

**Manipulate custom device aliases**

- Within OpenBoot, you'll need to understand how to set and display permanent and temporary device aliases.

**Set up OpenBoot security**

- This chapter will describe how to set up security so only those authorized have access to the OpenBoot interface and commands.

CHAPTER 2

# OpenBoot

## OBJECTIVES

**Use OpenBoot PROM commands to perform basic hardware testing**

- You'll learn how to perform diagnostics on system hardware, from the OpenBoot PROM, to verify connectivity to peripherals.

**Use the `boot` command**

- You'll learn the various methods used to start the system up into single- and multiuser mode.

**Load the kernel**

- As system administrator, you'll need to understand all of the steps necessary to load the kernel so that you are equipped to troubleshoot startup problems.
- The system administrator needs to understand the primary functions of the OpenBoot environment, which includes the programmable read-only memory (PROM). A complete understanding of how to use many of the OpenBoot commands and how to set and modify all of the configuration parameters that control system bootup and hardware behavior is required.

## OUTLINE

## Study Strategies

The following strategies will help you prepare for the exam:

- When studying this chapter, I suggest that you practice each step-by-step process that I've outlined on a Sun system. Unfortunately, an Intel-based system running Solaris 8 does not provide the OpenBoot environment necessary to practice every topic that is described in this chapter. Practice working in the OpenBoot environment using the various OpenBoot commands presented in this chapter.
- Check out the hardware configuration of your Sun system using the various OpenBoot commands presented in this chapter. Familiarize yourself with all the devices associated with your system. You should be able to identify each hardware component by its device path name.
- Practice creating both temporary and permanent device aliases. In addition, practice setting the various OpenBoot system parameters that I've described in this chapter.
- Finally, practice booting the system using the various methods described. Understand how to boot to an alternate kernel or system file.

## INTRODUCTION

Chapter 1, "System Startup and Shutdown," provided a general overview of the startup process, presented an introduction to OpenBoot, and gave specifics on /sbin/init, run levels, and run control scripts. This chapter provides more details on the OpenBoot firmware and kernel loading.

## OPENBOOT ENVIRONMENT

The hardware-level user interface that you see before the operating system starts is called the OpenBoot PROM (OBP). OpenBoot is based on an interactive command interpreter that gives you access to an extensive set of functions for hardware and software development, fault isolation, and debugging. The OBP firmware is stored in the socketed startup PROM (Programmable Read-Only Memory). The OpenBoot PROM consists of two 8KB chips on the system board: the startup PROM itself, which contains extensive firmware allowing access to user-written startup drivers and extended diagnostics, and an NVRAM (Non-Volatile Random-Access Memory) chip.

The NVRAM chip has user-definable system parameters and writeable areas for user-controlled diagnostics, macros, and device aliases. The NVRAM is where the system identification information is stored, such as the hostid, Ethernet address, and time of day (TOD) clock. A single lithium battery backup provides backup for the NVRAM and clock. Many software packages use this hostid for licensing purposes; therefore, it is important that this chip can be removed and placed into any replacement system board.

OpenBoot is currently at version 3, which is the version I describe in this chapter. Depending on the age of your system, you could have PROM version 1, 2, or 3 installed. The original boot PROM firmware, version 1, was first introduced on the Sun SPARCstation 1. The first version of the OpenBoot PROM was version 2, which first appeared on the SPARCstation 2 system. OpenBoot version 3 is the version currently available on the Ultra series systems. Version 3 of the OpenBoot architecture provides a significant increase in functionality over the boot PROMs in earlier Sun systems. One notable feature of the OpenBoot firmware is a programmable user interface, based on the interactive programming language Forth. In Forth, sequences of user commands can be combined to form complete programs. This capability provides a powerful tool for debugging hardware and software. Another benefit of version 3 is the flash update feature. You can update the version 3 firmware without replacing the PROM chip.

> **NOTE**
> The Intel environment has no OpenBoot PROM or NVRAM. On Intel systems, before the kernel is started, the system is controlled by the read-only-memory (ROM) Basic Input/Output System (BIOS), the firmware interface on a PC.

## Single Versus Multiple CPU Systems

The following system types have only one system board, and hold only one boot PROM and NVRAM chip:

- SPARCstation 4, 5, 10, and 20
- ULTRA 1, 2, 5, 10, 30, 60, 80, 220, 250, 240, 420, and 450

All other systems can be configured with multiple system boards, and have a special boot PROM and NVRAM arrangement. The following list provides some things of which you should be aware on multiple CPU systems:

- These systems have a clock board to oversee the backplane communications.
- The HOSTID and Ethernet address are on the clock board, and are automatically downloaded to the NVRAM on all CPU boards when the Power-On Self-Test (POST) is complete.
- PROM contents on each CPU are compared and verified by checksums.
- The CPU located in the lower most card cage slot is the master CPU board.
- Each CPU runs its own individual POST.

## Accessing the OpenBoot Environment

You can get to the OpenBoot environment by using any one of the following commands previously discussed in Chapter 1:

- By halting the operating system.
- By pressing the Stop and A keys simultaneously (Stop+A). On terminals connected to the serial port, press the Break key.

NOTE

Solaris 8 introduced a new feature, which gives the ability to force a hanging system to halt. The new sequence to stop the system is Enter+~+Ctrl+B, which is equivalent to the Stop+A. There must be an interval of more than 0.5 seconds between characters, and the entire string must be entered in less than five seconds. This is true only with serial devices acting as consoles, and not for systems with keyboards of their own. If your console is connected to the serial port via a modem, you can send a break (Stop+A or L1+A) through the tip window by typing ~# (tilde+pound sign).

CAUTION

Forcing the system into the OpenBoot PROM using STOP+A or BREAK abruptly breaks execution of the operating system. It should be used only as a last effort to restart the system.

- When the system is initially powered on. If your system is not configured to start up automatically, it will stop at the user interface. If automatic startup is configured, you can make the system stop at the user interface by pressing the Stop+A keys after the display console banner is displayed, but before the system begins starting the operating system.
- If the system hardware detects an error from which it cannot recover. (This is known as a Watchdog Reset.)

## OpenBoot Firmware Tasks

The primary tasks of the OpenBoot firmware are as follows:

- Test and initialize the system hardware.
- Determine the hardware configuration.
- Start the operating system from either a mass storage device or a network.
- Provide interactive debugging facilities for testing hardware and software.
- Allow modification and management of system startup configuration, such as NVRAM parameters.

Specifically, OpenBoot will perform the following tasks necessary to initialize the operating system kernel:

1. Display system identification information and then run self-test diagnostics to verify the system's hardware and memory. These checks are known as POST (Power-On Self-Test).
2. Load the primary startup program, `bootblk`, from the default startup device.
3. The `bootblk` program finds and executes the secondary startup program, `ufsboot`, and loads it into memory.

   The `ufsboot` program loads the operating system kernel.

## OpenBoot Architecture

The OpenBoot architecture provides an increase in functionality and portability when compared to the proprietary systems of some other hardware vendors. Although this architecture was first implemented by Sun Microsystems as OpenBoot on SPARC (Scaleable Processor Architecture) systems, its design is processor-independent. Following are some notable features of OpenBoot firmware:

- Plug-in device drivers. A device driver that can be loaded from a plug-in device, such as an SBus card. The plug-in device driver can be used to boot the operating system from that device or to display text on the device before the operating system has activated its own software device drivers. This feature lets the input and output devices evolve without changing the system PROM.
- FCode interpreter. Plug-in drivers are written in a machine-independent interpreted language called FCode. Each OpenBoot system PROM contains an FCode interpreter. This allows the same device and driver to be used on machines with different CPU instruction sets.
- Device tree. Devices called nodes are attached to a host computer through a hierarchy of interconnected buses on the device tree. A node representing the host computer's main physical address bus forms the tree's root node. Both the user and the operating system can determine the system's hardware configuration by viewing the device tree.

  Nodes with children usually represent buses and their associated controllers, if any. Each such node defines a physical address space that distinguishes the devices connected to the node from one another. Each child of that node is assigned a physical address in the parent's address space. The physical address generally represents a physical characteristic unique to the device (such as the bus address or the slot number where the device is installed). The use of physical addresses to identify devices prevents device addresses from changing when other devices are installed or removed.

NOTE

Refer to ANSI X3.215-1994 (American National Standards Institute) if you're interested in more information on Forth.

- Programmable user interface. The OpenBoot user interface is based on the programming language Forth, which provides an interactive programming environment. It is a language that is used for direct communication between humans and machines. It can be quickly expanded and adapted to special needs and different hardware systems. You'll see Forth used not only by Sun, but also by other hardware vendors, such as Hewlett-Packard.

# OpenBoot Interface

The OpenBoot firmware provides a command-line interface for the user at the system console. On older Sun systems, such as the SPARCstation10 and SPARCstation20, this command-line interface had two modes: the Restricted Monitor and the Forth Monitor.

## The Restricted Monitor

The Restricted Monitor provides a simple set of commands to initiate booting of the system, resume system execution, or enter the Forth Monitor. The Restricted Monitor is also used to implement system security.

The Restricted Monitor prompt is >. When you enter the Restricted Monitor, the following screen is displayed, showing the commands you can enter:

```
Type b (boot), c (continue), or n (new command mode) >
```

The Restricted Monitor commands are listed in Table 2.1.

**TABLE 2.1**

**Restricted Monitor Commands**

| *Command* | *Description* |
|---|---|
| b | Boots the operating system. |
| c | Resumes the execution of a halted program. |
| n | Enters the Forth Monitor (commonly referred to as "new command mode"). |

## The Forth Monitor

The Forth Monitor, the default mode in OpenBoot, is an interactive command interpreter that gives you access to an extensive set of functions for hardware and software diagnosis. These functions are available to anyone who has access to the system console.

The Forth Monitor prompt is `ok`. When you enter the Forth Monitor mode, the following line is displayed:

```
Type help for more information ok
```

On older SPARCstations, if you want to leave the Forth Monitor mode and get into the Restricted Monitor mode, type the following:

```
ok old-mode
```

Old mode is not available on UltraSparc systems.

> **NOTE** When the system is halted, the PROM monitor prompt is displayed. The type of prompt depends on your system type. Older Sun systems, such as the Sun4/nnn series, use the greater-than sign (>) as the PROM prompt. Newer Sun systems use `ok` as the PROM prompt but support the > prompt. To switch from the > prompt to the `ok` prompt on newer Sun systems, type `n` at the > prompt.

# GETTING HELP IN OPENBOOT

You can obtain help at any time on the various Forth commands supported in OpenBoot by using the `help` command. The syntax for using help from the `ok` prompt is any of the choices listed in Table 2.2.

**TABLE 2.2**

**OPENBOOT HELP**

| *Command* | *Description* |
|---|---|
| `help` | Displays instructions about using the help system, and lists the available help categories. |
| `help <category>` | Shows help for all commands in the category. Use only the first word of the category description. |
| `help <command>` | Shows help for the individual command. |

Because of the large number of commands, help is available only for commands that are used frequently.

The following example shows the `help` command with no arguments:

```
ok help
```

The system responds with the following:

```
Enter 'help command-name' or 'help category-name' for more help
(Use ONLY the first word of a category description)
Examples:  help select -or- help line
    Main categories are:
Repeated loops
Defining new commands
Numeric output
Radix (number base conversions)
Arithmetic
Memory access
Line editor
System and boot configuration parameters
Select I/O devices
Floppy eject
Power on reset
Diag (diagnostic routines)
Resume execution
File download and boot
nvramrc (making new commands permanent)
ok
```

If you want to see the help messages for all commands in the category `diag`, for example, type the following:

```
ok help diag
```

The system responds with this:

```
test  <device-specifier>   Run selftest method for specified device
  Examples:
    test floppy   - test floppy disk drive
    test net      - test net
    test scsi     - test scsi
test-all        Execute test for all devices with selftest method
watch-clock     Show ticks of real-time clock
watch-net       Monitor network broadcast packets
watch-net-all   Monitor broadcast packets on all net interfaces
```

```
probe-scsi      Show attached SCSI devices
probe-scsi-all  Show attached SCSI devices for all host adapters
ok
```

If you want help for a specific command, type the following:

```
ok help test
```

Help responds with the following:

```
test  <device-specifier>   Run selftest method for specified device
  Examples:
    test floppy    - test floppy disk drive
    test net       - test net
    test scsi      - test scsi
test-all        Execute test for all devices with selftest method
watch-clock     Show ticks of real-time clock
watch-net       Monitor network broadcast packets
watch-net-all   Monitor broadcast packets on all net interfaces
probe-scsi      Show attached SCSI devices
probe-scsi-all  Show attached SCSI devices for all host adapters
ok
```

## PROM Full Device Names

OpenBoot deals directly with hardware devices in the system. Each device has a unique name, representing both the type of device and the location of that device in the system-addressing structure called the device tree. The OpenBoot firmware builds a device tree for all devices from information gathered at POST. The device tree is loaded into memory to be used by the kernel during boot to identify all configured devices. The following example shows a full device pathname for a system with SBus architecture, such as a SPARCstation20:

```
/sbus@1f,0/esp@0,40000/sd@3,0:a
```

This example shows a full device pathname for a PCI bus system, such as an Ultra5:

```
/pci@1f,0/pci@1,1/ide@3/disk
```

The next example shows the disk device on an Ultra system with a PCI-SCSI bus:

```
/pci@1f,0/pci@1/isptwo@4/sd@3,0
```

A full device pathname is a series of node names separated by slashes (/). The root of the tree is the machine node, which is not named explicitly, but is indicated by a leading slash (/). Each device pathname has this form:

```
driver-name@unit-address:device-arguments
```

The components of the device pathname are described in Table 2.3.

**TABLE 2.3**

**DEVICE PATHNAME PARAMETERS**

| *Parameter* | *Description* |
|---|---|
| `driver-name` | A human-readable string consisting of 1 to 31 letters, digits, and the following punctuation characters: , . _ + -.<br><br>Uppercase and lowercase characters are distinct. In some cases, the driver name includes the name of the device's manufacturer and the device's model name, separated by a comma. Typically, the manufacturer's uppercase, publicly listed stock symbol is used as the manufacturer's name (that is, SUNW,hme0). For built-in devices, the manufacturer's name is usually omitted (that is, sbus or pci).<br><br>@ must precede the address parameter, and serves as a separator between the driver name and unit address. |
| `unit-address` | A text string representing the physical address of the device in its parent's address space. The exact meaning of a particular address depends on the bus to which the device is attached. In this example:<br><br>`/sbus@1f,0/esp@0,40000/sd@3,0:a`<br><br>`1f,0` represents an address on the main system bus, because the SBus is directly attached to the main system bus in this example.<br><br>`0,40000` is an SBus slot number. The example shows that the device is in SBus slot 0 and the offset is `40000`.<br><br>`3,0` is a SCSI target and logical unit number. In the example, the disk device is attached to a SCSI bus at target 3, logical unit 0. |

| *Parameter* | *Description* |
|---|---|
| `device-arguments` | A text string whose format depends on the particular device. It can be used to pass additional information to the device's software. In this example: `/sbus@1f,0/scsi@2,1/sd@3,0:a` The argument for the disk device is "a." The software driver for this device interprets its argument as a disk partition, so the device pathname refers to partition "a" on that disk. |

The OpenBoot command `show-devs` is used to obtain information about devices and to display device pathnames. This command displays all the devices known to the system directly beneath a given device in the device hierarchy. `show-devs` used by itself shows the entire device tree. The syntax is as follows:

```
show-devs [device path]
```

An example is as follows:

```
ok show-devs
```

The system outputs the following information:

```
/TI,TMS390Z50@f,f8fffffc
/eccmemctl@f,0
/virtual-memory@0,0
/memory@0,0
/obio
/iommu@f,e0000000
/openprom
/aliases
/options
/packages
/obio/power@0,a01000
/obio/auxio@0,800000
/obio/SUNW,fdtwo@0,700000
/obio/interrupt@0,400000
/obio/counter@0,300000
/obio/eeprom@0,200000
/obio/zs@0,0
/obio/zs@0,100000
/iommu@f,e0000000/sbus@f,e0001000
/iommu@f,e0000000/sbus@f,e0001000/cgsix@2,0
/iommu@f,e0000000/sbus@f,e0001000/SUNW,DBRIe@f,8010000
/iommu@f,e0000000/sbus@f,e0001000/SUNW,bpp@f,4800000
/iommu@f,e0000000/sbus@f,e0001000/ledma@f,400010
/iommu@f,e0000000/sbus@f,e0001000/espdma@f,400000
/iommu@f,e0000000/sbus@f,e0001000/SUNW,DBRIe@f,8010000/mmcodec
/iommu@f,e0000000/sbus@f,e0001000/ledma@f,400010/le@f,c00000
```

```
/iommu@f,e0000000/sbus@f,e0001000/espdma@f,400000/esp@f,800000
/iommu@f,e0000000/sbus@f,e0001000/espdma@f,400000/esp@f,800000/st
/iommu@f,e0000000/sbus@f,e0001000/espdma@f,400000/esp@f,800000/sd
/packages/obp-tftp
/packages/deblocker
/packages/disk-label
```

Commands used to examine the device tree are listed in Table 2.4.

**TABLE 2.4**

**COMMANDS FOR BROWSING THE DEVICE TREE**

| *Command* | *Description* |
|---|---|
| `.properties` | Displays the names and values of the current node's properties. |
| `dev device-path` | Chooses the specified device node, making it the current node. |
| `dev node-name` | Searches for a node with the specified name in the subtree below the current node, and chooses the first such node found. |
| `dev ..` | Chooses the device node that is the parent of the current node. |
| `dev /` | Chooses the root machine node. |
| `device-end` | Leaves the device tree. |
| `"device-path" find-device` | Chooses the specified device node, similar to `dev`. |
| `ls` | Displays the names of the current node's children. |
| `pwd` | Displays the device pathname that names the current node. |
| `see wordname` | Decompiles the specified word. |
| `show-devs [device-path]` | Displays all the devices known to the system directly beneath a given device in the device hierarchy. `show-devs` used by itself shows the entire device tree. |
| `words` | Displays the names of the current node's methods. |
| `"device-path" select-dev` | Selects the specified device and makes it the active node. |

## OpenBoot Device Aliases

Device pathnames can be long and complex to enter. The concept of device aliases, like UNIX aliases, allows a short name to be substituted for a long name. An alias represents an entire device pathname, not a component of it. For example, the alias `disk0` might represent the following device pathname:

```
/sbus@1,f8000000/esp@0,40000/sd@3,0:a
```

OpenBoot has the predefined device aliases listed in Table 2.5 for commonly used devices, so you rarely need to type a full device pathname.

**TABLE 2.5**

**PREDEFINED DEVICE ALIASES**

| *Alias* | *Device Pathname* |
|---|---|
| disk | /pci@1f,0/pci@1,1/ide@3/disk@0,0 |
| disk0 | /pci@1f,0/pci@1,1/ide@3/disk@0,0 |
| disk1 | /pci@1f,0/pci@1,1/ide@3/disk@1,0 |
| disk2 | /pci@1f,0/pci@1,1/ide@3/disk@2,0 |
| disk3 | /pci@1f,0/pci@1,1/ide@3/disk@3,0 |
| cdrom | /pci@1f,0/pci@1,1/ide@3/cdrom@2,0:f |

NOTE: Device pathnames can vary on each platform. The device aliases shown in Table 2.5 are from a Sun Ultra5 system.

If you add disk drives or change the target of the startup drive, you might need to modify these device aliases. Table 2.6 describes the `devalias` command, which is used to examine, create, and change OpenBoot aliases.

**TABLE 2.6**

**devalias**

| *Command* | *Description* |
|---|---|
| devalias | Displays all current device aliases. |
| devalias_alias | Displays the device pathname corresponding to alias. |
| devalias_alias device-path | Defines an alias representing device-path. |

NOTE: If an alias with the same name already exists, the new value overwrites the old.

The following example creates a device alias named `disk3`, which represents a SCSI disk with a target ID of 3 on a SPARCstation10 system:

```
devalias disk3 /iommu/sbus/espdma@f,400000/esp@f,800000/sd@3,0
```

To confirm the alias, type `devalias`, and the system will print all the aliases:

```
ok devalias
screen          /iommu@f,e0000000/sbus@f,e0001000/cgsix@2,0
disk5           /iommu/sbus/espdma@f,400000/esp@f,800000/sd@0,0
floppy          /obio/SUNW,fdtwo
scsi            /iommu/sbus/espdma@f,400000/esp@f,800000
net-aui         /iommu/sbus/ledma@f,400010:aui/le@f,c00000
net-tpe         /iommu/sbus/ledma@f,400010:tpe/le@f,c00000
net             /iommu/sbus/ledma@f,400010/le@f,c00000
disk            /iommu/sbus/espdma@f,400000/esp@f,800000/sd@3,0
cdrom           /iommu/sbus/espdma@f,400000/esp@f,800000/sd@6,0:d
tape            /iommu/sbus/espdma@f,400000/esp@f,800000/st@4,0
tape0           /iommu/sbus/espdma@f,400000/esp@f,800000/st@4,0
tape1           /iommu/sbus/espdma@f,400000/esp@f,800000/st@5,0
disk3           /iommu/sbus/espdma@f,400000/esp@f,800000/sd@3,0
disk2           /iommu/sbus/espdma@f,400000/esp@f,800000/sd@2,0
disk1           /iommu/sbus/espdma@f,400000/esp@f,800000/sd@1,0
disk0           /iommu/sbus/espdma@f,400000/esp@f,800000/sd@3,0
ttyb            /obio/zs@0,100000:b
ttya            /obio/zs@0,100000:a
keyboard!       /obio/zs@0,0:forcemode
keyboard        /obio/zs@0,0
```

User-defined aliases are lost after a system reset or power cycle unless you create a permanent alias. If you want to create permanent aliases, you can either manually store the `devalias` command in a portion of non-volatile RAM (NVRAM) called `nvramrc`, or use the `nvalias` and `nvunalias` commands. The following section describes how to configure permanent settings in the NVRAM on a Sun system.

# OPENBOOT NON-VOLATILE RAM (NVRAM)

System configuration variables are stored in the system NVRAM. These OpenBoot variables determine the startup machine configuration and related communication characteristics. You can modify the values of the configuration variables, and any changes you make remain in effect, even after a power cycle. Configuration variables should be adjusted cautiously, however.

Table 2.7 describes OpenBoot's NVRAM configuration variables, their default values, and their functions.

**TABLE 2.7**

**NVRAM VARIABLES**

| *Variable* | *Default* | *Description* |
|---|---|---|
| `auto-boot?` | true | If true, start up automatically after power on or reset. |
| `boot-command` | boot | Command that is executed if `auto-boot?` is true. |
| `boot-device` | disk or net | Device from which to start up. |
| `boot-file` | Empty string | Arguments passed to the started program. |
| `diag-device` | net | Diagnostic startup source device. |
| `diag-file` | Empty string | Arguments passed to the startup program in diagnostic mode. |
| `diag-switch?` | false | If true, run in diagnostic mode. |
| `fcode-debug?` | false | If true, include name fields for plug-in device FCodes. |
| `input-device` | keyboard | Console input device (usually keyboard, ttya, or ttyb). |
| `nvramrc` | Empty | Contents of NVRAMRC. |
| `oem-banner` | Empty string | Custom OEM banner (enabled by `oem-banner?` true). |
| `oem-banner?` | false | If true, use custom OEM banner. |

*continues*

**TABLE 2.7** *continued*

**NVRAM VARIABLES**

| *Variable* | *Default* | *Description* |
|---|---|---|
| `oem-logo` | No default | Byte array custom OEM logo (enabled by `oem-logo?` true). Displayed in hexadecimal. |
| `oem-logo?` | false | If true, use custom OEM logo; otherwise, use Sun logo. |
| `output-device` | screen | Console output device (usually screen, ttya, or ttyb). |
| `sbus-probe-list` | 0123 | Which SBus slots to probe and in what order. |
| `screen-#columns` | 80 | Number of onscreen columns (characters/line). |
| `screen-#rows` | 34 | Number of onscreen rows (lines). |
| `security-#badlogins` | No default | Number of incorrect security password attempts. |
| `security-mode` | none | Firmware security level (options: none, command, or full). |
| `security-password` | No default | Firmware security password (never displayed). |
| `use-nvramrc?` | false | If true, execute commands in NVRAMRC during system startup. |

**NOTE** Older SPARC systems, because they use older versions of OpenBoot, might use different defaults or different configuration variables. As mentioned earlier, this text describes OpenBoot version 3.

The NVRAM configuration variables can be viewed and changed using the commands listed in Table 2.8.

**TABLE 2.8**

**VIEWING OR MODIFYING CONFIGURATION VARIABLES**

| *Command* | *Description* |
|---|---|
| `password` | Sets the security password. |
| `printenv` | Displays the current value and the default value for each variable. To show the current value of a named variable, type `printenv <parameter name>`. |
| `setenv variable value` | Sets the variable to the given decimal or text value. Changes are permanent, but they often take effect only after a reset. |

| *Command* | *Description* |
|---|---|
| `set-default variable` | Resets the value of the variable to the factory default. |
| `set-defaults` | Resets variable values to the factory defaults. |

The following examples illustrate the use of the commands described in Table 2.8.

All commands are entered at the `ok` OpenBoot prompt.

```
ok printenv
```

The system responds with this:

```
Variable Name          Value                            Default Value
tpe-link-test?         true                             true
scsi-initiator-id      7                                7
keyboard-click?        false                            false
keymap
ttyb-rts-dtr-off       false                            false
ttyb-ignore-cd         true                             true
ttya-rts-dtr-off       false                            false
ttya-ignore-cd         true                             true
ttyb-mode              9600,8,n,1,-                     9600,8,n,1,-
ttya-mode              9600,8,n,1,-                     9600,8,n,1,-
pcia-probe-list        1,2,3,4                          1,2,3,4
pcib-probe-list        1,2,3                            1,2,3
mfg-mode               off                              off
diag-level             max                              max
#power-cycles          89
system-board-serial#
system-board-date
fcode-debug?           false                            false
output-device          screen                           screen
input-device           keyboard                         keyboard
load-base              16384                            16384
boot-command           boot                             boot
auto-boot?             false                            true
watchdog-reboot?       false                            false
diag-file
diag-device            net                              net
boot-file
boot-device            disk:a disk net                  disk net
local-mac-address?     false                            false
ansi-terminal?         true                             true
```

> **NOTE**
> Depending on the version of OpenBoot you have on your system, the `printenv` command might show slightly different results. For this example, I used a system running OpenBoot version 3.15.

```
screen-#columns        80           80
screen-#rows           34           34
silent-mode?           false        false
use-nvramrc?           false        false
nvramrc
security-mode          none
security-password
security-#badlogins    0
oem-logo
oem-logo?              false        false
oem-banner
oem-banner?            false        false
hardware-revision
last-hardware-update
diag-switch?           false        false
```

To set the `auto-boot?` variable to false, type the following:

```
ok setenv auto-boot? false
```

Verify the setting by typing the following:

```
ok printenv auto-boot?
```

The system will respond with this:

```
auto-boot?     false     true
```

To reset the variable to its default setting, type the following:

```
ok set-default auto-boot?
```

Verify the setting by typing the following:

```
ok printenv auto-boot?
```

The system will respond with this:

```
auto-boot?     true     true
```

To reset all variables to their default settings, type the following:

```
ok set-defaults
```

It's also possible to set these variables from the UNIX command line by issuing the `eeprom` command. You must be logged-in as root to issue these commands, and although anyone can view a parameter, only root can change the value of a parameter. For example, to set the `auto-boot?` variable to true, type the following at the UNIX prompt:

```
eeprom auto-boot?=true
```

Any user can view the OpenBoot configuration variables from a UNIX prompt by typing the following:

```
/usr/sbin/eeprom
```

For example, to change the OpenBoot parameter `security-password` from the command line, you must be logged in as root and issue the following command:

```
example# eeprom security-password=
Changing PROM password:
New password:
Retype new password:
```

The security password you assign must be between zero and eight characters. Any characters after the eighth are ignored. You do not have to reset the system; the security feature takes effect as soon as you type the command.

With no parameters, the `eeprom` command will display all the OpenBoot configuration settings, similar to the OpenBoot `printenv` command.

The NVRAM commands listed in Table 2.9 can be used to modify devaliases so that they remain permanent, even after a restart.

**CAUTION**

Setting the security mode and password can leave a system unable to boot if you forget the password. It is impossible to break in without sending the CPU to Sun to have the PROM reset. OpenBoot security is discussed more in the next section.

**NOTE**

If you change an NVRAM setting on a SPARC system and the system will no longer start up, it is possible to reset the NVRAM variables to their default settings by holding down the Stop+N keys simultaneously while the machine is powering up. When issuing this command, hold down Stop+N immediately after turning on the power to the SPARC system; keep these keys pressed for a few seconds or until you see the banner (if the display is available). This is a good technique to force a system's NVRAM variables to a known condition.

**TABLE 2.9**

### NVRAM Commands

| *Command* | *Description* |
|---|---|
| `nvalias alias device-path` | Stores the command `devalias alias device-path` in NVRAMRC. (The alias persists until the `nvunalias` or `set-defaults` commands are executed.) Turns on `use-nvramrc`? |
| `nvunalias alias` | Deletes the corresponding alias from NVRAMRC. |

For example, to permanently create a devalias named `disk3`, which will represent a SCSI disk with a target ID of 3 on a SPARCstation10 system, type the following:

```
nvalias disk3/iommu/sbus/espdma@f,400000/esp@f,800000/sd@3,0
```

## nvedit

On systems with a PROM version of 1.x or 2.x, the `nvalias` command might not be available. On these systems, you'll need to use the `nvedit` command to create custom device aliases. `nvedit` is a line editor that edits the NVRAMRC directly, has a set of editing commands, and operates in a temporary buffer. The following is a sample `nvedit` session:

```
ok setenv use-nvramrc? true
```

The system responds with the following:

```
use-nvramrc? =     true
ok nvedit
  0: devalias pgx24 /pci@1f,0/pci@1,1/SUNW,m64B
  1: devalias disk0 /pci@1f,0/pci@1,1/ide@3/disk@0,0
  2: <Control-C>
ok nvstore
ok reset
   Resetting ......
ok boot disk0
```

In the previous session, I used `nvedit` to create a permanent device alias named disk0. I used `<control-C>` to exit the editor. I used the `nvstore` command to make the change permanent in the NVRAMRC. I issued the `reset` command to reset the system and then booted the system from disk0 using the `boot disk0` command.

Table 2.10 lists some of the basic commands that you can use while in the `nvedit` line editor.

**TABLE 2.10**

**nvedit COMMANDS**

| *Command* | *Meaning* |
|---|---|
| `control+c` | Exits the editor |
| `control+u` | Deletes the current line |
| `delete` | Erases the previous characters |
| `return` | Closes the current line and opens a new line |
| `control+b` | Goes back one character |

| *Command* | *Meaning* |
|---|---|
| `control+f` | Goes forward one character |
| `control+p` | Goes back one line |
| `control+n` | Goes forward one line |

# OpenBoot Security

Anyone who has access to the computer keyboard can access OpenBoot and modify parameters, unless you set up your security variables. These variables are listed in Table 2.11.

**TABLE 2.11**

**OpenBoot Security Variables**

| *Variable* | *Description* |
|---|---|
| `security-mode` | Restricts the set of operations that users are allowed to perform at the OpenBoot prompt. |
| `security-password` | The firmware security password. (It is never displayed.) Do not set this variable directly. This variable is set using `password`. |
| `security-#badlogins` | The number of incorrect security password attempts. |

**CAUTION** It is important to remember your security password and to set the security password before setting the security mode. If you forget this password, you cannot use your system; you must call your vendor's customer support service to make your machine bootable again.

To set the security password, type the following at the `ok` prompt:

```
ok password
ok New password (only first 8 chars are used): <enter password>
ok Retype new password: <enter password>
```

Earlier, I showed how to change the OpenBoot parameter `security-password` from the command line.

After assigning a password, you can set the security variables that best fit your environment.

security-mode is used to restrict the use of OpenBoot commands. When you assign one of the three values shown in Table 2.12, access to commands is protected by a password. The syntax for setting security-mode is as follows:

```
setenv security-mode <value>
```

The value that you enter for security-mode is one of the three values listed in Table 2.12.

**TABLE 2.12**

**OPENBOOT SECURITY VALUES**

| *Value* | *Description* |
|---|---|
| full | All OpenBoot commands except go require a password. This security mode is the most restrictive. |
| command | All OpenBoot commands except boot and go require the password. |
| none | No password is required (default). |

The following example sets the OpenBoot environment so that all commands except boot and go require a password:

```
setenv security-mode command
```

With security-mode set to command, a password is not required if you type the boot command by itself or type the go command. Any other command will require a password, including the use of the boot command with an argument.

Following are examples of when a password might be required when security-mode is set to command:

| | |
|---|---|
| ok boot | No password is required. |
| ok go | No password is required. |
| ok boot vmunix | A password is required. |

The system displays a password prompt as follows:

| | |
|---|---|
| Password | The password is not echoed as it is typed. |
| ok reset-all | A password is required. |

The system displays a password prompt as follows:

| | |
|---|---|
| `Password` | Type the password. |
| `Note` | The password is not echoed as it is typed. |

If you enter an incorrect security password, there will be a delay of about 10 seconds before the next startup prompt appears. The number of times that an incorrect security password can be typed is stored in the `security-#badlogins` variable. The syntax is as follows:

```
setenv security-#badlogins <variable>
```

For example, you can set the number of attempts to four with the following command:

```
setenv security-#badlogins 4
```

# OPENBOOT DIAGNOSTICS

Various hardware diagnostics can be run in OpenBoot. These can be used to troubleshoot hardware and network problems. These diagnostic commands are listed in Table 2.13.

**TABLE 2.13**

**OPENBOOT DIAGNOSTICS**

| *Command* | *Description* |
|---|---|
| `probe-scsi` | Identifies devices attached to a SCSI bus. |
| `probe-ide` | Identifies IDE devices attached to the PCI bus. |
| `test device-specifier` | Executes the specified device's self-test method. For example:<br>`test floppy` tests the floppy drive (if installed).<br>`test net` tests the network connection. |
| `test-all [device-specifier]` | Tests all devices that have a built-in self-test method below the specified device tree node. If `device-specifier` is absent, all devices beginning from the root node are tested. |
| `watch-clock` | Tests the clock function. |
| `watch-net` | Monitors the network connection. |

> **TIP**
>
> Use the `probe-scsi` command to obtain a free open SCSI target ID number before adding a tape unit, CD-ROM drive, disk drive, or any other SCSI peripheral. Only devices that are powered on will be located, so make sure that everything is turned on. Use this command after installing a SCSI device to ensure that it has been connected properly and that the system can see it. Also, use this command if you suspect a faulty cable or connection. If you have more than one SCSI bus, use the `probe-scsi-all` command.

The following examples use some of the diagnostic features of OpenBoot. The first example uses `probe-scsi` to identify all the SCSI devices attached to a particular SCSI bus. This command is useful for identifying SCSI target IDs that are already in use, or to check to make sure that all devices are connected and identified by the system.

```
ok probe-scsi
```

The system will respond with this:

```
Target 1
       Unit 0   Disk        SEAGATE ST1120N 833400093849
                            Copyright    1992 Seagate
                            All rights reserved 0000
Target 3
       Unit 0   Disk  MAXTOR LXT-213S SUN2074.20
```

This example uses the `probe-ide` command to identify all IDE devices connected to the PCI bus:

```
ok probe-ide
  Device 0  ( Primary Master )
          ATA Model: ST34321A
  Device 1  ( Primary Slave )
         Not Present
  Device 2  ( Secondary Master )
         Removable ATAPI Model: CRD-8322B
  Device 3  ( Secondary Slave )
         Not Present
```

The next example tests the system video and performs various other tests:

```
ok test all
```

To test the disk drive to determine whether it is functioning properly, put a formatted, high-density disk into the drive and type the following:

```
ok test floppy
```

The system should respond with this:

```
Testing floppy disk system. A formatted disk should be in
the drive.
Test succeeded.
```

Type `eject-floppy` to remove the disk.

Table 2.14 describes other OpenBoot commands that you can use to gather information about the system.

**TABLE 2.14**

**SYSTEM INFORMATION COMMANDS**

| *Command* | *Description* |
|---|---|
| banner | Displays the power-on banner. |
| show-sbus | Displays a list of installed and probed SBus devices. |
| .enet-addr | Displays the current Ethernet address. |
| .idprom | Displays ID PROM contents, formatted. |
| .traps | Displays a list of SPARC trap types. |
| .version | Displays the version and date of the startup PROM. |
| .speed | Displays CPU and bus speeds. |
| show-devs | Displays all installed and probed devices. |

The following example uses the `banner` command to display the CPU type, the installed RAM, the Ethernet address, the hostid, and the version and date of the startup PROM:

```
ok banner
```

The system responds with this:

```
Sun Ultra 5/10 UPA/PCI (UltraSPARC-IIi 270MHz), No Keyboard
OpenBoot 3.15, 128 MB memory installed, Serial #10642306.
Ethernet address 8:0:20:a2:63:82, Host ID: 80a26382.
```

**NOTE** For Solaris 8 to work properly, your PROM release must be version 1.1 or higher. Use the `banner` command to find out the PROM release for your system.

The next example uses the `.version` command to display the OpenBoot version and date of the startup PROM.

Type the following:

```
ok .version
```

The system responds with this:

```
Release 3.15 Version 2 created 1998/11/10 10:35
OBP 3.15.2 1998/11/10 10:35
POST 2.3.1 1998/08/07 16:33
```

The next example shows how to use the `.enet-addr` command to display the Ethernet address.

Type the following:

```
ok .enet-addr
```

The system responds with this:

```
8:0:20:1a:c7:e3
```

To display the CPU information, type

```
.speed
```

The system responds with this:

```
CPU  Speed : 270.00MHz
UPA  Speed : 090.00MHz
PCI  Bus A : 33MHz
PCI  Bus B : 33MHz
```

## Input and Output Control

The console is used as the primary means of communication between OpenBoot and the user. The console consists of an input device used for receiving information supplied by the user and an output device used for sending information to the user. Typically, the console is either the combination of a text/graphics display device and a keyboard or an ASCII terminal connected to a serial port.

The configuration variables relating to the control of the console are listed in Table 2.15.

**TABLE 2.15**

**CONSOLE CONFIGURATION VARIABLES**

| *Variable* | *Description* |
|---|---|
| `input-device` | Console input device (usually keyboard, ttya, or ttyb). |
| `output-device` | Console output device (usually screen, ttya, or ttyb). |
| `screen-#columns` | Number of onscreen columns (the default is 80 characters per line). |
| `screen-#rows` | Number of onscreen rows (the default is 34 lines). |

You can use these variables to assign the console's power-on defaults. These values do not take effect until after the next power cycle or system reset.

If you select `keyboard` for `input-device` and the device is not plugged in, input is accepted from the ttya port as a fallback device. If the system is powered on and the keyboard is not detected, the system will look to ttya—the serial port—for the system console and will use this port for all input and output.

The communication parameters on the serial port can be defined by setting the configuration variables for that port. These variables are shown in Table 2.16.

**TABLE 2.16**

**PORT CONFIGURATION VARIABLES**

| *Variable* | *Current Value* | *Default Value* |
|---|---|---|
| `ttyb-rts-dtr-off` | false | false |
| `ttyb-ignore-cd` | true | true |
| `ttya-rts-dtr-off` | false | false |
| `ttya-ignore-cd` | true | true |
| `ttyb-mode` | 9600,8,n,1,- | 9600,8,n,1,- |
| `ttya-mode` | 9600,8,n,1,- | 9600,8,n,1,- |

Following are the values for `ttya-mode` from left to right:

Baud rate: 110, 300, 1200, 4800, 9600, 19200

Data bits: 5, 6, 7, 8

Parity: n (none), e (even), o (odd), m (mark), s (space)

Stop bits: 1, 1.5, 2

Handshake: - (none), h (hardware: rts/cts), s (software: xon/xoff)

## BOOT

The primary function of the OpenBoot firmware is to start up the system. Starting up is the process of loading and executing a stand-alone program. An example of a stand-alone program is the operating system or the diagnostic monitor. In this discussion, the stand-alone program is the operating system kernel. After the kernel is loaded, it starts the UNIX system, mounts the necessary file systems, and runs /sbin/init to bring the system to the "initdefault" state specified in /etc/inittab. This process was discussed in Chapter 1.

Starting up can be initiated either automatically or by typing a command at the user interface. It is commonly referred to as the bootstrap procedure. On most SPARC-based systems, the bootstrap procedure consists of the following basic phases:

1. The system hardware is powered on.
2. The system firmware (the PROM) executes a POST. (The form and scope of these tests depends on the version of the firmware in your system.)
3. After the tests have been completed successfully, the firmware attempts to autoboot if the appropriate OpenBoot configuration variable (`auto-boot?`) has been set.

The OpenBoot startup process is shown here:

```
Sun Ultra 5/10 UPA/PCI (UltraSPARC-IIi 270MHz), No Keyboard
OpenBoot 3.15, 128 MB memory installed, Serial #10642306.
Ethernet address 8:0:20:a2:63:82, Host ID: 80a26382.
Rebooting with command: boot
Boot device: disk:a  File and args:
SunOS Release 5.8 Version Generic_108621-04 64-bit
Copyright 1983-2000 Sun Microsystems, Inc.  All rights reserved.
configuring IPv4 interfaces: hme0.
configuring IPv6 interfaces: hme0.
Hostname: ultra
metainit: unknown: there are no existing databases
The system is coming up.  Please wait.
checking ufs filesystems
/dev/rdsk/c0t0d0s5: is clean.
/dev/rdsk/c0t0d0s7: is clean.
/dev/rdsk/c0t0d0s6: is clean.
Starting IPv6 neighbor discovery.Setting default IPv6 interface\
for
```

```
 multicast: add net ff00::/8: gateway fe80::a0 0:20ff:fea2:6382
starting rpc services: rpcbind done.
Setting default IPv4 interface for multicast: add net 224.0/4: gateway
 unknown
syslog service starting.
syslogd: line 24: WARNING:loghost could not be resolved
Print services started.
volume management starting.
Mar 23 13:19:33 unknown snmpdx:
The system is ready.
ultra console login:
```

The startup process is controlled by a number of configuration variables. The ones that affect the startup process are described in Table 2.17.

**TABLE 2.17**

**BOOT CONFIGURATION VARIABLES**

| *Variable* | *Description* |
|---|---|
| `auto-boot?` | Controls whether the system automatically starts up after a system reset or when the power is turned on. The default for this variable is true. When the system is powered on, the system automatically starts up to the default run level. |
| `boot-command` | Specifies the command to be executed when `auto-boot?` is true. The default value of `boot-command` is `boot` with no command-line arguments. |
| `diag-switch?` | If the value is true, runs in the diagnostic mode. This variable is false by default. |
| `boot-device` | Contains the name of the default startup device that is used when OpenBoot is not in diagnostic mode. |
| `boot-file` | Contains the default startup arguments that are used when OpenBoot is not in diagnostic mode. The default is no arguments. (See Table 2.18 for details of when this variable is used.) |
| `diag-device` | Contains the name of the default diagnostic mode startup device. The default is `net`. (See Table 2.18 for details of when this variable is used.) |

*continues*

**TABLE 2.17** *continued*

**BOOT CONFIGURATION VARIABLES**

| *Variable* | *Description* |
|---|---|
| `diag-file` | Contains the default diagnostic mode startup arguments. The default is no arguments. (See Table 2.18 for details of when this variable is used.) |

Typically, `auto-boot?` will be true, `boot-command` will be `boot`, and OpenBoot will not be in diagnostic mode. Consequently, the system will automatically load and execute the program, and arguments described by `boot-file` from the device described by `boot-device` when the system is first turned on or following a system reset. The `boot` command and its options are described in Table 2.18.

`boot` has the following syntax:

```
boot [OBP name] [filename] [options] [flags]
```

[OBP name], `[filename]`, `[options]`, and `[flags]` are optional.

**TABLE 2.18**

**boot COMMAND**

| *Option* | *Description* |
|---|---|
| `OBP name` | Specifies the OpenBoot PROM designations. For example, on Desktop SPARC-based systems, the designation /sbus/esp@0,800000/sd@3,0:a indicates a SCSI disk (sd) at target 3, lun0 on the SCSI bus, with the esp host adapter plugged into slot 0. This OBP name can be a devalias, such as disk0 (floppy 3 1/2-inch diskette drive), net (Ethernet), or tape (SCSI tape). If OBP name is not specified and `diagnostic-mode?` returns true, boot uses the device specified by the `diag-device` configuration variable. |
| `filename` | The name of the stand-alone program to be started up (for example, kernel/unix). The default is to start up /platform/platform-name/kernel/unix from the root partition. If specified, `filename` is relative to the root of the selected device and partition. If not, the boot program uses the value of the `boot-file` or `diag-file` based on the `diag-switch?` parameter. |

| *Option* | *Description* |
|---|---|
| `options` | `-a`<br>The startup program interprets this flag to mean "Ask me," so it prompts for the name of the stand-alone program to load.<br>`-f`<br>When starting an Autoclient system, this option forces the `boot` program to bypass the client's local cache and read all files over the network from the client's file server. This option is ignored for all non-Autoclient systems. The `-f` option is then passed to the stand-alone program.<br>`-r`<br>Triggers device reconfiguration during startup. (This option is covered in Chapter 16, "Device Administration and Disk Management.") |
| `flags` | The `boot` program passes all startup flags to `filename`. They are not interpreted by `boot`. (See the next section for information on the options available with the default stand-alone program, `kernel/unix`.) |

If you want to start up the default program when `auto-boot?` is false, a few options are available for starting up the system from the `ok` prompt.

When you type the following:

```
boot
```

the machine will start up from the default startup device using no startup arguments. This is set in the `boot-device` variable.

Type the following:

```
boot [OBP name]
```

When you specify an explicit OBP name, such as disk3, the machine will start up from the specified startup device using no startup arguments.

Here's an example:

```
boot disk3
```

The system will boot from the disk drive defined by the devalias named disk3. It will then load `kernel/unix` as the default stand-alone startup program.

Type

```
boot [options]
```

When you specify explicit options with the `boot` command, the machine will use the specified arguments to start up from the default startup device.

Here's an example:

```
boot -a
```

The system will then ask for the name of the stand-alone program to load. If you specify `kernel/unix`, which is the default, you will be prompted to enter the directory that contains the kernel modules. (See the next section for details on kernel modules.)

Type

```
boot [OBP name] [options]
```

When you specify the `boot` command with an explicit startup device and explicit arguments, the machine will start up from the specified device with the specified arguments.

Here's an example:

```
boot disk3 -a
```

This example will give the same prompts as the previous example, except that you are now specifying a different startup device. The system will start up the bootblock from the disk drive defined by the devalias named `disk3`.

During the startup process, OpenBoot performs the following tasks:

1. The firmware can reset the machine if a client program has been executed since the last reset. The client program is normally an operating system or an operating system's loader program, but `boot` can also be used to load and execute other kinds of programs, such as diagnostics. For example, if you have just issued the `test net` command, when you next type `boot`, the system will reset before starting up.

2. The boot program is loaded into memory using a protocol that depends on the type of the selected device. You can start up from disk, tape, floppy, or the network. A disk startup might read a fixed number of blocks from the beginning of the disk, whereas a tape startup might read a particular tape file.
3. The loaded boot program is executed. The behavior of the boot program can be further controlled by the `argument` string, if one was passed to the `boot` command on the command line.

The program loaded and executed by the startup process is a secondary boot program, the purpose of which is to load the stand-alone program. The second-level program is either `ufsboot`, when starting up from a disk, or `inetboot`, when starting up across the network.

If starting up from disk, the bootstrap process consists of two conceptually distinct phases: primary startup and secondary startup. The PROM assumes that the program for the primary startup (`bootblk`) is in the primary bootblock, which resides in sectors 1–15 of the startup device. The bootblock is created using the `installboot` command. The software installation process typically installs the bootblock for you, so you won't need to issue this command unless you're recovering a corrupted bootblock.

To install a bootblock on disk c0t3d0s0, type the following:

```
installboot /usr/platform/'uname -i'/lib/fs/ufs/bootblk \
/dev/rdsk/c0t3d0s0
```

You cannot see the bootblock. It resides in a protected area of the disk that cannot be viewed. The program in the bootblock area will load the secondary startup program, named `ufsboot`.

When executing the `boot` command, if a filename was specified, this filename is the name of the stand-alone startup program to be loaded. If the pathname is relative (does not begin with a slash), `ufsboot` will look for the program in a platform-dependent search path. In other words, the relative path to the stand-alone program will be prefixed with */platform/<platform-name>*. *<platform-name>* will be specific to your hardware.

> **NOTE**
>
> Use the `uname -i` command to determine your system's platform name. For example, on a SPARCstation10, the path will be /platform/SUNW,SPARCstation-10. Use the command `uname -m` to find the hardware-class-name of a system; for a SPARCstation10, the hardware-class-name will be sun4m. If you look in the /platform directory, you'll see that /platform/SUNW,SPARCstation-10 is merely a link to /platform/sun4m.

On the other hand, if the path to filename is absolute, `boot` will use the specified path. The startup program then loads the stand-alone program and transfers control to it.

The following example shows how to specify the stand-alone startup program from the OpenBoot `ok` prompt:

```
ok boot disk5 kernel/unix -s
```

In the example, the PROM will look for the primary boot program (`bootblk`) on disk5 (/iommu/sbus/espdma@f,400000/esp@f,800000/sd@0,0). The primary startup program will then load `ufsboot`. This will load the stand-alone startup program named /platform/SUNW, SPARCstation-10/kernel/unix using the `-s` flag. Typical secondary startup programs, such as `kernel/unix`, accept arguments of the form `filename -flags`, in which `filename` is the path to the stand-alone program and `-flags` is a list of options to be passed to the stand-alone program. The example will start up the operating system kernel, which is described in the next section. The `-s` flag will instruct the kernel to start up in single-user mode.

## KERNEL

The secondary startup program, `ufsboot`, which was described in the preceding section, loads the operating system kernel. The platform-specific kernel used by `ufsboot` is named /platform/`uname -m`/kernel/unix.

The kernel initializes itself and begins loading modules, using `ufsboot` to read the files. After the kernel has loaded enough modules to mount the root file system, it unmaps the `ufsboot` program and continues, using its own resources. The kernel creates a user process and starts the `/sbin/init` process, which starts other processes by reading the /etc/inittab file. (The `/sbin/init` process is described in Chapter 1.)

The kernel is dynamically configured in Solaris 8. It consists of a small static core and many dynamically loadable kernel modules. A kernel module is a hardware or software component that is used to perform a specific task on the system. An example of a loadable kernel module is a device driver that is loaded when the device is accessed. Drivers, file systems, STREAMS modules, and other modules are loaded automatically as they are needed, either at startup or at runtime. After these modules are no longer in use, they can be unloaded. Modules are kept in memory until that memory is needed. The `modinfo` command provides information about the modules currently loaded on a system.

When the kernel is loading, it reads the /etc/system file where system configuration information is stored. This file modifies the kernel's parameters and treatment of loadable modules. It specifically controls the following:

- The search path for default modules to be loaded at boot time, as well as the modules not to be loaded at boot time
- The modules to be forcibly loaded at boot time rather than at first access
- The root type and device
- The new values to override the default kernel parameter values

The following is an example of the default /etc/system file:

```
*ident     "@(#)system       1.18    97/06/27 SMI" /* SVR4 1.5 */
*
* SYSTEM SPECIFICATION FILE
*
* moddir:
*
*Set the search path for modules. This has a format similar to the
*csh path variable. If the module isn't found in the first directory
*it tries the second and so on. The default is /kernel /usr/kernel
*
*Example:
*moddir: /kernel /usr/kernel /other/modules
* root device and root filesystem configuration:
*
*The following may be used to override the defaults provided by
*the boot program:
*
*rootfs:          Set the filesystem type of the root.
*
*rootdev:         Set the root device. This should be a fully
*                 expanded physical pathname. The default is the
*                 physical pathname of the device where the boot
*                 program resides. The physical pathname is
*                 highly platform and configuration dependent.
```

```
*
*Example:
*          rootfs:ufs
*          rootdev:/sbus@1,f8000000/esp@0,800000/sd@3,0:a
*
*(Swap device configuration should be specified in /etc/vfstab.)
* exclude:
*
*Modules appearing in the moddir path which are NOT to be loaded,
*even if referenced. Note that `exclude' accepts either a module name,
*or a filename which includes the directory.
*
*Examples:
*          exclude: win
*          exclude: sys/shmsys
* forceload:
*
*Cause these modules to be loaded at boot time, (just before mounting
*the root filesystem) rather than at first reference. Note that
*forceload expects a filename which includes the directory. Also
*note that loading a module does not necessarily imply that it will
*be installed.
*
*Example:
*          forceload: drv/foo
* set:
*
*Set an integer variable in the kernel or a module to a new value.
*This facility should be used with caution. See system(4).
*
*Examples:
*
*To set variables in 'unix':
*
*          set nautopush=32
* set maxusers=40
*
*To set a variable named 'debug' in the module named 'test_module'
*
*          set test_module:debug = 0x13
```

The /etc/system file contains commands of this form:

```
set parameter=value
```

> **NOTE** Commands must be 80 characters or fewer in length, and comment lines must begin with an asterisk (*) and end with a newline character.

For example, the setting for the kernel parameter MAXUSERS is set in the /etc/system file with the following line:

```
set maxusers = 40
```

Commands that affect loadable modules are of this form:

```
set module:variable=value
```

If a system administrator needs to change a tunable parameter in the /etc/system file, the `sysdef` command can be used to verify the change. `sysdef` lists all hardware devices, system devices, loadable modules, and values of selected kernel-tunable parameters. The following is the output produced from the `sysdef` command:

```
*
* Hostid
*
  80a26382
*
  sun4m  Configuration

*
*
* Devices
*
packages (driver not attached)
        terminal-emulator (driver not attached)
        deblocker (driver not attached)
        obp-tftp (driver not attached)
        disk-label (driver not attached)
        SUNW,builtin-drivers (driver not attached)
        sun-keyboard (driver not attached)
        ufs-file-system (driver not attached)
chosen (driver not attached)
openprom (driver not attached)
        client-services (driver not attached)
options, instance #0
aliases (driver not attached)
memory (driver not attached)
virtual-memory (driver not attached)
```

```
pci, instance #0
        pci, instance #0
                ebus, instance #0
                        auxio (driver not attached)
                        power, instance #0
                        SUNW,pll (driver not attached)
                        se, instance #0
                        su, instance #0
                        su, instance #1
                        ecpp (driver not attached)
                        fdthree, instance #0
                        eeprom (driver not attached)
                        flashprom (driver not attached)
                        SUNW,CS4231 (driver not attached)
                network, instance #0
                SUNW,m64B, instance #0
                ide, instance #0
                        disk (driver not attached)
                        cdrom (driver not attached)
                        dad, instance #0
                        sd, instance #0
        pci, instance #1
                pci (driver not attached)
                        pci108e,1000 (driver not attached)
                        SUNW,qfe (driver not attached)
                        pci108e,1000 (driver not attached)
                        SUNW,qfe (driver not attached)
                        pci108e,1000 (driver not attached)
                        SUNW,qfe (driver not attached)
                        pci108e,1000 (driver not attached)
                        SUNW,qfe (driver not attached)
SUNW,UltraSPARC-IIi (driver not attached)
pseudo, instance #0
        clone, instance #0
        ip, instance #0
        ip6, instance #0
        tcp, instance #0
        tcp6, instance #0
        udp, instance #0
        udp6, instance #0
<Truncated output>
*
* Loadable Objects
*
```

```
* Loadable Object Path = /platform/SUNW,Ultra-5_10/kernel
*
misc/platmod
misc/sparcv9/platmod
*
* Loadable Object Path = /platform/sun4u/kernel
*
dacf/sparcv9/consconfig_dacf
drv/db21554
drv/dma
drv/ebus
drv/fd
drv/ledma
drv/pci_pci
drv/pcipsy
drv/power
......
<List of devices truncated>
*
* System Configuration
*
  swap files
swapfile             dev  swaplo blocks   free
/dev/dsk/c0t0d0s1   136,1      16 1048928 976384
*
* Tunable Parameters
*
 2482176        maximum memory allowed in buffer cache (bufhwm)
    1898        maximum number of processes (v.v_proc)
      99        maximum global priority in sys class (MAXCLSYSPRI)
    1893        maximum processes per user id (v.v_maxup)
      30        auto update time limit in seconds (NAUTOUP)
      25        page stealing low water mark (GPGSLO)
       5        fsflush run rate (FSFLUSHR)
      25        minimum resident memory for avoiding deadlock (MINARMEM)
      25        minimum swapable memory for avoiding deadlock (MINASMEM)
*
* Utsname Tunables
*
     5.8  release (REL)
 unknown  node name (NODE)
   SunOS  system name (SYS)
Generic_108528-07  version (VER)
*
```

```
* Process Resource Limit Tunables (Current:Maximum)
*
          Infinity:Infinity             cpu time
          Infinity:Infinity             file size
          Infinity:Infinity             heap size
0x0000000000800000:Infinity             stack size
          Infinity:Infinity             core file size
0x0000000000000100:0x0000000000000400   file descriptors
          Infinity:Infinity             mapped memory
*
* Streams Tunables
*
     9  maximum number of pushes allowed (NSTRPUSH)
 65536  maximum stream message size (STRMSGSZ)
  1024  max size of ctl part of message (STRCTLSZ)
*
* IPC Messages module is not loaded
*
*
* IPC Semaphores
*
    10  semaphore identifiers (SEMMNI)
    60  semaphores in system (SEMMNS)
    30  undo structures in system (SEMMNU)
    25  max semaphores per id (SEMMSL)
    10  max operations per semop call (SEMOPM)
    10  max undo entries per process (SEMUME)
 32767  semaphore maximum value (SEMVMX)
 16384  adjust on exit max value (SEMAEM)
*
* IPC Shared Memory
*
  1048576       max shared memory segment size (SHMMAX)
     1  min shared memory segment size (SHMMIN)
   100  shared memory identifiers (SHMMNI)
     6  max attached shm segments per process (SHMSEG)
*
* Time Sharing Scheduler Tunables
*
60      maximum time sharing user priority (TSMAXUPRI)
SYS     system class name (SYS_NAME)
```

The adb (absolute debugger) command can also be used to verify that a change was actually made after the system has been started up, but be careful using it.

**CAUTION**

adb can change kernel parameters on a running system, and could potentially crash your system if used improperly. Undertake the following procedures with caution. Improper entries in the /etc/system file or improper use of adb can result in a corrupted system, causing the system to crash or be unable to restart.

If the kernel parameter you're looking for is not displayed with sysdef (for example, MAXUSERS), use adb. At the UNIX command prompt, when you're logged in as root, execute the following command:

```
adb -k /dev/ksyms  /dev/mem
```

/dev/ksyms is a special driver that provides an image of the kernel's symbol table. This can be used to examine the information in memory. adb will reply with the amount of physical memory (hex, in 4KB pages) as follows:

```
physmem 3dec
```

You will not receive a prompt after this, but adb is running and is ready for a command. To check a tunable parameter while in adb, use the following syntax:

| | |
|---|---|
| <parameter>/D | Displays the integer parameter in decimal |
| <parameter>/X | Displays the integer parameter in hexadecimal |

<parameter> is replaced with the kernel symbol being examined. For example:

```
maxusers/D
```

will display the MAXUSERS parameter in decimal notation, as follows:

```
maxusers:     40
```

Type shminfo_shmmax/D to display the max shared memory segment size. The system responds with this:

```
shminfo_shmmax: 1048576
```

Exit adb by typing $q and pressing Enter.

MDB, the Modular Debugger, is a new general-purpose debugging tool for the Solaris Operating Environment, which is backward compatible with adb. Refer to the Solaris Modular Debugger Guide for more information.

## CHAPTER SUMMARY

### KEY TERMS

- OpenBoot
- Bootblock
- ufsboot
- OBP
- NVRAM
- PROM
- POST
- Device tree
- Full device name
- Device Alias
- Boot
- Kernel

This chapter provided a complete description of the OpenBoot environment; the PROM, the NVRAM, and the kernel.

In this chapter, I described how to access OpenBoot and the various commands available to test and provide information about the hardware.

I described the OpenBoot architecture. I explained how OpenBoot controls many of the hardware devices. Using the programmable user interface available in OpenBoot, the system administrator can set several parameters that control system hardware and peripherals.

Device names were also explained in this chapter. Throughout this book, I will be referring to various device names used in Solaris. It's important that you understand each one of them. I'll revisit this topic in Chapter 16, where devices and device drivers are covered in depth. Along with device names, I explained how to set temporary and permanent device aliases.

Finally, I described how to secure the OpenBoot environment from unauthorized access and I took you deeper into the topic we discussed in the previous chapter—booting and loading the kernel.

This chapter and Chapter 1 covered system startup, assuming that the operating system was installed and configured. In the next chapter, I'll describe how to install the Solaris operating system from the OpenBoot PROM.

## APPLY YOUR KNOWLEDGE

# Exercises

### 2.1 Using OpenBoot Commands

In the following exercises, you will halt the system and use the following OpenBoot commands to set parameters and gather basic information about your system.

**Estimated time**: 15 minutes

1. Issue the correct OpenBoot command to display the banner as follows:

   ```
   banner
   ```

2. Set parameters to their default values as follows:

   ```
   reset-all
   ```

3. Display the list of OpenBoot help topics as follows:

   ```
   help
   ```

4. Use the `banner` command to get the following information from your system:

   ROM revision:

   MB of installed memory:

   System type:

   System serial number:

   Ethernet address:

   Host ID:

5. Display the following list of OBP parameters using the `printenv` command:

   ```
   output-device
   input-device
   auto-boot?
   boot-device
   ```

6. Set the `auto-boot?` parameter to false to prevent the system from booting automatically after a reset.

   From the OpenBoot `ok` prompt, type the following:

   ```
   setenv auto-boot? false
   ```

   Verify it has been set by typing the following:

   ```
   printenv auto-boot?
   ```

   Now, from the UNIX prompt, set the `auto-boot?` parameter back to true as follows:

   ```
   eeprom auto-boot?=true
   ```

   Take the system back down to init level 0, and verify that that the `auto-boot?` paramater is set to true.

7. Use the following commands to display the list of disk devices attached to your system:

   ```
   probe-scsi
   probe-scsi-all
   probe-ide
   ```

   Explain the main difference between these commands.

> **CAUTION**
>
> If any of these commands returns a message warning that your system will hang if you proceed, enter `n` to avoid running the command. Run `reset-all` before running `probe` again and then respond `y` to this message.

## APPLY YOUR KNOWLEDGE

8. List the target number and the device type of each SCSI device attached to your system using the OpenBoot commands in step 7.
9. From the OpenBoot prompt, identify your default boot device as follows:

```
printenv boot-device
```

10. Use the `show-disks` OpenBoot command to get a listing of the disk drives on your system as follows:

```
show-disks
```

Display the full device path for the disk4 devalias as follows:

```
devalias disk4
```

Create a permanent device alias named disk4 that points to SCSI target 4 as follows.

```
nvalias disk4 /iommu/sbus/espdma@f,400000/
esp@f,800000/sd@4,0
```

Reset the system, and verify the devalias is still set by typing the following:

```
reset
devalias disk4
```

11. Boot the system, log on as root, and use the `eeprom` command to list all NVRAM parameters using the `eeprom` command.
12. Use the `eeprom` command to list only the setting of the `boot-device` parameter as follows:

```
eeprom boot-device
```

13. Reset the `boot-device` to its default parameter from the OpenBoot prompt as follows:

```
set-default boot-device
```

14. From the OpenBoot prompt, remove the alias disk4 as follows:

```
nvunalias disk4
```

15. Reset the system, and verify disk4 is no longer set as follows:

```
reset
printenv
```

16. Set all the OpenBoot parameters back to their default values as follows:

```
set-defaults
```

## Review Questions

1. The hardware-level user interface that you see before the operating system has been started is called:

   A. OpenBoot

   B. EEPROM

   C. Firmware

   D. Boot PROM

2. Which of the following is where the system identification information is stored, such as the hostid?

   A. Firmware

   B. OpenBoot

   C. NVRAM

   D. Kernel

3. What task(s) is/are performed by OpenBoot? (Select two.)

   A. Executing POST

   B. Loading the `bootblk`

   C. Executing `ufsboot`

   D. Loading the OS kernel

## APPLY YOUR KNOWLEDGE

4. Which of the following is *not* a task of the OpenBoot firmware?

   A. Testing and initializing the system hardware

   B. Loading the kernel

   C. Starting up the operating system from either a mass storage device or from a network

   D. Allowing modification and management of system startup configuration, such as NVRAM parameters

5. Which of the following is attached to a host computer through a hierarchy of interconnected buses on the device tree.

   A. SBUS cards

   B. SCSI peripherals

   C. Plug-in device drivers

   D. Nodes

6. /pci@1f,0/pci@1,1/ide@3/disk is what type of device?

   A. Full device pathname

   B. Physical device

   C. Logical device

   D. Instance

7. Which of the following is used to obtain information about devices and to display device path names in OpenBoot?

   A. `show-devs`

   B. `dmesg`

   C. `pwd`

   D. `sysdef`

8. Which command creates a temporary device alias named `disk3`?

   A. `setenv disk3 /iommu/sbus/espdma@f,400000/esp@f,800000/sd@3,0`

   B. `set disk3 /iommu/sbus/espdma@f,400000/esp@f,800000/sd@3,0`

   C. `nvalias disk3 /iommu/sbus/espdma@f,400000/esp@f,800000/sd@3,0`

   D. `devalias disk3 /iommu/sbus/espdma@f,400000/esp@f,800000/sd@3,0`

9. If you want to create permanent aliases in NVRAM (that show up after a reboot), which of the following commands should you use?

   A. `devalias`

   B. `nvalias`

   C. `setenv`

   D. `eeprom`

10. Which NVRAM variable specifies the device from which to start up?

    A. `boot-device`

    B. `boot-file`

    C. `output-device`

    D. `input-device`

11. Which command cannot be used to modify NVRAM variables?

    A. `set-defaults`

    B. `setenv`

    C. `nvalias`

    D. `set-default`

## APPLY YOUR KNOWLEDGE

12. If a system will not start due to a bad NVRAM variable, which of the following, performed at the OpenBoot prompt, resets the NVRAM variables to their default settings?

    A. `set-default <variable>`

    B. Stop–N

    C. `set-defaults`

    D. Ctrl-N

13. Which of the following can restrict the set of operations that users are allowed to perform at the OpenBoot prompt?

    A. `security-password`

    B. `security-mode`

    C. `set-secure`

    D. `set-security`

14. Which of the following is used in OpenBoot to test all devices that have a built-in self-test method below the specified device tree node?

    A. `diag`

    B. `probe-scsi`

    C. `test-all`

    D. `test`

15. Which option is used with the OpenBoot `boot` command so that you are prompted for the name of the standalone program to load?

    A. `-v`

    B. `-f`

    C. `-s`

    D. `-a`

16. What resides in blocks 1–15 of the startup device?

    A. `bootblk`

    B. `superblock`

    C. `kernel`

    D. `ufsboot`

17. Which of the following loads the operating system kernel?

    A. `ufsboot`

    B. `openBoot`

    C. `bootblk`

    D. `init`

18. Which of the following commands lists all hardware devices, system devices, loadable modules, and the values of selected kernel tunable parameters?

    A. `more /var/adm/messages`

    B. `adb`

    C. `dmesg`

    D. `sysdef`

19. Which directory stores the physical device names?

    A. /var

    B. /dev

    C. /kernel

    D. /devices

    E. /etc

## APPLY YOUR KNOWLEDGE

20. What key combination would you enter to interrupt a system that is not responding?

    A. Ctrl+B

    B. Ctrl+C

    C. Stop+A

    D. Ctrl+Alt+Delete

    E. Ctrl+Break

21. What does the `ufsboot` program do?

    A. Loads bootblock from the default startup device

    B. Loads the kernel

    C. Finds and executes the secondary startup program

    D. Runs self-test diagnostics (POST) to verify the system's hardware and memory

22. What is the function of the `auto-boot?` parameter set in the OpenBoot PROM?

    A. Boots automatically after power-on or reset

    B. Sets the default boot device

    C. Reboots after watchdog reset

    D. Automatically performs a system reboot when a system core file has been generated

23. Which of the following commands is used to set the auto-boot parameter?

    A. `setenv auto-boot?=false`

    B. `set auto-boot=false`

    C. `eeprom auto-boot?=false`

    D. `nvset`

24. To display all OpenBoot parameter settings, such as boot-device and ttya-mode, what should you type?

    A. `nvalias`

    B. `devalias`

    C. `printenv`

    D. `show all`

25. To check the target IDs on all of the SCSI devices connected to all of the SCSI controllers, what should you type?

    A. `test-all`

    B. `probe-scsi`

    C. `probe-scsi-all`

    D. `test-scsi`

26. The kernel reads which of the following files when loading? (It is where system configuration information is stored.)

    A. /etc/system

    B. /platform/<arch>/kernel/unix

    C. /etc/inittab

    D. /kernel/unix

## Answers to Review Questions

1. **A.** The hardware-level user interface that you see before the operating system starts is called the OpenBoot PROM (OBP).

2. **C.** The NVRAM is where the system identification information is stored, such as the hostid, Ethernet address, and time of day (TOD) clock.

## APPLY YOUR KNOWLEDGE

3. **A, B**. The two primary tasks of the OpenBoot firmware are to run POST and load the bootblock.

4. **B**. OpenBoot runs POST to initialize the system hardware. It also loads the primary startup program, `bootblk`, from the default startup device. The `bootblk` program finds and executes the secondary startup program, `ufsboot`, and loads it into memory. From that point, the `ufsboot` program loads the operating system kernel.

5. **D**. Devices called nodes are attached to a host computer through a hierarchy of interconnected buses on the device tree. A node representing the host computer's main physical address bus forms the tree's root node.

6. **A**. A full device pathname is a series of node names separated by slashes (/). The root of the tree is the machine node, which is not named explicitly, but is indicated by a leading slash (/). Each device pathname has this form:

```
driver-name@unit-address:device-arguments
```

7. **A**. The OpenBoot command `show-devs` is used to obtain information about devices and to display device pathnames.

8. **D**. Use the `devalias` command to create a temporary device alias named `disk3` as follows:

```
devalias disk3 /iommu/sbus/espdma@f,400000/
esp@f,800000/sd@3,0
```

9. **B**. Use the `nvalias` command from the OpenBoot PROM on the eeprom command from the Unix prompt to create a permanent alias in NVRAM that remains in effect even after a reboot.

10. **A**. The NVRAM variable `named boot-device` contains the name of the default startup device.

11. **C**. Use one of the following commands to modify NVRAM parameters: `setenv`, `set-default`, or `set-defaults`.

12. **B**. To reset the NVRAM variables to their default settings, hold down the Stop+N keys simultaneously while the machine is powering up.

13. **B**. The `OpenBoot` command security-mode restricts the set of operations that users are allowed to perform at the OpenBoot prompt.

14. **C**. The OpenBoot command `test-all` tests all devices that have a built-in self-test method below the specified device tree node.

15. **D**. Issue the OpenBoot `boot` command with the `-a` option so that you are prompted for the name of the stand-alone program to load.

16. **A**. The `bootblk` resides in blocks 1–15 of the startup device.

17. **A**. The secondary startup program, `ufsboot`, loads the operating system kernel.

18. **D**. Use the `sysdef` command to list all hardware devices, system devices, loadable modules, and the values of selected kernel tunable parameters.

19. **D**. Physical device names are stored in the /devices directory.

20. **C**. Interrupt a system that is not responding by pressing the Stop+A keys simultaneously (Stop+A).

21. **B**. The `ufsboot` program loads the operating system kernel.

## APPLY YOUR KNOWLEDGE

22. **A.** `auto-boot?` controls whether the system automatically starts up after a system reset or when the power is turned on. The default for this variable is true. When the system is powered on, the system automatically starts up to the default run level.

23. **C.** `eeprom auto-boot?=false` is used to set the `auto-boot?` parameter.

24. **C.** At the OpenBoot prompt, use the `printenv` command to display all OpenBoot parameter settings.

25. **C.** Use the `probe-scsi-all` command to check the target IDs on all of the SCSI devices connected to all of the SCSI controllers.

26. **A.** When the kernel is loading, it reads the /etc/system file where system configuration information is stored. This file modifies the kernel's parameters and treatment of loadable modules.

# CHAPTER 3

# Installing the Solaris 8 Software

## OBJECTIVES

This chapter describes the steps that the system administrator must follow to install the Solaris 8 Operating System on a networked standalone. These steps include the following:

**Prepare to install the Solaris 8 software**

- When you install the operating system, you will be prompted for a checklist of items. It's important that you compile this information before you begin the installation.

**Verify the minimum Solaris 8 software system requirements**

- To install and run Solaris 8 on a system, you must verify that the hardware meets a minimum set of requirements.

**Understand Solaris software terminology**

- To understand the dialog box that will be presented by the installation program, you need to understand Sun's terminology and how it bundles its software modules.

**Select a system configuration to install**

- You need to select the type of system configuration that you want to install. This chapter will describe each type of configuration that is available.

**Understand disk storage systems and partitions**

- During the installation, you need to set up the disks and disk partitions. To properly set them up, you first need to understand the concepts behind disk storage and partitioning. You then need to think about how you want data stored on your system's disks.

## OBJECTIVES

**Understand device drivers**

- Device drivers control every device connected to your system, and some devices use multiple device drivers. Before installing the operating system, you must verify that all devices are connected and functioning. This chapter explains device drivers so you can recognize and verify all devices connected to your system.

**Understand methods of installing the Solaris 8 software**

- This chapter identifies five methods that can be used to install the operating system. They are described so that you can determine which method works best for your installation.

**Install Solaris 8**

- The process of installing the operating system is outlined in this chapter.

## OUTLINE

## Outline



## Study Strategies

The following strategies will help you prepare for the exam:

- Understand each of the five methods used to install the operating system. Primarily, you need to know the difference between each method, as well as where and when to use each one.
- Know all of the requirements for installing the Solaris 8 operating environment.
- Understand all of the terminology and concepts described in this chapter, as well as the terms outlined at the end of the chapter. Each turn and concept is likely to appear on the exam.
- Understand everything I describe in the "Disk Storage Systems" section. Understand all the various device drivers and the various device names. Make sure that you understand the issues related to disk partitioning.
- Finally, practice all of the commands presented in this chapter until you can perform them and describe them from memory. In addition, practice installing the Solaris 8 operating environment on a Sun or Intel system no fewer than three times or until you can perform all the tasks from memory.

## Introduction

The Solaris installation process consists of three phases: system configuration, system installation, and post-installation tasks such as setting up printers, users, and networking. This chapter describes the various system configurations and the installation of the Solaris operating system on a workstation. Chapter 15, “Installing a Server,” describes the installation process in more detail, especially on servers.

## Requirements and Preparation for Installing the Solaris 8 Software

The first step in the installation is to determine whether your system type is supported under Solaris 8. Second, you need to decide which system configuration you want to install and whether you have enough disk space to support that configuration.

In preparation for installing Solaris 8 on a system, use Table 3.1 to check whether your system type is supported. Also, make sure you have enough disk space for Solaris and all of the packages you plan to install. (The section “Software Terminology” later in this chapter will help you estimate the amount of disk space required to hold the Solaris operating system.)

To determine your system type, use the `uname -m` command. The system will respond with the platform group and the platform name for your system. Compare the system response to the Platform Group column in Table 3.1. For example, to check for Sun platforms that support the Solaris 8 environment, use the command `uname -m`. On a Sun Ultra5, the system returns sun4u as the platform name.

**TABLE 3.1**

**SUN PLATFORMS THAT SUPPORT THE SOLARIS 8 ENVIRONMENT**

| *System* | *Platform Name* | *Platform Group* |
|---|---|---|
| x86-based | i86pc | i86pc |
| SPARCserver 1000/1000E | SUNW, SPARCserver-1000 | sun4d |
| SPARCcenter 2000/2000E | SUNW, SPARCcenter-2000 | sun4d |
| SPARCstation 4 | SUNW, SPARCstation-4 | sun4m |
| SPARCstation 5 | SUNW, SPARCstation-5 | sun4m |
| SPARCstation 10 | SUNW, SPARCstation-10 | sun4m |
| SPARCstation 10SX | SUNW, SPARCstation-10SX | sun4m |
| SPARCstation 20 | SUNW, SPARCstation-20 | sun4m |
| SPARCstation LX | SUNW, SPARCstation-LX | sun4m |
| SPARCclassic | SUNW, SPARCclassic | sun4m |
| Ultra 1 systems | SUNW, Ultra-1 | sun4u |
| Ultra Enterprise 1 systems | SUNW, Ultra-1 | sun4u |
| Ultra 2 systems | SUNW, Ultra-2 | sun4u |
| Ultra Enterprise 2 systems | SUNW, Ultra-2 | sun4u |
| Ultra Enterprise 150 | SUNW, Ultra-1 | sun4u |
| Ultra Enterprise 250 | SUNW, Ultra-2 | sun4u |
| Ultra 450 | SUNW, Ultra-4 | sun4u |
| Ultra Enterprise 450 | SUNW, Ultra-4 | sun4u |
| Ultra Enterprise 3000, 3500,4000, 4500, 5000, 5500, 6000, 6500, 10000 | SUNW, Ultra-Enterprise | sun4u |
| Ultra 5 | SUNW, Ultra-5/10 | sun4u |
| Ultra 10 | SUNW, Ultra-5/10 | sun4u |
| Ultra 30 | SUNW, Ultra-30 | sun4u |
| Ultra 60 | SUNW, Ultra-60 | sun4u |
| Ultra 80 SUNW, Ultra-60 | | sun4u |

*continues*

> **NOTE** Sun states that not all platforms and peripheral devices listed in this chapter are compatible. Contact your authorized Sun support provider for support information.

**TABLE 3.1** *continued*

**SUN PLATFORMS THAT SUPPORT THE SOLARIS 8 ENVIRONMENT**

| *System* | *Platform Name* | *Platform Group* |
|---|---|---|
| Sun Blade 100, 1000 | SUNW, Blade-100 | sun4u |
| Sun Blade 1000 | SUNW, Blade-1000 | sun4u |
| Sun Fire 280R, 880, 6800, 4810, 4800, 3800 | SUNW, Sun-Fire | sun4u |

## Unsupported Sun4c Architectures

The following sun4c architecture systems are no longer supported:

- SPARCstation SLC
- SPARCstation ELC
- SPARCstation IPC
- SPARCstation IPX
- SPARCstation 1
- SPARCstation 1+
- SPARCstation 2
- SPARCstation Voyager
- SPARC Xterminal 1

Check partition 2 by using the `format` command to determine whether your disk drive is large enough to load Solaris. See Chapter 6, "Introduction to File Systems," for the correct use of this command. As described in Chapter 6, partition 2 represents the entire disk.

## Minimum System Requirements

The computer must meet the following requirements before you can install Solaris 8 using the interactive installation method:

- The system must have a minimum of 64MB of RAM. Sufficient memory requirements are determined by several factors, including the number of active users and applications you plan to run.
- The media is distributed on CD-ROM only, so a CD-ROM is required either locally or on the network.
- A minimum of 2.3GB of disk space is required. See the next section for disk space requirements for the specific Solaris software that you plan to install. Also, add disk space to support your environment's swap space requirements.
- The system must be a SPARC-based or an INTEL-based system.

# SOFTWARE TERMINOLOGY

The Solaris operating system comes on a CD-ROM, and is bundled in packages. Packages are grouped into clusters. The following sections describe the Solaris bundling scheme.

## Software Package

A software package is a collection of files and directories in a defined format. It describes a software application, such as manual pages and line printer support. Solaris 8 contains approximately 80 software packages that total approximately 900MB of disk space.

A Solaris software package is the standard way to deliver bundled and unbundled software. Packages are administered by using the package administration commands, and are generally identified by a SUNWxxx naming convention.

## Software Clusters and Configuration Clusters

Software packages are grouped into software clusters, which are logical collections of software packages. For example, the online manual pages cluster contains one package. Some clusters contain multiple packages, such as the JavaVM 1.0 cluster, which contains the Java JIT compiler, JavaVM demo programs, JavaVM developers package, JavaVM man pages, and JavaVM runtime environment.

For SPARC systems, clusters are grouped into five configuration clusters to make the software installation process easier. During the installation process, you will be asked to install one of the five configuration clusters. These five configuration clusters are core system support, end-user support, developer system support, entire distribution, and entire distribution plus OEM system support. The following list describes each configuration cluster:

- Core system support. 258MB of disk space is required for the software only. Sun, however, recommends 718MB to support the software, swap, and disk overhead required to support this cluster. This configuration cluster contains the minimum software required to boot and run Solaris on a system. It includes some networking software and the drivers required to run the OpenWindows environment, but it does not include the OpenWindows software.
- End-user system support. 767MB of disk space is required for the software only. Sun, however, recommends 1.6GB to support the software, swap, and disk overhead required to support this cluster. This configuration cluster contains the core system support software plus end user software, which includes OpenWindows and the Common Desktop Environment software.
- Developer system support. 1.8GB of disk space is required for the software only. Sun, however, recommends 1.9GB to support the software, swap, and disk overhead required to support this cluster. This configuration cluster contains the end-user software plus libraries, include files, man pages, and programming tools for developing software. Compilers and debuggers are purchased separately and are not included.

- Entire distribution. 1.9GB of disk space is required for the software only. Sun, however, recommends 2.3GB to support the software, swap, and disk overhead required to support this cluster. This configuration cluster contains the entire Solaris 8 release.
- Entire distribution plus OEM system support. 1.6GB of disk space is required for the software only. Sun, however, recommends 2.4GB to support the software, swap, and disk overhead required to support this cluster. This configuration cluster contains the entire Solaris 8 release software plus extended hardware support.

  This cluster is available only on Sun systems, not on the Intel version of Solaris.

> **NOTE** Swap space and necessary file system overhead is included in the disk space recommendations for each configuration cluster. A minimum of 320MB is required for swap space, but more space might be needed. By default, Solaris Web Start allocates 512MB for swap space.

## Solaris Media

The Solaris 8 operating system software is distributed on CD-ROM, and is referred to as "the installation media kit." The media kit comes in two versions: an Intel version and a SPARC version. If you have a Sun system, install the SPARC version. If you plan to install Solaris on a personal computer, use the Intel version. In addition, each platform type has a domestic version and an international version of the media kit. The domestic version of the SPARC media kit has four CDs, which are labeled as follows:

- Solaris 8 Installation English SPARC Platform Edition
- Solaris 8 Software CD 1 of 2 SPARC Platform Edition
- Solaris 8 Software CD 2 of 2 SPARC Platform Edition
- Solaris 8 Documentation CD (English SPARC / Intel Platform Edition)

An international version of the media kit is also available for use outside of the United States. This international version contains everything in the domestic version with the following additional CDs:

- Solaris 8 Documentation European SPARC / Intel Platform Edition
- Solaris 8 Documentation Asian SPARC / Intel Platform Edition

The Intel version of the Solaris 8 media kit includes the same CDs as the SPARC version, plus a disk labeled "Solaris 8 Device Configuration Assistant Intel Platform Edition." To begin the installation on an Intel system, you'll first boot from the Device Configuration floppy disk. This step is unnecessary on a Sun system. The Device Configuration Assistant will configure the devices on the PC and instruct you when to install the Solaris 8 Installation CD.

## System Configuration to Be Installed

Before installing the operating system, you need to determine the system configuration to be installed. The configurations are defined by the way they access the root (/) and /usr file systems and the swap area. The system configurations are as follows:

- Server
- Clients, which include the following:
  - Diskless clients
  - JavaStation clients
  - Solstice AutoClients
  - Stand-alone systems

### Server

A server system has the following file systems installed locally:

- The root (/) and /usr file systems, plus swap space
- The /export, /export/swap, and /export/home file systems, which support client systems and provide home directories for users
- The /opt directory or file system for storing application software

Servers can also contain the following software to support other systems:

- Operating system services for diskless clients and AutoClient systems

- Solaris CD image and boot software for networked systems to perform remote installations
- A JumpStart directory for networked systems to perform custom JumpStart installations

> **NOTE** Many system administrators have questioned whether support is available for AutoClients and diskless clients in Solaris 8. Sun's own documentation has confused many of us. As I write this chapter, "Solaris 8 System Administration Guide Volume 1" says the following: "AutoClient and diskless systems are not supported in the Solaris 8 release." However, in the Solaris 8 July 2001 Release Notes, Sun says, "Solstice AdminSuite 2.3 software is no longer supported. Any attempt to run Solstice AdminSuite 2.3 to configure a Solstice AutoClient or diskless client will result in a failure for which no patch is available or planned. Solaris 8 July 2001 includes new commands for diskless client management. See smosservice(1M) and smdiskless(1M) for more information." Therefore, AutoClient and diskless client support is still available in Solaris 8, even though the Solaris 8 System Administration Guide Volume 1 states that it is not. AutoClients and diskless clients are simply not supported in the Solstice AdminSuite package.

## Client

A client is a system that uses remote services from a server. Some clients have limited disk storage capacity, or perhaps none at all, so they must rely on remote file systems from a server to function. Diskless clients, JavaStation clients, and AutoClients are examples of this type of client.

Other clients might use remote services (such as installation software) from a server, but they don't rely on a server to function. A stand-alone system, which has its own hard disk containing the root (/), /usr, and /export/home file systems and swap space, is a good example of this type of client.

### Diskless Client

A diskless client is a system with no local disk. It is dependent on a server for all of its software and storage area. The operating system is located on a server on the network. The diskless client boots from the server, remotely mounts its root (/), /usr, and /export/home file systems from a server, allocates swap space on the server, and obtains all its data from the server. Any files created are stored on the server.

A diskless client generates significant network traffic because of its need to continually access the server for operating system functions and to access virtual memory space across the network. A diskless client cannot operate if it is detached from the network, or if its server is unavailable.

### JavaStation Client

The JavaStation is a client designed for zero administration. This client optimizes Java. The JavaStation client takes full advantage of the network to deliver everything from Java applications and services to complete, integrated system and network management. This type of client can create much network traffic, so make sure your network has the needed capacity. The JavaStation has no local administration; booting, administration, and data storage are handled by servers via the network.

## AutoClient

An AutoClient system is nearly identical to a diskless client, except that it caches all of its needed system software from a server. AutoClient systems use Solaris diskless and CacheFS technologies. CacheFS is a general-purpose, file-system caching mechanism that improves performance and scalability by reducing server and network load. (See Chapter 17, "The NFS Environment," for a complete description of how CacheFS works.) An AutoClient system has the following characteristics:

- It requires a 100MB or larger local disk for swapping and caching. Its root (/) file system and the /usr file system are on a server somewhere on the network, but they are cached locally.
- It can be set up so that it can continue to access its cached root (/) and /usr file systems when the server is unavailable.
- It relies on servers to provide other file systems and software applications.
- It contains no permanent data, making it a field-replaceable unit (FRU).

An AutoClient system uses its local disk for swap space and to cache its individual root (/) file system and the /usr file system from a server's file systems. With the AutoClient configuration, administration is streamlined because the system administrator can maintain many AutoClient systems from a central location. Changes do not have to be made on individual systems. You must obtain a license for each AutoClient system you want to add to your network.

Table 3.2 gives a brief overview of each system configuration. It outlines which file systems are local and which are accessed over the network.

TABLE 3.2

**SYSTEM CONFIGURATIONS**

| *System Type* | *Local File Systems* | *Local Swap* | *Remote File Systems* |
|---|---|---|---|
| Server | root (/), /usr, /home, /opt/export, /export/home | Yes | Optional |
| JavaStation | None | No | /home |
| Diskless client | None | No | root (/), swap, /usr, /home |
| AutoClient | cached root (/), cached/usr | Yes | /var |
| Stand-alone | root (/), /usr, /export/home | Yes | Optional |

## Stand-Alone

On a stand-alone system, the operating system is loaded on a local disk, and the system is set to run independently of other systems for portions of the operating system. The operating system might be networked to other stand-alone systems. A networked stand-alone system can share information with other systems on the network, but it can function autonomously because it has its own hard disk with enough space to contain the root (/), /usr, and /home file systems and swap space. The stand-alone system has local access to operating system software, executables, virtual memory space, and user-created files. Sometimes, the stand-alone system will access the server for data or access a CD-ROM or tape drive from a server if one is not available locally.

### Performance of Clients Relative to a Stand-Alone System

A system administrator decides which system configuration to use based on available hardware and how much to streamline the administration of the network. For example, does the system have a large enough local disk to hold all the operating system? Also, would the features of the AutoClient, diskless, or JavaStation system configurations facilitate the administration of remote systems? For the most part, AutoClient configurations are used to ease system administration in a large network of systems. Because the operating system is downloaded from a server at bootup, maintaining the workstation's operating system from a centralized location is easy. Diskless clients, on the other hand, are used when disk space on the workstation is limited, but because swapping is done across the network, network bandwidth needs to be considered.

Looking at each system type from a performance and ease-of-management point of view, you see that the stand-alone system has the best performance, but it is the most difficult to administer. The diskless client is easy to administer, but has the poorest performance of the other client types.

The AutoClient system is also easy to administer and has better performance than the diskless client. With the cost of disk drives decreasing, and network bandwidth at a premium these days, this is usually a better alternative than the diskless client or even the JavaStation.

The JavaStation is the easiest to administer, but requires more network bandwidth than the AutoClient. Also, the applications and services you plan to run must be Java-based.

## Disk Storage Systems

Before you begin to install a system, you need to think about how you want data stored on your system's disks. With one disk, the decision is easy. When multiple disks are installed, you must decide which disks to use for the operating system, the swap area, and the user data.

Solaris breaks disks into pieces called partitions, or slices. A Solaris disk can be divided into a maximum of seven partitions.

Why would you want to divide the disk into multiple partitions? Some administrators don't; they use the entire disk with one partition. By using one partition, all the space on the disk is available for anyone to use. When the system administrator creates a partition, the space in that partition is available only to the file system that is mounted on it. If another file system on the same disk runs out of space, it cannot borrow space from the other partition without repartitioning the disk. However, partitioning can provide some advantages. The following list describes some of the reasons why you might want to consider partitioning disks:

- Partitions allow finer control over such tasks as creating backups. UNIX commands, such as `ufsdump`, work on entire file systems. For backups, you might want to separate data and swap space from the application software so that backups are completed faster with a `ufsdump`. For example, you might want to back up only data on a daily basis. On the other hand, you'll need to take down the system to single-user mode to back up / and /usr, so separating the data will make your backup complete much more quickly and result in less downtime.
- If one file system becomes corrupted, the others remain intact. If you need to perform a recovery operation, you can restore a smaller file system more quickly. Also, when data is separated from system software, you can modify file systems without shutting down the system or reloading operating system software.
- Partitions allow you to control the amount of disk storage allocated to an activity or type of use.
- If file systems are mounted remotely from other systems, you can share only the data that needs to be accessed, not the entire system disk.

The installation process gives you the option of creating partitions. Start with the default partition scheme supplied with the installation program, which is to set up a file system for root (/), /usr, and swap. This scheme sets up the required partitions, and provides you with the sizes required, based on the software cluster you select to install. The following is a typical partitioning scheme for a system with a single disk drive:

- root (/) and /usr. Solaris normally creates two partitions for itself: root (/) and /usr. The installation program determines how much space you need. Most of the files in these two partitions are static. Information in these file systems will not increase in size unless you add software packages later. If you plan to add third-party software after the installation of Solaris, make sure you increase this partition to accommodate the additional files you plan to load. If the root (/) file system fills up, the system will not operate properly.
- swap. This area on the disk doesn't have files in it. In UNIX, you're allowed to have more programs than will fit into memory. The pieces that aren't currently needed in memory are transferred into swap to free up physical memory for other active processes. Swapping into a dedicated partition is a good idea for two reasons: swap partitions are isolated so that they aren't put on tape with the daily backups, and a swap partition can be laid out on a disk in an area to optimize performance.
- /home. On a single-disk system, everything not in root (/), /usr, or swap should go into a separate partition. /home is where you would put user-created files.
- /var (optional). Solaris uses this area for system log files, print spoolers, and email. The name /var is short for variable because this file system contains system files that are not static, but are variable in size. One day, the print spooler directory might be empty; another day, it might contain several 1MB files. This separate file system is created to keep the root (/) and /usr file systems from filling up with these files. If the /var file system does not exist, make sure you make root (/) larger.

- /opt (optional). By default, the Solaris installation program loads optional software packages here. Also, third-party applications are usually loaded into /opt. If this file system does not exist, the installation program puts the optional software in the root file system. If the /opt file system does not exist, make sure you make root (/) larger.

File systems provide a way to segregate data, but when a file system runs out of space, you can't increase it or "borrow" from a file system that has some unused space. Therefore, the best plan is to create a minimal number of file systems with adequate space for expansion. See Chapter 6 and Chapter 7, "Solaris File Systems: Advanced Topics," for additional information on planning and creating file systems.

## Basic Considerations for Planning Partition Sizes

Planning disk and partition space depends on many factors: the number of users, the application requirements, and the number and size of files and databases. Following are some basic considerations for determining your disk space requirements:

- Allocate additional disk space for each language selected (for example, Chinese, Japanese, Korean).
- If you need printing or mail support, create a partition for a separate /var file system and allocate additional disk space. You need to estimate the number and size of email messages and print files to size this partition properly.
- Allocate additional disk space on a server that will provide home file systems for users. Again, the number of users and the size of their files will dictate the size of this file system. By default, home directories are usually located in the /export file system.
- Allocate additional disk space on an operating system server for diskless clients or Solstice AutoClient systems.

- Make sure you allocate enough swap space. Factors that dictate the amount of swap space are the number of users and the application requirements. Consult with your application vendor for swap-space requirements. Vendors usually give you a formula to determine the amount of swap space you need for each application.
- Determine the software packages you will be installing, and calculate the total amount of disk space required. When planning disk space, remember that the Solaris Interactive Installation program lets you add or remove individual software packages from the software cluster you select.
- Create a minimum number of file systems. By default, the Solaris Interactive Installation program creates only root (/), /usr, and swap, although /export is also created when space is allocated for operating system services. Creating a minimum number of file systems helps with future upgrades and file system expansion because separate file systems are limited by their slice boundaries. Be generous with the size of your file systems, especially root (/) and /usr. These file systems cannot be increased without completely reloading the operating system.
- Calculate additional disk space for copackaged or third-party software.

## Partition Arrangements on Multiple Disks

> **NOTE** You cannot split a partition between two or more disks.

Although a single large disk can hold all partitions and their corresponding file systems, two or more disks are often used to hold a system's partitions and file systems.

For example, a single disk might hold the root (/) file system, a swap area, and the /usr file system; and a second disk might be used for the /export/home file system and other file systems containing user data. In a multiple-disk arrangement, the disk containing the root (/) and /usr file systems and swap space is referred to as the system disk. Disks other than the system disk are called secondary disks or nonsystem disks.

Locating a system's file systems on multiple disks allows you to modify file systems and partitions on the secondary disks without shutting down the system or reloading the operating system software. Also, multiple disks allow you to distribute the workload as evenly as possible among different I/O systems and disk drives, such as distributing the /home and swap partitions evenly across disks.

Having more than one disk increases input/output (I/O) volume. By distributing the I/O load across multiple disks, you can avoid I/O bottlenecks.

> **NOTE** A good way to improve system performance is to create more than one swap partition, and assign each of them to separate disk drives. When the system needs to access swap, the disk I/O is spread across multiple drives.

# Device Drivers

A computer typically uses a wide range of peripheral and mass-storage devices, such as a SCSI disk drive, a keyboard, a mouse, and some kind of magnetic backup medium. Other commonly used devices include CD-ROM drives, printers, and plotters.

Solaris communicates with peripheral devices through device files. Before Solaris can communicate with a device, it must have a device driver, a low-level program that allows the kernel to communicate with a specific piece of hardware. The driver serves as the operating system's "interpreter" for that piece of hardware.

When a system is booted for the first time, the kernel creates a device hierarchy to represent all devices connected to the system. Devices are described in three ways in the Solaris environment, using three distinct naming conventions: the physical device name, the instance name, and the logical device name. System administrators need to understand the device names when using commands to manage disks, file systems, and other devices.

## Physical Device Name

A physical device name represents the full device pathname of the device. Physical device files are found in the /devices directory and have the following naming convention:

```
/devices/sbus@1,f8000000/esp@0,40000/sd@3,0:a
```

You can display physical device names by using one of the commands listed in Table 3.3.

> **TIP**
>
> Use the output of the `prtconf` and `sysdef` commands to identify which disk, tape, and CD-ROM devices are connected to the system. The output of these commands displays the `driver not attached` message next to the device instances. Because some system process is always monitoring these devices, the `driver not attached` message is usually a good indication that no device is physically at that device instance.

**TABLE 3.3**

**DISPLAYING PHYSICAL DEVICE NAMES**

| *Command* | *Description* |
|---|---|
| `prtconf` | Displays system configuration information, including the total amount of memory and the device configuration as described by the system's hierarchy. The output displayed by this command depends on the type of system. |
| `sysdef` | Displays device configuration information, including system hardware, pseudo devices, loadable modules, and selected kernel parameters. |
| `dmesg` | Displays system diagnostic messages and a list of devices attached to the system since the last reboot. |

If you need to remind yourself of the meanings of the fields of a physical device name, refer to Chapter 1, " System Startup and Shutdown," for a detailed discussion. In addition, Chapter 16, "Device Administration and Disk Management," includes additional information about devices.

## Instance Name

The instance name represents the kernel's abbreviated name for every possible device on the system. For example, `sd0` and `sd1` represent the instance names of two SCSI disk devices. Instance names are mapped in the /etc/path_to_inst file, and are displayed by using the commands `dmesg`, `sysdef`, and `prtconf`.

## Logical Device Name

Logical device names are used with most Solaris file system commands to refer to devices. Logical device files in the /dev directory are symbolically linked to physical device files in the /devices directory. Logical device names are used to access disk devices in the following circumstances:

- Adding a new disk to the system
- Moving a disk from one system to another
- Accessing (or mounting) a file system residing on a local disk
- Backing up a local file system
- Repairing a file system

Logical devices are organized in subdirectories under the /dev directory by their device types, as shown in Table 3.4.

**TABLE 3.4**

**DEVICE LOCATIONS**

| *Directory* | *Device Type* |
|---|---|
| /dev/dsk | Block interface to disk devices |
| /dev/rdsk | Raw or character interface to disk devices |
| /dev/rmt | Tape devices |
| /dev/term | Serial-line devices |
| /dev/cua | Dial-out modems |
| /dev/pts | Pseudo terminals |
| /dev/fbs | Frame buffers |
| /dev/sad | STREAMS administrative driver |

Logical device files have major and minor numbers that indicate device drivers, hardware addresses, and other characteristics. Furthermore, a device filename must follow a specific naming convention. A logical device name for a disk drive has the following format:

```
/dev/[r]dsk/cxtxdxsx
```

The fields of the logical device name are described in Table 3.5.

**TABLE 3.5**

**DISK DRIVE LOGICAL DEVICE NAME**

| *Field* | *Description* |
|---|---|
| `cX` | Refers to the SCSI controller number |
| `tX` | Refers to the SCSI bus target number |
| `dX` | Refers to the disk number (always 0, except on storage arrays) |
| `sX` | Refers to the slice or partition number |

Following are two examples of logical device filenames for disk drives:

- `/dev/dsk/c0t3d0s0`. Refers to slice 0 on a SCSI disk drive with a target ID of 3 on SCSI controller 0. Buffered device.
- `/dev/rdsk/c0t3d0s0`. Refers to slice 0 on a SCSI disk drive with a target ID of 3 on SCSI controller 0. Raw device.

## Block and Character Device Files

Some devices, such as disk drives, have an entry under both the /dev/dsk directory and the /dev/rdsk directory. The /dsk directory refers to the block or buffered device file, and the /rdsk directory refers to the character or raw device file. The "r" in rdsk stands for "raw." Disk and file administration commands require the use of either a raw device interface or a block device interface. The device file used specifies whether I/O is to be handled in block or character mode, commonly referred to as I/O type.

Block device files transfer data by using system buffers to speed up I/O transfer. Storage devices—such as tape drives, disk drives, and CD-ROMs—use block device files. Under most circumstances, Solaris accesses the disk via the block device. Data is buffered or cached in memory until the buffer is full, and then it is written to disk.

Character device interfaces transfer only small amounts of data, one character at a time. With a character device file, data is written directly to the disk, bypassing system I/O buffers. The application program controls buffering. Terminals, printers, plotters, and storage devices use character I/O.

Different commands require different device file interfaces. When a command requires the character device interface, specify the /dev/rdsk subdirectory. When a command requires the block device interface, specify the /dev/dsk subdirectory. When you're not sure whether a command requires the use of /dev/dsk or /dev/rdsk, check the online manual page for that command.

# METHODS OF INSTALLING THE SOLARIS 8 SOFTWARE

You can use one of five methods to install the Solaris software: Interactive, JumpStart, Custom JumpStart, Web Start, or installation over the network.

## Interactive

The Solaris Interactive Installation program guides you step-by-step through installing the Solaris software. The Interactive program does not allow you to install all of the software (Solaris software and copackaged software) in your product box at once; it installs only the SunOS software. After you install the Solaris software, you must install the other copackaged software by using the copackaged installation programs.

## JumpStart

JumpStart provides the capability to install Solaris on a new system by inserting the CD into the CD-ROM and turning on power to the system. No interaction is required. The software components installed are specified by a default profile that is selected based on the model and disk size of the system.

All new SPARC-based systems have the JumpStart software (a preinstalled boot image) preinstalled on the boot disk. You can install the JumpStart software on existing systems by using the `re-preinstall` command.

NOTE

On a new system that Sun shipped, the installation software is specified by a default profile that is based on the system's model and the size of its disks; you don't have a choice of the software to be installed. Make sure this JumpStart configuration is suited to your environment. The system loads the end-user distribution group and sets up minimal swap space. Partitions and their sizes are set up by using default parameters that might not be suitable for the applications you plan to install.

## Custom JumpStart

This method, formerly called Auto-Install, allows you to automatically—and identically—install many systems with the same configuration without having to configure each of them individually. Custom JumpStart requires up-front setup of configuration files before the systems can be installed, but it's the most cost-effective way to automatically install Solaris software for a large installation.

When might you want to use JumpStart? For example, suppose you need to install the Solaris software on 50 systems. Of these 50 systems to be installed, 25 are in engineering as stand-alone systems with the entire distribution configuration cluster, and 25 are in the IS group with the developer distribution configuration cluster. JumpStart allows you to set up a configuration file for each department and install the operating system identically on all the systems. This process facilitates the installation by automating it, ensuring consistency between systems.

JumpStart, an objective on the second exam, is covered in detail in Chapter 21, "JumpStart."

## Web Start

Solaris Web Start is Sun's browser-based "virtual assistant" for installing software. Using Solaris Web Start and Sun's web browser, you select either a default installation or a customize option to install only the software you want, including the Solaris configuration cluster, Solstice utilities, and other copackaged software. From Sun's web browser, an installation profile is created that is used by Solaris JumpStart to install the Solaris software and the other selected software products with minimal intervention. Web Start simplifies the creation of the JumpStart configuration file.

New in Solaris 8 is the Web Start Flash installation feature that enables you to create a single reference installation of the Solaris operating environment on a machine, which is called the master machine. After installing the operating system onto the master machine, you can add or delete software and modify system configuration information as needed. Then, you can replicate that installation on a number of systems, which are called clone machines.

Web Start, an objective on the second exam, is covered in Appendix A, "Web Start."

## Installing Over the Network

Because the Solaris software is distributed on a CD, a system must have access to a CD-ROM drive to install it. However, if you don't have a local CD-ROM, you can set up the system to install from a remote CD or CD image on a remote disk drive. The remote Solaris CD image must be provided by an installation server that has either the Solaris CD copied to its hard disk or the Solaris CD mounted from its CD-ROM drive. Installing the operating system across the network is handy when a local CD-ROM is not available.

# THE SOLARIS INSTALLATION PROCESS

Solaris is installed by using the Solaris Install tool, a GUI that is friendly and easy to use. This section provides an overview of the installation process using the interactive installation program on a Sun system. For a more detailed overview of the Solaris 8 interactive installation procedure, see Chapter 15.

**CAUTION**

The following procedure reinstalls your operating system. That means it destroys all data on the target file systems.

The interactive installation program brings up various menus, and asks for your input. The Install tool allows you to go back to previous screens if you make a mistake, and it doesn't actually do anything to your system until the installation program reaches the end and tells you it is about to start the loading process. During the installation, help is always available via the Help button.

If you're upgrading or installing Solaris on a running system, use the following steps to shut down and then perform the installation.

> **NOTE** This installation is for a Sun system. To begin the installation on an Intel-based PC, insert the Device Configuation Assistant floppy, and boot to the floppy disk. You'll be instructed to install the Solaris media after the devices are configured.

## STEP BY STEP

### 3.1 Shutting Down and Starting a Solaris 8 Installation

1. Become root.
2. Issue the `shutdown` command. This command brings the system to a single-user state by halting the window system and leaving you with a single root prompt on the console. It takes about a minute.
3. Issue the `halt` command. This command puts you into the PROM. You'll know you're in the PROM when you receive either an `ok` or a `>` prompt.
4. Put the Solaris 8 Software CD 1 of 2 into the CD player and boot from the CD.
5. At the `ok` prompt, type `boot cdrom`.

The system boots from the CD-ROM. The process is slow, but the flashing light on the CD player shows activity. Eventually, the system starts the GUI and presents you with the Solaris Installation program. Follow the instructions onscreen to install the software on the system. Have the following information available because the installation tool will ask for it:

- Hostname. The name for the system. Hostnames should be short, easy to spell, and lowercase; and they should have no more than 64 characters. If the system is on a network, the hostname should be unique.
- IP address. This information must come from your site IP coordinator. 192.9.200.1 is one example of an IP address. IP addresses must be unique for every system on your network. For a large site or a site that has a presence on the Internet, you should apply for a unique IP address from the NIC to ensure that no other network shares your address. On workstations, some sites use DHCP, described in Chapter 18, "Name Services," to automatically set the IP address.

- Subnet mask. Along with the IP address, make sure that you also get the subnet mask used at your site. On an existing system, this information can be obtained from the /etc/netmasks file.
- Ipv6. You'll be asked if support for Ipv6, the next-generation Internet protocol, should be installed.
- NIS, NIS+, DNS, LDAP, or NONE. You'll need to specify which name service your system will be using, or NONE if you're not using one. Refer to Chapter 18 for more information.
- Security. You'll be asked if Kerberos security should be configured. Kerberos provides selectable strong user- or server-level authentication based on symmetric key cryptography. Ask your in-house security personnel if Kerberos security is required.
- Timezone. You'll need to know the geographic region and timezone in which this system will be operated.
- Root password. During the installation, you will be asked to assign a password to the root user account.
- Language. Determine the language to be used to install the Solaris 8 Operating environment.

When the installation program is finished gathering information, it asks you if it's okay to begin the installation. When the installation is complete, you are asked to supply a root password. Make sure you complete this step and supply a secure password.

This completes the installation of the Solaris operating system.

## CHAPTER SUMMARY

### KEY TERMS

- Platform group
- Platform name
- Installation media
- Software package
- Software cluster
- Configuration clusters
- Swap space
- Server
- Client
- Diskless client
- AutoClient
- Stand-alone
- Disk partition
- Device driver
- Physical device name
- Instance name
- Logical device name
- Block device
- Character device
- Hostname
- IP address
- IPV6

This chapter described the fundamentals of installing a system. It described the steps of preparation that the system administrator must perform before installing Solaris 8. The chapter also addressed the topics and terms you'll need to know when taking the first Solaris certified system administrator exam.

Other chapters in this book discuss the various installation procedures—such as JumpStart, Web Start, and installation of a server using the Interactive Installation program—in more detail to prepare you for taking the second exam. Subsequent chapters also discuss post-installation procedures, such as setting up print queues, adding users, and setting up a backup procedure.

## APPLY YOUR KNOWLEDGE

# Exercises

### 3.1 Preparing to Install the Solaris 8 Operating Environment

In this exercise, you will perform the steps necessary to prepare for a Solaris 8 operating system install on a networked, stand-alone system.

**Estimated Time**: 15 minutes

1. Identify your system type using the following command:

   ```
   uname -m
   ```

   Is it a supported platform type listed in Table 3.1, and do you have the Solaris 8 Installation media kit for that platform?

2. Identify the peripherals connected to your system, and determine the device name for the CD-ROM and the disk drive that will be used as the boot device. Use the `prtconf`, `sysdef`, and `dmesg` commands described in this chapter to identify these devices.

   Make sure your system meets the minimum system requirements for Solaris 8. If it does not meet the minimum requirements, you will not be able to install Solaris 8. Check the amount of RAM as follows:

   ```
   prtconf|grep Memory
   ```

   Does the system have a CD-ROM?

   Check the amount of disk space using the `format` command and listing the size of partition 2, making sure that you select the correct device name for your boot disk.

> **NOTE**
> Chapter 7 describes the use of the `format` command.

3. Determine the software cluster that you want to install, and determine the amount of disk space it will require. Compare this value with the total size of your disk, which was determined in the previous step. For example, if the size of disk slice 2 was 1.3GB, and I want to install the Entire Distribution cluster, I do not have enough disk space to complete the installation.

4. Plan your storage requirements, as described in the "Disk Storage Systems" section. Determine the file systems and partition sizes that you want the installation program to create.

5. Obtain the following information that will be required by the Solaris 8 installation program:

   - What is the hostname of the system? Use the `hostname` command to determine the hostname on an existing system, or ask your network administrator to assign a hostname.
   - Does it have a static IP address or DHCP? Use the `ifconfig` command to determine the IP address on an existing system, or ask your IP coordinator to assign an IP address. For more information on using the `ifconfig` command to determine a system's IP address, see Chapter 13, "The Solaris Network Environment."
   - Does Ipv6, the next-generation Internet protocol, need to be enabled?

## APPLY YOUR KNOWLEDGE

> **NOTE** Enabling IPV6 will have no effect if this machine is not on a network that provides IPV6 service. IPV4 service will not be affected if IPV6 is enabled.

- Is a name service used, such as NIS, NIS+, DNS, or LDAP? See Chapter 18 for more information on name services.
- Should Kerberos security be configured? Ask your in-house security personnel if this is required.
- What is the geographic region of your time-zone (Eastern, Central, Alaska)?
- During the installation, you will be asked to assign a password to the root user account.
- Determine the language to be used to install the Solaris 8 operating environment.

## Review Questions

1. What is the minimum amount of RAM required to install Solaris 8?

   A. 16MB

   B. 32MB

   C. 64MB

   D. 128MB

2. What is the best command used to find out the name of your hardware's platform group and name?

   A. `uname -a`

   B. `sysdef`

   C. `arch`

   D. `uname -m`

3. What is a software cluster?

   A. A group of files and directories that describe a software application

   B. A logical collection of software packages

   C. Any software that can be installed on Solaris

   D. A collection of files that make up a software application

4. What is a software package?

   A. A group of files and directories that describe a software application

   B. A logical collection of software packages

   C. A collection of files that make up a software application

   D. A collection of files and directories

5. Which of the following does an AutoClient system have?

   A. A local disk and local swap; (/) and /usr are cached from a networked server

   B. No local disk; (/) and /usr are cached into RAM from a remote server

   C. A local disk and a local root (/), but /usr is cached from a remote server

   D. A local disk, a local root (/), and a local /usr, but swap is on a remote server

6. Which is *not* one of the five configuration clusters in Solaris 8?

   A. Entire system support

   B. End user support

## APPLY YOUR KNOWLEDGE

C. Developer system support

D. Entire distribution plus OEM system support

7. What are the default file systems created by the Solaris installation program?

A. /, /opt, /usr, /var, and swap

B. /, /usr, /var, and swap

C. /, /usr, /var, /usr/openwin, /opt, and swap

D. /, /usr, and swap

8. Which of the following best describes a physical device name?

A. It represents the full device pathname of a device.

B. It is equivalent to the SCSI target ID of a device.

C. It represents the actual name of a device, such as a disk, tape, and so on.

D. It represents the kernel's abbreviated name for a device on the system.

9. Which of the following is the command used to display device configuration information, such as system hardware, pseudo devices, loadable modules, and kernel parameters?

A. `dmesg`

B. `sysdef`

C. `prtconf`

D. `uname`

10. In the standard device filenaming convention "cXtYdZ," what does the "tY" portion of the filename identify?

A. The controller card to which this device is attached

B. The SCSI target address of the device

C. The LUN of the device

D. The function number as contained on the "Core I/O" board

11. Which of the following is a character device name?

A. /dev/dsk/c0t3d0s0

B. /dev/rdsk/c0t3d0s0

C. /dev/cua

D. /devices/sbus@1,f8000000/esp@0,40000/sd@3,0:a

12. What best describes an instance name?

A. The kernel's abbreviated name for every possible device on the system

B. A symbolic link to a physical device file

C. The full device pathname of a device

D. The SCSI address of a disk drive

## Apply Your Knowledge

13. Logical devices are organized in subdirectories under which directory?

    A. /dev

    B. /devices

    C. /kernel

    D. /

14. Which of the following is not a valid method of installing Solaris 8?

    A. Installing over a subnet

    B. Interactive

    C. Installing from a remote CD-ROM on a system on the same subnet

    D. Web Start

15. What best describes a logical device name?

    A. It is a symbolic link to a physical device file.

    B. It represents the kernel's abbreviated name for every possible device on the system.

    C. It represents the full device pathname of a device.

    D. It defines the SCSI address of a disk drive.

16. Which of the following are characteristics of a character device?

    A. Character device interfaces transfer only small amounts of data, one character at a time.

    B. With a character device file, data is written directly to the disk, bypassing system I/O buffers.

    C. The application program controls buffering.

    D. All of the above.

17. Which of the following statements is *not* true of a software package?

    A. A software package is a group of files and directories that describe a software application, such as manual pages and line printer support.

    B. A software package is a standard way to deliver bundled and unbundled software.

    C. Software packages are grouped into software clusters.

    D. Software packages are administered using the `installf` command.

18. On a UNIX workstation, what is the first step in installing a new operating system?

    A. Informing the users

    B. Repartitioning the hard drive

    C. Finding the source distribution media

    D. Performing a full backup

19. Which is *not* a valid software configuration cluster to choose during installation of the Solaris 8 operating environment?

    A. Core

    B. Client

    C. End User

    D. Developer

20. For which of the following is Custom JumpStart used?

    A. To install the Solaris software on 50 identical systems

    B. To start a system that refuses to boot

## APPLY YOUR KNOWLEDGE

C. To set up AutoClient systems on a server

D. To interactively guide you, step-by-step, in installing the Solaris software

21. For which of the following is Web Start used?

A. To set up your server as a web server

B. To start up a default Internet browser, such as Netscape

C. To simplify the creation of the JumpStart configuration file

D. To set up software on a remote system via the web

22. Which of the following commands is the *best* way to shut down a system?

A. `shutdown`

B. `halt`

C. `reboot`

D. `Stop+A`

## Answers to Review Questions

1. **C.** The system on which you will be installing Solaris 8 must have a minimum of 64MB of RAM.

2. **D.** To determine your system type, use the `uname -m` command. The system will respond with the platform group and the platform name for your system.

3. **B.** Software packages are grouped into software clusters, which are logical collections of software packages.

4. **A.** A software package is a collection of files and directories in a defined format. It is a group of files and directories that describe a software application.

5. **A.** An AutoClient system uses its local disk for swap space, and to cache its individual root (/) file system and the /usr file system from a server's file systems.

6. **A.** The five configuration clusters are core system support, end-user support, developer system support, entire distribution, and entire distribution plus OEM system support.

7. **D.** The default partition scheme supplied with the installation program, which is to set up a file system, includes root (/), /usr, and swap.

8. **A.** A physical device name represents the full device pathname of the device. Physical device files are found in the /devices directory and have the following naming convention:

```
/devices/sbus@1,f8000000/esp@0,40000/sd@3,0:a
```

9. **B.** The `sysdef` command displays device configuration information, including system hardware, pseudo devices, loadable modules, and selected kernel parameters.

10. **B.** The fields of the logical device name cXtYdZ are as follows:

`cX` Refers to the SCSI controller number

`tY` Refers to the SCSI bus target number

`dZ` Refers to the disk number (always 0, except on storage arrays)

11. **B.** In the following character device name, /dev/rdsk/c0t3d0s0, the /rdsk directory refers to the character or raw device file. The *r* in rdsk stands for *raw*.

## Apply Your Knowledge

12. **A.** The instance name represents the kernel's abbreviated name for every possible device on the system. For example, `sd0` and `sd1` represent the instance names of two SCSI disk devices.

13. **A.** Logical device names are used with most Solaris file system commands to refer to devices. Logical device files in the /dev directory are symbolically linked to physical device files in the /devices directory.

14. **A.** The Solaris 8 operating environment cannot be installed over a subnet.

15. **A.** Logical device files in the /dev directory are symbolically linked to physical device files in the /devices directory.

16. **D.** Character device interfaces transfer only small amounts of data, one character at a time. With a character device file, data is written directly to the disk, bypassing system I/O buffers. The application program controls buffering. Terminals, printers, plotters and storage devices use character I/O.

17. **D.** The `installf` command is used to add a file to the software installation database, not to administer software packages.

18. **D.** The first step in installing the operating system is to run a full backup to tape because the installation process destroys all data on the disk.

19. **B.** The five configuration clusters are core system support, end-user support, developer system support, entire distribution, and entire distribution plus OEM system support.

20. **A.** Custom JumpStart allows you to automatically and identically install many systems with the same configuration without having to configure each of them individually.

21. **C.** Web Start simplifies the creation of the JumpStart configuration file.

22. **A.** Shutting down a Solaris system with the `shutdown` command is the recommended and best method of shutting down a system.

# Chapter 4

# Software Package Administration

## Objectives

The following is the test objective for this chapter:

**Understand the tools for managing software**

- Sun provides several standard tools for managing software on Solaris. This chapter describes all of these tools for performing the following tasks:
  - Add and remove software packages
  - List and verify installed software packages
  - Install and remove software patches

- One of the system administrator's primary responsibilities is to add and remove Solaris software packages, including software patches. A complete understanding of the methods and commands used to accomplish these tasks is critical.

## OUTLINE



## STUDY STRATEGIES

The following strategies will help you study for the exam:

- ▶ When studying this chapter, I suggest that you practice the step-by-step examples that I've outlined on either a Sun system or an Intel-based system running the Solaris 8 operating system. Practice all of the step-by-step examples until you can perform them from memory.
- ▶ Become familiar with all the tools used to manage software on a Solaris system. Understand which tool is best for a particular circumstance.
- ▶ Understand the terms used in this chapter to describe how Sun packages their software. For your convenience, the important terms are listed at the end of this chapter. Many of these terms will be on the actual exam.
- ▶ Finally, make sure you understand the operating system patching process. Pay special attention to how to obtain patches, how to install them, and how to verify patches on your system.

# INTRODUCTION

The system administrator is responsible for managing all software installed on a system. Installing and removing software is a routine task that is performed frequently. Chapter 3, "Installing the Solaris 8 Software," described the installation of the Solaris operating system. This chapter explains how to add and remove additional applications after the operating system has already been installed.

Sun and its third-party vendors deliver software products in a form called a software package. The term *package* refers to a method of distributing and installing software to systems where the products will be used. A package is a collection of files and directories in a defined format that conforms to the Application Binary Interface (ABI), a supplement to the System V Interface Definition. The Solaris operating environment provides a set of utilities that interpret the ABI format, and provides the means to install or remove a package or to verify its installation.

# TOOLS FOR MANAGING SOFTWARE

Solaris provides the tools for adding and removing software from a system. These are described in Table 4.1.

**TABLE 4.1**

**TOOLS FOR MANAGING SOFTWARE**

| *Command* | *Description* |
|---|---|
| ***Managing Software from the Command Line*** | |
| `pkgadd` | Adds software packages to the system |
| `pkgrm` | Removes software packages from the system |
| `pkgchk` | Checks the accuracy of a software package installation |
| `pkginfo` | Displays software package information |
| `pkgask` | Stores answers in a response file so that they can be supplied automatically during an installation |
| `pkgparam` | Displays package parameter values |

*continues*

**TABLE 4.1** *continued*

**TOOLS FOR MANAGING SOFTWARE**

| *Command* | *Description* |
|---|---|
| ***Managing Software from the Graphical User Interface*** | |
| `admintool` | Invokes from within CDE or Openwindows |
| Solaris Product Registry | Manages all of your Solaris sofware. |

Use the `pkgadd` or `pkgrm` commands directly from the command line to load or remove software packages. The `pkgadd` and `pkgrm` commands can be incorporated into scripts to automate the software installation process. Many third-party vendors use `pkgadd` in scripts as a means of installing their software.

Admintool, on the other hand, provides an easy-to-use interface for installing and removing software packages. It is simply a graphical user interface to the `pkgadd` and `pkgrm` commands. Using the Admintool graphical interface is a convenient way to view software already installed on a system or to view the software that resides on the installation media. If you're unfamiliar with software-package naming conventions, if you are uncomfortable using command-line options, or if you're managing software on only one system at a time, you'll find Admintool an easy way to add and remove software packages.

New in Solaris 8 is the Solaris Product Registry, a system for maintaining records of the software products installed on a Solaris system. The Product Registry includes a GUI tool to make managing your Solaris software easier. The Product Registry allows you to install, list, or uninstall Solaris software packages or clusters.

## ADDING AND REMOVING SOFTWARE PACKAGES

When you add a software package, the `pkgadd` command decompresses and copies files from the installation media, such as the CD-ROM, to a local system's disk. When you use packages, files are delivered in package format, and are unusable as they are delivered.

The pkgadd command interprets the software package's control files and then decompresses the product files and installs them on the system's local disk.

You should know the following things before installing additional application software:

- Sun packages always begin with the prefix SUNW, as in SUNWvolr, SUNWadmap, and SUNWab2m. Third-party packages usually begin with a prefix that corresponds to the company's stock symbol.
- You can use the pkginfo command or Admintool to view software already installed on a system.
- Clients might have software that resides partially on a server and partially on the client. If this is the case, adding software for the client requires adding packages to both the server and the client.
- You need to know where the software will be installed, and you need to make sure you have a file system that has enough disk space to store the application software. If you know the name of the software package, you can use the pkgparam command to determine where the package will be loaded. For example, to find out information about the SUNWvolr package, type the following:

```
pkgparam -d /cdrom/cdrom0/s0/Solaris_2.8/Product SUNWvolr  SUNW_PKGTYPE
```

SUNW_PKGTYPE is a special parameter that reports where a Solaris software package will be installed. If the package does not have the SUNW_PKGTYPE parameter set, the pkgparam command returns an empty string. For Sun packages, this usually means that the package will be installed in /opt.

The system responds with the location where the application will be stored:

```
root
```

**NOTE** It's not always clear what the pkgid is for a particular software package or application until it is actually installed. Sometimes the release documentation that came with the package will tell you the name of the pkgid. Other times you might need to call the vendor to get the pkgid information.

CAUTION

When you remove a package, the `pkgrm` command deletes all the files associated with that package unless those files are also shared with other packages. If the files are shared with another package, a system message will warn you that other packages use these files, and you will be prompted if you want to remove them anyway. Be sure you do not delete application software without using `pkgrm`. For example, some system administrators delete an application simply by removing the directory containing the application software. With this method, files belonging to the application that might reside in other directories are missed. With `pkgrm`, you'll be assured of removing all files associated with the application.

NOTE

Copying packages to a spool directory is not the same as installing the packages on a system.

Although the `pkgadd` and `pkgrm` commands do not log their output to a standard location, they do keep track of the product installed or removed. The `pkgadd` and `pkgrm` commands store information in a software product database about a package that has been installed or removed. By updating this database, the `pkgadd` and `pkgrm` commands keep a record of all software products installed on the system.

## Using a Spool Directory

For convenience, you can copy frequently installed packages to a spool directory. If you copy packages to the default spool directory, /var/spool/pkg, you do not need to specify the source location of the package when using the `pkgadd` command. The `pkgadd` command, by default, will look in the /var/spool/pkg directory for any packages specified on the command line.

### STEP BY STEP

#### 4.1 Adding a Package to the Spool Directory

To add a package to the spool directory named /var/spool/pkg, follow these steps:

1. Log in as root.
2. Make sure the spool directory exists.
3. Add a software package to a spool directory using the `pkgadd` command as follows:

```
pkgadd -d <device-name> -s <spool directory> <pkgid>
```

in which

- `-d <device-name>` specifies the absolute path to the software package. *`<device-name>`* can be the path to a device, a directory, or a spool directory.
- `-s <spooldir>`. Specifies the name of the spool directory where the software package will be spooled. You must specify a *`<spooldir>`*, a directory where the software will be put.

- `<pkgid>` *(Optional).* This is the name of one or more packages, separated by spaces, to be added to the spool directory. If omitted, `pkgadd` copies all available packages.

4. Verify that the package has been copied to the spool directory, using the `pkginfo` command, as follows:

   ```
   pkginfo -d <spooldir> | grep <pkgid>
   ```

   The `pkginfo` command will return a line of information about the package if it has been copied to the spool directory properly. If it returns an empty command line, the package has not been successfully copied to the spool directory.

The following is an example of how to copy a software package:

```
# pkgadd -d /cdrom/sol_8_sparc/s0/Solaris_8/Product -s /var/spool/pkg SUNWaudio
  Transferring <SUNWaudio> package instance
# pkginfo -d /var/spool/pkg   system   SUNWaudio   Audio/ applications
```

## Adding Software Packages Using Admintool

This section describes how you add software packages using Admintool.

### STEP BY STEP

#### 4.2 Installing Additional Application Software with Admintool

The procedure for installing additional application software with Admintool follows:

1. Start Admintool as the user root by typing `admintool` at the command prompt.

*continues*

*continued*

2. The Users main menu appears, as shown in Figure 4.1.

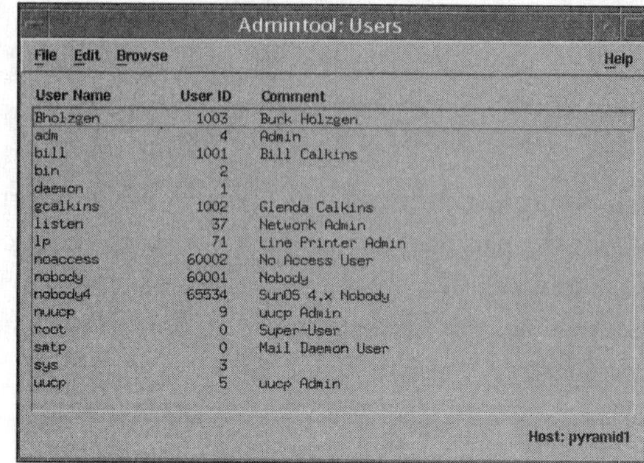


**FIGURE 4.1**
The Users main menu.

3. Choose Browse, Software. The Software window appears, as shown in Figure 4.2.

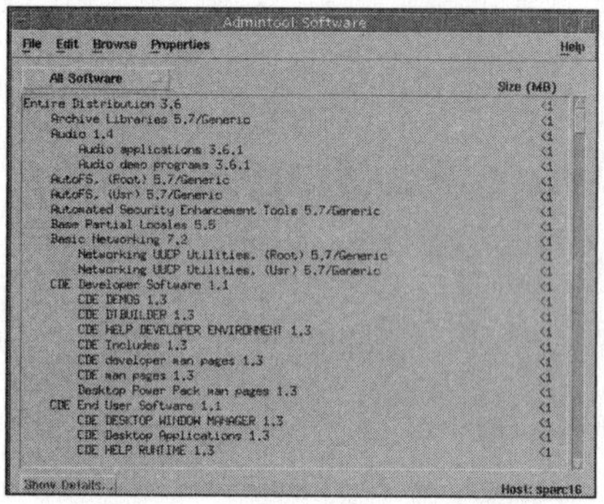

**FIGURE 4.2**
The Software window.

4. Choose Edit, Add. The Set Source Media window appears, as shown in Figure 4.3.

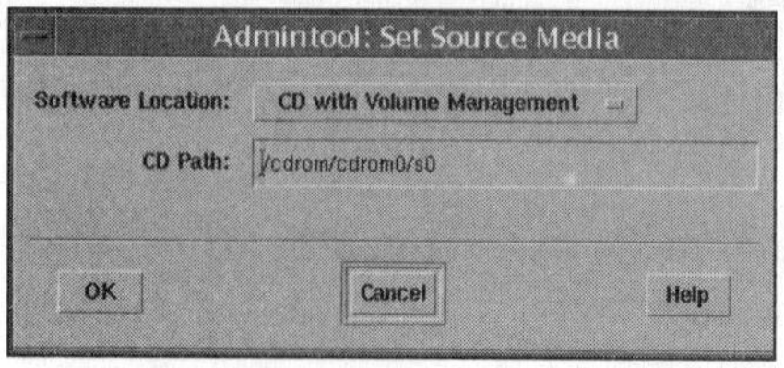

**FIGURE 4.3**
The Set Source Media window.

5. Specify the path to the installation medium. The default path from which to install the application is the mounted SPARC Solaris CD. Click OK to display the Add Software window, shown in Figure 4.4.

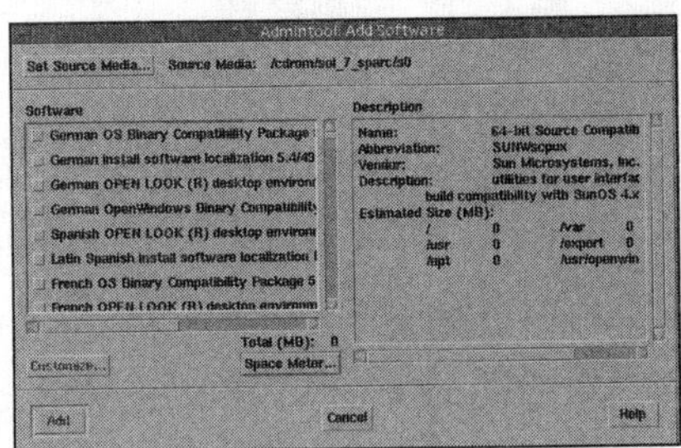


**FIGURE 4.4**
The Add Software window.

6. In the Software portion of the window, click the check boxes corresponding to the software you want to install. When you have selected all the packages, click the Add button.

A command tool window appears for each package being installed, displaying the installation output. When the installation is complete, the Software window refreshes to display the packages just added.

## Removing Software Packages Using Admintool

To remove software packages using Admintool, follow the procedures in the following steps.

**STEP BY STEP**

### 4.3 Removing Application Software

The procedure for removing application software is as follows:

1. Start Admintool, if it's not already running, and choose Browse, Software. The Software window opens, as shown in Figure 4.5.

*continues*

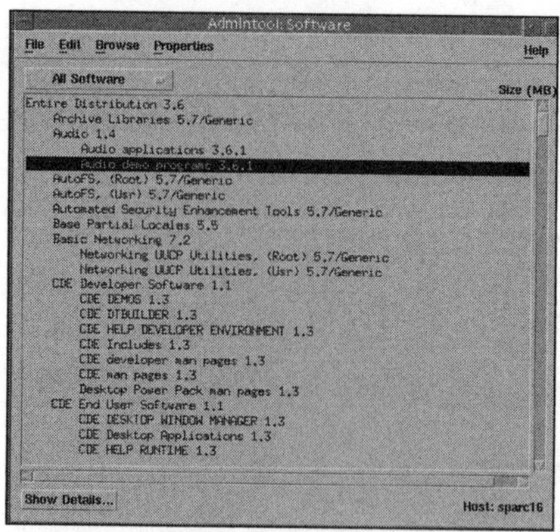


**FIGURE 4.5**
The Software window.

2. Select the software package you want to remove, and choose Edit, Delete. A message appears, asking you to confirm that you want to remove the software (see Figure 4.6).

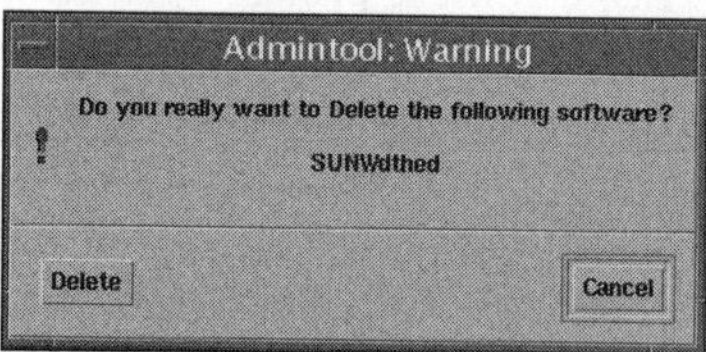


**FIGURE 4.6**
Confirm the software removal.

For each package being deleted, a command tool window is displayed, asking for confirmation before deleting the software. Type `y`, `n`, or `q`. If you choose to delete the software, the output from the removal process is displayed in the command tool window.

## SOLARIS PRODUCT REGISTRY

The Solaris Product Registry enables you to do the following:

- View a list of installed and registered software and some software attributes
- Find and launch an installer
- Install additional software products
- Uninstall software

The main difference between the Product Registry and the other tools is that the product registry is designed to be compatible with more of the newer installation wizards and Web Start 3.0.

To start up the Solaris Product Registry, type the following:

```
/usr/bin/prodreg
```

The product registry window shown in Figure 4.7 will appear.

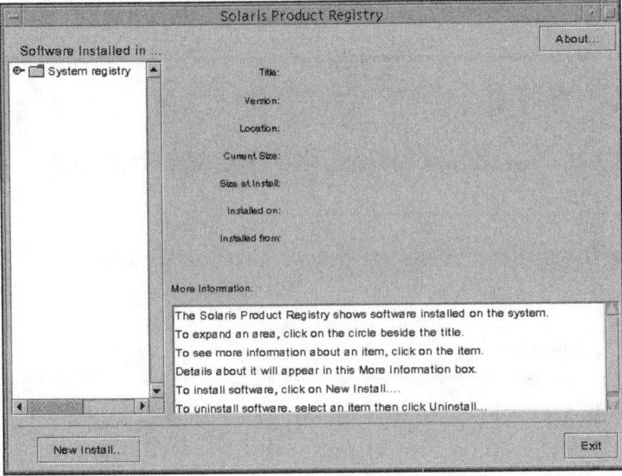


**FIGURE 4.7**
Product registry window.

To view the contents of the System Registry, double-click the folder next to System Registry with the left mouse button. The Registry will be expanded and the contents will be listed. Click any folder listed to get more information on that package. In Figure 4.7, I clicked on System Registry, then DiskSuite 4.2.1, and the information shown in Figure 4.8 was displayed.

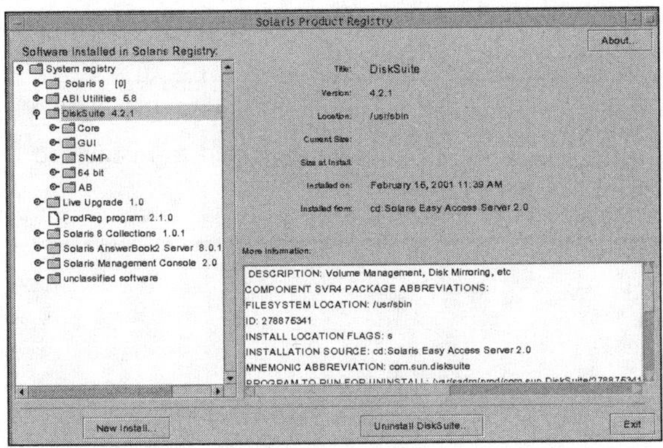


**FIGURE 4.8**
System Registry: DiskSuite Information.

Along with listing information about all installed software products on your system, use the Solaris Product Registry to check the integrity of software products installed on the system. Follow the steps outlined for listing installed software. After you see the package you want to check, click its name in the window titled Software Installed in Solaris Registry. If all or part of the product is missing, the message `Missing files in one or more components` is displayed after the Installed From attribute.

## STEP BY STEP

### 4.4 Installing Software Using the Solaris Product Registry

To install software using the Solaris Product Registry, follow these steps:

1. Log in as root.
2. Insert the CD-ROM that contains the software you want to add to the system. When you insert the CD, the Volume Manager automatically mounts the CD.
3. Start the Solaris Product Registry, as outlined earlier in this section.
4. Click the New Install button at the bottom of the Solaris Product Registry window. The Product Registry displays the Select Installer dialog box, which initially points to the /cdrom directory.
5. When you find the installer you want, click its name in the Files box and then click OK.
6. The installer you selected is launched. Follow the directions displayed by the installer you selected to install the software.

You can also use the Product Registry to remove software by following these steps:

## STEP BY STEP

### 4.5 Uninstalling Software Using the Solaris Product Registry

To uninstall software, go into the Solaris Product Registry window and follow these steps:

1. Click the System Registry folder in the window titled Software Installed in Solaris Registry, and click the software package you want to remove. Read the software attributes to make sure this is the software you want to uninstall.
2. Click the Uninstall <software_product_name> button at the bottom of the Solaris Product Registry window. The software product you selected is uninstalled.

# Listing and Verifying Installed Packages

At any time, you can use the Software Product Registry, Admintool, or issue the `pkginfo` command from the command line to obtain a complete listing of the software installed on a system. The Product Registry GUI interface will display information about installed software as described in the previous section and shown in Figure 4.8. The Software window in Admintool displays all the installed software when you choose Browse, Software (see Figure 4.9).

You can obtain more information about individual software packages by double-clicking any of the listed software packages in Admintool.

Figure 4.10 illustrates the `pkginfo` command used from the command line, with `more` used to show the display of information one page at a time.

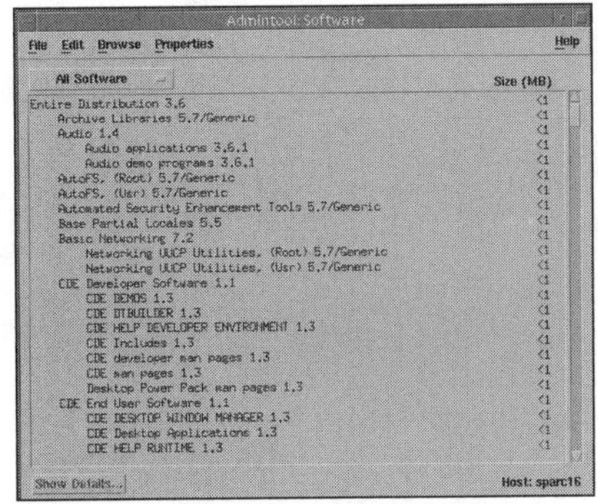

**FIGURE 4.9**
The Software window.

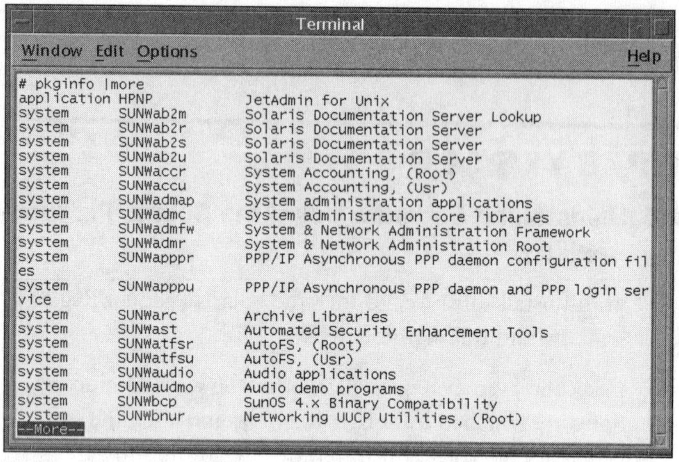

```
Terminal
Window  Edit  Options                                              Help
# pkginfo |more
application HPNP          JetAdmin for Unix
system      SUNWab2m      Solaris Documentation Server Lookup
system      SUNWab2r      Solaris Documentation Server
system      SUNWab2s      Solaris Documentation Server
system      SUNWab2u      Solaris Documentation Server
system      SUNWaccr      System Accounting, (Root)
system      SUNWaccu      System Accounting, (Usr)
system      SUNWadmap     System administration applications
system      SUNWadmc      System administration core libraries
system      SUNWadmfw     System & Network Administration Framework
system      SUNWadmr      System & Network Administration Root
system      SUNWapppr     PPP/IP Asynchronous PPP daemon configuration fil
es
system      SUNWapppu     PPP/IP Asynchronous PPP daemon and PPP login ser
vice
system      SUNWarc       Archive Libraries
system      SUNWast       Automated Security Enhancement Tools
system      SUNWatfsr     AutoFS, (Root)
system      SUNWatfsu     AutoFS, (Usr)
system      SUNWaudio     Audio applications
system      SUNWaudmo     Audio demo programs
system      SUNWbcp       SunOS 4.x Binary Compatibility
system      SUNWbnur      Networking UUCP Utilities, (Root)
--More--
```

**FIGURE 4.10**
The pkginfo output.

Table 4.2 lists some of the files and directories used with package administration.

**TABLE 4.2**

**SOFTWARE PACKAGE FILES AND DIRECTORIES**

| *File or Directory Name* | *Description* |
|---|---|
| /var/sadm/install/contents | Software package map of the entire system. This file shows information about each software component, such as its default permission level and the package to which it belongs. |
| /opt/<pkgname> | The preferred location for the installation of unbundled packages. |
| /etc/opt/<pkgname> | The preferred location for log files of unbundled packages. |

## SOFTWARE PATCHES

Another system administration task is managing system software patches. A patch is a fix to a reported software problem. Sun will ship several software patches to customers so that problems can be resolved before the next release of software. The existing software is derived from a specified package format that conforms to the ABI.

Patches are identified by unique alphanumeric strings. The patch base code comes first, then a hyphen, and then a number that represents the patch revision number. For example, patch 110453-01 is a Solaris 8 patch to correct an Admintool problem.

You might want to know more about patches that have previously been installed. Table 4.3 shows commands that provide useful information about patches already installed on a system.

**TABLE 4.3**

**HELPFUL COMMANDS FOR PATCH ADMINISTRATION**

| *Command* | *Function* |
|---|---|
| `showrev -p` | Shows all patches applied to a system. |
| `pkgparam <pkgid> PATCHLIST` | Shows all patches applied to the package identified by `pkgid`. |
| `pkgparam <pkgid> PATCH INFO <patch-number>` | Shows the installation date and name of the host from which the patch was applied. `<pkgid>` is the name of the package (for example, SUNWadmap) and `<patch-number>` is the specific patch number. |
| `patchadd -R client_root_path -p` | Shows all patches applied to a client, from the server's console. |
| `patchadd -p` | Shows all patches applied to a system. |
| `patchrm <patchname>` | Removes a specified patch. `<patchname>` is the name of the patch to be removed. |

## Installing a Patch

Sun customers can access security patches and other recommended patches via the World Wide Web or anonymous FTP. Sun customers who have purchased a service contract can access an extended set of patches and a complete database of patch information. (This information is also available via the World Wide Web or anonymous FTP, and it is regularly distributed on CD-ROM.

Detailed information about how to install and remove a patch is provided in the Install.info file included with each patch. Each patch also contains a README file that contains specific information about the patch.

Patches come in three different formats. Solaris 8 patches come in zip format, such as 104945-02.zip. For Solaris 8 patches, use the `unzip` command to extract the patch files as follows:

```
/usr/bin/unzip 104945-02.zip
```

For Solaris 2.6 and earlier operating environments, patches might come in compressed tar format, such as 104945-02.tar.Z. Use the `zcat` command to decompress this type of patch file and the `tar` command to create the patch directories, as follows:

```
/usr/bin/zcat 104945-02.tar.Z | tar xvf -
```

Other Solaris patches might come as gzip compressed tar files, such as 102945-02.tar.gz. To extract a gzip compressed tar file, use the `gzcat` command to decompress and create the patch directories as follows:

```
/usr/bin/gzcat 104945-02.tar.gz | tar xvf -
```

The `patchadd` command is used to install directory-format patches to a Solaris 8 system. It must be run as root. The syntax is as follows:

```
patchadd [ -d ] [ -u ] [ -B backout_dir ]
```

The `patchadd` command is described in Table 4.4.

**TABLE 4.4**

**patchadd COMMAND OPTIONS**

| *Common Option* | *Description* |
|---|---|
| `-d` | Does not create a backup of the files to be patched. The patch cannot be removed when this option has been used to install the patch. By default, `patchadd` saves a copy of all files being updated so that the patch can be removed if necessary. Do not use the -d option unless you're positive the patch has been tested. |
| `-p` | Displays a list of the patches currently applied. |

| *Common Option* | *Description* |
|---|---|
| -u | Installs the patch unconditionally, with file validation turned off. The patch is installed, even if some of the files to be patched have been modified since their original installation. |
| -B *<backout_dir>* | Saves backout data to a directory other than the package database. Specify <backout_dir> as an absolute pathname. |
| -M <patch_dir> <patch_id> | Specifies the patches to be installed. Specify patches to the -M option by directory location and by patch number |
| *or* | |
| -M <patch_dir> <patch_file list> | by directory location and patch number. To use the directory location and patch number, specify <patch_dir> as the absolute pathname of the directory that contains spooled patches. Specify <patch_id > as the patch number of a given patch. You can also specify multiple patch_ids. By directory location and the name of a file containing a patch list. To use the directory location and a file containing a patch list, specify <patch_dir > as the absolute pathname of the directory containing the file with a list of patches to be installed. Specify <patch_list > as the name of the file containing the patches to be installed. See the example later in this section. |
| -R <client_root_path> | Locates all patch files generated by patchadd under the directory <client_root_path>. <client_root_path> is the directory that contains the bootable root of a client from the server's perspective. Specify <client_root_path > as the absolute pathname to the beginning of the directory tree under which all patch files generated by patchadd are to be located. See the example later in this section. |

The following examples describe how to add patches to your system. A word of caution is in order before you install patches, however. It has been my personal experience, Murphy's Law you might say, that things can go wrong. Because you're modifying the operating system with a patch, I highly recommend that you back up your file systems before loading patches. Although it can be a time-consuming and seemingly unnecessary task, I once encountered a power failure during a patch installation that completely corrupted my system. Another time, the patch-installation script was defective and the patch did not load properly. Without a backup, I would have had to reinstall the entire operating system.

> **NOTE**
> Additional options to the `patchadd` command security can be found online in the Solaris system manual pages.

The following example installs a patch to a stand-alone machine:

```
patchadd /var/spool/patch/104945-02
```

The following example installs multiple patches. The patchlist file specifies a file containing a list of patches to install:

```
patchadd -M /var/spool/patch patchlist
```

The following example displays the patches installed on a client system named client1:

```
patchadd -R /export/root/client1 -p
```

When you're installing a patch, the `patchadd` command copies files from the patch directory to the local system's disk. More specifically, `patchadd` does two things:

- It determines the Solaris version number of the managing host and the target host.
- It updates the patch package's pkginfo file with information about patches made obsolete by the patch being installed, other patches required by this patch, and patches incompatible with this patch.

The `patchadd` command will not install a patch under the following conditions:

- The package is not fully installed on the host.
- The patch architecture differs from the system architecture.
- The patch version does not match the installed package version.
- An installed patch already exists with the same base code and a higher version number.
- The patch is incompatible with another, already installed patch. (Each installed patch keeps this information in its pkginfo file.)

- The patch being installed requires another patch that is not installed.

## Removing a Patch

Sometimes, a patch does not work as planned and needs to be removed from the system. The utility used to remove, or "back out of," a patch is the `patchrm` command, described in Table 4.5. Its syntax is as follows:

```
patchrm [ -f ] [ -B backout_dir ]
```

**TABLE 4.5**

**`patchrm` COMMAND OPTIONS**

| *Common Options* | *Description* |
|---|---|
| `-f` | Forces the patch removal, regardless of whether the patch was superseded by another patch. |
| `-B backout_dir` | Removes a patch whose backout data has been saved to a directory other than the package database. This option is needed only if the original backout directory, supplied to the `patchadd` command at installation time, has been moved. Specify `backout_dir` as an absolute pathname. |

The following example removes a patch from a stand-alone system:

```
patchrm 104945-02
```

The `patchrm` command removes a Solaris 8 patch package, and restores previously saved files, restoring the file system to its state before a patch was applied, unless any of the following four conditions exist:

- The patch was installed with `patchadd -d`. (The `-d` option instructs `patchadd` not to save copies of files being updated or replaced.)

- The patch has been made obsolete by a later patch.
- The patch is required by another patch already installed on the system.
- The `patchrm` command calls `pkgadd` to restore packages saved from the initial patch installation.

## General Guidelines

Some software packages do not conform to the ABI; therefore, they cannot be installed by using Admintool or the `pkgadd` command. For installation of products that do not conform to the ABI, follow the vendor's specific installation instructions. Following are a few additional guidelines to follow when installing new software on a system:

> **NOTE** For each release of software, Sun usually has a prebundled set of patches called "Recommended and Security Patches." These patches have been thoroughly tested, and Sun recommends adding these patches to every system after the initial software installation is completed.

- Always be cautious with third-party or public-domain software. Make sure that the software has been tested and is free of viruses before installing it on a production system.
- Make sure the software package is supported under Solaris 8.
- Always read the vendor's release notes for special loading instructions. They might contain kernel parameters that need to be modified or suggest software patches that need to be applied.
- Do not install patches unless directed by Sun or one of your software providers. Some patches have not been tested thoroughly, especially when used in conjunction with other software patches. Adverse system performance problems could result.

Adding and removing software packages is one of the simpler tasks you will encounter in system administration. As with all computer software, you should first load new software packages or patches on a nonproduction system for test purposes. Only after the software has been thoroughly tested should you install it on a production system.

This chapter described Software Package Administration. It began by describing the methods Sun uses to package its bundled and unbundled operating system software. Then it described the tools and methods used to install, verify, and remove these software packages on a Solaris system.

## CHAPTER SUMMARY

It also explained that occasionally, software deficiencies are discovered and need to be repaired. You learned how to obtain, install, and, if necessary, uninstall software patches.

Chapter 11, "Backup and Recovery," describes how to create a tape backup of everything you've installed. A good backup can save you time in the event of a hardware malfunction. With a good backup, you won't need to retrace the steps of installing software packages or patches and setting up users.

Some of the subsequent chapters describe how to configure some of the software packages you've installed, such as the LP Print Service (Chapter 10, "The LP Print Service"), NFS (Chapter 17, "The NFS Environment"), NIS (Chapter 18, "Name Services"), Solstice AdminSuite (Chapter 19, "Solaris Management Console and Solstice AdminSuite"), and the Common Desktop Environment (Appendix B, "Administration and Configuration of the CDE").

### KEY TERMS

- Software package
- Software patch
- Software spool directory
- Bundled software package
- Unbundled software package
- Compressed tar file
- Patchlist file

## Exercises

## APPLY YOUR KNOWLEDGE

# Exercises

### 4.1 Software Package Administration

This exercise takes you through the task of installing, verifying, and removing software on a Solaris system using the command line.

**Estimated Time**: 20 minutes

1. List the software packages that are currently installed on your system by typing the following:

   ```
   pkginfo
   ```

2. Display a long-format listing of information for the SUNWman package installed on your system.

   ```
   pkginfo -l SUNWman
   ```

   What is listed for the status, install date, number of files, and number of blocks used by this package?

3. Remove the SUNWdoc package from your system with the following:

   ```
   pkgrm SUNWdoc
   ```

   Verify that the software package has been removed by repeating step 1.

   Now, we'll reinstall the software package. Log in as root, and insert the Solaris 8 Installation CD into the CD-ROM drive. Use `pkgadd` to spool the SUNWdoc package into the default spool area as follows:

   ```
   pkgadd -d \
   /cdrom/sol_8_u3_sparc/s0/Solaris_8/Product \
   -s /var/spool/pkg SUNWdoc
   ```

4. Use the following commands to verify the presence of SUNWdoc in the default spool area:

   ```
   pkginfo -d /var/spool/pkg
   ```

5. Observe the messages displayed, and verify that the package is installed in /var/spool/pkg.

6. Reinstall the SUNWdoc package from the spool area as follows:

   ```
   pkgadd
   ```

7. Select the SUNWdoc package when you are prompted, and the package will be reinstalled.

8. To remove the SUNWdoc package from the spool area, type the following:

   ```
   pkgrm -s /var/spool/pkg
   ```

   Select the SUNWdoc package, and it will be removed from the spool directory.

9. You can now use the `pkgchk` command to check the completeness, pathname, file contents, and file attributes of the SUNWdoc package:

   ```
   pkgchk SUNdoc
   ```

# Review Questions

1. Which of the following commands is used to show software package information?

   A. `pkgadd`

   B. `pkgchk`

   C. `pkgparam`

   D. `pkginfo`

2. Which of the following commands verifies the accuracy of a software package installation?

   A. `pkgadd`

   B. `pkgchk`

   C. `pkgask`

   D. `pkginfo`

## APPLY YOUR KNOWLEDGE

3. Which of the following methods are used to remove software packages from a system?

   A. `pkgrm`

   B. `rm -r`

   C. Admintool

   D. All of the above

4. What do software packages usually start with?

   A. An abbreviation of the software package

   B. The company's stock symbol

   C. SUNW

   D. Anything the vendor chooses

5. Which of the following commands prepares a compressed tar patch file (with a ".Z" extension) for installation and saves approximately 25% on temporary disk space usage?

   A. `installpatch -u 104945-02.tar.Z`

   B. `installpatch -f 104945-02.tar.Z`

   C. `/usr/bin/zcat 104945-02.tar.Z | tar xvf -`

   D. `unzip 104945-02.tar.Z | tar xvf -`

6. Which of the following commands show(s) all patches applied to a system? Choose all that apply.

   A. `patchadd -p`

   B. `pkginfo`

   C. `showrev -p`

   D. All of the above

7. Which of the following commands is used to remove a patch from a system?

   A. `uninstall`

   B. `pkgrm -s`

   C. `patchrm`

   D. `rm -r`

8. Sun distributes software patches in which of the following forms? Choose all that apply.

   A. Sun FTP site

   B. Email

   C. CD-ROM

   D. Magnetic tape

9. The Solaris Product Registry enables you to do which of the following? Choose all that apply.

   A. View a list of installed software

   B. Uninstall software

   C. Launch the installer

   D. Directly edit software packages with the registry editor

10. When installing a patch using the `patchadd` command, which of the following options does not create a backup of the files to be patched?

    A. `-f`

    B. `-p`

    C. `-B`

    D. `-d`

## Apply Your Knowledge

11. Which of the following conditions will prevent a patch from being installed?

    A. The patch being installed requires another patch that is not installed.

    B. The patch is incompatible with another, already installed patch.

    C. The patch was removed.

    D. The patch version is not the most up-to-date version.

    E. All of the above

## Answers to Review Questions

1. **D**. The `pkginfo` command displays software package information.

2. **B**. The `pkgchk` command checks the accuracy of a software package installation.

3. **A**. The `pkgrm` command removes software packages from the system.

4. **B**. Software package names usually start with the company's stock symbol.

5. **C**. Patches might come in compressed tar format, for example, 104945-02.tar.Z. Use the `zcat` command to decompress this type of patch file.

6. **A**., **C**. Use the `patchadd -p` command or the `showrev -p` command to show all patches that have been applied to a system.

7. **C**. Use the `patchrm` command to remove a patch from a system.

8. **A**., **B**., **C**. Software patches are delivered to the customer in the following ways: from Sun's FTP site, via email, or on CD-ROM.

9. **A**., **B**., **C**. The Solaris Product Registry enables you to view all installed software, uninstall software, or launch the installer to install additional software.

10. **D**. The `-d` option for the `patchadd` command does not create a backup of the files to be patched.

11. **A**., **B**. The following conditions can prevent a patch from being installed:

    - The patch being installed requires another patch that is not installed.
    - The patch is incompatible with another, already installed patch.

## Objectives

The following are the test objectives for this chapter:

**Use Admintool or the command line to add, delete, and modify user accounts**

- Administering user accounts using Admintool is an efficient way to add, modify, and remove user account information. This is a routine activity for system administrators, so a complete understanding of this functionality within Admintool is required.

**Set up, customize, and administer initialization files**

- User sessions are customized using initialization files that are referenced each time the user logs in. Administration of each initialization file will be described.

**Administer user home directories**

- Administering the system involves close monitoring and administration of the user personal directories. It's the system administrator's responsibility to protect public and personal data in these directories.

CHAPTER 5

# Setting up User Accounts

## OUTLINE



## STUDY STRATEGIES

The following strategies will help you prepare for the exam:

- ▶ As you read this chapter, practice the step-by-step examples that I've provided on a Sun or Intel-based system running Solaris 8. Practice the steps until you are able to perform them from memory.
- ▶ Make sure that you understand each of the attributes associated with a user account (described in Table 5.3), such as UID, Primary group, default shell, and so on.
- ▶ Use Admintool to add a few users to your system and set up the initialization files I describe in this chapter. Modify the account attributes, such as the default shell, group, and UID value. Modify variables in the initialization files for each user to see the results.
- ▶ Practice using the command-line tools for adding, modifying, and removing user accounts. These commands will appear on the Sun exam, so make sure you understand them thoroughly. Continue practicing these commands until you can perform them from memory.

## INTRODUCTION

Access to a system is allowed only through user login accounts set up by the system administrator. A user account includes information that a user needs to log in and use a system—a user login name, a password, the user's home directory, and login initialization files. User accounts can range from occasional guests needing read-only access to a few files, to regular users who need to share information between several departments.

Table 5.1 lists the methods and tools available in Solaris for adding new user accounts to the system.

**TABLE 5.1**

**ADDING NEW USER ACCOUNTS**

| *Environment* | *Recommended Tool* | *Availability* |
|---|---|---|
| On remote and/ or local systems in a networked name service (NIS, NIS+) | User and Group Manager (graphical user interface) from the Solstice AdminSuite | Available as a separate product |
| Local system | Admintool (graphical user interface) | Provided with Solaris 8 |
| Command line | Terminal window (CDE environment) or shell tool or command tool (OpenWindows environment) | Provided with Solaris 8 |

As with many UNIX commands, the command-line method of adding user accounts is cumbersome and confusing. For this reason, Sun has added user account administration to the Solaris Admintool. Admintool is a graphical user interface designed to ease several routine system administration tasks. When using Admintool, the system administrator is presented with a menu-like interface that is much easier to use than the ASCII interface supplied at the command prompt. Admintool does not change name service maps or tables when NIS or NIS+ is being used; this task is accomplished by an unbundled product called Solstice AdminSuite. For instructions on using AdminSuite, refer to Chapter 19, "Solaris Management Console and Solstice AdminSuite." This chapter describes how to use Solaris Admintool and command line to administer user accounts on the system.

## Adding a User Account with Admintool

> **NOTE**
> When you're adding or modifying user accounts, Admintool edits the files /etc/passwd, /etc/shadow, and /etc/group. As root, you could edit these files directly, but this is not recommended. Errors in any of the files could cause adverse effects on the system. See Chapter 8, "System Security," for a complete description of these files.

To perform administrative tasks such as adding user accounts, the administrator must be logged in as superuser (root) or be a member of GID 14 (sysadmin).

The first step in setting up a new user account is to have the user provide the information you will need to administer this account. You'll also need to set up proper permissions so that the user can share information with other members of his department. To start, you'll need to know the user's full name, department, and any groups with which the user will be working. I like to sit down with the user and fill out an information sheet like the one shown in Table 5.2 so that I have all the information I'll need when I set up the account.

**TABLE 5.2**

**User Information Data Sheet**

| *Item* | *Description* |
|---|---|
| User Name: | |
| UID: | |
| Primary Group: | |
| Secondary Groups: | |
| Comment: | |
| Default Shell: | |
| Password Status and Aging: | |
| Home Directory Server Name: | |
| Home Directory Path Name: | |
| Mail Server: | |
| Department Name: | |

| *Item* | *Description* |
|---|---|
| Department Administrator: | |
| Manager: | |
| Employee Name: | |
| Employee Title: | |
| Employee Status: | |
| Employee Number: | |
| Start Date: | |
| Desktop System Name: | |

# STEP BY STEP

## 5.1 Adding a New Login User

To add a new user login account, follow this procedure:

1. Start up Admintool as a member of the sysadmin group by typing `admintool` at the command prompt.

   The Users main menu appears, as shown in Figure 5.1.

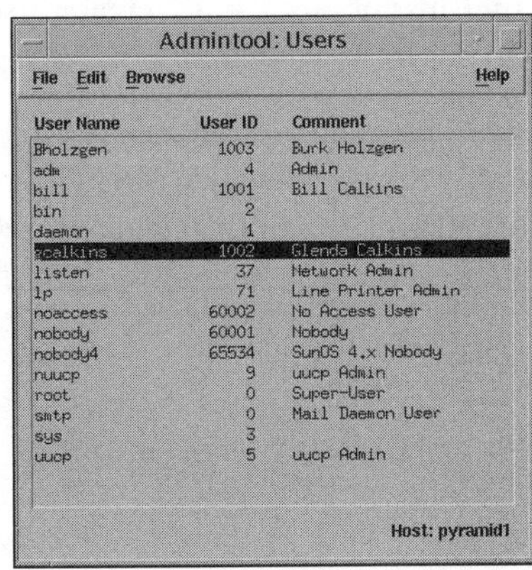


**FIGURE 5.1**
The Users main menu.

*continues*

*continued*

2. Choose Edit, Add to display the Add User window, shown in Figure 5.2.

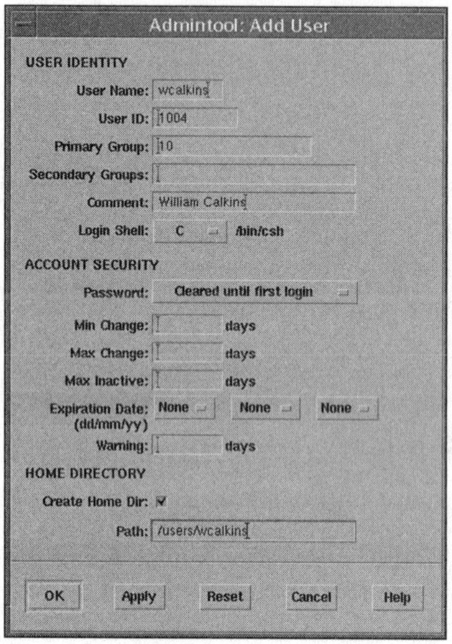

**FIGURE 5.2**
The Add User window.

3. Fill in the text boxes in the Add User window. Table 5.3 describes the information needed. If you aren't sure how to complete a field, click the Help button to see field definitions for this window.

4. After entering the information, click OK. The current list of user accounts is displayed in the Users main window.

**TABLE 5.3**

## Add User Fields

| *Item* | *Description* |
|---|---|
| User Name | Enter a unique login name that will be entered at the Solaris login prompt. Choose a name unique to your organization. The name can contain 2–8 uppercase characters (A–Z), lowercase characters (a–z), or digits (0–9), but no underscores or spaces. The first character must be a letter, and at least one character must be a lowercase letter. |

| *Item* | *Description* |
|---|---|
| User ID | Enter the unique user ID (discussed in Chapter 8). Admintool automatically assigns the next available UID; however, in a networked environment, make sure that this number is not duplicated by another user on another system. All UIDs must be consistent across the network. The UID is typically a number between 100 and 60002, but it can go as high as 2147483647. See the note in the description for "Primary Group" regarding UIDs greater than 60000. |
| Primary Group | Enter the primary group name or GID (group ID) number for the group to which the user will belong. This is the group the operating system will assign to files created by the user. Group 10 (staff) is a predefined group that is sufficient for most users. GIDs can range from 0 to 60002, but they can go as high as 2147483647.<br><br>Note: Previous Solaris software releases used 32-bit data types to contain the user IDs (UIDs) and group IDs (GIDs), but UIDs and GIDs were constrained to a maximum useful value of 60000. Starting with the Solaris 2.5.1 release and compatible versions, the limit on UID and GID values has been raised to the maximum value of a signed integer, or 2147483647. UIDs and GIDs over 60000 do not have full functionality and are incompatible with many Solaris features, so avoid using UIDs or GIDs over 60000. |
| Secondary Groups | (Optional) Enter the names or GIDs, separated by spaces, of any additional groups to which the user belongs. A user can belong to as many as 16 secondary groups. |
| Comment | (Optional) Enter any comments, such as the full username or phone number. |
| Login Shell | Click this button to select the shell the user will use, such as /bin/csh. If nothing is selected, the default shell is the Bourne shell (/bin/sh). |
| Password | Click this button to specify the password status. Selectable options are as follows:<br><br>• Cleared until first login. This is the default. The account does not have a password, assigned. The user is prompted for a password on first login, unless `passreq=no` is set in /etc/default/login.<br><br>• Account is locked. The account is disabled with an invalid password, and can be unlocked by assigning a new password. This type of account allows a user to own files, but not to log in. |

*continues*

**TABLE 5.3** *continued*

**ADD USER FIELDS**

| *Item* | *Description* |
|---|---|
| | • No password; `setuid` only. The account cannot be logged into directly. This allows programs such as `lp` and `uucp` to run under an account without allowing a user to log in.<br>• Normal password. The account will have a password that you set in the pop-up window that appears. |
| Min Change | (Optional) Enter the minimum number of days allowed between password changes. This is intended to prevent a user from changing the password and then changing it back a few seconds later, which would defeat the concept of password aging. The default is 0. |
| Max Change | (Optional) Enter the maximum number of days the password is valid before it must be changed; otherwise, the account is locked. Leaving the field blank means the password never has to be changed. |
| Max Inactive | (Optional) Enter the maximum number of days an account can go without being accessed before it is automatically locked. A blank field means the account remains active, no matter how long it goes unused. |
| Expiration Date | (Optional) Enter the date when the user account expires. `None` means no expiration. |
| Warning | (Optional) Enter the number of days to begin warning the user before the password expires. A blank means no warning is given. |
| Create Home Dir Check Box | Check this box to have the user's home directory automatically created. |
| Path | Use the Path field to point to an existing directory or to specify a new directory to create. |

**NOTE**

Users can type the UNIX command `passwd` at the command prompt to change their passwords. Refer to Chapter 8 for additional information on setting passwords.

# DELETING A USER ACCOUNT WITH ADMINTOOL

When a user account is no longer needed on a system, delete it from the system. The following procedure describes how to perform this task.

## STEP BY STEP

### 5.2 Using Admintool to Delete an Existing User Account

Use Admintool to delete an existing user account. The procedure to delete a user account is as follows:

1. Start Admintool if it's not already running, and choose Browse, Users.
2. In the Users window, select the user account entry you want to remove.
3. Choose Edit, Delete.
4. A message is displayed to confirm the removal of the user account (see Figure 5.3).

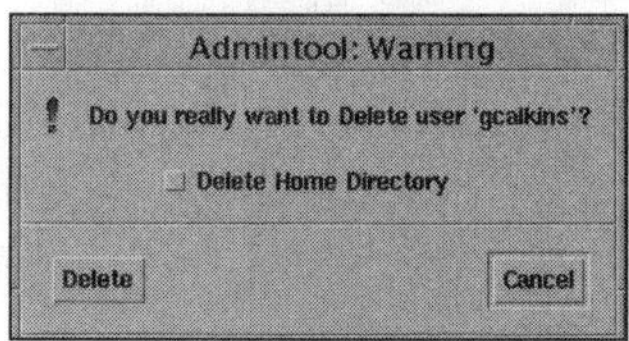


**FIGURE 5.3**
Confirmation that you want to delete the user account.

5. (Optional) Click the Delete Home Directory check box to delete the user's home directory and its contents. If you don't check the box, the user account will be deleted, but the contents of the user's home directory will remain.
6. Click OK when you are ready to delete the user account. The user account entry is deleted from the Users main window.

# MODIFYING A USER ACCOUNT WITH ADMINTOOL

If a login needs to be modified—to change a password or disable an account, for example—use Admintool to modify these user account settings.

## STEP BY STEP

### 5.3 Modifying a User Account with Admintool

The process for modifying a user account follows:

1. Start Admintool if it's not already running, and choose Browse, Users.
2. Select the user account entry to be modified.
3. Choose Edit, Modify.
4. The Modify User window is displayed, containing the selected user account entry (see Figure 5.4).

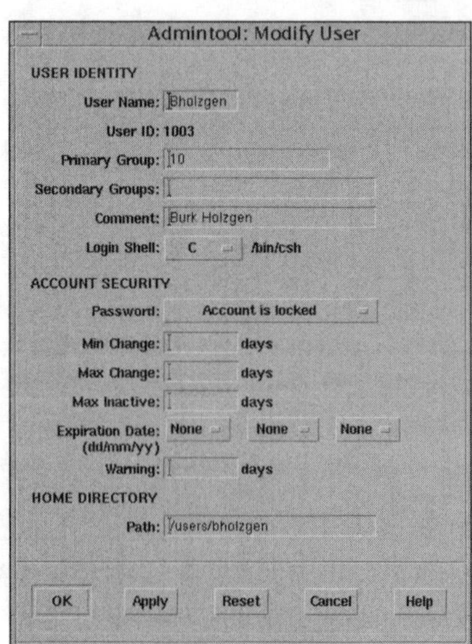


**FIGURE 5.4**
The Modify User window.

5. The following are descriptions of some of the modifications allowed:

   - Locking a login

     Choose Password: Account is locked.

   - Changing a user's password

     Enable a user account by changing the password status to Normal Password or Cleared Until First Login.

6. Click OK, and the modification is made.

## Adding a Group with Admintool

You might need to add a group that does not already exist on the system. Perhaps a new group of users called "engrg" (from the engineering department) needs to be added.

### STEP BY STEP

#### 5.4 Adding a Group with Admintool

The following steps describe how to add the new "engrg" group:

1. Start Admintool if it's not already running, and choose Browse, Groups.
2. The Groups window is displayed, as shown in Figure 5.5.

*continues*

*continued*

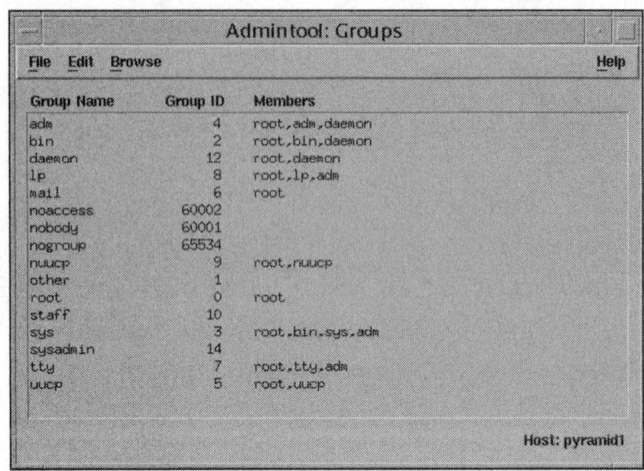


**FIGURE 5.5**
The Groups window.

3. Choose Edit, Add.

4. The Add Group window is displayed, as shown in Figure 5.6. If you're not sure how to complete a field, click the Help button to see field definitions for this window.

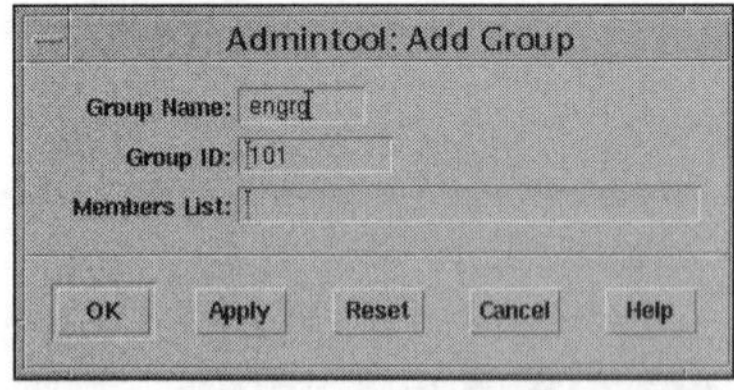


**FIGURE 5.6**
The Add Group window.

5. Type the name of the new group in the Group Name text box.

6. Type the group ID number for the new group in the Group ID text box. This should be a unique number.

7. (Optional) Type usernames in the Members List text box. These are the users who belong to the new group. Usernames must be separated by commas. The list of users will be added to the group.

8. Click OK. The list of groups displayed in the Groups window is updated to include the new group.

# Managing User and Group Accounts from the Command Line

Another way to manage user accounts is from the command line. Although using the command line is more complex than using the Admintool GUI interface, the command line provides a little more flexibility. Solaris supplies the user administration commands described in Table 5.4 for setting up and managing user accounts.

**TABLE 5.4**

**Account Administration Commands**

| *Command* | *Description* |
|---|---|
| `useradd` | Adds a new user account |
| `userdel` | Deletes a user account |
| `usermod` | Modifies a user account |
| `groupadd` | Adds a new group |
| `groupmod` | Modifies a group (for example, changes the group ID or name) |
| `groupdel` | Deletes a group |

## Adding User Accounts from the Command Line

You can add new user accounts on the local system using the `useradd` command. This command adds an entry for the new user into the /etc/passwd and /etc/shadow files, which are described in Chapter 8.

Just like Admintool, the `useradd` command also copies all the user initialization files found in the /etc/skel directory into the new user's home directory. User initialization files are covered in the next section of this chapter.

I'll begin by describing the useradd command. The syntax for the useradd command is as follows:

```
useradd [-u <uid>] [-g <gid>] [-G <gid,gid,…>] [-d <dir>] -m [-s <shell>] [-c <comment>][-f <inactive>] \
[-e <expiration>] <loginname>
```

Table 5.5 describes these options:

**TABLE 5.5**

**useradd COMMAND OPTIONS**

| *Option* | *Description* |
|---|---|
| -u <uid> | Sets the unique UID for the user. |
| -g <gid> | Specifies a predefined GID or name for the user. This will be the user's primary group. |
| -G <gid> | Defines the new user's secondary group memberships. Multiple groups can be entered, but must be separated by commas. |
| -m | Creates a new home directory if one does not already exist. |
| -s <shell> | Defines the full pathname for the shell program to be used as the user's login shell. The default is /bin/sh if a shell is not specified. |
| -c <comment> | This is only a comment and is typically used to specify the user's full name, location, and phone number. |
| -d <directory> | The home directory of the new user. It defaults to *<base_dir>*/*<account_name>*, in which *<base_dir>* is the base directory for new login home directories, and *<account_name>* is the new login name. |
| -e <expire> | Sets an expiration date on the user account. Specifies the date on which the user can no longer log in and access the account. After the specified date, the account is locked. Use the following format to specify the date: *mm/dd/yy*. |
| -f <inactive> | Sets the number of inactive days allowed on a user account. If the account is not logged into during the specified number of days, the account is locked. |
| -k <skeldir> | Specifies an alternate location for the user initialization template files. Files from this directory will be copied into the user's home directory. The default location is /etc/skel. |

Many additional options are also available, although most are not used as often. See the online manual pages for a listing of all the options to the `useradd` command.

The following example creates a new login account for Bill Calkins. The login name will be "bcalkins," the UID will be 3000, and the group will be "other." I'm going to instruct the system to create a home directory name /export/home/bcalkins. The default shell will be /bin/ksh, and the initialization files are to be copied from the /etc/skel directory:

```
useradd -u 3000 -g other -d /export/home/bcalkins -m -s /bin/ksh -c "Bill Calkins, ext. 1111" bcalkins
```

## Modifying User Accounts from the Command Line

Use the `usermod` command to modify existing user accounts from the command line. `usermod` can be used to modify most of the options that were used when the account was originally created.

The command syntax for `usermod` is as follows:

```
usermod [-u <uid>] -o [-g <gid>] [-G <gid,gid,…>] [-d <dir>] -m [-s <shell>] [-c <comment>] \
[-l <newloginname>] [-f <inactive>] [-e <expiration>] <loginname>
```

The options used with the `usermod` command are the same as those described for the `useradd` command, except for those listed in Table 5.6.

**TABLE 5.6**

**`usermod` Command Options**

| *Option* | *Description* |
|---|---|
| `-l <newloginname>` | Change a user's login name on a specified account. |
| `-m` | Moves the user's home directory to the new location specified with the `-d` option. |

**NOTE**

Although the new home directory has been changed, existing files still must be manually moved from the old home directory to the new home directory.

The following example changes the login name for user bcalkins to wcalkins. It also changes the home directory to /export/home/wcalkins and default shell to /bin/ksh.

```
usermod -d /export/home/wcalkins - m -s /bin/ksh -l
➥wcalkins bcalkins
```

## Deleting User Accounts from the Command Line

Use the `userdel` command to delete a user's login account from the system. Options can be specified to save or remove the user's home directory. The syntax for the `userdel` command is as follows:

```
userdel [-r] <loginname>
```

in which `-r` removes the user's home directory from the local file system. If this option is not specified, only the login is removed; the home directory remains intact.

The following example removes the login account for bcalkins, but does not remove the home directory:

```
userdel bcalkins
```

## Adding Group Accounts from the Command Line

Use the `groupadd` command to add new group accounts on the local system. This command adds an entry to the /etc/group file. The syntax for the `groupadd` command is as follows:

```
groupadd [-g <gid>] -o <groupname>
```

in which

`-g <gid>` assigns the group ID `<gid>` for the new group.

-o allows the gid to be duplicated. In other words, more than one groupname can share the same GID.

The following example adds a new group named acct with a GID of 1000 to the system:

```
groupadd -g 1000 acct
```

## Modifying Group Accounts from the Command Line

Use the `groupmod` command to modify the definitions of a specified group. The syntax for the `groupmod` command is as follows:

```
groupmod [-g <gid>] -o [-n <name>] <groupname>
```

in which

`-g <gid>` assigns the new group ID <gid> for the group.

`-o` allows the gid to be duplicated. In other words, more than one groupname can share the same GID.

`-n <name>` specifies a new name for the group.

The following example changes the acct group GID to 2000:

```
groupmod -g 2000 acct
```

## Deleting Group Accounts from the Command Line

Use the `groupdel` command to delete a group account from the local system. The syntax for the `groupdel` command is as follows:

```
groupdel <groupname>
```

The following example deletes the group named "acct" from the local system:

```
groupdel acct
```

# Setting Up User Initialization Files

Part of setting up a user's home directory is providing user initialization files for the user's login shell. A user initialization file is a shell script that sets up a work environment for a user after the user logs in to a system. You can perform any task in a user initialization file that you can perform in a shell script, but its primary job is to define the characteristics of the user's work environment, such as search path, environment variables, and windowing environment. Each login shell has its own user initialization file (or files) located in the user's home directory. These files are run automatically when the user logs in.

Default user initialization files, such as .cshrc, .profile, and .login, are created automatically in the user's home directory when a new user account is added. The system administrator can predefine the contents of these files or can choose to use the system default files. The Solaris 8 system software provides default user initialization files for each shell in the /etc/skel directory on each system. These files are listed in Table 5.7.

**TABLE 5.7**

**Default Initialization Files**

| *Name* | *Description* |
|---|---|
| local.cshrc | The default .cshrc file for the C shell |
| local.login | The default .login file for the C shell |
| local.profile | The default .profile file for the Bourne and Korn shells |

You can use these initialization files as a starting point, and modify them to create a standard set of files that will provide a work environment common to all users. You can also modify them to provide the working environment for different types of users.

# Customizing User Initialization Files

When a user logs into a system, the shell initialization files determine the work environment. The shell startup scripts can be modified to set environment variables and directory paths needed by a specific user. These startup scripts are located in the user's home directory.

When you are setting up user initialization files, it might be important to allow the users to customize their own initialization files. This can be accomplished with centrally located and globally distributed user initialization files called site initialization files. These files let you continually introduce new functionality to all of the user work environments by editing one initialization file. The local initialization file, located in the user's home directory, allows user-specific configuration.

A local initialization file lets users further customize their own work environment. Site initialization files are located in the /etc directory, and can be edited only by root. They are designed to distribute site-wide changes to all user work environments. Individual user initialization files are located in each user's home directory, and can be customized by the owner of that directory. When a user logs in, the site initialization file is run first, and then the initialization file located in the user's home directory is run.

> **NOTE**
> Do not use system initialization files located in the /etc directory (/etc/profile, /etc/.login) to manage an individual user's work environment. These are site initialization files, considered to be global files, meant to be generic and used to set work environments for all users. The system will run this startup file first, and will then run the user's startup file located in the home directory.

The most common customizations to shell startup scripts are environment variables. Table 5.8 describes environment and shell variables you might want to customize in a user initialization file.

**TABLE 5.8**

**SHELL AND ENVIRONMENT VARIABLE DESCRIPTIONS**

| *Variable* | *Description* |
|---|---|
| `ARCH` | Sets the user's system architecture (for example, sun4, i386). This variable can be set with `ARCH = `uname -p`` (in Bourne or Korn shells) or `setenv ARCH `uname -p`` (in the C shell). The shell has no built-in behavior that depends on this variable; it's just a useful variable for branching within shell scripts. |
| `history` | Sets the history for the C shell. |
| `HOME` | Sets the path to the user's home directory. |
| `LPDEST` | Sets the user's default printer. |
| `PATH` (or `path` in the C shell) | Lists, in order, the directories the shell searches to find the program to run when the user types a command. If the directory is not in the search path, users must type the complete pathname of a command.<br>The default `PATH` is automatically defined in .profile (Bourne or Korn shell) or .cshrc (C shell) as part of the login process.<br>The order of the search path is important. When identical commands exist in different locations, the first command found with that name is used. For example, suppose `PATH` is defined (in Bourne and Korn shell syntax) as `PATH=/bin:/usr/bin:/usr/sbin:$HOME/bin` and a file named "sample" resides in both /usr/bin and /home/glenda/bin. If the user types the command `sample` without specifying its full pathname, the version found in /usr/bin is used. |
| `prompt` | Defines the shell prompt for the C shell. |
| `TERM` (or `term` in the C shell) | Defines the terminal. This variable should be reset in /etc/profile or /etc/.login. When the user invokes an editor, the system looks for a file with the same name as the definition of this environment variable. The system searches the directory /usr/share/lib/terminfo to determine the terminal characteristics. |
| `MAIL` | Sets the path to the user's mailbox. |
| `MANPATH` | Sets the search path for system manual pages. |
| `umask` | Sets the default user mask. |

## STEP BY STEP

### 5.5 Verifying and Changing a User's Environment

The following example illustrates how to verify a user's environment settings and how to change them:

1. Log in as the user. This step lets you see the user's environment as the user will see it.

2. Edit the user's initialization files. The following steps suggest some changes and show the shell-specific syntax to use.

3. Set the user's default path to include the home directory and directories or mount points for the user's windowing environment and applications. To change the path setting, add or modify the line for `PATH` as follows:

   For the Bourne or Korn shell, the syntax is as follows:

   ```
   PATH=/dirname1:/dirname2:/dirname3:.; export PATH
   ```

   For example, enter the following line in the user's $HOME/.profile file:

   ```
   PATH=$PATH:/usr/bin:/$HOME/bin:/net/glrr/files1/bin:.;export PATH
   ```

   For the C shell, the syntax is as follows:

   ```
   set path =(/dirname1 /dirname2 /dirname3 .)
   ```

   For example, enter the following line in the user's $HOME/.cshrc file:

   ```
   set path=($path /usr/bin $HOME/bin /net/glrr/files1/bin .)
   ```

4. Check that the environment variables are set to the correct directories for the user's windowing environments and third-party applications. Type `env` and press Enter:

   ```
   $ env

   HOME=/home/ncalkins
   HZ=100
   LOGNAME=ncalkins
   MAIL=/var/mail/ncalkins
   PATH=/usr/bin
   ```

*continues*

NOTE

Prefixing $PATH (K shell) or $path (C shell) appends changes to the user's path settings already set by the site initialization file. When you set the PATH variable with this procedure, initial path settings are not overwritten and lost. Also note the "dot" (.) at the end of the list to denote the current working directory. The dot should always be at the end of the path, as discussed in Chapter 8.

*continued*

```
SHELL=/bin/sh
TERM=sun
TZ=EST5EDT
$
```

5. Add or change the settings of environment variables by entering either of the following lines:

   For the Bourne or Korn shell, the syntax is as follows:

   ```
   VARIABLE=value;export VARIABLE
   ```

   The following example sets the user's default mail directory:

   ```
   MAIL=/var/mail/ncalkins;export MAIL
   ```

   For the C shell, the syntax is as follows:

   ```
   setenv VARIABLE value
   ```

   The following example sets the history to record the last 100 commands:

   ```
   setenv HISTORY 100
   ```

# THE HOME DIRECTORY

The home directory is the portion of a file system allocated to a user for storing private files. The amount of space you allocate for home directories depends on the kinds of files the user creates and the type of work performed. An entire file system is usually allocated specifically for home directories, and the users all share this space. The system administrator needs to monitor user home directories so that one user does not use more than his fair share of space. Disk quotas are used to control the amount of disk space a user can occupy. They are discussed in Chapter 6, "Introduction to File Systems."

A home directory can be located on either the user's local system or on a remote file server. Although any directory name can be used, the home directory in either case is, by convention, /export/home/<username>. When you put the home directory in /export/home, it is available across the network in case the user logs in from several different stations. For a large site, you should store home directories on a server.

Regardless of where their home directory is located, users usually access it through a mount point named /home/<username>. When Autofs is used to mount home directories, you are not permitted to create any directories under the /home mount point on any system. The system recognizes the special status of /home when Autofs is active. For more information about Autofs and automounting home directories, refer to Chapter 17, "The NFS Environment."

To access the home directory anywhere on the network, you should always refer to it as `$HOME`, not as /export/home/<username>. The latter is machine-specific and should be discouraged. In addition, any symbolic links created in a user's home directory should use relative paths (for example, ../../../x/y/x) so that the links will be valid no matter where the home directory is mounted. The location of user home directories might change. By not using machine-specific names, you maintain consistency and reduce system administration.

## Name Services

If you are managing user accounts for a large site, you might want to consider using a name service, such as NIS or NIS+. A name service lets you store user account information in a centralized manner instead of storing it in every system's /etc files. When using a name service for user accounts, users can move from system to system using the same user account without having site-wide user account information duplicated in every system's /etc files. Using a name service also promotes centralized and consistent user account information. NIS and NIS+ are discussed in Chapter 18, "Name Services."

## CHAPTER SUMMARY

### KEY TERMS

- Admintool
- User ID (UID)
- Group
- Group ID (GID)
- Primary group
- Secondary group
- Login Shell
- Password aging
- Home directory
- User initialization file
- Shell variable

This concludes the discussion of how to add user login accounts to the system. I described how to add, modify, and remove user accounts using both the Admintool and the command line. The graphical user interface of Admintool makes managing user accounts much easier than the command-line method.

Secondly, I described the user shell initialization files. I described how to use these files to customize the user work environment. In addition, many of the default shell environment variables that control the user shell environment were described.

Finally, I described the home directory—the portion of a file system allocated to a user for storing private files.

This chapter described the tasks associated with managing user accounts. Because most users will be using the Common Desktop Environment (CDE) window interface, as the system administrator, you'll also need to be familiar with the setup and customization of the CDE. As of this writing, this is a topic that is not covered on either examination, but is described later in Appendix B, "Administration and Configuration of the CDE."

The next chapter switches gears a bit and introduces you to Solaris file systems.

## APPLY YOUR KNOWLEDGE

# Exercises

### 5.1 Managing User Accounts

In the following exercise, you will use Admintool to add new users to your system, lock user accounts, and set up password aging.

**Estimated Time**: 20 minutes

1. After the Admintool GUI appears, use Admintool to add the following list of users:

| login | password | shell | UID | Pri GID | Secondary GID |
|---|---|---|---|---|---|
| user3 | trng | Korn | 1003 | 10 | 14 |
| user4 | trng | C | 1004 | 10 | 14 |
| user5 | trng | Bourne | 1005 | 10 | |
| locked1 | (lock accnt) | Korn | 1006 | 10 | |
| cleared1 | (cleared until 1st) login | Bourne | 1007 | 10 | |
| nopass1 | (no password) | Korn | 1008 | 10 | |

2. Logout.
3. Can you log in as the user `locked1`?

   Try logging in as `cleared1`- what happens?

   Can `root` su to become user `cleared1`?

### 5.2 User Initialization Files

In the following exercise, you'll work with user initialization files.

**Estimated Time**: 20 minutes

1. Use the vi editor to edit the /etc/skel/local.profile, and add the following entries to set the following variables:

```
EDITOR=/usr/bin/vi; export EDITOR
PATH=$PATH:/usr/lib/lp; export EDITOR
```

2. Use Admintool to create a new user called `user9` that uses the Korn shell. Log in as `user9`, and verify that all the variables you set in /etc/skel/local.profile are set correctly in the user's environment by typing the following:

```
env
```

3. Create a .profile file for user9 that includes two aliases and sets the primary prompt to display the current working directory. Use the vi editor to add the following three lines to the .profile file located in user9's home directory:

```
alias del='rm -i'
alias hi='echo hello'
PS1=\$PWD' $'
```

4. Log out and log back in as the same user to verify that the .profile works. Do you have a new shell prompt?

## APPLY YOUR KNOWLEDGE

5. Verify that your new aliases are defined by typing the following:

```
alias
```

6. Log out and log back in again as root.

7. Use `useradd` to create a new user named user10, specify the korn shell as the default shell, and assign a password of `trng`.

```
Example:
# useradd -u 1010 -g 10 -d \
/export/home/user10 -m -s /bin/ksh -c \
"Solaris Student" user10
# passwd user10
 New Passwd:
 Re-enter new passwd:
```

8. Log out and log back in as `user10`. Record the list of initialization files in your home directory with the `ls -la` command.

   Which of these files is the same as /etc/skel/local.profile?

   Copy /etc/skel/local.profile to .profile.

9. Log out and log back in as `user10`. Verify that the variables set in the .profile for user9 are also set in this login (`PATH` and `EDITOR`).

   Are they correct?

## Review Questions

1. What is the maximum length of a username?

   A. 1 to 8 characters

   B. 2 to 8 characters

   C. 1 to 7 characters

   D. Unlimited

2. UID 0 is typically which of the following?

   A. root

   B. daemon

   C. adm

   D. lpr

3. How many secondary groups can a user belong to?

   A. 1

   B. 32

   C. Unlimited

   D. 16

4. What does the Max Change field in Admintool do when adding a new user ID?

   A. Sets the minimum number of days before a user can use the new login

   B. Sets the maximum number of days allowed between password changes

   C. Sets the maximum number of days an account can go without being accessed before it is automatically locked

   D. Sets the maximum number of days of inactivity before the account is turned inactive

5. When adding a new user account in AdminTool, which of the following options is/are not available for setting the password?

   A. Password is cleared until first login

   B. Account is locked

   C. No password assigned

   D. Have the system generate a password

## APPLY YOUR KNOWLEDGE

6. What is the best way to delete a login but retain the user's files?

   A. Delete the login, but unselect the Delete Home Directory check box.

   B. Change the password on the login.

   C. Change the UID of the login.

   D. Delete the login, but don't delete files with the `rm` command.

7. Which of the following are not default user initialization files?

   A. .cshrc

   B. .login

   C. .profile

   D. .exrc

8. Which directory contains the Solaris default initialization files?

   A. /etc/default

   B. /etc/skel

   C. /etc/dfs

   D. /home

9. What is the proper syntax to set the default path in the Korn shell?

   A. `PATH=/dirname1:/dirname2:/dirname3:.; \`
   `export PATH`

   B. `setenv path =(/dirname1 /dirname2 \`
   `/dirname3 .)`

   C. `set path =(/dirname1 /dirname2 /dirname3 .)`

   D. `setenv PATH /dirname1:/dirname2:/dirname3`

10. What is the proper syntax to set the default path in the C shell?

    A. `set path = (/dirname1 /dirname2 / \`
    `dirname3 .)`

    B. `PATH=/dirname1:/dirname2:/dirname3:.; \`
    `export PATH`

    C. `setenv path =(/dirname1 /dirname2 \`
    `/dirname3 .)`

    D. `setenv PATH /dirname1:/dirname2:/dirname3`

11. Which of the following files contains the encrypted password information?

    A. /etc/shadow

    B. /etc/passwd

    C. /etc/default/password

    D. /etc/password

12. What is the site-wide initialization file for the Korn shell called?

    A. /etc/profile

    B. $HOME/.profile

    C. /etc/.profile

    D. /etc/skel/local.profile

13. What is the site-wide initialization file for the C shell called?

    A. /etc/.login

    B. /etc/login

    C. $HOME/.login

    D. /etc/skel/local.login

APPLY YOUR KNOWLEDGE

## Answers to Review Questions

1. **B**. A user login name can contain two to eight uppercase characters (A–Z) or lowercase characters (a–z) or digits (0–9), but no underscores or spaces. The first character must be a letter, and at least one character must be a lowercase letter.
2. **A**. The UID for the root login is always 0.
3. **D**. A user can belong to as many as 16 secondary groups.
4. **B**. The Max Change field sets the maximum number of days allowed between password changes.
5. **D**. Admintool cannot automatically generate a password for a user account.
6. **A**. When deleting a user account in Admintool, deselect the Delete Home Directory check box to retain all of the user's files.
7. **D**. The following are default user initialization files that get put into a user's home directory when their account is created: .cshrc, .login,. profile.
8. **B**. The /etc/skel directory contains the Solaris default initialization files.
9. **A**. To set the default path in the Korn shell, issue the following command:

   ```
   PATH=/dirname1:/dirname2:/dirname3:.; \
   export PATH
   ```

10. **A**. To set the default path in the C-shell, issue the following command: `set path = (/dirname1 \ /dirname2 /dirname3.)`
11. **A**. The /etc/shadow file contains the encrypted password information for each user account.
12. **A**. The site-wide initialization file for the Korn shell is /etc/profile.
13. **A**. The site-wide initialization file for the C shell is /etc/.login.

## Objectives

The following are the test objectives for this chapter:

**Define and understand the Solaris 8 file systems**

- This is an introduction to the various types of file systems available in Solaris. Solaris has several utilities and options for creating file systems. The system administrator needs to know how to use these utilities and understand the affect that the various options will have on performance and functionality.

**Understand disk geometry**

- To properly configure disk storage systems, the system administrator needs to understand the physical geometry of disk storage devices.

**Understand disk slicing**

- In addition to installing disk storage systems, the system administrator needs to understand concepts of allocating disk space.

**Compare the Logical Volume Manager to standard Solaris file systems**

- In addition to conventional methods of allocating disk space on smaller systems, you'll be introduced to advanced methods of disk allocation on servers.

**Manage and control disk space use**

- After storage systems are in place and configured, the system administrator needs to monitor this disk space regularly so that it is allocated and utilized efficiently.

**Understand custom file system parameters**

- After you install and partition the storage hardware, you need to understand the type of file system to utilize and how to administer it. Solaris provides many utilities for creating, checking, mounting, and displaying information about file systems.

CHAPTER 6

# Introduction to File Systems

## OUTLINE



## STUDY STRATEGIES

The following study strategies will help you prepare for the exam:

- As with every chapter of this book, you'll need a Solaris 8 system on which to practice. Practice every step-by-step example that is presented until you can perform the steps from memory. Also, as you practice creating file systems, you'll need some unused disk space with which to practice. I recommend an empty, secondary disk drive for this purpose.
- Become familiar with all the terms presented at the end of this chapter. You'll see them used throughout the exams. In addition, familiarize yourself with the various types of file systems described in this chapter, but specifically, pay close attention to the UFS file system type and UFS file system parameters. Most questions on the exam revolve around the UFS file system. In addition, make sure you understand the Logical Volume Manager. You don't need to know how to use it—just understand what it does and why you would use it.
- Make sure that you practice disk slicing. Understand how to create and delete disk slices, and pay close attention to the limitations inherent with standard disk slices. Practice partitioning a disk using the `format` utility until you have the process memorized.
- Finally, understand how to mount and unmount a file system as well as how to configure the /etc/vfstab file. Make sure that you understand all of the commands described in this chapter that are used to manage and display information about file systems, such as `df`, `fsck`, and `prtvtoc`.

# INTRODUCTION

This chapter introduces you to Solaris file systems, and provides some of the fundamental concepts you'll need for the first exam. After reading this chapter, you'll understand the fundamentals of disk drives and their geometry. You'll also understand how Solaris uses a disk for file storage through its file systems. Finally, you'll understand how to manage Solaris file systems and control disk space usage. Chapter 7, "Solaris File Systems: Advanced Topics," provides more details on constructing and tuning Solaris file systems.

NOTE: A few topics covered in this chapter are required for the second exam, but are more appropriate in this chapter. A notation will be made when a particular topic is an objective for the second exam.

# A FILE SYSTEM DEFINED

A *file system* is a structure of directories used to organize and store files on disk. A file system is a collection of files and directories stored on disk in a standard UNIX file system format. All disk-based computer systems have a file system. In UNIX, file systems have two basic components: files and directories. A *file* is the actual information as it is stored on the disk, and a *directory* is a listing of the filenames. In addition to keeping track of filenames, the file system must also keep track of files' access dates and ownership. Managing the UNIX file systems is one of the system administrator's most important tasks. Administration of the file system involves the following:

- Ensuring that users have access to data. This means that systems are up and operational, file permissions are set up properly, and data is accessible.
- Protecting file systems against file corruption and hardware failures. This is accomplished by checking the file system regularly and maintaining proper system backups.
- Securing file systems against unauthorized access. Only authorized users should have access to files. The data must be protected from intruders.
- Providing users with adequate space for their files.

- Keeping the file system clean. In other words, data in the file system must be relevant and not wasteful of disk space. Procedures are needed to make sure that users follow proper naming conventions and that data is stored in an organized manner.

You'll see the term "file system" used in several ways. Usually, "file system" describes a particular type of file system (disk-based, network-based, or virtual file system). It might also describe the entire file tree from the root directory downward. In another context, the term "file system" might be used to describe the structure of a disk slice, described later in this chapter.

The Solaris system software uses the virtual file system (VFS) architecture, which provides a standard interface for different file system types. The VFS architecture lets the kernel handle basic operations, such as reading, writing, and listing files, without requiring the user or program to know about the underlying file system type. Furthermore, Solaris provides file system administrative commands that allow you to maintain file systems.

## Defining a Disk's Geometry

Before creating a file system on a disk, you need to understand the basic geometry of a disk drive. Disks come in many shapes and sizes. The number of heads, tracks, sectors, and the disk capacity vary from one model to another.

A *hard disk* consists of several separate disk platters mounted on a common spindle. Data stored on each platter surface is written and read by *disk heads*. The circular path that a disk head traces over a spinning disk platter is called a *track*.

Each track is made up of a number of sectors laid end-to-end. A sector consists of a header, a trailer, and 512 bytes of data. The *header* and *trailer* contain error-checking information to help ensure the accuracy of the data. Taken together, the set of tracks traced across all the individual disk platter surfaces for a single position of the heads is called a *cylinder*.

## Disk Controller

Associated with every disk is a *controller*, an intelligent device responsible for organizing data on the disk. Some disk controllers are located on a separate circuit board (such as SCSI), and some are integrated with the disk drive (such as IDE/EIDE).

## Defect List

Disks might contain areas where data cannot be written and retrieved reliably. These areas are called *defects*. The controller uses the error-checking information in each disk block's trailer to determine whether a defect is present in that block. When a block is found to be defective, the controller can be instructed to add it to a defect list and avoid using that block in the future. The last two cylinders of a disk are set aside for diagnostic use and for storing the disk defect list.

## Disk Label

A special area of every disk is set aside for storing information about the disk's controller, geometry, and slices. This information is called the disk's *label*, or *Volume Table of Contents* (VTOC).

To label a disk means to write slice information onto the disk. You usually label a disk after defining its slices. If you fail to label a disk after creating slices, the slices will be unavailable because the operating system has no way of knowing about them.

## Partition Table

An important part of the disk label is the *partition table*, which identifies a disk's slices, the slice boundaries (in cylinders), and the total size of the slices. A disk's partition table can be displayed by using the `format` utility.

# SOLARIS FILE SYSTEM TYPES

Solaris file systems can be put into three categories: disk-based, network-based, and virtual.

## Disk-Based File Systems

*Disk-based* file systems reside on the system's local disk. Following are the four types of disk-based file systems:

- UFS. The UNIX file system, which is based on the BSD FAT Fast file system (the traditional UNIX file system). The UFS file system is the default disk-based file system used in Solaris.
- HSFS. The High Sierra and ISO 9660 file system. The HSFS file system is used on CD-ROMs, and is a read-only file system.
- PCFS. The PC file system, which allows read/write access to data and programs on DOS-formatted disks written for DOS-based personal computers.
- UDF. New in Solaris 8 is the UDF (Universal Disk Format) file system. UDF is the new industry-standard format for storing information on the optical media technology called *DVD* (Digital Versatile Disc or Digital Video Disc).

## Network-Based File Systems

*Network-based* file systems are file systems accessed over the network. Typically, they reside on one system and are accessed by other systems across the network.

The Network File System (NFS) or remote file systems are file systems made available from remote systems. NFS is the only available network-based file system. (NFS is discussed in detail in Chapter 17, "The NFS Environment," and is covered on the second exam.)

## Virtual File Systems

*Virtual file systems,* previously called *pseudo file systems,* are virtual or memory-based file systems that create duplicate paths to other disk-based file systems or provide access to special kernel information and facilities. Most virtual file systems do not use file system disk space, although a few exceptions exist. Cache file systems, for example, use a file system to contain the cache.

Some virtual file systems, such as the temporary file system, might use the swap space on a physical disk. The following is a list of some of the more common types of virtual file systems:

- SWAPFS. A file system used by the kernel for swapping. Swap space is used as a virtual memory storage area when the system does not have enough physical memory to handle current processes.
- PROCFS. The Process File System resides in memory. It contains a list of active processes, by process number, in the /proc directory. Commands such as `ps` use information in the /proc directory. Debuggers and other development tools can also access the processes' address space by using file system calls.
- LOFS. The Loopback File System lets you create a new virtual file system. You can access files by using an alternative path name. The entire file system hierarchy looks as if it is duplicated under /tmp/newroot, including any file systems mounted from NFS servers. All files are accessible with a pathname starting from either / or /tmp/newroot.
- CacheFS. The Cache File System lets you use disk drives on local workstations to store frequently used data from a remote file system or CD-ROM. The data stored on the local disk is the cache.
- TMPFS. The temporary file system uses local memory for file system reads and writes. Because TMPFS uses physical memory and not the disk, access to files in a TMPFS file system is typically much faster than to files in a UFS file system. Files in the temporary file system are not permanent; they are deleted when the file system is unmounted and when the system is shut down or rebooted. TMPFS is the default file system type for the /tmp directory in the SunOS system software. You can

copy or move files into or out of the /tmp directory just as you would in a UFS /tmp file system. When memory is insufficient to hold everything in the temporary file system, the TMPFS file system uses swap space as a temporary backing store as long as adequate swap space is present.

- /var/run. /var/run is a new temporary file system in Solaris 8. /var/run is the repository for temporary system files that are not needed across systems. The /tmp directory continues to be a repository for non-system temporary files.

  Because /var/run is mounted as a memory-based file system rather than a disk-based file system, updates to this directory do not cause unnecessary disk traffic that interferes with systems that are running power-management software.

  The /var/run directory requires no administration and cannot be unmounted with the `umount -a` or the `umountall` command.

  For security reasons, root owns /var/run.

- MNTFS. New in Solaris 8, this file system type maintains information about currently mounted file systems. MNTFS is described later in this chapter.

## Disk Slices

> **NOTE** Solaris device names use the term "slice" (and the letter 's' in the device name) to refer to the slice number. Slices were called "partitions" in SunOS 4.x. This book attempts to use the term "slice" whenever possible; however, certain interfaces, such as the `format` and `prtvtoc` commands, refer to slices as partitions.

Disks are divided into regions called disk slices, or disk partitions. A *slice* is composed of a single range of contiguous blocks. It is a physical subset of the disk (except for slice 2, which represents the entire disk). A UNIX file system is built within these disk slices. The boundaries of a disk slice are defined when a disk is formatted by using the Solaris `format` utility, and the slice information for a particular disk can be viewed by using the `prtvtoc` command. Each disk slice appears to the operating system (and to the system administrator) as if it were a separate disk drive.

A physical disk consists of a stack of circular platters. Data is stored on these platters in a cylindrical pattern. Cylinders can be grouped and isolated from one another. A group of cylinders is referred to as a slice. A slice is defined with start and end points, defined from the center of the stack of platters, which is called the *spindle*.

To define a slice, the administrator provides a starting cylinder and an ending cylinder. A disk can have up to eight slices, named 0 to 7, but it is uncommon to use partition 2 as a file system. (See Chapter 3, "Installing the Solaris 8 Software," for a discussion of disk-storage systems and sizing partitions.)

> **NOTE** Sometimes a relational database uses an entire disk and requires one single raw partition. It's convenient in this circumstance to use slice 2 because it represents the entire disk.

When setting up slices, remember these rules:

- Each disk slice holds only one file system.
- No file system can span multiple slices.
- After a file system is created, its size cannot be increased or decreased without repartitioning the entire disk and restoring all data from a backup.
- Slices cannot span multiple disks; however, multiple swap slices on separate disks are allowed.

When I discuss logical volumes in the next chapter, I'll describe how to get around some of these limitations in file systems.

Also, follow these guidelines when planning the layout of file systems:

- Distribute the workload as evenly as possible among different I/O systems and disk drives. Distribute /home and swap directories evenly across disks. A single disk has limitations on how quickly data can be transferred. By spreading this load across more than one disk, you can improve performance exponentially. This concept is described in Chapter 16, "Device Administration and Disk Management," in which I describe striping using DiskSuite.
- Keep projects or groups within the same file system. This allows you to keep better track of data for backups, recovery, and security reasons. Some disks might have better performances than others.
- Use the faster drives for file systems that need quick access and the slower drives for data that might not need to be retrieved as quickly.

- Use as few file systems per disk as possible. On the system (or boot) disk, you usually have three slices: /, /usr, and a swap area. On other disks, create one or (at most) two slices. Fewer, roomier slices cause less file fragmentation than many small, overcrowded slices. Higher-capacity tape drives and the capability of `ufsdump` to handle multiple volumes facilitate backing up larger file systems.
- It is not important for most sites to be concerned about keeping similar types of user files in the same file system.
- Occasionally, you might have some users who consistently create small or large files. You might consider creating a separate file system with more inodes for users who consistently create small files. (See the sections on inodes and changing the number of bytes per inode later in this chapter.)

## Displaying Disk Configuration Information

As described earlier, disk configuration information is stored in the disk label. If you know the disk and slice number, you can display information for a disk by using the print volume table of contents (`prtvtoc`) command. You can specify the volume by specifying any non-zero-size slice defined on the disk (for example, /dev/rdsk/c0t3d0s2 for all of disk 3 or /dev/rdsk/c0t3d0s5 for just the sixth slice). If you know the target number of the disk, but do not know how it is divided into slices, you can show information for the entire disk by specifying either slice 2 or slice 0. The following Step by Step shows how you can examine information stored on a disk's label by using the `prtvtoc` command.

### STEP BY STEP

#### 6.1 Examining a Disk's Label Using the *prtvtoc* Command

1. Become superuser.
2. Type `prtvtoc /dev/rdsk/cntndnsn` and press Enter.

Information for the disk and slice you specify is displayed. In the following steps, information is displayed for all of disk 3:

3. Type `prtvtoc /dev/rdsk/c0t3d0s2` and press Enter.

   The system responds with this:

```
* /dev/rdsk/c0t3d0s2 (volume "") partition map
*
* Dimensions:
*     512 bytes/sector
*      36 sectors/track
*       9 tracks/cylinder
*     324 sectors/cylinder
*    1272 cylinders
*    1254 accessible cylinders
*
* Flags:
*   1: unmountable
*  10: read-only
*
*                         First   Sector  Last
* Partition Tag Flags     Sector  Count   Sector  Mount Directory
  2           5   01      0       406296  406295
  6           4   00      0       242352  242351
  7           0   00      242352  163944  406295  /files7
```

   The `prtvtoc` command shows the number of cylinders and heads, as well as how the disk's slices are arranged.

## Using the `format` Utility to Create Slices

Before you can create a file system on a disk, the disk must be formatted, and you must divide it into slices by using the Solaris `format` utility. Formatting involves two separate processes:

- Writing format information to the disk
- Completing a surface analysis, which compiles an up-to-date list of disk defects

When a disk is formatted, header and trailer information is superimposed on the disk. When the `format` utility runs a surface analysis, the controller scans the disk for defects. It should be noted that defects and formatting information reduce the total disk space available for data. This is why a new disk usually holds only 90–95 percent of its capacity after formatting. This percentage varies according to disk geometry and decreases as the disk ages and develops more defects.

> **CAUTION**
> Formatting and creating slices is a destructive process, so make sure user data is backed up before you start.

The need to perform a surface analysis on a disk drive has dropped as more manufacturers ship their disk drives formatted and partitioned. You should not need to use the `format` utility when adding a disk drive to an existing system unless you think disk defects are causing problems. The only other reason you should need to use `format` is if you want to change the partitioning scheme.

The `format` utility searches your system for all attached disk drives, and reports the following information about the disk drives it finds:

- Target location
- Disk geometry
- Whether the disk is formatted
- Whether the disk has mounted partitions

In addition, the `format` utility is used in disk repair operations to do the following:

- Retrieve disk labels
- Repair defective sectors
- Format and analyze disks
- Partition disks
- Label disks (write the disk name and configuration information to the disk for future retrieval)

The Solaris installation program partitions and labels disk drives as part of installing the Solaris release. However, you might need to use the `format` utility when doing the following:

- Displaying slice information
- Dividing a disk into slices

- Formatting a disk drive when you think disk defects are causing problems
- Repairing a disk drive

The main reason a system administrator uses the `format` utility is to divide a disk into disk slices.

## STEP BY STEP

### 6.2 Formatting a Disk

The process of creating slices follows:

1. Become superuser.
2. Type `format`.

   The system responds with this:

   ```
   AVAILABLE DISK SELECTIONS:
   0. c0t0d0 at scsibus0 slave 24
   sd0: <SUN0207 cyl 1254 alt 2 hd 9 sec 36>
    .c0t3d0 at scsibus0 slave 0: test
   sd3: <SUN0207 cyl 1254 alt 2 hd 9 sec 36>
   ```

3. Specify the disk (enter its number).

   The system responds with this:

   ```
   FORMAT MENU:
       disk - select a disk
       type - select (define) a disk type
       partition - select (define) a partition table
       current - describe the current disk
       format - format and analyze the disk
       repair - repair a defective sector
       label - write label to the disk
       analyze - surface analysis
       defect - defect list management
       backup - search for backup labels
       verify - read and display labels
       save - save new disk/partition definitions
       inquiry - show vendor, product and revision
       volname - set 8-character volume name
       !<cmd> - execute <cmd>, then return
       quit
   ```

**NOTE** It is unnecessary to type the entire command. After you type the first two characters of a command, the `format` utility recognizes the entire command.

*continues*

*continued*

4. Type `partition` at the `format` prompt. The partition menu is displayed.

```
format> partition
PARTITION MENU:
    0 - change '0' partition
    1 - change '1' partition
    2 - change '2' partition
    3 - change '3' partition
    4 - change '4' partition
    5 - change '5' partition
    6 - change '6' partition
    7 - change '7' partition
    select - select a predefined table
    modify - modify a predefined partition table
    name - name the current table
    print - display the current table
    label - write partition map and label to the disk
    !<cmd> - execute <cmd>, then return
    quit
```

5. Type `print` to display the current partition map.

   The system responds with this:

```
partition> print
Current partition table (original):
Total disk cylinders available: 2733 + 2 (reserved cylinders)

Part Tag        Flag Cylinders     Size     Blocks
0    root       wm   0 -   202     150.66MB (203/0/0)  308560
1    swap       wu   203 - 332     96.48MB  (130/0/0)  197600
2    backup     wm   0 - 2732      1.98GB   (2733/0/0) 4154160
3    unassigned wm   333 - 390     43.05MB  (58/0/0)   88160
4    unassigned wm   391 - 443     39.34MB  (53/0/0)   80560
5    unassigned wm   444 - 801     265.70MB (358/0/0)  544160
6    usr        wm   802 - 2182    1.00GB   (1381/0/0) 2099120
7    home       wm   2183 - 2732   408.20MB (550/0/0)  836000
```

**NOTE** If you don't label the drive, your partition changes will not be retained.

6. After you partition the disk, you must label it by typing `label` at the partition prompt:

```
partition> label
```

7. After labeling the disk, type `quit` to exit the partition menu:

```
partition> quit
```

8. Type `quit` again to exit the format utility:

```
format> quit
```

**CAUTION**

You will lose all data when changing partition sizes. Make sure that you either copy your data to another disk or to tape before continuing.

It's important to point out a few undesirable things that can happen when defining disk partitions with the `format` utility if you're not careful. First, be careful not to waste disk space. Wasted disk space can occur when you decrease the size of one slice and do not adjust the starting cylinder number of the next adjoining disk slice.

Second, don't overlap disk slices. Overlapping occurs when one or more cylinders are allocated to more than one disk slice. For example, increasing the size of one slice without decreasing the size of the adjoining slice will create overlapping partitions. The `format` utility will not warn you of wasted disk space or overlapping partitions.

One more item of note: On standard UFS file systems, don't change the size of disk slices that are currently in use. When a disk with existing slices is repartitioned and relabeled, any existing data will be lost. Before repartitioning a disk, first copy all the data to tape or to another disk.

## The Free Hog Slice

When using the format utility to change the size of disk slices, a temporary slice is automatically designated that expands and shrinks to accommodate the slice resizing operations. This temporary slice is referred to as the "free hog," and it represents the unused disk space on a disk drive. If a slice is decreased, the free hog expands. The free hog is then used to allocate space to slices that have been increased. It does not, however, prevent the overlapping of disk slices as described in the previous section.

The free hog slice exists only when you run the `format` utility. It is not saved as a permanent slice.

## Using the Format Utility to Modify Partitions

If you need to change the size of slices on a particular disk, you can either re-create the disk slices as outlined in the previous section or use the `modify` option of the `format` utility.

The `modify` option allows the root to create slices by specifying the size of each slice without having to keep track of starting cylinder boundaries. It will also keep track of any excess disk space in the temporary free hog slice.

**NOTE**

If you try to modify mounted partitions, you receive an error that states `Cannot modify disk partitions while it has mounted partitions.`

## STEP BY STEP

### 6.3 Modifying a Disk Slice

To modify a disk slice, follow these steps:

1. Make a backup of your data. This process will destroy the data on this disk.
2. As root, enter the partition menu of the `format` utility as described in the 6.2 Step by Step.
3. After printing the existing partition scheme, type `modify` and press Enter.

   When typing `modify`, you'll see the following output on a disk that does not have mounted partitions:

   ```
   Select partitioning base:
           0. Current partition table (original)
           1. All Free Hog
   Choose base (enter number) [0]?
   ```

4. Press Enter to select the default selection. The following is displayed:

```
Part      Tag    Flag   Cylinders     Size        Blocks
0          usr    wm    0 -   194     100.26MB   (195/0/0)    205335
1 unassigned      wu    195 - 1167    500.28MB   (973/0/0)   1024569
2       backup    wm    0 - 3983      2.00GB     (3984/0/0)  4195152
3 unassigned      wm    0              0         (0/0/0)           0
4 unassigned      wm    0              0         (0/0/0)           0
```

```
5 unassigned    wm     0             0          (0/0/0)          0
6 unassigned    wm     0             0          (0/0/0)          0
7 unassigned    wm     0             0          (0/0/0)          0

Do you wish to continue creating a new partition
table based on above table[yes]?
```

5. Press Enter to select the default selection. The following message will be displayed:

   ```
   Free Hog partition[6]?
   ```

6. Press Enter to select the default selection. If all the disk space is in use, the following message will be displayed:

   ```
   Warning: No space available from Free Hog partition.
   Continue[no]?
   ```

> **NOTE** Slice 6 is not displayed because that is the temporary free hog.

7. Type yes. You'll be prompted to type the new size for each partition:

```
Enter size of partition '0' [205335b,195c,100.26mb,0.10gb]: 90m
Enter size of partition '1' [1024569b,973c,500.28mb 0.49gb]:450m
Enter size of partition '3' [0b, 0c, 0.00mb, 0.00gb]: <cr>
Enter size of partition '4' [0b, 0c, 0.00mb, 0.00gb]: <cr>
Enter size of partition '5' [0b, 0c, 0.00mb, 0.00gb]: <cr>
Enter size of partition '7' [0b, 0c, 0.00mb, 0.00gb]: <cr>
```

> **NOTE** Slice 6, the free hog, represents the unused disk space. You might want to allocate this space to another partition so it does not go unused, or you can save it and allocate it another time to an unused partition.

When you are finished resizing the last partition, the following will be displayed, showing you the revised partition map:

```
Part      Tag    Flag     Cylinders       Size        Blocks
0         usr    wm        0 -  175      90.49MB     (176/0/0)  185328
1 unassigned     wu      176 - 1051     450.40MB     (876/0/0)  922428
2       backup   wm        0 - 3983       2.00GB     (3984/0/0) 4195152
3 unassigned     wm        0               0         (0/0/0)          0
4 unassigned     wm        0               0         (0/0/0)          0
5 unassigned     wm        0               0         (0/0/0)          0
6 unassigned     wm     1052 - 3983      1.47GB     (2932/0/0)  3087396
7 unassigned     wm        0               0         (0/0/0)          0
Okay to make this the current partition table[yes]?
```

*continues*

*continued*

8. Press Enter to confirm your modified partition map. You'll see the following message displayed:

   ```
   Enter table name (remember quotes):
   ```

9. Name the modified partition `table` and press Enter:

   ```
   Enter table name (remember quotes): c0t3d0.2gb
   ```

10. After entering the name, the following message will be displayed:

    ```
    Ready to label disk, continue?
    ```

11. Type `yes` and press Enter to continue.
12. Type `quit` (or `q`) and press Enter to exit the partition menu. The main menu will be displayed.
13. Type `quit` and press Enter to exit the `format` utility.

## Recovering Disk Partition Information

It's always a good idea to save a disk's VTOC (Volume Table of Contents) to a file using the `prtvtoc` command described earlier. This information can then be used later to restore the disk label if your current VTOC becomes corrupted or accidentally changed or you need to replace the disk drive.

By saving the output from the `prtvtoc` command into a file on another disk, you can reference it when running the `fmthard` command. The `fmthard` command updates the VTOC on hard disks.

## STEP BY STEP

### 6.4 Recovering a VTOV (Volume Table of Contents)

To recover a VTOC, follow these steps:

1. Run the `format` utility on the disk, and label it with the default partition table.

2. Use the `fmthard` command to write the backup VTOC information back to the disk drive. The following example uses the `fmthard` command to recover a corrupt label on a disk named /dev/rdsk/c0t3d0s2. The backup VTOC information is in a file named c0t3d0 in the /vtoc directory:

```
fmthard -s /vtoc/c0t3d0s0 /dev/rdsk/c0t3d0s2
```

---

Another use for the `fmthard` command is if you need to partition several disks with the same partitioning scheme. Get the VTOC information from the disk you want to copy (c0t0d0), and write the information to the new disk (c1t0d0) as follows:

```
prtvtoc /dev/rdsk/c0t0d0s0 | fmthard -s - /dev/rdsk/c1t0d0s2
```

## Logical Volumes

On a large server with many disk drives, standard methods of disk slicing are inadequate and inefficient. Limitations imposed by standard disk slices include the slices' inability to be larger than the file system that holds them. Because file systems cannot span multiple disks, the size of the file system is limited to the size of the disk. Another problem with standard file systems is that they cannot be increased in size without destroying data on the file system.

Sun has addressed these issues with two software packages: Solstice DiskSuite and Sun Enterprise Volume Manager. Both packages allow file systems to span multiple disks, and provide for improved I/O and reliability compared to the standard Solaris file system. We refer to these types of file systems as *logical volumes* (LVMs).

Solstice DiskSuite is now part of Solaris 8. The Enterprise Volume Manager is purchased separately and is not part of the standard Solaris operating system distribution. Typically, DiskSuite is used on Sun's multipacks, and the Enterprise Volume Manager package is used on the Sparc StorEdge arrays. (LVMs, DiskSuite, and Enterprise Volume Manager are discussed in detail in Chapter 16, "Device Administration and Disk Management," and are covered on the second exam.)

> **NOTE**
>
> When using Web Start to install the operating system, the swap partition is placed at the start of the disk, but is still called partition 1, followed by root, which is still called partition 0. It's a bit confusing, but disk slices do not necessarily need to be laid out consecutively on the disk. In other words, slice 1 can start at cylinder 0 and end at cylinder 1271, whereas slice 0 can start at cylinder 1272 and end at cylinder 1495. A marginal performance increase is achieved by putting swap at the starting cylinder because of the faster rotation speeds on the outside perimeter of the disk. Web Start is described in Appendix A, "Web Start."

## PARTS OF A UFS FILE SYSTEM

UFS is the default disk-based file system used in the Solaris system software. It provides the following features:

- State flags. Shows the state of the file system as clean, stable, active, or unknown. These flags eliminate unnecessary file system checks. If the file system is clean or stable, `fsck` (file system check) is not run when the system boots.
- Extended fundamental types (EFT). 32-bit user ID (UID), group ID (GID), and device numbers.
- Large file systems. A UFS file system can be as large as 1 terabyte (TB) and can have regular files up to 2 gigabytes (GB). By default, the Solaris system software does not provide striping, which is required to make a logical slice large enough for a 1TB file system. Optional software packages, such as Solstice DiskSuite, provide this capability.

During the installation of the Solaris software, several UFS file systems are created on the system disk. These are Sun's default file systems. Their contents are described in Table 6.1.

**TABLE 6.1**

**SOLARIS DEFAULT FILE SYSTEMS**

| *Slice* | *File System* | *Description* |
|---|---|---|
| 0 | root | Root (/) is the top of the hierarchical file tree. It holds files and directories that make up the operating system. The root directory contains the directories and files critical for system operation, such as the kernel, the device drivers, and the programs used to boot the system. It also contains the mount point directories, in which local and remote file systems can be attached to the file tree. The root (/) file system is always in slice 0. |

| *Slice* | *File System* | *Description* |
|---|---|---|
| 1 | swap | Provides virtual memory or swap space. Swap space is used when you're running programs too large to fit in the computer's memory. The Solaris operating environment then "swaps" programs from memory to the disk and back, as needed. Although it is not technically required, it is common for the swap slice to be located in slice 1 unless /var is set up as a file system. If /var is set up, it uses slice 1, and swap is usually put on slice 4. The /var file system is for files and directories likely to change or grow over the life of the local system. These include system logs, vi and ex backup files, printer spool files, and uucp files. On a server, it's a good idea to have these files in a separate file system. |
| 2 | Entire Disk | Refers to the entire disk, and is defined automatically by Sun's `format` utility and the Solaris installation programs. The size of this slice should not be changed. |
| 3 | /export | Holds alternative versions of the operating system. These alternative versions are required by client systems whose architectures differ from that of the server. Clients with the same architecture type as the server obtain executables from the /usr file system, usually slice 6. /export is also where user home directories or file systems are located that will be shared across the network. This is discussed in more detail in Chapter 17, "The NFS Environment." |
| 4 | /export/swap | Provides virtual memory space for client systems. |
| 5 | /opt | Holds additional Sun software packages such as AdminSuite and optional third-party software that has been added to a system. If a slice is not allocated for this file system during installation, the /opt directory is put in slice 0, the root (/) file system. |

*continues*

**TABLE 6.1** *continued*

**SOLARIS DEFAULT FILE SYSTEMS**

| *Slice* | *File System* | *Description* |
|---|---|---|
| 6 | /usr | Holds operating system commands—also known as executables—designed to be run by users. This slice also holds documentation, system programs (`init` and `syslogd`, for example), and library routines. The /usr file system also includes system files and directories that can be shared with other users. Files that can be used on all types of systems (such as man pages) are in /usr/share. |
| 7 | /home | Holds files created by users (also named /export/home). On a standard system, /home is a mount point that AutoFS manages. See Chapter 17 for more information. |

You need to create (or re-create) a UFS file system only when you do the following:

- Add or replace disks
- Change the slices of an existing disk
- Do a full restore on a file system
- Change the parameters of a file system, such as block size or free space

When you create a UFS file system, the disk slice is divided into cylinder groups. The slice is then divided into blocks to control and organize the structure of the files within the cylinder group. Each block performs a specific function in the file system. A UFS file system has the following four types of blocks:

- Boot block. Stores information used when booting the system.
- Superblock. Stores much of the information about the file system.
- Inode. Stores all information about a file except its name.
- Storage or data block. Stores data for each file.

## The Boot Block

The *boot block* stores the procedures used in booting the system. Without a boot block, the system does not boot. If a file system is not to be used for booting, the boot block is left blank. The boot block appears only in the first cylinder group (cylinder group 0) and is the first 8KB in a slice.

## The Superblock

The superblock stores much of the information about the file system. Following are a few of the more important items contained in a superblock:

- Size and status of the file system
- Label (file system name and volume name)
- Size of the file system's logical block
- Date and time of the last update
- Cylinder group size
- Number of data blocks in a cylinder group
- Summary data block
- File system state (clean, stable, or active)
- Pathname of the last mount point

Without a superblock, the file system becomes unreadable. The superblock is located at the beginning of the disk slice and is replicated in each cylinder group. Because it contains critical data, multiple superblocks are made when the file system is created.

A copy of the superblock for each file system is kept up-to-date in memory. If the system gets halted before a disk copy of the superblock gets updated, the most recent changes are lost, and the file system becomes inconsistent. The `sync` command forces every superblock in memory to write its data to disk. The file system check program `fsck` can fix problems that occur when the `sync` command hasn't been used before a shutdown.

A summary information block is kept with the superblock. It is not replicated, but is grouped with the first superblock, usually in cylinder group 0. The summary block records changes that take place as the file system is used, listing the number of inodes, directories, fragments, and storage blocks within the file system.

## The Inode

An *inode* contains all of the information about a file except its name, which is kept in a directory. An inode is 128 bytes. The inode information is kept in the cylinder information block and contains the following:

- The type of the file (regular, directory, block special, character special, link, and so on)
- The mode of the file (the set of read/write/execute permissions)
- The number of hard links to the file
- The user-id of the file's owner
- The group-id to which the file belongs
- The number of bytes in the file
- An array of 15 disk-block addresses
- The date and time the file was last accessed
- The date and time the file was last modified
- The date and time the file was created

The maximum number of files per UFS file system is determined by the number of inodes allocated for a file system. The number of inodes depends on the amount of disk space that is allocated for each inode and the total size of the file system. By default, one inode is allocated for each 2KB of data space. You can change the default allocation by using the `-i` option of the `newfs` command. This is discussed in Chapter 7, "Solaris File Systems: Advanced Topics."

## The Storage Block

*Storage blocks*, also called data blocks, occupy the rest of the space allocated to the file system. The size of these storage blocks is determined at the time a file system is created. Storage blocks are allocated, by default, in two sizes: an 8KB logical block size and a 1KB fragmentation size.

For a regular file, the storage blocks contain the contents of the file. For a directory, the storage blocks contain entries that give the inode number and the filename of the files in the directory.

## Free Blocks

Blocks not currently being used as inodes, indirect address blocks, or storage blocks are marked as *free* in the cylinder group map. This map also keeps track of fragments to prevent fragmentation from degrading disk performance.

# Creating a UFS File System

Use the `newfs` command to create UFS file systems. `newfs` is a convenient front end to the `mkfs` command, the program that creates the new file system on a disk slice. (Please note that `newfs` is a topic covered on the second exam.)

On Solaris 8 systems, information used to set some of the parameter defaults, such as number of tracks per cylinder and number of sectors per track, is read from the disk label. `newfs` determines the file system parameters to use, based on the options you specify and information provided in the disk label. Parameters are then passed to the `mkfs` (make file system) command, which builds the file system. Although you can use the `mkfs` command directly, it's more difficult to use, and you must supply many of the parameters manually. (The use of the `newfs` command is discussed more in the next section.)

You must format the disk and divide it into slices before you can create UFS file systems on it. `newfs` removes any data on the disk slice and creates the skeleton of a directory structure, including a directory named `lost+found`. After you run `newfs` successfully, it's essential to run the `fsck` command to check the integrity of the file system before mounting it for the first time. (The `fsck` command is described later in this chapter.) After you run `fsck`, the slice is ready to be mounted as a file system.

To create a UFS file system on a formatted disk that has already been divided into slices, you need to know the raw device filename of the slice that will contain the file system.

**CAUTION**

Be sure you have specified the correct device name for the slice before performing the next step. You will erase the contents of the slice when the new file system is created, and you don't want to erase the wrong slice.

## STEP BY STEP

### 6.5 Creating a UFS File System

If you are re-creating or modifying an existing UFS file system, back up and unmount the file system before performing these steps.

1. Become superuser.
2. Type `newfs /dev/rdsk/<device-name>`, and press Enter. You are asked if you want to proceed. The `newfs` command requires the use of the raw device name and not the buffered device name. Refer to Chapter 16, "Device Administration and Disk Management," for more information on raw and buffered devices.
3. Type `y` to confirm.

The following example creates a file system on `/dev/rdsk/c0t3d0s7`:

1. Become superuser by typing `su`, and enter the root password.
2. Type `newfs /dev/rdsk/c0t3d0s7`.

   The system responds with this:

```
newfs: construct a new file system /dev/rdsk/c0t3d0s7 (y/n)? y
/dev/rdsk/c0t3d0s7:  163944 sectors in 506 cylinders of 9 tracks, 36 sectors
83.9MB in 32 cyl groups (16 c/g, 2.65MB/g, 1216 i/g)
super-block backups (for fsck -b #) at:
32, 5264, 10496, 15728, 20960, 26192, 31424, 36656, 41888,
47120, 52352, 57584, 62816, 68048, 73280, 78512, 82976, 88208,
93440, 98672, 103904, 109136, 114368, 119600, 124832, 130064, 135296,
140528, 145760, 150992, 156224, 161456,
```

The `newfs` command uses conservative and safe default values to create the file system. I describe how to modify these values in the next chapter. Here are the default parameters used by the `newfs` command:

- The file system block size is 8,192.
- The file system fragment size (the smallest allocable unit of disk space) is 1,024 bytes.
- The percentage of free space is now calculated as follows: (64MB/partition size) * 100, rounded down to the nearest integer and limited to between 1% and 10%, inclusive.
- The number of inodes or bytes per inode is 2,048. This controls how many inodes are created for the file system (one inode for each 2KB of disk space).

# Understanding Custom File System Parameters

Before you choose to alter the default file system parameters assigned by the `newfs` command, you need to understand them. This section describes each of these parameters:

- Logical block size
- Fragment size
- Minimum free space
- Rotational delay (gap)
- Optimization type
- Number of inodes and bytes per inode

## Logical Block Size

The *logical block size* is the size of the blocks that the UNIX kernel uses to read or write files. The logical block size is usually different from the physical block size (usually 512 bytes), which is the size of the smallest block that the disk controller can read or write.

You can specify the logical block size of the file system. After the file system is created, you cannot change this parameter without rebuilding the file system. You can have file systems with different logical block sizes on the same disk.

By default, the logical block size is 8192 bytes (8KB) for UFS file systems. The UFS file system supports block sizes of 4096 or 8192 bytes (4KB or 8KB, with 8KB being the recommended logical block size).

To choose the best logical block size for your system, consider both the performance desired and the available space. For most UFS systems, an 8KB file system provides the best performance, offering a good balance between disk performance and use of space in primary memory and on disk.

As a general rule, a larger logical block size increases efficiency for file systems in which most of the files are large. Use a smaller logical block size for file systems in which most of the files are small. You can use the `quot -c` file system command on a file system to display a complete report on the distribution of files by block size.

## Fragment Size

As files are created or expanded, they are allocated disk space in either full logical blocks or portions of logical blocks called *fragments*. When disk space is needed to hold data for a file, full blocks are allocated first, and then one or more fragments of a block are allocated for the remainder. For small files, allocation begins with fragments.

The ability to allocate fragments of blocks to files rather than whole blocks saves space by reducing the fragmentation of disk space that results from unused holes in blocks.

You define the fragment size when you create a UFS file system. The default fragment size is 1KB. Each block can be divided into one, two, four, or eight fragments, resulting in fragment sizes from 512 bytes to 8192 bytes (for 4KB file systems only). The lower boundary is actually tied to the disk sector size, typically 512 bytes.

> **NOTE** The upper boundary might equal the full block size, in which case the fragment is not a fragment at all. This configuration might be optimal for file systems with large files when you are more concerned with speed than with space.

When choosing a fragment size, look at the trade-off between time and space: A small fragment size saves space, but requires more time to allocate. As a general rule, a larger fragment size increases efficiency for file systems in which most of the files are large. Use a smaller fragment size for file systems in which most of the files are small.

## Minimum Free Space

The *minimum free space* is the percentage of the total disk space held in reserve when you create the file system. Before Solaris 7, the default reserve was always 10%. In Solaris 7 and now Solaris 8, the minimum free space is automatically determined. This new method of calculating free space results in less wasted disk space on large file systems.

Free space is important because file access becomes less and less efficient as a file system gets full. As long as the amount of free space is adequate, UFS file systems operate efficiently. When a file system becomes full, using up the available user space, only `root` can access the reserved free space.

Commands such as `df` report the percentage of space available to users, excluding the percentage allocated as the minimum free space. When the command reports that more than 100% of the disk space in the file system is in use, some of the reserve has been used by `root`.

If you impose quotas on users, the amount of space available to the users does not include the free space reserve. You can change the value of the minimum free space for an existing file system by using the `tunefs` command.

## Rotational Delay (Gap)

The *rotational delay* is the expected minimum time (in milliseconds) that it takes the CPU to complete a data transfer and initiate a new data transfer on the same disk cylinder. The default delay depends on the type of disk and is usually optimized for each disk type.

When writing a file, the UFS allocation routines try to position new blocks on the same disk cylinder as the previous block in the same file. The allocation routines also try to optimally position new blocks within tracks to minimize the disk rotation needed to access them.

To position file blocks so that they are "rotationally well-behaved," the allocation routines must know how fast the CPU can service transfers and how long it takes the disk to skip over a block. By using options to the `mkfs` command, you can indicate how fast the disk rotates and how many disk blocks (sectors) it has per track. The allocation routines use this information to figure out how many milliseconds the disk takes to skip a block. Then, by using the expected transfer time (rotational delay), the allocation routines can position or place blocks so that the next block is just coming under the disk head when the system is ready to read it.

Place blocks consecutively only if your system is fast enough to read them on the same disk rotation. If the system is too slow, the disk spins past the beginning of the next block in the file and must complete a full rotation before the block can be read, which takes a lot of time. You should try to specify an appropriate value for the gap so that the head is located over the appropriate block when the next disk request occurs.

You can change the value of this parameter for an existing file system by using the `tunefs` command. The change applies only to subsequent block allocation, not to blocks already allocated. (`tunefs` is described in detail in the next chapter.)

## Optimization Type

The *optimization type* is either space or time. When you select space optimization, disk blocks are allocated to minimize fragmentation and optimize disk use. Space optimization is the default.

When you select time optimization, disk blocks are allocated as quickly as possible, with less emphasis on their placement. Time is the default when you set the minimum free space to 10 percent or greater. With enough free space, the disk blocks can be allocated effectively with minimal fragmentation.

You can change the value of the optimization type parameter for an existing file system by using the `tunefs` command.

### Number of Inodes and Bytes Per Inode

The number of inodes determines the number of files you can have in the file system because each file has one inode. The number of bytes per inode determines the total number of inodes created when the file system is made: the total size of the file system divided by the number of bytes per inode. After the inodes are allocated, you cannot change the number without re-creating the file system.

> **NOTE** Having too many inodes is much better than running out of them. If you have too few inodes, you could reach the maximum number of files on a disk slice that is practically empty.

The default number of bytes per inode is 2048 (2KB), which assumes that the average size of each file is 2KB or greater. Most files are larger than 2KB. A file system with many symbolic links will have a lower average file size. If your file system will have many small files, you can give this parameter a lower value.

## File System Operations

This section describes the Solaris utilities used for creating, checking, repairing, and mounting file systems. Use these utilities to make file systems available to the user and to ensure their reliability.

### Synchronizing a File System

The UFS file system relies on an internal set of tables to keep track of inodes as well as used and available blocks. When a user performs an operation that requires data to be written to the disk, the data to be written is first copied into a buffer in the kernel. Normally, the disk update is not handled until long after the write operation has returned. At any given time, the file system, as it resides on the disk, might lag behind the state of the file system represented by the buffers located in physical memory. The internal tables finally get updated when the buffer is required for another use or when the kernel automatically runs the `fsflush` daemon (at 30-second intervals).

If the system is halted without writing out the memory-resident information, the file system on the disk will be in an inconsistent state. If the internal tables are not properly synchronized with data on the disk, inconsistencies result, and file systems need repairing. File systems can be damaged or become inconsistent because of abrupt termination of the operating system in these ways:

- Power failure
- Accidental unplugging of the system
- Turning off the system without the proper shutdown procedure
- Performing a Stop+A (L1+A)
- A software error in the kernel
- A hardware failure that halts the system unexpectedly

To prevent unclean halts, the current state of the file system must be written to disk (that is, synchronized) before you halt the CPU or take a disk offline.

## Repairing File Systems

During normal operation, files are created, modified, and removed. Each time a file is modified, the operating system performs a series of file system updates. When a system is booted, a file system consistency check is automatically performed. Most of the time, this file system check repairs any problems it encounters. File systems are checked with the `fsck` (file system check) command.

The Solaris `fsck` command uses a state flag, which is stored in the superblock, to record the condition of the file system. This flag is used by the `fsck` command to determine whether a file system needs to be checked for consistency. The flag is used by the `/etc/bcheckrc` script during booting, and by the `fsck` command when run from a command line using the `-m` option. Following are the possible state values:

- FSCLEAN. If the file system was unmounted properly, the state flag is set to FSCLEAN. Any file system with an FSCLEAN state flag is not checked when the system is booted.
- FSSTABLE. The file system is (or was) mounted but has not changed since the last check point—`sync` or `fsflush`—which normally occurs every 30 seconds. For example, the kernel periodically checks to see if a file system is idle and, if it is, flushes the information in the superblock back to the disk and marks it FSSTABLE. If the system crashes, the file system structure is stable, but users might lose a small amount of data. File systems marked as FSSTABLE can skip the checking before mounting.
- FSACTIVE. When a file system is mounted and then modified, the state flag is set to FSACTIVE, and the file system might contain inconsistencies. A file system is marked as FSACTIVE before any modified data is written to the disk. When a file system is unmounted gracefully, the state flag is set to FSCLEAN. A file system with the FSACTIVE flag must be checked by `fsck`, because it might be inconsistent. The system does not mount a file system for read/write unless its state is FSCLEAN or FSSTABLE.
- FSBAD. If the root file system is mounted when its state is not FSCLEAN or FSSTABLE, the state flag is set to FSBAD. The kernel does not change this file system state to FSCLEAN or FSSTABLE. A root file system flagged FSBAD as part of the boot process is mounted as read-only. You can run `fsck` on the raw root device and then remount the `root` file system as read/write.
- FSLOG. If the file system was mounted with UFS logging, the state flag is set to FSLOG. Any file system with an FSLOG state flag is not checked when the system is booted. See the section titled "Mounting a File System with UFS Logging Enabled," in which I describe mounting a file system from the command line.

`fsck` is a multipass file system check program that performs successive passes over each file system, checking blocks and sizes, pathnames, connectivity, reference counts, and the map of free blocks (possibly rebuilding it). `fsck` also performs cleanup. The phases (passes) performed by the UFS version of `fsck` are described in Table 6.2.

**TABLE 6.2**

**`fsck` PHASES**

| `fsck` *Phase* | *Task Performed* |
|---|---|
| Phase 1 | Checks blocks and sizes |
| Phase 2 | Checks pathnames |
| Phase 3 | Checks connectivity |
| Phase 4 | Checks reference counts |
| Phase 5 | Checks cylinder groups |

Normally, `fsck` is run noninteractively at bootup to preen the file systems after an abrupt system halt in which the latest file system changes were not written to disk. Preening automatically fixes any basic file system inconsistencies, but does not try to repair more serious errors. While preening a file system, `fsck` fixes the inconsistencies it expects from such an abrupt halt. For more serious conditions, the command reports the error and terminates. It then tells the operator to run `fsck` manually.

## Determining Whether a File System Needs Checking

File systems must be checked periodically for inconsistencies to avoid unexpected loss of data. As stated earlier, checking the state of a file system is automatically done at bootup; however, it is not necessary to reboot a system to check if the file systems are stable.

## STEP BY STEP

### 6.6 Determining the Current State of the File System

The following procedure outlines a method for determining the current state of the file systems and whether they need to be fixed:

1. Become a superuser.
2. Type `fsck -m /dev/rdsk/cntndnsn` and press Enter. The state flag in the superblock of the file system you specify is checked to see whether the file system is clean or requires checking. If you omit the device argument, all the UFS file systems listed in /etc/vfstab with a `fsck` pass value of greater than 0 are checked.

In the following example, the first file system needs checking, but the second file system does not:

```
fsck -m /dev/rdsk/c0t0d0s6

** /dev/rdsk/c0t0d0s6
ufs fsck: sanity check: /dev/rdsk/c0t0d0s6 needs checking
fsck -m /dev/rdsk/c0t0d0s7
** /dev/rdsk/c0t0d0s7
ufs fsck: sanity check: /dev/rdsk/c0t0d0s7 okay
```

## Running `fsck` Manually

You might need to manually check file systems when they cannot be mounted or when you've determined that the state of a file system is unclean. Good indications that a file system might need to be checked are error messages displayed in the console window or system crashes that occur for no reason.

When you run `fsck` manually, it reports each inconsistency found and fixes innocuous errors. For more serious errors, the command reports the inconsistency and prompts you to choose a response. Sometimes corrective actions performed by `fsck` result in some loss of data. The amount and severity of data loss can be determined from the `fsck` diagnostic output.

**NOTE** The `fsck` command has a `-y` option that automatically answers "yes" to every question. But be careful: If `fsck` asks to delete a file, it will answer yes, and you will have no control over it. If it doesn't delete the file, however, the file system remains unclean and cannot be mounted.

**NOTE** Occasionally, the file system's superblock can become corrupted and `fsck` will ask you for the location of an alternate superblock. This information can be obtained by typing:

```
newfs -Nv <raw device name>
```

## STEP BY STEP

### 6.7 Manually Checking File Systems

To check all file systems manually, follow these steps:

1. Become a superuser.
2. Unmount the file system.
3. Type `fsck` and press Enter.

   All file systems in the `/etc/vfstab` file with entries greater than 0 in the `fsck pass` field are checked. You can also specify the mount point directory or `/dev/rdsk/`*`cntndnsn`* as arguments to `fsck`. The `fsck` command requires the raw device filename.

   Any inconsistency messages are displayed. The only way to successfully change the file system and correct the problem is to answer "yes" to these messages.
4. If you corrected any errors, type `fsck` and press Enter. `fsck` might not be able to fix all errors in one execution. If you see the message `FILE SYSTEM STATE NOT SET TO OKAY`, run the command again and continue to run `fsck` until it runs clean with no errors.
5. Rename and move any files put in `lost+found`. Individual files put in the `lost+found` directory by `fsck` are renamed with their inode numbers, so figuring out what they were named originally can be difficult. If possible, rename the files and move them where they belong. You might be able to use the `grep` command to match phrases with individual files and use the `file` command to identify file types, ownership, and so on. When entire directories are dumped into `lost+found`, it is easier to figure out where they belong and move them back.

# Mounting File Systems

After you create a file system, you need to make it available. You make file systems available by mounting them. Using the `mount` command, you attach a file system to the system directory tree at the specified mount point, and it becomes available to the system. The root file system is mounted at boot time, and cannot be unmounted. Any other file system can be mounted or unmounted from the root file system at any time.

The various methods used to mount a file system are described in the next sections.

## Creating an Entry in the /etc/vfstab File to Mount File Systems

The /etc/vfstab (virtual file system table) file contains a list of file systems to be automatically mounted when the system is booted to the multiuser state. The system administrator places entries in the file, specifying what file systems are to be mounted at bootup. The following is an example of the /etc/vfstab file:

```
#device             device              mount FS    fsck  mount    mount
#to mount           to fsck             point type  pass  at boot  options
/dev/dsk/c0t0d0s0   /dev/rdsk/c0t0d0s0  /     ufs   1     no       -
/proc               -                   /proc proc        no       -
/dev/dsk/c0t0d0s1   -                   -     swap        no       -
swap                -                   /tmp  tmpfs -     yes      -
/dev/dsk/c0t0d0s6   /dev/rdsk/c0t0d0s6  /usr  ufs    2    no       -
/dev/dsk/c0t3d0s7   /dev/rdsk/c0t3d0s7  /data ufs    2    no       -
```

Each column of information follows this format:

- `device to mount`. The buffered device that corresponds to the file system being mounted.
- `device to fsck`. The raw (character) special device that corresponds to the file system being mounted. This determines the raw interface used by `fsck`. Use a dash (-) when there is no applicable device, such as for swap, /proc, tmp, or a network-based file system.
- `mount point`. The default mount point directory.
- `FS type`. The type of file system.

> **NOTE** A common misconception is that the `fsck pass` field specifies the order in which file systems are to be checked. In SunOS system software, the `fsck pass` field does not specify the order in which file systems are to be checked. During bootup, a preliminary check is run on each file system to be mounted from a hard disk, using the boot script `/sbin/rcS`, which checks the / and /usr file systems. The other rc shell scripts then use the `fsck` command to check each additional file system sequentially. They do not check file systems in parallel. File systems are checked sequentially during booting even if the `fsck` pass numbers are greater than `1`. The values can be any number greater than `1`.

- `fsck pass`. The pass number used by `fsck` to decide whether to check a file. When the field contains a dash (-), the file system is not checked. When the field contains a value of 1 or greater, the file system is checked sequentially. File systems are checked sequentially in the order that they appear in the /etc/vfstab file. The value of the pass number has no effect on the sequence of file system checking.
- `mount at boot`. Specifies whether the file system should be automatically mounted when the system is booted. The rc scripts located in the /etc directory specify which file system gets mounted at each run level.
- `mount options`. A list of comma-separated options (with no spaces) used when mounting the file system. Use a dash (-) to show no options.

## Using the Command Line to Mount File Systems

File systems can be mounted from the command line by using the `mount` command. The commands in Table 6.3 are used from the command line to mount and unmount file systems.

> **NOTE** File systems are automatically unmounted as part of the system shutdown procedure.

**TABLE 6.3**

**FILE SYSTEM COMMANDS**

| *Command* | *Description* |
|---|---|
| `mount` | Mounts specified file systems and remote resources. |
| `mountall` | Mounts all file systems specified in a file system table (vfstab). |
| `umount` | Unmounts specified file systems and remote resources. |
| `umountall` | Unmounts all file systems specified in a file system table. |

CD-ROMs containing file systems should be automatically mounted when the CD-ROM is inserted if Volume Manager is running. Disks containing file systems that have not yet been automatically mounted can be manually mounted by running the `volcheck` command.

As a general rule, local disk slices should be included in the /etc/vfstab file so that they automatically mount at bootup.

Unmounting a file system removes it from the file system mount point. Some file system administration tasks cannot be performed on mounted file systems. You should unmount a file system when

- It is no longer needed.
- You check and repair it by using the `fsck` command.
- You are about to do a complete backup of it.

## Displaying Mounted File Systems

Whenever you mount or unmount a file system, the /etc/mnttab (mount table) file is modified to show the list of currently mounted file systems.

In previous Solaris releases, /etc/mnttab was a text-based file that stored information about mounted file systems. The downside of being a file was that it could get out of sync with the actual state of mounted file systems. With /etc/mnttab implemented as a file system, the information on mounted file systems and mount options can be more accurately kept in the kernel. Therefore, this file now will always reflect the in-kernel mount table. The /etc/mnttab is now a MNTFS file system that provides read-only information directly from the kernel about mounted file systems for the local system. The kernel maintains the list in order of mount time. That is, the first mounted file system is first in the list, and the most recently mounted file system is last.

You can display the contents of the mount table by using the `cat` or `more` commands, but you cannot edit them as you would the /etc/vfstab file. Here is an example of a mount table file:

```
/dev/dsk/c0t3d0s0               ufs    rw,suid  693186371
/dev/dsk/c0t1d0s6     /usr      ufs    rw,suid  693186371
/proc                 /proc     proc   rw,suid  693186371
swap                  /tmp      tmpfs  rw,dev=0  693186373
```

> **NOTE** Is it ever necessary to run fsck on a file system that has UFS logging enabled? The answer is yes. It is usually unnecessary to run fsck on a file system that has UFS logging enabled. The one exception to this is when the log is bad. An example of this is when a media failure causes the log to become unusable. In this case, logging will put the file system in an "error state," and you will be unable to mount it and use it until fsck is run. The safest option is to always run fsck. It will bail out immediately if logging is there and the file system is not in an error state.

You can also view a mounted file system by typing /etc/mount from the command line. The system displays the following:

```
/ on /dev/dsk/c0t3d0s0 read/write/setuid/largefiles on ...
/usr on /dev/dsk/c0t3d0s6 read/write/setuid/largefiles on ...
/proc on /proc read/write/setuid on Fri May 16 11:39:05 1997
/dev/fd on fd read/write/setuid on Fri May 16 11:39:05 1997
/export on /dev/dsk/c0t3d0s3 setuid/read/write/largefiles on ...
/export/home on /dev/dsk/c0t3d0s7 setuid/read/write/largefiles on ...
/export/swap on /dev/dsk/c0t3d0s4 setuid/read/write/largefiles on ...
/opt on /dev/dsk/c0t3d0s5 setuid/read/write/largefiles on ...
/tmp on swap read/write on Fri May 16 11:39:07 1997
```

## Mounting a File System with Large Files

The largefiles mount option lets users mount a file system containing files larger than 2GB. The largefiles mount option is the default state for the Solaris 8 environment. The largefiles option means that a file system mounted with this option might contain one or more files larger than 2GB.

You must explicitly use the nolargefiles mount option to disable this behavior. The nolargefiles option provides total compatibility with previous file system behavior, enforcing the 2GB maximum file size limit.

> **NOTE** File systems at or above 90 percent of capacity should be cleared of unnecessary files. You can do this by moving them to a disk, or you can remove them after obtaining the user's permission.

## Mounting a File System with UFS Logging Enabled

The new UFS logging feature eliminates file system inconsistency, which can significantly reduce the time of system reboots. Use the -o logging option in the /etc/vfstab file or as an option to the mount command to enable UFS logging on a file system.

UFS logging is the process of storing file system operations to a log before the transactions are applied to the file system. Because the file system can never become inconsistent, fsck can usually be bypassed, which reduces the time to reboot a system if it crashes, or after an unclean halt.

The UFS log is allocated from free blocks on the file system. It is sized at approximately 1MB per 1GB of file system, up to a maximum of 64MB. The default is `nologging`.

## Displaying a File System's Disk Space Usage

Use the `df` command and its options to see the capacity of each file system mounted on a system, the amount of space available, and the percentage of space already in use. Use the `du` (directory usage) command to report the number of free disk blocks and files.

The following is an example of how to use the `df` command to display disk space information. The command syntax is as follows:

```
df -F fstype -g -k -t <directory>
```

Table 6.4 explains the `df` command and its options.

**TABLE 6.4**

**THE df COMMAND**

| *Command* | *Description* |
|---|---|
| `df` | The `df` command with no options lists all mounted file systems and their device names. It also lists the total number of 512-byte blocks used and the number of files. |
| `<directory>` | The directory whose file system you want to check. The device name, blocks used, and number of files are displayed. |
| `-F fstype` | The unmounted file systems, their device names, the number of 512-byte blocks used, and the number of files on file systems of type `fstype` are displayed. |
| `-k` | A list of file systems, kilobytes used, free kilobytes, percent capacity used, and mount points are displayed. |
| `-t` | Displays total blocks as well as blocks used for all mounted file systems. |

The following example illustrates how to display disk space information with the `df` command. Type the following:

```
df -k
```

The system responds with this:

```
Filesystem          kbytes   used    avail   capacity  Mounted on
/proc               0        0       0       0%        /proc
/dev/dsk/c0t3d0s0   144799   23880   106440  19%       /
/dev/dsk/c0t3d0s6   1016455  496362  459106  52%       /usr
fd                  0        0       0       0%        /dev/fd
/dev/dsk/c0t3d0s3   41151    11      37025   1%        /export
/dev/dsk/c0t3d0s7   392503   9       353244  1%        /export/home
/dev/dsk/c0t3d0s4   37351    9       33607   1%        /export/swap
/dev/dsk/c0t3d0s5   255319   187031  42757   82%       /opt
swap                107584   272     107312  1%        /tmp
```

You'll see disk usage information displayed for each currently mounted file system.

## Displaying Directory Size Information

By using the `df` command, you display file system disk usage. You can use the `du` command to display the disk usage of a directory and all its subdirectories in 512-byte blocks.

The `du` command shows you the disk usage of each file in each subdirectory of a file system. To get a listing of the size of each subdirectory in a file system, type `cd` to the pathname associated with that file system, and run the following pipeline:

```
du -s* | sort -r -n
```

This pipeline, which uses the reverse and numeric options of the `sort` command, pinpoints large directories. Use `ls -l` to examine the size (in bytes) and modification times of files within each directory. Old files or text files over 100KB often warrant storage offline.

The following example illustrates how to display the amount of disk space being consumed by the /var/adm directory using the `du` command. The largest files are displayed first, and the `-k` option displays the file size in 1024 bytes. Type the following:

```
du -k /var/adm|sort -r -n
```

The system responds with this:

```
92    /var/adm
4     /var/adm/acct
1     /var/adm/sa
```

```
1     /var/adm/passwd
1     /var/adm/log
1     /var/adm/acct/sum
1     /var/adm/acct/nite
1     /var/adm/acct/fiscal
```

## Controlling User Disk Space Usage

Quotas let system administrators control the size of UFS file systems by limiting the amount of disk space that individual users can acquire. Quotas are especially useful on the file systems where user home directories reside. After the quotas are in place, they can be changed to adjust the amount of disk space or number of inodes users can consume. Additionally, quotas can be added or removed as system needs change. Also, quota status can be monitored. Quota commands allow administrators to display information about quotas on a file system or search for users who have exceeded their quotas.

After you have set up and turned on disk and inode quotas, you can check for users who exceed their quotas. You can also check quota information for entire file systems by using the commands listed in Table 6.5.

**TABLE 6.5**

**COMMANDS TO CHECK QUOTAS**

| *Command* | *Description* |
|---|---|
| `quota` | Displays the quotas and disk usage within a file system for individual users on which quotas have been activated. |
| `repquota` | Displays the quotas and disk usage for all users on one or more file systems. |

You won't see quotas in use much today because the cost of disk space continues to fall. In most cases, the system administrator simply watches disk space to identify users who might be using more than their fair share. As you saw in this section, you can easily do this by using the `du` command. On a large system with many users, however, disk quotas can be an effective way to control disk space usage.

## CHAPTER SUMMARY

This chapter described the fundamentals of disk file systems and how they are managed. I described important terms related to disk geometry that you need to understand before creating a file system.

This chapter also introduced all the file system types available on Solaris. You should understand which file system to use for the various circumstances you might encounter.

Preparing a disk for a file system by partitioning it into disk slices using the format utility was described. The Solaris commands used for displaying and recovering this disk information were also discussed.

The process of creating a file system onto a disk partition was described. Many file system creation parameters that affect performance were presented. This section also detailed all the parts of a file system so that, as you create file systems, you are familiar with terminology you'll encounter.

Finally, the system administrator must monitor all file systems regularly. Commands and utilities used to accomplish this task were described in detail.

Chapter 7 will introduce some advanced topics in file system management, including managing removable media, advanced topics in creating and tuning file systems, DiskSuite, and the Solstice Volume Manager. System administrators spend a great deal of time managing and fine-tuning file systems to improve system efficiency. Therefore, understanding these topics is critical for system administrators.

### KEY TERMS

- File system
- Disk label
- Partition table
- Disk-based file system
- Network-based file system
- Virtual file system
- Disk slice
- Free hog slice
- Swap
- Logical volume
- Superblock
- Inode
- Storage block
- Free block
- UFS logging
- Disk quota

## APPLY YOUR KNOWLEDGE

# Exercises

### 6.1 Displaying Disk Configuration Information

In this exercise, you determine the disk geometry and slice information of your disk drive.

**Estimated Time**: 20 minutes

1. Log in as root.
2. Display and record your current disk configuration information using the `prtvtoc` command, as shown here:

   ```
   prtvtoc <raw disk device name>
   ```

   How are the disk slices arranged? What disk geometry does it display?
3. Now, follow these steps to look at your disk information using the format utility:

A. Type `format`. The Main Menu appears, displaying your disk drives. You're going to select the disk numbered 0, so note all of the information on that line.

B. Type `0`. This will select the first disk listed. The Format Menu will appear.

C. Type `partition`. The Partition menu will appear.

D. Type `print`. All of your disk partition information will be displayed.

E. Press Ctrl+D. You'll exit the format utility.

### 6.2 Creating a File System

The following exercise requires that you have a spare disk drive connected to your system or a spare, unused slice on a disk. You will practice creating a disk slice and creating a file system.

**Estimated Time**: 30 minutes

1. Practice creating a slice on your spare disk drive using the steps outlined in the earlier section titled "Using the `format` Utility to Create Slices."
2. Create a file system on the new or unused slice using the `newfs` command as follows:

   ```
   newfs <raw device name>
   ```
3. Create a directory in the root partition named /test, as shown here:

   ```
   mkdir /test
   ```
4. Mount the new file system using the following command:

   ```
   mount <block device name> /test
   ```
5. Unmount the file system, as shown here:

   ```
   umount /test
   ```
6. View the contents of the /etc/vfstab file on your system by typing `cat /etc/vfstab`.
7. Add the following line to the /etc/vfstab file for the file system you've just created so that it gets mounted automatically at boot time:

   ```
   <Raw device name>    <block device name> \
   /test   ufs    2      yes
   ```
8. Reboot the system:

   ```
   /usr/sbin/shutdown -y -g0 -i6
   ```
9. Verify that the file system was mounted automatically:

   ```
   mount
   ```

## APPLY YOUR KNOWLEDGE

## Review Questions

1. What statement is *not* true about disk slices on standard Solaris?

   A. Each slice can hold only one file system.

   B. A file system cannot span multiple disk slices.

   C. A file system cannot be increased or decreased.

   D. Slices can span multiple disks.

2. Where is disk configuration information stored?

   A. On the disk label

   B. In several locations on the disk

   C. In the superblock

   D. In the partition table

3. Which of the following stores the procedures used to boot the system?

   A. Bootblock

   B. Superblock

   C. Inode

   D. Disk label

4. Which of the following commands will display partition information about a disk?

   A. `prtvtoc`

   B. `sysdef`

   C. `df -k`

   D. `sysinfo`

5. Which of the following is not a virtual file system?

   A. /export/home

   B. Tmpfs

   C. Cachefs

   D. Procfs

6. Which of the following tasks cannot be performed with the format utility?

   A. Repairing defective sectors

   B. Partitioning

   C. Retrieving corrupted disk labels

   D. Displaying disk usage

7. Which of the following does the superblock not contain?

   A. Size and status of the file system

   B. Cylinder group size

   C. Pathname of the last mount point

   D. Boot information

8. What information does the inode contain?

   A. The type of file

   B. File directory information

   C. The number of bytes in the file

   D. Logical volume information

9. What is the recommended command used to create file systems?

   A. `AdminTool`

   B. `newfs`

## APPLY YOUR KNOWLEDGE

C. `mkfs`

D. `format`

10. What is *not* true about logical block sizes?

    A. The logical block size is the size of the blocks the Unix kernel uses to read or write files.

    B. By default, the logical block size is 8192 bytes.

    C. A larger logical block size increases efficiency for file systems in which most of the files are large.

    D. A small logical block size increases efficiency for file systems in which most of the files are large.

11. What is the default number of bytes per inode?

    A. 2048

    B. 1024

    C. 8192

    D. 64

12. In Solaris, which of the following is referred to as the smallest allocable unit of disk space?

    A. Fragment

    B. Data block

    C. Logical block

    D. Byte

13. What is another name for swap space?

    A. Virtual memory

    B. Random Access Memory

    C. Partition C or Slice 2

    D. Static memory

14. When should a file system be checked with `fsck`?

    A. If the file system was unmounted properly

    B. After a power outage

    C. Whenever a file system cannot be mounted

    D. When data has been accidentally deleted

15. What does `fsck` do when it preens a file system?

    A. Forces checking of the file system

    B. Checks and fixes the file system non-interactively

    C. Checks writeable file systems only

    D. Only checks to determine if a file system needs checking

16. Which of the following files contains a list of file systems to be automatically mounted at bootup?

    A. /etc/fstab

    B. /etc/dfs/dfstab

    C. /etc/vfstab

    D. /etc/rc2.d/S74autofs

17. What does the `mountall` command do?

    A. Mounts the CD-ROM and floppy automatically

    B. Mounts all file systems specified in a file system table

    C. Shares all files systems so that they can be mounted

    D. Mounts the tape in the tape drive

## APPLY YOUR KNOWLEDGE

18. What command(s) is/are used to display disk space information?

    A. `du`

    B. `df`

    C. `quota`

    D. `repquota`

    E. All of the above

19. Which of the following mount options is used to mount file systems that have files larger than 2GB?

    A. `largefiles`

    B. `nolargefiles`

    C. `lf`

    D. `nlf`

20. What should you do to enable UFS logging on a file system?

    A. Use the `-o` logging option with the `mount` command.

    B. Use the `-l` option with the `mount` command.

    C. Use the `ufslog` option with the `mount` command.

    D. Use the logging feature in the `newfs` command when creating the file system.

21. Which of the following represents the correct format for an entry in the /etc/vfstab file?

    A. device to mount, device to `fsck`, mount point, FS type, `fsck` pass, mount at boot, mount options.

    B. device to `fsck` , device to mount, mount point, FS type, `fsck` pass, mount at boot, mount point

    C. mount point, device to mount, device to `fsck`, mount point, FS type, `fsck` pass, mount at boot

    D. mount point, device to `fsck`, device to mount, mount point, FS type, `fsck` pass, mount at boot

22. Which of the following commands shows you the disk usage of each file in each subdirectory of a file system?

    A. `du`

    B. `df`

    C. `ls`

    D. `printenv`

23. Which of the following commands displays disk space occupied by mounted file systems?

    A. `df`

    B. `du`

    C. `ls`

    D. `printenv`

## APPLY YOUR KNOWLEDGE

## Answers to Review Questions

1. **D**. On a standard Solaris file system, a file system cannot span multiple disks or slices. It's only possible when using virtual file systems (that is, DiskSuite).
2. **A**. Disk configuration information is stored on the disk label.
3. **A**. The boot block stores the procedures used in booting the system. Without a boot block, the system does not boot.
4. **A**. The slice information for a particular disk can be viewed by using the `prtvtoc` command.
5. **A**. The following are virtual file systems: swapfs, procfs, lofs, cachefs, tmpfs, /var/run, and mntfs.
6. **D**. The format utility is used to retrieve corrupted disk labels, repair defective sectors, format and analyze disks, partition disks, and label disks.
7. **D**. Here are a few of the more important things contained in a superblock:
    - Size and status of the file system
    - Label (file system name and volume name)
    - Size of the file system's logical block
    - Date and time of the last update
    - Cylinder group size
    - Number of data blocks in a cylinder group
    - Summary data block
    - File system state (clean, stable, or active)
    - Pathname of the last mount point
8. **A.**, **C**. An inode contains all of the information about a file except its name, which is kept in a directory. The inode information is kept in the cylinder information block and contains the following:
    - The type of the file (regular, directory, block special, character special, link, and so on)
    - The mode of the file (the set of read/write/execute permissions)
    - The number of hard links to the file
    - The user-id of the file's owner
    - The group-id to which the file belongs
    - The number of bytes in the file
    - An array of 15 disk-block addresses
    - The date and time the file was last accessed
    - The date and time the file was last modified
    - The date and time the file was created
9. **B**. `newfs` is the recommended command to create file systems.
10. **D**. As a general rule, a larger logical block size increases efficiency for file systems in which most of the files are large. Use a smaller logical block size for file systems in which most of the files are small.
11. **A**. The default number of bytes per inode is 2048 (2KB), which assumes that the average size of each file is 2KB or greater.
12. **A.**The file system fragment size is the smallest allocable unit of disk space, which is 1,024 bytes.

## Apply Your Knowledge

13. **A.** Swap space is also referred to virtual memory.

14. **A.**, **B.**, **C.** `fsck` should be run after a power outage, when a file system is unmounted improperly, or whenever a file system cannot be mounted.

15. **B.** Normally, `fsck` is run noninteractively at bootup to preen the file systems after an abrupt system. Preening automatically fixes any basic file system inconsistencies and does not try to repair more serious errors. While preening a file system, `fsck` fixes the inconsistencies it expects from such an abrupt halt. For more serious conditions, the command reports the error and terminates.

16. **C.** The /etc/vfstab file contains a list of file systems to be automatically mounted when the system is booted to the multiuser state.

17. **B.** The `mountall` command mounts all file systems specified in a file system table (vfstab).

18. **E.** The following commands can be used to display disk space usage: `du`, `df`, `quota`, `repquota`

19. **A.** The `largefiles` mount option lets users mount a file system containing files larger than 2GB.

20. **A.** Use the `-o logging` option to the `mount` command to enable UFS logging on a file system.

21. **A.** The correct format for the /etc/vfstab file is as follows:

    device to mount, device to `fsck`, mount point, FS type, `fsck` pass, mount at boot, mount point

22. **A.** Use the `du` (directory usage) command to report the number of free disk blocks and files.

23. **A.** The `df` command with no options lists all mountedfile systems and their device names. It also lists the total number of 512-byte blocks used and the number of files.

## Objectives

The following test objectives are covered in this chapter:

**Construct a file system**

- Constructing file systems is a routine task for system administrators. A complete understanding of when to utilize and how to construct each type of file system found in Solaris 8 is required.

**Tune a file system**

- Solaris provides a method for fine-tuning many of the parameters assigned to file systems. The system administrator needs to understand these parameters and adjust them to achieve optimum performance.

**Use large file systems**

- Solaris can accommodate applications that will be supporting large files that are larger than 2GB. However, the proper file system parameters must be set to accommodate these large files.

**Use additional options when mounting and unmounting file systems**

- Each file system type supports many options that control how the file system will function and perform. The system administrator needs to be familiar with all of these options when mounting and unmounting file systems.

**Work with removable media and Volume Manager**

- Solaris has accommodations for managing removable media, such as removable disk and CD-ROM, via the Volume Manager. The system administrator needs to know how to enable and disable this facility as well as understand the associated configuration files.

CHAPTER 7

# Solaris File Systems: Advanced Topics

## Objectives

**Get information on file systems**

- The system administrator must monitor and administer file systems on a regular basis, and needs to be familiar with the various tools used to accomplish this task.

## Outline

## Study Strategies

The following strategies will help you prepare for the test:

- As you study this chapter, make sure you practice all of the commands that are introduced on a Sun or Intel system that runs Solaris 8. Practice the commands and each of the options I've described. Practice the examples and step-by-steps until you can perform them from memory. These are scenarios that you are likely to encounter on the exam.
- Understand all of the terms outlined at the end of this chapter. On the exam, you'll encounter some of these terms and will be required to match them to a description.
- Pay particular attention to the `newfs` and `mount`/`umount` commands. Understand all of the options and examples. These topics are covered heavily on the exam.

# Introduction

> **NOTE**
> This chapter covers objectives for exams Part I and Part II; however, the majority of the information relates to the first exam. (The second exam has limited questions related to file systems.) I'll make a notation when the material relates to the Part II exam.

In Chapter 6, "Introduction to File Systems," I described how to create, check, mount, and display file systems with Solaris 8. I explained file system structure, disk geometry, disk slices, and the `format` utility. In Chapter 16, "Device Administration and Disk Management," disk devices and device names are covered in detail. (Although Chapter 16 covers objectives for the Part II exam, I recommend reading that chapter to answer questions you might have after reading this chapter. File systems and devices go hand-in-hand but are not covered on the same exam; therefore, device configuration and naming are covered in Section II of this book.)

In this chapter, I continue the discussion of file systems. Specifically, I cover the objectives outlined at the beginning of this chapter.

# Constructing a File System

Constructing file systems is a topic covered on both exams. In Chapter 6, I described how `newfs` was the friendly front end to the `mkfs` command. The `newfs` command automatically determines all the necessary parameters to pass to `mkfs` to construct new file systems. `newfs` was added in Solaris to make the creation of new file systems easier. It's highly recommended that the `newfs` command be used to create file systems, but it's also important to see what is happening "behind the scenes" with the `mkfs` utility. The syntax for `mkfs` is as follows:

```
/usr/sbin/mkfs [options] <character device name>
```

Its options are described in Table 7.1.

**TABLE 7.1**

**THE `mkfs` COMMAND**

| *Option* | *Description* |
|---|---|
| `-F` | Used to specify the file system type. If this option is omitted, the /etc/vfstab and /etc/default/fs files are checked to determine a file system type. |

| *Option* | *Description* |
|---|---|
| `-m` | Shows the command line that was used to create the specified file system. No changes are made to the file system. |
| `-v` | Verbose. Shows the command line, but does not execute anything. |
| `-o <specific options>` | A list of options specific to the type of file system. The list must have the following format: `-o` followed by a space, followed by a series of `keyword [=value]` pairs, separated by commas, with no intervening spaces. |
| `apc=<n>` | Reserved space for bad block replacement on SCSI devices. The default is 0. |
| `N` | Prints the file system parameters without actually creating the file system. |
| `nsect=<n>` | The number of sectors per track on the disk. The default is 32. |
| `ntrack=<n>` | The number of tracks per cylinder on the disk. The default is 16. |
| `bsize=<n>` | Logical block size, either 4096 (4KB) or 8192 (8KB). The default is 8192. The sun4u architecture does not support the 4096-block size. |
| `fragsize=<bytes>` | The smallest amount of disk space, in bytes, to allocate to a file. The value must be a power of 2 selected from the range 512 to the logical block size. If the logical block size is 4096, legal values are 512, 1024, 2048, and 4096. If the logical block size is 8192, 8192 is also a legal value. The default is 1024. |
| `cgsize=<cyls>` | The number of cylinders per cylinder group. The default is 16. |
| `free=<n>` | The minimum percentage of free space to maintain in the file system. This space is off-limits to normal users. After the file system is filled to this threshold, only the superuser can continue writing to the file system. This parameter can be subsequently changed using the `tunefs` command. The default is 10 percent, however, on large file systems; the `minfree` value is determined automatically. |
| `rps=<rps>` | The rotational speed of the disk, specified in revolutions per second. The default is 60. |

*continues*

**TABLE 7.1** *continued*

**THE mkfs COMMAND**

| *Option* | *Description* |
|---|---|
| `nbpi=<value>` | The `value` specified is the number of bytes per inode, which specifies the density of inodes in the file system. The number is divided into the total size of the file system to determine the fixed number of inodes to create. It should reflect the expected average size of files in the file system. If fewer inodes are desired, a larger number should be used. To create more inodes, a smaller number should be given. The default is 2048. |
| `opt=<value>` | Space or time optimization preference. The `value` can be `s` or `t`. Specify `s` to optimize for disk space. Specify `t` to optimize for speed (time). The default is `t`. Generally, you should optimize for time unless the file system is more than 90 percent full. |
| `gap=<milliseconds>` | Rotational delay, specified in milliseconds. Indicates the expected time (in milliseconds) required to service a transfer completion interrupt and to initiate a new transfer on the same disk. The `value` is used to decide how much rotational spacing to place between successive blocks in a file. The actual disk used determines the default. |
| `nrpos=<n>` | The number of different rotational positions into which to divide a cylinder group. The default is 8. |
| `maxcontig=<blocks>` | The maximum number of blocks, belonging to one file, that is allocated contiguously before inserting a rotational delay. For a 4KB file system, the default is 14; for an 8KB file system, the default is 7. This parameter can subsequently be changed using the `tunefs` command. |

`mkfs` constructs a file system on the character (or raw) device found in the /dev/rdsk directory. Again, it is highly recommended that you do not run the `mkfs` command directly, but instead use the friendlier `newfs` command, which automatically determines all the necessary parameters required by `mkfs` to construct the file system. In the following example, the `-v` option to the `newfs` command will output all the parameters passed to the `mkfs` utility. Type the following:

```
newfs -v /dev/rdsk/c0t0d0s0
```

The system outputs the following information and creates a new file system on /dev/rdsk/c0t0d0s0:

```
newfs: construct a new file system /dev/rdsk/c0t0d0s0: (y/n)? y
mkfs -F ufs /dev/rdsk/c0t0d0s0 2097576 117 9 8192 1024 32 6 90 4096 t 0 -1 8 15
/dev/rdsk/c0t0d0s0: 2097576 sectors in 1992 cylinders of 9 tracks, 117 sectors
1024.2MB in 63 cyl groups (32 c/g, 16.45MB/g, 4096 i/g)
super-block backups (for fsck -F ufs -o b=#) at:
32, 33856, 67680, 101504, 135328, 169152, 202976, 236800, 270624, 304448,
338272, 372096, 405920, 439744, 473568, 507392, 539168, 572992, 606816,
640640, 674464, 708288, 742112, 775936, 809760, 843584, 877408, 911232,
945056, 978880, 1012704, 1046528, 1078304, 1112128, 1145952, 1179776, 1213600,
1247424, 1281248, 1315072, 1348896, 1382720, 1416544, 1450368, 1484192,
1518016, 1551840, 1585664, 1617440, 1651264, 1685088, 1718912, 1752736,
1786560, 1820384, 1854208, 1888032, 1921856, 1955680, 1989504, 2023328,
2057152, 2090976,
```

You'll see in the output that all of the `mkfs` parameters used to create the file system are displayed, as well as the location of each backup copy of the superblock.

## The `labelit` Command

After you create the file system with `newfs`, you can use the `labelit` utility to write or display labels on unmounted disk file systems. The syntax for `labelit` is as follows:

```
labelit [-F ufs] [-V] <special> [ fsname volume ]
```

Labeling a file system is optional. It's required only if you're using a program such as `volcopy`, which will be covered soon. The `labelit` command is described in Table 7.2.

> **NOTE**
> If fsname and volume are not specified, labelit prints the current values of these labels. Both fsname and volume are limited to six or fewer characters.

**TABLE 7.2**

**THE labelit COMMAND**

| *Parameter* | *Description* |
|---|---|
| special | This name should be the physical disk section (for example, /dev/dsk/c0t0d0s6). |
| fsname | This represents the mount point (for example, root (/), /home, and so on) of the file system. |
| volume | This can be used to represent the physical volume name. |
| -F | This specifies the file system type on which to operate. The file system type should either be specified here or be determinable from the /etc/vfstab entry. If no matching entry is found, the default file system type specified in /etc/default/fs is used. |
| -V | This prints the command line but does not perform an action. |

The following is an example of how to label a disk partition using the labelit command. Type the following:

```
labelit -F ufs /dev/rdsk/c0t0d0s6 disk1 vol1
```

The system responds with this:

```
fsname:  disk1
volume:  vol1
```

## The volcopy Command

The administrator (root) can use the volcopy command to make a copy of a labeled file system. This command works with ufs file systems, but the file system must be labeled with the labelit utility before the volcopy command is issued. To determine if a file system is a ufs file system, issue this command:

```
fstyp  /dev/rdsk/c0t0d0s6
```

The system responds with this:

```
ufs
```

The volcopy command can be used to copy a file system from one disk to another.

The syntax for `volcopy` is as follows:

```
volcopy [options] <fsname> <srcdevice> <volname1> <destdevice> <volname2>
```

`volcopy` is described in Table 7.3.

**TABLE 7.3**

**THE volcopy COMMAND**

| *Option* | *Description* |
|---|---|
| `-F` | This specifies the file system type on which to operate. This should either be specified here or be determinable from the /etc/vfstab entry. If no matching entry is found, the default file system type specified in /etc/default/fs is used. |
| `-V` | This prints the command line, but does not perform an action. |
| `-a` | This requires the operator to respond "yes" or "no." If the `-a` option is not specified, `volcopy` pauses 10 seconds before the copy is made. |
| `-o <options>` | This is a list of options specific to the type of file system. The list must have the following format: `-o` followed by a space, followed by a series of `keyword [=value]` pairs, separated by commas, with no intervening spaces. |
| `<fsname>` | This represents the mount point (for example, /, u1, and so on) of the file system being copied. |
| `<srcdevice> / <destdevice>` | This is the disk partition specified using the raw device (for example, /dev/rdsk/clt0d0s7, /dev/rdsk/clt0d1s7, and so on). |
| `<srcdevice> / <volname1>` | This is the device and physical volume from which the copy of the file system is being extracted. |
| `<destdevice> / <volname2>` | This is the target device and physical volume. |

**NOTE**

`fsname` and `volname` are limited to six or fewer characters, and are recorded in the superblock. `volname` can be a dash (—) to use the existing volume name.

The following example copies the contents of /home1 (/dev/rdsk/c0t0d0s6) to /home2 (/dev/rdsk/c0t1d0s6):

```
volcopy -F ufs disk1 /dev/rdsk/c0t0d0s6 vol1 /dev/rdsk/c0t1d0s6 vol2
```

Other commands can also be used to copy file systems—`ufsdump`, `cpio`, `tar`, and `dd`, to name a few. These commands are discussed in Chapter 11, "Backup and Recovery."

## Tuning File Systems

A situation might arise in which you want to change some of the parameters that were set when you originally created the file system. Perhaps you want to change the `minfree` value to free some additional disk space on a large disk drive. Using the `tunefs` command, you can modify the following file system parameters:

- `maxcontig`
- `rotdelay`
- `maxbpg`
- `minfree`
- `optimization`

**CAUTION**

`tunefs` can destroy a file system in seconds. Always back up the entire file system before using `tunefs`.

See Table 7.1 for a description of these options.

The syntax for `tunefs` is as follows:

```
tunefs [ -a <maxcontig> ] [ -d <rotdelay> ] [ -e <maxbpg> ] [ -m <minfree> ] [ -o [ <value> ] \
special/filesystem
```

The `tunefs` command is described in Table 7.4.

**TABLE 7.4**

**The tunefs Command**

| *Option* | *Description* |
|---|---|
| `-a <maxcontig>` | Specifies the maximum number of contiguous blocks that are laid out before forcing a rotational delay (see the `-d` option). The default value is 1 because most device drivers require an interrupt per disk transfer. For device drivers that can chain several buffers into a single transfer, set this to the maximum chain length. |

| *Option* | *Description* |
| --- | --- |
| `-d <rotdelay>` | Specifies the expected time (in milliseconds) to service a transfer completion interrupt and to initiate a new transfer on the same disk. It is used to decide how much rotational spacing to place between successive blocks in a file. |
| `-e <maxbpg>` | Sets the maximum number of blocks that any single file can allocate from a cylinder group before it is forced to begin allocating blocks from another cylinder group. Typically, this value is set to approximately one-quarter of the total blocks in a cylinder group. The intent is to prevent any single file from using up all the blocks in a single cylinder group. The effect of this limit is to cause big files to do long seeks more frequently than if they were allowed to allocate all the blocks in a cylinder group before seeking elsewhere. For file systems with exclusively large files, this parameter should be set higher. |
| `-m <minfree>` | Specifies the percentage of space held back from normal users (the minimum free space threshold). The default value is 10 percent; however, on large file systems, the `minfree` value is determined automatically. |
| `-o <value>` | Changes the optimization strategy for the file system. The `value` is either `space` or `time`. Use `space` to conserve space; use `time` to organize file layout and minimize access time. Generally, optimize a file system for time unless it is more than 90 percent full. |
| `<special>/<filesystem>` | Enters either the special device name (such as /dev/rdsk/c0t0d0s6) or the file system name (such as /home). |

The file system must be unmounted before you use `tunefs`.

To change the minimum free space (`minfree`) on a file system from 10 percent to 5 percent, type the following:

```
tunefs -m5 /dev/rdsk/c0t0d0s6
minimum percentage of free space changes from 10% to 5%
```

The manual page of `tunefs` recommends that `minfree` be set at 10 percent, and that if you set the value under that, you lose performance. This means that 10 percent of the disk is unusable. This might not have been too bad in the days when disks were a couple hundred megabytes in size, but on a 9GB disk, you're losing 900MB of disk space. The mention of loss of performance in the manual

> **NOTE** On large file systems, the minfree is automatically determined so that disk space is not wasted. Use the `mkfs -m` command described next if you want to see the actual minfree value that `newfs` used.

page is misleading. With such large disk drives, you can afford to have `minfree` as low as 1 percent. This has been found to be a practical and affordable limit. In addition, performance does not become an issue because locating free blocks even within a 90MB area is efficient. A rule of thumb is to use the default 10 percent `minfree` value for file systems up to 1GB, and adjust the `minfree` value so that your `minfree` area is no larger than 100MB. As for the performance, applications do not complain about the lower `minfree` value. The one exception would be the root (/) file system, in which the system administrator can use his judgment to allow more free space just to be conservative, in case root (/) ever becomes 100 percent full.

Later, if you want to see what parameters were used when creating a file system, issue the `mkfs` command:

```
mkfs -m /dev/rdsk/c0t0d0s6
```

The system responds with this:

```
mkfs -F ufs -o nsect=117,ntrack=9,bsize=8192,fragsize=1024,cgsize=16,free=5,rps=90,nbpi=2062,opt=t,\
apc=0,gap=0,nrpos=8,maxcontig=15 /dev/rdsk/c0t0d0s6 205334
```

## The `fstyp` Command

Another good command to use to view file system parameters is the `fstyp` command. Use the `-v` option to obtain a full listing of a file system's parameters:

```
fstyp -v /dev/rdsk/c0t0d0s6
```

The system responds with this:

```
ufs
magic  11954  format dynamic      time   Sat Oct      2 10:11:06 1999
sblkno 16     cblkno 24     iblkno 32     dblkno 528
sbsize 3072   cgsize 2048   cgoffset      64     cgmask 0xfffffff0
ncg    13     size   102667 blocks95994
bsize  8192   shift  13     mask   0xffffe000
fsize  1024   shift  10     mask   0xfffffc00
frag   8      shift  3      fsbtodb       1
minfree       5%     maxbpg 2048   optim  time
maxcontig 15  rotdelay  0ms rps    90
csaddr 528    cssize 1024   shift 9       mask   0xfffffe00
ntrak  9      nsect  117    spc    1053   ncyl   195
cpg    16     bpg    1053   fpg    8424   ipg    3968
nindir 2048   inopb  64     nspf   2
nbfree 11995  ndir   2      nifree 51577 nffree 1
cgrotor       0      fmod   0      ronly 0
fs_reclaim is not set
```

```
file system state is valid, fsclean is 1
blocks available in each rotational position
cylinder number 0:
   position 0:   0    8   15   22   30   37   44   52   59
   position 1:   1    9   16   23   31   38   45   53   60
   position 2:   2   10   17   24   39   46   61
   position 3:   3   18   25   32   40   47   54   62
   position 4:   4   11   19   26   33   41   48   55   63
   position 5:   5   12   20   27   34   42   49   56
   position 6:   6   13   21   28   35   50   57   64
   position 7:   7   14   29   36   43   51   58   65
cylinder number 1:
   position 0:  66   74   81   88  103  110  117  125
   position 1:  67   82   89   96  104  111  118  126
   position 2:  68   75   83   90   97  105  112  119  127
   position 3:  69   76   84   91   98  106  113  120
   position 4:  70   77   85   92   99  114  121  128
   position 5:  71   78   93  100  107  115  122  129
   position 6:  72   79   86   94  101  108  116  123  130
   position 7:  73   80   87   95  102  109  124  131
...
...
```

**NOTE** It's always a good idea to print the `mkfs` options used on a file system along with information provided by the `prtvtoc` command. Put the printout in your system log so that if you ever need to rebuild a file system because of a hard drive failure, you can re-create it exactly as it was before.

# Large Versus Small Files

On a 32-bit system, a *large file* is a regular file whose size is greater than or equal to 2.31GB. A *small file* is a regular file whose size is less than 2GB. Some utilities can handle large files, and others cannot. A utility is called *large-file-aware* if it can process large files in the same manner that it does small files. A large-file-aware utility can handle large files as input and can generate large files as output. The `newfs`, `mkfs`, `mount`, `umount`, `tunefs`, `labelit`, and `quota` utilities are all large-file-aware for `ufs` file systems.

On the other hand, a utility is called *large-file-safe* if it causes no data loss or corruption when it encounters a large file. A utility that is large-file-safe is unable to properly process a large file, so it returns an appropriate error. Some examples of utilities that are not large-file-aware but are large-file-safe include the `vi` editor and the `mailx` and `lp` commands.

# MOUNTING A FILE SYSTEM

In Chapter 6, I described the basics of how to mount file systems. (I purposely did not bring up all the many options available in the mount command until you had more time to use it.) The syntax for mount is as follows:

```
mount -F <fstype> [generic_options] [ -o specific_options ] [ -O ]
```

Table 7.5 describes these options.

**TABLE 7.5**

**THE mount COMMAND**

| *Option* | *Description* | |
|---|---|---|
| -F <fstype> | Used to specify the file system type (fstype) on which to operate. If fstype is not specified, it must be determined from the /etc/vfstab file or by consulting /etc/default/fs or /etc/dfs/fstypes. | |
| generic_options | Can be any of the following: | |
| | -m | Mounts the file system without making an entry in /etc/mnttab. |
| | -r | Mounts the file system as read-only. |
| | -O | Overlay mount. Allows the file system to be mounted over an existing mount point, making the underlying file system inaccessible. If a mount is attempted on a pre-existing mount point without setting this flag, the mount fails, producing the error device busy. |
| | -p | Prints the list of mounted file systems in the /etc/vfstab format. This must be the only option specified. |
| | -v | Prints the list of mounted file systems in verbose format. This must be the only option specified. |
| | -V | Echoes the complete command line, but does not execute the command. umount generates a command line by using the options and arguments provided by the user and adding to them information derived from /etc/mnttab. This option should be used to verify and validate the command line. |

| Option | Description |
|---|---|
| `-o` | Specifies fstype-specific options. These options can be specified with the `-o` option. If you specify multiple options, separate them with commas (no spaces)—for example, `-o ro,nosuid`. |
| `-rw\|ro` | Specifies read/write or read-only. The default is read/write. |
| `-nosuid` | Disallows `setuid` execution, and prevents devices on the file system from being opened. The default is to enable `setuid` execution and to allow devices to be opened. |
| `-remount` | With `rw`, remounts a file system with read/write access. |
| `-f` | Fakes an entry in /etc/mnttab, but doesn't really mount any file systems. |
| `-n` | Mounts the file system without making an entry in /etc/mnttab. |
| `-largefiles` | Specifies that a file system might contain one or more files larger than 2GB. It is not required that a file system mounted with this option contain files larger than 2GB, but this option allows such files within the file system. |
| `-nolargefiles` | Provides total compatibility with previous file system behavior, enforcing the 2GB maximum file size limit. |

The following examples illustrate the options described in Table 7.5.

A file system has been created on disk c0t0d0 on slice s0. The directory to be mounted on this disk slice is /home2. To mount the file system, first create the directory called /home2, and then type the following:

```
mount /dev/dsk/c0t0d0s0 /home2
```

If the file system has been mounted, you return to a command prompt. No other message is displayed.

In the next example, the `-v` option is used with the `mount` command to display a list of all mounted file systems:

```
mount -v
```

The system responds with this:

```
/dev/dsk/c0t3d0s0 on / type ufs read/write/setuid/largefiles on Fri Oct  1 13:04:06 1999
/dev/dsk/c0t3d0s6 on /usr type ufs read/write/setuid/largefiles on Fri Oct  1 13:04:06 1999
/proc on /proc type proc read/write/setuid on Fri Oct  1 13:04:06 1999
fd on /dev/fd type fd read/write/setuid on Fri Oct  1 13:04:06 1999
/dev/dsk/c0t3d0s1 on /var type ufs read/write/setuid/largefiles on Fri Oct  1 13:04:06 1999
/dev/dsk/c0t3d0s3 on /export type ufs setuid/read/write/largefiles on Fri Oct  1  13:04:08 1999
/dev/dsk/c0t3d0s5 on /opt type ufs setuid/read/write/largefiles on Fri Oct  1 13:04:08 1999
swap on /tmp type tmpfs read/write on Fri Oct  1 13:04:08 1999
sparc4:/usr on /net/sparc4/usr type nfs nosuid/remote on Fri Oct  1 13:39:00 1999
```

Type the `mount` command with the `-p` option to display a list of mounted file systems in /etc/vfstab format:

```
mount -p
```

The system responds with this:

```
/dev/dsk/c0t3d0s0 - / ufs - no rw,suid,largefiles
/dev/dsk/c0t3d0s6 - /usr ufs - no rw,suid,largefiles
/proc - /proc proc - no rw,suid
fd - /dev/fd fd - no rw,suid
/dev/dsk/c0t3d0s1 - /var ufs - no rw,suid,largefiles
/dev/dsk/c0t3d0s3 - /export ufs - no suid,rw,largefiles
/dev/dsk/c0t3d0s5 - /opt ufs - no suid,rw,largefiles
swap - /tmp tmpfs - no
sparc4:/usr - /net/sparc4/usr nfs - no nosuid
/dev/dsk/c0t0d0s0 - /home2 ufs - no suid,rw,largefiles
```

The `-p` option is useful for obtaining the correct settings if you're making an entry in the /etc/vfstab file.

The following example mounts a file system as read-only:

```
mount -o ro /dev/dsk/c0t0d0s0 /home2
```

The next example uses the `mount` command to mount a directory to a file system as read/writeable, disallow `setuid` execution, and allow the creation of large files:

```
mount -o rw,nosuid,largefiles /dev/dsk/c0t0d0s0 /home2
```

Type mount with no options to verify that the file system has been mounted and to review the mount options that were used:

```
mount
```

The system responds with information about all mounted file systems, including /home2:

```
/home2 on /dev/dsk/c0t0d0s0 read/write/nosuid/largefiles \
on Tue Oct 5 06:56:33 1999
```

NOTE

After you mount a file system with the default largefiles option, and large files have been created, you cannot remount the file system with the nolargefiles option until you remove any large files and run fsck to reset the state to nolargefiles.

# /etc/mnttab

When a file system is mounted, an entry is maintained in the mounted file system table called /etc/mnttab. The file /etc/mnttab is really a file system that provides read-only access to the table of mounted file systems for the current host. The mount command adds entries to this table, and umount removes entries from this table. The kernel maintains the list in order of mount time. For example, the first mounted file system is first in the list and the most recently mounted file system is last. When mounted on a mount point, the file system appears as a regular file containing the current mnttab information. Each entry in this table is a line of fields separated by spaces in this form:

```
<special> <mount_point> <fstype>  <options>  <time>
```

Table 7.6 describes each field.

**TABLE 7.6**

**/ETC/MNTTAB FIELDS**

| *Field* | *Description* |
|---|---|
| <special> | The resource to be mounted (that is, /dev/dsk/c0t0d0s0) |
| <mount_point> | The pathname of the directory on which the file system is mounted |
| <fstype> | The file system type |
| <options> | The list of mount options used to mount the file system |
| <time> | The time at which the file system was mounted |

Following is a sample /etc/mnttab file:

```
more /etc/mnttab
/dev/dsk/c0t0d0s0    /     ufs    rw,intr,largefiles,onerror=panic,suid,dev=2200000    985708256
/dev/dsk/c0t0d0s3    /usr   ufs    rw,intr,largefiles,onerror=panic,suid,dev=2200003    985708257
/proc   /proc   proc    dev=2dc0000     985708254
fd      /dev/fd fd      rw,suid,dev=2e80000     985708258
mnttab  /etc/mnttab     mntfs   dev=2f80000     985708260
/dev/dsk/c0t0d0s4       /var    ufs     rw,intr,largefiles,onerror=panic,suid,dev=2200004    985708260
swap    /var/run        tmpfs   dev=1   985708260
swap    /tmp    tmpfs   dev=2   985708263
/dev/dsk/c0t0d0s6       /data   ufs     rw,intr,largefiles,\onerror=panic,suid,dev=2200006    985708263
/dev/dsk/c0t0d0s5       /opt    ufs     rw,intr,largefiles,\onerror=panic,suid,dev=2200005\
985708263/dev/dsk/c0t0d0s7       /export/home    ufs
rw,intr,largefiles,onerror=panic,suid,dev=2200007  985708263
-hosts  /net    autofs  indirect,nosuid,ignore,nobrowse,dev=3040001     985708269
auto_home       /home   autofs  indirect,ignore,nobrowse,dev=3040002    985708269
-xfn    /xfn    autofs  indirect,ignore,dev=3040003     985708269
```

In previous versions of Solaris, the /etc/mnttab file was a text file. The downside of being a text file was that it could get out of sync with the actual state of mounted file systems ,or it could be manually edited. In Solaris 8, this file is an `mntfs` file system that provides read-only information directly from the kernel about mounted file systems for the local hosts.

# UNMOUNTING A FILE SYSTEM

To unmount a file system, use the `umount` command:

```
umount <mount-point>
```

`<mount-point>` is the name of the file system you want to unmount. This can be either the directory name in which the file system is mounted or the device name path of the file system. For example, to unmount the /home2 file system, type the following:

```
umount /home2
```

Alternatively, you can specify the device name path for the file system:

```
umount /dev/dsk/c0t0d0s0
```

Unmounting a file system removes it from the file system mount point, and deletes the entry from /etc/mnttab. Some file system administration tasks cannot be performed on mounted file systems, such as `labelit`, `fsck`, and `tunefs`. You should unmount a file system if any of the following three conditions exist:

- The file system is no longer needed or has been replaced by a file system that contains software that is more current.
- You need to check and repair the file system using the `fsck` command.
- You plan to do a complete backup.

**NOTE** File systems are automatically unmounted as part of the system shutdown procedure.

## The `fuser` Command

Before you can unmount a file system, you must be logged in as the administrator (root), and the file system must not be busy. A file system is considered busy if a user is in a directory in the file system or if a program has a file open in that file system. You can make a file system available for unmounting by changing to a directory in a different file system or by logging out of the system. If something is causing the file system to be busy, you can use the `fuser` command, described in Table 7.7, to list all the processes that are accessing the file system and to stop them if necessary.

**NOTE** Always notify users before unmounting a file system.

The syntax for `fuser` is as follows:

```
/usr/sbin/fuser [options] <file>|<filesystem>
```

Replace `<file>` with the filename you are checking, or replace `<filesystem>` with the name of the file system you are checking.

**TABLE 7.7**

**THE `fuser` COMMAND**

| *Option* | *Description* |
|---|---|
| `-c` | Reports on files that are mount points for file systems and on any files within that mounted file system. |
| `-f` | Prints a report for the named file, but not for files within a mounted file system. |
| `-k` | Sends the SIGKILL signal to each process. Because this option spawns kills for each process, the kill messages might not show up immediately. |
| `-u` | Displays the user login name in parentheses following the process ID. |

The following example uses the `fuser` command to find out why /home2 is busy:

```
fuser -u /home2
```

The system displays each process and user login name that is using this file system:

```
/home2:     8448c(root)    8396c(root)
```

The following command stops all processes that are using the /home2 file system by sending a `SIGKILL` to each one. Don't use it without first warning the users.

```
fuser -c -k /home2
```

Using the `fuser` command as described is the preferred method for determining who is using a file system before unmounting it. New in Solaris 8 is another, less desirable, method for unmounting a file system using the `umount` command with the `-f` option as follows:

```
umount -f /home2
```

The `-f` option will forcibly unmount a file system. Using this option can cause data loss for open files and programs that access files after the file system has been unmounted and will return an error (EIO). The `-f` option should be only used as a last resort.

# Volume Manager

Volume Manager (not to be confused with Enterprise Volume Manager, described in Chapter 18, "Name Services"), with the `vold` daemon, is the mechanism that manages removable media, such as the CD-ROM and floppy disk drives. Mounting and unmounting a file system requires root privileges. How do you let users insert, mount, and unmount CD-ROMs and floppy disks without being the administrator (root)? After a file system has been mounted and you remove the medium, what happens to the mount? Usually, when you disconnect a disk drive while it is mounted, the system begins displaying errors and messages. The same thing happens if you remove a floppy disk or CD-ROM while it is mounted.

Volume Manager, with its `vold` daemon, provides assistance to overcome these problems. The `vold` daemon simplifies the use of disks and CDs by automatically mounting them. Volume Manager provides three major benefits:

- By automatically mounting floppy disks and CDs, Volume Manager simplifies their use.
- Volume Manager allows the user to access floppy disks and CDs without having to be logged in as root.
- Volume Manager lets the administrator (root) give other systems on the network automatic access to any floppy disks and CDs that the users insert into your system.

To begin, let's look at the two devices the system administrator needs to manage: the floppy disk drive and the CD-ROM. Volume Manager provides access to both devices through the /vol/dev directory. In addition, Volume Manager creates links to the floppy disk and CD-ROM devices through various directories, as shown in Table 7.8.

**TABLE 7.8**

**VOLUME MANAGER DIRECTORIES AND LINKS**

| *Link* | *Description* |
|---|---|
| /vol/dev/diskette0 | The directory providing block device access for the medium in floppy drive 0 |
| /vol/dev/rdiskette0 | The directory providing character device access for the medium in floppy drive 0 |
| /vol/dev/aliases/floppy0 | The symbolic link to the character device for the medium in floppy drive 0 |
| /dev/rdiskette | The directory providing character device access for the medium in the primary floppy drive, usually drive 0 |
| /vol/dev/aliases/cdrom0 | The directory providing character device access for the medium in the primary CD-ROM drive |
| /vol/dev/dsk/ | The directory providing access to the CD-ROM buffered, or block, device |
| /vol/dev/rdsk/ | The directory providing access to the CD-ROM character, or raw, device |
| /cdrom/cdrom0 | The symbolic link to the buffered device for the medium in CD-ROM drive 0 |
| /floppy/floppy0 | The symbolic link to the buffered device for the medium in floppy drive 0 |

The `vold` daemon automatically mounts CD-ROM and file systems when removable media containing recognizable file systems are inserted into the devices. When a CD is inserted, `vold` automatically mounts the CD-ROM file system into the /vol/dev directories just described. With a floppy disk, however, the floppy's file system is not automatically mounted until you issue the `volcheck` command. The `volcheck` command instructs `vold` to look at each device and determine if new media has been inserted into the drive. On floppy disks, don't have `vold` continually poll the disk drive like it does on a CD because of the hardware limitation in floppy drives. Continuously polling of a floppy disk for media causes a mechanical action in the floppy disk drive and causes the drive to wear out prematurely.

The `vold` daemon is the workhorse behind Volume Manager. It is automatically started by the /etc/init.d/volmgt script. `vold` reads the /etc/vold.conf configuration file at startup. The vold.conf file contains the Volume Manager configuration information that `vold` uses.

This information includes the database to use, labels that are supported, devices to use, actions to take if certain media events occur, and the list of file systems that are unsafe to eject without unmounting. The vold.conf file looks like this:

```
# @(#)vold.conf 1.25     99/11/11 SMI
#
# Volume Daemon Configuration file
#
# Database to use (must be first)
db db_mem.so
# Labels supported
label cdrom label_cdrom.so cdrom
label dos label_dos.so floppy rmdisk pcmem
label sun label_sun.so floppy rmdisk pcmem
# Devices to use
use cdrom drive /dev/rdsk/c*s2 dev_cdrom.so cdrom%d
use floppy drive /dev/rdiskette[0-9] dev_floppy.so floppy%d
use pcmem drive /dev/rdsk/c*s2 dev_pcmem.so pcmem%d forceload=true
use rmdisk drive /dev/rdsk/c*s2 dev_rmdisk.so rmdisk%d
# Actions
eject dev/diskette[0-9]/* user=root /usr/sbin/rmmount
eject dev/dsk/* user=root /usr/sbin/rmmount
insert dev/diskette[0-9]/* user=root /usr/sbin/rmmount
insert dev/dsk/* user=root /usr/sbin/rmmount
notify rdsk/* group=tty user=root /usr/lib/vold/volmissing -p
remount dev/diskette[0-9]/* user=root /usr/sbin/rmmount
remount dev/dsk/* user=root /usr/sbin/rmmount
# List of file system types unsafe to eject
unsafe ufs hsfs pcfs udfs
```

Each section in the vold.conf file is labeled with its function. Of these sections, you can safely modify the devices to use, which are described in Table 7.9, and actions, which are described in Table 7.10.

The “Devices to Use” section describes the devices for `vold` to manage. `vold` has the following syntax:

```
use <device> <type> <special> <shared_object> <symname> [ options ]
```

**TABLE 7.9**

**VOLD.CONF DEVICES TO USE**

| *Parameter Field* | *Description* |
|---|---|
| `device` | The type of removable media device to be used. Legal values are `cdrom` and `floppy`. |
| `type` | The device's specific capabilities. The legal value is `drive`. |
| `special` | Specifies the device or devices to be used. The path usually begins with /dev. |
| `shared_object` | The name of the program that manages this device. `vold` expects to find this program in /usr/lib/vold. |
| `symname` | The symbolic name that refers to this device. The `symname` is placed in the device directory. |
| `options` | The user, group, and mode permissions for the medium inserted (optional). |

The `special` and `symname` parameters are related. If `special` contains any shell wildcard characters (that is, has one or more asterisks or question marks in it), `symname` must have a `%d` at its end. In this case, the devices that are found to match the regular expression are sorted and then numbered. The first device has a 0 filled in for the `%d`, the second device found has a 1, and so on.

If the special specification does not have shell wildcard characters, the `symname` parameter must explicitly specify a number at its end.

The "Actions" section specifies which program should be called if a particular event (action) occurs. The syntax for the Actions field is as follows:

```
insert regex [ options ] <program> <program_args>
eject regex [ options ] <program> <program_args>
notify regex [ options ] <program> <program_args>
```

The different actions are listed in Table 7.10.

**TABLE 7.10**

**VOLD.CONF ACTIONS**

| *Parameter* | *Description* |
|---|---|
| `insert|eject|notify` | The media action prompting the event. |
| `regex` | This Bourne shell regular expression is matched against each entry in the /vol file system that is being affected by this event. |
| `[options]` | Specifies which user or group name this event is to run (optional). |
| `<program>` | The full pathname of an executable program to be run if `regex` is matched. |
| `program_args` | Arguments to the program. |

In the default vold.conf file, you see the following entries under the "Devices to Use" and "Actions" sections:

```
# Devices to use
use cdrom drive /dev/rdsk/c*s2 dev_cdrom.so cdrom%d
use floppy drive /dev/rdiskette[0-9] dev_floppy.so floppy%d
use pcmem drive /dev/rdsk/c*s2 dev_pcmem.so pcmem%d forceload=true
use rmdisk drive /dev/rdsk/c*s2 dev_rmdisk.so rmdisk%d
# Actions
eject dev/diskette[0-9]/* user=root /usr/sbin/rmmount
eject dev/dsk/* user=root /usr/sbin/rmmount
insert dev/diskette[0-9]/* user=root /usr/sbin/rmmount
insert dev/dsk/* user=root /usr/sbin/rmmount
notify rdsk/* group=tty user=root /usr/lib/vold/volmissing -p
remount dev/diskette[0-9]/* user=root /usr/sbin/rmmount
remount dev/dsk/* user=root /usr/sbin/rmmount
```

When a CD is inserted into the CD-ROM named /dev/dsk/c0t6d0, the following happens:

1. `vold` detects that the CD has been inserted, and runs the `/usr/sbin/rmmount` command. `rmmount` is the utility that automatically mounts a file system on a CD-ROM and floppy. It determines the type of file system, if any, that is on the medium. If a file system is present, `rmmount` mounts the file system (for a CD-ROM, in /cdrom0).

   If the medium is read-only (either a CD-ROM or a floppy with the write-protect tab set), the file system is mounted as read-only. If a file system is not identified, `rmmount` does not mount a file system.

2. After the mount is complete, the `action` associated with the media type is executed. The `action` allows other programs to be notified that a new medium is available. For example, the default `action` for mounting a CD-ROM or a floppy is to start File Manager.

   These `actions` are described in the configuration file /etc/rmmount.conf. Following is an example of the default /etc/rmmount.conf file:

   ```
   # @(#)rmmount.conf 1.10     00/02/14 SMI
   #
   # Removable Media Mounter configuration file.
   #

   # File system identification
   ident udfs ident_udfs.so cdrom floppy rmdisk
   ident hsfs ident_hsfs.so cdrom
   ident ufs ident_ufs.so cdrom floppy rmdisk pcmem
   ident pcfs ident_pcfs.so floppy rmdisk pcmem

   # Actions
   action cdrom action_filemgr.so
   action floppy action_filemgr.so
   action rmdisk action_filemgr.so

   # Mount
   mount * hsfs udfs ufs -o nosuid
   ```

3. If the user issues the `eject` command, `vold` sees the media event, and executes the `action` associated with that event. In this case, it runs `/usr/sbin/rmmount`. `rmmount` unmounts mounted file systems, and executes actions associated with the media type called out in the /etc/rmmount.conf file. If a file system is "busy" (that is, it contains the current working directory of a live process), the eject action fails.

The system administrator can modify vold.conf to specify which program should be called if media events happen, such as eject or insert. If the vold.conf configuration file is modified, `vold` must be told to reread the /etc/vold.conf file. Do this by stopping and starting `vold` as follows. Type the following:

```
/etc/init.d/volmgt stop
```

Then type the following:

```
/etc/init.d/volmgt start
```

Several other commands help you administer Volume Manager on your system. They are described in Table 7.11.

**TABLE 7.11**

**VOLUME MANAGER COMMANDS**

| *Command* | *Description* |
|---|---|
| `rmmount` | Removable media mounter. Used by `vold` to automatically mount /cdrom and /floppy if a CD or floppy disk is installed. |
| `volcancel` | Cancels a user's request to access a particular CD-ROM or floppy file system. This command, issued by the system administrator, is useful if the removable medium containing the file system is not currently in the drive. |
| `volcheck` | The system administrator issues this command to check the drive for installed media. By default, it checks the drive pointed to by /dev/diskette. |
| `volmissing` | This action, which is specified in vold.conf, notifies the user if an attempt is made to access a CD or floppy disk that is no longer in the drive. |
| `vold` | The Volume Manager daemon, controlled by /etc/vold.conf. |

To some, volume management might seem more trouble than it's worth. To disable volume management, remove (or rename) the file named /etc/rc2.d/S92volmgt. Then issue the command `/etc/init.d/volmgt stop`. If you want to have volume management on the CD but not the floppy disk, comment out the entries in the "Devices to Use" and "Actions" sections of the vold.conf file with a `#` as follows:

```
# Devices to use
use cdrom drive /dev/rdsk/c*s2 dev_cdrom.so cdrom%d
#use floppy drive /dev/rdiskette[0-9] dev_floppy.so floppy%d
use pcmem drive /dev/rdsk/c*s2 dev_pcmem.so pcmem%d forceload=true
# use rmscsi drive /dev/rdsk/c*s2 dev_rmscsi.so rmscsi%d

# Actions
#insert dev/diskette[0-9]/* user=root /usr/sbin/rmmount
insert dev/dsk/* user=root /usr/sbin/rmmount
#eject dev/diskette[0-9]/* user=root /usr/sbin/rmmount
eject dev/dsk/* user=root /usr/sbin/rmmount
notify rdsk/* group=tty user=root /usr/lib/vold/volmissing -p
```

With the changes made to /etc/vold.conf, when the `vold` daemon starts up, it manages only the CD-ROM and not the floppy disk.

`vold` is picky. Knowing this is the key to keeping `vold` from crashing or not working for some reason. With other computers, such as PCs, you can eject CD-ROMs with no problems. With Solaris, `vold` isn't that robust, so the system administrator needs to follow a few ground rules when using Volume Manager:

- Always use `vold` commands for everything to do with CD-ROMs and floppy disks. Use the commands listed in Table 5.11 to accomplish your task.
- Before pressing the button on the outside of the box to eject a CD-ROM disk, be sure to type `eject cdrom`. This is to ensure that you don't already have a CD in the reader.
- Never press the button to eject a CD when a CD is already in the machine. This could cause `vold` to stop working. Again, use the `eject cdrom` command instead.
- If you can't stop or start `vold` using the /etc/init.d/volmgt script, you need to restart the system to get `vold` working properly.

## STEP BY STEP

### 7.1 Using the Removable Media Manager GUI

I have found that the most reliable way to use floppy disks is via the removable media manager GUI in CDE (Common Desktop Environment). Problems seem to be minimized when using floppy disks if I go through the media manager GUI versus the command line. To use the removable media manager, follow these steps:

1. Open the File Manager GUI from the CDE front panel located at the bottom of the screen, as shown in Figure 7.1.

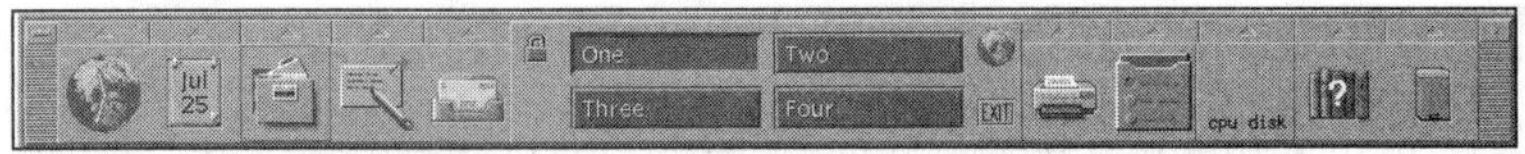


**FIGURE 7.1**
Front panel.

The File Manager will appear.

2. Click the File menu located in the menu bar, as shown in Figure 7.2.

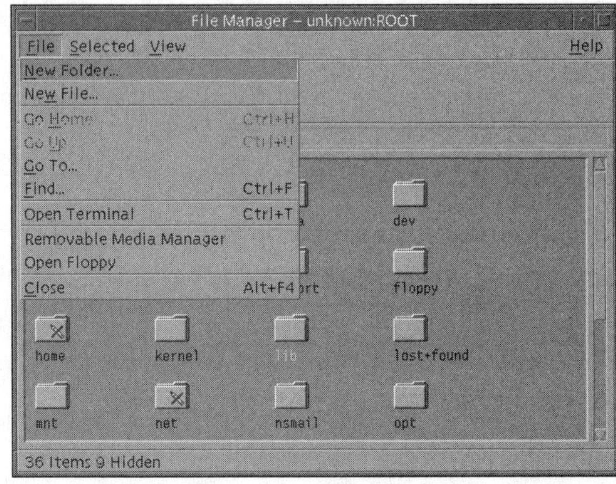


**FIGURE 7.2**
File Manager.

A pull-down menu will appear.

3. Select Removable Media Manager from the pull-down menu, and the Removable Media Manager will appear, as shown in Figure 7.3.

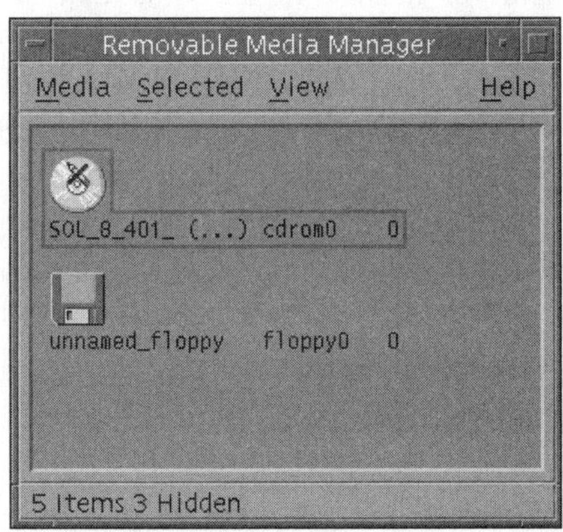


**FIGURE 7.3**
Removable Media Manager.

## Troubleshooting Volume Manager

You might sometimes have problems with mounting a floppy or a CD-ROM. First, check to see if Volume Manager knows about the device. The best way to do this is to look in /vol/dev/rdiskette0, and see if something is there. If not, the `volcheck` command has not been run or a hardware problem exists. If references to /vol lock up the system, it means that the daemon has died, and you need to restart the `vold` daemon as described earlier.

If `vold` is working properly, insert a formatted floppy disk, and type the following:

```
ls -l /vol/dev/rdiskette0
```

The system responds with this:

```
total 0
crw-rw-rw-   1 nobody   nobody    91,  7 Oct 13 14:56 unlabeled
```

NOTE: The volume is unlabeled; therefore, the file in /vol/dev/rdiskette0 is called unlabeled.

Check to make sure that a link exists in /floppy to the character device in /vol/dev/rdiskette0. Type the following:

```
ls -l /floppy0
```

The system responds with this:

```
total 18
lrwxrwxrwx   1 root     nobody        11 Oct 13 14:56 \
floppy0 -> ./unlabeled
```

If a name is in /vol/dev/rdiskette0, as previously described, and nothing is mounted in /floppy/<name_of_media>, it's likely that data on the medium is an unrecognized file system. For example, perhaps it's a `tar` archive, a `cpio` backup, or a Macintosh file system. Don't use Volume Manager to get to these file types. Instead, access them through the block or character devices found in /vol/dev/rdiskette0 or /vol/dev/diskette0, with user tools to interpret the data on them, such as `tar`, `dd`, or `cpio`. For example, if you're trying to access a `tar` archive on a floppy disk, use this command:

```
tar tvf /vol/dev/rdiskette0/unlabeled
```

All `tar` files on the floppy disk will be listed.

To create a tar file on a floppy disk, the disk must contain a SunOS volume label. Use the fdformat command to format a floppy disk and add a volume label. The syntax of the fdformat command is as follows:

```
fdformat [options] [<devname>]
```

This command is described in Table 7.12.

**TABLE 7.12**

**THE fdformat COMMAND**

| *Option* | *Description* |
|---|---|
| -b <label> | Labels the medium with a volume label. A SunOS volume label is restricted to eight characters. A DOS volume label is restricted to all uppercase characters. |
| -B <filename> | Installs a special startup loader in <filename> on an MS-DOS disk. This option is meaningful only when the -d option (or -t dos) is also specified. |
| -d | Formats MS-DOS media. |
| -D | Formats a 720KB (3 1/2-inch) or 360KB (5 1/4-inch) double-density disk. This is the default for double-density-type drives. It is needed if the drive is a high or extended density type. |
| -e | Ejects the disk when it is finished. |
| -E | Formats a 2.88MB (3 1/2-inch) extended-density disk. This is the default for extended-density-type drives. |
| -f | Force. Does not ask for confirmation before starting format. |
| -H | Formats a 1.44MB (3 1/2-inch) or 1.2MB (5 1/4-inch) high-density disk. This is the default for high-density-type drives; it is needed if the drive is the extended-density type. |
| -l | Formats a 720KB (3 1/2-inch) or 360KB (5 1/4-inch) double-density disk. |
| -L | Formats a 720KB (3 1/2-inch) or 360KB (5 1/4-inch) double-density disk. |
| -m | Formats a 1.2MB (3 1/2-inch) medium-density disk. |
| -M | Writes a 1.2MB (3 1/2-inch medium-density format on a high-density disk (use only with the -t nec option). |
| -U | Unmounts any file systems and then formats the disk. |
| -q | Quiet; does not print status messages. |

*continues*

**TABLE 7.12** *continued*

**THE fdformat COMMAND**

| *Option* | *Description* |
|---|---|
| `-v` | Verifies each block of the disk after the format. |
| `-x` | Skips the format, and only writes a SunOS label or an MS-DOS file system. |
| `-t dos` | Installs an MS-DOS file system and startup sector formatting. This is equivalent to the DOS `format` command or the `-d` option. |
| `-t nec` | Installs an NEC-DOS file system and startup sector on the disk after formatting. This should be used only with the `-M` option. |

In Table 7.12, the device specified for `<devname>` depends on whether you're using Volume Manager. On systems using Volume Manager, replace `<devname>` with `floppy0`. If you're not using Volume Manager, replace `<devname>` with `rdiskette0`.

If `<devname>` is omitted, the default disk drive (/vol/dev/rdiskette0/unlabeled), if one exists, is used.

By default, `fdformat` uses the configured capacity of the drive to format the disk. For example, a 3 1/2-inch high-density drive uses disks with a formatted capacity of 1.44MB. After formatting and verifying, `fdformat` writes an operating-system label on block 0. Use the `-t dos` option (the same as the `-d` option) to put an MS-DOS file system on the disk after the format is done. Otherwise, `fdformat` writes a SunOS label in block 0.

To format the default disk device with a SunOS label so that it can be used to create a `tar` archive, insert the floppy disk, and issue the following command:

```
fdformat <cr>
```

The system responds with this:

```
Formatting 1.44 MB in /vol/dev/rdiskette0/unlabeled
Press return to start formatting floppy
```

Press the Enter key. The system displays a series of dots, as follows, until formatting is complete:

```
..................................
```

You can then create a `tar` archive on the disk. Type the following:

```
tar cvf /vol/dev/rdiskette0/unlabeled /etc/hosts
```

The /etc/hosts file is written to the disk in `tar` format.

If you're still having problems with Volume Manager, one way to gather debugging information is to run the `rmmount` command with the debug (`-D`) flag. To do this, edit /etc/vold.conf and change the lines that have `/usr/sbin/rmmount` to include the `-D` flag. For example:

```
insert /vol*/dev/diskette[0-9]/* user=root \
/usr/sbin/rmmount -D
```

This causes various debugging messages to appear on the console.

To see debugging messages from the Volume Manager daemon, run the daemon, `/usr/sbin/vold`, with the `-v -L 10` flags. It logs data to /var/adm/vold.log. This file might contain information that could be useful in troubleshooting.

You might also want to mount a CD-ROM on a different mount point using volume management. `vold`, by default, mounts the CD-ROM on the mount point /cdrom/cdrom0, but the user can mount it on a different mount point by following these instructions.

## STEP BY STEP

### 7.2 Mounting a CD-ROM on a Different Mount Point

1. If Volume Manager is running, bring up File Manager, and eject the CD-ROM by issuing the following command:
   ```
   eject cdrom
   ```
2. Stop the volume management daemon by typing the following:
   ```
   /etc/init.d/volmgt stop
   ```
3. Create the directory called /test:
   ```
   mkdir /test
   ```
4. Insert the CD-ROM into the CD drive, and issue this command:
   ```
   /usr/sbin/vold -d /test &
   ```

Now, instead of using the /vol directory, `vold` will use /test as the starting directory.

## INFORMATION ON FILE SYSTEMS

In Chapter 6, I described the `df` and `fsck` commands. The `df` command gives you capacity information on each mounted file system. The output of `df` and `fsck` is often misunderstood. This section goes into more detail about these two commands, and describes their output so that you can better understand the information displayed. I begin with the `fsck` command. Remember, run `fsck` only on unmounted file systems, as shown in the following example. Type the following:

```
umount /home2
fsck /dev/rdsk/c0t0d0s6
```

The system responds with this:

```
** /dev/rdsk/c0t0d0s0
** Last Mounted on /home2
** Phase 1 - Check Blocks and Sizes
** Phase 2 - Check Pathnames
** Phase 3 - Check Connectivity
** Phase 4 - Check Reference Counts
** Phase 5 - Check Cyl groups
5 files, 19 used, 95975 free (15 frags, 11995 blocks,  0.0% \
fragmentation)
```

`fsck` first reports some things related to usage, as shown in Table 7.13.

> **NOTE** A fragment is one data block in size, and a block consists of a number of data blocks, typically eight.

**TABLE 7.13**

**`fsck` OUTPUT**

| *Field* | *Description* |
|---|---|
| `files` | Number of files in the file system. |
| `used` | Number of data blocks used. |
| `free` | Number of data blocks free (fragments and whole blocks). |

Then `fsck` reports more details of the free space, as shown in Table 7.14.

**TABLE 7.14**

**fsck OUTPUT**

| *Field* | *Description* |
|---|---|
| `frags` | The number of free fragments (from fragmented blocks). |
| `blocks` | The number of free blocks (whole unfragmented blocks). |
| `% fragmentation` | Free fragments as a percentage of the whole disk size. |

Fragmentation does not refer to fragmentation in the sense of a file's disk blocks being inefficiently scattered across the whole file system, as you see in a DOS file system.

In Solaris, a high percentage of fragmentation implies that much of the free space is tied up in fragments. In the previous example, fragmentation was 0 percent. High fragmentation affects creation of new files—especially those larger than a few data blocks. Typically, high fragmentation is caused by creating large numbers of small files. The solution is to either create a larger file system or decrease the block size (finer granularity).

For example, in a file system that creates predominantly 5KB files on an 8KB block size, many 3KB fragments are free and are never used. In the extreme case, this would result in a file system that is effectively full, despite only 5/8 of the file system being used. If the block size is decreased to 4KB, which is the smallest block size available in Solaris 8, the file system is improved. The solution is summarized in Table 7.15.

**TABLE 7.15**

**BLOCK SIZES**

| *Block Size* | *Typical Pattern* |
|---|---|
| 8KB blocks | Many 5KB fragment blocks and 3KB fragments are wasted. |
| 4KB blocks | Many full blocks plus one full fragment block per four full blocks, which is much better. |

Now, let's review the output from the `df` command:

```
mount /dev/dsk/c0t0d0s6 /home2
df  -k /home2
```

The system responds with this:

```
Filesystem                 Kbytes    used     avail \
capacity       Mounted on
/dev/dsk/c0t0d0s6          95994     19       91176      1% \
/home2
```

The 95994 value in the output represents the total file system size in KB. It includes the 5 percent `minfree` that you specified earlier with the `tunefs` command. The solution is summarized in Table 7.16.

**TABLE 7.16**

**OUTPUT FROM df**

| *Field* | *Description* |
|---|---|
| 19KB used | The amount of space used in the file system. |
| 91176KB available | Space available in the file system. This value is equal to the file system size, minus the `minfree%`, less the space used (95994–5%–19). |
| 1% capacity | Space used as a percentage, calculated as follows: kilobytes used/(kilobytes available – `minfree%`) |

## CHAPTER SUMMARY

This concludes the discussion of local file systems. This chapter introduced you to the many options available for constructing file systems using the `mkfs` and `newfs` commands. Other Solaris utilities for labeling, copying, and tuning file systems were also presented.

Advanced options of the `mount` command were described. The chapter also explained how to display mount options currently in use on a particular file system. In addition, the chapter showed you how to determine what process or user is using a file system before you unmount it.

In addition to manually mounting file systems, this chapter described the Volume Manager for automatically mounting file systems on CD-ROM and diskette. All of the Volume Manager commands and associated configuration files were presented and explained.

Chapter 16, "Device Administration and Disk Management," discusses disk devices in detail. Although this topic is covered on the Part II exam, you might want to review that chapter for a detailed description of the various device configurations that make up file systems. Chapter 13, "The Solaris Network Environment," and Chapter 17, "The NFS Environment," discuss how to share file systems with other hosts on the network. The next chapter discusses system security and describes how to protect your systems and the data on them.

**KEY TERMS**

- Block size
- File system minfree space
- Volume name
- File system type
- Large files
- Large-file-aware
- Large-file-safe
- Mounted file system table (mnttab)
- Volume manager
- Fragment

## APPLY YOUR KNOWLEDGE

## Exercises

In the previous chapter, you created a new file system. In the following exercises, we'll continue where we left off by performing more complex tasks on this file system.

### 7.1 Tuning a File System

In this exercise, you'll modify some of the file system parameters that were specified when the file system was originally created with the `newfs` command.

**Estimated Time**: 15 minutes

1. Log in as root.
2. List all of the parameters currently in use on the file system by typing the following:

```
newfs -v <raw device name>
```

3. Open another window. Leave the information just displayed in step 2 in the window for referencing later. In the new window, type the `tunefs` command to change the minfree value to 5% on the file system as follows:

```
tunefs -m5 <raw device name>
```

4. View the new file system parameters, but this time you'll use the `mkfs` command as follows:

```
mkfs -m <raw device name>
```

   Compare the parameters displayed with the parameters that were displayed earlier in the other window.

5. Try the `fstyp` command for viewing file system parameters as follows:

```
fstyp -v <raw device name>
```

### 7.2 Mounting and Unmounting a File System

In this exercise, you'll mount a file system that will support files larger than 2GB.

## Apply Your Knowledge

**Estimated Time**: 5 minutes

1. Log in as root.
2. If the file system is mounted already, unmount it using the `umount` command. You can check which file systems are mounted by typing `mount` with no options.
3. Mount the file system to support large files as follows:

```
mount -o largefiles <block device name> /test
```

4. Verify that it worked by typing `mount` with no options, and checking the output.

### 7.3 Using Volume Manager

In this exercise, you'll utilize Volume Manager to automatically mount a CD-ROM.

**Estimated Time**: 10 minutes

1. Insert a CD-ROM disc into the CD-ROM player.
2. Type the `mount` command with no options to verify that the device was mounted. What is the mount point that was used?
3. Eject the CD-ROM as follows:

```
eject cdrom
```

4. Type the following command to look for the Volume Manager process named vold:

```
pgrep -l vold
```

5. Turn off the Volume Manager by typing the following:

```
/etc/init.d/volmgt stop
```

6. Type the following command to look for the Volume Manager process named vold:

```
pgrep -l vold
```

7. Insert the CD into the CD-ROM player. Did it mount the CD?
8. Restart the Volume Manager daemon by typing the following:

```
/etc/init.d/volmgt start
```

9. Type the `mount` command with no options to list all mounted file systems. Is the CD mounted now?

## Review Questions

1. Which of the following causes high fragmentation?

   A. Creating large numbers of small files

   B. Creating large numbers of large files

   C. Not enough disk space

   D. A file's disk blocks being inefficiently scattered across the whole file system

2. Output from `df` does not contain which of the following fields?

   A. Total size in kilobytes

   B. Fragmentation

   C. Capacity

   D. Kilobytes available

3. Which of the following is the recommended way to create a file system?

   A. `mkfs`

   B. `format`

   C. `tunefs`

   D. `newfs`

## APPLY YOUR KNOWLEDGE

4. Which of the following commands do you use to write or display labels on unmounted disk file systems?

   A. `format`

   B. `prtvtoc`

   C. `newfs`

   D. `labelit`

5. Which of the following commands does the administrator (root) use to copy a labeled file system from one disk to another?

   A. `volcopy`

   B. `ufsdump`

   C. `tar`

   D. All of the above

6. Which of the following commands do you issue to determine whether a file system is a UFS file system?

   A. `fstyp`

   B. `prtvtoc`

   C. `format`

   D. `newfs -v`

7. Which of the following commands is used to change the minfree value of a file system?

   A. `mkfs`

   B. `tunefs`

   C. `newfs`

   D. `format`

8. Which of the following commands do you use to view a full listing of file system parameters?

   A. `fstyp`

   B. `mkfs`

   C. `newfs`

   D. `prtvtoc`

9. A large file is a regular file whose size is greater than or equal to:

   A. 100MB

   B. 1GB

   C. 5GB

   D. 2GB

10. Which of the following is *not* large-file-aware?

    A. `labelit`

    B. `vi`

    C. `mkfs`

    D. `mount`

11. Which of the following types of utility is able to handle large files as input and to generate large files as output?

    A. Large-file-compatible

    B. Large-file-safe

    C. Large-file-aware

    D. Large-file-capable

## Apply Your Knowledge

12. Which of the following options to the mount command provides total compatibility with previous file system behavior, enforcing the 2GB maximum file size limit?

    A. `-o compat`

    B. `-largefiles`

    C. `-nolargefiles`

    D. `-o large`

13. Which of the following options do you type the `mount` command with to display a list of mounted file systems in /etc/vfstab format?

    A. `-p`

    B. `-v`

    C. `-f`

    D. `-a`

14. Which of the following examples uses the `mount` command to map a directory to a file system as read/writeable, disallows `setuid` execution, and enables the creation of large files:

    A. `mount -o rw,nosuid,large /dev/dsk/c0t0d0s0 /home2`

    B. `mount -o rw,nosuid,largefiles /dev/dsk/c0t0d0s0 /home2`

    C. `mount -o rw,nosuid,largefiles /dev/rdsk/c0t0d0s0 /home2`

    D. `mount -o rw,suid,largefiles /dev/dsk/c0t0d0s0 /home2`

15. When a file system is mounted, where are entries maintained?

    A. /etc/mnttab

    B. /etc/vfstab

    C. /etc/fstab

    D. /mnt

16. Which of the following tasks can be performed on a mounted file system?

    A. `labelit`

    B. `fsck`

    C. `tunefs`

    D. `shutdown`

17. If something is causing the file system to be busy, which of the following commands can you use to list all the processes accessing the file system?

    A. `fuser`

    B. `mount`

    C. `ps`

    D. `finger`

18. Which of the following commands stops all processes that are using the /home2 file system?

    A. `fuser -c -k /home2`

    B. `fuser -k /home2`

    C. `kill -9 /home2`

    D. `umount /home2`

## APPLY YOUR KNOWLEDGE

19. Which of the following is the mechanism that manages removable media, such as the CD-ROM and floppy disk drives?

    A. `autofs`

    B. `NFS`

    C. `vold`

    D. `init`

20. `vold` does all of the following except what?

    A. Gives other systems on the network automatic access to any disks and CDs the users insert into your system

    B. Automatically mounts disks and CDs

    C. Enables the user to access disks and CDs without having to be logged in as root

    D. Automatically mounts a file system located on another system when that file system is accessed

21. Which of the following is the directory that provides character device access for the media in the primary floppy drive?

    A. /vol/dev/diskette0

    B. /dev/rdiskette

    C. /vol/dev/aliases/floppy0

    D. /floppy/floppy0

22. Which of the following contains the volume management configuration information used by `vold`?

    A. /etc/init.d/volmgt

    B. /etc/vfstab

    C. /etc/vold.conf

    D. /etc/inittab

23. Which of the following files can the system administrator modify to specify which program should be called if media events happen, such as eject or insert?

    A. /etc/vold.conf

    B. /etc/rmmount.conf

    C. /etc/inittab

    D. /etc/mnttab

24. Which of the following actions notifies the user if an attempt is made to access a CD or disk that is no longer in the drive?

    A. `vold`

    B. `volcheck`

    C. `volmissing`

    D. `rmmount`

25. Which of the following commands is used to format a floppy disk and add a volume label?

    A. `format -d`

    B. `labelit`

    C. `format`

    D. `fdformat`

26. Which of the following do you issue to stop the `volume management` daemon?

    A. `vold stop`

    B. `/etc/init.d/volmgt stop`

    C. `ps -ef|grep vold, then kill the process ID for vold`

    D. `volcancel`

## Apply Your Knowledge

27. Which of the following commands displays capacity information on each mounted file system?

    A. `du`

    B. `format`

    C. `prtvtoc`

    D. `df`

28. Which of the following commands is typed to have the system mount the floppy automatically?

    A. `volcheck`

    B. `vold`

    C. `mount`

    D. `automount`

29. You can type `mount /opt` on the command line and not get an error message if which of the following conditions exits?

    A. /opt is listed in the /etc/rmtab.

    B. /opt is listed in the /etc/mnttab.

    C. /opt is listed in the /etc/vfstab.

    D. /opt is listed in the /etc/dfs/dfstab.

30. Volume Manager provides access to the CD-ROM and floppy devices through which of the following directories?

    A. /vol/dev

    B. /dev/vol

    C. /dev

    D. /vold

31. Which of the following is *not* true about Volume Manager?

    A. Volume Manager is started via the /etc/init.d/volmgt script.

    B. Volume Manager automatically mounts CDs and floppy disks.

    C. Volume Manager reads the /etc/vold.conf configuration file at startup.

    D. Volume Manager automatically mounts file systems at bootup.

## Answers to Review Questions

1. **A.** Typically, creating large numbers of small files causes high fragmentation. The solution is to either create a larger file system or to decrease the block size (finer granularity).

2. **B.** The `df` command does not display the percentage of fragmentation.

3. **D.** `newfs` is the friendly front end to the `mkfs` command. The `newfs` command automatically determines all the necessary parameters to pass to `mkfs` to construct new file systems. `newfs` was added in Solaris to make the creation of new file systems easier. It's highly recommended that the `newfs` command be used to create file systems.

4. **D.** After you create the file system with `newfs`, you can use the `labelit` utility to write or display labels on unmounted disk file systems.

## APPLY YOUR KNOWLEDGE

5. **D**. Use `volcopy`, `ufsdump`, `cpio`, `pax`, or `tar` to copy a labeled file system from one disk to another.

6. **A**. Use the `fstyp` command to determine a file system type. For example, use it to check if a file system is a `ufs` file system.

7. **B**. Use the `tunefs` command to change the min-free value of a file system.

8. **A**. Use the `fstyp` command to view file system parameters. Use the `-v` option to obtain a full listing of a file system's parameters.

9. **D**. A large file is a regular file whose size is greater than or equal to 2GB.

10. **B**. A utility is called large-file-aware if it can process large files in the same manner that it does small files. A large-file-aware utility can handle large files as input, and can generate large files as output. The `vi` command is not large-file-aware.

11. **C**. As stated in the previous question and answer, a utility is called large-file-aware if it can process large files in the same manner that it does small files. A large-file-aware utility can handle large files as input and can generate large files as output.

12. **C**. `The -nolargefiles` option to the `mount` command provides total compatibility with previous file system behavior, enforcing the 2GB maximum file size limit.

13. **A**. Type the `mount` command with the `-p` option to display a list of mounted file systems in /etc/vfstab format.

14. **B**. The following command:

```
mount -o rw,nosuid,largefiles \
/dev/dsk/c0t0d0s0 /home2
```

uses the `mount` command to map a directory to a file system as read/writeable, disallows `setuid` execution, and enables the creation of large files more than 2GB in size.

15. **A**. When a file system is mounted, an entry is maintained in the mounted file system table called /etc/mnttab. This file is actually a read-only file system, and contains information about devices that are currently mounted.

16. **D**. Do not perform the following commands on a mounted file system: `fsck`, `tunefs`, and `labelit`.

17. **A**. If something is causing the file system to be busy, you can use the `fuser` command to list all of the processes accessing the file system and to stop them if necessary.

18. **A**. The following command stops all processes that are using the /home2 file system by sending a `SIGKILL` to each one: `fuser -c -k /home2`

19. **C**. The `vold` daemon is the mechanism that manages removable media, such as the CD-ROM and floppy disk drives.

20. **D**. `vold` does not automatically mount a file system located on another system when that file system is accessed. The facility responsible for that task is AutoFS.

21. **B**. /dev/rdiskette and /vol/dev/rdiskette0 are the directories providing character device access for the medium in the primary floppy drive, usually drive 0.

22. **C**. `vold` reads the /etc/vold.conf configuration file at startup. The vold.conf file contains the Volume Manager configuration information used by `vold`.

## APPLY YOUR KNOWLEDGE

23. **A.** The "Actions" section of the vold.conf file specifies which program should be called if a particular event (action) occurs, such as eject or insert.

24. **C.** The volmissing action in the vold.conf file notifies the user if an attempt is made to access a CD or diskette that is no longer in the drive.

25. **D.** Use the `fdformat` command to format a floppy disk, and then add a volume label.

26. **B.** Run the following run control script to stop the `volume management` daemon:

    `/etc/init.d/volmgt stop`

27. **D.** The `df` command gives you capacity information on each mounted file system.

28. **A.** The `volcheck` command instructs `vold` to look at each device and determine if new media has been inserted into the drive. The system administrator issues this command to check the drive for installed media. By default, it checks the drive to which /dev/diskette points.

29. **C.** You can type `mount /opt` on the command line and not get an error message if /opt is listed in the /etc/vfstab file.

30. **A.** Volume Manager provides access to the floppy disk and CD-ROM devices through the /vol/dev directory.

31. **D.** Volume Manager does not automatically mount file systems at bootup. It does, however, automatically mount CD-ROM and file systems when removable media containing recognizable file systems are inserted into the devices.

CHAPTER 8

# System Security

## Objectives

Describing processes and procedures to keep your Solaris system secure involves discussing the following test objectives:

**Understand physical security**

- Many procedures focus on keeping the data and operating system secure. The system administrator cannot ignore keeping the hardware secure and limiting physical access to the equipment.

**Control system access**

- The system administrator will control access to the operating system via the user logins. Only those users with active logins will have access to the system and the data. The system administrator will control the level of access that each user will have.

**Control file access**

- The system administrator will assign access to directories and files using the standard Solaris permission scheme. Understanding this permission scheme and applying it to user and group IDs is necessary for controlling access to critical system data.

**Understand network security**

- Most Solaris systems are on a network, connected to systems outside the local premises, and accessible by a multitude of users from other sites. Keeping the system secure in this type of environment can be difficult, but it is a critical part of the system administrator's job.

**Secure superuser access**

- Reserve superuser privileges for only those system administrators who are authorized to use them and understand the risk of performing system tasks using the superuser privileges.

## Objectives

**Understand the Automated Security Enhancement Tool (ASET)**

- Solaris provides the Automated Security Enhancement Tool (ASET) for keeping your operating system secure. ASET is a tool for setting up and monitoring security on a Solaris system. The system administrator will use it to make specific checks and adjustments to system files and permissions to ensure system security.

**Employ common-sense security techniques**

- Many of the concepts described and Solaris tools provided are useless if common-sense security measures are overlooked.

In addition to the objectives listed for this chapter, we will discuss auditing users. Although this topic appears on the second exam, I have included it in this chapter because the material fits well with the topics discussed and does not warrant a chapter of its own.

## Outline

## Outline



## Study Strategies

The following strategies will help you prepare for the exam:

- ▶ You'll find several questions on the exam regarding Solaris security. I advise you to study this chapter carefully, and pay attention to the details. Practice each step-by-step, and memorize each command. It's important that you practice what you've learned on a Solaris 8 system until you can perform the task from memory.
- ▶ Pay special attention to the section "Controlling File Access." Make sure you understand everything discussed because the exam will test heavily on topics from this section. Know the commands described and understand permission values that have been set on a file or directory.
- ▶ Memorize all the configuration files described in this chapter. You won't need to understand how they are structured—just understand for what they are used and how they can be used to monitor and control security on your system.
- ▶ Various commands and files are described in the section on auditing users. Make sure you understand the commands and log files that are described. Also, as you read through the "Network Security" section, pay special attention to the concept of trusted hosts and restrictions on superuser access.
- ▶ Finally, study the terms at the end of the chapter. These terms might appear in questions, so you need to understand what they mean.

# Introduction

Keeping the system's information secure is one of the system administrator's primary tasks. System security involves protecting data against loss due to a disaster or system failure. In addition, it is the system administrator's responsibility to protect systems from the threat of an unauthorized intruder and to protect data on the system from unauthorized users. Some of the worst disasters I've seen have come from authorized personnel—even system administrators—destroying data unintentionally. Therefore, the system administrator is presented with two levels of security: protecting data from accidental loss, and securing the system against intrusion or unauthorized access.

The first scenario—protecting data from accidental loss—is easy to achieve with a full system backup scheme you run regularly. Regular backups provide protection in the event of a disaster. If a user accidentally destroys data, if the hardware malfunctions, or if a computer program simply corrupts data, the system administrator can restore files from the backup media. (Backup and recovery techniques are covered in Chapter 11, "Backup and Recovery.")

The second form of security—securing the system against intrusion or unauthorized access—is more complex. This book cannot cover every security hole or threat, but it does discuss UNIX security fundamentals. Protection against intruders involves the following:

- Physical security. Limit physical access to the computer equipment.
- Controlling system access. Limit user access via passwords and permissions.
- Controlling file access. Limit access to data by assigning file access permissions.
- Auditing users. Monitor user activities to detect a threat before damage occurs.
- Network security. Protect against access through phone lines, serial lines, or the network.
- Securing superuser access. Reserve superuser access for system administration use only.

## PHYSICAL SECURITY

Physical security is simple: Lock the door. Limit who has physical access to the computer equipment to prevent theft or vandalism. In addition, limit access to the system console. Anyone who has access to the console ultimately has access to the data. If the computer contains sensitive data, keep it locked in a controlled environment with clean power and adequate protection against fire, lightning, flood, and other building disasters. Restrict access to protect against tampering with the system and its backups. Anyone with access to the backup media could steal it and access the data. Furthermore, if a system is logged in and left unattended, anyone who can use that system can gain access to the operating system and the network. Make sure your users log out or "lock" their screens before walking away. In summary, you need to be aware of your users' computer surroundings, and you need to physically protect them from unauthorized access.

## CONTROLLING SYSTEM ACCESS

Controlling access to systems involves using passwords and appropriate file permissions. To control access, all logins must have passwords, and the passwords must be changed frequently. Password aging is a system parameter set by the system administrator that requires users to change their passwords after a certain number of days. Password aging lets you force users to change their passwords periodically or prevent users from changing their passwords before a specified interval. Set an expiration date for a password to prevent an intruder from gaining undetected access to the system through an old and inactive account. For a high level of security, require users to change their passwords every six weeks. Changing passwords once every three months is adequate for lower levels of security. Change system administration logins (such as root and sys) monthly, or whenever a person who knows the root password leaves the company or is reassigned.

Several files that control default system access are stored in the /etc/default directory. These files limit access to specific systems on a network. Table 8.1 summarizes the files in the /etc/default directory.

**TABLE 8.1**

**FILES IN THE /ETC/DEFAULT DIRECTORY**

| *Filename* | *Description* |
|---|---|
| /etc/default/passwd | Controls default policy on password aging. |
| /etc/default/login | Controls system login policies, including root access. The default is to limit root access to the console. |
| /etc/default/su | Specifies where attempts to su to root are logged and where these log files are located. The file also specifies whether attempts to su to root are displayed on a named device (such as a system console). |

You can set default values in the /etc/default/passwd file to control user passwords. Table 8.2 lists the options that can be controlled through the /etc/default/passwd file.

**TABLE 8.2**

**FLAGS IN /ETC/DEFAULT/PASSWD**

| *Flags* | *Description* |
|---|---|
| MAXWEEKS | Specifies the maximum time period that a password is valid. |
| MINWEEKS | Specifies the minimum time period before the password can be changed. |
| PASSLENGTH | Specifies a minimum password length for all regular users. The value can be 6, 7, or 8. |
| WARNWEEKS | Specifies a time period warning of the password's ensuing expiration date. |

The system administrator's job is to ensure that all users have secure passwords. A system cracker can break improper passwords and put the entire system at risk. Enforce the following guidelines on passwords:

- Passwords should contain a combination of six to eight letters, numbers, or special characters.
- A phrase such as "beammeup" works well as a password.
- Nonsense words made up of the first letter of every syllable in a phrase, such as "swotrb" for "Somewhere Over the Rainbow," work well for a password.
- Words with numbers or symbols substituted for letters, such as "sn00py" for "snoopy," also make good passwords.

On the other hand, the following are poor choices for passwords:

- Proper nouns, names, login names, and other passwords a person might guess just by knowing something about you (the user)
- Your name forward, backward, or jumbled
- Names of family members or pets
- Car license plate numbers
- Telephone numbers
- Social Security numbers
- Employee numbers
- Names related to a hobby or interest
- Seasonal themes, such as Santa in December
- Any word in the dictionary
- Simple keyboard patterns (asdfgh)
- Passwords you've used previously

# Where User Account Information Is Stored

User account and group information is stored in files located in the /etc directory.

Most of the user account information is stored in the /etc/passwd file; however, password encryption and password aging details are stored in the /etc/shadow file. Group information is stored in the /etc/group file. Users are put together into groups based on their file access needs; for example, the "acctng" group might be users in the accounting department.

Each line in the /etc/passwd file contains several fields, separated by a colon (:), and is formatted as follows:

```
username:password:uid:gid:comment:home-directory:login-shell
```

Table 8.3 defines each field in the /etc/passwd file.

**TABLE 8.3**

**FIELDS IN THE /ETC/PASSWD FILE**

| *Field Name* | *Description* |
|---|---|
| `username` | Contains the information user or login name. Usernames should be unique and consist of one to eight letters (A–Z, a–z) and numerals (0–9), but no underscores or spaces. The first character must be a letter, and at least one character must be a lowercase letter. |
| `password` | Contains an x, which is a placeholder for the encrypted password that is stored in the /etc/shadow file and is used by the `pwconv` command described later in this section. |
| `uid` | Contains a user identification (UID) number that identifies the user to the system. UID numbers for regular users should range from 100–60000, but they can go as high as 2147483647 (see the following Note).<br><br>All UID numbers should be unique. UIDs less than 100 are reserved. To minimize security risks, avoid reusing UIDs from deleted accounts. |
| `gid` | Contains a group identification (GID) number that identifies the user's primary group. Each GID number must be a whole number between 0–60000 (60001 and 60002 are assigned to `nobody` and `noaccess`, respectively). GIDs can go as high as 2147483647 (see the following Note). GID numbers under 100 are reserved for system default group accounts. |

| *Field Name* | *Description* |
|---|---|
| `comment` | Usually contains the user's full name. |
| `home-directory` | Contains the user's home directory pathname. |
| `login-shell` | Contains the user's default login shell. |

Each line in the /etc/shadow file contains several fields separated by colons (:). This line is formatted as follows:

```
username:password:lastchg:min:max:warn:inactive:expire
```

Table 8.4 defines each field in the /etc/shadow file.

**TABLE 8.4**

**FIELDS IN THE /ETC/SHADOW FILE**

| *Field Name* | *Description* |
|---|---|
| `username` | Contains the user or login name. |
| `password` | Might contain the following entries: a 13-character encrypted user password; the string *LK*, which indicates an inaccessible account; or the string NP, which indicates no password on the account. |
| `lastchg` | Indicates the number of days between January 1, 1970, and the last password modification date. |
| `min` | Contains the minimum number of days required between password changes. |
| `max` | Contains the maximum number of days the password is valid before the user is prompted to specify a new password. |
| `inactive` | Contains the number of days a user account can be inactive before being locked. |
| `expire` | Contains the absolute date when the user account expires. Past this date, the user cannot log into the system. |

Some experienced system administrators will edit the /etc/passwd file directly for various reasons, but only after creating a backup copy of the original /etc/passwd file. In Chapter 18, "Name Services," I describe this procedure. An example would be when you might want to restore an /etc/passwd file from backup—perhaps the original was corrupted or incorrectly modified. After modifying the /etc/passwd file, run the `pwconv` command. This command updates the /etc/shadow file with information from the /etc/passwd file.

**NOTE**

Previous Solaris software releases used 32-bit data types to contain the UIDs and GIDs, but UIDs and GIDs were constrained to a maximum useful value of 60000. Starting with the Solaris 2.5.1 release and compatible versions, the limit on UID and GID values has been raised to the maximum value of a signed integer, or 2147483647. UIDs and GIDs over 60000 do not have full functionality and are incompatible with many Solaris features, so avoid using UIDs or GIDs greater than 60000.

**NOTE**

Refrain from editing the /etc/passwd file directly, and never edit the /etc/shadow file directly. Any incorrect entry can prevent you from logging into the system. These files are updated automatically using one of the Solaris account administration commands, or Admintool, which are described in Chapter 5, "Setting Up User Accounts."

It is the pwconv command that relies on the special value of "x" in the password field of the /etc/passwd file. The "x" indicates that the password for the user already exists in the /etc/shadow file. If the /etc/shadow file does not exist, pwconv re-creates everything in it from information found in the /etc/passwd file. If the /etc/shadow file does exist, the following is performed:

- Entries that are in the /etc/passwd file and not in the /etc/shadow file are added to the shadow file.
- Entries that are in the /etc/shadow file and not in the /etc/passwd file are removed from the shadow file.

Each line in the /etc/group file contains several fields, separated by colons (:). This line is formatted as follows:

```
group-name:group-password:gid:user-list
```

Table 8.5 defines each field in the /etc/group file.

**TABLE 8.5**

**FIELDS IN THE /ETC/GROUP FILE**

| *Field Name* | *Description* |
|---|---|
| group-name | Contains the name assigned to the group. For example, members of the accounting department might be called acct. Group names can have a maximum of nine characters. |
| group-password | Usually contains an asterisk or is empty. The group-password field is a relic of earlier versions of UNIX. |
| gid | Contains the group's GID number. It must be unique on the local system, and should be unique across the entire organization. Each GID number must be a whole number between 0–60002, but it can go as high as 2147483647. Numbers less than 100 are reserved for system default group accounts. User-defined groups can range from 100–60000 (60001 and 60002 are reserved and assigned to nobody and noaccess, respectively). See the previous Note regarding the use of UIDs and GIDs greater than 60000. |
| user-list | Contains a list of groups and a comma-separated list of user names, representing the user's secondary group memberships. Each user can belong to a maximum of 16 secondary groups. |

By default, all Solaris 8 systems have the following groups already defined in the /etc/group file. Do not use the following groups for users. Also, some system processes and applications might rely on these groups, so do not change the GID or remove these groups from the /etc/group file unless you are absolutely sure of the effect on the system.

root::0:root

other::1:

bin::2:root,bin,daemon

sys::3:root,bin,sys,adm

adm::4:root,adm,daemon

uucp::5:root,uucp

mail::6:root

tty::7:root,tty,adm

lp::8:root,lp,adm

nuucp::9:root,nuucp

staff::10:

daemon::12:root,daemon

sysadmin::14:

nobody::60001:

noaccess::60002:

nogroup::65534:

> **NOTE** Members of the `sysadmin` group (group 14) are allowed to use the Admintool utility and the Solstice AdminSuite software for the purpose of adding and removing users' accounts, groups, software, printers, and serial devices. A system administrator might assign this group to a backup system administrator or power user. Unless you are a member of the UNIX `sysadmin` group, you must become superuser on your system to use Admintool or AdminSuite.

## Restricted Shells

System administrators can use restricted versions of the Korn shell (`rksh`) and Bourne shell (`rsh`) to limit the operations allowed for a particular user account. Restricted shells are especially useful for ensuring that time-sharing users, or users' guests on a system, have restricted permissions during login sessions. When an account is set up with a restricted shell, users cannot do the following:

- Change directories
- Set the `$PATH` variable

NOTE

Do not confuse the restricted shell /usr/lib/rsh with the remote shell /usr/bin/rsh. When specifying a restricted shell, you should not include the user's path—/bin, /sbin, or /usr/bin. Doing so allows the user to start another shell (a nonrestricted shell).

- Specify path or command names beginning with /
- Redirect output

You can also provide the user with shell procedures that have access to the full power of the standard shell but impose a limited menu of commands.

## Controlling File Access

After you have established login restrictions, you need to control access to the data on the system. Some users only need to look at files; others need the ability to change or delete files. You might have data that you do not want anyone else to see. You control data access by assigning permission levels to a file or directory.

Three levels of access permission are assigned to a UNIX file to control access by the owner, the group, and all others. Display permissions with the `ls -la` command. The following example shows the use of the `ls -la` command to display permissions on files in the /users directory:

```
ls -la    /users
```

The system responds with this:

```
drwxr-xr-x   2   bill   staff   512   Sep 23 07:02        .
drwxr-xr-x   3   root   other   512   Sep 23 07:02        ..
-rw-r--r--   1   bill   staff   124   Sep 23 07:02        .cshrc
-rw-r--r--   1   bill   staff   575   Sep 23 07:02        .login
```

The first column of information displays the type of file and its access permissions for the user, group, and others. The r, w, and x are described in Table 8.6. The third column displays the owner of the file—usually the user who created the file. The owner of a file (and superuser) can decide who has the right to read it, to write to it, or—if it is a command—to execute it. The fourth column displays the group to which this file belongs—normally the owner's primary group.

**TABLE 8.6**

**FILE ACCESS PERMISSIONS**

| *Symbol* | *Permission* | *Means that Designated Users...* |
|---|---|---|
| r | Read | Can open and read the contents of a file |
| w | Write | Can write to the file (modify its contents), add to it, or delete it |
| x | Execute | Can execute the file (if it is a program or shell script) |
| - | Denied | Cannot read, write to, or execute the file |

When listing the permissions on a directory, all columns of information are the same as for a file, with one exception. The r, w, and x found in the first column are treated slightly differently than for a file. They are described in Table 8.7.

**TABLE 8.7**

**DIRECTORY ACCESS PERMISSIONS**

| *Symbol* | *Permission* | *Means that Designated Users...* |
|---|---|---|
| r | Read | Can list files in the directory. |
| w | Write | Can add or remove files or links in the directory. |
| x | Execute | Can open or execute files in the directory. Also can make the directory and the directories beneath it current. |
| - | Denied | Cannot read, write, or execute. |

Use the commands listed in Table 8.8 to modify file access permissions and ownership, but remember that only the owner of the file or root can assign or modify these values.

**TABLE 8.8**

**File Access Commands**

| *Command* | *Description* |
|---|---|
| `chmod` | Changes access permissions on a file. You can use either symbolic mode (letters and symbols) or absolute mode (octal numbers) to change permissions on a file. |
| `chown` | Changes the ownership of a file. |
| `chgrp` | Changes the group ownership of a file. |

## Effective User ID and Group ID

The `su` (switch user) command allows a user to become another user without logging off the system. To use the `su` command, you must supply the password for the user you are attempting to log in as, unless you are already logged in as root. The root user can run `su` without being prompted for passwords.

System administrators often use the `su` command. For example, as a safety precaution, rather than using the superuser password as a regular login, a system administrator might use a regular, non-root login whenever he is not performing administration functions. When root access is required, the system administrator quickly switches to superuser using the `su` command. When the administrator is finished performing the task, he exits the superuser account and continues working using his normal, non-root account.

If the user enters the correct password, `su` creates a new shell process as specified in the shell field of the /etc/passwd file for that particular user. In the following example, user1 will run the `su` command to become user2:

```
su user2
```

An option to the `su` command is the – (dash). This option specifies a complete login. The specified user's .profile will be run and the environment will be changed to what would be expected if the user actually logged in as the specified user.

Without the -, the environment is passed along from the original login, with the exception of `$PATH`, which is controlled by PATH and SUPATH in the /etc/default/su file described later in this chapter.

## Default umask

When a user creates a file or directory, the user mask controls the default file permissions assigned to the file or directory. The `umask` command should set the user mask in a user initialization file, such as /etc/profile or .cshrc. You can display the current value of the user mask by typing `umask` and pressing Enter.

The user mask is set with a three-digit octal value, such as 022. The first digit sets permissions for the user, the second sets permissions for the group, and the third sets permissions for others. To set the `umask` to 022, type the following:

```
umask 022
```

By default, the system sets the permissions on a file to 666, granting read and write permission to the user, group, and others. The system sets the default permissions on a directory or executable file to 777, or `rwxrwxrwx`. The value assigned by `umask` is subtracted from the default. To determine the `umask` value you want to set, subtract the value of the permissions you want from 666 (for a file) or 777 (for a directory). The remainder is the value to use with the `umask` command. For example, suppose you want to change the default mode for files to 644 (`rw-r--r--`). The difference between 666 and 644 is 022, which is the value you would use as an argument to the `umask` command.

Setting the `umask` value has the effect of granting or denying permissions in the same way `chmod` grants them. For example, the command `chmod 022` grants write permission to group and others, and `umask 022` denies write permission to group and others.

## Sticky Bit

The sticky bit is a permission bit that protects the files within a directory. If the directory has the sticky bit set, a file can be deleted only by the owner of the file, the owner of the directory, or root. This prevents a user from deleting other users' files from public directories. A `t` or `T` in the access permissions column of a file listing indicates that the sticky bit has been set:

```
drwxrwxrwt   2 uucp   uucp   512 Feb 12 07:32 \
/var/spool/uucppublic
```

Use the `chmod` command to set the sticky bit. The symbols for setting the sticky bit by using the `chmod` command in symbolic mode are listed in Table 8.9.

**TABLE 8.9**

**STICKY BIT MODES**

| *Symbol* | *Description* |
|---|---|
| t | Sticky bit is on; execution bit for others is on. |
| T | Sticky bit is on; execution bit for others is off. |

## Access Control Lists (ACLs)

ACLs (pronounced *ackls*) can provide greater control over file permissions when the traditional UNIX file protection in the Solaris operating system is not enough. The traditional UNIX file protection provides read, write, and execute permissions for the three user classes: owner, group, and other. An ACL provides better file security by allowing you to define file permissions for the owner, owner's group, others, specific users and groups, and default permissions for each of these categories.

For example, assume you have a file you want everyone in a group to be able to read. To give everyone access, you would give "group" read permissions on that file. Now, assume you want only one person in the group to be able to write to that file. Standard UNIX doesn't let you set that up; however, you can set up an ACL to give only one person in the group write permissions on the file. Think of ACL entries as an extension to regular UNIX permissions.

ACL entries are the way to define an ACL on a file, and they are set through the ACL commands. ACL entries consist of the following fields, separated by colons:

```
entry_type:uid¦gid:perms
```

ACL entries are defined in Table 8.10.

**TABLE 8.10**

**ACL ENTRIES**

| *ACL Field* | *Description* |
|---|---|
| `entry_type` | The type of ACL entry on which to set file permissions. For example, `entry_type` can be user (the owner of a file) or mask (the ACL mask). |
| `uid` | The username or identification number. |
| `gid` | The group name or identification number. |
| `perms` | The permissions set on `entry_type`. Permissions are indicated by the symbolic characters `rwx` or an octal number, as used with the `chmod` command. |

The ACL mask entry indicates the maximum permissions allowed for users, other than the owner, and for groups. The mask is a quick way to change permissions on all users and groups. For example, the `mask:r--` mask entry indicates that users and groups cannot have more than read permissions, even though they might have write/execute permissions.

## Setting ACL Entries

Set ACL entries on a file by using the `setfacl` command:

```
$ setfacl -s \
user::perms,group::perms,other:perms,mask:perms, \
acl_entry_list filename ...
```

The `-s` option replaces the entire ACL with the new ACL entries, if an ACL already exists on the file.

The following example sets the user permissions to read/write, group permissions to read-only, and other permissions to none on the txt1.doc file. In addition, the user bill is given read/write permissions on the file, and the ACL mask permissions are set to read/write, which means that no user or group can have execute permissions.

```
$ setfacl -s user::rw-,group::r--,other:---,mask: \
rw-,user:bill:rw- txt1.doc
```

In addition to the ACL entries for files, you can set default ACL entries on a directory that apply to files created within the directory. For example, I'll use the `setfacl` command to set execute privileges on the /home/bholzgen directory for user bcalkins. Execute privileges on a directory allow a user to change to that directory and do a long listing with the `ls -l` command on that directory. Before I set the ACL on this directory, let's look at the default permission that currently exists on that directory:

```
drwxr-xr-x   2 bholzgen   staff    512 Jul 30 12:41, \
bholzgen
```

> **NOTE** When you set default ACL entries for specific users and groups on a directory for the first time, you must also set default ACL entries for the file owner, file group, others, and ACL mask.

Now, issue the command to set the ACL privileges:

```
setfacl -s user::rwx,g::r--,o:---,m:rwx,user:bcalkins:rwx \
/export/home/bholzgen
```

Use the `getfacl` command to display the ACL entry for the /export/home/bholzgen directory as follows:

```
getfacl /export/home/bholzgen
```

The system responds with the following:

```
# file: /export/home/bholzgen
# owner: bholzgen
# group: staff
user::rwx
user:bcalkins:rwx                  #effective:rwx
group::r--              #effective:r--
mask:rwx
other:---
```

Now, the only persons allowed to change into the /export/home/bholzgen directory are bholzgen and bcalkins. No other members, except root, will be able to access this directory—not even members of the same group.

## Checking the New File Permissions

Check the new file permissions with the `ls -l` command. The plus sign (+) to the right of the mode field indicates that the file has an ACL:

```
$ ls -l
 total 210
```

```
-rw-r-----+   1 mike  sysadmin   32100  Sep 11 13:11 txt1.doc
-rw-r--r--    1 mike  sysadmin   1410   Sep 11 13:11 txt2.doc
-rw-r--r--    1 mike  sysadmin   1700   Sep 11 13:11 labnotes
```

## Verifying ACL Entries

To verify which ACL entries were set on the file, use the `getfacl` command:

```
$ getfacl txt1.doc
```

The system responds with this:

```
# file: txt1.doc
# owner: mike
# group: sysadmin
user::rw-
user:bill:rw-         #effective:rw-
group::r--            #effective:r--
mask:rw-
other:---
```

## Copying a File's ACL to Another File

Copy a file's ACL to another file by redirecting the `getfacl` output as follows:

```
getfacl <filename1>: | setfacl  -f  -  <filename2>
```

In the following example, I copy the ACL from file1 to file2:

```
getfacl file1 | setfacl -f - file2
```

Issuing the `getfacl` command, I can verify that the change has been made:

```
getfacl file*

# file: file1
# owner: root
# group: other
user::rw-
user:bcalkins:rw-                 #effective:rw-
group::r--               #effective:r--
mask:rw-
other:---

# file: file2
# owner: root
# group: other
user::rw-
user:bcalkins:rw-                 #effective:rw-
group::r--               #effective:r--
mask:rw-
other:---
```

## Modifying ACL Entries on a File

Modify ACL entries on a file by using the `setfacl` command:

```
setfacl -m <acl_entry_list> <filename1> [filename2 ...]
```

The arguments for the `setfacl` command are described in Table 8.11.

**TABLE 8.11**

**setfacl ARGUMENTS**

| *Argument* | *Description* |
|---|---|
| `-m` | Modifies the existing ACL entry. |
| `<acl_entry_list>` | Specifies the list of one or more ACL entries to modify on the file or directory. You can also modify default ACL entries on a directory. (See Table 8.12 for the list of ACL entries.) |
| `<filename>` | Specifies the file or directory. |

The ACL entries that can be specified with the `setfacl` command are described in Table 8.12.

**TABLE 8.12**

**ACL ENTRIES FOR FILES**

| *ACL Entry* | *Description* |
|---|---|
| `u[ser]::<perms>` | File owner permissions. |
| `g[roup]::<perms>` | File group permissions. |
| `o[ther]:<perms>` | Permissions for users other than the file owner or members of the file group. |
| `m[ask]:<perms>` | The ACL mask. The mask entry indicates the maximum permissions allowed for users (other than the owner) and for groups. The mask is a quick way to change permissions on all the users and groups. For example, the `mask:r-- mask` entry indicates that users and groups cannot have more than read permissions, even though they might have write/execute permissions. |
| `u[ser]:uid:<perms>` | Permissions for a specific user. For `uid`, you can specify either a username or a numeric UID. |
| `g[roup]:gid:<perms>` | Permissions for a specific group. For `gid`, you can specify either a group name or a numeric GID. |

## Deleting ACL Entries from a File

To delete an ACL entry from a file, use the `setfacl -d <acl_entry_list>` command. The following example illustrates how to remove an ACL entry for user bcalkins on file1 and file2:

```
setfacl -d u:bcalkins file1 file2
```

Use the `getfacl` command, described earlier, to verify that the entries have been deleted.

# Setting the Correct Path

Setting your path variable correctly is important; otherwise, you might accidentally run a program introduced by someone else that harms the data or your system. This kind of program, which creates a security hazard, is called a "Trojan horse." For example, a substitute `su` program could be placed in a public directory where you, as system administrator, might run it. Such a script would look just like the regular `su` command. The script would remove itself after execution, and you would have trouble knowing that you actually ran a Trojan horse.

The path variable is automatically set at login time through the startup files .login, .profile, and .cshrc. Setting up the user search path so that the current directory (.) comes last prevents you and your users from running this type of Trojan horse. The path variable for superuser should not include the current directory (.).

> **NOTE** Solaris provides a utility called ASET (Automated Security Enhancement Tool) that examines the startup files to ensure that the path variable is set up correctly and does not contain a dot (.) entry for the current directory. ASET is discussed later in this chapter.

# The `setuid` and `setgid` Programs

When set-user identification (`setuid`) permission is set on an executable file, a process that runs the file is granted access based on the file's owner (usually root) rather than the user who created the process. This allows a user to access files and directories that normally are available only to the owner. For example, the `setuid` permission on the `passwd` command makes it possible for a user to edit the /etc/passwd file to change passwords. When a user executes the `passwd` command, that user assumes the permissions of the root ID, which is UID 0. The `setuid` permission can be identified by using the `ls -l` command. The s in the permissions field of the following example indicates the use of `setuid`:

```
ls -l /usr/bin/passwd
  -r-sr-sr-x   1 root     sys     10332 May  3 08:23 /usr/bin/passwd
```

Many executable programs must be run as root (that is, as superuser) to work properly. These executables run with the user ID set to 0 (`setuid=0`). Anyone running these programs runs them with the root ID, which creates a potential security problem if the programs are not written with security in mind.

On the other hand, the use of `setuid` on an executable program presents a security risk. A determined user can usually find a way to maintain the permissions granted to him by the `setuid` process, even after the process has finished executing. For example, a particular command might grant root privileges through the `setuid`. If a user can break out of this command, he could still have the root privileges granted by the `setuid` on that file. An intruder who accesses a system will look for any files that have the `setuid`.

> **TIP**
>
> To find files that have `setuid` permissions, become superuser. Then use the `find` command to find files that have `setuid` permissions set:
>
> ```
> # find [directory] -user root \
> -perm -4000 -exec ls -ldb {} \
> ; >/tmp/filename
> ```

Except for the executables shipped with Solaris that have their `setuid` to root, you should disallow the use of `setuid` programs—or at least restrict and keep them to a minimum.

The set-group identification (`setgid`) permission is similar to `setuid`, except that the process's effective GID is changed to the group owner of the file, and a user is granted access based on permissions granted to that group. Using the `ls -l` command, you can see that the file /usr/bin/mail has `setgid` permissions:

```
-r-x--s--x   1 bin   mail   64376 Jul  16 1997 /usr/bin/mail
```

The following example illustrates how to set the UID on an executable file named myprog1:

```
chmod 4744  myprog1
```

Verify the change by typing the following:

```
ls -l myprog1
```

The system responds with this:

```
-rwsr--r--   1   root   other   25   Mar   6   11:52  myprog
```

The following example illustrates how to set the GID on an executable file named myprog1:

```
chmod 2070 myprog1
```

Verify the change by typing the following:

```
ls -l myprog1
```

The system responds with this:

```
----rws---   1   root   other   25   Mar   6   11:58   myprog
```

A user can set the UID or GID permission for any file he owns.

# AUDITING USERS

The next two sections describe a few of the commands used to view information about users who have logged into the system. (Please note that auditing is covered on the Part II exam.)

## Monitoring Users and System Usage

As the system administrator, you'll need to monitor system resources and watch for unusual activity. Having a method to monitor the system is useful when you suspect a breach in security. For example, you might want to monitor the login status of a particular user. Use the `logins` command to monitor a particular user's activities as follows:

**STEP BY STEP**

### 8.1 Monitoring a User's Activity

1. Become superuser.
2. Display a user's login status by using the `logins` command:

   ```
   # logins -x -l username
   ```

   For example, to monitor login status for the user calkins, type the following:

   ```
   # logins -x -l calkins
   ```

The system displays the following information:

```
calkins        200      staff           10   Bill S. Calkins
                       /export/home/calkins
                       /bin/sh
                       PS 030195 10 7 -1
```

Table 8.13 describes the information output of the `logins` command.

**TABLE 8.13**

**OUTPUT FROM THE `logins` COMMAND**

| *Field* | *Description* |
|---|---|
| `calkins` | The login name. |
| `200` | The UID. |
| `staff` | The primary group. |
| `10` | The GID. |
| `Bill S. Calkins` | The comment field of the /etc/passwd file. |
| `/export/home/calkins` | The user's home directory. |
| `/bin/sh` | The user's default login shell. |
| `PS 030195 10 7 -1` | Specifies the password aging information: the last date the password was changed, the number of days required between changes, the number of days allowed before a change is required, and the warning period. |

You'll want to monitor user logins to ensure that their passwords are secure. A potential security problem is to have users without passwords (in other words, users who use a carriage return for a password). Periodically check user logins by using the following method:

## STEP BY STEP

### 8.2 Checking for Users with Blank Passwords

1. Become superuser.
2. Display users who have no passwords by using the `logins` command:

```
# logins -p
```

The system responds with a list of users who do not have passwords.

---

Another good idea is to watch anyone who has tried to access the system, but failed. You can save failed login attempts by creating the /var/adm/loginlog file with read and write permission for root only. After you create the loginlog file, all failed login activity is written to this file automatically after five failed attempts. This file does not exist by default; the system administrator must create it. To enable logging to this file as root, create the file as follows:

```
touch /var/adm/loginlog
```

The loginlog file contains one entry for each failed attempt. Each entry contains the user's login name, the tty device, and the time of the failed attempt. If a person makes fewer than five unsuccessful attempts, none of the attempts is logged.

The following is an example of an entry in which someone tried to log in as root, but failed:

```
# more /var/adm/loginlog
root:/dev/pts/5:Wed Apr 11 11:36:40 2001
root:/dev/pts/5:Wed Apr 11 11:36:47 2001
root:/dev/pts/5:Wed Apr 11 11:36:54 2001
root:/dev/pts/5:Wed Apr 11 11:37:02 2001
```

The loginlog file might grow quickly. To use the information in this file and to prevent the file from getting too large, you must check it and clear its contents occasionally. If this file shows a lot of activity, someone might be attempting to break into the computer system.

## Checking Who Is Logged In

Use the Solaris `who` command to find out who is logged in to a system. To obtain this information, the `who` command examines the /var/adm/utmpx file, which contains a history of all logins since the file was last created.

Without arguments, the who command lists the login account name, terminal device, login date and time, and where the user logged in from. Here is an example:

```
# who
root        pts/3        May 11 14:47     (10.64.178.2)
root        pts/1        May 10 15:42     (sparc1.PDESIGNINC.COM)
root        pts/2        May 10 15:53     (sparc1.PDESIGNINC.COM)
root        pts/4        May 11 14:48     (pluto)
```

Here are some of the more common options used with the who command:

-a Processes /var/adm/utmpx or the named file with -b, -d, -l, -p, -r, -t, -T, and -u options turned on. The following example shows the output you'll see with the -a option:

```
who -a
NAME        LINE      TIME    IDLE    PID  COMMENTS
   .        system boot       May 10 09:56
   .        run-level 3       May 10 09:56 3         0  S
rc2             .    May 10 09:56 old     70   id=  s2 term=0 \
exit=0
rc3             .    May 10 09:57 old     270  id=  s3 term=0 \
exit=0
sac             .    May 10 09:57 old     294  id=  sc
LOGIN       console  May 10 09:57 0:13    295
zsmon           .    May 10 09:57 old     297
LOGIN       console  May 10 09:57 0:13    299     (:0)
root      + pts/3    May 11 14:47         505     (10.64.178.2)
root      + pts/1    May 10 15:42 0:13    366 \
(ovserv.PDESIGNINC.COM)
root      + pts/2    May 10 15:53 22:02   378 \
(ovserv.PDESIGNINC.COM)
root      + pts/4    May 11 14:48 0:13    518     (holl300s)
```

-b Indicates the time and date of the last reboot, as shown in the following example:

```
who -b
The system responds with:
.         system boot  May 10 09:56
```

-m Outputs only information about the current terminal:

```
who -m
The system responds with:
root        pts/3          May 11 14:47     (10.64.178.2)
```

-n <x> Takes a numeric argument, <x>, which specifies the number of users to display per line. <x> must be at least 1. The -n option can only be used with the -q option (described next).

-q (Quick who) Displays only the names and the number of users currently logged on. When this option is used, all other options are ignored. Following is an example of the -q and -n options:

```
who -q -n2
The system responds with:
root      root
root      root
# users=4
```

-r Indicates the current run level of the init process:

```
who -r
The system responds with:
.       run-level 3  May 10 09:56     3       0  S
```

-s Lists only the name, line, and time fields. This is the default when no options are specified.

## The *whodo* Command

The whodo command produces formatted and dated output from information in the /var/adm/utmpx, /tmp/ps_data, and /proc/pid files. It displays each user logged in and the active processes owned by that user. The output shows the date, time, and machine name. For each user logged in, the system displays the device name, UID, and login time, followed by a list of active processes associated with the UID. The process list includes the device name, process-ID, CPU minutes and seconds used, and process name. The following is an example of the whodo command:

```
whodo
```

The system responds with:

```
Thu May 11 15:16:56 EDT 2000
holl300s

pts/3         root      14:47
    pts/3           505     0:00 sh
    pts/3           536     0:00 whodo

pts/1         root      15:42
    pts/1           366     0:00 sh
    pts/1           514     0:00 rlogin
    pts/1           516     0:00 rlogin

pts/2         root      15:53
    pts/2           378     0:00 sh

pts/4         root      14:48
    pts/4           518     0:00 sh
```

Use the -l option with the whodo command to get a long listing:

```
whodo -l
```

The system responds with:

```
   3:23pm  up 1 day(s), 5 hr(s), 27 min(s)  4 user(s)
User      tty             login@  idle   JCPU   PCPU      what
root      pts/3           2:47pm     6       whodo -l
root      pts/1          Wed 3pm    35       rlogin holl300s
root      pts/2          Wed 3pm 22:24       -sh
root      pts/4           2:48pm    35       -sh
```

The fields displayed are the user's login name; the name of the tty the user is on; the time of day the user logged in (in hours:minutes); the idle time, which is the time since the user last typed anything (in hours:minutes); the CPU time used by all processes and their children on that terminal (in minutes:seconds); the CPU time used by the currently active processes (in minutes:seconds); and the name and arguments of the current process.

## The *last* Command

The Solaris last command looks in the /var/adm/wtmpx file for information about users who have logged in to the system. The last command displays the sessions of the specified users and terminals in chronological order. For each user, last displays the time when the session began, the duration of the session, and the terminal where the session took place. The last command also indicates whether the session is still active or if it was terminated by a reboot.

For example, the command last root console lists all of root's sessions, as well as all sessions on the console terminal:

```
# last root console |more
```

The system responds with this:

```
root    pts/2    10.64.178.2          Tue May 30 11:24   still logged in
root    pts/1    10.64.178.2          Fri May 26 14:26 - 15:47  (01:20)
root    pts/1    10.64.178.2          Fri May 26 11:07 - 13:37  (02:29)
root    pts/1    10.64.178.2          Fri May 26 10:12 - 10:23  (00:11)
root    pts/1    10.64.178.2          Fri May 26 09:40 - 09:42  (00:02)
root    console :0     Wed May 24 16:36 - 16:38  (00:01)
root    console :0     Wed May 24 16:20 - 16:36  (00:15)
root    pts/3    10.64.178.2     Wed May 24 13:52 - 14:22 (1+00:30)
root    pts/1    ultra5.PDESIGNINC       Mon May 22 15:14 - 15:15  (00:00)
root    pts/2    sparc21.PDESIGNINC      Wed May 10 15:53 - 15:47  (23:53)
```

# Network Security

The most difficult system administration issue to address is network security. When you connect your computer to the rest of the world via a network such as the Internet, someone could find an opening.

## Firewalls

A way to protect your network from unauthorized users accessing hosts on your network is to use a firewall, or a secure gateway system. A firewall is a dedicated system separating two networks, each of which approaches the other as not trusted—a secure host that acts as a barrier between your internal network and outside networks. The firewall has two primary functions: It acts as a gateway to pass data between the networks, and it acts as a barrier to block the passage of data to and from the network. In addition, the firewall system receives all incoming email and distributes it to the hosts on the internal network.

## Securing Network Services

Solaris is a powerful operating system that executes many useful services. However, some of these services aren't needed and can pose a potential security risk, especially for a system connected to the Internet. The first place to start is /etc/inetd.conf. This file specifies for which services the `/usr/sbin/inetd` daemon will listen. `inetd` is the daemon that provides many of the Internet-related services. By default, /etc/inetd.conf is configured for 30 or more services, but you probably need only two: ftp and telnet. You eliminate the remaining unnecessary services by commenting them out. For example, to disallow telnet logins, you would want to disable the following service in the /etc/inetd.conf file:

```
#telnet  stream  tcp     nowait  root /usr/sbin/in.telnetd \
in.telnetd
```

ftpd, tftpd, fingerd, and many other Internet services can all be disabled in a similar manner. Afterward, you must restart the `inetd` daemon as follows:

```
# kill -HUP <inetd pid>
```

It is critical to turn off all unneeded network services because many of the services run by inetd, such as rexd, pose serious security threats. rexd is the daemon responsible for remote program execution. On a system connected to the rest of the world via the Internet, this could create a potential entry point for a hacker. TFTP should absolutely be disabled if you don't have diskless clients taking advantage of it. Many sites will also disable finger, so that external users can't figure out the usernames of your internal users. Everything else pretty much depends on the needs of your site.

The next place to start disabling unneeded processes is in the /etc/rc2.d and /etc/rc3.d startup directories. As stated in Chapter 1, "System Startup," here you will find startup scripts launched by the init process. Again, some of these processes might not be needed. To keep a script from starting during the boot process, replace the capital S with a small s. Table 8.14 lists some of the startup scripts that might not be needed and could pose security threats to your system.

**TABLE 8.14**

**STARTUP SCRIPTS**

| *Startup Script* | *Description* |
|---|---|
| /etc/rc2.d/S73nfs.client | Used for NFS mounting a system. A firewall should never mount another file system. |
| /etc/rc2.d/S74autofs | Used for automounting. Again, a firewall should never mount another file system. |
| /etc/rc2.d/S80lp | Used for printing. (Your firewall should never need to print.) |
| /etc/rc2.d/S88sendmail | Listens for incoming email. Your system can still send mail (such as alerts) with this disabled. |
| /etc/rc2.d/S71rpc | Portmapper daemon. A highly insecure service. Required if you are running CDE. |
| /etc/rc2.d/S99dtlogin | The CDE daemon. Starts CDE by default. |
| /etc/rc3.d/S15nfs.server | Used to share file systems. (A bad idea for firewalls.) |
| /etc/rc3.d/S76snmpdx | The snmp daemon. |

Firewalls are one of the fastest-growing technical tools in the field of information security. However, a firewall is only as secure as the operating system on which it resides.

## TCP Wrappers

Another issue is TCP Wrappers. TCP Wrappers is a tool commonly used on UNIX systems to monitor and filter connections to network services. Although it does not encrypt, TCP Wrappers does log and control who can access your system. It is a binary that wraps itself around inetd services, such as telnet or ftp. With TCP Wrappers, the system launches the wrapper for inetd connections, logs all attempts, and then verifies the attempt against an ACL. If the connection is permitted, TCP Wrappers hands the connection to the proper binary, such as telnet. If the connection is rejected by the access control list, the connection is dropped.

Why would a firewall need TCP Wrappers? Doesn't the firewall do all of that for you? First, in case the firewall is compromised or crashes, TCP Wrappers offers a second layer of defense. No firewall is 100 percent secure. Second, TCP Wrappers protects against firewall misconfigurations that could provide a point of entry for a hacker. Third, TCP Wrappers adds a second layer of logging—verifying other system logs.

**NOTE** Be sure to use a system other than the firewall to retrieve and compile TCP Wrappers. You should not have compilers on the firewall.

## The /etc/default/login File

One last way to protect your system from unauthorized access—regardless of whether it's on the Internet—is via the /etc/default/login file. Make sure the following line is uncommented:

```
CONSOLE=/dev/console
```

With this entry, root is allowed to log in only from the secure system console, and not via the network by using `telnet` or `rlogin`. However, this entry does not disallow a user from using the `su` command to switch to root after logging in as a regular user.

## Modems

Modems are always a potential point of entry for intruders. Anyone who discovers the phone number can attempt to log in. Low-cost computers can be turned into automatic calling devices that search for modem lines and then try endlessly to guess passwords and break in. If you must use a modem, use it for outgoing calls only. An outgoing modem will not answer the phone. If you allow calling in, implement a callback system. The callback system guarantees that only authorized phone numbers can connect to the system. Another option is to have two modems that establish a security key between one and the other. This way, only modems with the security key can connect with the system modem and gain access to the computer.

## The Trusted Host

Along with protecting the password, you need to protect your system from a root user coming in from across the network. For example, systemA is a trusted host from which a user can log in without being required to type a password. Be aware that a user who has root access on systemA could access the root login on systemB simply by logging in across the network if systemA is set up as a trusted host on systemB. When systemB attempts to authenticate root from systemA, it relies on information in its local files—specifically, /etc/hosts.equiv and /.rhosts.

## The /etc/hosts.equiv File

The /etc/hosts.equiv file contains a list of trusted hosts for a remote system, one per line. A /etc/hosts.equiv file has the following structure:

```
system1
system2 user_a
```

If a user (root) attempts to log in remotely by using `rlogin` from one of the hosts listed in this file, and if the remote system can access the user's password entry, the remote system allows the user to log in without a password.

When an entry for a host is made in /etc/hosts.equiv, such as the sample entry for system1, this means that the host is trusted, and so is any user at that machine. If the username is also mentioned, as in the second entry in the same file, the host is trusted only if the specified user is attempting access. A single line of + in the /etc/hosts.equiv file indicates that every known host is trusted.

The /etc/hosts.equiv file presents a security risk. If you maintain an /etc/hosts.equiv file on your system, this file should include only trusted hosts in your network. The file should not include any host that belongs to a different network or any machines that are in public areas.

> **TIP** Change the root login to something other than "root," and never put a system name into the /etc/hosts.equiv file without a username or several names after it.

## The .rhosts File

The .rhosts file is the user equivalent of the /etc/hosts.equiv file. It contains a list of hosts and users. If a host-user combination is listed in this file, the specified user is granted permission to log in remotely from the specified host without having to supply a password. Note that an .rhosts file must reside at the top level of a user's home directory because .rhosts files located in subdirectories are not consulted. Users can create .rhosts files in their home directories—another way to allow trusted access between their own accounts on different systems without using the /etc/hosts.equiv file.

The .rhosts file presents a major security problem. Although the /etc/hosts.equiv file is under the system administrator's control and can be managed effectively, any user can create an .rhosts file granting access to whomever the user chooses—without the system administrator's knowledge.

When all of the users' home directories are on a single server, and only certain people have superuser access on that server, a good way to prevent a user from using an .rhosts file is to create (as superuser) an empty .rhosts file in the user's home directory. Then, change the permissions in this file to 000 so that changing it would be difficult, even as superuser. This would effectively prevent a user from risking system security by using an .rhosts file irresponsibly.

The only secure way to manage .rhosts files is to completely disallow them. One possible exception to this policy is the root account, which might need to have an .rhosts file to perform network backups and other remote services.

## Restricting FTP

Solaris 8's File Transfer Protocol (FTP) is a common tool for transferring files across the network. Although most sites leave FTP enabled, you need to limit who can use it. Solaris 8 contains a file named /etc/ftpusers, which is used to restrict access via FTP. The /etc/ftpusers file contains a list of login names that are prohibited from running an FTP login on the system. Following is an example of the default /etc/ftpusers file:

```
# more /etc/ftpusers
root
daemon
bin
sys
adm
lp
uucp
nuucp
listen
nobody
noaccess
nobody4
```

> **NOTE** The default in Solaris 8 is to not allow FTP logins by root. If you choose to allow FTP logins by root, remove "root" from the /etc/ftpusers file. In addition, make sure that the /etc/default/login file allows remote root login privileges. This procedure is described later in the section titled "Restricting Root Access."

Names in this file must match login names in your /etc/passwd file.

The FTP server called `in.ftpd` daemon reads the /etc/ftpusers file each time an FTP session is invoked. If the login name of the user trying to gain access matches a name in the /etc/ftpusers file, access is denied.

Another file called /etc/shells contains a list of the shells on the system. Whereas the /etc/ftpusers file contains a list of users not allowed to use FTP, the /etc/shells file will allow FTP connections only to those users running shells that are defined in this file. If this file exists, and an entry for a shell does not exist in this file, any user running the undefined shell is not allowed FTP connections to this system.

The /etc/shells file does not exist by default. If the file does not exist, the system default shells will be used. The system default shells are as follows:

| | |
|---|---|
| /bin/bash | /sbin/sh |
| /bin/csh | /usr/bin/bash |
| /bin/jsh | /usr/bin/csh |
| /bin/ksh | /usr/bin/jsh |
| /bin/pfcsh | /usr/bin/ksh |
| /bin/pfksh | /usr/bin/pfcsh |
| /bin/pfsh | /usr/bin/pfksh |
| /bin/sh | /usr/bin/pfsh |
| /bin/tcsh | /usr/bin/sh |
| /bin/zsh | /usr/bin/tcsh |
| /sbin/jsh | /usr/bin/zsh |

You can create this file using the vi editor and listing each shell that you want to be recognized by the system. Following is an example /etc/shells file:

```
# more /etc/shells
        /sbin/sh
        /bin/sh
        /bin/ksh
```

NOTE: If you don't also list all of the default shells in the /etc/shells file, as I have done in the previous example, users using these shells will not be allowed access.

## Securing Superuser Access

The UNIX superuser identity is immune from restrictions placed on other users of the system. Any UNIX account with a UID of zero (0) is the superuser. All UNIX systems have a default superuser login named root. The user of this account can access any file and run any command. This login is valuable because any user who might have gotten himself into trouble by removing access permissions, forgetting his password, or simply needing a file from an area to which he doesn't have access can be helped by root.

However, root access can be dangerous. Root can delete anything, including the operating system (most system administrators have deleted the entire root file system at one time or another). The root login is both dangerous and necessary. System administrators must not give this password to anyone and should use it themselves only when required.

## Restricting Root Access

Root access needs to be safeguarded against unauthorized use. Assume that any intruder is looking for root access. You can protect the superuser account on a system by restricting access to a specific device through the /etc/default/login file. For example, if superuser access is restricted to the console, the superuser can log in only at the console, which should be in a locked room. Anybody who remotely logs in to the system to perform an administrative function must first log in with his login and then use the `su` command to become superuser.

---

### STEP BY STEP

#### 8.3 Restricting Root Access

Do the following to restrict superuser (root) from logging in to the system console from a remote system:

1. Become superuser.
2. Edit the /etc/default/login file.
3. Uncomment the following line:

```
CONSOLE=/dev/console
```

---

The previous example set the variable CONSOLE to /dev/console. If the variable CONSOLE were set as follows:

```
CONSOLE=
```

with no value defined, then root could not log in from anywhere, not even the console. The only way to get into the system as root is to first log in as a regular user and become root by issuing the su command. If the system console is not in a controlled environment, this option might be useful.

## Monitoring Superuser Access

Solaris provides a utility for monitoring all attempts to become superuser. These logs are useful when you're trying to track down unauthorized activity. Whenever someone issues the su command to switch from user and become root, this activity is logged in a file called /var/adm/sulog. The sulog file lists all uses of the su command, not only those used to switch user to superuser. The entries show the date and time the command was entered, whether it was successful, the port from which the command was issued, and the name of the user and the switched identity.

**STEP BY STEP**

### 8.4 Monitoring Superuser Access

To monitor who is using the su command, you must first turn on this logging utility. To turn on logging of the su command, follow these steps:

1. Become superuser.
2. Edit the /etc/default/su file.
3. Uncomment the following line:

```
SULOG=/var/adm/sulog
```

Through the /etc/default/su file, you can also set up the system to display a message on the console each time an attempt is made to use the su command to gain superuser access from a remote system. This is a good way to immediately detect someone trying to gain superuser access to the system on which you are working.

## STEP BY STEP

### 8.5 Monitoring Superuser (root) Access Attempts

Do the following to display superuser (root) access attempts to the console:

1. Become superuser.
2. Edit the /etc/default/su file.
3. Uncomment the following line:
   `CONSOLE=/dev/console`
4. Use the su command to become root, and verify that a message is printed on the system console.

## SUDO

SUDO, an acronym for "superuser do," is a public-domain software package that allows a system administrator to give certain users (or groups of users) the ability to run some (or all) commands as root, or as another user while logging the commands and arguments to a log file for auditing. SUDO allows the system administrator to give access to and track specific root commands without actually giving out the root password. To give a user access to a command that requires root privileges, the system administrator configures the access list or sudoers file. Here is a sample sudoers file:

```
# sample sudoers file.
# This file MUST be edited with the 'visudo' command as \
root.
# See the man page for the details on how to write a \
sudoers file.

# Host alias specification
```

```
# User alias specification
User_Alias      DBA=oracle
User_Alias      APPLMGR=applmgr
User_Alias      SA=tej1,wbc4,wck2,wbp9
User_Alias \
OPER=tbw1,tdk1,tss1,wcs6,wjsh,yhq1,yjsd,ylb7

# Cmnd alias specification
Cmnd_Alias      MOUNT=/sbin/mount,/sbin/umount
Cmnd_Alias      BACKUP=/usr/sbin/ufsdump
Cmnd_Alias      RESTORE=/usr/sbin/ufsrestore
Cmnd_Alias      SHUTDOWN=/sbin/shutdown
Cmnd_Alias      KILL=/usr/bin/kill
Cmnd_Alias      CRONTAB=/usr/bin/crontab
# User privilege specification
root    ALL=(ALL) ALL
DBA     ALL=MOUNT,KILL,BACKUP
APPLMGR ALL=MOUNT,KILL
OPER    ALL=SHUTDOWN
```

To run a command, simply add `sudo` to your command as follows:

```
sudo shutdown
```

You'll be prompted for your personal password, not root's password. SUDO confirms that you are allowed to execute the command, and logs what you did to the SUDO log file.

**NOTE** SUDO will cache your password so that you don't need to keep entering it for successive `sudo` commands. The default is five minutes for the caching of the password.

The following are the advantages of SUDO:

- You don't have to give out the root password to everyone. It's a handy way to give users controlled access for commands they need to get their work done.
- It's a good tool to get beginning system administrators started without giving them full access.
- The audit logs are quite handy to track root activities. If something changes, you can go to the log to see when it happened and who did it.
- It works well, and is a simple but effective point solution.

SUDO is not part of the Solaris 8 operating system, but it is distributed freely on the Internet. Visit my web site, `www.pdesigninc.com`, for an up-to-date site from which to download SUDO.

New to Solaris 8, and similar to the functionality provided by SUDO, is the Role-Based Access Control (RBAC) facility. RBAC is an objective covered on the Part II exam, so it is described in detail in Section II, Chapter 20, "Role-Based Access Control."

# AUTOMATED SECURITY ENHANCEMENT TOOL (ASET)

The Solaris 8 system software includes the Automated Security Enhancement Tool (ASET), which helps you monitor and control system security by automatically performing tasks you would otherwise do manually. ASET performs the following seven tasks, each making specific checks and adjustments to system files and permissions to ensure system security:

- Verifies appropriate system file permissions
- Verifies system file contents
- Checks the consistency and integrity of /etc/passwd and /etc/group entries
- Checks on the contents of system configuration files
- Checks environment files (.profile, .login, .cshrc)
- Verifies appropriate `eeprom` settings
- Builds a firewall on a router

The ASET security package provides automated administration tools that let you control and monitor your system's security. You specify a low, medium, or high security level at which ASET will run. At each higher level, ASET's file-control functions increase to reduce file access and tighten your system security.

ASET tasks are disk-intensive and can interfere with regular activities. To minimize the impact on system performance, schedule ASET to run when the system activity level is lowest—for example, once every 24 or 48 hours at midnight.

The syntax for the `aset` command is as follows:

```
/usr/aset/aset -l <level> -d <pathname>
```

Options to the `aset` command are described in Table 8.15.

**TABLE 8.15**

### aset Command Options

| *Option* | *Description* | |
|---|---|---|
| <level> | Specifies the level of security. Valid values are low, medium, and high. | |
| | Low security | This level ensures that attributes of system files are set to standard release values. ASET performs several checks and reports potential security weaknesses. At this level, ASET takes no action and does not affect system services. |
| | Medium security | This level provides adequate security control for most environments. ASET modifies some of the settings of system files and parameters, restricting system access to reduce the risks from security attacks. ASET reports security weaknesses and any modifications it makes to restrict access. At this level, ASET does not affect system services. |
| | High security | This level renders a highly secure system. ASET adjusts many system files and parameter settings to minimum access permissions. Most system applications and commands continue to function normally, but at this level, security considerations take precedence over other system behavior. |
| <pathname> | Specifies the working directory for ASET. The default is /usr/aset. | |

The following example runs ASET at low security using the default working directory /usr/aset:

```
# /usr/aset/aset -l low
======= ASET Execution Log =======
ASET running at security level low
Machine = holl300s; Current time = 0530_14:03
aset: Using /usr/aset as working directory
Executing task list ...
        firewall
        env
        sysconf
        usrgrp
        tune
```

```
        cklist
        eeprom
All tasks executed. Some background tasks may still be \
running.
Run /usr/aset/util/taskstat to check their status:
     /usr/aset/util/taskstat     [aset_dir]
where aset_dir is ASET's operating \
directory,currently=/usr/aset.
When the tasks complete, the reports can be found in:
     /usr/aset/reports/latest/*.rpt
You can view them by:
     more /usr/aset/reports/latest/*.rpt
#
```

## Common-Sense Security Techniques

A system administrator can have the best system security measures in place, but without the users' cooperation, system security will be compromised. The system administrator must teach common-sense rules regarding system security, such as the following:

- Use proper passwords. Countless sites use passwords such as "admin" or "supervisor" for their root accounts.
- Don't give your password to anyone, no matter who he says he is. One of the best system crackers of our time said that he would simply pose as a system support person, ask a user for his password, and get free reign to the system.
- If you walk away from the system, log out or lock the screen. Think of the damage if someone walked up to your station and sent a scathing email to the president of your company—with your name attached!
- Don't connect modems to your system without approval from the system administrator.

## CHAPTER SUMMARY

This chapter discussed fundamental concepts in system security. When considering security, begin by securing the hardware in a secure location. Remember: Anyone who has physical access to the computer can access the operating system and data, regardless of how secure you've made everything else.

Keep your data secure by controlling the user logins on the system. Make sure users have secure passwords and are not making their logins and passwords public. Implement password aging and restricted shells where they make sense.

Set up file and directory permissions to ensure that users only have access to the data that they are authorized to see. Utilize secure `umask` values, and if necessary, ACLs. Monitor all user activities using the Solaris utilities described in this chapter. Finally, do not set `setuid` and `setgid` permissions unless absolutely necessary.

If your system is on a network, implement network security measures that were described in this chapter. Turn off unneeded services. Use the "deny first, then allow" rule. In other words, turn off as many services and applications as possible and then selectively turn on those that are essential. Utilize trusted systems carefully. Also, keep your operating system security patches up to date. As new threats are discovered, they are quickly fixed through a security patch. Chapter 4, "Software Package Administration," describes the process of obtaining and loading system patches.

Lastly, secure the superuser password. Keep it under tight control, and make sure it is never made available to anyone except those who are authorized. Limit using the superuser login unless the task to be performed requires root privileges.

Although system crackers seem to always find new ways to break into systems, the concepts described in this chapter provide a strong defense against an attack. Also, refer to Chapter 5 for putting these concepts to practical use as you set up and manage user accounts.

In the next chapter, we'll switch gears a little, and I'll describe all of the details behind a system process. As system administrator, your primary responsibility will be to manage all processes that run on the system.

### KEY TERMS

- Password aging
- Password encryption
- Default shells
- Restricted shell
- File access permissions
- User mask
- Sticky bit
- Access control list
- Trojan horse
- Set-user identification permission
- Set-group identification permission
- Firewall
- Network service
- Trusted host
- Automated Security Enhancement Tool
- Low security (as it pertains to ASET)
- Medium security (as it pertains to ASET)
- High security (as it pertains to ASET)

# APPLY YOUR KNOWLEDGE

## Exercises

### 8.1 Monitoring Users

In this exercise, you'll use the various utilities to monitor users who are accessing your system.

**Estimated Time**: 5 minutes

1. Log in as root.
2. Create a file called loginlog in the /var/adm directory:

```
cd /var/adm
touch loginlog
```

3. Log out and log back in. Do not log in using CDE; log in using the command line.
4. Enter `root` after the login prompt, and supply an incorrect password. Do this five times. After the fifth attempt, log in as root using the correct password and examine the /var/adm/loginlog file as follows:

```
more /var/adm/loginlog
```

5. Use the `finger` command to display information about the user named user9 as follows:

```
finger user9
finger -m user9
```

6. User the `finger` command to display information about a user on another system as follows:

```
finger user9@<hostname>
finger -m user9@<hostname>
```

7. Use the `last` command to display user and reboot activity.
8. Use the `logins` command to obtain information on the user9 login account as follows:

```
logins -x -l user9
```

### 8.2 File Access

In this exercise, you'll use UNIX permissions to control file access by allowing/disallowing access to files and directories.

**Estimated Time**: 20 minutes

1. Log in as `user9`.
2. Type the `umask` command to determine your current umask value:

```
umask
```

If the umask is not 002, change it by typing the following:

```
umask 002
```

3. Create a file in your home directory as follows:

```
cd $HOME
touch file1
```

4. Type `ls -l` to see the default permission that was assigned to this file.
5. Set your umask to 022 as follows:

```
umask 022
```

6. Create a file named file2, and look at the default permission value.

```
touch file2
ls -l
```

7. Create a new user called newuser as follows:

```
useradd -u 3001 -g 10 -d /export/home/ \
user20 -m -s /bin/ksh -c \
"Temporary User" user20
```

Set the password to user20 as follows:

```
passwd user20
```

8. Log out and back in as `user9`. You'll be placed in your home directory /export/home/user9.

## APPLY YOUR KNOWLEDGE

9. Create a new file named file10, and list the permissions:

```
touch file10
ls -l
```

10. Use `chmod` to `setuid` permissions on file10, and list the permissions:

```
chmod 4555 file10
ls -l
```

11. Use `chmod` to `setuid` and `setgid` permissions on file10 and then display the permissions:

```
chmod 6555 file10
ls -l
```

What changed?

12. Use `chmod` to remove all execute permissions from file10 and then display the new permissions:

```
chmod 6444 file10
ls -l
```

13. List the directory permissions on /tmp as follows:

```
ls -ld /tmp
```

Note the sticky bit is set on /tmp.

14. As user9, change to the /tmp directory and create a file called file1.

```
cd /tmp
touch file1
ls -l
```

Note the permissions on the file. They should be 644 (rw-r—-r—).

15. Switch to user20. In the /tmp directory, remove the file named file1:

```
su user20
cd /tmp
rm file1
```

What message did you receive?

16. Exit the current shell to return back to the user9 ID. Change to the user9 home directory and set the ACL on file10 so that user20 has read and write permissions on the file:

```
exit
cd $HOME
setfacl -m user:user20:6 file10
```

17. Now, list the file permissions on file10 with `ls -l`. Note the +, which indicates that ACL is set on the file.

18. List the ACL entry on file10 as follows:

```
getfacl file10
```

19. Remove the ACL on file10 as follows:

```
setfacl -d u:user20 file10
```

### 8.3 Restricting Root Access

In this exercise, you'll make changes to the system to restrict root logins.

**Estimated Time**: 10 minutes

1. Try to log into your system as `root` from a remote system. If the /etc/default/login file has not been modified from its default settings, you should not be able to log in.

2. Log into your system from the console as `root`.

3. Use `vi` to edit the file called /etc/default/login and add a pound sign (#) at the beginning of the following line:

```
#CONSOLE=/dev/console
```

4. Try to log into your system as root from a remote system. Does it work?

5. Now, try to open an FTP connection from a remote system as follows:

```
ftp <hostname>
```

## APPLY YOUR KNOWLEDGE

6. When prompted with a login name, try to get in as root. If the /etc/ftpusers file has not been modified from its default settings, you'll get a `Login Incorrect` message and will not be able to log in.

7. Remove root from the /etc/ftpusers files. Does the FTP session work now?

8. Disallow all FTP connections by commenting out the following line in the /etc/inetd.conf file:

```
#ftp    stream  tcp6    nowait  root \
/usr/sbin/in.ftpd       in.ftpd
```

9. Afterward, you must restart the `inetd` daemon. Get the process ID of the `inetd` daemon using the following:

```
pgrep inetd
```

10. Restart the process as follows:

```
kill -HUP <inetd pid>
```

11. Try to connect from a remote system using FTP.

## Review Questions

1. What is the maximum UID number in Solaris 8?

   A. 2147483647

   B. 60000

   C. 120000

   D. Unlimited

2. What can you do if CONSOLE= is included in the /etc/default/login file?

   A. Log in as `root` from the network and console.

   B. Log in as a regular user and then `su` to root.

   C. Log in as `root` from the console, but not from the network.

   D. Log in as `root` from the network, but not from the console.

3. Which are functions of the /etc/group file?

   A. Assigns users to secondary groups

   B. Assigns a name to a group ID number

   C. Provides a special group for `su` privileges

   D. Specifies which users can access network resources, such as printers

4. You are a system administrator, and suspect that one of your users has repeatedly tried to use `su` to gain root privileges. Which of the following files would you look at to see if your suspicion is correct?

   A. /usr/adm/syslog

   B. /usr/adm/lastlog

   C. /usr/adm/utmpx

   D. /usr/adm/sulog

5. What effect does the sticky bit have if it is set on the /tmp directory as drwxrwxrwt 2 sys sys 512 May 26 11:02 /tmp?

   A. It permits superuser access only.

   B. It prohibits all read/write permissions.

   C. It restricts only the owner to removing and renaming of the files.

   D.It is a security risk because any user can delete another user's files.

6. Which of the following files controls the default policy on password aging?

   A. /etc/default/login

   B. /etc/default/passwd

## APPLY YOUR KNOWLEDGE

C. /etc/shadow

D. /etc/passwd

7. Which of the following do not make secure passwords?

A. Phrases

B. Nonsense words

C. Words with numbers or symbols

D. Employee numbers

8. Which of the following makes a secure password?

A. Combination of six or more letters

B. Your name forward, backward, or jumbled

C. Keyboard patterns (asdfgh)

D. Any word in the dictionary

9. Password aging and encryption are stored in which of the following files?

A. /etc/passwd

B. /etc/shadow

C. /etc/default/passwd

D. /etc/default/login

10. Which group(s) has/have privileges to run Solstice AdminSuite?

A. `root`

B. `sysadmin`

C. `staff`

D. `sys`

11. On file permissions, what does the w in the example -rwxr-xr-x mean?

A. Write privileges for the owner

B. Write privileges for the owner and group

C. Write privileges for everyone

D. Write privileges for root only

12. What command is used to change read, write, and execute permissions on a file?

A. `chgrp`

B. `chown`

C. `chmod`

D. `passwd`

13. When a user creates a file or directory, which of the following controls the default file permissions assigned to the file or directory?

A. `chmod`

B. `permissions assigned`

C. `umask`

D. `chown`

14. To what does a `umask` value of 022 set the default permission on a directory?

A. 644

B. 755

C. 022

D. 533

## APPLY YOUR KNOWLEDGE

15. To what does a `umask` value of 022 set the default permission on a file?

    A. 644

    B. 755

    C. 022

    D. 533

16. What does the permission dr-xr—r— on a directory mean?

    A. Only the owner and group member can list files in this directory.

    B. Only the owner can open files in this directory.

    C. Neither read, write, nor execute privileges have been assigned.

    D. Only the owner can remove files in this directory.

17. What does the "s" in the permission field mean?

    ```
    -r-sr--r--   2 bcalkins staff 512 May 26 \
    11:57 script.1
    ```

    A. When a user executes this script, that user assumes the permissions of the root ID.

    B. The access permissions column of this file indicates the sticky bit has been set.

    C. Only bcalkins has permission to run this command.

    D. When a user executes this script, that user assumes the permissions of bcalkins.

18. What is the difference between `chmod` and `umask`?

    A. A `chmod` value can be set by individual users, whereas `umask` operates on the system level.

    B. `chmod` uses the sticky bit and umask doesn't.

    C. `umask` permissions are stored in a directory rather than in the files.

    D. `umask` changes the default permissions for every file and directory created in the future, whereas `chmod` works on a specific directory or file that already exists.

19. What does a restricted shell not allow the user to do?

    A. Change directories

    B. Redirect output

    C. Remove files

    D. Execute scripts

20. To what can rsh refer?

    A. The default system shell or the remote shell command

    B. A combination of the Bourne and C shell or a restricted shell

    C. The variable used to limit the number of login attempts or a restricted shell

    D. A restricted shell or the remote shell command

## APPLY YOUR KNOWLEDGE

21. Which of the following commands displays users that don't have a password?

    A. Do a more on the /etc/passwd file

    B. `logins -p`

    C. `passwd`

    D. `attributes`

22. Which of the following files contains a list of trusted hosts for a remote system?

    A. /.rhosts

    B. /etc/hosts.equiv

    C. /etc/default/login

    D. /etc/hosts

23. Which of the following files allows a specified user permission to log in remotely from the specified host without having to supply a password?

    A. .rhosts

    B. /etc/hosts.equiv

    C. /etc/default/login

    D. /etc/hosts

24. You can protect the superuser account on a system by restricting access to a specific device through what file?

    A. /etc/hosts.equiv

    B. /etc/default/login

    C. /etc/default/passwd

    D. /etc/default/su

25. Which of the following files lists all uses of the `su` command?

    A. /var/adm/wtmpx

    B. /var/adm/messages

    C. /var/adm/lastlog

    D. /var/adm/sulog

26. Which of the following makes specific checks and adjustments to system files and permissions to assure system security?

    A. `chmod`

    B. ASET

    C. ACL

    D. Making the proper entry in the /etc/default/login file

27. Shell scripts that run SUID or SGID can be sufficiently secure.

    A. True

    B. False

28. Which of the following commands is used to set ACL entries on a file?

    A. `setfacl`

    B. `chmod`

    C. `chown`

    D. `getfacl`

**APPLY YOUR KNOWLEDGE**

29. What does the plus sign (+) to the right of the permission mode field indicate (-rw-r———+ )?

    A. The file has an ACL.

    B. The sticky bit is set.

    C. When a user executes this script, that user assumes the permissions of owner (setuid).

    D. It sets group ID on execution.

30. Which of the following commands is used to delete an ACL?

    A. `setfacl -d <acl_entry_list>`

    B. `delfacl`

    C. `chown -acl`

    D. `setfacl -m`

31. Which of the following commands displays each user logged in and the active processes owned by that user?

    A. `whodo`

    B. `who`

    C. `w`

    D. `who -a`

32. Which of the following commands displays the time and date of the last reboot?

    A. `who -b`

    B. `who -i`

    C. `uptime`

    D. `uname`

## Answers to Review Questions

1. **A.** AUID numbers for regular users should range from 100–60000, but they can go as high as 2147483647.
2. **B.** In the /etc/default/login file, with no value defined for the variable CONSOLE, root cannot log in from anywhere—not even the console. The only way to get in to the system as root is to first log in as a regular user and become root by issuing the `su` command.
3. **A.**, **B.** The /etc/group file assigns users to secondary groups and assigns a name to a group ID number.
4. **D.** Whenever someone issues the `su` command to switch from user and become root, this activity is logged in a file called /var/adm/sulog. The sulog file lists all uses of the `su` command, not only those used to switch user to superuser. The entries show the date and time the command was entered, whether it was successful, the port from which the command was issued, and the name of the user and the switched identity.
5. **C.** If the sticky bit is set on the /tmp directory as rwxrwxrwx, it restricts only the owner to removing and renaming of his files.
6. **B.** The /etc/default/passwd file controls the default policy on password aging.
7. **D.** Employee numbers are not secure passwords.
8. **A.** Ensure that passwords contain a combination of 6–8 letters, numbers, or special characters.
9. **B.** Password encryption and password aging details are stored in the /etc/shadow file.

## APPLY YOUR KNOWLEDGE

10. **A.**, **B.** Root has full privileges under AdminSuite. Members of the `sysadmin` group (group 14) are allowed to use the Admintool utility and the Solstice AdminSuite software for the purpose of adding and removing users accounts, groups, software, printers, and serial devices.

11. **A.** On files, the "w" in the first field of the permissions list designates write privileges for the owner.

12. **C.** The `chmod` command changes access permissions on a file. You can use either symbolic mode (letters and symbols) or absolute mode (octal numbers) to change permissions on a file.

13. **C.** When a user creates a file or directory, the `umask` value controls the default file permissions assigned to the file or directory.

14. **B.** A `umask` value of 022 sets the default permission on a directory to 755 (rwxr-xr-x).

15. **A.** A umask value of 022 sets the default permission on a file to 644 (rwxr-xr-x).

16. **B.** The following permissions on a directory (r-xr—r—) allow only the owner to open files in this directory.

17. **D.** The following permission on a file (-r-sr—r—) means that when a user executes this script, that user assumes the permissions of bcalkins.

18. **D.** `umask` changes the default permissions for every file and directory created in the future, whereas `chmod` works on a specific directory or file that already exists.

19. **A.**, **B.** A restricted shell does not allow the user to change directories or redirect output.

20. **D.** rsh is an acronym that refers to either a restricted shell or the remote shell command. Do not confuse the restricted shell /usr/lib/rsh with the remote shell /usr/bin/rsh. When specifying a restricted shell, you should not include the user's path—/bin, /sbin, or /usr/bin. Doing so allows the user to start another shell (a nonrestricted shell).

21. **B.** Use the `logins -p` command to display usernames that do not have a password associated with them.

22. **B.** The /etc/hosts.equiv file contains a list of trusted hosts for a remote system, one per line.

23. **A.** The .rhosts file is the user equivalent of the /etc/hosts.equiv file. It contains a list of trusted hosts for a remote system, as well as a list of users. If a host-user combination is listed in this file, the specified user is granted permission to log in remotely from the specified host without having to supply a password.

24. **B.** You can protect the superuser account on a system by restricting access to a specific device through the CONSOLE variable located in the /etc/default/login file.

25. **D.** The sulog file lists all uses of the `su` command, not only those used to switch user to superuser. The entries show the date and time the command was entered, whether it was successful, the port from which the command was issued, and the name of the user and the switched identity.

26. **B.** The Solaris 8 system software includes the Automated Security Enhancement Tool (ASET), which helps you monitor and control system security by automatically performing tasks you would otherwise do manually. ASET performs the seven tasks, each making specific checks and adjustments to system files and permissions to ensure system security.

## Apply Your Knowledge

27. **A.** Shell scripts that run SUID or SGID can be sufficiently secure. However, extreme caution must be exercised because if a user can break out of a program that has these permission levels, he could still have the root privileges.
28. **A.** Use the `setfacl` command to set ACL entries on a file or directory.
29. **A.** The plus sign (+) to the right of the permission mode field (-rw-r———-+ ) indicates that the file has an ACL.
30. **A.** Use the `setacl -f` command to delete an ACL on a file or directory.
31. **A.**, **D.** Use the `whodo` command and the `who -a` command to display each user logged in and the active processes owned by that user.
32. **A.** The `who -b` command displays the time and date of the last reboot.

## OBJECTIVES

The following test objectives are covered in this chapter:

### Manage Solaris processes

- Managing system processes is a common task for any system administrator. You should know how to list the commands that display information for all active processes on the system, and you should be able to list commands that terminate an active process. You should also be able to state the effect of sending a specified signal to a process.

#### View a Solaris process

- A Solaris system runs hundreds of processes per hour. The system administrator must understand how to view information for all the active processes on the system.

#### Understand how processes react to signals

- Processes interact with each other via signals. The system administrator needs to understand the various signals, how to send them to a process, and how a process will react to each of them.

#### Understand how Solaris schedules processes

- Hundreds of processes will compete for execution time on the system. Scheduling is one of the key elements of effectively managing a Solaris system.

#### Use the Solaris batch-processing facilities

- Many processes compete for execution time so scheduling jobs to run at off-peak hours can dramatically improve system performance. The system administrator needs to understand how to use the Solaris batch-processor to schedule processes.

CHAPTER 9

# Process Control

## Outline



## Study Strategies

The following strategies will help you prepare for the test:

- Understand each of the commands I've introduced in this chapter enough so that you can match the command and option with a description. I suggest that you practice them on a Solaris system so that you can become familiar with the output they produce.
- Know all the commands used to display information about a process. When viewing processes, understand each of the fields that are displayed in the output.
- Finally, understand what a signal is, how it is sent to a process, and what the effect on the process is. Pay special attention to commands and signals used to terminate or restart processes.

## INTRODUCTION

This chapter covers Solaris processes—how to view processes, understanding the effects signals have on processes, and how to manage processes.

In addition to the test objectives outlined at the beginning of this chapter, I've included a section on syslog. Although syslog is an objective that's covered on the Part II exam, it fits well with the material in this chapter and did not warrant a chapter of its own.

## VIEWING A PROCESS

> **NOTE** The term "fork" is used to describe a process started from another process. As with a fork in the road, one process turns into two. You'll also see the term "spawn" used—the two words are interchangeable.

Solaris is a multitasking environment in which a number of programs run at the same time. Each Solaris program can start and stop multiple processes while it is running. A Parent process forks a child process, which in turn can fork other processes.

A *process* is a single program running in its own address space. A process under Solaris consists of an address space and a set of data structures in the kernel to keep track of that process. The address space is a section of memory that contains the code to execute a task. The kernel must keep track of the following data for each process on the system:

- Address space
- Current status of the process
- Execution priority of the process
- Resource usage of the process
- Current signal mask
- Ownership of the process

A process is distinct from a job, command, or program that may be composed of many processes working together to perform a specific task. For example, a computer-aided design application is a single program. When this program starts, it spawns other processes as it runs. When a user logs into the program, it spawns yet other processes. Each process has a process ID associated with it and is referred to as a pid. You can monitor processes that are currently executing by using one of the commands listed in Table 9.1.

**TABLE 9.1**

**COMMANDS TO DISPLAY PROCESSES**

| *Command* | *Description* |
|---|---|
| `ps` | Executed from the command line to display information about active processes. |
| `pgrep` | Executed from the command line to find processes by a specific name or attribute. |
| `prstat` | Executed from the command line to display information about active processes on the system. |
| `CDE Process Manager` | A GUI used to display and control processes on a system. This utility requires a terminal capable of displaying graphics. |

Before getting into the commands used to monitor processes, you first need to become familiar with process attributes. A process has certain attributes that directly affect execution. These are listed in Table 9.2.

**TABLE 9.2**

**PROCESS ATTRIBUTES**

| *Attribute* | *Description* |
|---|---|
| `PID` | The process identification (a unique number that defines the process within the kernel). |
| `PPID` | The parent `PID` (the creator of the process). |
| `UID` | The user ID number of the user who owns the process. |
| `EUID` | The effective user ID of the process. |
| `GID` | The group ID of the user who owns the process. |
| `EGID` | The effective group ID that owns the process. |
| `Priority` | The priority at which the process runs. |

Use the `ps` command to view processes currently running on the system. Use the `ps` command when you're on a character-based terminal and don't have access to a graphical display. Adding the `-l` option to the `ps` command displays a variety of other information about the processes currently running, including the state of each process (listed under S). The codes used to show the various process states are listed in Table 9.3.

**TABLE 9.3**

**PROCESS STATES**

| *Code* | *Process State* | *Description* |
|---|---|---|
| O | Running | The process is running on a processor. |
| S | Sleeping | The process is waiting for an event to complete. |
| R | Runnable | The process is on run queue. |
| Z | Zombie state | The process was terminated, and the parent is not waiting. |
| T | Traced | The process was stopped by a signal because the parent is tracing it. |

To see all the processes that are running on a system, type

```
ps -el
```

The system responds with the following output:

```
 F  S  UID  PID  PPID  C  PRI  NI  ADDR      SZ   WCHAN     TTY      TIME  CMD
19  T  0    0    0     0  0    SY  f0274e38  0    ?                  0:01  sched
 8  S  0    1    0     0  41   20  f5af4888  162  f5af4a80  ?        0:01  init
19  S  0    2    0     0  0    SY  f5af41c8  0    f02886a4  ?        0:00  pageout
19  S  0    3    0     1  0    SY  f5af3b08  0    f028aeb4  ?        9:57  fsflush
 8  S  0    299  1     0  65   20  f5af26c8  368  f597e0ce  console  0:00  ttymon
 8  S  0    101  1     0  41   20  f5af3448  340  f5d5bfae  ?        0:00  in.route
 8  S  0    298  1     0  41   20  f5af2d88  350  f5982c78  ?        0:00  sac
 8  S  0    111  1     0  41   20  f5af2008  455  f5d5bf5e  ?        0:01  rpcbind
 8  S  0    164  1     0  41   20  f5d5e890  691  f5d5ef38  ?        0:01  syslogd
 8  S  0    138  1     0  41   20  f5d5e1d0  450  f5d5be96  ?        0:00  inetd
 8  S  0    113  1     0  79   20  f5d5db10  462  f5d5bee6  ?        0:00  keyserv
 8  S  0    160  1     0  41   20  f5d5d450  650  f5d5bcb6  ?        0:00  automoun
 8  S  0    143  1     0  74   20  f5d5cd9   502  f5d5bebe  ?        0:00  statd
 8  S  0    145  1     0  77   20  f5d5c6d0  409  f5d5be1e  ?        0:00  lockd
 8  S  0    242  1     0  41   20  f5d5c010  514  f5d5b8a6  ?        0:01  vold
 8  S  0    184  1     0  46   20  f5e4a898  480  f5e4aa90  ?        0:01  nscd
 8  S  0    178  1     0  51   20  f5e4a1d8  360  f5982eb8  ?        0:01  cron
```

The manual page for the ps command describes all the fields displayed with the ps command as well as all the command options. Table 9.4 lists some important fields.

**TABLE 9.4**

**PROCESS FIELDS**

| *Field* | *Description* |
|---|---|
| F | Flags associated with the process. |
| S | The state of the process. The two most common values are S for sleeping and R for running. An important value to look for is X, which means that the process is waiting for memory to become available. When you frequently see this on your system, you are out of memory. Refer to Table 9.3 for a complete list of the process states. |
| UID | The user ID of the process owner. For many processes, this is 0 because they run setuid. |
| PID | The process ID of each process. This value should be unique. Generally, PIDs are allocated lowest to highest, but wrap at some point. This value is necessary for you to send a signal, such as the kill signal, to a process. |
| PPID | The parent process ID. This identifies the parent process that started the process. Using the PPID allows you to trace the sequence of process creation that took place. |
| PRI | The priority of the process. Without the -c option, higher numbers mean lower priority. With the -c option, higher numbers mean higher priority. |
| NI | The nice value, used in priority computation. This is not printed when the -c option is used. The process's nice number contributes to its scheduling priority. Making a process nicer means lowering its priority. |
| ADDR | The memory address of the process. |

| *Field* | *Description* |
|---|---|
| SZ | The SIZE field. This is the total number of pages in the process. Each page is 4096 bytes. |
| WCHAN | The address of an event for which the process is sleeping (if it's –, the process is running). |
| STIME | The starting time of the process (in hours, minutes, and seconds). |
| TTY | The terminal assigned to your process. |
| TIME | The cumulative CPU time used by the process in minutes and seconds. |
| CMD | The command that generated the process. |

You often want to look at all processes. You can do this using the command `ps -el`. A number of options available with the `ps` command control what information gets printed. A few of them are listed in Table 9.5.

**TABLE 9.5**

**ps COMMAND OPTIONS**

| *Option* | *Description* |
|---|---|
| -A | Lists information for all processes. Identical to `-e`. |
| -a | Lists information about all processes most frequently requested. Processes not associated with a terminal will not be listed. |
| -f | Generates a full listing. |
| -P | Prints the number of the processor to which the process is bound, if any, under an additional column header PSR. This is a useful option on systems that have multiple processors. |
| -u <username> | Lists only process data for a particular user. In the listing, the numerical user ID will be printed unless you give the `-f` option, which prints the login name. |

**NOTE** The UNIX `sort` command is useful when you're looking at system processes. Use the `sort` command as the pipe output to sort by size or PID. For example, to sort by the SZ field, use the command `ps -el | sort +9` (remember, `sort` starts numbering fields with 0).

For a complete list of options to the `ps` command, refer to the Solaris online manual pages.

## pgrep

Solaris 8 provides the `pgrep` command, which replaces the combination of the `ps`, `grep`, `egrep`, and `awk` commands that were used to manage processes in releases prior to Solaris 7. The `pgrep` command examines the active processes on the system, and reports the process IDs of the processes whose attributes match the criteria you specify on the command line. The command syntax for the `pgrep` command is

```
pgrep <options> <pattern>
```

`pgrep` options are described in Table 9.6.

**TABLE 9.6**

**pgrep OPTIONS**

| *Option* | *Description* |
|---|---|
| `-d <delim>` | Specifies the output delimiter string to be printed between each matching process ID. If no `-d` option is specified, the default is a newline character. |
| `-f` | The regular expression pattern should be matched against the full process argument string. If no `-f` option is specified, the expression is matched only against the name of the executable file. |
| `-g <pgrplist>` | Matches only processes whose process group ID is in the given list. |
| `-G <gidlist>` | Matches only processes whose real group ID is in the given list. Each group ID may be specified as either a group name or a numerical group ID. |
| `-l` | Long output format. Prints the process name along with the process ID of each matching process. |
| `-n` | Matches only the newest (most recently created) process that meets all other specified matching criteria. |
| `-P <ppidlist>` | Matches only processes whose parent process ID is in the given list. |
| `-s <sidlist>` | Matches only processes whose process session ID is in the given list. |
| `-t <termlist>` | Matches only processes that are associated with a terminal in the given list. Each terminal is specified as the suffix following /dev/ of the terminal's device path name in /dev (for example, term/a or pts/0). |

| *Option* | *Description* |
|---|---|
| `-u <euidlist>` | Matches only processes whose effective user ID is in the given list. Each user ID may be specified as either a login name or a numerical user ID. |
| `-U <uidlist>` | Matches only processes whose real user ID is in the given list. Each user ID may be specified as either a login name or a numerical user ID. |
| `-v` | Matches all processes except those that meet the specified matching criteria. |
| `-x` | Considers only processes whose argument string or executable filename exactly matches the specified pattern. |
| `<pattern>` | A pattern to match against either the executable filename or full process argument string. |

For example, the following `pgrep` example finds all processes that have `"dt"` in the process argument string:

```
pgrep -l -f "dt"
```

The system responds with this:

```
258 /usr/openwin/bin/Xsun :0 -nobanner -auth /var/dt/A:0-3YaaGa
256 /usr/dt/bin/dtlogin -daemon
280 /bin/ksh /usr/dt/bin/Xsession
259 /usr/dt/bin/dtlogin -daemon
327 /usr/dt/bin/dsdm
342 /usr/dt/bin/dtsession
3067 /usr/dt/bin/dtterm -C -ls -name Console
325 /usr/dt/bin/sdt_shell -c      unset DT;      DISPLAY=:0;      /usr/dt/bin/dt
328 -sh -c      unset DT;      DISPLAY=:0;      /usr/dt/bin/dtsession_res -merge
341 /usr/dt/bin/ttsession
349 dtwm
351 /usr/dt/bin/sdtperfmeter -f -H -t cpu -t disk -s 1 -name fpperfmeter
353 /bin/ksh /usr/dt/bin/sdtvolcheck -d -z 5 cdrom
730 /usr/dt/bin/dtterm -C -ls -name Console
1312 /bin/sh -c dtfile -noview
1313 dtfile -noview
1316 dtfile -noview
6886 /usr/dt/bin/dtscreen -mode blank
```

To find the process ID for the `lpsched` process, issue this command:

```
pgrep -l lpsched
```

The system responds with this:

```
6899 lpsched
```

## prstat

Use the `prstat` command from the command line to monitor system processes. Again, like the `ps` command, it provides information on active processes. The difference is that you can specify whether you want information on specific processes, UIDs, CPU IDs, or processor sets. By default, `prstat` displays information about all processes sorted by CPU usage. Another nice feature with `prstat` is that the information remains onscreen, and is updated periodically. The information displayed by the `prstat` command is described in Table 9.7.

**TABLE 9.7**

**COLUMN HEADINGS FOR THE prstat COMMAND**

| *Column Heading* | *Description* |
|---|---|
| PID | The process identification (a unique number that defines the process within the kernel). |
| USERNAME | The login ID name of the owner of the process |
| SIZE | The total virtual memory size of the process in kilobytes (K), megabytes (M), or gigabytes (G). |
| RSS | The resident set size of the process in kilobytes, megabytes, or gigabytes. |
| STATE | The state of the process:<br><br>cpu<n> – Process is running on CPU <n><br>sleep – Process is waiting for an event to complete.<br>run – Process is in run queue<br>zombie – Process terminated and parent not waiting<br>stop – Process is stopped |
| PRI | The priority of the process |
| NICE | The value used in priority computation. |
| TIME | The cumulative execution time for the process. |
| CPU | The percentage of recent CPU time used by the process. |
| PROCESS | The name of the process. |
| NLWP | The number of lightweight processes (LWPs) in the process. |

I've introduced some new terminology in this section, so Table 9.8 defines a few terms related to processing in general.

**TABLE 9.8**

**PROCESS TERMINOLOGY**

| *Term* | *Description* |
|---|---|
| Multitasking | A technique used in an operating system for sharing a single processor between several independent jobs.<br><br>Multitasking introduces overheads because the processor spends some time in choosing the next job to run and in saving and restoring tasks' state, but it reduces the worst-case time from job submission to completion compared with a simple batch system where each job must finish before the next one starts. Multitasking also means that while one task is waiting for some external event, the CPU is free to do useful work on other tasks.<br><br>A multitasking operating system should provide some degree of protection of one task from another to prevent tasks from interacting in unexpected ways, such as accidentally modifying the contents of each other's memory areas.<br><br>The jobs in a multitasking system may belong to one or many users. This is distinct from parallel processing, in which one user runs several tasks on several processors. Time-sharing is almost synonymous with multitasking, but implies that there is more than one user. |
| Parallel processing | The simultaneous use of more than one computer to solve a problem. The processors may either communicate to cooperate in solving a problem, or they may run completely independently, possibly under the control of another processor, which distributes work to the others and collects results from them. |
| Multithreaded | Sharing a single CPU between multiple tasks (or "threads") in a way designed to minimize the time required to switch threads. Multithreading differs from multitasking in that threads share more of their environment with each other than do tasks under multitasking. |
| Lightweight process (LWP) | A single-threaded subprocess. LWPs are scheduled by the kernel to use available CPU resources based on their scheduling class and priority. LWPs include a kernel thread, which contains information that has to be in memory all the time and a LWP, which contains information that is swappable. A process can consist of multiple LWPs and multiple application threads. A lightweight process is somewhere between a thread and a full process. |

*continues*

**TABLE 9.8** *continued*

**PROCESS TERMINOLOGY**

| *Term* | *Description* |
|---|---|
| Application thread | A series of instructions with a separate stack that can execute independently in a user's address space. The threads can be multiplexed on top of LWPs. |
| Address space | The range of addresses that a processor or process can access, or at which a device can be accessed. The term may refer to either physical address or virtual address. The size of a processor's address space depends on the width of the processor's address bus and address registers. |
| Shared memory | Usually refers to RAM, which can be accessed by more than one process in a multitasking operating system with memory protection. |

> **NOTE** The `psrinfo` command displays information about all processors installed in the system. `psrinfo` displays one line for each configured processor, displaying whether it is on-line, non-interruptible, off-line, or powered off, and when that status last changed.

The syntax for the `prstat` command is as follows:

```
prstat [options] <count> <interval>
```

Table 9.9 describes the `prstat` command options and arguments.

**TABLE 9.9**

**`prstat` OPTIONS AND ARGUMENTS**

| ***prstat Options*** *Option* | *Description* |
|---|---|
| `-a` | Displays separate reports about processes and users at the same time. |
| `-c` | Continuously prints new reports below previous reports instead of overwriting them. |
| `-n <nproc>` | Restricts the number of output lines. The `<nproc>` argument specifies how many lines of process or LWP statistics are reported. |
| `-p <pidlist>` | Reports only processes that have a PID in the given list. |
| `-P <cpulist>` | Reports only processes or LWPs that have most recently executed on a CPU in the given list. The `<cpulist>` argument identifies each CPU by an integer as reported by `psrinfo`. |

| ***prstat* Options** *Option* | *Description* |
|---|---|
| `-S <key>` | Sorts output lines by `<key>` in descending order. Values for `<key>` can be<br>`cpu` – Sort by process CPU usage – This is the default.<br>`time` – Sort by process execution time.<br>`size` – Sort by size of process image.<br>`rss` – Sort by resident set size.<br>`pri` – Sort by process priority. |
| `-s <key>` | Sorts output lines by `<key>` in ascending order. See the `-S` option for a list of valid `keys` to use. |
| `-t` | Reports total usage summary for each user. |
| `-u <euidlist>` | Reports only processes whose effective user ID is in the given list. The value for `<euidlist>` may be specified as either a login name or a numerical user ID. |
| `-U <euidlist>` | Reports only processes whose real user ID is in the given list. The value for `<euidlist>` may be specified as either a login name or a numerical user ID. |
| ***prstat* Arguments** | ***Arguments/Description*** |
| *<count>* | Specifies the number of times that the statistics are repeated. By default, `prstat` reports statistics until a termination signal is received. |
| *<interval>* | Specifies the sampling interval in seconds; the default interval is FIVE seconds. |

The following example uses the `prstat` command to view the four most active root processes running:

```
prstat -u root -n 4 1 1
```

The system displays the following output:

```
PID USERNAME      SIZE   RSS    STATE    PRI    NICE    TIME    CPU
     PROCESS/NLWP          3998   root    1464K         1088K          cpu0
     48   0    0:00.00          0.2%          prstat/1
763  root 6864K           4464K         sleep       58   0          0:00.01
     0.2%       dtterm/1
3299 root 1504K           1208K         sleep       48   0          0:00.12
     0.1%       prstat/1
602  root 7208K           4816K         sleep       49   0          0:00.03
     0.1%       dtterm/1
Total: 51 processes, 114 lwps, load averages: 0.00, 0.01, 0.02
```

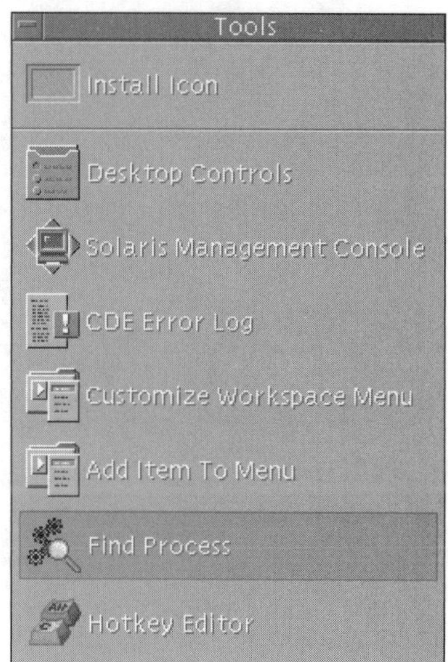


**FIGURE 9.1**
Front panel.

## CDE Process Manager

New in Solaris 8 is CDE Process Manager, `sdtprocess`, a graphical Common Desktop Environment (CDE) tool that provides a Process Manager window for monitoring and controlling system processes.

The advantage of using Process Manager is that you can view and control processes without knowing all the complex options associated with the `ps` and `kill` commands. For example, you can display processes that contain specific character strings, and you can sort the process list alphabetically or numerically. You can initiate a search using the `find` command, or you can terminate a process simply by highlighting it and clicking kill.

To open Process Manager, you need to log into the CDE windowing environment. You can start the GUI either by executing the command `sdtprocess` as follows:

```
sdtprocess &
```

or click Find Process on the front panel Tools subpanel, as shown in Figure 9.1.

The Process Manager window opens as shown in Figure 9.2.

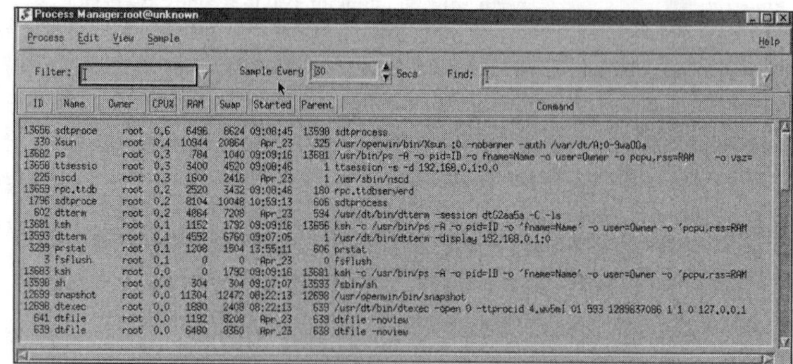


**FIGURE 9.2**
Process Manager window.

Each process attribute in the header of the Process Manager window provides detailed information about the process, and is described in Table 9.10.

**TABLE 9.10**

## Process Manager Window

| *Column Heading* | *Description* |
|---|---|
| ID | Process ID |
| Name | Process name |
| Owner | The login ID name of the owner of the process |
| CPU% | Ratio of CPU time available in the same period, expressed as a percentage |
| RAM | Amount of RAM currently occupied by this process |
| Swap | Total size in virtual memory |
| Started | Actual start time (or date if other than current) |
| Parent | Process ID of parent process, or PPID |
| Command | Actual UNIX command (truncated) being executed |

Click any of the column headings to sort the processes by that attribute. For example, click the CPU heading to sort all processes by their CPU usage. The list updates every 30 seconds, but you can enter a value in the Sampling field to update the list as frequently as you like. Finally, you can enter a text string in the Find drop-down menu that is common to the process entries of all of the processes you want to display. In Figure 9.3, I entered `root` in the Find field to display all processes owned by root. I also changed the sampling to every 5 seconds, and clicked the CPU heading to sort processes by their CPU usage.

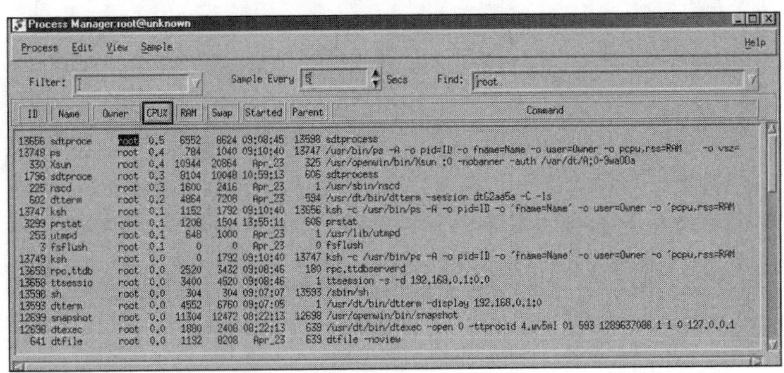


**FIGURE 9.3**
Sorted Process Manager window.

Another nice feature of the Process Manager is the capability to display the ancestry of a process. When a UNIX process initiates one or more processes, we call them child processes, or children. Child and parent processes have the same user ID. To view the parent process and all the child processes that belong to it, highlight the process in the Process Manager window. Click Process from the toolbar at the top of the window, and select Show Ancestry, as shown in Figure 9.4.

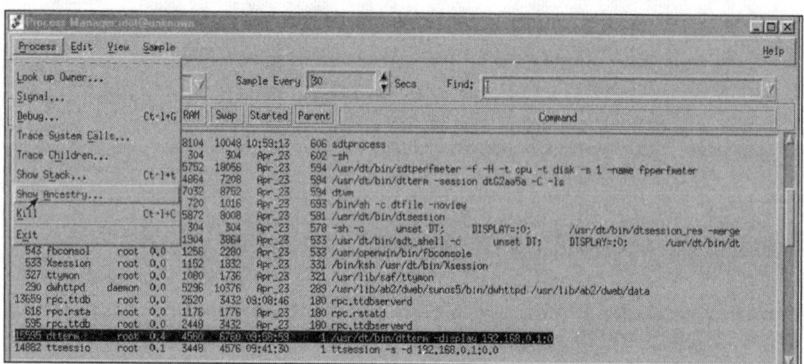

**FIGURE 9.4**
Selecting Show Ancestry.

The window shown in Figure 9.5 displays showing all the processes belonging to the parent.

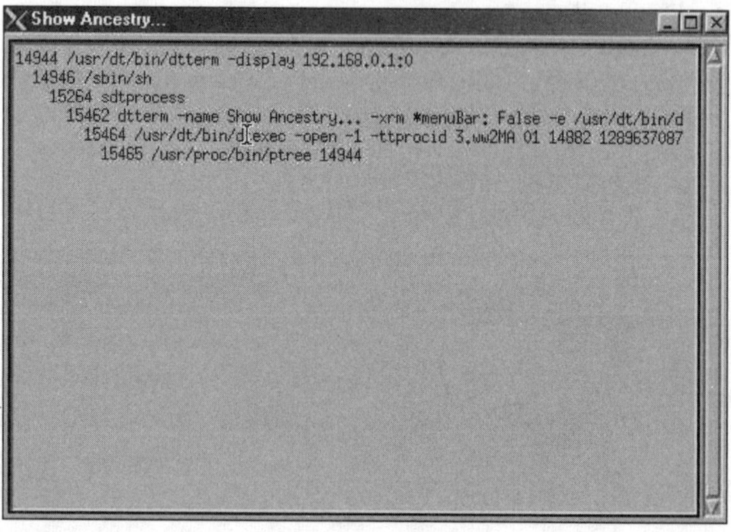


**FIGURE 9.5**
Show Ancestry window.

The command line equivalent to the Ancestry selection in Process Manager is the `ptree` command. Use this command when you don't have a graphical display terminal. The `ptree` command displays the process ancestry trees containing the specified PIDs or users. The child processes are displayed indented from their respective parent processes. For example, here is the process tree for the `dtlogin` process, which has a PID of 331:

```
ptree 331
```

The system responds with:

```
331   /usr/dt/bin/dtlogin -daemon
  533   /bin/ksh /usr/dt/bin/Xsession
    543   /usr/openwin/bin/fbconsole
    578   /usr/dt/bin/sdt_shell -c unset DT;  DISPLAY=:0;  /usr/d
      581   -sh -c  unset DT;  DISPLAY=:0;  /usr/dt/bin/dtsession_
        594   /usr/dt/bin/dtsession
          601   dtwm
          602   /usr/dt/bin/dtterm -session dtG2aa5a -C -ls
            606   -sh
              1796  sdtprocess
              3299  prstat
          603   /usr/dt/bin/sdtperfmeter -f -H -t cpu -t disk -s 1 -name fpperfme
          16461 /usr/dt/bin/dtexec -open 0 -ttprocid 1.wv5mI 01 593 1289637086 1
            16462 /usr/dt/bin/dtscreen -mode blank
```

# USING SIGNALS

Solaris supports the concept of sending software signals to a process. These signals are ways for other processes to interact with a running process outside the context of the hardware. The `kill` command is used to send a signal to a process. System administrators most often use the signals SIGHUP, SIGKILL, and SIGSTOP. The SIGHUP signal is used by some utilities as a way to notify the process to do something, such as reread its configuration file. The SIGHUP signal is also sent to a process if the telephone connection is lost or hangs up. The SIGKILL signal is used to abort a process, and the SIGSTOP signal is used to pause a process. Table 9.11 describes the most common signals an administrator is likely to use.

**TABLE 9.11**

## SIGNALS AVAILABLE UNDER SOLARIS

| *Signal* | *Number* | *Description* |
|---|---|---|
| SIGHUP | 1 | Hangup. Usually means that the controlling terminal has been disconnected. |
| SIGINT | 2 | Interrupt. The user can generate this signal by pressing Ctrl+C or Delete. |
| SIGQUIT | 3 | Quits the process and produces a core dump. |
| SIGILL | 4 | Illegal instruction. |
| SIGTRAP | 5 | Trace or breakpoint trap. |
| SIGABRT | 6 | Abort. |
| SIGEMT | 7 | Emulation trap. |
| SIGFPE | 8 | Arithmetic exception. Informs a process of a floating-point error. |
| SIGKILL | 9 | Killed. Forces the process to terminate. This is a sure kill. |
| SIGBUS | 10 | Bus error. |
| SIGSEGV | 11 | Segmentation fault. |
| SIGSYS | 12 | Bad system call. |
| SIGPIPE | 13 | Broken pipe. |
| SIGALRM | 14 | Alarm clock. |
| SIGTERM | 15 | Terminated. A gentle kill that gives processes a chance to clean up. |
| SIGUSR1 | 16 | User signal 1. |
| SIGUSR2 | 17 | User signal 2. |
| SIGCHLD | 18 | Child status changed. |
| SIGPWR | 19 | Power fail or restart. |
| SIGWINCH | 20 | Window size change. |
| SIGURG | 21 | Urgent socket condition. |
| SIGPOLL | 22 | Pollable event. |
| SIGSTOP | 23 | Stopped (signal). Pauses a process. |
| SIGTSTP | 24 | Stopped (user). |
| SIGCONT | 25 | Continued. |
| SIGTTIN | 26 | Stopped (tty input). |

| *Signal* | *Number* | *Description* |
|---|---|---|
| SIGTTOU | 27 | Stopped (tty output). |
| SIGVTALRM | 28 | Virtual timer expired. |
| SIGPROF | 29 | Profiling timer expired. |
| SIGXCPU | 30 | CPU time limit exceeded. |
| SIGXFSZ | 31 | File size limit exceeded. |
| SIGWAITING | 32 | Concurrency signal reserved by threads library. |
| SIGLWP | 33 | Inter-LWP signal reserved by threads library. |
| SIGFREEZE | 34 | Checkpoint freeze. |
| SIGTHAW | 35 | Checkpoint thaw. |
| SIGCANCEL | 36 | Cancellation signal reserved by threads library. |

In addition, you can write a signal handler in a program to respond to a signal being sent. For example, many system programs, such as the name server daemon, respond to the SIGHUP signal by rereading their configuration files. This signal can then be used to update the process while running, without having to terminate and restart the process. For many signals, however, nothing can be done other than printing an appropriate error message and terminating the process.

The `kill` command sends a terminate signal (signal 15) to the process, and the process is terminated. Signal 15, which is the default when no options are used with the `kill` command, is a gentle kill that allows a process to perform cleanup work before terminating. Signal 9, on the other hand, is called a sure, unconditional kill because it cannot be caught or ignored by a process. If the process is still around after a `kill -9`, it is either hung up in the UNIX kernel, waiting for an event such as disk I/O to complete, or you are not the owner of the process.

The `kill` command is routinely used to send signals to a process. You can kill any process you own, and superuser can kill all processes in the system except those that have process IDs 0, 1, 2, 3, and 4. The `kill` command is poorly named, because not every signal sent by it is used to kill a process. This command gets its name from its most common use—terminating a process with the `kill -15` signal.

> **NOTE** A common problem occurs when a process continually starts up new copies of itself—referred to as forking or spawning. Users have a limit on the number of new processes they can fork. This limit is set in the kernel with the MAXUP (maximum number of user processes) value. Sometimes, through user error, a process keeps forking new copies of itself until the user hits the MAXUP limit. As a user reaches this limit, the system appears to be waiting. If you kill some of the user's processes, the system resumes creating new processes on behalf of the user. It can be a no-win situation. The best way to handle these runaway processes is to send the STOP signal to suspend all processes and then send a KILL signal to terminate the processes. Because the processes were first suspended, they can't create new ones as you kill them off.

You can send a signal to a process you own with the `kill` command. Many signals are available, but you need to worry about only two right now: 9 and 15. To send a signal to a process, first use the `ps` command to find the process ID (PID) number. For example, type `ps -ef` to list all processes and find the PID of the process you want to terminate:

```
ps -ef

UID     PID  PPID  C    STIME  TTY       TIME  CMD
root      0     0  0   Nov 27  ?         0:01  sched
root      1     0  0   Nov 27  ?         0:01  /etc/init -
root      2     0  0   Nov 27  ?         0:00  pageout
root      3     0  0   Nov 27  ?        12:52  fsflush
root    101     1  0   Nov 27  ?         0:00
/usr/sbin/in.routed -q
root    298     1  0   Nov 27  ?         0:00
/usr/lib/saf/sac -t 300
root    111     1  0   Nov 27  ?         0:02
/usr/sbin/rpcbind
root    164     1  0   Nov 27  ?         0:01
/usr/sbin/syslogd -n -z 12
root    138     1  0   Nov 27  ?         0:00
/usr/sbin/inetd -s
root    113     1  0   Nov 27  ?         0:00
/usr/sbin/keyserv
root    160     1  0   Nov 27  ?         0:01
/usr/lib/autofs/automountd
.
.
.
root    439   424  0   Nov 27  ?        0:00  /bin/cat
/tmp/.removable/notify0
root   5497   433  1 09:58:02  pts/4     0:00  script psef
```

To kill the process with a PID number of 5497, type

```
kill -15 5497
```

Another way to kill a process is to use the `pkill` command. `pkill` functions identically to `pgrep`, which was described earlier, except instead of displaying information about each process, the process is terminated. A signal name or number may be specified as the first command-line option to `pkill`. The value for the signal can be any value described in Table 9.11. For example, to kill a process named `test`, issue the following command:

```
pkill -9 test
```

If no signal is specified, SIGTERM (15) is sent by default.

In addition, the CDE Process Manager, which was described earlier, can be used to kill processes. In the Process Manager window, highlight the process that you want to terminate, click Process from the toolbar at the top of the window, and then select Kill from the pull-down menu as shown in Figure 9.6.

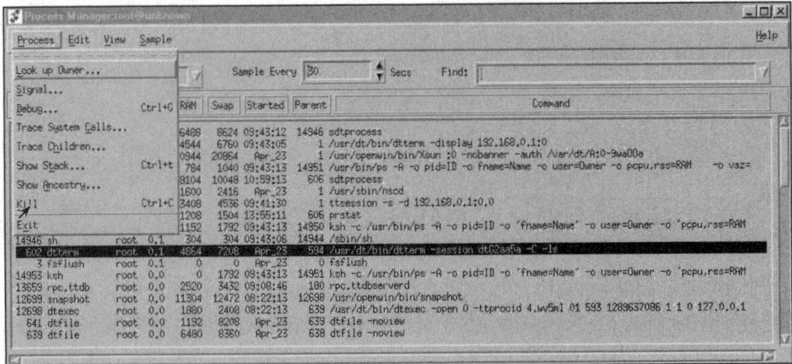


**FIGURE 9.6**
Killing processes

The equivalent UNIX command used by the Process Manager to terminate a process is

```
kill -9 <PID>
```

where *<PID>* is the process ID of the selected process.

> **NOTE**
>
> You can redefine the command performed by the Kill menu item to a different command by redefining the action labeled "Kill" in the file:
>
> `/usr/dt/appconfig/types/C/sdtprocess.dt`
>
> See Appendix B "Administration and Configuration of the CDE" for details on configuring CDE.

## Scheduling Processes

Processes compete for execution time. Scheduling, one of the key elements in a time-sharing system, determines which of the processes will execute next. Although hundreds of processes might be present on the system, only one actually uses the CPU at any given time. Time-sharing on a CPU involves suspending a process and then restarting it later. Because the suspension and resumption of active processes occurs several times each second, it appears to the user that the system is performing many tasks simultaneously.

UNIX attempts to manage the priorities of processes by giving a higher priority to those that have used the least amount of the CPU. In addition, processes that are sleeping on an event, such as a keyboard press, get higher priority than processes that are purely CPU-driven.

On any large system with a number of competing user groups, the task of managing resources falls on the system administrator. This task is both technical and political. As a system administrator, you must understand your company goals in order to manage this task successfully. When you understand the political implications of who should get priority, you are ready to manage the technical details. As root, you can change the priority of any process on the system by using the `nice` or `priocntl` command. Before you do this, you must understand how priorities work.

## Scheduling Priorities

All processes have an execution priority assigned to them—an integer value that is dynamically computed and updated on the basis of several different factors. Whenever the CPU is free, the scheduler selects the most favored process to resume executing. The process selected is the one with the lowest-priority number, because lower numbers are defined as more favored than higher ones. Multiple processes at the same priority level are placed in the run queue for that priority level. Whenever the CPU is free, the scheduler starts the processes at the head of the lowest-numbered, non-empty run queue. When the process at the top of a run queue stops executing, it goes to the end of the line, and the next process moves up to the front. After a process begins to run, it continues to execute until it needs to wait for an I/O operation to complete, receives an interrupt signal, or exhausts the maximum execution time slice defined on that system. A typical time slice is 10 milliseconds.

A UNIX process has two priority numbers associated with it. One of the priority numbers is its requested execution priority with respect to other processes. This value (its nice number) is set by the process's owner and by root; it appears in the `NI` column in a `ps -l` listing. The other priority assigned to a process is the execution priority. This priority is computed and updated dynamically by the operating system, taking into account such factors as the process's nice number, how much CPU time it has had recently, and what other processes are running and their priorities. The execution priority value appears in the `PRI` column on a `ps -l` listing.

Although the CPU is the most-watched resource on a system, it is not the only one. Memory use, disk use, I/O activity, and the number of processes all tie together in determining the computer's throughput. For example, suppose you have two groups, A and B. Both groups require large amounts of memory—more than is available when both are running simultaneously. Raising the priority of Group A over Group B might not help if Group B does not fully relinquish the memory it is using. Although the paging system will do this over time, the process of swapping a process out to disk can be intensive and can greatly reduce performance. A better alternative might be to completely stop Group B with a signal and then continue it later, when Group A has finished.

## Changing the Priority of a Time-Sharing Process with `nice`

The `nice` command is supported only for backward compatibility with previous Solaris releases. The `priocntl` command provides more flexibility in managing processes. The priority of a process is determined by the policies of its scheduling class and by its nice number. Each time-sharing process has a global priority that is calculated by adding the user-supplied priority, which can be influenced by the `nice` or `priocntl` commands and the system-calculated priority.

The execution priority number of a process is assigned by the operating system, and is determined by several factors, including its schedule class, how much CPU time it has used, and its nice number. Each time-sharing process starts with a default nice number, which it inherits from its parent process. The nice number is shown in the `NI` column of the `ps` report.

A user can lower the priority of a process by increasing its user-supplied priority number. Only the superuser can increase the priority of a process by lowering its nice value. This prevents users from increasing the priorities of their own processes, thereby monopolizing a greater share of the CPU.

In UNIX, nice numbers range from 0 to +19. The highest priority is 0. Two versions of the command are available: the standard version, `/usr/bin/nice`, and a version that is integrated into the C shell as a C shell built-in.

Use the `nice` command as described in Table 9.12 when submitting a program or command.

**TABLE 9.12**

## SETTING PRIORITIES WITH NICE

| *Command* | *Description* |
|---|---|
| ***Lowering the Priority of a Process*** | |
| `nice <command_name>` | Increases the nice number by four units (the default). |
| `nice +4 <command_name>` | Increases the nice number by four units. |
| `nice +10 <command_name>` | Increases the nice number by 10 units. |
| ***Increasing the Priority of a Process*** | |
| `nice -10 <command_name>` | Raises the priority of the command by lowering the nice number. |

As system administrator, you can use the `renice` command to change the priority of a process after it has been submitted. The `renice` command has the following form:

```
renice priority -n <value> -p <pid>
```

Use the `ps -el` command to find the PID of the process for which you want to change the priority. The process you want to change in the following example is named "largejob":

```
F S   UID   PID  PPID  C PRI NI      ADDR      SZ    WCHAN TTY     TIME  CMD
9 S     0  8200 4100  0  84 20  f0274e38    193            ?      0:00  largejob
```

Issue the following command to increase the priority of PID 8200:

```
renice -n -4 -p 8200
```

Issuing the `ps -el` command again shows the process with a higher priority:

```
F S  UID   PID  PPID  C PRI NI      ADDR    SZ    WCHAN  TTY      TIME   CMD
9 S  0     8200 4100  0 60  16   f0274e38  193            ?       0:00   largejob
```

## Changing the Scheduling Priority of Processes with `priocntl`

The standard priority scheme has been improved beginning with Solaris n as part of its support for real-time processes. Real-time processes are designed to work in applications areas in which nearly immediate response to events is required. These processes are given nearly complete access to all system resources when they are running. Solaris uses time-sharing priority numbers ranging from –20 to 20. Solaris uses the `priocntl` command, intended as an improvement over the `nice` command, to modify process priorities. To use `priocntl` to change a priority on a process, type

```
priocntl -s -p <new-priority>  -i pid <process-id>
```

where `new-priority` is the new priority for the process, and `process-id` is the PID of the process you want to change.

The following example sets the priority level for process 8200 to –5:

```
priocntl -s -p -5 -i pid 8200
```

The following example is used to set the priority (`nice` value) for every process created by a given parent process:

```
priocntl -s -p -5 -I ppid 8200
```

As a result of this command, all processes forked from process 8200 will have a priority of –5.

The priority value assigned to a process can be displayed using the `ps` command, which was described earlier in this chapter.

The functionality of the `priocntl` command goes much further than what I've described in this section, but for the certification exam, I've described what you will need to know. Consult the online manual pages for more information about the `priocntl` command.

# Using the Solaris Batch-Processing Facility

A way to divide processes on a busy system is to schedule jobs so that they run at different times. A large job, for example, could be scheduled to run at 2 a.m., when the system would normally be idle. Solaris supports two methods of batch processing: the `crontab` and `at` commands. The `crontab` command schedules multiple system events at regular intervals, and the `at` command schedules a single system event.

## Configuring Crontab

The `cron` daemon schedules system events according to commands found in each crontab file. A crontab file consists of commands, one per line, which will be executed at regular intervals. The beginning of each line contains five date and time fields that tell the `cron` daemon when to execute the command. The sixth field is the full pathname of the program you want to run. These fields, described in Table 9.13, are separated by spaces.

**TABLE 9.13**

**The Crontab File**

| *Field* | *Description* | *Values* |
|---|---|---|
| 1 | Minute | 0 to 59. An * in this field means every minute. |
| 2 | Hour | 0 to 23. An * in this field means every hour. |
| 3 | Day of month | 1 to 31. An * in this field means every day of the month. |
| 4 | Month | 1 to 12. An * in this field means every month. |
| 5 | Day of week | 0 to 6 (0 = Sunday). An * in this field means every day of the week. |
| 6 | Command | Enter the command to be run. |

Follow these guidelines when making entries in the crontab file:

- Use a space to separate fields.
- Use a comma to separate multiple values in any of the date or time fields.
- Use a hyphen to designate a range of values in any of the date or time fields.
- Use an asterisk as a wildcard to include all possible values in any of the date or time fields. For example, an asterisk (*) can be used in the time field to mean all legal values.
- Use a comment mark (#) at the beginning of a line to indicate a comment or a blank line.
- Each command within a crontab file must consist of one line, even if it is very long, because `crontab` does not recognize extra carriage returns.

The following sample `crontab` command entry displays a reminder in the user's console window at 5 p.m. on the 1st and 15th of every month:

```
0 17 1,15 * * echo Hand in Timesheet > /dev/console
```

Crontab files are found in the /var/spool/cron/crontabs directory. Several crontab files besides root are provided during the SunOS software installation process; they are also located in this directory. Other crontab files are named after the user accounts for which they are created, such as bill, glenda, miguel, or nicole. They also are located in the /var/spool/cron/crontabs directory. For example, a crontab file named root is supplied during software installation. Its contents include these command lines:

```
10  3  *  *  0,4 /etc/cron.d/logchecker
10  3  *  *  0   /usr/lib/newsyslog
15  3  *  *  0 /usr/lib/fs/nfs/nfsfind
1   2  *  *  * [ -x /usr/sbin/rtc ] && /usr/sbin/rtc -c
> /dev/null 2>&1
```

The first command line instructs the system to run `logchecker` at 3:10 a.m. on Sunday and Thursday. The second command line schedules the system to run `newsyslog` at 3:10 a.m. every Sunday. The third command line orders the system to execute `nfsfind` on

Sunday at 3:15 a.m. The fourth command line instructs the system to check for daylight savings time and make corrections if necessary. If there is no RTC time zone or no /etc/rtc_config file, this entry will do nothing.

The `cron` daemon handles the automatic scheduling of crontab commands. Its function is to check the /var/spool/cron/crontab directory every 15 minutes for the presence of crontab files. It checks for new crontab files or changes to existing ones, reads the execution times listed within the files, and submits the commands for execution at the proper times.

## Creating and Editing a Crontab File

Creating an entry in the crontab file is as easy as editing a text file using your favorite editor. Use the steps described next to edit this file; otherwise, your changes are not recognized until the next time the `cron` daemon starts up. `cron` only examines crontab configuration files during its own process initialization phase or when the `crontab` command is run. This reduces the overhead of checking for new or changed files at regularly scheduled intervals.

**NOTE** The `crontab` command chooses the system default editor, which is `ed`, unless you've set the `EDITOR` variable to /usr/bin/vi as follows:

```
EDITOR=vi;export EDITOR
```

## STEP BY STEP

### 9.1 Creating or Editing a Crontab File

1. (Optional) To create or edit a crontab file belonging to root or another user, become superuser.
2. Create a new crontab file, or edit an existing one, by typing
   ```
   crontab -e
   ```
3. Add command lines to the file, following the syntax described in Table 9.13.
4. Save the changes and exit the file. The crontab file is placed in /var/spool/cron/crontabs.
5. Verify the crontab file by typing
   ```
   crontab -l
   ```
   The system responds by listing the contents of the crontab file.

## Controlling Access to Crontab

You can control access to crontab by modifying two files in the /etc/cron.d directory: cron.deny and cron.allow. These files permit only specified users to perform crontab tasks such as creating, editing, displaying, and removing their own crontab files. The cron.deny and cron.allow files consist of a list of usernames, one per line. These access control files work together in the following manner:

- If cron.allow exists, only the users listed in this file can create, edit, display, and remove crontab files.
- If cron.allow doesn't exist, all users may submit crontab files, except for users listed in cron.deny.
- If neither cron.allow nor cron.deny exists, superuser privileges are required to run crontab.

Superuser privileges are required to edit or create cron.deny and cron.allow.

During the Solaris software installation process, a default /etc/cron.d/cron.deny file is provided. It contains the following entries:

- daemon
- bin
- smtp
- nuucp
- listen
- nobody
- noaccess

None of the users listed in the cron.deny file can access `crontab` commands. The system administrator can edit this file to add other users who will be denied access to the `crontab` command. No default cron.allow file is supplied. This means that, after the Solaris software installation, all users (except the ones listed in the default cron.deny file) can access crontab. If you create a cron.allow file, only those users can access crontab commands.

## Scheduling a Single System Event (at)

The at command is used to schedule jobs for execution at a later time. Unlike crontab, which schedules a job to happen at regular intervals, a job submitted with at executes once, at the designated time.

To submit an at job, type at. Then specify an execution time and a program to run, as shown in the following example:

```
at 07:45am today
at> who > /tmp/log
at> <Press Control-d>
job 912687240.a at Thu Jun 1 07:14:00 2000
```

When you submit an at job, it is assigned a job identification number, which becomes its filename along with the .a extension. The file is stored in the /var/spool/cron/atjobs directory. In much the same way as it schedules crontab jobs, the cron daemon controls the scheduling of at files.

The command syntax for at is

```
at -m <time> <date>
```

The at command is described in Table 9.14.

**TABLE 9.14**

**at COMMAND SYNTAX**

| *Option* | *Description* |
|---|---|
| -m | Sends you mail after the job is completed. |
| <time> | The hour when you want to schedule the job. Add am or pm if you do not specify the hours according to a 24-hour clock. midnight, noon, and now are acceptable keywords. Minutes are optional. |
| <date> | The first three or more letters of a month, a day of the week, or the keywords today or tomorrow. |

You can set up a file to control access to the at command, permitting only specified users to create, remove, or display queue information about their at jobs. The file that controls access to at is

/etc/cron.d/at.deny. It consists of a list of user names, one per line. The users listed in this file cannot access `at` commands. The default at.deny file, created during the SunOS software installation, contains the following usernames:

- daemon
- bin
- smtp
- nuucp
- listen
- nobody
- noaccess

With superuser privileges, you can edit this file to add other user names whose `at` access you want to restrict.

## Checking Jobs in Queue (`atq` and *at* `-l`)

To check your jobs that are waiting in the `at` queue, use the `atq` command. This command displays status information about the `at` jobs you created. Use the `atq` command to verify that you have created an `at` job. The `atq` command confirms that `at` jobs have been submitted to the queue, as shown in the following example:

```
atq
Rank  Execution Date        Owner   Job            Queue   Job Name
1st   Jun  1, 2000 08:00    root    912690000.a     a      stdin
2nd   Jun  1, 2000 08:05    root    912690300.a     a      stdin
```

Another way to check an `at` job is by issuing the `at -l` command. This command shows the status information on all jobs submitted by a user, as shown in this example:

```
at -l
user = root    912690000.a    Thu Jun  1 08:00:00 2000
user = root    912690300.a    Thu Jun  1 08:05:00 2000
```

## Removing and Verifying Removal of at Jobs

To remove the at job from the queue before it is executed, type

```
at -r [job-id]
```

where job-id is the identification number of the job you want to remove.

Verify that the at job is removed by using the at -l (or atq) command to display the jobs remaining in the at queue. The job whose identification number you specified should not appear. In the following example, we'll remove an at job that was scheduled to execute at 08:00 a.m. on June 1. First, check the at queue to locate the job identification number:

```
at -l
user = root    912690000.a    Thu Jun  1 08:00:00 2000
user = root    912690300.a    Thu Jun  1 08:05:00 2000
```

Next, remove the job from the at queue:

```
at -r 912690000.a
```

Finally, verify that this job has been removed from the queue:

```
at -l
user = root    912690300.a    Thu Jun  1 08:05:00 2000
```

NOTE: Syslog is covered on the Part II exam.

# SYSLOG

A critical part of the system administrator's job is monitoring the system. Solaris uses the syslog message facility to do this. syslogd is the daemon responsible for capturing system messages. The messages can be warnings, alerts, or simply informational messages. As the system administrator, you'll customize syslog to specify where and how system messages are to be saved.

The syslogd daemon receives messages from applications on the local host or from remote hosts, and directs messages to a specified log file. To each message that syslog captures, it adds a timestamp, the message type keyword at the beginning of the message, and a newline at the end of the message. For example, the following message was logged in the /var/adm/messages file:

```
May 12 06:50:36 ultra5 unix: NOTICE: alloc: /opt: file
system full
```

Syslog allows you to capture messages by facility (the part of the system that generated the message) and by level of importance. Facility is considered to be the service area generating the message or error (such as printing, email, or network), whereas the level can be considered the level of severity (such as notice, warning, error, or emergency). Syslog also allows you to forward messages to another machine so that all your messages can be logged in one location. The `syslogd` daemon reads and logs messages into a set of files described by the configuration file /etc/syslog.conf. An entry in the /etc/syslog.conf file is composed of two fields:

```
selector     action
```

The `selector` field contains a semicolon-separated list of priority specifications of this form:

```
facility.level [ ; facility.level ]
```

The `action` field indicates where to forward the message.

There are many defined facilities; they are described in Table 9.15.

**TABLE 9.15**

**RECOGNIZED VALUES FOR FACILITY**

| *Value* | *Description* |
|---|---|
| `user` | Messages generated by user processes. This is the default priority for messages from programs or facilities not listed in this file. |
| `kern` | Messages generated by the kernel. |
| `mail` | The mail system. |
| `daemon` | System daemons, such as `in.ftpd`. |
| `auth` | The authorization system, such as login, su, getty, and others. |
| `lpr` | The line printer spooling system, such as lpr, lpc, and others. |
| `news` | Reserved for the USENET network news system. |
| `uucp` | Reserved for the UUCP system. It does not currently use the syslog mechanism. |
| `cron` | The cron/at facility, such as `crontab`, `at`, `cron`, and others. |
| `local0-7` | Reserved for local use. |
| `mark` | For timestamp messages produced internally by `syslogd`. |
| `*` | An asterisk indicates all facilities except the mark facility. |

Table 9.16 lists recognized values for the syslog `level` field. They are listed in descending order of severity.

**TABLE 9.16**

**RECOGNIZED VALUES FOR `level`**

| *Value* | *Description* |
|---|---|
| `emerg` | For panic conditions that would normally be broadcast to all users. |
| `alert` | For conditions that should be corrected immediately, such as a corrupted system database. |
| `crit` | For warnings about critical conditions, such as hard device errors. |
| `err` | For other errors. |
| `warning` | For warning messages. |
| `notice` | For conditions that are not error conditions, but may require special handling. |
| `info` | Informational messages. |
| `debug` | For messages that are normally used only when debugging a program. |
| `none` | Does not send messages from the indicated facility to the selected file. For example, the entry `*.debug;mail.none` in /etc/syslog.conf will send all messages except mail messages to the selected file. |

Values for the `action` field can have one of four forms:

- A filename, beginning with a leading slash. This indicates that messages specified by the selector are to be written to the specified file. The file will be opened in append mode.
- The name of a remote host, prefixed with an @. An example is @server, which indicates that messages specified by the selector are to be forwarded to `syslogd` on the named host. The hostname "loghost" is the hostname given to the machine that will log `syslogd` messages. Every machine is "loghost" by default. This is specified in the local /etc/hosts file. It is also possible to specify one machine on a network to be "loghost" by making

the appropriate host table entries. If the local machine is designated as "loghost," `syslogd` messages are written to the appropriate files. Otherwise, they are sent to the machine "loghost" on the network.

- A comma-separated list of usernames, which indicates that messages specified by the selector are to be written to the named users if they are logged in.
- An asterisk, which indicates that messages specified by the selector are to be written to all logged-in users.

Blank lines are ignored. Lines in which the first non-whitespace character is a # are treated as comments.

All of this becomes much clearer when you look at sample entries from an /etc/syslog.conf file:

```
*.err    /dev/console
*.err;daemon,auth.notice;mail.crit    /var/adm/messages
mail.debug    /var/spool/mqueue/syslog
*.alert    root
*.emerg    *
kern.err    @server
*.alert;auth.warning    /var/log/auth
```

In this example, the first line prints all errors on the console.

The second line sends all errors, daemon and authentication system notices, and all critical errors from the mail system to the file /var/adm/messages.

The third line sends mail system debug messages to /var/spool/mqueue/syslog.

The fourth line sends all alert messages to user root.

The fifth line sends all emergency messages to all users.

The sixth line forwards kernel messages of err (error) severity or higher to the machine named server.

The last line logs all messages from the authorization system of alert level or higher in the file /var/log/auth.

The level `none` may be used to disable a facility. This is usually done in the context of eliminating messages. For example:

```
*.debug;mail.none /var/adm/messages
```

selects debug messages from all facilities except those from mail. In other words, mail messages are disabled. The mail system, sendmail, logs a number of messages. This information can be extremely large, so some system administrators disable mail messages or send them to another file that they clean out frequently. Before disabling mail messages, however, remember that sendmail messages come in very handy when you're diagnosing mail problems or tracking mail forgeries.

`syslogd` is started in the early stages of multiuser bootup from the /etc/rc2.d directory with a script called S74syslog. To restart the syslog facility, issue this:

```
/etc/rc2.d/S74syslog stop
/etc/rc2.d/S74syslog start
```

The syslog facility reads its configuration information from /etc/syslog.conf whenever it receives the HUP signal (such as `kill -HUP`). The first message is always logged by the `syslog` daemon itself when it places a timestamp on when the daemon was started.

## Other Important Files Where Information Is Logged

Solaris has many files that hold logging information. Most of these files are stored in the /var/adm directory. The following list of these log files briefly describes the information they contain:

- /var/adm/messages. The messages file holds information that prints to the console. These might include root logins and `su` attempts.
- /var/adm/lastlog. This file holds the most recent login time for each user in the system.

- /var/adm/utmpx. The utmpx database file contains user access and accounting information for commands such as `who`, `write`, and `login`. The utmpx file is where information such as the terminal line and login time are stored for access by the `who` command.
- /var/adm/wtmpx. The wtmpx file contains the history of user access and accounting information for the utmpx database. The wtmpx file keeps track of logins and logouts since reboot. The `last` command, described in Chapter 8, "System Security," reads that file and processes the information.
- /var/adm/acct. This is the system accounting file. If enabled, the accounting file records a record for every process listing the following information: the name of the user who ran the command, the name of the command, the CPU time used, the completion timestamp of the process, and a flag indicating completion status. Accounting information can be very useful in monitoring who is doing what on your system.
- /var/adm/sulog. The sulog file holds records for everyone who has used the `su` command on the system. Here is a sample:

```
SU 04/29 09:39 + console root-daemon
SU 04/29 15:29 + console root-daemon
SU 05/02 05:38 + console root-daemon
SU 05/12 06:20 + console root-daemon
SU 05/12 07:59 + pts/1 root-bcalkins
```

- /var/cron/log. Keeps a record of all cron activity.

Good system administration requires that you look over your system logs frequently and keep their size in check. Some of these files can grow extremely large and fill up a file system quickly.

## Chapter Summary

### KEY TERMS

- process
- `ps` command
- `pgrep` command
- Syslog
- crontab file
- `priocntl` command
- `nice` command
- `prstat` command
- `ps` command
- CDE Process Manager

This chapter described Solaris processes and the various Solaris utilities available to monitor them. Using commands such as `ps`, `prstat`, and `sdtprocess`, you can view all the attributes associated with a process.

The concept of sending signals to a process was described. A signal is a message sent to a process to interrupt it and cause a response. You also learned how to send signals to processes to cause a response such as terminating a process.

Setting process priorities was described. The various commands, such as `nice` and `priocntl`, which are used to set and change process priorities, were described. In addition, I described how to use the `crontab` and `at` facilities. Use these facilities to submit batch jobs and schedule processes to run when the system is less busy to reduce the demand on resources such as the CPU and disks.

Finally, I described the syslog messaging facility. `syslogd` is the daemon responsible for capturing system messages such as warnings, alerts, or informational messages. You'll monitor these messages proactively to resolve problems that may be occurring on your system.

The system administrator needs to be aware of the processes that belong to each application. As users report problems, the system administrator can quickly locate the processes being used, and look for irregularities. By keeping a close watch on system messages and processes, you'll become familiar with what is normal and what is abnormal. Don't wait for problems to happen—watch system messages and processes daily. Create shell scripts to watch processes for you and to look for irregularities in the system log files. By taking a proactive approach to system administration, you'll find problems before they affect the users.

In Chapter 10, "The LP Print Service," we'll explore another topic that you'll need to become very acquainted with—the LP Print Service, the facility responsible for all printing within the Solaris environment.

APPLY YOUR KNOWLEDGE

# Exercises

## 9.1 Displaying Process Information

In this exercise, you'll use the various utilities described in the chapter to display information about active processes.

**Estimated Time:** 10 minutes

1. Log in as root into the Common Desktop Environment (CDE).
2. Open a new window, and display the active processes using the `ps` command:

   ```
   ps -ef <cr>
   ```

3. Open another new window, and display the active processes using the `prstat` command:

   ```
   prstat <cr>
   ```

   Notice that the `ps` command took a snapshot of the active processes, but the `prstat` command continues to update its display.

4. Type `q` to exit `prstat`.
5. Display the dtlogin process and all of its child processes. First, obtain the PID of the `dtlogin` process with the `pgrep` command:

   ```
   pgrep dtlogin
   ```

   Now use the `ptree` command with the PID of the `dtlogin` process to display the ancestry tree:

   ```
   ptree 331
   ```

6. Now start the Process Manager.

   ```
   sdtprocess &
   ```

   Notice that the window updates periodically.

7. In the sample field at the top of the window, change the sample period from 30 to 5 seconds.
8. Sort the processes by ID by clicking on the ID button in the header.

## 9.2 Using Signals

In this exercise, you'll use signals to terminate a process.

**Estimated Time:** 10 minutes

1. Log in as root.
2. Find the process ID for the `sdtprocess`.

   ```
   pgrep sdtprocess
   ```

3. Kill the process.

   ```
   kill -9 <PID of sdtprocess>
   ```

4. Restart the Process Manager.

   ```
   sdtprocess &
   ```

5. Kill the `vold` process from the Process Manager.
6. Find the `vold` process by typing `vold` in the Filter field at the top of the Process Manager window.
7. Highlight the `vold` process.
8. Select Process from the toolbar at the top of the screen.
9. Select Kill from the pull-down menu.

## 9.3 Using the Batch Process

In this exercise, you'll use `crontab` to configure a process to execute everyday at a specified time.

**Estimated Time:** 10 minutes

1. Log in as root into a CDE session.
2. Open a new window and edit the `crontab` entry:

   ```
   crontab -e
   ```

## Apply Your Knowledge

3. Enter the following after the last line at the end of the file:

```
0 11 * * * echo Hand in Timesheet > \
/dev/console
```

4. Save and close the file.

   Open a console window and at 11:00 a.m., you'll see the message "Hand in Timesheet" displayed.

## Review Questions

1. Which of the following commands finds all processes that have "dt" in the process argument string? Choose all that apply.

   A. `pgrep -l -f "dt"`

   B. `ps -ef "dt"`

   C. `ps -el "dt`

   D. `ps -ef¦grep dt`

2. Which commands can be used to monitor system processes:

   A. `prstat`

   B. `psrset`

   C. `ptree`

   D. `sdtprocess`

3. Which one of the following commands kills a process named `test`?

   A. `pkill -9 test`

   B. `kill -9 test`

   C. `ps -ef¦¦grep kill¦ kill -9`

   D. `kill test`

4. Which commands display active system processes and update at a specified interval? Choose all that apply.

   A. `ps`

   B. `prstat`

   C. `sdtprocess`

   D. `ptree`

5. In output from the `ps` command, what does an "R" stand for in the S field:

   A. The process is on the run queue.

   B. The process is receiving input.

   C. It is a regular process.

   D. The process is sleeping, so it must be restarted.

6. In output from the `ps` command, which of the following does the UID field display?

   A. The parent process

   B. The process id

   C. The process owner

   D. The priority of the process

7. Which one of the following options to the `ps` command lists only processes for a particular user?

   A. `-P`

   B. `-f`

   C. `-l`

   D. `-u`

8. Which one of the following options to the `ps` command lists only processes associated with the local terminal?

## APPLY YOUR KNOWLEDGE

A. `-l`

B. `-a`

C. `-f`

D. `-t`

9. Which one of the following sends a terminate signal (signal 15) to a process with a PID of 2930?

A. kill 2930

B. stop 2930

C. Ctrl+C

D. cancel 2930

10. Which one of the following signals stops a process unconditionally?

A. 9

B. 0

C. 15

D. 1

11. Which one of the following commands is used to change the priority on a process?

A. `nice`

B. `priocntl`

C. `ps`

D. `hup`

12. Which one of the following commands is issued to increase the priority of PID 8200?

A. `renice -n -4 -p 8200`

B. `nice -n -4 -p 8200`

C. `nice -i 8200`

D. `renice -I -p 8200`

13. Which utilities can be used to show the process ancestry tree? Choose all that apply.

A. `ps`

B. `ptree`

C. `sdtprocess`

D. `prstat`

15. Which two of the following commands schedules a command to run once at a given time?

A. `crontab`

B. `priocntl`

C. `at`

D. `cron`

16. Which one of the following commands shows the jobs queued up by the `at` command?

A. `atq`

B. `at -l`

C. `ps`

D. `crontab`

17. Which one of the following crontab entries instructs the system to run logchecker at 3:10 on Sunday and Thursday nights?

A. 0 4 * * 10,3 /etc/cron.d/logchecker

B. 10 3 * * 0,4 /etc/cron.d/logchecker

C. * 10 3 0,4 /etc/cron.d/logchecker

D. 10 3 * * 0-4 /etc/cron.d/logchecker

## Apply Your Knowledge

18. Which one of the following is the daemon responsible for capturing system messages?

    A. `syslogd`

    B. `messaged`

    C. `init`

    D. `msgd`

19. Which one of the following is the line in the /etc/syslog.conf file that sends all alert messages to user root?

    A. *.alert root

    B. alert root

    C. root *.alert

    D. *.emerg root

20. Which one of the following logs keeps a record of all cron activity?

    A. /var/cron/log

    B. /var/spool/cron/log

    C. /var/adm/cron

    D. /var/adm/messages

21. At which run level is the syslog daemon started?

    A. 2

    B. 1

    C. 3

    D. It runs at all run levels.

22. Which one of the following files holds the most recent login time for each user in the system?

    A. /var/adm/lastlog

    B. /var/adm/messages

    C. /var/adm/acct

    D. /var/adm/utmpx

23. A user wants to execute a command later today, after leaving work. Which one of the following commands will allow him to do this?

    A. `runat`

    B. `at`

    C. `submit`

    D. None of the above

## Answers to Review Questions

1. **A., D.** Use the `pgrep` and `ps` commands to view processes running on your system. The commands `pgrep -l -f "dt"` and `ps -ef¦grep dt` find all the processes that have "dt" in the process argument string and display them.

2. **D.** New in Solaris 8 is CDE Process Manager, `sdtprocess`, a graphical Common Desktop Environment (CDE) tool that provides a process manager window for monitoring and controlling system processes.

3. **A.** The command `pkill -9 test` kills a process named test.

4. **B., C.** The `prstat` and `sdtprocess` commands display active system processes, and can be configured to update at a specified interval.

5. **A.** In output from the `ps` command, the "R" in the "S" field means that the process is on the run queue.

6. **C.** In output from the `ps` command, the UID field displays the process owner.

## APPLY YOUR KNOWLEDGE

7. **D.** The `-u` option to the `ps` command lists only processes for a particular user.

8. **B.** The `-a` option to the `ps` command lists only processes associated with the local terminal.

9. **A.** The command `kill 2930` sends a terminate signal (signal 15) to a process with a PID of 2930.

10. **A.** Signal 9 stops a process unconditionally.

11. **A., B.** The commands `nice` and `priocntl` are used to change the priority on a process.

12. **A.** The `renice -n -4 -p 8200` command is issued to increase the priority of a process with a PID of 8200.

13. **B., C.** The utilities `ptree` and `sdtprocess` are used to show the process ancestry tree.

14. **C.** The `at` command schedules a command to run once at a given time.

15. **A., B.** The `atq` and `at -l` commands show the jobs queued up by the `at` command.

16. **B.** The crontab entry 10 3 * * 0,4 /etc/cron.d/logchecker instructs the system to run logchecker at 3:10 on Sunday and Thursday nights.

17. **A.** The `syslogd` is the daemon responsible for capturing system messages.

18. **A.** The entry `*.alert  root` in the /etc/syslog.conf file, tells `syslogd` to send all alert messages to user root.

19. **A.** The log file named /var/cron/log keeps a record of all `cron` activity.

20. **A.** The `syslog` daemon is started at run level 2.

21. **A.** The file /var/adm/lastlog holds the most recent login time for each user in the system.

22. **B.** Use the `at` command to execute a command or script at a later time.

## OBJECTIVES

The following are the test objectives for this chapter.

**Understand the Solaris LP print service**

- Setting up and administering printers in Solaris requires an understanding of the print spooler, the print daemons, and the printer configuration files. Each of these will be described in this chapter.

**Manage printers**

- Managing printers in Solaris 8 involves using several utilities and commands. These commonly used utilities and commands will be described in this chapter.

CHAPTER 10

# LP Print Service

# OUTLINE

## STUDY STRATEGIES

The following strategies will help you prepare for the test:

- In this chapter, you'll notice that I don't show many lengthy step-by-step procedures, but I do introduce several commands used to manage printers, along with examples on how to use the commands. Practice the step-by-steps as well as the commands, and make sure that you understand where and when to use them.
- Pay close attention to the differences between the SVR4 and the BSD style print services.
- Make sure that you understand the difference between a print server and a print client. Understand the differences between local and networked printers, and pay close attention to the various configuration files that are used to define a printer.

## Introduction

Printers are a standard peripheral for any computer system. One of the first devices added to any new system is a printer. The multiuser nature of the Solaris operating environment means that the Solaris printer software is more complex than that of a single-user operating system. This means that adding a printer to a Solaris system requires more than just plugging it in.

This chapter describes how to set up local printers, set up access to remote printers, and perform some printer administration tasks by using the Admintool GUI or the command line. Most of the system administrator's needs for setting up printing services, adding printers to servers, or adding access from print clients to remote printers on print servers should be met by Admintool. Setting up a printer from the command line can be a complex task. This chapter examines the hardware issues involved in connecting a printer to a Solaris system before moving on to examine the more complex part of the process—configuring the software.

## The Solaris Print Service

The Solaris print service is a default cluster that is installed when the operating system is initially installed. To verify that the package is installed, look for the following software packages by issuing the `pkginfo` command that was described in Chapter 4, "Software Package Administration."

| | |
|---|---|
| SUNWlpmsg | ToolTalk programs for passing printer alerts. |
| SUNWfdl | Solaris Desktop Font Downloader for Adobe PostScript printers. |
| SUNWscplp | SunSoft Print-Source Compatibility, (Usr). Print utilities for user interface and source build compatibility with SunOS 4.x. |
| SUNWslpr | root (/) file system portion of the Service Location Protocol (SLP) framework; includes the SLP configuration file and start scripts for the SLP daemon. |

| | |
|---|---|
| SUNWslpu | usr file system portion of the Service Location Protocol (SLP) framework. |
| SUNWslpx | Service Location Protocol (SLP) 64-bit developer libraries. |
| SUNWmp | MP (make pretty) Print Filter. |
| SUNWpcr | Client configuration files and utilities for the print service. |
| SUNWpcu | Client configuration files and utilities for the print service. |

> **NOTE** The Service Location Protocol (SLP) is an Internet Engineering Task Force (IETF) protocol for discovering shared resources (such as printers, file servers, networked cameras, and so on) in an enterprise network. The Solaris 8 operating environment contains a full implementation of SLP that includes APIs that enable developers to write SLP-enabled applications; it also provides system administrators with a framework for ease of network extensibility.

Setting up a Solaris printer involves setting up the spooler, the print daemon, and the hardware (the printer and the printer port). The system administrator needs to verify that the computer has at least 8MB of disk space available for /var/spool/lp. Print files will be sent to this location to prepare them for printing. Other configuration files are created, but Solaris takes care of that part for you. When setting up a printer, Solaris makes the appropriate changes in the system's /etc/printers.conf file and the /etc/lp directory as required.

## LP Print Service Directories

The LP print service includes the following directory structure, files, and logs:

- /usr/bin. This directory contains the LP print service user commands.
- /usr/sbin. This directory contains the LP print service administrative commands.
- /usr/share/lib/terminfo. This directory contains the terminfo database, which describes the capabilities of devices, such as printers and terminals. The terminfo database is discussed later in this chapter.
- /usr/lib/lp. This directory contains the LP print service daemons, binary files used by the print service, PostScript filters, and default printer interface programs.

- /usr/lib/lp/postscript. This directory contains all the PostScript filter programs that the Solaris LP print service provides. Print filters are used to convert the content of the print request to a format accepted by the destination printer.
- /etc/lp. This directory contains the LP service configuration files. These files are edited using the print service configuration tools described later in this chapter.
- /etc/lp/interfaces. This directory contains each printer interface program file. Entries in this directory are specific for each printer installed on the system.
- /etc/lp/printers. In this directory are subdirectories for each local printer attached to the system. Each subdirectory contains configuration information and alert files for each printer.
- /var/spool/lp. All current print requests are stored here until they are printed.
- /var/lp/logs. This directory contains a history log of print requests.

## The Print Spooler

Spool stands for Simultaneous Peripheral Operations OnLine. The spooler is also referred to as the queue. Users execute the print spooler `lp` program when they want to print something. The print spooler then takes what the user wants to print and places it in the predefined /var/spool/lp print spooling directory.

Spooling space is the amount of disk space used to store and process requests in the print queue. The size of the /var directory depends on the size of the disk and how the disk is partitioned. If /var is not created as a separate partition, the /var directory uses some root partition space, which is likely to be quite small. A large spool directory could consume 600MB of disk space. Look at the size and partitioning of the disks available on systems that could be designated as print servers.

When connecting printers, first carefully evaluate the users' printing needs and usage patterns. If users typically print only short ASCII files without sophisticated formatting requirements, a print server with 20–25MB of disk space allocated to /var is probably sufficient. However, if many users are printing lengthy PostScript files, they will probably fill up the spooling space quite frequently. When /var fills up and users cannot queue their jobs for printing, workflow is interrupted. The size of /var is set when the operating system is loaded and disks are partitioned.

> **CAUTION** Some print jobs consume large amounts of disk space. In fact, one of my clients had a report that consumed more than 800MB when it was spooled to the printer. When /var runs out of disk space, many system functions cannot continue, such as printing, message logging, and mail. Make sure you provide adequate space in /var when setting up your system.

For SunOS users, the SVR4 `lp` program is equivalent to the BSD `lpr` print program. In SunOS, the print spooler is located in /usr/spool. When Sun switched from SunOS 4.x (which was based on BSD UNIX) to SunOS 5.x (which is based on SVR4 UNIX), print systems between BSD and SVR4 were quite different. Throughout this chapter, I'll make reference to the BSD print system for system administrators who might be familiar with it. The BSD printing protocol is an industry standard. It is widely used and provides compatibility between different types of systems from various manufacturers. For sites that have a mix of BSD and SVR4 UNIX, Sun has provided compatibility for both print systems in Solaris.

## The LP Print Daemons

The /usr/lib/`lpsched` daemon is the UNIX utility responsible for scheduling and printing in Solaris 8. Sometimes this is referred to as the `lp` daemon. The `lpsched` print daemon is the UNIX process responsible for taking output from the spooling directory and sending it to the correct printer. `lpsched` also tracks the status of printers and filters on the print server. Again, for SunOS users, `lpsched` is equivalent to `lpd` in BSD UNIX.

> **NOTE** /usr/lp/lpsched is actually a soft link to the binary named /usr/lib/lp/lpsched.

The /usr/sbin/`inetd` daemon is started at bootup and listens for service requests on all the ports associated with each of the services listed in its configuration file /etc/inetd.conf, which was described in Chapter 8, "System Security". When a request arrives, `inetd` executes the server program associated with the service.

The /usr/lib/print/`in.lpd` daemon is started by `inetd` and implements the network listening service for the print protocol. When `inetd` receives a print request, `in.lpd` is started to service the connection. The `in.lpd` daemon exits after the request has been serviced.

Many methods can be used to define a printer on a Solaris system. Table 10.1 describes the tools Solaris provides for adding printers.

**TABLE 10.1**

**SOLARIS PRINTER UTILITIES**

| *Utility* | *Description* |
|---|---|
| SunSoft Print Client Software | An interface that was previously available only with the Solstice AdminSuite set of administration tools. It is now available as part of the standard Solaris distribution software and is used to set up print clients. |
| Admintool | A graphical user interface used to create, modify, and delete printers on a local system. This is the recommended way for novice users to add printers. |
| Solstice Print Manager | A graphical user Print Manager interface used to manage printers in a name service environment. Available only with the Solaris 8 server software distribution. |
| LP Print Service Commands | The command-line utilities used to set up and manage printers. These commands provide complete functionality; Admintool and the AdminSuite packages are somewhat limited for advanced tasks. |

# SETTING UP THE HARDWARE

Connecting printers to a UNIX system is no one's favorite activity because it can quickly become a time-consuming task. Many printers are on the market, each with a slightly different interface. When connecting a printer locally to a Sun system, you have one of three options:

- An Ethernet connection
- A parallel connection
- A serial connection

The type of connection depends on the connectivity options available on the printer. If the printer supports the option, an Ethernet connection will be the best. If Ethernet connectivity is not an option, a parallel connection is the preferred method. Most, if not all, printers have a parallel port. If no parallel option exists, the final choice is a serial connection.

## Ethernet Connection

Many new printers provide an option to add an Ethernet interface. A printer with an Ethernet connection is referred to as a network printer. A network printer is a hardware device that provides printing services to print clients without being directly cabled to a print server. It is a print server with its own system name and IP address and is connected directly to the network. The Ethernet interface might be internal or external to the printer. Using an Ethernet interface to install a printer is recommended because of its speed.

## Parallel Connection

Most printers, with a few rare exceptions, have a parallel interface. A parallel interface can have a tremendous advantage over a serial interface, especially if it uses a Centronics interface. The Centronics interface completely defines all wires used in the parallel connection between the printer and the computer. Simply connect the printer to the back of the Sun system by using a Centronics parallel cable. Some Sun systems do not have a DB25 parallel connector, and require a special cable from Sun. Other older Sun systems do not have a parallel interface, so you must add one by purchasing an SBUS parallel interface from Sun.

## Serial Connection

Some printers support both parallel and serial connections. Sometimes, a printer is connected via the serial interface because the Sun station does not have an available parallel interface. Connecting a device using a serial interface requires a thorough understanding of serial transmission. This method of connecting a printer is the most difficult because of the complexity in establishing the proper "handshake," or means of communication, between the computer and the printer.

## SETTING UP THE SOFTWARE

For network printers, use the vendor's software to configure the operating system. After you have completed the vendor software installation, you don't need a further software configuration. You must obtain software from the printer manufacturer to install the printer on your system. Most are easy to configure. The HP Jetdirect print server is the most popular, but it is by no means the only print server available.

> **CAUTION**
>
> Don't use Admintool or Print Manager to add, modify, or delete a network-based printer that is connected directly to the Ethernet with its own network interface card. You won't damage anything, but your printer will not be recognized by the system, even though the printer might appear in the printer tool window. Always use the manufacturer-supplied software to manage the printer.

The first step is to connect the print server to the network and set the IP address. This process varies on print servers, so follow the manufacturer's guidelines on how to do this. Next, install the print server software and follow the manufacturer's guidelines for configuring the printer. The vendor's software configures everything; no additional software configuration is required.

For printers that have a parallel or serial connection, you must use the Solaris tools to configure the operating system to recognize the printer.

### BSD Versus SVR4 Printing Software

The software that drives the UNIX printing process is an area in which the two UNIX versions, BSD and SVR4, are similar and yet different. The two print systems are similar in that both are based on the concept of spooling. Both SVR4 and BSD print services support the concept of an interface program, which acts as a filter through which all output sent to the printer is passed. The following are some sample uses of an interface program:

- Adding a banner page. Most UNIX systems automatically add a banner page to the front of a print job. The purpose of the page is to identify the owner of the printer output.

- Adding or removing a line-feed character. UNIX uses just the line-feed character to separate lines. The first problem you might encounter when testing a printer is that the text comes out in a stair-step manner. Most printers have a carriage return/line feed and auto line-feed dip switch that controls what the printer will use. The stair-step problem can be fixed by modifying the interface program that performs the necessary translation on all output going to the printer or by setting the printer's dip switch to the setting recommended by the hardware manufacturer.

The differences between BSD and SVR4 are in the configuration files and the spooling directories, which the Solaris operating environment configured automatically. Differences also exist in the way that the `lpsched` daemon handles print jobs as compared to the `lpd` daemon in BSD.

## BSD Print Service

Each printer connected to a BSD system must have its own spooling directory that is serviced by one `lpd` daemon. The spool directories are located in the /var/spool/lpd directory. Each printer has its own `lpd` daemon. In BSD, `lpd` accesses the file /etc/printcap for any information it requires concerning the printer. The printcap file is the system's printer database file that stores all the necessary information about all printers connected to the system. To use a printer, that printer must have an entry in the /etc/printcap file. The `lpr` function is BSD's equivalent to `lp` under SVR4. If users want to print something, they use the `lpr` command, which sends the necessary information to a specified spooling directory.

## SVR4 Print Service

In SVR4, one `lpsched` daemon services all printers. The `lpsched` daemon is continually running and provides the "power" for the print service. Only one instance of `lpsched` should be running at any one time.

The LP print service performs the following functions:

- Administers files and schedules local print requests
- Receives and schedules network requests

- Filters files (if necessary) so that they print properly
- Starts programs that interface with the printers
- Tracks the status of jobs
- Tracks forms mounted on the printer
- Tracks print wheels currently mounted
- Delivers alerts to mount new forms or different print wheels
- Delivers alerts about printing problems

Most of the LP configuration files are located in the /var/spool/lp directory, except for the interface files, which are located in the /etc/lp/interfaces directory. A SCHEDLOCK file should be in /var/spool/lp that is responsible for ensuring that only one instance of `lpsched` runs. You use the `lpadmin` command to add, configure, and delete printers from the system.

Information about printers can be found in the /etc/printers.conf file and files located in the /etc/lp directory. Solaris Admintool provides a graphical interface to many of the `lp` commands listed in Table 10.2.

**TABLE 10.2**

**SOLARIS lp COMMANDS**

| *Command* | *Description* |
|---|---|
| `accept/reject` | Enables or disables any further requests for a printer or class entering the spooling area. |
| `cancel` | Lets the user stop the printing of information |
| `enable/disable` | Enables or disables more output from the spooler to the printer |
| `lp` | The user's print command. Places information to be printed into the spooler |
| `lpadmin` | Allows the configuration of the print service |
| `lpmove` | Moves print requests between destinations |
| `lpsched` | Starts the print service |
| `lpshut` | Stops the print service |
| `lpstat` | Displays the status of the print service |

Although Solaris uses the SVR4 print model, it still supports BSD-style printing to provide interoperability. The widely used BSD printing protocol provides compatibility between different types of systems from various manufacturers.

## Print Server Versus Print Client

The print server is a system that has a local printer connected to it and makes the printer available to other systems on the network. The print client is a remote system that can send print requests to a print server. A system becomes a print client when you install the print client software and enable access to remote printers on the system. Any networked system with a printer can be a print server, as long as the system has adequate resources to manage the printing load.

The print client issues print commands that allow it to initiate print requests. The `print` command locates a printer and printer configuration information.

When a print job is sent from the print client, the user issues either the SVR4-style `lp` command or the BSD-style `lpr` command. Any one of the styles shown in Table 10.3 can be used.

**TABLE 10.3**

**VALID PRINT STYLES**

| *Style* | *Description* |
|---|---|
| Atomic | The `print` command and option followed by the printer name or class. For example: `lp -d neptune filename` |
| POSIX | The `print` command and option followed by server:printer. For example: `lpr -P galaxy:neptune filename` |
| Context | Defined in the Federated Naming Service Programming Guide. For example: `lpr -d thisdept/service/printer/printer-name filename` |

If the user doesn't specify a printer name or class in a valid style, the command checks the user's `PRINTER` or `LPDEST` environment variable for a default printer name. These variables can be set in the user's startup file to specify a default printer to use. If neither environment variable for the default printer is defined, the command checks the .printers file in the user's home directory for the default printer alias. If the command does not find a default printer alias in the .printers file, it then checks the print client's /etc/printers.conf file for configuration information. If the printer is not found in the /etc/printers.conf file, the command checks the name service (NIS or NIS+), if any.

## Configuring Software for a Solaris Printer

> **NOTE**
>
> If you're sitting at systemA and you want to connect a printer to systemB, you don't need to get into your car and drive to that location to run Admintool on systemB. From systemA, simply rlogin to systemB and type the following:
>
> ```
> admintool -display systemA:0.0
> ```
>
> SystemB's Admintool should now be displayed on systemA just as if you were sitting at systemB.

The print client software and the Printer Manager application offer a graphical solution for setting up and managing printers in a networked environment. The advantage of the Printer Manager software is that it supports a name service (NIS or NIS+) that lets you centralize print administration for a network. If you're using a name service, Solaris Printer Manager is the preferred method for managing printer configuration information. Using a name service for storing printer configuration information is desirable because it makes printer information available to all systems on the network, making printing administration easier. You can also use the `lpadmin` command on the command line to configure printers on individual systems. Admintool provides an alternative method for installing printers in the Solaris environment. It provides a graphical interface to the `lp` commands listed in Table 10.2. This section describes how to use Admintool to set up the printer software.

You must run Admintool on the system to which you have attached the printer because it doesn't allow you to make changes to a remote system. When setting up a printer, Admintool makes the appropriate changes in the system's /etc/printers.conf file and /etc/lp directory.

## STEP BY STEP

### 10.1 Configuring a Printer Using Admintool

Follow these steps to configure a printer by using Admintool:

1. Type `admintool` to bring up the Admintool menu. The Admintool window appears.
2. Select Browse, Printers, as shown in Figure 10.1.

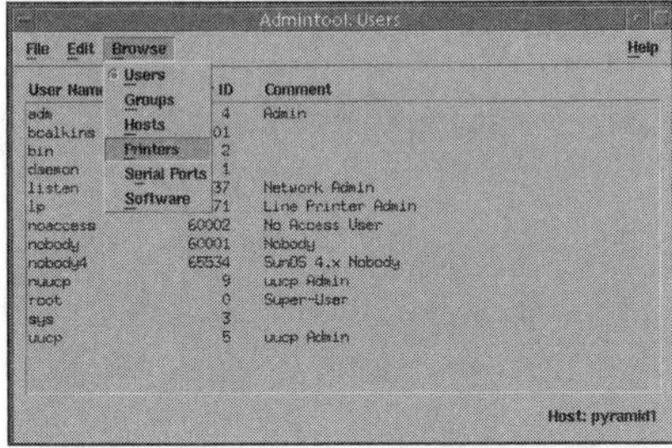


**FIGURE 10.1**
Selecting printers with Admintool.

The Printers configuration window, shown in Figure 10.2, appears. Existing printers are displayed.

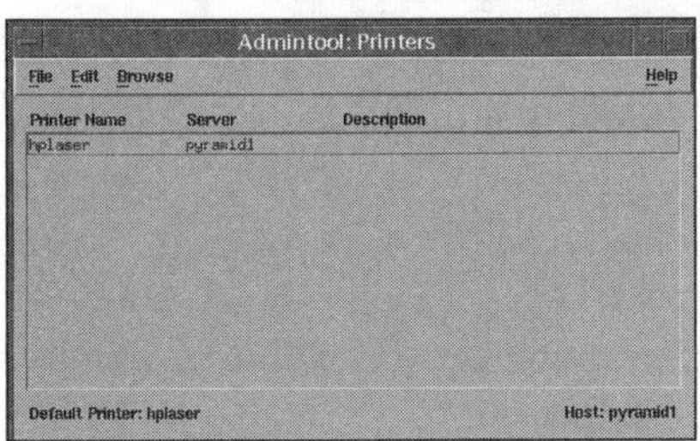


**FIGURE 10.2**
The Printers configuration window.

3. Choose Edit, Add.
4. If you're configuring a print client and the print server is located across the network, physically connected to another system, select Access to Printer from the pull-down menu. The Add Access to Printer window appears, as shown in Figure 10.3.

*continues*

*continued*

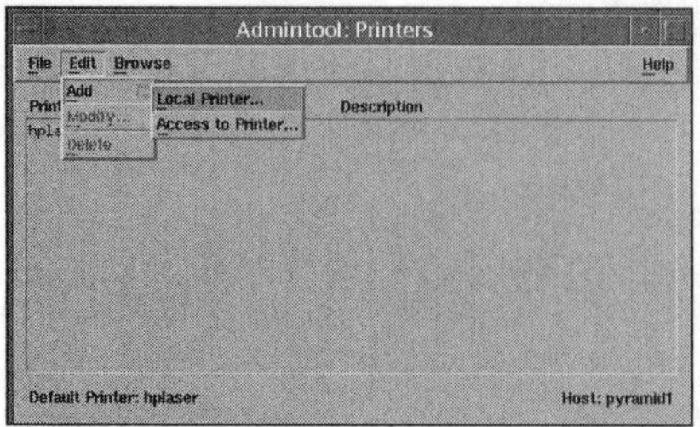


**FIGURE 10.3**
Printers window pop-up menu.

The Add Access to Printer window appears, as shown in Figure 10.4.

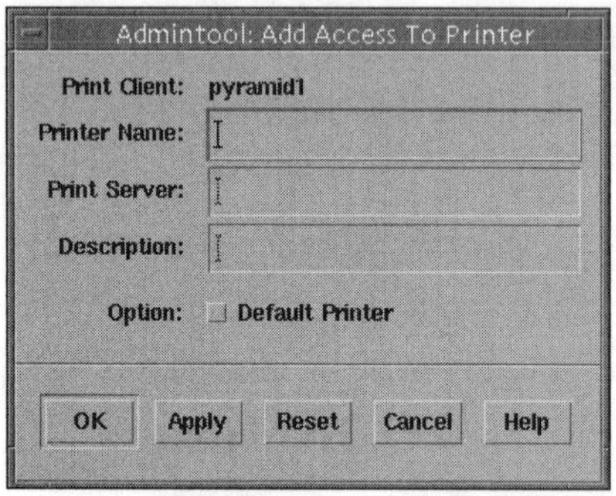

Admintool: Add Access To Printer
Print Client: pyramid1
Printer Name:
Print Server:
Description:
Option: Default Printer
OK Apply Reset Cancel Help

**FIGURE 10.4**
The Add Access to Printer window.

5. Fill in the information in the window as follows:
   - Printer Name. Enter the name of the printer on the remote system you want to access.
   - Print Server. Enter the name of the system to which the printer is connected.
   - Description. If you want to, enter a brief description of the printer.
   - Option. Check this option if you want to make this the system default printer.
6. Click the OK button. The window closes, and the information is added to the appropriate LP print system files.
7. If you're configuring a print server and the printer will be connected to the local system, select Local Printer from the pop-up menu shown in Figure 10.3. The window shown in Figure 10.5 is displayed.

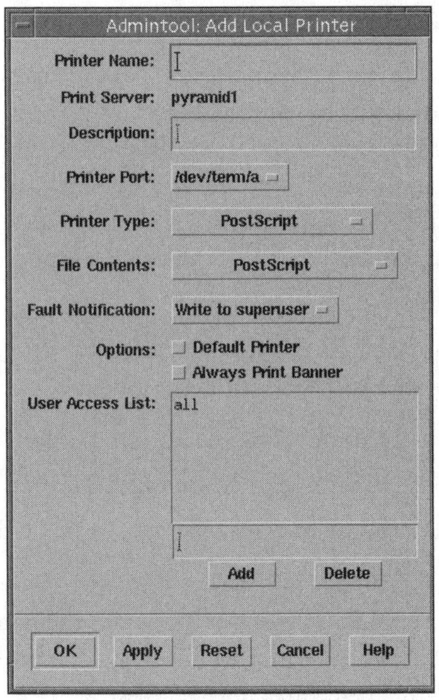


**FIGURE 10.5**
The Add Local Printer window.

**8.** Fill in the fields as follows:

- Printer Name. Enter the name you want to call this printer.
- Description. If you want to, enter a brief description of the printer.
- Printer Port. Click the button and select the port to which the printer is connected:

  /dev/term/a is serial port A.

  /dev/term/b is serial port B.

  /dev/bpp0 is the parallel port.

  Select Other if you've connected an SBUS card with another device name.

- Printer Type. Click the button to select the printer type that matches your printer. The printer types here corresponds to printers listed in the /usr/share/lib/terminfo directory. The printer type you select must correspond to an entry in the terminfo database. UNIX works best

*continues*

NOTE

One printer can be identified as the default printer for the system. If a user does not specify a printer when printing, the job will go to the default printer.

*continued*

with PostScript printers because page formatting of text and graphics from within CDE is for a PostScript printer. If you want to select a PostScript printer, your printer must be able to support PostScript. If you're using an HP LaserJet printer, choose HPLaserJet as the print type unless your LaserJet printer supports PostScript.

- File Contents. Click the button to select the format of the files that will be sent to the printer.
- Fault Notification. Click the button to select how to notify the superuser in case of a printer error.
- Options. Choose to print a banner, or make this the default printer.
- User Access List. If you want to, enter the names of the systems allowed to print to this printer. If nothing is entered, all clients are allowed access.

9. After filling in all the fields, click the OK button. The window closes, and the new printer name appears in the Printers window, shown in Figure 10.2.

## Using a Printer Not Listed on the Printer Types Menu

Printer types listed in the Print Manager window correspond to printers listed in the /usr/share/lib/terminfo directory. If a printer type is not available for the type of printer you are adding, you might need to add an entry in the /usr/share/lib/terminfo database. Each printer is identified in the terminfo database by a short name; for example, an HP LaserJet printer is listed under the /usr/share/lib/terminfo/h directory as HPLaserJet. The entries for PostScript printers are in /usr/share/lib/terminfo/P. The name found in the directory is the printer type you specify when setting up a printer.

If you cannot find a terminfo entry for your printer, you can try selecting a similar type of printer; however, you might have trouble keeping the printer set in the correct modes for each print request. If no terminfo entry exists for your type of printer, and you want to keep the printer set in the correct modes, you can either customize the interface program used with the printer or add an entry to the terminfo database. You'll find the printer interface program located under the /etc/lp/interfaces directory. Editing an interface file or adding an entry to the terminfo database is beyond the scope of this *Training Guide*. A printer entry in the terminfo database contains and defines hundreds of items. Refer to the Solaris 8 System Administration Guide, Volume II in the Answerbook2 online manuals for information on performing this task. Another good reference on this topic is John Strang and Tim O'Reilly's book "termcap & terminfo" published by O'Reilly & Associates, Inc. (ISBN: 0937175226).

# ADMINISTERING PRINTERS

Managing the print system involves monitoring the `lp` system and uncovering reasons why it might not be working properly. Other routine tasks involve canceling print jobs and enabling or disabling a printer while it's being serviced. This section provides instructions for the daily tasks you will perform to manage printers and the print scheduler. All of the following commands require superuser access.

## Deleting Printers and Managing Printer Access

Use Admintool to delete a printer from the system. In the Print Manager window of Admintool, highlight the printer you want to delete and select Edit, Delete, as shown in Figure 10.6. The printer queue will be deleted from the system.

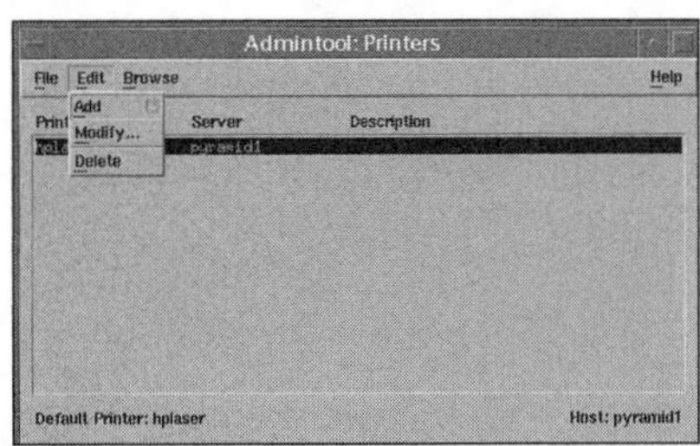


**FIGURE 10.6**
Deleting a printer.

To delete a printer at the command line, issue the following command on the system where the printer is connected:

```
lpadmin -x <printer-name>
```

The printer is deleted from the system.

Perhaps you do not want to remove the printer from the print server, but you want to keep a particular system from printing to the print server. Issue the following command on the print client from which you want to delete the printer:

```
lpsystem -r <print-server>
```

The print server is deleted from the print client's /etc/lp/Systems file.

Perhaps a printer will be going offline for repairs. To stop accepting print requests on a particular printer, type the following command on the system where the printer is physically connected:

```
reject <printer-name>
```

This step prevents any new requests from entering the printer's queue while you are in the process of removing the printer.

To allow a printer to keep taking requests, but to stop the printer from printing the requests, type the following command on the system where the printer is physically connected:

```
disable <printer-name>
```

When stopping or disabling a printer, you might need to move existing jobs that have been queued to that printer. To move print jobs from one printer to another, use the `lpmove` command as follows:

```
lpmove <printer1> < printer2>
```

The arguments for the `lpmove` command are described in Table 10.4.

**TABLE 10.4**

**lpmove ARGUMENTS**

| *Argument* | *Description* |
|---|---|
| <printer1> | The name of the printer from which all print requests will be moved. |
| <printer2> | The name of the printer to which all print requests will be moved. |

If you move all the print requests to another printer, the `lpmove` command automatically stops accepting print requests for printer1. This next step is necessary if you want to begin accepting new print requests for the printer:

```
accept printer1
```

In the following example, the `lpmove` command moves print requests from the printer eps1 to the printer eps2, for example, when eps1 is being taken down for maintenance. After the printer is ready to start accepting print jobs again, use the `accept` command to resume accepting print requests on eps1:

```
lpmove eps1 eps2
accept eps1
```

## Creating Printer Classes

You can put several locally attached printers into a group called a printer class. This might be helpful if you have several printers sitting next to each other, and it doesn't matter which printer your job goes to. When you have set up a printer class, users can then specify the class (rather than individual printers) as the destination for a print request. The first printer in the class that is free to print is used. The result is faster turnaround because all printers are utilized. You create printer classes with the `lpadmin` command as follows:

```
lpadmin -c
```

No default printer classes are known to the print service; printer classes exist only if you define them. Following are three ways you can define printer classes:

- By printer type (for example, PostScript)
- By location (for example, 5th floor)
- By work group or department (for example, Accounting)

Alternatively, a class might contain several printers that are used in a particular order. The LP print service always checks for an available printer in the order in which printers were added to a class. Therefore, if you want a high-speed printer to be accessed first, you would add it to the class before you add a low-speed printer. As a result, the high-speed printer would handle as many print requests as possible. The low-speed printer would be reserved as a backup printer when the high-speed printer was in use.

Printer class names must be unique and can contain a maximum of 14 alphanumeric characters and underscores. You are not obligated to define printer classes. You should add them only if you determine that using printer classes would benefit the users on the network.

## STEP BY STEP

### 10.2 Defining Printer Classes

To define a printer class, follow these steps:

1. Log in as superuser or `lp` on the print server.
2. Define a class of printers by using the `lpadmin` command:
   `lpadmin -p <printer-name> -c <printer-class>`

The arguments for `lpadmin` are described in Table 10.5.

**TABLE 10.5**

**`lpadmin` ARGUMENTS**

| *Argument* | *Description* |
|---|---|
| `-p <printer-name>` | The name of the printer you are adding to a class of printers |
| `-c <printer-class>` | The name of a class of printers |

The specified printer is added to the end of the list in the class in the print server's /etc/lp/classes/<printer-class> file. If the printer class does not exist, it is created. Verify the printers in a printer class by using the `lpstat` command:

```
lpstat -c printer-class
```

In the following example, the command adds the printer luna to the class roughdrafts:

```
lpadmin -p luna -c roughdrafts
```

## Checking Printer Status

The lpstat command is used to verify the status of a printer. You can use this command to determine which printers are available for use or to examine the characteristics of a particular printer. The lpstat command syntax is as follows:

```
lpstat [-d] [-p <printer-name> [-D] [-l]] [-t]
```

The lpstat command options are described in Table 10.6.

**TABLE 10.6**

**lpstat Command Syntax and Options**

| *Option* | *Description* | |
|---|---|---|
| -a | Reports whether printers are accepting requests. You can also specify a specific list of printers, as shown in the example lpstat -a eps1 eps2 eps3. | |
| -d | Shows the system's default printer. | |
| -p <printer-name> | Shows whether a printer is active or idle, when it was enabled or disabled, and whether it is accepting print requests. You can specify multiple printer names with this command. Use a space or a comma to separate printer names. If you use spaces, enclose the list of printer names in quotes. If you don't specify the printer name, the status of all printers is displayed. | |
| -D | Shows the description of the specified printer. | |
| -l | Shows the characteristics of the specified printer. | |
| -t | Shows status information about the LP print service, including the status of all printers—whether they are active and whether they are accepting print requests. | |
| -u <logon-IDs> | Print the status of output requests for users, in which <logon-IDs> can be one or all of the following: | |
| | <user> | A user on the local system, as shown in the example lpstat -u bcalkins |
| | <host!user> | A user on a system, as shown in the example lpstat -u systema!bcalkins |
| | <host!all> | All users on a particular system, as shown in the example lpstat -u systema!all |
| | <all!user> | A particular user on all systems, as shown in the example lpstat -u all!bcalkins |
| | all | All users on all systems specified as follows: lpstat -u all |

Following are a few examples of the `lpstat` command:

```
lpstat -p hplaser
```

The system responds with this:

```
printer hplaser is idle. enabled since Jun 16 10:09 1998.
available.
```

In the following example, the command requests a description of the printers hplaser1 and hplaser2:

```
lpstat -p "hplaser1 hplaser2" -D
printer hplaser1 faulted. enabled since Jun 16 10:09 1998.
available.
unable to print: paper misfeed jam

Description: Printer by finance.
printer hplaser2 is idle. enabled since Jun 16 10:09 1998.
available.
Description: Printer in computer room.
```

In the following example, the command requests the characteristics of the printer hplaser:

```
lpstat -p hplaser -l
 printer hplaser is idle. enabled since Jun 16 10:11 1998.
 available.
  Content types: any
  Printer types: unknown
  Description: Printer by computer room.
  Users allowed:
   (all)
  Forms allowed:
   (none)
  Banner not required
  Character sets:
   (none)
  Default is pitch:
  Default page size:
```

## Managing Printer Queues

Part of the routine task of managing printers is managing their queues. Occasionally, large jobs are submitted that are not needed and can be aborted. Other times, you might want to put a high-priority job ahead of other jobs that are waiting to be printed. The following outlines some of the routine tasks you might want to perform on the printer queues.

## Deleting a Print Job

To remove someone else's print job from the print queue, you first need to become root. Then, determine the request ID of the print request to cancel by using the `lpstat` command as follows:

```
lpstat -u bcalkins
eps1-1    bcalkins     1261    Mar 16 17:34
```

In this example, user bcalkins has one request in the queue. The request ID is eps1-1.

## Canceling a Print Request

Cancel a print request by using the `cancel` command. The command syntax is as follows:

```
cancel <request-id> | <printer-name>
```

The arguments for the `cancel` command are described in Table 10.7.

**TABLE 10.7**

**`cancel` ARGUMENTS**

| *Argument* | *Description* |
|---|---|
| `<request-id>` | The request ID of a print request to be canceled. You can specify multiple request IDs. Use a space or a comma to separate request IDs. If you use spaces, enclose the list of request IDs in quotes. |
| `<printer-name>` | Specifies the printer for which you want to cancel the currently printing print request. You can specify multiple printer names with this command. Use a space or a comma to separate printer names. |

In the following example, the command cancels the eps1-3 and eps1-4 print requests:

```
cancel eps1-3 eps1-4
 request "eps1-3" cancelled
 request "eps1-4" cancelled
```

In the next example, the command cancels the print request that is currently printing on the printer eps1:

```
cancel eps1
 request "eps1-9" cancelled
```

## Sending a Print Job at a Higher Priority

The `lp` command with the `-q` option assigns the print request a priority in the print queue. Specify the priority level as an integer from 0–39. Use 0 to indicate the highest priority and 39 to indicate the lowest. If no priority is specified, the LP administrator assigns the default priority for a print service.

The following example illustrates how to send a print job to printer eps1 with the highest priority:

```
lp -deps1 -q0 file1
```

## Limiting User Access to a Printer

Allow or deny users access to a printer by using the `lpadmin` command. The command syntax is as follows:

```
lpadmin -p <printer-name> -u allow:<user-list> \
[ deny:<user-list>]
```

The arguments for the `lpadmin` command are described in Table 10.8.

**TABLE 10.8**

**`lpadmin` ARGUMENTS**

| *Argument* | *Description* |
|---|---|
| `-p <printer-name>` | The name of the printer to which the allow or deny user access list applies. |
| `-u allow:<user-list>` | Usernames to be added to the allow user access list. You can specify multiple usernames with this command. Use a space or a comma to separate names. If you use spaces, enclose the list of names in quotes. |
| `-u deny:<user-list>` | Usernames to be added to the deny user access list. You can specify multiple usernames with this command. Use a space or a comma to separate names. If you use spaces, enclose the list of names in quotes. Table 10.9 provides the valid values for `user-list`. |

The specified users are added to the allow or deny user access list for the printer in one of the following files on the print server:

/etc/lp/printers/printer-name/users.allow

/etc/lp/printers/printer-name/users.deny

**TABLE 10.9**

**VALUES FOR ALLOW AND DENY LISTS**

| *Value for* `user-list` | *Description* |
|---|---|
| `user` | A user on any system. |
| `all` | All users on all systems |
| `none` | No user on any system |
| `system!user` | A user on the specified system only |
| `!user` | A user on the local system only |
| `all!user` | A user on any system |
| `all!all` | All users on all systems |
| `system!all` | All users on the system |
| `!all` | All users on the local system |

**NOTE**

If you specify `none` as the value for `user-list` in the allow user access list, the following files are not created for the print server:

/etc/lp/printers/printer-name/alert.sh

/etc/lp/printers/printer-name/alert.var

/etc/lp/printers/printer-name/users.allow

/etc/lp/printers/printer-name/users.deny

In the following example, the command allows only the users bcalkins and bholzgen access to the printer eps1:

```
lpadmin -p eps1 -u allow:bcalkins,bholzgen
```

In the next example, the command denies the users bcalkins and bholzgen access to the printer eps2:

```
lpadmin -p eps2 -u deny:"bcalkins bholzgen"
```

Use the `lpstat` command to view access information about a particular printer. The following command displays access information for the printer named eps1:

```
lpstat -p eps1 -l
```

The system responds with this:

```
printer eps1 is idle. enabled since Mon Mar 20 14:39:48 EST
2000. available.

        Form mounted:
        Content types: postscript
```

```
Printer types: PS
Description: epson
Connection: direct
Interface: /usr/lib/lp/model/standard
On fault: write to root once
After fault: continue
Users allowed:
bcalkins
bholzgen
Forms allowed:
      (none)
Banner not required
Character sets:

Default pitch:
Default page size: 80 wide 66 long
Default port settings:
```

## Accepting or Rejecting Print Requests for a Printer

As root, you can stop accepting print requests for the printer by using the `reject` command. The command syntax is as follows:

```
reject [-r "reason"] <printer-name>
```

The arguments for the `reject` command are described in Table 10.10.

**TABLE 10.10**

**reject ARGUMENTS**

| *Argument* | *Description* |
|---|---|
| `-r "reason"` | Tells the users why the printer is rejecting print requests. The reason is stored and displayed whenever a user checks on the status of the printer using `lpstat -p`. |
| `<printer-name>` | The name of the printer that will stop accepting print requests. |

The following example stops the printer eps1 from accepting print requests:

```
reject -r "eps1 is down for repairs" eps1
destination "eps1" will no longer accept requests
```

Any queued requests will continue printing as long as the printer is enabled. In the following example, the command sets the printer eps1 to accept print requests again:

```
accept eps1
destination "eps1" now accepting requests
```

## Canceling a Print Request from a Specific User

Change to the root or `lp` user if you want to cancel print requests of other users. Cancel a print request from a specific user with the `cancel` command. The command syntax is as follows:

```
cancel -u <user-list> <printer-name>
```

The arguments for the `cancel` command are described in Table 10.11.

**TABLE 10.11**

**`cancel` ARGUMENTS**

| *Argument* | *Description* |
|---|---|
| `-u <user-list>` | Cancels the print request for a specified user. `<user-list>` can be one or more usernames. Use a space or a comma to separate usernames. If you use spaces, enclose the list of names in quotes. |
| `<printer-name>` | Specifies the printer for which you want to cancel the specified user's print requests. `<printer-name>` can be one or more printer names. Use a space or a comma to separate printer names. If you use spaces, enclose the list of printer names in quotes. If you don't specify `<printer-name>`, the user's print requests will be canceled on all printers. |

In the following example, the command cancels all the print requests submitted by the user bcalkins on the printer luna:

```
cancel -u bcalkins  luna
request "luna-23" cancelled
```

In the following example, the command cancels all the print requests submitted by the user bcalkins on all printers:

```
cancel -u bcalkins
request "asteroid-3" cancelled
request "luna-8" cancelled
```

## Changing the Priority of a Print Request

Change the priority of a print request by using the following `lp` command:

```
lp -i <request-id> -H <change-priority>
```

The options for the `lp` command are described in Table 10.12.

**TABLE 10.12**

**lp OPTIONS**

| Option | Description | |
|---|---|---|
| `-i <request-id>` | The request ID of a print request you want to change. You can specify multiple request IDs with this command. Use a space or a comma to separate request IDs. If you use spaces, enclose the list of request IDs in quotation marks. | |
| `-H <change-priority>` | One of the three ways to change the priority of a print request: `hold`, `resume`, or `immediate`: | |
| | `hold` | Places the print request on hold until you cancel it or instruct the LP print service to resume printing the request. |
| | `resume` | Places a print request that has been on hold in the queue. It will be printed according to its priority and placement in the queue. If you put a hold on a print job that is already printing, `resume` puts the print request at the head of the queue so that it becomes the next request printed. |
| | `immediate` | Places a print request at the head of the queue. If a request is already printing, you can put that request on hold to allow the next request to print immediately. |

| *Option* | *Description* |
|---|---|
| `-q < priority-level >` | Assigns the print request a priority in the print queue. Specify `<priority-level>` as an integer from 0–39. Use 0 to indicate the highest priority and 39 to indicate the lowest priority. |

In the following example, the command changes a print request with the request ID eps1-29 to priority level 1:

```
lp -i eps1-29 -q 1
```

## Restarting the Print Scheduler

The print scheduler, `lpsched`, handles print requests on print servers. If printouts are not coming out of the printer, you might need to restart the print scheduler. To restart the print scheduler, you use the `lpsched` command. If a print request was printing when the print scheduler stopped running, that request would be printed in its entirety when you restarted the print scheduler.

First, stop the scheduler by typing the following:

```
/usr/lib/lp/lpshut
```

To restart the scheduler, type the following:

```
/usr/lib/lp/lpsched
```

The `lp` system is started by the /etc/init.d script named `lp`. There is a link from this file to the /etc/rc2.d directory so that the `lp` service starts automatically every time the system is booted. The same script can be used to reset the entire `lp` service by issuing the following command:

```
/etc/init.d/lp stop
```

The `lp` service will be stopped. You can restart the `lp` service with the following command:

```
/etc/init.d/lp start
```

**NOTE** The /etc/init.d/lp script starts and stops the entire print service and not just the scheduler. Use `lpshut` and `lpsched` to stop and restart the scheduler only.

## Setting a User's Default Printer

When you added the printer, you were given the option of selecting that printer as the default printer for that particular system. You might want to set the default printer at the user level so that, on a particular system, users can specify their own default printer. If users don't provide a printer name when sending a print job, the print command searches for the default printer in the following order:

1. `LPDEST` variable
2. `PRINTER` variable
3. System's default printer

These variables can be set in the user's .profile file. The `lp` command checks LPDEST and then PRINTER. If neither variable has been set, then the variable named _default is checked for in the following files:

$HOME/.printers

An entry in this file naming printer1 as the default printer looks like this:

```
default printer1
```

If the $HOME/.printers file does not exist, the /etc/printers.conf file is checked. An entry in this file would look like this:

```
_default¦lp:
        :use=system1:
        :bsdaddr=system1,printer1
```

If the _default variable is not set in the /etc/printers.conf file, then the name service database is checked if you're running a name service, as described in Chapter 18, "Name Services." If the destination printer name cannot be located in any of these files, the print request cannot be processed.

# Modifying the Printer with Admintool

Solaris Admintool can be used to modify a printer after it has been added to the system. Modifications that can be made to a printer via Admintool include the following:

- Giving the printer description
- Indicating the printer port
- Listing file contents
- Providing fault notification
- Selecting a default printer
- Printing a banner
- Accepting and processing print requests
- Providing a user access list

To modify a printer via Admintool, select Edit, Modify from the Printers window, as shown in Figure 10.7.

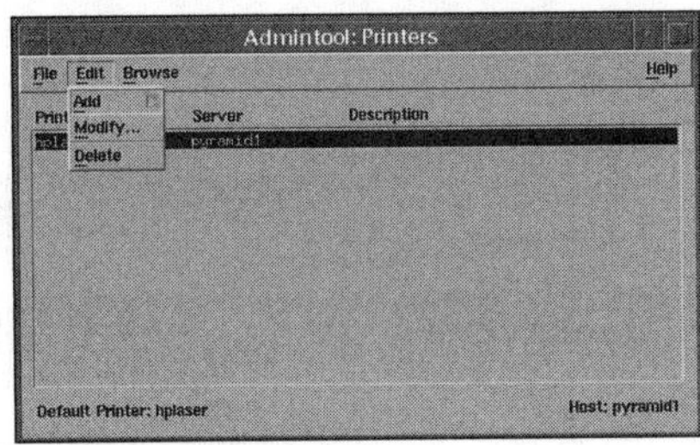


**FIGURE 10.7**
The Printers window.

The Modify Printer window appears, as shown in Figure 10.8.

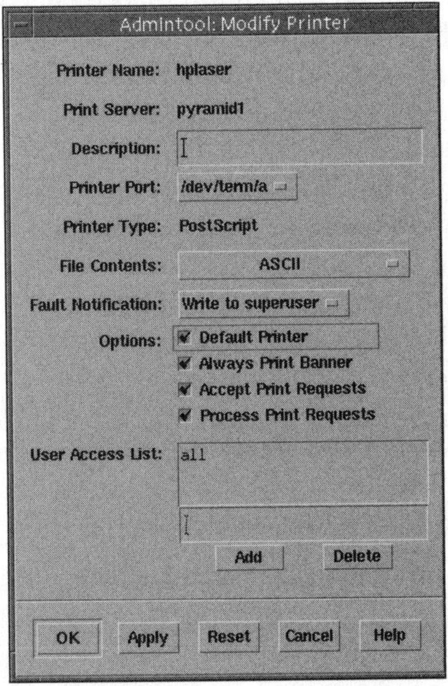


**FIGURE 10.8**
The Modify Printer window.

Modify the selected printer by selecting or filling in the appropriate fields in the Modify Printer window.

## CHAPTER SUMMARY

### KEY TERMS

- Spool
- Print daemon
- Network printer
- Print queue
- Local printer
- Lpsched
- Lpd
- Print server
- Print client
- Default printer
- Terminfo database
- Printer class
- Print scheduler

We could spend a great deal of time describing the LP print service. We could explore a more in-depth discussion on configuring printer filters, creating terminfo databases, and troubleshooting printing problems, but that's beyond the scope of this *Training Guide.* To prepare for the certification exam and basic system administration, you need to understand the basics of the LP print service. This includes the print spooler, print daemons, and printer configuration files. Also, you need to know where these files and programs are stored in the Solaris 8 directory structure.

In addition to understanding the LP print service, you need to know how to use all the utilities and programs that are used to manage the LP print service.

The majority of system problems I respond to are printer-related. You should also become familiar with your third-party applications and how they prepare print jobs to be sent to the spooler. Many of the problems I encounter are not with the Solaris print service, but in the way that the application formats the print job. This chapter introduced you to the Solaris print system and the `lpsched` daemon. Printers can also be administered in a networked environment using Solstice AdminSuite, described in Chapter 19, "Solaris Management Console and Solstice AdminSuite." Chapter 9, "Process Control," explores all the Solaris processes. For a more detailed discussion of the `lpsched` daemon, refer to the Solaris 8 System Administration Guide, Volume II in the Answerbook2 online manuals.

APPLY YOUR KNOWLEDGE

## Exercises

### 10.1 Configuring a Printer Using *lpadmin* (Command Line)

This exercise will show you how to add and remove a local LaserJet 5M printer on a print server. The commands in this example must be executed on the print server where the printer is connected. The following information is available for the installation:

Printer name: `hp1`

Port device: `/dev/ecpp0`

System type: `Ultra5`

Printer type: `HP LaserJet5M`

File content type: `PostScript/PCL`

**Estimated Time**: 10 minutes

1. As root, use the `lpadmin` command to add the printer named `hp1` to the parallel port (`/dev/ecpp0` on an ultra system, and `/dev/bpp0` on a sparc system), set the printer type as `hplaser`, and specify the file content types as `any`:

   ```
   lpadmin -p hp1 -v /dev/ecpp0 -T hplaser -I \
   any
   ```

   Now, start accepting print requests for the printer and enable the printer.

   ```
   enable hp1
   accept hp1
   ```

2. Verify that the printer is set up and ready:

   ```
   lpstat -p hp1 -l
   ```

3. Now send a print job to the printer to test it:

   ```
   lp -d hp1 /etc/hosts
   ```

4. Remove the printer:

   ```
   lpadmin -x hp1
   ```

5. Verify that it has been removed:

   ```
   lpstat -t
   ```

### 10.2 Configuring a Printer Using AdminTool (GUI)

In this exercise, add a LaserJet 5M printer to the print server using Admintool.

**Estimated Time**: 5 minutes

1. As root, start up Admintool.

   ```
   admintool &
   ```

2. From the Browse button at the top of Admintool window, select `Printers` from the pull-down menu.

3. From the `Edit` button at the top of Admintool window, select `Add`, then `Local Printer` from the pull-down menu. Fill in the fields as follows:

   Printer Name: `hp1`

   Description: `Hplaser 5M`

   Printer Port: `/dev/eccp0` (/dev/bpp0 on a Sparc system)

   Printer Type: `HP Printer`

   File Contents: `Any`

   Click on `OK` when finished, then exit Admintool.

4. Verify the printer is set up and ready by typing the following:

   ```
   lpstat -p hp1 -l
   ```

## Apply Your Knowledge

### 10.3 Stopping and Starting the LP Print Service

In this exercise, use the `lpshut` and `lpsched` commands to stop and start the LP print service.

**Estimated Time**: 5 minutes

1. Halt the LP print service. Any printers that are currently printing when the command is invoked will be stopped.

```
/usr/lib/lpshut
```

2. Use the `lpsched` command to start the LP print service. Printers that are restarted using this command will reprint jobs in their entirety that were interrupted with the `lpshut` command.

```
/usr/lib/lpsched
```

### 10.4 Setting Up a Network-Based Printer

The following exercise illustrates how to configure a printer that is connected directly to the network via its own network interface card. In the example, the printer is utilizing an HP Jet direct interface, and I'm going to use Hewlett-Packard's JetAdmin software to configure the printer.

**Estimated Time**: 15 minutes

1. Obtain the JetAdmin software from Hewlett-Packard's web site (`www.hp.com`), and install it using the `pkgadd` command described in Chapter 5, "Setting Up User Accounts." Make sure you get the correct version of JetAdmin. As of this writing, the current version is named SOLd621.PKG. Put the downloaded file in the /tmp directory.

2. Install the JetAdmin package into the /opt/hpnp directory using the `pkgadd` command:

```
pkgadd -d /tmp/SOLd621.PKG
```

You'll see the following output:

```
The following packages are available:
  1  HPNP      JetAdmin for Unix
               (sparc) D.06.21
Select package(s) you wish to process (or/
'all' to process all packages).
(default: all) [?,??,q]: 1
```

3. Type the following:

```
1 <return>
Processing package instance <HPNP> from
</var/spool/pkg/SOLd621.PKG>

JetAdmin for Unix
(sparc) D.06.21
(c)Copyright Hewlett-Packard Company 1991,
1992, 1993. All Rights Reserved.
(c)Copyright 1983 Regents of the University
of California
(c)Copyright 1988, 1989 by Carnegie Mellon
University
RESTRICTED RIGHTS LEGEND
Use, duplication, or disclosure by the U.S.
Government is subject to restrictions as set
forth in sub-paragraph (c)(1)(ii) of the
Rights in Technical Data and Computer
Software clause in DFARS 252.227-7013.
                        Hewlett-Packard
                        Company
                        3000 Hanover Street
                        Palo Alto, CA 94304
                        U.S.A.
Where should HPNP be installed?
(<return> for /opt/hpnp) [?,q] <enter>
```

4. Enter `<return>` to install in the /opt/hpnp directory.

```
HPNP will be installed in /opt/hpnp.
Please configure the sub-packages you would
like to install.
    ------------------------------------
---------
Done altering installation configuration
    1. [ N/A ]  JetPrint
    2. [ On  ]  JobMonitor
    3. [ On  ]  HPNPF
    4. [ On  ]  HPNPD
    5. [ On  ]  CONVERT
    ?.          Help
    ------------------------------------
---------
```

## APPLY YOUR KNOWLEDGE

```
Select a number to toggle an installation
option.
When done select 0.  Select ? for help
information: 0
```

5. Enter: `0 <return>`

```
Select a number to toggle an installation
option.
When done select 0.  Select ? for help
information: 0
Using </> as the package base directory.
## Processing package information.
## Processing system information.
## Verifying disk space requirements.
## Checking for conflicts with packages
already installed.
The following files are already installed on
the system and are being used by another
package:
  /etc <attribute change only>
  /etc/init.d <attribute change only>
  /etc/rc1.d <attribute change only>
  /etc/rc2.d <attribute change only>
  /usr <attribute change only>
  /usr/bin <attribute change only>
Do you want to install these conflicting
files [y,n,?,q] y
```

6. Enter: `y <return>`

```
This package contains scripts which will be
executed with super-user permission
during the process of installing this
package.
Do you want to continue with the installation
of <HPNP> [y,n,?] y
```

7. Enter: `y <return>`

   You'll see a list of files being installed followed by the message:

```
Installation of <HPNP> was successful.
```

   The following information is available regarding the printer that is going to be installed:

   Printer name: hplaser

   IP address: 192.168.1.10

8. Configure the HP LaserJet printer using the JetAdmin utility that was just installed:

```
/opt/hpnp/jetadmin
```

   The following dialog box will be displayed:

```
*********************************************
        *                   MAIN MENU
*
        *  HP JetAdmin Utility for UNIX
(Rev. D.06.21)  *

*********************************************
       1) Configuration (super-user only):
            - configure printer, add printer
to spooler
       2) Diagnostics:
            - diagnose printing problems
       3) Administration (super-user only):
            - manage HP printer, JetDirect
       4) Administration (super-user only):
            - manage JetAdmin
       5) Printer Status:
            - show printer status, location,
and contact
                    ?) Help        q) Quit
Please enter a selection (q - quit):1
```

   Enter: `1 <return>`

```
Printer Network Interface:
                   1) Create printer
                      configuration in
                      BOOTP/TFTP database
                   2) Remove printer
                   configuration from
                   BOOTP/TFTP
          Spooler:
                   2) Add printer to local
                      spooler
                   3) Delete printer from
                      local/ spooler
                   4) Modify existing
                      spooler queue(s)
               ?) Help          q) Quit
Please enter a selection: 3
```

## Apply Your Knowledge

Enter: `3 <return>`

```
Enter the network printer name or IP address
(q - quit): 192.168.1.10
```

Enter: `<IP Address>`

```
Following is a list of suggested parameter
values for this queue. You can change any
settings by selecting the corresponding non-
zero numbers. The values will be used to
configure this queue when '0' is selected.
To abort the operation, press 'q'.
Configurable Parameters:                Current
Settings
-----------------------                ---------
   1) Lp destination (queue) name       [192_1]
   2) Status log                        [(No
                                         log)]
   3) Queue class                       [(not
                                      assigned)]
   4) JobMonitor                        [OFF]
   5) Default queue                     [NO]
   6) Additional printer configuration...
Select an item for change, or '0' to
configure (q-quit):1
```

Enter: `1 <return>`

```
Currently used names:
hp1
Enter the lp destination name (default=192_1,
q - quit): hplaser
```

Enter: `hplaser <return>`

```
Following is a list of suggested parameter
values for this queue. You can change
any settings by selecting the corresponding
non-zero numbers. The values will be
used to configure this queue when '0' is
selected. To abort the operation, press
 'q'.
Configurable Parameters:                Current
                                        Settings
-----------------------                ---------
1) Lp destination (queue) name       [hplaser]
2) Status log                        [(No log)]
3) Queue class                       [(not
                                      assigned)]
   4) JobMonitor                              [OFF]
   5) Default queue                           [NO]
   6) Additional printer configuration...
Select an item for change, or '0' to/
configure (q-quit):0
```

Enter: `0 <return>`

```
Ready to configure hplaser.
OK to continue? (y/n/q, default=y)y
```

Enter: `y <return>`

The system will display the following:

```
Finished adding "hplaser" to the spooler.
Press the return key to continue ...
```

Enter `<return>`, followed by "q", and another "q" to exit the JetAdmin utility.

9. Verify that the printer is enabled and ready:

```
lpstat -p hplaser -l
```

## Review Questions

1. Which of the following is the UNIX utility responsible for printing in SRV4 UNIX?

   A. `lpr`

   B. `lp`

   C. `lpd`

   D. `spool`

2. Where is the spool directory located in Solaris?

   A. /var/spool/lpd

   B. /var/spool/lp

   C. /usr/spool/lp

   D. /usr/spool/lpd

## APPLY YOUR KNOWLEDGE

3. Which of the following commands prevents queuing of print requests?

   A. `disable`

   B. `cancel`

   C. `reject`

   D. `lpshut`

4. Which of the following can be used to add a local printer to a print server:

   A. Admintool

   B. Printer Manager

   C. `lpadmin`

   D. `lp`

5. Which of the following commands stops the print service?

   A. `lpsched`

   B. `lpshut`

   C. `cancel`

   D. `disable`

6. Which of the following commands places information to be printed into the spooler?

   A. `lpr`

   B. `print`

   C. `lpsched`

   D. `lp`

7. Which of the following statements is true of a print server?

   A. It is a system that has a local printer connected to it.

   B. It is a remote system that can send print requests to another system for printing.

   C. It is a system that makes a printer available to other systems on the network.

   D. Prints can be initiated from it.

8. If the user doesn't specify a printer name, which of the following environmental variables tells it where to print?

   A. $HOME

   B. $LPDEST

   C. $PRINTER

   D. $DEFAULT_DEST

9. When adding a printer in AdminTool, what is the Print Server field used for?

   A. It defines the name of the system to which the printer is connected.

   B. It defines the system as a print server.

   C. It selects a system from which to download the print software.

   D. It defines a system that can spool to the local printers.

10. Which of the following is a serial port device?

    A. /dev/bpp0

    B. /dev/ttya

    C. /dev/term/a

    D. /dev/fd

## APPLY YOUR KNOWLEDGE

11. Which of the following are valid printer ports?

    A. /dev/terma

    B. /dev/term/a

    C. /dev/ecpp0

    D. /dev/term/ttya

12. Which of the following commands cancels all print requests for the user bcalkins on the printer jetprint?

    A. `lprm -bcalkins jetprint`

    B. `cancel -Pjetprint bcalkins`

    C. `cancel -u bcalkins jetprint`

    D. `lpremove -Pjetprint bcalkins`

13. Which of the following methods can be used to delete a printer?

    A. `lpadmin -x<printername>`

    B. `lpshut <printername>`

    C. Admintool

    D. `lpadmin -D <printername>`

14. Which of the following commands removes a job from the print queue?

    A. `lpmove`

    B. `cancel`

    C. `lprm`

    D. `reject`

15. Which of the following daemons services all printers?

    A. `lpsched`

    B. `lpd`

    C. `lpr`

    D. `spoold`

16. Where is information on printers found?

    A. /etc/printers.conf

    B. /etc/lp

    C. /var/spool/lp

    D. /etc/print

17. Which of the following is a system that has a local printer connected to it and makes the printer available to other systems on the network?

    A. Print server

    B. Print client

    C. Client

    D. Server

18. If the user doesn't specify a printer name or class when printing, which of the following variables is checked for a default printer to use?

    A. `PRINTER` and `LPDEST`

    B. `LPDEST`

    C. `PRINT`

    D. `DEFAULT_DEST`

19. In which directory are the terminfo entries for PostScript printers?

    A. /usr/share/lib/terminfo/P

    B. /var/spool/lp/postscript

    C. /etc/lp/interfaces

    D. /etc/lp/printers

## APPLY YOUR KNOWLEDGE

20. Which of the following commands adds the printer luna to the class roughdrafts?

    A. `lpadmin -p luna -c roughdrafts`

    B. `lpadmin -class roughdrafts -p luna`

    C. `lpadmin luna -c roughdrafts`

    D. `lpadmin -cp roughdrafts luna`

21. Which of the following commands displays the characteristics of the printer hplaser?

    A. `lpstat -p hplaser -l`

    B. `lpstat -p hplaser`

    C. `lpadmin -p hplaser -l`

    D. `lpstat -a -p hplaser -l`

22. Which of the following commands changes a print request with the request ID eps1-29 to priority level 1?

    A. `lp -i eps1-29 -q 1`

    B. `lpadmin -i eps1 -q 0`

    C. `lp -i eps1-29 -q 39`

    D. `lpadmin -i eps1 -q 39`

## Answers to Review Questions

1. **B**. The UNIX utility responsible for printing in SRV4 UNIX is called `lp`.
2. **B**. For Solaris, the spool directory is located in /var/lp/spool.
3. **C**. The `reject` command disables any further requests for a printer or class entering the spooling area.
4. **A**., **B**., **C**. Use one of the following tools to add a local printer to a print server: Admintool, Printer Manager, or `lpadmin`.
5. **B**. The `lpshut` command stops the print service.
6. **D**. The `lp` command places information to be printed into the spooler.
7. **A**., **C**. A print server is a system that has a local printer connected to it. A print server makes a printer available to other systems on the network.
8. **B**., **C**. If the user doesn't specify a printer name or class in a valid style, the command checks the user's `PRINTER` or `LPDEST` environment variable for a default printer name.
9. **A**. When using Admintool to add a printer, the Print Server field defines the name of the system to which the printer is connected.
10. **C**. /dev/term/a is the serial port device.
11. **B**., **C**. Valid printer ports on a Solaris system include /dev/term/a, /dev/term/b, and /dev/ecpp0.
12. **C**. The following command cancels all print requests for the user bcalkins on the printer named jetprint:

    ```
    cancel -u bcalkins jetprint
    ```

13. **A**., **C**. To delete a printer from the system, you can use either the `lpadmin -x` command or the Admintool interface.
14. **B**. Use the `cancel` command to remove a job from the print queue.
15. **A**. The print scheduler, `lpsched`, handles print requests on print servers.

## APPLY YOUR KNOWLEDGE

16. **A.**, **B.** When setting up a printer with Admintool or `lpadmin`, Solaris makes the appropriate changes in the system's /etc/printers.conf file and the /etc/lp directory as required.

17. **A.** The print server is a system that has a local printer connected to it and makes the printer available to other systems on the network.

18. **A.** If the user doesn't specify a printer name or class in a valid style, the `lp` command checks the user's `PRINTER` or `LPDEST` environment variable for a default printer name.

19. **A.** The terminfo entries for PostScript printers are stored in the /usr/share/lib/terminfo/P directory.

20. **A.** To add a printer to a class, use the following command syntax: `lpadmin -p <printer-name> -c <printer-class>`.

21. **A.** Use the `lpstat` commands to display the characteristics of a particular printer, as follows: `lpstat -p <printername> -l`

22 **A.** Use the lp command to change the priority of a print job to priority level 1: `lp -i <job name> -q 1`.

## OBJECTIVES

The following are the test objectives for this chapter:

**Match the backup, archive, and restore utilities to their respective functional capabilities.**

- Solaris 8 provides several utilities for copying data between disks, tapes, or other types of media. A system administrator needs to understand the capabilities of each utility, and determine which is best for a particular circumstance. This chapter will describe all of the utilities and commands used to back up and restore data on a Solaris system.

**Identify the commands and steps required to back up a file system to tape.**

- You'll need to understand all of the steps required to back up a file or file system to tape for each of the various Solaris backup utilities.

**Identify the commands and steps required to restore a file system from tape.**

- You'll need to understand all of the steps required to restore a file or file system from tape for each of the various Solaris backup utilities.

CHAPTER 11

# Backup and Recovery

## OUTLINE



## STUDY STRATEGIES

The following strategies will help you prepare for the test:

- As you study this chapter, make sure that you thoroughly understand the various backup tools available in Solaris. On the exam, you'll need to match the correct tool to the task it can perform or the correct description.
- Practice the commands and all of the options on a live Solaris 8 system (Sun or Intel). Try to memorize the examples I've provided. The examples illustrate the command and options most likely to appear on the exam. It's best if you have a tape drive with which to practice, but if you don't have one, practice using the commands to move files between two partitions on a disk.
- Familiarize yourself with the step-by-steps in this chapter. Memorize them—they are on the exam.

## INTRODUCTION

Backing up a system involves copying data from the system's hard disks onto removable media that can be safeguarded in a secure area. Backing up system data is one of the most crucial system administration functions, and should be performed regularly. Backups are used to restore data if files become corrupted or if system failure or a building disaster destroys data. Having a fault-tolerant disk array is not enough. Disk mirroring and RAID 5 protect your data in case of a hardware failure, but they do not protect against file corruption, natural disaster, or accidental deletion of a file. In other words, disk mirroring does not protect against flood damage or fire. In addition, if a program corrupts a particular file, it will be just as corrupt on the mirrored copy as well. Therefore, some type of offsite backup of your data must be in place. Backing up system data—the most important task you will perform—must be done on a regular basis. Although even a comprehensive backup scheme can't guarantee against loss of information, you can make sure the loss will be minimal.

This chapter describes methods available to perform a backup, types of backups, development of a solid backup strategy, and restoration of data if you encounter a loss. First, you'll find an explanation of the `tar`, `dd`, `cpio`, and `pax` commands, which are used to copy data from disk to disk or from disk to tape. Then you'll learn that the `ufsdump` and `ufsrestore` utilities are the preferred method of backing up data from a Solaris system to tape on a regular basis.

## BACKUP MEDIA

Selecting your backup media is as critical as selecting the program to perform the backup. Your backup media should be removable so that the information can be taken to another site for safe storage in case of fire, flood, or other natural disaster. In some cases, the backup medium is simply another system on the network located in an alternate building. Most backup systems, however, use tape media. Magnetic tape still provides the lowest cost per megabyte for storing data. Table 11.1 shows some typical tape devices used for storing backed up data.

**TABLE 11.1**

**TAPE DEVICE TYPES**

| *Media Type* | *Capacity* |
|---|---|
| 1/2-inch reel tape | 140MB (6250 BPI) |
| 1/4-inch cartridge tape (QIC) | 8GB |
| 8mm cartridge tape | 40–70GB |
| 4mm DAT cartridge tape (DDs-DDS4) | 1–40GB |
| DLT 1/2-inch cartridge tape (DLT2000-DLT7000) | 20–80GB |

To achieve higher capacity, one or more of these tape drives are combined into cabinets, called tape libraries or tape silos, capable of storing several terabytes of data spread across tens or even hundreds of tapes. Operating with robotic arms, tapes are located, retrieved, and loaded into a tape drive automatically to eliminate human intervention.

## Solaris Backup and Restoration Utilities

Solaris provides the utilities listed in Table 11.2. The backup utilities can be used to copy data from disk to removable media, and restore it.

**TABLE 11.2**

**BACKUP UTILITIES**

| *Utility* | *Description* |
|---|---|
| `tar` | Archives data to another directory, system, or medium. |
| `dd` | Copies data quickly. |
| `cpio` | Copies data from one location to another. |
| `pax` | Copies files and directory subtrees to a single tape. This utility provides better portability than `tar` or `cpio`, so it can be used to transport files to other types of UNIX systems. |
| `ufsdump` | Backs up all files in a file system. |
| `ufsrestore` | Restores some or all of the files archived with the `ufsdump` command. |

## tar

The primary use of the tar (tape archiver) command is to copy file systems or individual files from a hard disk to a tape or from a tape to a hard disk. You can also use tar to create a tar archive on a hard disk or floppy disk, and to extract files from a tar archive on a hard disk or floppy disk. The tar command is popular because it's available on most UNIX systems; however, it is limited to a single tape. If the data you are backing up requires more than one tape, use the cpio, pax, or ufsdump commands, which I will describe later.

The tar command has the following syntax:

```
tar <options> <tar filename> <file list>
```

in which options is the list of command options listed in Table 11.3.

**TABLE 11.3**

**COMMAND OPTIONS FOR tar**

| *Option* | *Description* |
|---|---|
| c | Creates a tar file. |
| t | Table of contents. Lists the names of the specified files each time they occur in the tar filename. If no file argument is given, the names of all files in the tar filename are listed. When used with the v function modifier, it displays additional information for the specified files. |
| x | Extracts or restores files from a tar filename. |
| v | Verbose. Outputs information to the screen as tar reads or writes the archive. |
| f | Uses the tar filename argument as the name of the tar archive. If f is omitted, tar uses the device indicated by the TAPE environment variable (if it is set). If the TAPE variable is not set, tar uses the default values defined in /etc/default/tar. If the name of the tar file is -, tar writes to the standard output or reads from the standard input. |

For a more complete listing of command options, refer to the Solaris online manual pages.

The `<tar filename>` is used with the `f` option, and can be any name you want. The filename can also be the name of a device, such as /dev/rmt/0 or /dev/rfd0. The `<file list>` is a list of files you want to include in the archive.

## tar Examples

The following examples illustrate the use of the `tar` command.

To create a tape archive of everything in the /home/bcalkins directory on tape device /dev/rmt/0, type the following:

```
tar cvf /dev/rmt/0 /home/bcalkins
```

To list the files in the archive, type the following:

```
tar tvf /dev/rmt/0
```

To restore the file /home/bcalkins/.profile from the archive, type the following:

```
tar xvf /dev/rmt/0 /home/bcalkins/.profile
```

Use `tar` to create an archive file on disk instead of tape. The `tar` filename will be files.tar, as follows:

```
tar cvf files.tar /home/bcalkins
```

To extract files that were created using the preceding example, type the following:

```
tar xvf files.tar
```

Notice the use of the full pathname. Using the full pathname to create the archive ensures that the files will be restored to their original location in the directory hierarchy. You will not be able to restore them elsewhere.

If you want to be able to restore files with a relative pathname in the preceding example, you can change to the /home/bcalkins directory and specify files to be archived as `./*`. This puts the files into the archive using a pathname relative to the current working directory rather than an absolute pathname (one beginning with a forward slash). Files can then be restored into any directory.

## dd

The main advantage of the dd command is that it quickly converts and copies files with different data formats, such as differences in block size or record length.

The most common use of dd is to transfer a complete file system or partition from your hard disk to a tape. You can also use it to copy files from one hard disk to another. When you're copying data, the dd command makes an image copy (an exact byte-for-byte copy) of any medium, which can be either tape or disk. The command arguments are described in Table 11.4. The syntax for the dd command is as follows:

```
dd if=<input-file> of=<output-file> <option=value>
```

**TABLE 11.4**

**dd COMMAND ARGUMENTS**

| *Argument* | *Description* |
|---|---|
| if | Used to designate an input file. The input file can be a filename or a device name, such as /dev/rmt/0. If no input file is specified, input for dd is taken from the UNIX standard input. |
| of | Used to designate an output file. The output file can be a filename or a device name, such as /dev/rmt/0. If no output file is specified, output from dd is sent to the UNIX standard output. |

Several other options can follow on the command line to specify buffer sizes, block sizes, and data conversions. See the Solaris online manual pages for a list of these options.

## dd Examples

The next few examples illustrate the use of the dd command to copy data. The first example shows how the dd command is used to duplicate tapes. This procedure requires two tape drives—a source tape and a destination tape:

```
dd if=/dev/rmt/0 of=/dev/rmt/1
```

The next example uses `dd` to copy one entire hard disk to another hard disk. In the example, you need two disks, and both must have the same geometry. Disk geometry was discussed in Chapter 6, "Introduction to File Systems."

```
dd if=/dev/rdsk/c0t1d0s2 of=/dev/rdsk/c0t4d0s2 bs=128
```

In this example, the option `bs=128` specifies a block size. A large block size, such as 128KB or 256KB, will decrease the time to copy by buffering large amounts of data. Notice also that the raw device is specified. For this technique to work properly, you must use the raw (character) device to avoid the buffered (block) I/O system.

You can use the `dd` command with `tar` to create an archive on a remote tape drive. In the next example, `tar` is used to create an archive on a remote system by piping the output to a tape drive called /dev/rmt/0 on a remote system named xena:

```
tar cvf - <files> | rsh xena dd of=/dev/rmt/0 obs=128
```

Another example would be to read `tar` data coming from another UNIX system, such as Silicon Graphics. Silicon Graphics swaps every pair of bytes, making a `tar` tape unreadable on a Solaris system. To read a `tar` tape from an SGI system, type the following:

```
dd if=/dev/nrst0 conv=swab | tar xvf -
```

In a similar way, a Solaris system can create a `tar` tape that an SGI system can read:

```
tar cvf - <files> | dd of=/dev/nrst0 conv=swab
```

## cpio

The `cpio` command is used to copy data from one place to another. `cpio` stands for "copy input to output." When copying files with `cpio`, you present a list of files to its standard input and write the file archive to its standard output. The principal advantage of `cpio` is its flexible syntax. The command acts as a filter program, taking input information from the standard input file and delivering its output to the standard output file. The input and output can be manipulated by using the shell to specify redirection and pipelines. Following are the advantages of `cpio` over other UNIX utilities:

- `cpio` can back up and restore individual files, not just whole file systems. (`tar` and `pax` also have this capability.)

- Backups made by `cpio` are smaller than those created with `tar` because the header is smaller.
- `cpio` can span multiple tapes; `tar` is limited to a single tape.

Because of its flexibility, `cpio` has more options, and is perceived as a more complex command than `tar`.

The `cpio` program operates in one of three modes: copy-out (`cpio -o`), copy-in (`cpio -i`), or pass (`cpio -p`). Use copy-out when creating a backup tape and copy-in when restoring or listing files from a tape. The pass mode is generally used to copy files from one location to another on disk. You must always specify one of these three modes. The command syntax for the `cpio` command is as follows:

```
cpio <mode> <option>
```

in which `mode` is `-i`, `-o`, or `-p`, and `option` is an option from Table 11.5.

**TABLE 11.5**

**COMMAND OPTIONS FOR cpio**

| *Option* | *Description* |
|---|---|
| `-c` | Writes header information in ASCII format for portability. |
| `-d` | Creates as many directories as needed. |
| `-B` | Specifies that the input has a blocking factor of 5120-byte records instead of the default 512-byte records. You must use the same blocking factor when you retrieve or copy files from the tape to the hard disk as you did when you copied files from the hard disk to the tape. You must use this option whenever you copy files or file systems to and from a tape drive. |
| `-v` | Verbose. Reports the names of the files as they are processed. |
| `-u` | Copies unconditionally. Without this option, an older file will not replace a newer file that has the same name. |
| `-m` | Retains the previous file modification time. This option is ineffective on directories that are being copied. |

## `cpio` Examples

The following example shows how to copy the directory /work and its subdirectories to a tape drive with the device name /dev/rmt/0. The `-o` option specifies copy-out mode, `-c` will output the header information in ASCII format, and I'm using the `-B` option to increase the blocking factor to 5120 bytes to improve the speed.

```
cd /work
ls -R ¦ cpio -ocB > /dev/rmt/0
```

The next example shows how to copy the files located on a tape back into the directory named /work on a hard disk:

```
cd /work
cpio -icvdB < /dev/rmt/0
```

The `-i` option specifies copy-in mode, `-d` will create directories as needed to restore the data to the original location, and `-v` will display all the output.

## Backing Up Files with Copy-Out Mode

To use copy-out mode to make backups, you send a list of files to the `cpio` command via the standard input of `cpio`. In practice, you'll use the UNIX `find` command to generate the list of files to be backed up. Copy-out mode is specified by using the `-o` option on the `cpio` command line. In the next example, a file named "list" contains a short list of files to be backed up to tape:

```
cpio -ovB list > /dev/rmt/1
```

Normally, as indicated in Table 11.5, `cpio` writes files to the standard output in 512-byte records. By specifying the `-B` option, you increase the record size to 5120 bytes to significantly speed up the transfer rate, as shown in the previous example. You can use UNIX commands to generate a list of files for `cpio` to back up in a number of other ways, as shown in the following examples.

You can back up files by entering filenames via the keyboard. Press Ctrl+D when you have finished typing filenames. Type the following:

```
cpio -o > /dev/rmt/1
File1.txt
File2.txt
```

You can use the `ls` command to generate the list of files to be backed up by `cpio`. Type the following:

```
cd /home/bcalkins
ls * | cpio -o >/dev/rmt/1
```

Use the `find` command to generate a list of files that the user bcalkins created and modified in the past five days. This is the list of files to be backed up:

```
find . -user bcalkins -mtime -5  -print | cpio -o >/
/dev/rmt/1
```

If the current tape fills up, the `cpio` program prompts you for another tape. You see a message that says the following:

```
If you want to go on, type device/file name when ready
```

You should then change the tape and enter the name of the backup device (for example, /dev/rmt/1).

## Restoring Files with Copy-In Mode

Use the copy-in mode of `cpio` to restore files from tape to disk. The following examples describe methods used to restore files from a `cpio` archive.

This first example restores all files and directories from tape to disk. The `cpio` options specified will restore files unconditionally (`-u`) to the /users directory, and will retain previous file modification times (`-m`). Type the following:

```
cd /users
cpio -icvumB < /dev/rmt/1
```

The next example selectively restores files that begin with "database." The `-d` option will create directories as needed. Type the following:

```
cpio -icvdumB 'database*' < /dev/rmt/1
```

> **NOTE** Single quotes must be used to pass the wildcard argument (`*`) to `cpio`.

To obtain a list of files that are on tape, follow the next example:

```
cpio -ictB < /dev/rmt/1
```

The list of files on /dev/rmt/1 will appear onscreen.

## Pass Mode

Pass mode generally is not used for backups. The destination must be a directory on a mounted file system, which means that pass mode cannot be used to transfer files to tape. However, you can use pass mode within cpio to copy files from one directory to another. The advantage of using cpio over cp is that original modification times and ownership are preserved. Specify pass mode by using the -p option in cpio. The following example copies all files from /users to /bkup:

```
cd /users
mkdir /bkup
ls * | cpio -pdumv bkup
```

Files will be listed to the screen as they are copied.

## pax

Included since Solaris 2.5 is the pax command, a POSIX-conformant archive utility that can read and write tar and cpio archives. It is available on all UNIX systems that are POSIX-compliant, including IBM's AIX, Hewlett-Packard's HP-UX, and Linux.

pax can read, write, and list the members of an archive file, and copy directory hierarchies. The pax utility supports a wide variety of archive formats, including tar and cpio.

If pax finds an archive that is damaged or corrupted while it is processing, pax attempts to recover from media defects. It searches the archive to locate and process the largest possible number of archive members.

The action to be taken depends on the presence of the -r and -w options, which are referred to as the four modes of operation: list, read, write, and copy (described in Table 11.6). The syntax for the pax command is as follows:

```
pax <mode> <options>
```

**TABLE 11.6**

**FOUR MODES OF OPERATION FOR pax**

| *Option* | *Operation Mode* | *Description* |
|---|---|---|
| -r | Read mode | When -r is specified but -w is not. pax extracts the filenames and directories found in the archive file. The archive file is read from disk or tape. If an extracted file is a directory, the file hierarchy is extracted as well. The extracted files are created relative to the current file hierarchy. |
| None | List mode | When neither -r nor -w is specified. pax displays the filenames or directories found in the archive file. The archive file is read from disk, tape, or the standard input. The list is written to the standard output. |
| -w | Write mode | When -w is specified, but -r is not. pax writes the contents of the file to the standard output in an archive format specified by the -x option. If no files are specified, a list of files to copy (one per line) is read from the standard input. A directory includes all the files in the file hierarchy rooted at the file. |
| -rw | Copy mode | When both -r and -w are specified. pax copies the specified files to the destination directory. |

In addition to selecting a mode of operation, you can select one or more options from Table 11.7.

**TABLE 11.7**

**COMMAND OPTIONS FOR pax**

| *Option* | *Description* |
|---|---|
| -r | Reads an archive file from standard input and extracts the specified files. If any intermediate directories are needed to extract an archive member, these directories are created. |
| -w | Writes files to the standard output in the specified archive format. When no file operands are specified, standard input is read for a list of pathnames—one per line, without leading or trailing blanks. |

*continues*

**TABLE 11.7** *continued*

**COMMAND OPTIONS FOR pax**

| *Option* | *Description* |
|---|---|
| -a | Appends files to the end of an archive that was previously written. |
| -b | Block size. The block size must be a multiple of 512 bytes, with a maximum of 32256 bytes. A block size can end with k or b to specify multiplication by 1024 (1K) or 512 bytes, respectively. |
| -c | Matches all file or archive members except those specified by the pattern and file operands. |
| -f <archive> | Specifies <archive> as the pathname of the input or output archive. A single archive can span multiple files and different archive devices. When required, pax prompts for the pathname of the file or device of the next volume in the archive. |
| -i | Interactively renames files or archive members. For each archive member matching a pattern operand or file matching a file operand, a prompt will be written to the terminal. |
| -n | Selects the first archive member that matches each pattern operand. No more than one archive member is matched for each pattern. |
| -p <string> | Specifies one or more file-characteristic options (privileges). The string option-argument is a string specifying file characteristics to be retained or discarded when extracted. The string consists of the specification characters a, e, m, o, and p. Multiple characteristics can be concatenated within the same string, and multiple -p options can be specified. The meanings of the specification characters are as follows:<br>a Does not preserve file access times<br>e Preserves everything: user ID, group ID, file mode bits, file access times, and file modification times<br>m Does not preserve file modification times<br>o Preserves the user ID and group ID<br>P Preserves the file mode bits<br>-v Verbose mode |
| -x <format> | Specifies the output archive format, with the default format being ustar. pax currently supports cpio, tar, bcpio, ustar, sv4crc, and sv4cpio. |

For additional options to the pax command, see the Solaris online manual pages.

When using pax, you can also specify file operands along with the options from Table 11.6. The operand specifies a destination directory or file pathname. If you specify a directory operand that does not exist, that the user cannot write, or that is not of type directory, pax exits with a nonzero exit status.

The file operand specifies the pathname of a file to be copied or archived. When a file operand does not select at least one archive member, pax writes these file operand pathnames in a diagnostic message to standard error and then exits with a nonzero exit status.

Another operand is the pattern operand, which is used to select one or more pathnames of archive members. Archive members are selected by using the filename pattern-matching notation described by fnmatch. The following are examples of pattern operands:

| | |
|---|---|
| ? | A question mark matches any character. |
| * | An asterisk matches multiple characters. |
| [ | The open bracket introduces a pattern bracket expression. |

When a pattern operand is not supplied, all members of the archive are selected. When a pattern matches a directory, the entire file hierarchy rooted at that directory is selected. When a pattern operand does not select at least one archive member, pax writes these pattern operands in a diagnostic message to standard error and then exits with a nonzero exit status.

## pax Examples

The following examples illustrate the use of the pax command. For example, to copy files to tape, issue this pax command, using -w to copy the current directory contents to tape and -f to specify the tape device:

```
pax -w -f /dev/rmt/0
```

To list a verbose table of contents for an archive stored on tape device /dev/rmt/0, issue the following command:

```
pax -v -f /dev/rmt/0
```

The tape device in these two examples could have been a filename to specify an archive on disk.

The following command can be used to interactively select the files to copy from the current directory to the destination directory:

```
pax -rw -i . <dest_dir>
```

As you become more familiar with the `pax` utility, you'll begin to use it in place of `tar` and `cpio` because of the following:

- Its portability to other UNIX systems
- Its capability to recover damaged archives
- Its capability to span multiple volumes

## ufsdump

Although the other Solaris utilities discussed in this chapter can be used to copy files from disk to tape, `ufsdump` is designed specifically for backups, and is the recommended method for backing up your Solaris file systems. The `ufsdump` command copies files, directories, or entire file systems from a hard disk to a tape or from disk to disk. The only drawback of using `ufsdump` is that the file systems must be inactive before you can conduct a full backup. If the file system is still active, nothing in the memory buffers is copied to tape.

You should back up any file systems critical to users, including file systems that change frequently. See Table 11.8 for suggestions on the file systems to back up and the suggested frequency.

**TABLE 11.8**

**FILE SYSTEMS TO BACK UP**

| *File System* | *Frequency* |
|---|---|
| root (/) | If you frequently add and remove clients and hardware on the network, or you have to change important files in root (/), this file system should be backed up. You should do a full backup of the root (/) file system between once a week and once a month. If /var is in the root (/) file system and your site keeps user mail in the /var/mail directory on a mail server, you might want to back up root (/) daily. |
| /usr | The contents of this file system are fairly static and need to be backed up only from once a week to once a month. |

| *File System* | *Frequency* |
|---|---|
| /export/home | The /export/home file system contains the home directories and subdirectories of all users on the system; its files are volatile and should be backed up daily. |
| Data | All data directories should be backed up daily. |

The `ufsdump` command has many built-in features that the other archive utilities don't have:

- The `ufsdump` command can be used to back up individual file systems to local or remote tape devices or disk drives. The device can be on any system in the network. This command works quickly because it is aware of the structure of the UFS file system, and it works directly through the raw device file.
- `ufsdump` has built-in options to create incremental backups that will back up only those files that were changed since a previous backup, saving tape space and time.
- `ufsdump` has the capability to back up groups of systems over the network from a single system. You can run `ufsdump` on each remote system through a remote shell or remote login, directing the output to the system on which the drive is located.
- The system administrator can restrict user access to backup tables.
- The `ufsdump` command has a built-in option to verify data on tape against the source file system.

Backing up a file system with `ufsdump` is referred to as "dumping" a file system. When a file system is dumped, a level between 0 and 9 is specified. A level 0 dump is a full backup, and contains everything on the file system. Level 1–9 dumps are incremental backups and contain only files that have changed since a previous dump at a lower level.

A good backup schedule involves a recommended three-level dump strategy: a level 0 dump at the start of the month (manually), automated weekly level 5 dumps, and automated daily level 9 dumps. The automated dumps are performed at 4:30 a.m., a time when most systems are typically idle. Automated daily dumps are performed Sunday through Friday mornings. Automated weekly dumps are performed on Saturday mornings. Backups are automated by creating a shell script and using `cron` to execute the script on a regular basis.

**NOTE**

See Chapter 9, "Process Control," for more information on `cron`.

Table 11.9 shows the dump level performed on each day of a typical month. Note that the level 0 dump at the start of the month is performed manually because the entire system must be idle before you can back up the root file system. One way to ensure that the system is not being used is to put the system in single-user mode. The level 9 and 5 dumps are automated with `cron`, but also must be conducted when the file systems are not being used.

**TABLE 11.9**

**FILE SYSTEM DUMP SCHEDULE**

| *Floating* | *Sun* | *Mon* | *Tues* | *Wed* | *Thur* | *Fri* | *Sat* |
|---|---|---|---|---|---|---|---|
| 1st of month | 0 | | | | | | |
| Week 1 | 9 | 9 | 9 | 9 | 9 | 9 | 5 |
| Week 2 | 9 | 9 | 9 | 9 | 9 | 9 | 5 |
| Week 3 | 9 | 9 | 9 | 9 | 9 | 9 | 5 |
| Week 4 | 9 | 9 | 9 | 9 | 9 | 9 | 5 |

The backup schedule in Table 11.9 accomplishes the following:

- Each weekday tape accumulates all files changed since the end of the previous week or the initial level 0 for the first week. All files that have changed since the lower-level backup at the end of the previous week are saved each day.
- Each Saturday tape contains all files changed since the last level 0.

This dump schedule requires at least four sets of seven tapes—one set for each week and one tape for the level 0 dump. Each set will be rotated each month. The level 0 tapes should not be overwritten, and should be saved for at least one year.

Be aware that even with the backup schedule outlined in Table 11.9, data can still be lost. If a hard disk fails at 3 p.m., all modifications since the 4:30 a.m. backup will be lost. Also, files that were deleted midweek will not appear on the level 5 tapes. Sometimes, a user accidentally deletes a file and does not realize it for several weeks. When the user wants to use the file, it is not there. If he asks you to restore it from backup, the only tape it appears on is the level 0, and it could be too far out of date to be useful. By not overwriting the daily level 9 tapes frequently, you can minimize this problem.

The syntax for the `ufsdump` command is as follows:

```
/usr/sbin/ufsdump <options> <arguments> <files to dump>
```

The options to the `ufsdump` command are described in Table 11.10.

**TABLE 11.10**

**ufsdump OPTIONS**

| *Option* | *Description* |
|---|---|
| `<options>` | A single string of one-letter option names. |
| `<arguments>` | Option arguments that can be multiple strings. The option letters and the arguments that go with them must be in the same order. |
| `<files to dump>` | The files to back up. This argument must always come last. It specifies the source or contents of the backup. It usually identifies a file system, but it can also identify individual files or directories. For a file system, specify the name of the file system or the raw device file for the disk slice where the file system is located. |

Table 11.11 describes the options and arguments for the `ufsdump` command.

**TABLE 11.11**

**OPTIONS FOR THE ufsdump COMMAND**

| *Option* | *Description* |
|---|---|
| 0 to 9 | Backup level. Specify level 0 for a full backup of the entire file system. Levels 1–9 are for incremental backups of files that have changed since the last lower-level backup. |

*continues*

**TABLE 11.11** *continued*

**OPTIONS FOR THE ufsdump COMMAND**

| *Option* | *Description* |
|---|---|
| a <archive-file> | Instructs `ufsdump` to create an archive file. Stores a backup table of the tape contents in a specified file on the disk. The file can be understood only by `ufsrestore`, which uses the table to determine whether a file to be restored is present in a backup file and, if so, on which volume of the medium it resides. |
| b <factor> | Blocking factor. Specifies the number of 512-byte blocks to write to tape per operation. |
| c | Instructs `ufsdump` to back up to cartridge tape. When end-of-media detection applies, this option sets the block size to 126. |
| d <bpi> | Tape density. Use this option only when `ufsdump` cannot detect the end of the medium. |
| D | Diskette. Backs up to floppy disk. |
| f <dump-file> | Dump file. Specifies the destination of the backup. The `dump-file` argument can be one of the following:<br>• A local tape drive or disk drive<br>• A remote tape drive or disk drive<br>• Standard output<br>Use this argument when the destination is not the default local tape drive /dev/rmt/0. If you use the `f` option, you must specify a value for `dump-file`. |
| l | Autoload. Use this option if you have an autoloading (stack-loader) tape drive. When the end of a tape is reached, this option takes the drive offline and waits up to two minutes for the tape drive to be ready again. If the drive is ready within two minutes, it continues. If the drive is not ready after two minutes, autoload prompts the operator to load another tape. |
| n | Notify. When intervention is needed, this option sends a message to all terminals of all users in the `sys` group. |
| o | Offline. When `ufsdump` is finished with a tape or disk, it takes the drive offline, rewinds it (if it's a tape), and removes the medium if possible (for example, it ejects a disk or removes an 8mm autoloaded tape). |
| s <size> | Size. Specifies the length of tape in feet or the size of disk in a number of 1024-byte blocks. You need to use this option only when `ufsdump` cannot detect the end of the medium. |

| Option | Description |
|---|---|
| S | Estimates the size of the backup. Determines the amount of space needed to perform the backup (without actually doing it) and outputs a single number indicating the estimated size of the backup in bytes. |
| t <tracks> | Tracks. Specifies the number of tracks for 1/4-inch cartridge tape. You need to use this option only when ufsdump cannot detect the end of the medium. |
| u | Updates the dump record. For a completed backup of a file system, adds an entry to the file /etc/dumpdates. The entry indicates the device name for the file system's disk slice, the backup level (0 to 9), and the date. No record is written when you do not use the u option or when you back up individual files or directories. If a record already exists for a backup at the same level, it is replaced. |
| v | Verify. After each tape or disk is written, verifies the contents of the medium against the source file system. If any discrepancies occur, prompts the operator to mount a new medium and then repeats the process. Use this option on an unmounted file system only; any activity in the file system causes it to report discrepancies. |
| w | Warning. Lists the file systems appearing in /etc/dumpdates that have not been backed up within a day. When you use this option, all other options are ignored. |
| W | Warning with highlight. Shows all file systems that appear in /etc/dumpdates, and highlights file systems that have not been backed up within a day. When you use this option, all other options are ignored. |

The ufsdump command uses these options by default:

```
ufsdump 9uf /dev/rmt/0 <files-to-back-up>
```

## ufsdump Examples

The following examples illustrate the use of the ufsdump command.

The following is an example of a full backup of the /users file system:

```
ufsdump 0ucf /dev/rmt/0 /users
  DUMP: Writing 63 Kilobyte records
  DUMP: Date of this level 0 dump: Sat Dec 12 13:13:22 1998
  DUMP: Date of last level 0 dump: the epoch
  DUMP: Dumping /dev/rdsk/c0t1d0s0 (pyramid1:/users) to /dev/rmt/0.
  DUMP: Mapping (Pass I) [regular files]
  DUMP: Mapping (Pass II) [directories]
  DUMP: Estimated 10168 blocks (4.96MB).
```

```
DUMP: Dumping (Pass III) [directories]
DUMP: Dumping (Pass IV) [regular files]
DUMP: Tape rewinding
DUMP: 10078 blocks (4.92MB) on 1 volume at 107 KB/sec
DUMP: DUMP IS DONE
```

In the following example, the local /export/home file system on a Solaris 8 system is backed up to a tape device on a remote Solaris 8 system called sparc1:

```
ufsdump 0ucf sparc1:/dev/rmt/0 /export/home
DUMP: Date of this level 0 dump: Sat Dec 12 11:50:1 3 1998
DUMP: Date of last level 0 dump: the epoch
DUMP: Dumping /dev/rdsk/c0t3d0s7 (/export/home) to \
/dev/rmt/0  on host sparc1
DUMP: mapping (Pass I) [regular files]
DUMP: mapping (Pass II) [directories]
DUMP: estimated 19574 blocks (9.56MB)
DUMP: Writing 63 Kilobyte records
DUMP: dumping (Pass III) [directories]
DUMP: dumping (Pass IV) [regular files]
DUMP: level 0 dump on Tue Oct 25 10:30:53 1994
DUMP: Tape rewinding
DUMP: 19574 blocks (9.56MB) on 1 volume
DUMP: DUMP IS DONE
```

If you want to see how much space a backup is going to require, issue the following command:

```
ufsdump 0s <filesystem>
```

The estimated number of bytes needed on tape to perform the level 0 backup is displayed.

## ufsrestore

The `ufsrestore` command copies files from backups created using the `ufsdump` command. You can use `ufsrestore` to reload an entire file system from a level 0 dump and incremental dumps that follow it, or to restore one or more single files from any dump tape. If `ufsrestore` is run by root, files are restored with their original owner, last modification time, and mode (permissions).

The syntax for the `ufsrestore` command is as follows:

```
ufsrestore  <options>  <arguments> < filename(s)>
```

The options for the `ufsrestore` command are described in Table 11.12.

**TABLE 11.12**

**ufsrestore OPTIONS**

| *Option* | *Description* |
|---|---|
| `<options>` | Gives you the choice of one and only one of these options: `i`, `r`, `R`, `t`, or `x`. |
| `<arguments>` | Follows the `options` string with the arguments that match the options. |
| `<filename(s)>` | Specifies files to be restored as arguments to the `x` or `t` options, and must always come last. |

Table 11.13 describes some of the more common options and arguments for the `ufsrestore` command.

**TABLE 11.13**

**COMMAND OPTIONS FOR ufsrestore**

| *Option* | *Description* |
|---|---|
| `i` | Interactive. Runs `ufsrestore` in interactive mode. In this mode, you can use a limited set of shell commands to browse the contents of the medium and select individual files or directories to restore. See Table 11.14 for a list of available commands. |
| `r` | Recursive. Restores the entire contents of the medium into the current working directory, which should be the top level of the file system. Information used to restore incremental dumps on top of the full dump is also included. To completely restore a file system, use this option to restore the full (level 0) dump and then each incremental dump. This is intended for a new file system that was just created with the `newfs` command. |
| `x <filename(s)>` | Extract. Selectively restores the files you specify using the `filename(s)` argument. `filename(s)` can be a list of files and directories. All files under a specified directory are restored unless you also use the `h` option. If you omit `filename(s)` or enter `.` for the root directory, all files on all volumes of the medium (or from standard input) are restored. Existing files are overwritten, and warnings are displayed. |

*continues*

**TABLE 11.13** *continued*

**COMMAND OPTIONS FOR ufsrestore**

| *Option* | *Description* |
|---|---|
| `t <filename(s)>` | Table of contents. Checks the files specified in the `<filename(s)>` argument against the medium. For each file, the full filename and the inode number (if the file is found) are listed. If the filename is not found, `ufsrestore` indicates that the file is not on the "volume," meaning any volume in a multivolume dump. If you do not enter the `<filename(s)>` argument, all files on all volumes of the medium are listed without distinguishing on which volume the files are located. When you use the `h` option, only the directory files specified in `<filename(s)>`—not their contents—are checked and listed. The table of contents is read from the first volume of the medium or (if you use the `a` option) from the specified archive file. This option is mutually exclusive with the `x` and `r` options. |
| `b <factor>` | Blocking factor. Specifies the number of 512-byte blocks to read from tape per operation. By default, `ufsrestore` tries to figure out the block size used in writing the tape. |
| `m` | Restores specified files into the current directory on the disk, regardless of where they are located in the backup hierarchy, and renames them with their inode number. For example, if the current working directory is /files, a file in the backup named ./database/test with inode number 156 is restored as /files/156. This option is useful when you are extracting only a few files. |
| `s<n>` | Skips to the nth backup file on the medium. This option is useful when you put more than one backup on a single tape. |
| `v` | Verbose. Displays the name and inode number of each file as it is restored. |

For a full listing, refer to the Solaris online manual pages.

Table 11.14 lists the commands that can be used with `ufsrestore` when using interactive mode (`ufsrestore -i`).

**TABLE 11.14**

## COMMANDS FOR AN INTERACTIVE RESTORATION

| *Command* | *Description* |
|---|---|
| `ls <directory-name>` | Lists the contents of either the current directory or the specified directory. Directories are suffixed with a /. Entries in the current list to be restored (extracted) are marked by an * prefix. If the verbose option is in effect, inode numbers are also listed. |
| `cd <directory-name>` | Changes to the specified directory in the backup hierarchy. |
| `add <filename>` | Adds the current directory or the specified file or directory to the list of files to extract (restore). If you do not use the `h` option, all files in a specified directory and its subdirectories are added to the list. Note that it's possible that not all the files you want to restore to a directory will be on a single backup tape or disk. You might need to restore from multiple backups at different levels to get all the files. |
| `delete <filename>` | Deletes the current directory or the specified file or directory from the list of files to extract (restore). If you do not use the `h` option, all files in the specified directory and its subdirectories are deleted from the list. Note that the files and directories are deleted only from the extract list you are building. They are not deleted from the medium. |
| `extract` | Extracts the files in the list and restores them to the current working directory on the disk. Specify 1 when asked for a volume number. If you are doing a multitape or multidisk restoration and you are restoring a small number of files, start with the last tape or disk. |
| `help` | Displays a list of the commands you can use in interactive mode. |
| `pwd` | Displays the pathname of the current working directory in the backup hierarchy. |
| `q` | Quits interactive mode without restoring additional files. |
| `verbose` | Turns the `verbose` option on or off. Verbose mode can also be entered as `v` on the command line outside interactive mode. When verbose is on, the interactive `ls` command lists inode numbers, and the `ufsrestore` command displays information on each file as it is extracted. |

## `ufsrestore` Examples

The following examples illustrate how to restore data from a tape by using `ufsrestore`.

Use the `ufsrestore` command to display the contents of the tape:

```
ufsrestore tf /dev/rmt/0
    2       .
 4249       ./users
12400       ./users/bill
12401       ./users/bill/.login
12402       ./users/bill/.cshrc
12458       ./users/bill/admin
12459       ./users/bill/junk
```

Use `ufsrestore` to restore a file from a backup that was created using `ufsdump`:

```
ufsrestore f /dev/rmt/0 filename
```

You can restore entire directories from a remote drive located on the system called sparc1 by adding `remote-host:` to the front of the tape device name, as illustrated in the next example:

```
ufsrestore rf sparc1:/dev/rmt/0 filename
```

Occasionally, a file system becomes so damaged that you must completely restore it from a backup. If you have faithfully backed up file systems, you can restore them to the state of the last backup. The first step in recovering a file system is to delete everything in the damaged file system and re-create the file system using the `newfs` command. To recover a damaged file system, perform the following steps:

## STEP BY STEP

### 11.1 Recovering and Restoring a Damaged File System

**1.** Unmount the file system as follows:

```
umount  /filesystem
```

in which `filesystem` is the name of the corrupted file system.

**2.** After unmounting the file system, issue the `newfs` command to create a new file system as follows:

```
newfs /dev/rdsk/<disk-partition-name>
```

in which `<disk-partition-name>` is the name of the raw disk partition containing the corrupted file system.

3. Check the new file system using `fsck` as follows:

   ```
   fsck /dev/rdsk/c?t?d?s?
   ```

4. Mount the file system to be restored, and change to that directory:

   ```
   mount /dev/dsk/c?t?d?s? <directory>
   cd /<directory>
   ```

5. Load the tape, and issue the following command:

   ```
   ufsrestore rf /dev/rmt/0
   ```

   The entire contents of the tape will be restored to the file system. All permissions, ownerships, and dates will remain as they were when the last incremental tape was created.

   The next two steps are optional.

6. Remove the `restoresymtable` file created by the `ufsrestore` command. This is a temporary file, and is not required after the file system has been successfully restored.

7. It's also a good idea to unmount the file system and run `fsck again` to check the repaired file system.

## Recovering the Root or /usr File System

Sometimes a careless administrator with root access accidentally deletes part or all of the root (/) or /usr file system. Other times, the file system can become unusable because of a faulty disk drive or a corrupted file system. Follow this procedure if you ever need to recover the root (/) or /usr file system:

### STEP BY STEP

#### 11.2 Recovering the Root or /usr File System

1. Replace and partition the disk if it has failed.

2. Re-create the file system by issuing the `newfs` command as follows:

   ```
   newfs /dev/rdsk/<disk-partition-name>
   ```

*continues*

*continued*

in which <disk-partition-name> is the name of the raw disk partition containing the corrupted file system.

3. Check the new file system using `fsck` as follows:

```
fsck /dev/rdsk/<disk-partiton-name>
```

4. Mount the new file system on a temporary mount point:

```
mount /dev/dsk/<disk-partition-name> /mnt
```

5. Change to the /mnt directory:

```
cd /mnt
```

6. Write-protect the tapes so that you don't accidentally overwrite them.

7. Load the tape, and issue the following command:

```
ufsrestore rf /dev/rmt/0
```

The entire contents of the tape will be restored to the file system. All permissions, ownerships, and dates will remain as they were when the last incremental tape was created.

8. Verify that the file system is restored:

```
ls
```

9. Remove the `restoresymtable` file that is created and used by `ufsrestore` to checkpoint the restoration:

```
rm restoresymtable
```

10. Change to the root (/) directory:

```
cd /
```

11. Unmount the newly created file system:

```
umount /mnt
```

12. Check the new file system with `fsck`:

```
fsck /dev/rdsk/< disk-partition-name>
```

The restored file system is checked for consistency.

13. If you are recovering the root (/) file system, create the boot blocks on the root partition by using the `installboot` command:

```
installboot  /usr/platform/`uname-i`/lib/fs/ufs/bootblk /dev/rdsk/< disk-partition-name>
```

The `installboot` command installs the boot blocks onto the boot disk. Without the boot blocks, the disk cannot boot. (`installboot` is covered again in Section II of this book.)

**14.** Insert a new tape into the tape drive, and back up the new file system:

```
ufsdump 0uf /dev/rmt/n /dev/rdsk/device-name
```

A level 0 backup is performed. Always do an immediate backup of a newly created file system because `ufsrestore` repositions the files and changes the inode allocation.

**15.** Reboot the system:

```
init 6
```

The system is rebooted.

The following example is an actual session that restores the root (/) file system from tape device /dev/rmt/0 to SCSI disk target 3 slice 0 on controller 0:

```
# mount /dev/dsk/c0t3d0s0 /mnt
# cd /mnt
# tapes
# ufsrestore rf /dev/rmt/0
```

Files are restored from tape:

```
# rm restoresymtable
# cd /
# umount /mnt
# fsck /dev/rdsk/c0t3d0s0
```

The system displays the `fsck` passes as the file system is checked:

```
# installboot \
 /usr/platform/sun4m/lib/fs/ufs/bootblk /dev/rdsk/c0t3d0s0
# ufsdump 0uf /dev/rmt/0 /dev/rdsk/c0t3d0s0
# shutdown -y -g0 -i0
```

The system is halted. At the `ok` prompt, perform a reconfiguration reboot as follows:

```
boot -r
```

This will ensure that all devices connected to the system have been configured properly in the kernel and in the /dev and /devices directories.

**NOTE**

The `tapes` command creates the /dev entries for the tape drive. It creates links in /dev/rmt to the actual tape device special files. The `tapes` command is covered in Chapter 16, "Device Administration and Disk Management."

## Additional Notes About Restoring Files

When you restore files in a directory other than the root directory of the file system, `ufsrestore` re-creates the file hierarchy in the current directory. For example, if you restore files to /home that were backed up from /users/bcalkins/files, the files are restored in the directory /home/users/bcalkins/files.

When restoring individual files and directories, it's a good idea to restore them to a temporary directory such as /var/tmp. After you verify the files, you can move them to their proper locations. You can restore individual files and directories to their original locations; however, if you do so, be sure you are not overwriting newer files with older versions from the backup tape.

Don't forget to make regular backups of your operating system. With all the customization you've done, such as adding user accounts, setting up printers, and installing application software, losing this information would be disastrous. Whenever you make modifications that affect the root (/), /usr, /opt, or other operating system directories, bring the system down into single-user mode and perform a level 0 dump.

## Chapter Summary

**KEY TERMS**

- Block size
- Tape archive
- File system dump
- Incremental backup
- Full backup

This chapter described the standard copy and backup utilities available in Solaris. It described the various types of backup media available. It discussed `tar`, `dd`, `cpio`, and `pax`, and described how to use them to copy and restore files, directories, and entire file systems.

This chapter also described how to use `ufsdump` and `ufsrestore` to perform regular backups on your system. In addition, it described a recommended backup schedule that could be implemented to safeguard any system from deliberate or accidental loss of data.

Finally, this chapter described how to recover data from your backup media. It described the procedure to restore single files or entire file systems.

Although these utilities do a good job of backing up your data, if your company has several servers and large storage pools, you might want to investigate some of the more robust backup packages available from third parties such as Veritas or Legato. Most of these packages provide a comprehensive suite of utilities for conducting and managing backups in a complex computing environment. In most cases, they allow single-point backups—not only for Solaris, but for other operating systems as well.

---

## APPLY YOUR KNOWLEDGE

## Exercises

Note that these exercises utilize a tape drive connected as /dev/rmt/0. If your system does not have a tape drive attached to it, substitute the device /dev/rmt/0 for a filename such as /tmp/foo.

### 11.1 Using `tar`

In this exercise, you'll use the `tar` command to copy files from disk to tape.

**Estimated Time**: 15 minutes (depends on the size of /export/home)

1. Create a tape archive of everything in the /export/home directory on tape device /dev/rmt/0:

   ```
   tar cvf /dev/rmt/0 /export/home
   ```

2. List the contents of the archive:

   ```
   tar tvf /dev/rmt/0
   ```

3. Now, add another tape archive to the same tape. This is referred to as a "stacked" tape. First, you need to advance the tape past the first archive using the `mt` command:

   ```
   mt  -f /dev/rmt/0 fsf 1
   ```

4. Now add the next archive of the /var/adm directory:

   ```
   tar xvf /dev/rmt/0 /var/adm
   ```

5. Now rewind the tape:

   ```
   mt -f /dev/rmt/0 rew
   ```

6. List the first archive on the tape. Notice the use of the "no rewind" device:

   ```
   tar tvf /dev/rmt/0n
   ```

7. Now list the contents of the second tape archive on the stacked tape:

   ```
   tar tvf /dev/rmt/0
   ```

   Note: It's important to make a notation on the tape label that this is a stacked tape and also to record the order of each archive on the tape.

### 11.2 Using *cpio* and *pax*

The exercise demonstrates how to copy user files that have been modified in the past 30 days to a tape drive with the device name /dev/rmt/0. Specify a larger than default blocking factor to increase the transfer speed.

**Estimated Time**: 15 minutes (depends on the size of /export/home)

1. `cd /export/home`

## APPLY YOUR KNOWLEDGE

2. Locate all files using the `find` command, and transfer them to tape using `cpio`:

   ```
   find . -mtime -30 -print | cpio -oB > \
   /dev/rmt/0
   ```

3. List all the files that were backed up in step 2:

   ```
   cpio -ict < /dev/rmt/0
   ```

4. Use the `pax` utility to list the contents of the tape that was created using `cpio`:

   ```
   pax -v -f /dev/rmt/0
   ```

### 11.3 Using *ufsdump* and *ufsrestore*

In this exercise, you'll use the `ufsdump` command to back up an entire file system. You'll then use the `ufsrestore` command to restore a file.

Caution: Don't do this exercise on a production system.

**Estimated Time**: 20 minutes

1. Log in as root.

2. Back up the entire /var file system to tape as follows:

   ```
   ufsdump 0ucf /dev/rmt/0 /var
   ```

3. Remove the /var/adm/messages file:

   ```
   rm /var/adm/messages
   ```

4. Restore the /var/adm/messages file using `ufsrestore`:

   ```
   cd /var
   ufsrestore -ivf /dev/rmt/0
   ```

5. At the `ufsrestore>` prompt, verify that the messages file is on the tape:

   ```
   ls adm/messages
   ```

6. Mark the file for extraction, and then extract the file:

   ```
   add adm/messages
   extract
   ```

   When the system asks you to "Specify the next volume", type `1`.

   When asked to "set owner/mode for '.'?[yn]", enter `y`

   Enter `q` to exit the `ufsrestore` utility.

7. Verify that the file has been restored to its proper location using the `ls -l` command.

## Review Questions

1. What will the following command sequence do?

   ```
   #cd /home/myjunk
   #tar cvf /dev/rmt/0 .
   ```

   A. Take all the files in /home/myjunk, package them into a single `tar` archive on /dev/rmt/0, and print out a commentary of the process.

   B. Extract the contents of the tape at /dev/rmt/0 to /home/myjunk.

   C. Tar all the files in /dev/rmt/0 to /home/myjunk, create a table of contents, and ignore checksum errors.

   D. Tar all the files in the current directory into two separate archives, one for the contents of myjunk and one for the rest of /home.

2. Given the following backup schedule, which tapes would be needed to fully restore the system if it goes down on a Saturday?

   - First Monday of the month—level 0 (tape 1)

## APPLY YOUR KNOWLEDGE

- All other Mondays—level 1 (tape 2)
- Wednesdays—level 2 (tape 3)
- Fridays—level 4 (tape 4)

A. All four of them

B. Tapes 2–4

C. Tapes 1, 2, and 4

D. Tapes 1, 3, and 4

3. Which of the following commands can be used in conjunction with `tar` and `cpio` to perform incremental archives?

   A. `sort`

   B. `find`

   C. `grep`

   D. `diff`

4. Which of the following utilities has a built-in function to perform incremental backups?

   A. `tar`

   B. `cpio`

   C. `ufsdump`

   D. `dd`

5. Which of the following commands lists the contents of a tar file?

   A. `tar -cvf`

   B. `tar -xvf`

   C. `tar -tvf`

   D. `tar -txf`

6. Which of the following is false of `dd`?

   A. It quickly converts and copies files with different data formats.

   B. It is a good backup tool.

   C. It is used to transfer a complete file system or partition from your hard disk to a tape.

   D. It is used to copy all data from one disk to another.

7. Which of the following is false regarding the `cpio` command?

   A. It is used to copy data from one place to another.

   B. It is not a good tool for backups.

   C. It can back up and restore individual files, not just entire file systems.

   D. Backups made by `cpio` are smaller than those created with `tar`.

8. After restoring the root file system from tape, which of the following steps is not necessary?

   A. `fsck`

   B. `installboot`

   C. `init 6`

   D. `ufsdump 0uf`

9. Which of the following statements regarding the `pax` utility is false?

   A. It supports a wide variety of archive formats, including `tar` and `cpio`.

   B. It is a POSIX-conformant archive utility.

## APPLY YOUR KNOWLEDGE

C. It does not have a built-in function to perform incremental backups.

D. It is old and not a recommended backup utility.

## Answers to Review Questions

1. **A.** The first command changes your working directory, and the second creates the `tar` file. The commands shown in the example will take all the files in the /home/myjunk directory, package them into a single `tar` archive on /dev/rmt/0, and print out a commentary of the process.

2. **A.** To restore the data from backups, you'll first load the level 1 tape created the first Monday of the month, followed by the level 2 tape, followed by the level 3 tape, and finally the level 4 tape.

3. **B.** Use the `find` command in conjunction with `tar` and `cpio` to perform incremental archives.

4. **C.** `ufsdump` has built-in options to create incremental backups that will back up only those files that were changed since a previous backup, saving tape space and time.

5. **C.** The `-t` option with the `tar` command lists the contents of a `tar` file.

6. **B.** The main advantage of the `dd` command is that it quickly converts and copies files with different data formats, such as differences in block size or record length. The most common use of this command is to transfer a complete file system or partition from your hard disk to a tape. You can also use it to copy files from one hard disk to another. `dd` does not make a good backup tool, however.

7. **B.** `cpio` can be used as an excellent tool to back up and restore individual files, not just entire file systems.

8. **D.** After restoring the root file system from tape, you must install the boot block with the `installboot command`, run `fsck` on the file system, and then reboot with the `init 6` or `shutdown` command.

9. **D.** `pax` is the newest of the backup utilities described in this chapter. It works well as a backup utility.

## OBJECTIVES

The following are the test objectives for this chapter:

**Understand Solaris Shells**

- Understanding the fundamentals of shell programming is key to being an effective system administrator. The shell is your interface to the Solaris 8 operating system; therefore, it's one of the tools you will need to be proficient in using. Specifically, you'll need to understand the following topics pertaining to the Solaris shells:

- Select which shell to use. The Solaris environment provides many shells from which to choose. As the system administrator, you'll need to make an informed decision as to which shells the users of your system will use.

- Set shell variables. Many aspects of your job will require an understanding of shell variables. You'll set shell variables to customize the user environment, and you'll use shell variables as you create scripts to automate your routine tasks.

- Understand shell built-ins, shell conditionals, repeat action statements, and shell functions. To write shell scripts, you must understand the tools available in the shell to perform the task at hand. This chapter will introduce and describe the tools that will help you build shell scripts to automate your tasks and become more productive.

CHAPTER 12

# Writing Shell Scripts and Programs

## Outline



## Study Strategies

The following strategies will help you prepare for the test:

- When studying shells and shell scripts, nothing can replace practice and experience. I've introduced some key topics pertaining to shell scripts. You will become efficient in using the shell or writing shell scripts only if you practice all of the topics presented in this chapter on a Solaris system.
- Make sure that you understand the differences between all the various default shells in Solaris, such as how to set a local and environmental variable in each shell. In addition, understand all of the default variables that are provided in each shell.

## INTRODUCTION

A thorough understanding of shell programming is a must for any system administrator. System administrators must be able to read and write shell programs because many tasks can and should be automated by using such scripts. An advantage of using a script or shell program to perform a particular task is that doing so ensures consistency—in other words, the task is performed the same way each time. Also, many software products come with installation scripts that have to be modified for your system before they will work. This chapter first introduces some shell basics, and then it describes some fundamentals of creating a shell script.

## SHELL SCRIPT BASICS

A UNIX script is a sequence of UNIX commands, either in a file or typed at the command line, that perform multiple operations. Such files are also known as batch files in some systems. Another term for a script that might be familiar to you is macro. Usually, script or macro refers to a simple command sequence, but shell program identifies a file containing a more complicated arrangement of commands. Shell programs use the shell's control and conditional commands, called built-ins, which are discussed later in this chapter.

To run a file as a script, you must set the file's execution bit, as discussed in Chapter 8, "System Security." In the following example, you can see the execution bit has been set for the user, the group, and others:

```
% ls -l
-rwxr-xr-x  1 bcalkins      425  Jul 10 11:10      program.1
```

If the execution bit is set, what happens next depends on the first line of the file. If the first two characters on the first line are anything other than `#!`, the file is interpreted as a Bourne shell script. If the characters `#!` are followed by an explicit program location, such as /bin/csh, that program is run as an interpreter on the contents of the file. In other words, the program is run in the shell that is specified after the `#!` characters.

NOTE It's a good idea to put scripts and shell programs into their own directory to separate them from standard UNIX programs. They are commonly put into a directory named /usr/local/bin. It's also a good practice to suffix the program names with .sh, .csh, or .ksh so that they are readily identified as shell scripts.

To create a C shell script, for example, type the following on the first line of the file:

```
#!/bin/csh
```

## Selecting a Shell to Use

The login shell is the command interpreter that runs when you log in. The Solaris 8 operating environment offers three commonly used shells:

- The Bourne shell (/sbin/sh). The default shell. It is a command interpreter that executes commands read from a terminal or a file.
- The C shell (/bin/csh). A command interpreter with a C-like syntax. The C shell provides a number of convenient features for interactive use that are not available with the Bourne shell, including filename completion, command aliasing, and history substitution.
- The Korn shell (/bin/ksh). A command interpreter that executes commands read from a terminal or a file.

When writing scripts, you can use any of these three shells. The basic features of each shell are described in Table 12.1.

**TABLE 12.1**

**Basic Features of the Bourne, C, and Korn Shells**

| *Feature* | *Bourne* | *C* | *Korn* |
|---|---|---|---|
| Syntax compatible with sh | Yes | No | Yes |
| Job control | Yes | Yes | Yes |
| History list | No | Yes | Yes |
| Command-line editing | No | Yes | Yes |
| Aliases | No | Yes | Yes |
| Single-character abbreviation for login directory | No | Yes | Yes |

| *Feature* | *Bourne* | *C* | *Korn* |
|---|---|---|---|
| Protect files from overwriting | No | Yes | Yes (noclobber) |
| Ignore Ctrl+D (ignoreeof) | No | Yes | Yes |
| Enhanced cd | No | Yes | Yes |
| Initialization file separate from profile | No | Yes | Yes |
| Logout file | No | Yes | No |

In addition to the commonly used shells described, Solaris 8 also provides five additional shells:

- The J-shell (/sbin/jsh). Provides all of the functionality of Bourne shell, but enables job control. When the J-shell is invoked, job control is enabled in addition to all of the other Bourne shell functionality.
- The Restricted Korn shell. A restricted version of the Korn shell used to set up login names and execution environments whose capabilities need to be more controlled than those of the standard shell.
- The T-shell (/usr/bin/tcsh). Enhanced, but compatible, version of the C-shell with filename completion and command-line editing. Type `man tcsh` to see a complete online listing of the enhancements.
- The GNU Bourne-Again shell (/usr/bin/bash). Bash incorporates useful features from the Korn and C shells.
- The Z-shell (/usr/bin/zsh). Command interpreter (shell) usable as an interactive login shell and as a shell script command processor.

> **NOTE**
>
> In addition to the three standard shells, the Common Desktop Environment (CDE), described in Appendix B, "Administration and Configuration of the CDE," provides the Desktop Korn shell (`dtksh`). This shell gives Korn shell scripts a way to easily access most of the existing Xt and Motif functions used in the CDE graphical interface. To successfully use `dtksh`, you should have experience with Xlib, the Xt Intrinsics, the Motif widgets, and Korn Shell programming. It is also helpful to know the C programming language.
>
> In addition, Solaris 8 includes PERL, the Practical Extraction Report Language, for creating programs.

Selecting a particular shell to use is personal preference. I find that most BSD UNIX users use the C shell because of its roots at Berkeley. Many of us old SunOS users still prefer to use the C shell because we've used it for so many years. On the other hand, I find that SystemV users prefer the Korn shell. These preferences stem from the early development days of UNIX. For system administration, the Bourne shell is best for writing scripts. It is the default shell in Solaris, and is the only shell found on all UNIX systems. All scripts that come with Solaris (that is, those that run control scripts located in /etc/init.d) and most third-party software are also written in the Bourne shell. In addition, because the Bourne shell is located in /sbin, it's the only shell available when /usr is not mounted (that is, in single-user mode). The Bourne shell was designed from the beginning for use as a programming language, which explains its breadth of programming features. An additional reason for using the Bourne shell is that its conditionals and controls are compatible with all other shells, including the `dtksh` shell used in the CDE environment. `dtksh` is discussed in Appendix B.

All examples in this chapter use the Bourne shell.

## Bourne Shell Variables

A variable is a name that refers to a temporary storage area in memory. A value such as a text string or number is assigned to a variable and can be changed at any time. The Bourne shell uses two types of variables to store values: local and environmental. Each is described in this chapter.

A variable is either set to some particular value or is said to be "unset," which means that it does not exist as a variable. Shell variables are an integral part of shell programming. The shell variable provides the capability to store and manipulate information within a shell program. The variables you use are completely under your control, and you can set or unset any number of variables as needed to perform a particular task.

A variable name must begin with a letter, and can contain letters, digits, and underscores, but no special characters. In the Bourne shell, environment variables are set with an assignment of `NAME=value`. In the following example, the `ME` and `BC` variables are set by entering the following at a command prompt:

```
ME=bill
BC="bill calkins"
```

Be sure not to have any white space before or after the equals sign (=). Double quotes, as used in the second example, are used when white space is present in the text string you are assigning to the variable. Whenever the shell sees a $variable, such as `$ME`, it substitutes into the command line the value stored for that variable.

## Quoting

Unfortunately, other programs also use many of the special characters that the shell uses—there simply are not enough characters to go around. When the special characters shown in Table 12.2 are used in the shell, they must be quoted. Quoting is used when an assigned value contains a special character, spaces, tabs, or newlines. Without the quotation marks, the special symbols will be interpreted as shell metacharacters instead of being passed as arguments to programs. The three methods of quoting used in the Bourne shell are described in Table 12.2.

**TABLE 12.2**

**QUOTING**

| *Character* | *Description* | *Functionality* |
|---|---|---|
| \ | Backslash | Quotes the next character (also known as "escaping"). |
| ' | Single quote marks | No interpretation occurs. |
| " | Double quotes | All characters enclosed in double quotation marks are quoted, except backslash, accent grave, double quote, and the currency symbol. |

**NOTE** Don't confuse the back tick with the single-quote character. A back tick is the symbol that appears on the same keyboard key as the ~ (tilde). The single-quote character appears on the same key as the " (double-quote) character.

Commands are read from the string between two back ticks (\` \`). The standard output from these commands can be used to set a variable.

With the back tick, no interpretation is done on the string before the string is read, except to remove backslashes (\) used to escape other characters. Escaping back ticks allows nested command substitutions like this one:

```
font=`grep font \`cat filelist\``
```

The backslashes inside the embedded command (`` \`cat filelist\` ``) protect the back ticks from immediate interpretation by the shell. With the back slash (\), the back tick just before `cat` fails to match the initial one before `grep`. The two "escaped" back ticks will be interpreted on the second pass, and the command will execute correctly.

In other words, because this example has two sets of back ticks, we need to show the shell which back tick pairs up with the other. We do this using the back slash (\). The shell will look at the command string twice—once to pair up the back ticks, and a second time to run the command.

## Delimiters

Some characters naturally act as delimiters in the Bourne shell. When encountered, such characters have the effect of separating one logical word from the next. The characters outlined in Table 12.3 have a special meaning to the shell and cause termination unless quoted.

**TABLE 12.3**

**DELIMITERS**

| *Character* | *Description* |
|---|---|
| ; | Command delimiter. Acts as a `<return>`, and executes the commands sequentially. |
| & | Runs commands asynchronously. |
| ( ) | Groups commands into a single logical word. |
| Newline | Separates records (the default). |
| Spaces, tabs | Separates fields (the default). |

## Shell Variables

To display the value of a variable, enter the following at the command prompt (the dollar sign informs the shell that the following name refers to a variable):

```
echo $BC
```

The following is displayed:

```
bill calkins
```

Variables you set are local to the current shell unless you mark them for export. Variables marked for export are called environment variables, and will be made available to any commands that the shell creates. The following command marks the variable `BC` for export:

```
export BC
```

You can list local variables by typing the `set` command. You can list variables that have been marked for export by typing the `env` command. The Bourne shell has several predefined variables, some of which are described in Table 12.4. These variables are assigned automatically when a user logs in, and are defined by the login program, the system initialization file, and the user's initialization files.

**TABLE 12.4**

### DEFAULT BOURNE SHELL VARIABLES

| *Variable* | *Description* |
|---|---|
| `ARCH` | Sets the user's system architecture (for example, sun4, sun4c, sun4u). |
| `CDPATH` | Sets the search path for the `cd` command. |
| `HOME` | Sets the value of the user's home directory. |
| `LANG` | Sets the locale. |
| `LOGNAME` | Defines the name of the user currently logged in. The default value of `LOGNAME` is automatically set by the login program to the username specified in the /etc/passwd file. You should only need to reference (not reset) this variable. |
| `LPDEST` | Sets the user's default printer. |
| `MAIL` | If this parameter is set to the name of a mail file and the `MAILPATH` parameter is not set, the shell informs the user of the arrival of mail in the specified file. |
| `MAILCHECK` | Specifies how often (in seconds) the shell will check for the arrival of mail in the files specified by the `MAILPATH` or `MAIL` parameters. The default value is 600 seconds (10 minutes). If set to 0, the shell will check after each prompt. |
| `MAILPATH` | Sets the mail path by defining a colon-separated list of filenames. If this parameter is set, the shell informs the user of the arrival of mail in any of the specified files. Each filename can be followed by `%`, and a message that will be printed when the modification time changes. The default message is `You have mail.` |

*continues*

> **NOTE** The order of the search path is important. When identical commands exist in different locations, the first command found with that name is used. For example, suppose that `PATH` is defined for user jean (in Bourne and Korn shell syntax) as `PATH=/bin:/usr/bin:/usr/sbin:$HOME/bin` and a file named "sample" resides in both /usr/bin and /home/jean/bin. If the user types the command `sample` without specifying its full pathname, the version found in /usr/bin is used.

**TABLE 12.4** *continued*

**DEFAULT BOURNE SHELL VARIABLES**

| *Variable* | *Description* |
|---|---|
| `MANPATH` | Sets the hierarchies of available man pages. |
| `OPENWINHOME` | Sets the path to the OpenWindows subsystem. |
| `PATH` | Lists, in order, the directories that the shell searches to find the program to run when the user types a command. If the directory is not in the search path, users must type the complete pathname of a command. The default `PATH` is automatically defined and set as specified in .profile (Bourne or Korn shell) or .cshrc (C shell) as part of the login process. |
| `PS1` | Sets the primary prompt string, by default `"$ "`. |
| `PS2` | Sets the secondary prompt string, by default `"> "`. |
| `SHELL` | Sets the default shell used by `make`, `vi`, and other tools. When the shell is invoked, it scans the environment for this name. |
| `TERM` | Defines the terminal. This variable should be reset in /etc/profile or /etc/.login. When the user invokes an editor, the system looks for a file with the same name as the definition of this environment variable. The system searches the directory referenced by `TERMINFO` to determine the terminal characteristics. |
| `TERMINFO` | Specifies the pathname for an unsupported terminal that has been added to the terminfo database. Use the `TERMINFO` variable in `$HOME/.profile` or `/$HOME/.login`. When the `TERMINFO` environment variable is set, the system first checks the `TERMINFO` path defined by the user. If it does not find a definition for a terminal in the `TERMINFO` directory defined by the user, it searches the default directory, /usr/share/lib/terminfo, for a definition. If it does not find a definition in either location, the terminal is identified as "dumb." |
| `TZ` | Sets the time zone used to display dates (for example, in the `ls -l` command). If `TZ` is not set in the user's environment, the system setting is used; otherwise, Greenwich Mean Time is used. |

# BUILT-INS

Built-ins are used in shell programs to make decisions and to add intelligence to the task to be performed. Built-ins for the Bourne shell are listed in Tables 12.5 and 12.6. More information on the built-ins described in Table 12.5 is available in the Solaris online manual pages. The shell conditionals listed in Table 12.6 are described in this chapter. Each shell has its own set of built-ins, with the Bourne shell having the fewest. For this reason, it is the smallest and fastest of the three shells.

**TABLE 12.5**

**BOURNE SHELL BUILT-INS**

| *Built-In* | *Description* |
|---|---|
| `break` | Exits a `for` or `while` loop. |
| `continue` | Continues the next iteration of a `for` or `while` loop. |
| `echo` | Writes arguments on standard output. |
| `eval` | Evaluates and executes arguments. |
| `exec` | Executes a program. Executes in place of the current process so that `exec` does not create a new process. |
| `exit` | Exits the shell program. |
| `export` | Creates a global variable. |
| `priv` | Sets or displays privileges. |
| `read` | Reads a line from standard input. |
| `readonly` | Changes a variable to read-only. |
| `set` | Sets shell options. |
| `test` | Evaluates conditional expressions. |
| `times` | Displays execution times. |
| `trap` | Manages execution signals. |
| `umask` | Sets default security for files and directories. |
| `unset` | Unsets a local variable. |
| `wait` | Waits for a background process to complete. |

**TABLE 12.6**

**BOURNE SHELL CONDITIONALS**

| *Conditional* | *Description* |
|---|---|
| `if-then-else-fi` | Tests a condition and selects an action based on the results of the test. |
| `case-esac` | Selects an action based on the value of the variable. |
| `for-do-done` | Repeats a sequence of commands until a predetermined condition is met. |
| `while-do-done` | Repeats a sequence of commands until a test condition is no longer true. |
| `until-do-done` | Repeats a sequence of commands until a test condition results in a successful status. |

# SHELL CONDITIONALS

In addition to the built-ins listed in Tables 12.5 and 12.6, the Bourne shell also contains some simple conditionals. A conditional command makes a choice depending on the outcome of a condition. Examples of simple conditionals are `&&` and ||, which I will discuss along with the `if` and `case` conditionals in this section.

## && and ||

The simplest conditional in the Bourne shell is the double ampersand (`&&`). When two commands are separated by a double ampersand, the second command executes only if the first command returns a zero exit status (an indication of successful completion).

Following is an example:

```
ls -ld /usr/bin > /dev/null && echo "Directory Found"
```

If the directory /usr/bin exists, the message `Directory Found` is displayed.

The opposite of `&&` is the double bar (||). When two commands are separated by ||, the second command executes only if the first command returns a nonzero exit status (indicating failure).

Following is an example:

```
ls -d  /usr/foo || echo "No directory found"
```

If the directory does not exist, the following message is displayed:

```
/usr/foo: No such file or directory
No directory found
```

## true and false Programs

The Bourne shell contains the special programs `true` and `false`. The only function of the `true` program is to return a true (zero) exit status. Similarly, the function of the `false` program is to return a false (nonzero) exit status.

Following is an example:

```
true && echo True
```

The system responds with `True`.

Following is another example:

```
False || echo False
```

The system responds with `False`.

True and false tests will be discussed later, when we discuss `if` and `while` conditionals.

> **NOTE** && and || are useful conditionals for creating simple scripts, but additional functionality is sometimes required. Therefore, the Bourne shell offers the if and case conditionals.

## if

One of the more important built-ins of the Bourne shell is the `if` conditional. The syntax of the `if` conditional is as follows:

```
if condition-list
       then list
      elif condition-list
       then list
    else list
    fi
```

The list following `if` is executed. If it returns a zero exit status, the list following the first `then` is executed. Otherwise, the list following `elseif` is executed. If its value is zero, the list following the next `then` is executed. Failing that, the `else` list is executed. If no list is executed, the `if` command returns a zero exit status.

The next example illustrates the use of an `if conditional statement`:

```
if  [ -f  /tmp/errlog ]
    then
        rm /tmp/errlog
        echo "Error log has been removed"
    else
        echo "No errorlog  has been found"
fi
```

In this example, the program checks for a file named /tmp/errlog. If the file is present and is a regular file, the program removes it. If the file is not present, the file prints a message.

## The Test Program

The previous example used the `if` test `[-f  /tmp/errlog]` to evaluate a conditional expression. At the heart of each control structure is a conditional test. The `test` command is commonly used in shell programs to perform various tests and to determine whether certain files and directories exist. The test program performs three types of tests:

- It can test files for certain characteristics, such as file type and permissions.
- It can perform string comparisons.
- It can make numeric comparisons.

`test` indicates the success or failure of its testing by its exit status. `test` evaluates an expression and, if its value is true, sets a zero (true) exit status. Otherwise, a nonzero (false) exit status is set. All shell commands return a true (0) value when they complete successfully or a false (1) value when they fail. You can display the exit status of the last shell command by looking at the `$?` variable with the `echo` command. Table 12.7 lists some of the common conditions that can be evaluated.

**TABLE 12.7**

## BUILT-IN TEST FUNCTIONS

| *Test Condition* | *Description* |
|---|---|
| `r <filename>` | True if the filename exists and is readable. |
| `w <filename>` | True if the filename exists and is writeable. |
| `x <filename>` | True if the filename exists and is executable. |
| `f <filename>` | True if the filename exists and is a regular file. |
| `d <filename>` | True if the filename exists and is a directory. |
| `h <filename>` | True if the filename exists and is a symbolic link. With all other primitives (except `-L filename`), the symbolic links are followed by default. |
| `c <filename>` | True if the filename exists and is a character special file. |
| `b <filename>` | True if the filename exists and is a block special file. |
| `u <filename>` | True if the filename exists and its set-user-ID bit is set. |
| `g <filename>` | True if the filename exists and its set-group-ID bit is set. |
| `k <filename>` | True if the filename exists and its sticky bit is set. |
| `n <filename>` | True if length of string is non-zero. |
| `s <filename>` | True if the filename exists and has a size greater than zero. |
| `z <filename>` | True if length of string is zero. |
| `<s1> = <s2>` | True if strings `s1` and `s2` are identical. |
| `<s1> != <s2>` | True if strings `s1` and `s2` are not identical. |
| `<n1> -eq <n2>` | True if the integers `n1` and `n2` are algebraically equal. Any of the comparisons `-ne`, `-gt`, `-ge`, `-lt`, and `-le` can be used in place of `-eq`. |
| `L <filename>` | True if the filename exists and is a symbolic link. With all other primitives (except `-h <filename>`), the symbolic links are followed by default. |
| ***These Test Functions Can Be Combined with the Following Operators*** | |
| `!` | Unary negation operator. |
| `a` | Binary and operator. |
| `o` | Binary or operator (`-a` has higher precedence than `-o`). |
| `(expression)` | Parentheses for grouping. Notice also that parentheses are meaningful to the shell and, therefore, must be quoted. |

Following is an example of where you might use a unary operator:

```
if  [ ! -f  /tmp/errlog ]
    then
        echo "No error log has been found"
fi
```

In this example, the statement `[ ! -f /tmp/errlog ]` tests whether the file `/tmp/errlog` does not exist.

## case

Many programs are menu-driven; that is, they offer the user a menu of choices from which to select. The `case` statement makes it easy to set up a menu of choices. The general syntax for a `case` statement is as follows:

```
case value in
choice1) commands;;
choice2) commands;;
...
esac
```

A `case` command executes the list associated with the first pattern that matches the choice. Following is an example to describe how a `case` statement works:

```
echo Please enter the letter next to the command that you \
want to select:
echo 'a  date'
echo 'b  ls'
echo 'c  who'
read choice
case $choice in
a) date;;
b) ls;;
c) who;;
*)   echo Invalid choice - Bye.
esac
```

The list of choices is scanned to find the one that matches the value input by the user. The choice `*)` matches any value, so it's usually added as a last option—a catch-all.

# Repeated-Action Commands

The Bourne shell provides three repeated-action commands, each of which corresponds to constructs you might have seen before in other programming languages:

- `for`
- `while`
- `until`

These commands cause a program to loop or repeat. They are described next.

## The `for` Loop

A useful shell command is the `for` loop, which is the simplest way to set up repetition in a shell script. The syntax of a `for` loop is as follows:

```
for name [ in wordlist . . . ]
do list
done
```

Each time a `for` command is executed, `name` is set to the next word taken from the `in word` list. If `in word . . .` is omitted, the `for` command executes the `do list` once for each positional parameter that is set. Execution ends when no more words are in the list. The following example illustrates a simple `for` loop:

```
for i in eat run jump play
do
    echo See spot $i
done
```

When the program is executed, the system responds with this:

```
See spot eat
See spot run
See spot jump
See spot play
```

If you want to enter data interactively, you can add the shell special command `read`:

```
echo Hello- What\'s your name\?
read name
for i in $name
do
    echo $i
done
```

When executing the program, the user is asked to enter the word `list`. Notice the use of the backslash (`\`) so that the `'` and the `?` are taken literally and are not used as special characters.

## The `while` Loop

A `while` loop repeats a set of commands continuously until a condition is met. The syntax for a `while` loop is as follows:

```
while condition-list
do commands
done
```

First, the `condition-list` is executed. If it returns a true exit status, the `do` list is executed, and the operation restarts from the beginning. If the `condition-list` returns a false exit status, the conditional structure is complete.

The following illustrates the `while` loop. The program checks to see if the file /tmp/errlog is present. If the file is not present, the program exits the loop. If the file is present, the program prints a message and runs again every five seconds until the file is removed.

**NOTE** The special command `sleep 5` instructs the system to wait five seconds before running again.

```
while [ -f /tmp/errlog ]
do echo The file is still there ; sleep 5
done
```

## The until Loop

The until loop is a variant of the while statement. Just as the while statement repeats as long as the condition-list returns a true value, the until statement repeats until the condition-list returns a false value. The following example continues to display a message every five seconds until the file is created:

```
until [ -f  /tmp/errlog ]
    do echo the file is missing; sleep 5
done
```

Conditional structures such as while and until are executed by the shell as if they were a single command. The shell scans the entire structure before any part of it is executed.

# Shell Functions

Any good programming language provides support for functions. A function is a bundle of statements that is executed as a group. The bundles are executed just like a "regular" command, and are used to carry out often-required tasks. An advantage of a function is that it is held in the computer's main memory, so execution is much quicker than with a script, which must be retrieved from disk. The current version of the Bourne shell supports shell functions; older versions of the Bourne shell did not. The syntax for shell functions is as follows:

```
name()
{
command-list
}
```

This command syntax defines a function named name. The body of the function is the command-list between { and }. This list is executed whenever name is specified as the name of a command. As an example, at the command prompt, type the following:

```
hello()
{
echo hello there
}
```

The function is named hello, and can be executed by typing hello. The output of the function is hello there. The exit status of a function is the exit status of the last command executed in the body.

# Chapter Summary

**KEY TERMS**

- Shell script
- Execution bit
- Restricted shell
- J-shell
- C-shell
- Korn shell
- Bourne shell
- Shell variable
- Quoting
- Shell built-ins
- Shell conditional
- Exit status
- Loop
- Shell function

Constructing your own commands with scripts and shell programs is a powerful and flexible tool to assist you in system administration. First, you need to select the shell that is the most comfortable for you to use. Choose from the Bourne shell, bash, C-shell, tcsh, or the Korn shell. An important note, however, is that most system administrators choose the Bourne shell because of its wide use and availability.

Shell variables were described in this chapter. As a system administrator, you'll be setting and using variables regularly. Most of your Solaris and third-party programs will rely on these variables. If they are set incorrectly, programs will go awry, and the system might not function properly.

Finally, shell built-ins and conditionals were described. You'll use these built-ins in your scripts to set variables, obtain input, and perform repetitive tasks and other operations necessary to automate routine tasks.

Using all of these tools, routine tasks can be simplified and automated to free up your time and allow you to attend to more demanding tasks. Shell programming is a skill that all UNIX system administrators must have and is one of the keys to becoming a sophisticated UNIX user.

This concludes Section I and the material that is covered on the Part I exam. The next section covers topics you'll need to know for the second exam. In many cases, Section II provides more details on topics that were introduced in this section but weren't objectives for the first exam.

## APPLY YOUR KNOWLEDGE

# Exercises

### 12.1 Using Bourne Shell Variables

In this exercise, you'll display and set Bourne shell variables.

**Estimated Time:** 10 minutes

1. Make sure you're in the Bourne shell by typing `/sbin/sh`. Verify you're in the Bourne shell by displaying the value of the $SHELL variable:

```
echo $SHELL
```

2. Print the values of the environmental variables in your environment:

```
env
```

3. Print the values of the local variables in your environment:

```
set
```

4. Change to your home directory:

```
cd $HOME
```

5. Create an environmental variable named ME. The value assigned to the variable should be your name.

```
ME='Bill Calkins'
export ME

echo $ME
```

6. Remove the variable:

```
unset ME
```

### 12.2 Creating a Bourne Shell Script

Write a Bourne shell script named search1 that prompts the user for a string to search for in all the files in his directory. Display the filenames of all the files that contain the string.

**Estimated Time:** 15 minutes

1. In your home directory, use vi to create a text file named *search1* with the following entries:

```
#!/bin/sh

echo "Please enter a string to search for: "

read string

echo The following files contain the string \
$string:

grep -l $string *
```

2. Set the execute permissions on the file:

```
chmod 744 search1
```

3. Execute the file as follows:

```
./search1
```

Make sure you have a text file in your home directory that has the string for which you plan to search. If you need to, use vi to create a couple of temporary files.

Use the vi editor to write the following shell script called *reverse* that will receive up to 10 arguments and list the arguments in reverse order.

4. In your home directory, use the vi editor to create the following script named *mylist*:

```
#!/sbin/sh
echo $(10) $9 $8 $7 $6 $5 $4 $3 $2 $1
```

5. Set execute permissions on the file:

```
chmod 744 mylist
```

6. Execute the script as follows, and view the results:

```
./mylist 1 2 3 4 5 6 7
```

# APPLY YOUR KNOWLEDGE

## 12.3 Using the case Conditional in a Script

This exercise demonstrates the use of the case conditional statement in a script. The script will display a list of options for the user to select from. A specific command will be run based on the option that is selected.

**Estimated Time**: 15 minutes

1. In your home directory, use the vi editor to create a file named *options* with the following entries:

```
#!/bin/sh
echo Please enter the letter next to the \
command that you want to select:
echo 'a  date'
echo 'b  ls'
echo 'c  who'
read choice
case $choice in
    a) date;;
    b) ls;;
    c) who;;
    *)   echo Invalid choice - Bye.
esac
```

2. Set execute permissions on the file named *options*:

```
chmod 744 options
```

3. Execute the script and enter a, b, or c and watch the results:

```
/.options
```

## 12.4 Creating an Interactive for Loop

This exercise will demonstrate how to set up repetition in a script using a for loop. This script will prompt the user to input names, and the script will generate a greeting for each name entered.

**Estimated Time**: 15 minutes

1. In your home directory, create a file named *users* using the vi editor with the following entries:

```
#!/bin/sh
echo "Hello- Please enter a list of names \
(ie. Bill Tom Mike)"
read LIST
for file in $LIST
do

echo Greetings $LIST

done
```

2. Set execute permissions on the file named *users*:

```
chmod 744 user
```

3. Execute the script:

```
./users
```

## 12.5 Using the *while* Conditional

This exercise will demonstrate how to use a while loop in a script. You'll create a program called *msg* that will display a message to the active window once every five seconds, for a minute.

**Estimated Time**: 15 minutes

1. In your home directory, use the vi editor to create a file named *msg* with the following contents:

```
#!/bin/sh
count=1
while
    [ count -lt 12 ]

do

    echo "Hello, I'm glad you're here"
    sleep 5
    let count=count+1

done
```

2. Set execute permissions on the file named msg:

```
chmod 744 msg
```

3. Execute the script:

```
./msg
```

## APPLY YOUR KNOWLEDGE

## Review Questions

1. Which of the following is the default shell on the Solaris system?

   A. Korn shell

   B. C shell

   C. Bourne shell

   D. dtksh

2. Which of the following is the correct method of setting a global variable in the Bourne shell?

   A. X=1; export X

   B. X=1; export $X

   C. export X=1

   D. setenv x 1

3. Which of the following is the correct method of setting a variable in the Bourne shell?

   A. x=1

   B. set x = 1

   C. setenv x 1

   D. export x=1

4. Which of the following shell conditionals repeats a sequence of commands until a test condition is no longer true?

   A. if-then-else-fi

   B. for-do-done

   C. while-do-done

   D. until-do-done

5. What does && do?

   A. The second command executes only if the first command returns a zero exit status.

   B. It runs a script or program in the background.

   C. The second command executes only if the first command returns a non-zero exit status.

   D. It executes the command twice.

6. Which of the following shell conditionals returns an exit status of 0 or 1?

   A. `set`

   B. `test`

   C. `echo $?`

   D. `case`

7. Which of the following are the Repeat Action commands found in the Bourne shell?

   A. `if`

   B. `for`

   C. `while`

   D. `case`

8. What are the main advantages of functions?

   A. They are easier to create than aliases.

   B. They are held in the computer's main memory, so execution is much quicker than it is for scripts.

   C. They are a bundle of statements executed as a group.

   D. They are more secure than scripts.

## APPLY YOUR KNOWLEDGE

9. How do you see the contents of a variable?

    A. `echo variable`

    B. `ls $variable`

    C. `set $variable`

    D. `echo $variable`

10. Which of the following is not a default shell variable that is automatically set when entering the Bourne shell?

    A. NAME

    B. CDPATH

    C. HOME

    D. LPDEST

11. Which of the following tests does the test program not perform?

    A. Testing whether a variable is set properly

    B. Testing files for certain characteristics, such as file type and permissions

    C. Performing string comparisons

    D. Making numeric comparisons

## Answers to Review Questions

1. **C.** The default shell on the Solaris system is the Bourne shell.

2. **A.** The correct method of setting a global variable in the Bourne shell is x=1; export x.

3. **A.** The correct method of setting a variable in the Bourne shell is x=1.

4. **C.** The shell conditional while-do-done repeats a sequence of commands until a test condition is no longer true.

5. **A.** When two commands are separated by a double ampersand, the second command executes only if the first command returns a zero exit status (an indication of successful completion).

6. **B., C.** `test` indicates the success or failure of its testing by its exit status. `test` evaluates an expression and, if its value is true, sets a zero (true) exit status. Otherwise, a nonzero (false) exit status is set. All shell commands return a true (0) value when they complete successfully or a false (1) value when they fail. You can display the exit status of the last shell command by looking at the `$?` variable with the `echo` command.

7. **B., C.** The Bourne shell provides three repeated-action commands: `for`, `while`, and `until`.

8. **B., C.** A function is a bundle of statements that is executed as a group. The bundles are executed just like a "regular" command, and are used to carry out often-required tasks. An advantage of a function is that it is held in the computer's main memory; therefore, execution is much quicker than with a script, which must be retrieved from disk.

9. **D.** The command `echo $variable` will show you the contents of a variable.

10. **A.** NAME is not a default shell variable that is automatically set when entering the Bourne shell. `LPDEST` sets the user's default printer, `CDPATH` sets the search path for the `cd` command, and `HOME` sets the value of the user's home directory.

## APPLY YOUR KNOWLEDGE

11. **A.** The test program performs three types of tests:

    - Testing files for certain characteristics, such as file type and permissions
    - Performing string comparisons
    - Making numeric comparisons

# SECTION II

# PART 2

## OBJECTIVES

The following test objectives are covered in this chapter:

**Define fundamental networking terms**

- This chapter will define some of the fundamental networking terms with which the system administrator must be familiar before attempting a network installation. Concepts pertaining to each layer within the seven-layer OSI model and the five-layer TCP/IP model are described.

**Plan and configure the network**

- Prior to implementing a network, the system administrator must gather information from all areas of the organization to develop an implementation plan. Various network configuration files must be customized for the specific environment.

**Understand IP addressing and name services**

- When planning a network, the system administrator must decide which IP addressing scheme and name service to use. This information is a required part of the network configuration; therefore, an understanding of these two topics is required.

**Understand network commands used to copy files and execute commands on remote systems**

- After the network is operational, you'll want to take advantage of the many Solaris commands and utilities to help you fully utilize your network. Tasks that once required a tape or floppy disk can now be completed over the network in a fraction of the time.

CHAPTER 13

# The Solaris Network Environment

## Objectives

**Perform network maintenance**

- Just like any other part of the system, the network requires regular monitoring and period maintenance. Starting and stopping network services, monitoring performance statistics, and troubleshooting problems are all in a day's work for the system administrator.

## Outline

## Outline



## Study Strategies

The following strategies will help you prepare for the exam:

- To practice the step-by-steps, the commands, and the exercises, you'll need two Solaris systems networked together. I highly recommend that you practice every command and step-by-step I've presented in this chapter until you can perform them from memory.
- Make sure that you understand each command in this section, and be prepared to match the command to the correct description.
- This chapter introduces more terms than any other chapter. Make sure that you know all of the terms listed in the Key Terms section at the end of this chapter. Be prepared to match the term with the correct description.

# Introduction

One chapter isn't enough to cover network administration; in fact, Sun has developed a certification exam specifically for this area. The Solaris 8 Administrator exam includes some questions on networking fundamentals, however, and this chapter provides you with that basic information. The topics include designing and planning, setting up, and maintaining the network.

# Network Fundamentals

Before you start, you need to know the definitions of some terms used in networking. You'll find numerous acronyms, which I'll try to sort out a bit here. I'll begin by describing the networking model that comes standard in Solaris 8. I'll describe the types of networks available and then I'll describe the various network protocols. Finally, I'll identify the physical components of the network hardware, including the network interfaces and cabling.

## Network Topologies

The term *network topology* refers to the overall picture of the network. The topology describes small and large networks, including LANs and WANs.

### LAN

A *local area network (LAN)* is a set of hosts, usually in the same building and on the same floor, connected by a high-speed medium such as Ethernet. A LAN might be a single IP network, or it might be a collection of networks or subnets connected through high-speed routers.

The network interface and cabling or wiring used for computer networks are referred to as *network media*. Some sort of thick or thin coaxial cable, twisted-pair telephone wire, or fiber-optic cable connects a Solaris LAN. In the Solaris LAN environment, twisted-pair wire is the most commonly used network medium, although fiber-optic cable is becoming a common medium as well.

### WAN

A *wide area network* (WAN) is a network that covers a potentially vast geographic area. An example of a WAN is the Internet. Other examples of WANs are enterprise networks linking the separate offices of a single corporation into one network spanning several floors, several buildings, an entire country, or perhaps an entire continent.

## Network Models

A *network model* refers to the common structure or protocol used to accomplish communication between systems. The two network models that provide the framework for network communication and that are the standards used in Solaris are the ISO/OSI reference model and the TCP/IP suite.

The models consist of different layers. Think of these as steps that must be completed before you can move on to the next step and ultimately communicate between systems.

## Network Protocols

The *network protocol* is the part of the network you configure but cannot see. It's the software portion of the network that controls data transmission between systems across the network. To understand protocols, you need to first understand network models.

### ISO/OSI Model

We first need to describe the seven-layered International Standards Organization (ISO)/Open Systems Interconnection (OSI) model that was devised the early 1980s. Although this model represents an ideal world and is somewhat meaningless in today's networking environment, it's quite helpful for identifying the distinct functions necessary for network communication to occur.

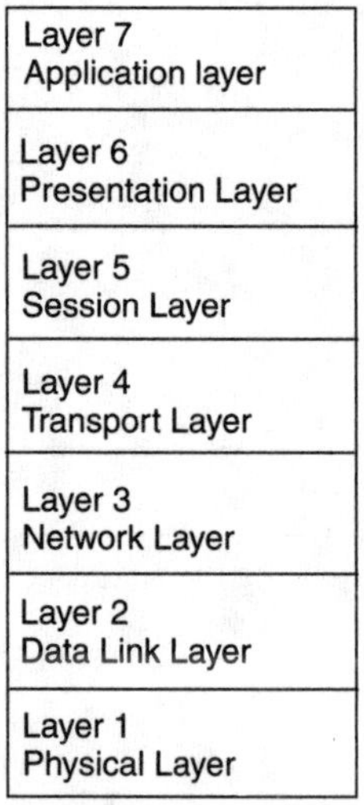

| Layer 7 Application layer |
|---|
| Layer 6 Presentation Layer |
| Layer 5 Session Layer |
| Layer 4 Transport Layer |
| Layer 3 Network Layer |
| Layer 2 Data Link Layer |
| Layer 1 Physical Layer |

**FIGURE 13.1**
Seven-layer ISO/OSI model.

In the ISO/OSI model, individual services that are required for communication are arranged in seven layers that build on one another. Each layer describes a specific network function described in Figure 13.1.

Table 13.1 describes the function of each individual layer.

**TABLE 13.1**

**ISO/OSI LAYERS**

| *ISO/OSI Layer* | *Function* |
|---|---|
| Physical | Layer 1 describes the network hardware, including electrical and mechanical connections to the network. |
| Data Link | Layer 2 splits data into frames for sending on the physical layer, and receives acknowledgement frames. It performs error checking, and retransmits frames not received correctly. |
| Network | Layer 3 manages the delivery of data via the Data Link layer, and is used by the Transport layer. The most common Network layer protocol is IP. |
| Transport | Layer 4 determines how to use the network layer to provide a virtually error-free, point-to-point connection so that host A can send messages to host B and they will arrive uncorrupted and in the correct order. |
| Session | Layer 5 uses the transport layer to establish a connection between processes on different hosts. It handles security and creation of the session. |
| Presentation | Layer 6 performs functions such as text compression, code, or format conversion to try to smooth out differences between hosts. It allows incompatible processes in the Application layer to communicate via the Session layer. |
| Application | Layer 7 is concerned with the user's view of the network (that is, formatting electronic mail messages). The Presentation layer provides the Application layer with a familiar local representation of data independent of the format used on the network. |

## TCP/IP Model

The Transmission Control Protocol/Internet Protocol (TCP/IP) model is a network communications protocol consisting of a set of formal rules that describe how software and hardware should interact within a network. TCP/IP uses five layers in the OSI reference model:

- Hardware layer
- Network Interface layer
- Internet layer
- Transport layer
- Application layer

## Hardware Layer

The Hardware layer corresponds to the ISO/OSI Physical layer, and describes the network hardware including electrical and mechanical connections to the network. This layer regulates the transmission of unstructured bit streams over a transmission medium, which might be one of the following:

- Ethernet IEEE802.3
- Token passing bus IEEE802.4
- Token ring IEEE802.5
- Metropolitan area networks IEEE802.6

Each medium is followed by its associated standard that was implemented by the Institute of Electrical and Electronics Engineers (IEEE) under project 802, which was named for the month (February) and year (1980) of its inception. Each medium is divided into its own substandard.

## Network Interface Layer

The Network Interface layer corresponds to the ISO/OSI Data Link layer, and manages the delivery of data across the physical network. This layer provides error detection and packet framing. *Framing* is a process of assembling bits into manageable units of data. A *frame* is a series of bits with a well-defined beginning and end.

Network Interface layer protocols consist of the following::

- Ethernet
- Fiber Distributed Data interface (FDDI)

- Point-to-Point Protocol (PPP)
- Token ring

These protocols are described later in this section.

## Internet Layer

The Internet layer corresponds to the ISO/OSI Network layer, and manages data addressing and delivery between networks, as well as fragmenting data for the Data Link layer. The Internet layer uses the following:

- Internet Protocol (IP). Determines the path a packet must take based on the destination host's IP address. Solaris 8 supports Ipv4 and Ipv6.
- Internet Control Message Protocol (ICMP). An extension to IP that allows for the generation of error messages, test packets, and informational messages related to IP.
- Address Resolution Protocol (ARP). Defines the method that maps a 32-bit IP address to a 48-bit Ethernet address.
- Reverse Address Resolution Protocol (RARP). The reverse of ARP. It maps a 48-bit Ethernet address to a 32-bit IP address.

## Transport Layer

The Transport layer corresponds to the ISO/OSI transport layer, and ensures that messages reach the correct application process using TCP and UDP.

Transmission Control Protocol (TCP) uses a reliable, connection-oriented circuit for connecting to application processes. A connection-oriented circuit allows a host to send data in a continuous stream to another host. It guarantees that all data is delivered to the other end in the same order as it was sent and without duplication. Communication proceeds through three well-defined phases: connection establishment, data transfer, and connection release.

User Datagram Protocol (UDP) is a connectionless protocol. It's faster than TCP because it does not require setting up a connection and handling acknowledgements. Because of this, it does not guarantee delivery. It is lightweight and efficient, but the application program must take care of all error processing and retransmission.

## Application Layer

The Application layer corresponds to the Session layer, Presentation layer, and the Application layer of the ISO/OSI model. The Application layer manages user-accessed application programs and network services. This layer is responsible for defining the way in which cooperating networks represent data. The Application layer protocols consist of the following:

- Network File system (NFS). A client server application that is described in Chapter 17, "The NFS Environment."
- Network Information System (NIS), Network Information System Plus (NIS+), and Domain Name System (DNS). Network services described in Chapter 18, "Name Services."
- rlogin, telnet, and FTP. Network services are described in the "Network Services" section later in this chapter.
- Hypertext Transfer Protocol (HTTP). Used by the World Wide Web to display text, pictures, and sound via a web browser.
- Simple Mail Transport Protocol (SMTP). Provides delivery of electronic mail messages.
- Remote Procedure Call (RPC). A protocol that one program can use to request services from another system on the network. RPC is described in the "Network Services" section later in this chapter.
- Routing Information Protocol (RIP).Provides for automated distribution of routing information between systems.
- Simple Network Management Protocol (SNMP). Used to manage and monitor all types of networking equipment, including computers, hubs, and routers.

For the network to function properly, information must be delivered to the intended destination in an intelligible form. Because different types of networking software and hardware need to interact to perform the network function, designers developed the TCP/IP communications protocol suite (it is a collection of protocols), now recognized as a standard by major international standards organizations and used throughout the world. Because it is a set of standards, TCP/IP runs on many different types of computers, making it easy for you to set up a heterogeneous network running any operating system that supports TCP/IP. The Solaris operating system includes the networking software to implement the TCP/IP communications protocol suite.

## Encapsulation and De-Encapsulation

When systems communicate via a network, think of the data progressing through each layer down from the Application layer to the Hardware layer, across the network, and then flowing back up from the Hardware layer to the Application layer. A header is added to each segment received on the way down the layers (encapsulation), and a header is removed from each segment on the way up through the layers (de-encapsulation). Each header contains specific address information so that the layers on the remote system know how to forward the communication.

As an example, in TCP/IP, a packet would contain a header from the physical layer, followed by a header from the network layer (IP), followed by a header from the transport layer (TCP), followed by the application protocol data.

## Packet

A *packet* is the basic unit of information to be transferred over the network. A packet is organized much like a conventional letter. Each packet has a header that corresponds to an envelope. The header contains the addresses of the recipient and the sender, plus information on how to handle the packet as it travels through each layer of the protocol suite. The message part of the packet corresponds to the letter itself. Packets can contain only a finite number of bytes of data, depending on the network medium in use. Therefore, typical communications such as email messages are sometimes split into packet fragments.

## Ethernet

Ethernet is a standard that defines the physical components a machine uses to access the network and the speed at which the network runs. It includes specifications for cabling, connectors, and computer interface components. Ethernet is a LAN technology that transmits information between computers at speeds of up to 10 million bits per second (Mbps). A newer version of Ethernet called 100Base-T, or Fast Ethernet, pushes the speed up to 100Mbps, and Gigabit Ethernet supports data transfer rates of 1 gigabit (1,000 megabits) per second. Ethernet can be run over four types of physical media, as described in Table 13.2.

**TABLE 13.2**

**ETHERNET MEDIA**

| *Media* | *Name* |
|---|---|
| Thick Ethernet | Type 10Base5 |
| Thin Ethernet | Type 10Base2 |
| Twisted-pair Ethernet | Type 10Base-T |
| Fiber-optic Ethernet | Types FOIRL and 10Base-F |

The 10Base-T type of Ethernet has been the most popular medium for years, but recently it has been replaced by 100Base-T.

Ethernet uses a protocol called CSMA/CD, which stands for Carrier Sense, Multiple Access, Collision Detect. The "Multiple Access" part means that every station is logically connected to a single cable. The "Carrier Sense" part means that before transmitting data, a station checks the cable to determine if any other station is already sending something. If the LAN appears to be idle, the station can begin to send data. When several computers connected to the same network need to send data, two computers might try to send at the same time, causing a collision of data. The Ethernet protocol senses this collision and notifies the computer to send the data again.

How can two computers send data at the same time? Isn't Ethernet supposed to check the network for other systems that might be transmitting before sending data across the network?

Here's what happens: An Ethernet station sends data at a rate of 10Mbps. This means it allows 100 nanoseconds per bit of information that is transmitted. The signal travels about one foot in a nanosecond. After the electrical signal for the first bit has traveled about 100 feet down the wire, the station begins sending the second bit. An Ethernet cable can run for hundreds of feet. If two stations are located 250 feet apart on the same cable, and both begin transmitting at the same time, they will be in the middle of the third bit before the signal from each reaches the other station.

This explains the need for the "Collision Detect" part of CSMA/CD. If two stations begin sending data at the same time, their signals will "collide" nanoseconds later. When such a collision occurs, the two stations stop transmitting and try again later after a randomly chosen delay period.

Although an Ethernet network can be built using one common signal wire, such an arrangement is not flexible enough to wire most buildings. Unlike an ordinary telephone circuit, Ethernet wire cannot be spliced to connect one copper wire to another. Instead, Ethernet requires a repeater, a simple station that is connected to two wires. When the repeater receives data on one wire, it repeats the data bit-for-bit on the other wire. When collisions occur, the repeater repeats the collision as well. In buildings that have two or more types of Ethernet cable, a common practice is to use media converters, switches, or repeaters to convert the Ethernet signal from one type of wire to another.

## FDDI

Fiber Distributed Data Interface (FDDI) is a standard for data transmission on fiber-optic lines in a LAN that can extend up to 200km (124 miles). The FDDI protocol is based on the token-ring protocol. In a token-ring network, all the computers are arranged schematically in a circle. A token, which is a special bit pattern, travels around the circle. To send a message, a computer catches the token, attaches a message to it, and then lets it continue to travel around the network to be delivered. In addition to being large geographically, an FDDI local area network can support thousands of users. FDDI also allows for larger packet sizes than lower-speed LANs using Ethernet.

An FDDI network usually contains two, dual-attached, counter-rotating token rings: a primary token ring and a secondary token ring for possible backup in case the primary ring fails. The primary ring offers up to 100Mbps capacity. If the secondary ring is not needed for backup, it can also carry data, doubling the capacity to 200Mbps. Normally, one ring is used for transmitting, and one is used for receiving. If either ring fails, FDDI will fall back to the other ring for both transmitting and receiving.

## Network Hardware

The network hardware is the physical part of the network you can actually see. The physical components connect the systems and include the NIC, host, cabling, connectors, hubs, and routers—some of which I will discuss here.

### NIC

The computer hardware that allows you to connect it to a network is known as a Network Interface Card (NIC), or network adapter. The network interface can support one or more communication protocols to specify how computers use the physical medium—the network cable—to exchange data. Many computers come with a preinstalled network interface (such as Sun workstations); others require you to purchase it separately (such as most PCs).

Each LAN media type has its own associated network interface. For example, if you want to use Ethernet as your network medium, you must have an Ethernet interface installed in each host that is to be part of the network. The connectors on the board to which you attach the Ethernet cable are referred to as Ethernet ports. The same is true if you plan to use FDDI, and so on.

### Host

If you are an experienced Solaris user, you are no doubt familiar with the term *host*, often used as a synonym for "computer" or "machine." From a TCP/IP perspective, only two types of entities exist on a network: routers and hosts. When a host initiates communication, it is called a sending host, or sender. For example, a host initiates communications when the user types `ping` or sends an email message to another user. The host that is the target of the communication is called the receiving host, or recipient.

Each host has a hostname, Internet address, and hardware address that helps identify it to its peers on the network. These are described in Table 13.3.

**TABLE 13.3**

**HOST INFORMATION**

| *Identity* | *Description* |
|---|---|
| Hostname | Every system on the network has a unique hostname. Hostnames let users refer to any computer on the network by using a short, easily remembered name rather than the host's network IP address. |
| Internet address | Each machine on a TCP/IP network has an Internet address (or IP address) that identifies the machine to its peers on the network. |
| Hardware address | Each host on a network will have a unique Ethernet address, also referred to as the Media Access Control (MAC) address. The manufacturer physically assigns this address to the machine's CPU or network interface. |

As root, you can use the `ifconfig -a` command to display both the system's IP and MAC addresses as follows:

```
ifconfig -a
lo0: flags=1000849<UP,LOOPBACK,RUNNING,MULTICAST,IPv4> mtu 8232 index 1 \
inet 127.0.0.1 netmask ff000000
hme0: flags=1004843<UP,BROADCAST,RUNNING,MULTICAST,DHCP,IPv4> mtu 1500 index 2 \
inet 192.168.1.106 netmask ffffff00 broadcast 192.168.1.255
ether 8:0:20:a2:63:82
```

You can also retrieve the MAC address from a system using the `banner` command at the OpenBoot prompt, as described in Chapter 2, "OpenBoot."

## Hub

Ethernet cabling is run to each system from a hub. The *hub* does nothing more than connect all the Ethernet cables so that the computers can connect to one another. It does not boost the signal or route packets from one network to another. When a packet arrives at one port, it is copied to the other ports so that all the computers on the LAN can see all the packets. Hubs can support from two to several hundred systems.

A *passive hub* serves as a conduit for the data, allowing it to go from one device, or segment, to another. *Intelligent hubs* include additional features that let an administrator monitor the traffic passing through the hub and to configure each port in the hub. Intelligent hubs are also called *manageable hubs*.

A third type of hub, called a *packet-switching hub* (or switch), is a special type of hub that forwards packets to the appropriate port based on the packet's address. Conventional hubs simply rebroadcast every packet to every port. Because switching hubs forward each packet only to the required port, they provide much better performance. Most switching hubs also support load balancing so that ports are dynamically reassigned to different LAN segments based on traffic patterns.

Some newer switching hubs support both traditional Ethernet (10Mbps) and Fast Ethernet (100Mbps) ports. This lets the administrator establish a dedicated Fast Ethernet channel for high-traffic devices such as servers.

## Router

A *router* is a machine that forwards Ethernet packets from one network to another. In other words, the router connects LANs, and the hub connects computers. To do this, the router must have at least two network interfaces. A machine with only one network interface cannot forward packets; it is considered a host. Most of the machines you set up on a network will be hosts.

Routers use headers and a forwarding table to determine where packets go, and they use ICMP (Internet Control Message Protocol) to communicate with each other and configure the best route between any two hosts. Very little filtering of data is done through routers. Routers do not care about the type of data they handle.

## Planning the Network

You need to do a great deal of planning before you set up your network. As part of the planning process, you must perform the following steps, which are described in this section:

1. Obtain a network number and, if applicable, register your network domain with the InterNIC addressing authority, as described in the section "Planning for IP Addressing," discussed later in this chapter.
2. After you receive your IP network number, devise an IP addressing scheme for your hosts, as described in section "IP Addressing (IPv4)" later in this chapter.
3. Create a list containing the IP addresses and hostnames of all machines to comprise your network. You will use this list as you build network databases.
4. Determine which name service to use on your network: NIS, NIS+, DNS, or the network databases in the local /etc directory. Name services are discussed later in this chapter.

Only after carefully planning your network are you ready to start setting it up.

## Setting Up the Network

During the installation of the operating system, you'll use the Solaris software installation program to configure your network. Following are the network configuration files set up by the Solaris installation program:

/etc/hostname.interface

/etc/nodename

/etc/defaultdomain

/etc/inet/hosts

/etc/defaultrouter

## /etc/hostname.interface

This file defines the network interfaces on the local host. At least one /etc/hostname.interface file should exist on the local machine. The Solaris installation program creates this file for you. In the filename, *interface* is replaced by the device name of the primary network interface.

The file contains only one entry: the hostname or IP address associated with the network interface. For example, suppose le0 is the primary network interface for a machine called system1. The file would be called /etc/hostname.le0, and the file would contain the entry `system1`.

## /etc/nodename

This file should contain one entry: the hostname of the local machine. For example, on a computer named xena, the file /etc/nodename would contain the entry `xena`.

## /etc/defaultdomain

This file is present only if your network uses a name service (described later in this chapter). This file should contain one entry: the fully qualified domain name of the administrative domain to which the local host's network belongs. You can supply this name to the Solaris installation program or edit the file at a later date.

For example, if the host is part of the domain pyramid, which is classified as a .com domain, /etc/defaultdomain should contain the entry `pyramid.com`.

## /etc/inet/hosts

The hosts database contains details of the machines on your network. This file contains the hostnames and IP addresses of the primary network interface and any other network addresses the machine must know about. When a user enters a command such as `ping xena`, the system needs to know how to get to the host named `xena`. The /etc/hosts file provides a cross-reference to look up and find xena's network IP address. For compatibility with BSD-based operating systems, the file /etc/hosts is a symbolic link to /etc/inet/hosts.

Each line in the /etc/inet/hosts file uses the following format:

```
address hostname <nickname> [#comment]
```

Each field in this syntax is described in Table 13.4.

**TABLE 13.4**

**/ETC/INET/HOSTS FILE FORMAT**

| *Field* | *Description* |
|---|---|
| address | The IP address for each interface the local host must know about. |
| hostname | The hostname assigned to the machine at setup and the hostnames assigned to additional network interfaces that the local host must know about. |
| <nickname> | An optional field containing a nickname or alias for the host. More than one nickname can exist. |
| [# comment] | An optional field where you can include a comment. |

When you run the Solaris installation program on a system, it sets up the initial /etc/inet/hosts file. This file contains the minimum entries the local host requires: its loopback address, its IP address, and its hostname.

For example, the Solaris installation program might create the following entries in the /etc/inet/hosts file for a system called xena:

```
127.0.0.1      localhost        loghost     #loopback address
192.9.200.3    xena                         #host name
```

In the /etc/inet/hosts file for machine xena, the IP address 127.0.0.1 is the loopback address, the reserved network interface used by the local machine to allow interprocess communication so that it sends packets to itself. The operating system, through the ifconfig command, uses the loopback address for configuration and testing. Every machine on a TCP/IP network must have an entry for the localhost, and must use the IP address 127.0.0.1.

If you've already installed your operating system and answered "no" to installing a network, you can either edit the network configuration files manually or reissue the network configuration portion of the installation program.

To reissue the program portion, you must first be superuser. Then type `sys-unconfig` at the command line to restore the system's configuration to an "as-manufactured" state. After you run the command, the system starts up again and prompts you for the system information described in Table 13.5.

**TABLE 13.5**

**SYSTEM INFORMATION**

| *Information* | *Action* |
|---|---|
| Hostname | Input a unique name for the computer. |
| Name service | Select NIS, NIS+, DNS, or NONE (in which case, a local file will be used). |
| Time zone | Input your local time zone. |
| IP address | Input the unique IP address for this host. |
| IP subnet mask | Input the subnet mask if your network uses them. |
| Root password | Enter a root password. |

When the system is finished prompting you for input, it continues the startup process. When the system is started, the network has been configured.

## /etc/defaultrouter

This file is present only when you need to define a router for a host. The /etc/defaultrouter file should contain an entry for each router directly connected to the network. The entry should be the name for the network interface that functions as a router between networks.

**NOTE** Chapter 8, "System Security," covered network security. If necessary, refer to that discussion of configuring the network security files /etc/hosts.equiv and /.rhosts.

> **NOTE** Due to deficiencies in the design of the IPv4 scheme, a revised protocol will gradually be phased in. The protocol, named IPv6 (IP version 6), has been designed to overcome the major limitations of the current approach. IPv6 is compatible with IPv4, but IPv6 makes it possible to assign many more unique Internet addresses, and offers support for improved security and performance.

# IP ADDRESSING (IPv4)

In IP Version 4, each host on the TCP/IP network has a unique 32-bit network address—referred to as the IP address—that is unique for each host on the network. If the host will participate on the Internet, this address must also be unique to the Internet. For this reason, Internet IP addresses are controlled by an administrative agency, such as the InterNIC.

The `IP address` is a sequence of four bytes, and is written in the form of four decimal integers separated by periods (for example, 0.0.0.0). Each integer is 8 bits long, and ranges from 0 to 255. The IP address consists of two parts: a network ID assigned by the InterNIC administrative agency and the host ID assigned by the local administrator. The first integer of the address (0.0.0.0) determines the address type, and is referred to as its *class*. Five classes of IP addresses exist: A, B, C, D, and E. Without going into great detail, the following is a brief description of each class.

## Class A Networks

Class A networks are used for very large networks with millions of hosts, such as the Internet. A class A network number uses the first 8 bits of the IP address as its network ID. The remaining 24 bits comprise the host part of the IP address. The values assigned to the first byte of class A network numbers fall within the range 0–127. For example, consider the IP address 75.4.10.4. The value 75 in the first byte indicates that the host is on a class A network. The remaining bytes, 4.10.4, establish the host address. The InterNIC assigns only the first byte of a class A number. Use of the remaining 3 bytes is left to the discretion of the owner of the network number. Only 126 class A networks can exist because 0 is reserved for the network and 127 is reserved for the loopback device, leaving 001–126 as usable addresses. Each of these networks can accommodate up to 16,777,214 hosts.

## Class B Networks

Class B networks are medium-sized networks, such as universities and large businesses with many hosts. A class B network number uses 16 bits for the network number and 16 bits for host numbers. The first byte of a class B network number is in the range 128–191. In the number 129.144.50.56, the first 2 bytes, 129.144, are assigned by the InterNIC and comprise the network address. The last 2 bytes, 50.56, make up the host address and are assigned at the discretion of the network's owner. A class B network can accommodate a maximum of 65,534 hosts. Again, the first and last addresses on the network are reserved. The 0 host address is reserved for the network, and the 255 address is reserved as the IP broadcast address; therefore, the actual number of hosts that can be assigned on a class B network is 65,534, not 65,536.

## Class C Networks

Class C networks are used for small networks containing fewer than 254 hosts. Class C network numbers use 24 bits for the network number and 8 bits for host numbers. A class C network number occupies the first 3 bytes of an IP address; only the fourth byte is assigned at the discretion of the network's owner. The first byte of a class C network number covers the range 192–223. The second and third bytes each cover the range 1–255. A typical class C address might be 192.5.2.5, with the first 3 bytes, 192.5.2, forming the network number. The final byte in this example, 5, is the host number. A class C network can accommodate a maximum of 254 hosts out of 256 addresses; again, this is because the first and last values are reserved.

## Class D and E Networks

Class D addresses cover the range 224–239 and are used for IP multicasting as defined in RFC 988. Class E addresses cover the range 240–255 and are reserved for experimental use.

> **NOTE**
> Do not arbitrarily assign network numbers to your network, even if you do not plan to attach it to other existing TCP/IP networks. As your network grows, you might decide to connect it to other networks. Changing IP addresses at that time can be a great deal of work and can cause downtime.

## Planning for IP Addressing

The first step in planning for IP addressing on your network is to determine which network class is appropriate for your network. After you have done this, you can obtain the network number from the InterNIC addressing authority. When you receive your network number, you can plan how you will assign the host parts of the IP address. You can reach the InterNIC Registration Services in several ways:

- Web site: `internic.net`

  Read the FAQ at this web site to learn more about domain name registration.
- The United States mailing address:

  Network Solutions Attn: InterNIC Registration Services 5
  05 Huntmar Park Drive
  Herndon, VA 22070
- Email: `hostmaster@rs.internic.net`.
- Phone: 703-742-4777. Phone service is available from 7 a.m. to 7 p.m. (Eastern Standard Time).
- You can also visit the Internet Corporation for Assigned Names and Numbers (ICANN). ICANN is the new nonprofit corporation that is assuming responsibility from the U.S. Government for coordinating certain Internet technical functions, including the management of the Internet domain name system. More information about ICANN can be found at `www.icann.org`.

# NETWORK SERVICES

Network services were discussed in Chapter 8. `inetd` is a network daemon that runs on the system, and listens on behalf of many server processes that are not started at boot time. The `inetd` daemon starts the appropriate server process when a request for that service is received. The /etc/inetd.conf file contains the list of services that `inetd` is to provide. Following is an entry from the /etc/inetd.conf file:

```
ftp     stream  tcp6    nowait  root    /usr/sbin/in.ftpd    in.ftpd
```

The syntax for the entry is as follows:

```
<service_name> tli <proto> <flags> <user> <server_pathname> <args>
```

Each network service uses a port that represents an address space, which is reserved for that service. Systems communicate to each other through these ports. Well-known ports are listed in the /etc/service file. Following are a few entries from the /etc/services file:

```
ftp-data        20/tcp
ftp             21/tcp
telnet          23/tcp
```

From these entries, we can see that the ftp service will communicate via port 21 and use the TCP protocol.

Each network service must have a unique port number that is used by all of the hosts on the network. Keeping track of these ports can be difficult, especially on a network supporting several network services.

Solaris utilizes a client-server model known as Remote Procedure Call (RPC). When using an RPC service, a client connects to a special server process, `rpcbind`, which is a well-known registered Internet service. `rpcbind` registers port numbers associated with each RPC service listed in the /etc/rpc file. The `rpcbind` process receives all RPC-based client application connection requests, and sends the client the appropriate server port number. For example, `mountd`, which is described in Chapter 17, is listed in the /etc/rpc file as follows:

```
mountd          100005  mount showmount
```

The `mountd` daemon has a program number of 100005, and is also known as `mount` and `showmount`.

Use the `rpcinfo` utility with the `-p` option to list registered RPC programs running on a system. For example, I can check on processes on another system as follows:

```
rpcinfo -p 192.168.1.21
```

The system responds with a list of all the registered RPC services found running on that system. The listing displays the program number, version, protocol, port, and service name. One of those listed is the `mountd` service:

```
program     vers     proto   port    service
100005      1        udp     32784   mountd
```

You can also use rpcinfo to unregister an RPC program. When used with the -d option, you can delete registration for a service. For example, sprayd is running on the local system. I could unregister it as follows:

```
rpcinfo  -d sprayd 1
```

The sprayd service would be stopped. In Chapter 9, "Process Control," I described how to send a signal to a process. I could restart sprayd by sending a HUP (hangup) signal to the inetd daemon as follows:

```
pkill -HUP inetd
```

# NAME SERVICE

When a user enters a command such as ping xena, one of the first things that must happen is translation of the hostname xena to an IP address. This can happen in one of two ways.

The IP address can be determined from the /etc/hosts file, or it can be resolved through a domain name service. For a small network, using just /etc/hosts is not a problem. For a larger network, trying to keep the /etc/hosts file in sync on all hosts can result in a great deal of work because these files must be exactly the same on each host. If the same address gets used on two different systems, the network could fail.

DNS relies on the named (pronounced *name d*) server to provide hostname-to-IP address translations. The named server is a host that permanently stores hostname and IP address information for a specific domain. A domain name is the network equivalent of a hostname. A hostname refers to a specific system on the network, and a domain name refers to a specific network. Sites and institutions are assigned a domain name for their network. In turn, they assign hostnames to systems within their domain. The Internet domain name system provides a scheme by which every site in the world has a unique name.

Name services and DNS are discussed again in more detail in Chapter 18.

# TCP/IP Commands

TCP/IP offers several commands and features that are supported on the Solaris operating environment. These commands are part of the TCP/IP networking package and are available on all UNIX systems that implement TCP/IP, unless specifically disabled by the administrator.

## telnet

`telnet` is used to log into another system on the network. The following is a sample session:

```
# telnet pyramid1
Trying 192.9.200.4...
Connected to pyramid1.
Escape character is '^]'.

SunOS 5.8
login: bill
Password:
Last login: Mon Jul 30 15:12:59 from 192.9.200.1
Sun Microsystems Inc.   SunOS 5.8       Generic February 2000
pyramid1%
```

## rlogin

`rlogin` is also a command for logging into another system on the network. Unlike `telnet`, `rlogin` has a mechanism whereby you don't have to enter a login name and password if the /.rhosts and /etc/hosts.equiv files are in place. These files are discussed in Chapter 9.

## ftp

The File Transfer Protocol (FTP) is used to transfer one or more files between two systems on the network. Following is a sample `ftp` session:

```
pyramid1% ftp pyramid1
Connected to pyramid1.
220 pyramid1 FTP server (SunOS 5.8) ready.
Name (pyramid1:bill): <cr>
331 Password required for bill.
Password: <enter password>
```

```
230 User bill logged in.
ftp> pwd
257 "/users/bill" is current directory.
ftp> ls
200 PORT command successful.
150 ASCII data connection for /bin/ls (192.9.200.4,47131) \
(0 bytes).
admin
file1
data
226 ASCII Transfer complete.
19 bytes received in 0.049 seconds (0.38 Kbytes/s)
ftp> get file1 /tmp/file1
200 PORT command successful.
150 ASCII data connection for file1 (192.9.200.4,47132) \
(31311 bytes).
226 ASCII Transfer complete.
local: /tmp/file1 remote: file1
31441 bytes received in 0.12 seconds (266.82 Kbytes/s)
ftp> bye
221 Goodbye.
pyramid1%
```

## rcp

You can also use the `rcp` (remote copy) command to transfer one or more files between two hosts on a network. The other system must trust your ID on the current host. This trust relationship was discussed in Chapter 8.

The `rcp` command is more convenient than `ftp`. First, `rcp` does not require a login or password if the proper trust relationship exists between the systems, which makes it suitable for scripts. Second, `rcp` allows complete directory trees to be copied from one system to another. However, `ftp` has more options and is considered more secure. Following is a sample use of `rcp`:

```
rcp /etc/hosts systemB:/etc/hosts
```

This example uses `rcp` to copy the file /etc/hosts from the local system to systemB.

## rsh

You use the `rsh` (remote shell) command to execute a shell on another system on the network. The other system must trust your ID on the current system. The following example uses `rsh` to get a long listing of the directory /etc on systemB:

```
rsh systemB ls -la /etc
```

## rexec

The `rexec` command is also used to execute a shell on a remote system. This command differs from `rsh` in that you must enter a password. At many sites, `rsh` is disabled for security reasons, and `rexec` is used as a replacement.

## rwho

The `rwho` command produces output similar to the `who` command, which was described in Chapter 9, but for all systems on the network.

## finger

The `finger` command displays information about users logged on to the local system or other systems. If `finger` is used without an argument, it gives information concerning users currently logged in. If `finger` is used with an argument (for example, the username glenda), it displays information about all users matching the argument. You can also use the `finger` command to look up users on a remote system by specifying the user as *`username@host`*. To protect user privacy, many remote systems do not allow remote fingering of their systems.

## rup

The rup command shows the host status of remote systems, similar to the uptime command. For example, to get uptime information about the remote host named sparc14, type the following:

```
rup sparc14
```

The system responds with this:

```
sparc14    up  2 days, 41 mins,  load average: 0.00, 0.00, 0.01
```

## ping

Use the ping command to test network connectivity to a particular host. The syntax for the ping command is as follows:

```
/usr/sbin/ping <options> <host> [timeout]
```

<host> is the hostname of the machine in question, and [timeout] is an optional argument to specify the time in seconds for ping to keep trying to reach the machine. 20 seconds is the default.

Some of the more common options to the ping command are described in Table 13.6.

**TABLE 13.6**

**ping OPTIONS**

| *Option* | *Description* |
|---|---|
| -v | Verbose output. Lists any ICMP packets, other than ECHO_RESPONSE, that are received. |
| -I <interval> | Specifies the interval between successive transmissions. The default is 1 second. |
| -s | When the -s flag is specified, ping sends one datagram per second (adjustable with -I), and prints one line of output for every ECHO_RESPONSE it receives. |

When you run ping, the ICMP protocol sends a datagram to the host you specify, asking for a response. ICMP is the protocol responsible for error handling on a TCP/IP network.

To test network connectivity between ultra5 and sparc14, type the following:

```
ping sparc14
```

If host sparc14 is up, this message is displayed:

```
sparc14 is alive
```

The message indicates that sparc14 responded to the ICMP request. However, if sparc14 is down or cannot receive the ICMP packets, you receive the following response:

```
no answer from sparc14
```

If you suspect that a machine might be losing packets even though it is up, you can use the `-s` option of `ping` to try to detect the problem. For example, type the following:

```
ping -s sparc14
```

`ping` continually sends packets to sparc14 until you send an interrupt character or a timeout occurs. The responses on your screen will resemble this:

```
PING sparc14: 56 data bytes
64 bytes from sparc14 (192.9.200.14): icmp_seq=0. time=1. ms
64 bytes from sparc14 (192.9.200.14): icmp_seq=1. time=0. ms
64 bytes from sparc14 (192.9.200.14): icmp_seq=2. time=0. ms
64 bytes from sparc14 (192.9.200.14): icmp_seq=3. time=0. ms
64 bytes from sparc14 (192.9.200.14): icmp_seq=4. time=0. ms
...
...
----sparc14 PING Statistics----
8 packets transmitted, 8 packets received, 0% packet loss
round-trip (ms)  min/avg/max = 0/0/1
```

The packet loss statistic at the end of the output indicates whether the host has dropped packets, which could indicate a network problem.

## spray

The `spray` command tests the reliability of your network. It can tell you whether packets are being delayed or dropped. `spray` sends a one-way stream of packets to a host using a Remote Procedure Call (RPC). It reports how many were received, as well as the transfer rate.

The syntax is as follows:

```
spray  [ -c <count> -d <interval> -l <packet_size>] <hostname>
```

Each option in this syntax is described in Table 13.7.

**TABLE 13.7**

**spray OPTIONS**

| *Field* | *Description* |
|---|---|
| -c <count> | Specifies the number of packets to send. |
| -d <interval> | Specifies the number of microseconds to pause between sending packets. If you don't use a delay, you might run out of buffers. |
| -l <packet_size> | Specifies the packet size. |
| <hostname> | Specifies the system to send packets to. The hostname argument can be either a name or an Internet address. |

spray is not useful as a networking benchmark because it uses unreliable connectionless transports, such as the User Datagram Protocol (UDP). spray can report a large number of packets dropped when the drops were caused by spray's sending packets faster than they could be buffered locally (before the packets got to the network medium). spray is used, however, to verify connectivity between two hosts and to test the operation of the network.

The following example illustrates the use of spray to send 100 packets to sparc14 (-c 100). Each packet is 2048 bytes (-l 2048). The packets are sent with a delay time of 20 microseconds between each burst (-d 20):

```
spray -c100 -d20 -l2048 sparc14
```

The system responds with this:

```
sending 100 packets of length 2048 to sparc14 ...
2 packets (2.000%) dropped by sparc14
567 packets/sec, 1161394 bytes/sec
```

# NETWORK MAINTENANCE

In addition to the TCP/IP set of commands, Solaris provides several network commands that the system administrator can use to check and troubleshoot the network.

## STEP BY STEP

### 13.1 Verifying that the Network Is Operational

**1.** Check the network connection to another system by typing the following:

```
ping <options> <ip address>
```

For example, to check the network between systemA and systemB, type `ping systemB` from systemA. If the check is successful, the remote system replies with this:

```
systemB is alive
```

If the network is not active, you get this message:

```
no answer from systemB
```

If this is the response, check your cabling and make sure the remote system is configured properly.

**2.** Use the `snoop` utility to determine what information is flowing between systems. The `snoop` utility can show what actually happens when one system pings another system as follows:

```
snoop 192.168.1.106 192.168.1.21
```

The system responds with the following:

```
Using device /dev/hme (promiscuous mode)
192.168.1.106 -> 192.168.1.21 ICMP Echo request \
(ID: 2677 Sequence number: 0)
192.168.1.21 -> 192.168.1.106 ICMP Echo reply \
(ID: 2677 Sequence number: 0)
```

**3.** Check for network traffic by typing the following:

```
netstat -i 5
```

The system responds with this:

```
input   le0   output  input   (Total) output
packets errs  packets errs colls packets errs  packets errs colls
95218   49983 189     1    0     218706  49983 123677  1    0
0       0     0       0    0     3       0     3       0    0
0       0     0       0    0     4       0     4       0    0
1       1     0       0    0     144     1     143     0    0
0       0     0       0    0     256     0     256     0    0
0       0     0       0    0     95      0     95      0    0
0       0     0       0    0     1171    0     1171    0    0
```

*continues*

*continued*

The `netstat` command is used to monitor the system's TCP/IP network activity. `netstat` can provide some basic data about how much and what kind of network activity is happening. The `-i` option shows the state of the network interface used for TCP/IP traffic. The last option, `5`, reissues the `netstat` command every 5 seconds to get a good sampling of network activity. Press Ctrl+C to break out of the `netstat` command.

4. Look in the `colls` column for a high number of collisions. To calculate the network collision rate, divide the number of output collisions (output colls) by the number of output packets. A network-wide collision rate of greater than 10% can indicate an overloaded network, a poorly configured network, or hardware problems.

5. Examine the `errs` column for a high number of errors. To calculate the input packet error rate, divide the number of input errors by the total number of input packets. If the input error rate is high—more than 25%—the host might be dropping packets due to transmission problems. Transmission problems can be caused by other hardware on the network, as well as heavy traffic and low-level hardware problems. Routers can drop packets, forcing retransmissions and causing degraded performance.

6. Type `ping -sRv <hostname>` from the client to determine how long it takes a packet to make a round trip on the network. If the round trip takes more than a few milliseconds, the routers on the network are slow, or the network is very busy. Issue the `ping` command twice, and ignore the first set of results. The `ping -sRv` command also displays packet losses. If you suspect a physical problem, use `ping -sRv` to find the response time of several hosts on the network. If the response time (in milliseconds) from one host is not what you expect, investigate that host.

## CHAPTER SUMMARY

Although networking is a topic that could consume many chapters in this book, I've described the fundamentals that you will need to know to set up a Solaris system on the network. All of the concepts that you will need to know for the Sun Certified System Administrator for the Solaris 8 Operating Environment exam (310-012) were described.

After reading this chapter, you should have an understanding of the two types of network models: ISO/OSI and TCP/IP. This chapter described all of the component layers of these two models.

The network hardware and software components were described along with all of the configuration files you might need to customize to get your network services operational.

Finally, this chapter discussed the network-related commands and utilities that you will use for monitoring and maintaining the network. In a networked environment, system performance depends on how well you've maintained your network. An overloaded network will disguise itself as a slow system and can even cause downtime. Monitor your network continuously. You need to know how the network looks when things are running well so that you know what to look for when the network is performing poorly. The network commands described in this chapter only report numbers. You're the one who decides if these numbers are acceptable for your environment. As stated earlier, when it comes to system administration, practice and experience will help you excel as a system administrator. The same holds true for administering a network.

The next chapter will describe some additional disk management topics so that, later on in this section, I can describe how to access these drives across the network using NFS.

**KEY TERMS**

- LAN
- WAN
- Network model
- Network protocol
- ISO/OSI Model (know each of the seven layers)
- TCP/IP
- UDP
- SMTP
- RPC
- Encapsulation
- De-Encapsulation
- Packet
- Ethernet
- FDDI
- Host
- Hub
- Hostname
- Internet address
- Router
- IP address
- Network class (Describe each class)
- Network service

## APPLY YOUR KNOWLEDGE

## Exercises

The following exercises require two hosts connected via Ethernet. You should have two hosts connected via a network, one named hostA and the other named hostB.

### 13.1 Obtaining Network Information

In this exercise, you'll use the various network commands and utilities to obtain information about your system and network.

**Estimated Time**: 15 minutes

1. Log in as root on hostA. Make sure you have an entry in your /etc/inet/hosts file for hostB.
2. As root, use the `ifconfig` command to display information about your network interface:

```
ifconfig -a
lo0: \
flags=1000849<UP,LOOPBACK,RUNNING,MULTICAST,\
IPv4> mtu 8232 index 1
inet 127.0.0.1 netmask ff000000
hme0: \
flags=1004843<UP,BROADCAST,RUNNING,MULTICAST,\
DHCP,IPv4> mtu 1500 index 2 \
inet 192.168.1.106 netmask ffffff00 broadcast\
192.168.1.255 \
ether 8:0:20:a2:63:82
```

   The `ifconfig` utility shows that the Ethernet address of the hme0 interface is 8:0:20:a2:63:82. The first half of the address is generally specific to the manufacturer. In this case, 8:0:20 is Sun Microsystems. The last half of the address, a2:63:82, is unique for every system.

3. Use `ping` to send ICMP echo requests from hostA to hostB.

```
ping hostB
```

   On hostA, use the `rpcinfo` utility with the `-p` option to list the registered RPC programs:

```
rpcinfo
```

4. Look for the `sprayd` service on your system:

```
rpcinfo | grep sprayd
```

5. Stop the `sprayd` service on your local system as follows:

```
rpcinfo -d sprayd 1
```

6. Verify that the `sprayd` service is gone:

```
rpcinfo | grep sprayd
```

7. Restart the `sprayd` service by sending a HUP (hangup) signal to the `inetd` daemon, as follows:

```
pkill -HUP inetd
```

8. Verify that the `sprayd` service is running:

```
rpcinfo | grep sprayd
```

### 13.2 Using *snoop* to Display Network Information

In this exercise, you'll use the `snoop`, `spray`, and `ping` commands to obtain information from your network.

**Estimated Time**: 10 minutes

1. On hostA, log in as root into a CDE session. In one window, start up the `snoop` utility as follows:

```
snoop hostA hostB
```

2. `snoop` will show what actually happens when hostA uses the `ping` command to communicate with hostB. In a second window on hostA, type the following:

```
ping hostB
```

3. Watch the information that is displayed in the first window that is running `snoop`.
4. Now issue the `spray` command to send a one-way

## APPLY YOUR KNOWLEDGE

stream of packets to hostB:

```
spray hostB
```

5. Watch the information that is displayed in the first window that is running snoop.

## Review Questions

1. Name and provide a brief description of each layer of the seven-layer OSI model.
2. Name and provide a brief description of each layer of the five-layer TCP/IP model.
3. In TCP/IP, a packet that contains a header from the Physical layer, followed by a header from the Network layer (IP), followed by a header from the Transport layer (TCP), followed by the application protocol data would be referred to as what?

   A. De-Encapsulation

   B. Encapsulation

   C. Encryption

   D. Decryption
4. By what other name is a host's unique Ethernet address referred to?

   A. IP address

   B. MAC address

   C. Internet address

   D. Hostname
5. Which of the following network configuration files does the Solaris installation program always set up? Choose all that apply.

   A. /etc/hostname.interface

   B. /etc/nodename

   C. /etc/inet/hosts

   D. /etc/defaultdomain
6. Which daemon starts the appropriate server process when a request for that service is received?

   A. `inetd`

   B. `init`

   C. `mountd`

   D. `nfsd`
7. What is TCP/IP?

   A. A general name for a set of protocols that allow computers to share resources across the network

   B. A network security specification used widely on the Internet

   C. One of the services provided by the domain name service

   D. Transfer control protocol/information protocol
8. Which of the following statements about IP addresses are true? Choose all that apply.

   A. IP addresses are written as four sets of numbers separated by periods.

   B. IP addresses provide a means of identifying and locating network resources.

   C. IP addresses are divided into three unique numbers: network, class, and host.

   D. The IP address identifies the machine to its peers on the network.
9. Which of the following statements is true about

## Apply Your Knowledge

the /etc/hostname.xxy file?

A. It is a system script file.

B. It is a SPARC executable file.

C. It contains the hostname of the local host.

D. It identifies the network interface on the local host.

10. Which of the following is a network component that forwards Ethernet packets from one network to another?

A. Hub

B. Switch

C. Network interface

D. Router

11. Which of the following contains the IP addresses and hostnames of machines on your network?

A. /etc/inet/hosts

B. /etc/hostname.xxy

C. /etc/defaultdomain

D. /etc/nodename

12. Which of the following network classes is for medium-sized networks such as campuses and large businesses with many hosts on their network?

A. Class A

B. Class B

C. Class C

D. Class D

13. Which of the following commands are used to transfer one or more files between two systems on the network? Choose all that apply.

A. `rexec`

B. `telnet`

C. `ftp`

D. `rcp`

E. `rsh`

14. Which of the following commands executes a shell on a remote system?

A. `rlogin`

B. `rexec`

C. `telnet`

D. `rcp`

E. `rsh`

15. Which of the following commands displays information on users logged on the local or other systems?

A. `who`

B. `logins`

C. `finger`

D. `rexec`

16. Which of the following commands can tell you whether packets are being delayed or dropped on your network?

A. `spray`

B. `ping`

C. `netstat`

D. `iostat`

## APPLY YOUR KNOWLEDGE

17. Which of the following commands is used to monitor the system's TCP/IP network activity?

    A. `iostat`

    B. `vmstat`

    C. `netstat`

    D. `ping`

18. Which command is used to determine the information that is flowing across the network between systems?

    A. `netstat`

    B. `snoop`

    C. `iostat`

    D. `ping`

## Answers to Review Questions

1. Physical. Layer 1 describes the network hardware, including electrical and mechanical connections to the network.

   Data Link. Layer 2 splits data into frames for sending on the Physical layer and receives acknowledgement frames. It performs error checking and retransmits frames not received correctly.

   Network. Layer 3 manages the delivery of data via the Data Link layer and is used by the Transport layer. IP is the most common Network layer protocol.

   Transport. Layer 4 determines how to use the Network layer to provide a virtually error-free, point-to-point connection so that host A can send messages to host B and they will arrive uncorrupted and in the correct order.

   Session. Layer 5 uses the Transport layer to establish a connection between processes on different hosts. It handles security and creation of the session.

   Presentation. Layer 6 performs functions such as text compression, code, or format conversion to try to smooth out differences between hosts. Allows incompatible processes in the Application layer to communicate via the Session layer.

   Application. Layer 7 is concerned with the user's view of the network (that is, formatting electronic mail messages). The Presentation layer provides the Application layer with a familiar local representation of data independent of the format used on the network.

2. The Hardware layer corresponds to the ISO/OSI Physical layer and describes the network hardware including electrical and mechanical connections to the network. This layer regulates the transmission of unstructured bit streams over a transmission medium.

   The Network Interface layer corresponds to the ISO/OSI Data Link layer and manages the delivery of data across the physical network. This layer provides error detection and packet framing.

   The Internet layer corresponds to the ISO/OSI Network layer and manages data addressing and delivery between networks, as well as fragmenting data for the Data Link layer.

   The Transport layer corresponds to the ISO/OSI Transport layer and ensures that messages reach the correct application process using TCP and UDP.

## APPLY YOUR KNOWLEDGE

The Application layer corresponds to the Session layer, Presentation layer, and Application layer of the ISO/OSI model. The Application layer manages user-accessed application programs and network services. This layer is responsible for defining the way in which cooperating networks represent data.

3. **B**. When systems communicate via a network, think of the data progressing through each layer down from the Application layer to the Hardware layer, across the network, and then flowing back up from the Hardware layer to the Application layer. A header is added to each segment received on the way down the layers. This is referred to as encapsulation.
4. **B**. A host's unique Ethernet address is also referred to as the MAC address.
5. **A.**, **B.**, **C**. The following network configuration files, /etc/hostname.interface, /etc/nodename, and /etc/inet/hosts, are initially set up by the Solaris installation program.
6. **A**. An `inetd` daemon starts the appropriate server process when a request for that service is received.
7. **A**. TCP/IP is a general name for a set of protocols that allow computers to share resources across the network.
8. **A.**, **B.**, **D**. The following are true of IP addresses: IP addresses are written as four sets of numbers separated by periods, IP addresses provide a means of identifying and locating network resources, IP addresses identify the machines to their peers on the network.
9. **D**. The /etc/hostname.xxy file identifies the network interface on the local host.
10. **D**. The router is a network component that forwards Ethernet packets from one network to another.
11. **A**. The /etc/inet/hosts file contains the IP addresses and hostnames of machines on your network.
12. **B**. Class B network classes are for medium-sized networks, such as campuses and large businesses with many hosts on their network. A class B network can accommodate a maximum of 65,534 hosts.
13. **C.**, **D**. The commands `ftp` and `rcp` are used to transfer one or more files between two systems on the network.
14. **E**. The `rsh` command executes a shell on a remote system.
15. **C**. The `finger` command displays information on users logged on the local or other systems.
16. **A**. The `spray` command tests the reliability of your network. It can tell you whether packets are being delayed or dropped. `spray` sends a one-way stream of packets to a host using a Remote Procedure Call (RPC). It reports how many were received, as well as the transfer rate.
17. **C**. The `netstat` command is used to monitor the system's TCP/IP network activity. `netstat` can provide some basic data about how much and what kind of network activity is happening.
18. **B**. The `snoop` command is used to determine what information is flowing across the network between systems.

## Objectives

The following test objectives are covered in this chapter:

**Utilize Solaris pseudo file systems**

- Besides the disk-based file systems that have been described in previous chapters, Solaris also utilizes file systems that reside in physical memory called pseudo file systems. The system administrator utilizes these file systems to increase performance. In this chapter, you'll learn about administering the various pseudo file systems available in Solaris 8.

**Understand the Swap File System (swapfs)**

- The Solaris operating environment can use disk space, called *swap areas*, for temporary memory storage when the system does not have enough physical memory to handle currently running processes. A system's memory requirements will change, and the system administrator must be knowledgeable in swap space management to monitor these resources and make ongoing adjustments as needed.

CHAPTER 14

# Solaris Pseudo File Systems and Swap Space

## Outline



## Study Strategies

The following strategies will help you prepare for the test:

- As you study this chapter, it's important that you practice each step-by-step example and each command that is presented on a Solaris system. Practice is very important on these topics, so practice until you can repeat the procedure from memory.
- Be sure that you understand each command in this section, and be prepared to match the command to the correct description.
- Be sure that you know all of the terms listed in the Key Terms section at the end of this chapter. Pay special attention to the types of file systems I've described, and know the characteristics of each. Be prepared to match all the terms presented in this chapter with the correct description.
- Finally, you must understand the concept of virtual memory. Know how it works, how to configure it, and learn the tools that are used to monitor it.

# INTRODUCTION

In Chapter 6, "Introduction to File Systems," and Chapter 7, "Solaris File Systems: Advanced Topics," I describe disk-based file systems; and in Chapter 18 "Names Services," I describe network-based file systems. In this chapter, I'm going to describe one more type of file system, the pseudo file system. Sometimes referred to as a ram-based or virtual file system, the distinguishing feature is that a pseudo file system does not reside on hard physical media. Pseudo file systems only reside in physical memory while the operating system is running.

Pseudo file systems are used to increase performance by providing access to data in physical memory instead of from disk. By now, you should know that accessing physical memory is much quicker than accessing the disk.

Consider that on an average system, it takes the CPU approximately 200ns (nanoseconds) to access RAM compared to 12,000,000ns to access the hard drive. To put this into perspective, this is equivalent to what's normally a 3 1/2 minute task taking 4 1/2 months to complete! Therefore, any time you can access something from RAM versus disk, the better. The pseudo file systems supported in the Solaris 8 operating environment are listed in Table 14.1 and described in the next section.

**TABLE 14.1**

**SOLARIS PSEUDO FILE SYSTEMS**

| *File System* | *Description* |
|---|---|
| procfs | The process file system contains a list of active processes, named according to process number, in the /proc directory. Images of active processes are stored here by their process ID number. Process tools, such as ptree, are available in the /usr/proc/bin directory that display highly detailed information about the processes listed in the /proc directory. |
| TMPFS | This is a temporary file system for file storage in memory without the overhead of writing to a disk-based file system. Data in this file system is destroyed every time the file system is unmounted or the system is rebooted. |
| fdfs | The file descriptor file system provides explicit names for opening files using file descriptors. |
| Swapfs | The swap file system is used by the kernel to manage swap space on disks. |

NOTE: The time from when a process starts to when it finishes is referred to as the *process life cycle*.

# PROCESS FILE SYSTEM (PROCFS)

The /proc file system contains detailed information about active processes. Many applications have been written to access this state information such as the ps command.

The process information stored in the /proc file system changes as the process moves through its *life cycle*.

The following is a listing of some of the directories and files found in /proc on a running system:

```
# cd /proc
# ls
0 225 262 327 365 3986 4037 4054 4200 4515 4785 4845 5169
1 230 275 330 3955 3990 4043 4056 4201 4516 4786 4860 5167
```

Each entry in the /proc directory is a decimal number corresponding to a process ID. Each directory in /proc has files that contain more detailed information about that process. The owner of each file in the /proc directory and below is determined by the userID of the process.

For example, the ps command shows that root has a process named dtterm with a PID of 5167. This process was started when I logged in as root and opened a dtterm window in CDE. In the /proc file system, I locate an image of that local process in a directory named 5167:

```
# ls -ld /proc/5167
dr-x--x--x   5 root   other   736 Jun 11 10:49 /proc/5167
```

In that directory, I find several files and subdirectories, owned by root, that contain various pieces of information relating to that process:

```
# ls -l /proc/5167
total 13819
-rw-------   1 root   other 7036928 Jun 11 10:49 as
-r--------   1 root   other     152 Jun 11 10:49 auxv
-r--------   1 root   other      72 Jun 11 10:49 cred
--w-------   1 root   other       0 Jun 11 10:49 ctl
lr-x------   1 root   other       0 Jun 11 10:49 cwd ->
dr-x------   2 root    other   1040 Jun 11 10:49 fd
-r--r--r--   1 root    other    120 Jun 11 10:49 lpsinfo
-r--------   1 root    other    912 Jun 11 10:49 lstatus
-r--r--r--   1 root    other    536 Jun 11 10:49 lusage
dr-xr-xr-x   3 root    other     48 Jun 11 10:49 lwp
-r--------   1 root    other   5376 Jun 11 10:49 map
dr-x------   2 root    other   1056 Jun 11 10:49 object
```

```
-r--------   1 root     other     6552 Jun 11 10:49 pagedata
-r--r--r--   1 root     other      336 Jun 11 10:49 psinfo
-r--------   1 root     other     5760 Jun 11 10:49 rmap
lr-x------   1 root     other        0 Jun 11 10:49 root ->
-r--------   1 root     other     1440 Jun 11 10:49 sigact
-r--------   1 root     other     1232 Jun 11 10:49 status
-r--r--r--   1 root     other      256 Jun 11 10:49 usage
-r--------   1 root     other        0 Jun 11 10:49 watch
-r--------   1 root     other     8512 Jun 11 10:49 xmap
```

The process tools that use the /proc file system are similar to some options of the `ps` command, except that the output provided by the tools is more detailed. For more information on managing processes, refer to Chapter 9, "Process Control."

The /proc directory is mounted at system bootup by scripts called from the /sbin/rcS script. The following entry in the /etc/vfstab file shows mounting of the proc file system on the /proc mount point:`/proc    -    /proc    proc    -    no    -`

## Temporary File System (TMPFS)

TMPFS is the default file system type for the /tmp directory in the Solaris operating environment—it is set up automatically when the operating system is installed. You can copy or move files into or out of the /tmp directory, just as you would in a UFS file system. In addition, the system administrator can create additional TMPFS file systems, which I'll describe later in this section.

The Temporary File System (TMPFS) uses local memory for file system reads and writes, which is typically much faster than a disk-based (UFS) file system. Using TMPFS can improve system performance by saving the cost of reading and writing temporary files to a local disk or across the network. For example, temporary files are created when you compile a program, and the operating system generates a lot of disk or network activity while manipulating these files. Using TMPFS to hold these temporary files can significantly speed up their creation, manipulation, and deletion.

Files in TMPFS file systems are not permanent. They are deleted when the file system is unmounted and when the system is shut down or rebooted.

The TMPFS file system uses swap space as a temporary storage area. If a system with a TMPFS file system does not have adequate swap space, two problems can occur:

- The TMPFS file system can run out of space, just as a regular file system can fill up.
- Because TMPFS allocates swap space to save file data (if necessary), some programs might not execute because there is not enough swap space. See the section later in this chapter describing swap space.

**CAUTION**

If you create multiple TMPFS file systems, be aware that they all use the same system resources. Files created under one TMPFS file system use up the physical memory space available for any other TMPFS, unless you limit TMPFS sizes using the `-o size=<size>` option of the `mount` command.

## STEP BY STEP

### 14.1 Creating a Temporary File System

To create a temporary file system, follow these steps:

1. Log in as root.
2. Create a directory, which will serve as the mount point for the TMPFS file system.

   There is no command, such as `newfs`, to create a TMPFS file system before mounting it. The TMPFS file system actually gets created in RAM when you execute the `mount` command and specify a file system type of TMPFS. The following example creates a new directory, /export/data, and mounts a TMPFS file system, limiting it to 25MB:

   ```
   mount -F tmpfs -o size=25m swap /export/data
   ```

The swap argument must be specified, but is disregarded and assumed to be the virtual memory resources within the system.

When issuing the `df -k` command, it shows the mounted TMPFS file system of 25MB:

```
# df -k
Filesystem           kbytes    used   avail capacity  Mounted on
/dev/dsk/c0t0d0s0    115417   44458   59418    43%     /
/dev/dsk/c0t0d0s6   1148982  700587  390946    65%     /usr
/proc                     0       0       0     0%     /proc
fd                        0       0       0     0%     /dev/fd
```

```
mnttab                    0       0       0     0%     /etc/mnttab
/dev/dsk/c0t0d0s1    288556   26134  233567    11%     /var
swap                  62816       0   62816     0%     /var/run
swap                  64408    1592   62816     3%     /tmp
/dev/dsk/c0t0d0s4    961257       9  903573     1%     /data
/dev/dsk/c0t0d0s5    192056    7598  165253     5%     /opt
/dev/dsk/c0t0d0s7   1164094  234689  871201    22%     /export/home
swap                  25600       0   25600     0%     /export/data
```

The following example from the local /etc/vfstab file shows an entry to enable the mounting of /tmpfs on the virtual memory subsystem at boot time:

```
swap    -       /tmp    tmpfs   -       yes     -
```

Because the size=<*number*> option is not specified, the size of the TMPFS file system on /tmp is limited only by the available system resources (physical memory and swap).

## File Descriptor File System (fdfs)

The fdfs file system is a pseudo file system, automatically configured when the operating system is installed, that maintains a repository of file descriptors for open files.

> **NOTE** A *file descriptor* is an integer that identifies a table of open files. This number is obtained as a result of opening a file. Operations that read, write, or close a file would take the file descriptor as an input parameter.

Active processes access files by using the file descriptors. The following example shows the list of file descriptors in the /dev/fd directory on a running system:

```
# ls /dev/fd
0   12 16 2  23 27 30 34 38 41 45 49 52 56 6  7
1   13 17 20 24 28 31 35 39 42 46 5  53 57 60 8
10  14 18 21 25 29 32 36 4  43 47 50 54 58 61 9
11  15 19 22 26 3  33 37 40 44 48 51 55 59 62
```

Some of the file descriptors that you may be familiar with are the following

```
/dev/fd/0      Standard input (stdin)
/dev/fd/1      Standard output (stdout)
/dev/fd/2      Standard error (stderr)
/dev/fd/3      Name of file (file)
```

The following example from the local /etc/vfstab file shows an entry to enable the mounting of the fdfs file system on the /dev/fd mount point at system bootup:

```
fd      -       /dev/fd fd      -       no      -
```

## The Swap File System (swapfs)

Physical memory is the random access memory (RAM) installed in your computer. To view the amount of physical memory installed in your computer, type the following:

```
prtconf¦ grep "Memory size"
```

The system displays a message similar to the following:

```
Memory size: 128 Megabytes
```

Not all physical memory is available for Solaris processes. Some memory is reserved for kernel code and data structures. The remaining memory is referred to as *available memory*. Processes and applications on your system may use available memory.

Physical memory is supplemented by specially configured space on the physical disk known as swap, or virtual memory. *Swap* is configured either on a special disk partition known as a swap partition or on a swap file system. In addition to swap partitions, special files called *swap files* can also be configured in existing UFS file systems to provide additional swap space when needed.

Every process running on a Solaris system requires space in memory. Space is allocated to processes in units known as *pages*. Some of a process' pages are used to store the process executable, whereas other pages are used to store the process' data.

Physical memory is a finite resource on any computer, and often times there are not enough pages in physical memory for all your system's processes. When a physical memory shortfall is encountered, the virtual memory system will begin moving data from physical memory out to the system's configured swap areas. When a process requests data that has been sent to swap, the virtual memory system brings that data back into physical memory. This process is known as *paging*.

The Solaris virtual memory system maps the files on disk to virtual addresses in memory—this is referred to as *virtual swap space*. As data in those files is needed, the virtual memory system maps the virtual addresses in memory to real physical addresses in memory. This mapping process greatly reduces the need for large amounts of physical swap on systems with large amounts of available memory. Here's how:

When the kernel runs a process, swap space for any private data or stack space used by the process must be reserved. This reservation is made just in case private data or stack information would need to be paged out of physical memory into swap. An example would be when under a heavy load, multiple processes are contending for a limited amount of RAM. Without the use of virtual swap, large amounts of physical swap space would need to be configured on systems just to accommodate these reservations. Even if your system has large amounts of RAM and never pages, you would still need large swap areas configured for these reservations just in case. Many programs will not even start if they cannot reserve the proper amount of swap at startup.

With the concept of virtual swap space provided by the swapfs file system, the need for configuring large amounts of disk-based swap on systems with large amounts of physical memory can be reduced. This is because swapfs provides virtual swap space addresses rather than real physical swap space addresses in response to the requests to reserve swap space.

With virtual swap space, provided by swapfs, real disk-based swap space is required only with the onset of paging, due to processes contending for memory. In this situation, swapfs must convert the virtual swap space addresses to physical swap space addresses for paging to actual disk-based swap space to occur.

## Swap Space and the TMPFS File System

The TMPFS file system stores files and their associated information in memory (in the /tmp directory) rather than on disk, which speeds up access to those files. This results in a major performance enhancement for applications such as compilers and DBMS products that use /tmp heavily.

The TMPFS file system allocates space in the /tmp directory from the system's swap resources. This means that as you use up space in /tmp, you are also using up swap space. So if your applications use /tmp heavily and you do not monitor swap space usage, your system could run out of swap space.

Follow these guidelines if you want to use TMPFS on a system with limited swap space:

- As described earlier in this chapter, mount the TMPFS file system with the `size` option `(-o size)` to control how much of the swap resources TMPFS can use.
- If you are close to running out of swap space, you can use your compiler's TMPDIR environment variable to point to a larger, real directory.
- Using your compiler's TMPDIR variable only controls whether or not the compiler is using /tmp. It has no effect on other programs' use of /tmp.

## Sizing Your Swap Space

The amount of swap space required on your system is based on the following criteria:

- Application programs need a minimum amount of swap space to operate properly. This information is usually contained in the documentation that came with the application. Follow the manufacturer's recommendation for swap space requirements.
- Determine whether large applications (like compilers) will be using the /tmp directory. Then allocate additional swap space to be used by TMPFS.
- To save any possible panic dumps resulting from a fatal system failure, there must be sufficient swap space to hold the necessary memory pages in RAM at the time of the failure. Therefore, if you have 1GB of physical memory, you'll need at least 1GB of disk-based space for a worst-case crash dump.

The amount of disk-based swap must be at least equal to the total amount of physical memory + the requirements of any concurrently running processes that include third-party applications and compilers. Many other factors also contribute to the amount of swap space you need to configure, such as the number of concurrent users and NIS+ to name a few.

If you are prepared to keep track of your swap space, and administer it regularly, then you can run with "just enough" swap space. I'll describe how to monitor swap space and how to add additional space to a running system in the next few sections. If you don't want the hassle and can spare some disk space in return for an easier life, then you should run with "lots" of swap space.

## Monitoring Swap Resources

If you run into a swap shortfall due to heavy demand on memory, you'll see errors appear on your system's console. The error may be something like this:

```
<application> is out of memory
 malloc error 0
 messages.1:Sep 21 20:52:11 mars genunix: [ID 470503 kern.warning]
WARNING: Sorry, no swap space to grow stack for pid 100295 (myprog)
```

This error means that an application was trying to get more memory and there was no swap space available to back it.

You could fill up a TMPFS file system due to the lack of available swap and get the following error:

```
<directory>: File system full, swap space limit exceeded
```

or

```
<directory>: File system full, memory allocation failed
```

This message is displayed if a page could not be allocated when writing a file. This can occur when TMPFS tries to write more than it is allowed, or TMPFS ran out of physical memory while attempting to create a new file or directory.

Monitor your swap space regularly. This will help you determine if you are running on the edge and need to increase the resource, or maybe you have too much swap space allocated and are wasting disk space. Most commercial performance-monitoring tools keep track of swap space, or can be configured to generate a warning when it gets low. For those of you that don't have access to these tools, Solaris provides some helpful tools, which are described briefly in Table 14.2. System performance monitoring however, is not a topic covered on the Administrator certification exams, so I will only describe the `/usr/sbin/swap` command in this chapter.

**TABLE 14.2**

**SWAP MONITORING TOOLS**

| *Command* | *Description* |
|---|---|
| /usr/sbin/swap | The /usr/sbin/swap utility provides a method of adding, deleting, and monitoring the system swap areas used by the memory manager. |
| /usr/bin/ps | Use the -al options of the /usr/bin/ps command to report the total size of a process currently in virtual memory. The value includes all mapped files and devices, and is reported in pages. These device mappings do not use swap space. |
| /usr/ucb/ps | Use this Berkley version of the ps command with the -alx options to report the total size of a process currently in virtual memory. The value includes all mapped files and devices, and is reported in kilobytes rather than pages. |
| /usr/bin/vmstat | Reports virtual memory statistics. |
| /usr/bin/sar | System activity reporter. |

The /usr/sbin/swap command has two options that can be used to monitor swap space. The -l option can be used to list swap space. For example:

```
swap -l
```

The system displays the following information listing the details of the systems physical swap space and is described in Table 14.3:

```
swapfile             dev  swaplo blocks   free
/dev/dsk/c0t0d0s3   136,3     16 302384  302384
```

**TABLE 14.3**

**OUTPUT FROM THE swap -l COMMAND**

| *Keyword* | *Description* |
|---|---|
| *<path>* | The pathname for the swap area. In the previous example, the pathname is swapfile. |
| dev | The major/minor device number is in decimal if it is a block special device; zeroes otherwise. |
| swaplo | The swaplo value for the area in 512-byte blocks. swaplo is a kernel parameter that can be modified by the system administrator and represents the offset, in 512-byte blocks, where usable swap space begins. |

| *Keyword* | *Description* |
|---|---|
| `blocks` | The `swaplen` value for the area in 512-byte blocks. `swaplen` is a kernel parameter that can be modified by the system administrator and defines the size of the swap area in 512-byte blocks. |
| `free` | The number of 512-byte blocks in this area that are not currently allocated. |

**NOTE** The list does not include swap space in the form of physical memory because this space is not associated with a particular swap area.

Use the `-l` option to determine the location of your system's swap areas.

Use the `-s` option to list a summary of the system's virtual swap space. For example:

```
swap -s
```

The system displays the following information that lists the details of the systems physical swap space and is described in Table 14.4:

```
total: 31760k bytes allocated + 5952k reserved = 37712k \
used, 202928k available
```

**TABLE 14.4**

**OUTPUT FROM THE `swap -s` COMMAND**

| *Keyword* | *Description* |
|---|---|
| `bytes allocated` | The total amount of swap space in 1024-byte blocks that is currently allocated as backing store (disk-backed swap space). |
| `reserved` | The total amount of swap space in 1024-byte blocks not currently allocated, but claimed by memory for possible future use. |
| `used` | The total amount of swap space in 1024-byte blocks that is either allocated or reserved. |
| `available` | The total amount of swap space in 1024-byte blocks that is currently available for future reservation and allocation. |

You can use the amount of swap space available and used (in the `swap -s` output) as a way to monitor swap space usage over time. If a system's performance is good, use `swap -s` to see how much swap space is available. When the performance of a system slows down, check the amount of swap space available to see if it has decreased.

> **NOTE**
>
> The `swap -l` command displays swap space in 512-byte blocks, and the `swap -s` command displays swap space in 1024-byte blocks. If you add up the blocks from `swap -l` and convert them to kilobytes, it will be less than used + available (in the `swap -s` output) because `swap -l` does not include physical memory in its calculation of swap space.

> **NOTE**
>
> A *crash dump* is a disk copy of the physical memory of the computer at the time of a fatal system error. When a fatal operating system error occurs, a message describing the error is printed to the console. The operating system then generates a crash dump by writing the contents of physical memory to a predetermined dump device, which is typically a local disk partition. This crash dump can then be analyzed to determine the cause of the system error. By default, the dump device is configured to be an appropriate swap partition. Therefore, it's necessary to make sure that your swap area is at least as large as your physical RAM; otherwise, the system will not have enough room to store the crash dump.

Then you can identify what changes to the system might have caused swap space usage to increase.

Keep in mind when using this command that the amount of physical memory available for swap usage changes dynamically as the kernel and user processes lock down and release physical memory.

## Setting Up Swap Space

As described in Chapter 15, "Installing a Server," swap space is configured during software installation through the installation program. If you use the installation program's automatic layout of disk slices and do not manually change the size of the swap slice, the Solaris installation program allocates default swap slices, as shown in Table 14.5, based on the amount of physical memory installed in your system.

**TABLE 14.5**

**DEFAULT SWAP SPACE ALLOCATIONS**

| *Physical RAM Installed* | *Default Swap Space Allocated* |
|---|---|
| 64–127 | 64MB |
| 128–511 | 128MB |
| Greater than 512 | 256MB |

The software installation program adds entries for swap slices and files in the /etc/vfstab file. These swap areas are activated each time the system is booted by the `/sbin/swapadd` script.

As system configurations change, more users are added, and new software packages are installed, you might need to add more swap space. There are two methods available for adding more swap to your system:

- Create a secondary swap partition.
- Create a swap file in an existing UFS file system.

Creating a secondary swap partition requires additional, unused disk space. You'll use the `format` command, as described in Chapter 6, to create a new partition and file system on a disk. After creating the swap partition, make an entry in the /etc/vfstab file so that the swap space is activated at bootup. The process is described next.

## STEP BY STEP

### 14.2 Creating a Secondary Swap File

1. You need to add an additional 175MB of swap space to your system. You don't have any more room on the disk for more swap space, but the /data directory (currently mounted on slice 5) is 200MB in size. Move all the data in /data to another server to free up the partition so you can use it as a swap partition. You can use any one of the methods described in Chapter 11, "Backup and Recovery," to do this.

2. After freeing up the /data directory and unmounting /dev/dsk/c0t0d0s5, use the `format` utility to set the tag name to `swap` and the permission flag to `wu` (writable and unmountable) as follows:

```
partition> 5

Part     Tag       Flag  Cylinders     Size      Block
5      unassigned  wm    3400 - 3833   200.26MB \
(434/0/0)    410130

Enter partition id tag[unassigned]: swap
Enter partition permission flags[wm]: wu
Enter new starting cyl[3400]: <return>
Enter partition size[410130b, 434c, 200.26mb, \
0.20gb]: <return>
```

   I then label the disk as follows:

```
Partition> la
Ready to label disk? y
```

3. Run the `newfs` command on that partition to remove all data and create a fresh file system on slice 5 as follows:

```
newfs /dev/rdsk/c0t0d0s5
```

*continues*

*continued*

4. Make an entry to the /etc/vfstab file where the fields are as follows:
   Device to mount: <name of swap block device or swap file>
   Device to fsck: –
   Mount Point: –
   FS-type: swap
   fsck pass: –
   Mount at boot: no
   Mount options: –
   Here's an example entry for the swap partition just added:
   ```
   /dev/dsk/c0t0d0s5       -       -       swap  -  no    -
   ```
5. Run the `swapadd` script to add the swap to your system as follows:
   ```
   /sbin/swapadd
   ```
6. Verify that the swap has been added as follows:
   ```
   swap -l
   ```
   The system responds with this:
   ```
   swapfile             dev  swaplo blocks   free
   /dev/dsk/c0t0d0s3   136,3      16 302384 302384
   /dev/dsk/c0t0d0s5   136,5      16 410112 410112
   ```
   /dev/dsk/c0t0d0s5 has been added to the list of available swap areas.

Here are a few additional notes on adding swap partitions:

- On systems running the 32-bit version of Solaris, swap areas must not exceed 2GB. If you wanted to add a 9GB disk to your swap area, you should slice it up into 2GB chunks. Then put separate entries in /etc/vfstab for each slice. On systems running the 64-bit version of Solaris 8, a block device larger than 2GB can be fully utilized.
- You get a large performance benefit from having swap partitions spread across separate disks. Swap space is allocated in a round-robin fashion from swap partition to swap partition, and it is not possible to prioritize usage of the various swap areas. Swap is allocated 1MB at a time from each swap partition in turn, unless one is full.

- It is not worth making a stripped metadevice to swap on, it just adds overhead and slows paging down.

The easiest way to add more swap space is to use the `mkfile` and `swap` commands to designate a part of an existing UFS file system as a supplementary swap area. Its intention is to be used as a temporary or semi-temporary solution to a swap shortage. Although this can be used for longer durations as well, it has a few disadvantages, which are the following:

- A swap file is considered a file within a file system, therefore, when backing up a file system, a rather large swap file (empty file) would also be backed up if you don't specifically exclude it.
- Because a swap file is simply a file in some file system, you will not ever be able to unmount that file system while the swap file is in use.

## STEP BY STEP

### 14.3 Adding Additional Swap Space

The following steps enable you to add more swap space without repartitioning a disk.

1. As root, use the `df -k` command to locate a file system with enough room to support the size swap file that you want to add:

```
# df -k
Filesystem            kbytes    used   avail capacity  Mounted

on
/dev/dsk/c0t0d0s0     115417   44452   59424    43%    /
/dev/dsk/c0t0d0s6    1148982  700587  390946    65%    /usr
/proc                      0       0       0     0%    /proc
fd                         0       0       0     0%    /dev/fd
mnttab                     0       0       0     0%    /etc/mnttab
/dev/dsk/c0t0d0s1     288556   26121  233580    11%    /var
swap                  200928       0  200928     0%    /var/run
swap                  201632     704  200928     1%    /tmp
/dev/dsk/c0t0d0s5     192056    7593  165258     5%    /opt
/dev/dsk/c0t0d0s7    1164094  234689  871201    22%    /export/home
/dev/dsk/c0t0d0s4     961257       9  903573     1%    /data
```

*continues*

> **NOTE** You can create a swap file without root permissions, but it is a good idea for root to be the owner of the swap file to avoid someone from accidentally overwriting it.

*continued*

2. Use the `mkfile` command to add a 50MB swap file named `swapfile` in the /data partition as follows:

```
mkfile 50m /data/swapfile
```

Use the `ls -l /data` command to verify that the file has been created:

```
ls -l /data/swapfile
-rw------T  1 root  other 52428800 Jun 13 13:28 \
/data/swapfile
```

The system shows the file named `swapfile` along with the file size. Notice that the sticky bit, described in Chapter 8, "System Security," has automatically been set.

3. Activate the swap area with the `swap` command as follows:

```
/usr/sbin/swap -a /data/swapfile
```

You must use the absolute pathname to specify the swap file. The swap file is added and available until the file system is unmounted, the system is rebooted, or the swap file is removed. Keep in mind that you can't unmount a file system while some process or program is swapping to the swap file.

4. Verify that the new swap area was added as follows:

```
swap -l
```

The system should respond with a message showing the swap file:

```
swapfile              dev  swaplo blocks   free
/dev/dsk/c0t0d0s3   136,3      16 302384 302384
/data/swapfile        -        16 102384 102384
```

5. If this will be a permanent swap area, add an entry for the swap file to the /ETC/VFSTAB file that specifies the full pathname of the swap file, and designate SWAP as the file system type as follows:

```
/data/swapfile - - swap - no -
```

There is some disagreement as to which type of swap area provides the best performance: a swap partition or a swap file. I've seen reasons stated in favor of both scenarios; however, two of the best I've seen in favor of a swap partition are as follows:

- A partition provides contiguous space, and can be positioned between specific cylinders that will provide the best performance.
- A swap file has to work through the file system when updates are made, whereas a swap partition has data written to it at a lower level, bypassing the interaction with the file system, making it slightly faster.

**NOTE** In an emergency, when no other local space is available, it's possible to add a swap file to a networked file system using NFS, which is described in Chapter 17, "The NFS Environment." Using NFS to access swap on another host is not recommended however, because it would put an increased load on your network, and performance would be unacceptable.

Sun's official statement, and the general consensus in the user community, is that there will be a performance impact by going the swap file versus the partition route, and recommend using swap files only as a temporary solution until a swap partition can be added.

## STEP BY STEP

### 14.4 Removing a Swap File

To remove swap from a system, follow these steps:

1. As root, use the `swap -d` command to remove the swap area as follows:

```
swap -d /dev/dsk/c0t0d0s5 for a swap partition or,
swap -d /data/swapfile  for a swap file.
```

2. Issuing the `swap -l` command shows that the swap area is gone.

```
swap -l
swapfile             dev  swaplo blocks   free
/dev/dsk/c0t0d0s3   136,3      16 302384 302384
```

The swap filename is removed from the list so that it is no longer available for swapping. The file itself is not deleted.

3. Edit the /etc/vfstab file and delete the entry for the swap file.

*continues*

*continued*

4. Remove the file to recover the disk space as follows:

```
rm /data/swapfile
```

If the swap area was in a partition, this disk space can now be allocated as a normal file system.

## CHAPTER SUMMARY

**KEY TERMS**

- Pseudo file system
- swapfs
- procfs
- TMPFS
- fdfs
- Process life cycle
- swap
- file descriptor
- physical memory
- virtual memory
- Virtual swap space
- Disk-based swap
- File system swap
- Crash dump
- Secondary swap

This chapter described the four types of pseudo file systems available in Solaris. I described the procfs file system and the relationship between system processes and the /proc directory. I also described the TMPFS file system, and how it can improve the performance of your applications by reading and writing temporary files to memory versus a local disk. You learned that the fdfs file system maintains a repository of file descriptors for open files. Finally, you learned how the operating system utilizes the swapfs file system as virtual memory storage when the system does not have enough physical memory to handle the needs of the currently running processes. I demonstrated how to add, monitor, and delete swap files and partitions.

In the next chapter, I'll describe the process of installing the Solaris operating system using the interactive installation program. The information you've learned in this chapter will be useful as you create TMPFS and swapfs file systems as part of the installation.

## APPLY YOUR KNOWLEDGE

## Exercises

### 14.1 Creating a TMPFS File System

In this exercise, you'll create a TMPFS file system and mount it to a directory named /training.

**Estimated Time**: 5 minutes

1. Log in as root.
2. Create a directory named /training, which will serve as the mount point for the TMPFS file system:

   ```
   mkdir /training:
   ```

3. Mount a TMPFS file system, limiting it to 20MB as follows:

   ```
   mount -F tmpfs -o size=20m swap /training
   ```

4. Verify that the new file system, exists by issuing the `df -k` command.

### 14.2 Adding Temporary Swap Space

In this exercise, you'll create a swap file to add additional, temporary swap space on your system.

**Estimated Time**: 15 minutes

1. As root, use the `df -k` command to locate a file system with enough room to support a swap file that is 20MB.
2. Use the `mkfile` command to add a 20MB swap file named "swapfile" in a directory as follows:

   ```
   mkfile 20m /<directory>/swapfile
   ```

3. Use the `ls -l /<directory>` command to verify that the file has been created.
4. Activate the swap area with the swap command as follows:

   ```
   /usr/sbin/swap -a /<directory>/swapfile
   ```

5. Use the `swap -l` command to verify that the new swap area was added.
6. Use the `swap -d` command to remove the swap area:

   ```
   swap -d /<directory>/swapfile
   ```

7. Issue the `swap -l` command to verify that the swap area is gone.

## Review Questions

1. Which file system is destroyed and created each time the system is booted?

   A. fdfs

   B. TMPFS

   C. procfs

   D. swapfs

2. After creating and adding additional swap space, what is the correct method to ensure the swap space is available following subsequent reboots?

   A. You can edit as a line entry to the /etc/vfstab file.

   B. You can modify the startup scripts to include a `swapadd` command.

   C. Swap cannot be added; therefore, you must adjust the size of the swap partition.

   D. Additional steps are required because the necessary changes are made to the start up file when the swap space is added.

## Apply Your Knowledge

3. Which file descriptor is used to identify standard error stderr?

   A. /dev/fd/0

   B. /dev/fd/1

   C. /dev/fd/2

   D. /dev/fd/3

4. Which command should be used to create a swap file?

   A. `cat`

   B. `touch`

   C. `mkfile`

   D. `swapadd`

   E. `newfs`

5. Which file system contains a list of active processes, named according to process number?

   A. TMPFS

   B. swapfs

   C. procfs

   D. fdfs

6. Why should you become a superuser prior to creating an additional swap file?

   A. You cannot create swap files unless you have root access permission.

   B. A swap file that has root permissions makes it more difficult to overwrite.

   C. The operation of growing a file system in the swap partition requires root access.

   D. All swap space resides in the swap partition on the root disk therefore root access is required.

7. This type of file system uses local memory for file system reads and writes:

   A. TMPFS

   B. swapfs

   C. nfs

   D. cachefs

8. Which option to the `mount` command limits the size of a TMPFS file system?

   A. `-o limit`

   B. `-o size`

   C. `-o <size>m`

   D. `-o nolargefiles`

9. Which command is used to show your available swap space?

   A. `prtconf`

   B. `swap -l`

   C. `swap -s`

   D. `vmstat`

   E. `/usr/bin/ps`

10. How are swap areas activated each time the system boots?

    A. The entry in the /etc/vfstab file does this.

    B. The /sbin/swapadd script does this.

    C. The `/usr/sbin/swap -a` command does this.

    D. The `swapon` command does this.

## APPLY YOUR KNOWLEDGE

11. Which command is used to create a TMPFS file system?

    A. `mount`

    B. `swap -a`

    C. `/sbin/swapadd`

    D. `newfs`

12. Which statements are true about swap areas? (Select all that apply.)

    A. An NFS file system can be used for a swap area.

    B. A swap file is the preferred method of adding swap on a permanent basis.

    C. A swap file is created in any ordinary file system.

    D. You cannot unmount a file system while a swap file is in use.

    E. Swap areas must not exceed 2GB on a Solaris 8 system.

    F. Using a stripped metadevice for swap space is very advantageous and improves performance.

## Answers to Review Questions

1. **B.** The TMPFS file system is destroyed and re-created each time the system is booted.

2. **A.** After creating and adding additional swap space, you can add an entry for that swap space in the /etc/vfstab file to ensure the swap space is available following subsequent reboots.

3. **C.** The /dev/fd/2 file descriptor is used to identify the standard error stderr.

4. **C.** Use the `mkfile` and `swap` commands to designate a part of an existing UFS file system as a supplementary swap area.

5. **C.** The process file system, procfs, contains a list of active processes, named according to process number, in the /proc directory. Images of active processes are stored here by their process ID number.

6. **B.** You should become a superuser prior to creating an additional swap file because a swap file that has root permissions makes it more difficult to accidentally overwrite.

7. **A.** The Temporary File System (TMPFS) uses local memory for file system reads and writes, which is typically much faster than a disk-based (UFS) file system. Using TMPFS can improve system performance.

8. **B.** The `-o` option to the `mount` command allows you to specify a `<size>` value to limit the maximum size of a TMPFS file system.

9. **C.** The `swap -s` command is used to display the available swap space on a system.

10. **B.** Swap areas are activated each time the system boots by the `/sbin/swapadd` script.

11. **A.** The `mount` command is used to create a TMPFS file system. There is no command, such as `newfs`, to create a TMPFS file system before mounting it. The TMPFS file system actually gets created in RAM when you execute the `mount` command and specify a file system type of TMPFS.

12. **A., C., D.** These statements are all true of a swap area: An NFS file system can be used for a swap area; a swap file is created in any ordinary file system; and you will not ever be able to unmount a file system while a swap file is in use.

## OBJECTIVES

The following test objectives are covered in this chapter:

**Understand the client-server environment**

- On the exam, you will be asked to define the types of servers and clients used in the Solaris network environment. This chapter describes all of the various types of servers and clients available in Solaris 8.

**Install software using the interactive installation program**

- The system administrator is responsible for the installation and setup of all servers and clients. This chapter describes the process of installing and configuring a server.

CHAPTER 15

# Installing a Server

## Outline



## Study Strategies

The following strategies will help you prepare for the test:

- ▶ This chapter requires a great deal of practice. The only way to really understand the software installation procedure is to do it over and over until you can perform the tasks in the step-by-steps I present from memory. You'll find that it's not so difficult after you understand how to set up your file systems. (You might need to refer to Chapter 6, "Introduction to File Systems," and Chapter 7, "Solaris File Systems: Advanced Topics," to refresh your memory. I recommend that you practice on a Sun system, but if you only have access to an Intel-based system, it will suffice.
- ▶ Understand the terminology presented in this chapter as it relates to the client-server relationship. Make sure that you understand the various types of servers and clients available in Solaris.
- ▶ Know the requirements for installing the operating system. Given a particular hardware configuration, you'll need to determine if it supports the Solaris 8 environment.
- ▶ Finally, I've put together a list of terms at the end of the chapter with which you need to be familiar. Study these terms and for the exam, be prepared to match each term to its description.

# INTRODUCTION

Chapter 3, "Installing the Solaris 8 Software," discussed setting up a single stand-alone system. In this chapter, the emphasis is on installing and configuring a server. I begin by describing a server, its role, and its relationship to other systems on the network. Then, I describe how to install the operating system.

# THE SERVER

A *server* is a system that provides services or file systems, such as home directories or mail files, to other systems on the network. An operating system (OS) server is a server that provides the Solaris software to other systems on the network. For diskless clients, operating system servers provide /usr, root (/), and swap file systems. For AutoClient systems, an operating system server provides all system software required to set up the individual root (/) and /usr file systems required for local swapping and caching. There are file servers, startup servers, database servers, license servers, print servers, installation servers, and even servers for particular applications. Each type of server has a different set of requirements based on the function it will serve. For example, a database server will be disk- and memory-intensive, but will probably not have many logged-in users. Therefore, when this system is configured, special thought needs to be put into setting up the file systems and fine-tuning kernel parameters that relate to disk I/O and memory usage to optimize system performance.

Systems that rely on servers are called *clients*. In other words, a client is a system that uses remote services from a server. Some clients have limited disk storage capacity, or perhaps none at all; these clients must rely on remote file systems from a server to function. Diskless and AutoClient clients are examples of this type of client. Other clients might use remote services, such as installation software, from a server. These clients don't rely on a server to function and are referred to as *stand-alone systems*.

System types are defined by how they access the root (/) and /usr file systems, including the swap area. Stand-alone and server systems mount these file systems from a local disk, whereas diskless and

AutoClient clients mount the file systems remotely, relying on servers to provide these services. A stand-alone system has all its Solaris software on its local disk and does not require services from an operating system server. Both networked and non-networked systems can be stand-alone systems in the Solaris operating environment.

The following is a brief description of the various clients you'll find in the Solaris 8 environment:

- Diskless client. A client that has no local disk or file systems. The diskless client boots from the server; remotely mounts its root (/), /usr, and /export/home file systems from a server; allocates swap space on the server; and obtains all its data from the server. Any files created are stored on the server.
- JavaStation. Also known as a zero-administration client, this client has no local file system and its /home is accessed from a server across the network. The JavaStation runs only applications that are 100% pure Java. All data, applications, and configuration information reside on a centralized server that is running Netra J software, a Solaris operating environment. Java applications are downloaded on demand and are executed locally.
- AutoClient. A client system type that caches (locally stores copies of data as it is referenced) all its needed system software from a server. The AutoClient system has a local disk, but the root (/) and /usr file systems are accessed across the network from a server and are loaded in a local disk cache. Files in the / and /usr file systems are copied to the cache disk as they are referenced. If a Solstice AutoClient client accesses an application that is not already in its disk cache, that application is downloaded. If the application already resides in the client's disk cache, the application is accessed locally. AutoClient replaced the dataless client in Solaris 2.6.

## Prerequisites for the Server

The server must meet a few minimum requirements before Solaris 8 can be installed:

- The Solaris 8 release supports all sun4d, sun4u, and sun4m platforms. Some sun4c systems might not be supported in future releases of Solaris 8 beyond the 11/99 release. Check with your hardware vendor if you have a sun4c system to make sure it is supported before proceeding.
- To run a graphical user interface (GUI) installation, the system must have a minimum of 32MB of RAM. As a server, however, it is typical to have 256MB of RAM or more.
- The disk needs to be large enough to hold the Solaris operating system, swap space, and additional software, such as Solstice AdminSuite and AutoClient. You'll also need to allocate additional disk space on an operating system server in the /export file system for diskless clients or Solstice AutoClient systems. Plan on a minimum of 1GB of disk space, but realistically you should have 2GB or more.

# Installing Solaris 8 on the Server

Before beginning the installation, let's go over a preinstallation checklist.

First, gather the system identification information about your server. If the system is running, you can gather all this information by using the commands listed in Table 15.1.

**TABLE 15.1**

**SYSTEM IDENTIFICATION INFORMATION**

| *Information Required* | *Command(s) Used to Gather the Information* |
|---|---|
| System name | /usr/bin/uname -u |
| Primary network interface | `ifconfig -a` |
| IP address | `ypmatch <system_name>`<br>`<host>nismatch <system_name>`<br>`more /etc/inet/hosts` |
| Domain name | `/usr/bin/domainname` |
| Whether part of a subnet | `more /etc/netmasks` |
| What name service is used | `more /etc/nsswitch.conf` |

Next, verify that you have enough disk space for Solaris 8 and all the copackaged and third-party software you plan to add. (Refer to Chapter 3 for the total size of each software configuration cluster.) Normally, a server would have several gigabytes (GB) of disk space available for the operating system, so you'll be installing the full distribution cluster. Also, you need to check with your software vendor regarding space requirements for any third-party software packages as well as swap space requirements.

In addition, make sure you have enough disk space if you plan to run the following software:

- AnswerBook2
- Desktop Power Pack
- Internet Mail Service
- ODBC Driver Manager
- OpenGL
- Solstice AdminSuite
- Solstice Backup
- Solstice DiskSuite
- Solaris 8 Documentation
- Sun Hardware AnswerBook

- Sun MediaCenter One
- Sun WebServer
- Sun Management Console

These packages occasionally change in size as they are updated, so contact Sun to obtain current disk space requirements for each of these packages.

**TIP** You can install software from a local CD or from a CD-ROM located on a system connected to the network. However, for speed, I recommend loading the software from a local CD-ROM drive.

## Installing Software Using the Interactive Installation Program

You are now ready to install your software. I recommend one of two methods to install the operating system: interactive or Web Start. The interactive installation process is described in this chapter. This option offers you the most flexibility when installing the operating system. Web Start is described in Appendix A, "Web Start."

### STEP BY STEP

#### 15.1 Installing the Interactive Software

The following steps provide an overview of the interactive software installation procedure:

1. Insert the Solaris 8 Installation CD into the CD-ROM drive.
2. At the OpenBoot ok prompt, type the following:

```
boot cdrom
```

The system starts from the CD-ROM, and begins by configuring devices. After a few minutes, you'll enter the system identification section of the installation. The installation program will begin a dialogue, asking you various questions about your system. It's best to gather this information ahead of time. Refer to section "The Solaris Installation Process" in Chapter 3, "Installing the Solaris 8 Software," for a list of the information you will need to

*continues*

*continued*

gather. Follow the system prompts, entering the information as it is presented. You are asked to select a language and locale. You'll also need to enter your system's hostname, IP address, and network information, so have this information available.

3. After the system identification section, you'll see the following dialogue:

```
Solaris Interactive Installation:

This system is upgradable, so there are two ways to install
the Solaris software.

The Upgrade option updates the Solaris software to the new
release, saving as many modifications to the previous version
of Solaris software as possible.  Back up the system before
using the Upgrade option.

The Initial option overwrites the system disks with the new
version of Solaris software.  This option allows you to
preserve any existing file systems.  Back up any modifications
made to the previous version of Solaris software before
starting the Initial option.

After you select an option and complete the tasks that follow,
a summary of your actions will be displayed.

F2_Upgrade    F4_Initial    F5_Exit    F6_Help
```

**CAUTION** All data on the operating system partitions will be lost. These partitions include / (root), /usr, /opt, and /var.

4. Press F4 to select a complete reinstallation of the software. You'll see the following dialog:

```
You'll be using the initial option for installing Solaris
software on the system. The initial option overwrites the
system disks when the new Solaris software is installed.

On the following screens, you can accept the defaults or you
can customize how Solaris software will be installed by:
        - Selecting the type of Solaris software to install
        - Selecting disks to hold software you've selected
        - Specifying how file systems are laid out on the
          disks
After completing these tasks, a summary of your selections
(called a profile) will be displayed.
```

**NOTE** Because you want a complete reinstallation of the software, you'll select F4. The upgrade option is available if you are currently running Solaris 7 and you want to upgrade to Solarls 8. With the upgrade option, all customizations you made in Solaris 7 will be saved.

5. Press F2 to continue.

You will be asked to select the geographical regions for which support should be installed, such as Asia, Eastern Europe, and so on. If you want to select a language other than English, select it here and then press F2 to continue.

**NOTE** The End User System Support cluster is selected by default. In the preceding example, I selected the Entire Distribution cluster, which is common for servers. After you select the software cluster you want to install, if you press F4, you will see an interactive menu that allows you to select and deselect software packages within a particular cluster.

6. You'll be asked if you want to install the Solaris 64-bit packages on this system. If your system is an UltraSparc (sun4u) system and it supports the 64-bit architecture, select this option to install the Solaris 64-bit packages on this system then press F2 to continue. You'll see the following dialog:

```
Select Software

Select the Solaris software to install on the system.

NOTE: After selecting a software group, you can add or remove
software by customizing it. However, this requires
understanding of software dependencies and how Solaris
software is packaged. The software groups displaying 64-bit
contain 64-bit support.

[ ]  Entire Distribution plus OEM support 64-bit  1158.00 MB
[ ]  Entire Distribution 64-bit ................. 1218.00 MB
[ ]  Developer System Support 64-bit ............ 1169.00 MB
[X]  End User System Support 64-bit ............. 855.00 MB
(F4 to Customize)
[ ]  Core System Support 64-bit ................. 269.00 MB

F2_Continue   F3_Go Back   F4_Allocate   F5_Exit   F6_Help
```

**NOTE** I always select the entire distribution on a server because it's frustrating to have to go back and install another package later, especially on a server supporting many users. Sometimes, the Entire Distribution cluster is not installed because of the lack of disk space. With disk space as inexpensive as it is today, add a larger disk and install the entire distribution.

7. Select the software cluster you want to install, and press F2. For a server, I recommend selecting the Entire Distribution cluster so that everything gets loaded.

After pressing F2, you'll see the following dialogue:

```
Select Disks:

On this screen you must select the disks for installing
Solaris software. Start by looking at the Suggested Minimum
field; this value is the approximate space needed to install
the software you've selected. Keep selecting disks until the
Total Selected value exceeds the Suggested Minimum value.
```

*continues*

*continued*

```
        Disk Device (Size)        Available Space
=============================================
        [X] c0t0d0   (4102 MB) boot disk      4102 MB  (F4 to
edit)

                             Total Selected:   4102 MB
                          Suggested Minimum:   851 MB

F2_Continue   F3_Go Back   F4_Edit   F5_Exit   F6_Help
```

**8.** Select your disks, and press F2. You'll see the following dialogue:

```
Preserve Data?
Do you want to preserve existing data? At least one of the
disks you've selected for installing Solaris software has file
systems or unnamed slices that you may want to save.


F2_Continue   F3_Go Back   F4_Preserve   F5_Exit   F6_Help
```

**9.** Press F2, and the data on all file systems is erased. You'll see the following dialogue:

```
Automatically Layout File Systems?
Do you want to use auto-layout to automatically layout file
systems? Manually laying out file systems requires advanced
system administration skills.

F2_Auto Layout   F3_Go Back   F4_Manual Layout  F5_Exit \
F6_Help
```

**10.** Press F2. The system automatically lays out the file systems. Sizes are determined by the software packages you selected. If you plan to add additional software, you can modify the file system sizes in later steps. You'll see the following dialogue:

```
Automatically Layout File Systems

On this screen you must select all the file systems you want
auto-layout to create, or accept the default file systems
shown.

NOTE: For small disks, it may be necessary for auto-layout to
break up some of the file systems you request into smaller
file systems to fit the
available disk space. So, after auto-layout completes, you may
find file systems in the layout that you did not select from
the list below.

            File Systems for Auto-layout
            ========================================
            [X]  /
            [ ]  /opt
            [ ]  /usr
```

```
        [ ]  /usr/openwin
        [ ]  /var
        [X]  swap

F2_Continue    F5_Cancel    F6_Help
```

**11.** Make your selection(s), and press F2.

For this example, I selected these additional file systems. You'll see the following dialogue:

```
File System and Disk Layout

The summary below is your current file system and disk layout,
based on the information you've supplied.

NOTE: If you choose to customize, you should understand file
systems, their intended purpose on the disk, and how changing
them may affect the operation of the system.

File system/Mount point            Disk/Slice           Size
=============================================================
/                                  c0t0d0s0             80 MB
/var                               c0t0d0s1             34 MB
overlap                            c0t0d0s2             4102 MB
swap                               c0t0d0s3             147 MB
/opt                               c0t0d0s5             25 MB
/usr                               c0t0d0s6             1159 MB
/export/home                       c0t0d0s7             2655 MB

F2_Continue   F3_Go Back   F4_Customize   F5_Exit   F6_Help
```

**12.** At this point, you can further customize the slice sizes by pressing F4. You'll then be given a menu to select new sizes for each partition. I'm going to change a few partition sizes, so I'm going to press F4. The following menu is displayed:

```
Customize Disk: c0t0d0
Boot Device: c0t0d0s0
====================================
Slice  Mount Point         Size (MB)
0       /                  80
1       /var               34
2       overlap            4102
3       swap               147
4                          0
5       /opt               25
6       /usr               1159
/export/home               2655
======================================
              Capacity:    4102 MB
             Allocated:    4100 MB
        Rounding Error:    2 MB
                  Free:    0 MB
```

*continues*

**NOTE**

I recommend adding /usr, /var, and /opt as separate file systems. /usr provides a separate file system for most of the Solaris binary files. /var allows space for system log files, spooled software packages, and many other things that can take up a large amount of disk space. It's not recommended that you make /var part of the root file system. /usr and /opt will provide space for additional software packages that you will add later. Again, it's not recommended that /opt and /usr be part of the root file system.

*continued*

**13.** I begin by decreasing the size of /export/home to 1174MB. I'll increase / to 120MB. I'll allocate 300MB to /var and 200MB to /opt. I'm then going to add another partition called /data, and make it 1000MB. When you're satisfied with the way the slices are sized, press F2 to continue. The following dialogue will be displayed:

```
File System and Disk Layout

The summary below is your current file system and disk layout,
based on the information you've supplied.

NOTE: If you choose to customize, you should understand file
systems, their intended purpose on the disk, and how changing
them may affect the operation of the system.

File system/Mount point    Disk/Slice          Size
/                          c0t0d0s0          120 MB
/var                       c0t0d0s1          300 MB
overlap                    c0t0d0s2         4102 MB
swap                       c0t0d0s3          147 MB
/data                      c0t0d0s4         1000 MB
/opt                       c0t0d0s5          200 MB
/usr                       c0t0d0s6         1159 MB
/export/home               c0t0d0s7         1174 MB
```

**14.** Double-check your selections, and press F2 when you're ready to go to the next step. This is a good time to verify all of your selections. Make sure swap is adequate for the type of server you are installing. It seems you can never be too large on swap space; or the /var, /opt, /usr file systems. In other words, error on the side of being too large, not too small.

Many servers today come with 18GB disk drives. I use the entire drive for the operating system. Most of my servers also run a third-party performance-monitoring package that can create huge log files in /var. Operating system patches can also use up a lot of space in /var. You'll find that you're constantly adding patches to a server because of the vast array of applications and hardware components that you're supporting. I usually go nuts and allocate a few gigabytes to each of the file systems.

Also, it's difficult to estimate your swap requirements on a server. These servers can run for months without a reboot and might be supporting several database applications or users. Again, allocate ample swap—no less than twice the amount of RAM. System performance will not be degraded if you allocate too much swap space. Too much excess swap space will simply waste disk space. Disk space is cheap, however, compared to the cost of running out of swap and crashing an application during peak production times. When you're satisfied with your selections, press F2, and the following dialogue, will be displayed:

```
Mount Remote File Systems?

Do you want to mount software from a remote file server? This
may be necessary if you had to remove software because of disk
space problems.

F2_Continue  F3_Go Back  F4_Remote Mounts  F5_Exit  F6_Help
```

**NOTE** I usually wait until after the initial software installation to set up these mounts. Many times ,the system is not connected to a production network at this point, so the mount points are unavailable. It's also a personal preference to save this task for the post-installation phase, when I set up users, printers, and so on. I have a checklist of all the things I need to do after software installation, and setting up mount points is one of them.

**15.** Press F2 to continue, unless you want to set up remote mounts.

You'll see the following dialogue:

```
Profile
The information shown below is your profile for installing Solaris
software.
It reflects the choices you've made on previous screens.

==================================================================

          Installation Option: Initial
                  Boot Device: c0t0d0
              Client Services: None

                     Software: Solaris 8, Entire Distribution 64-bit

File System and Disk Layout: /                   c0t0d0s0  120 MB
                             /var                c0t0d0s1  300 MB
                             swap                c0t0d0s3  147 MB
                             /data               c0t0d0s4 1000 MB
                             /opt                c0t0d0s5  200 MB
                             /usr                c0t0d0s6 1159 MB
                             /export/home        c0t0d0s7 1174 MB

F2_Continue    F4_Change    F5_Exit    F6_Help
```

**16.** Verify the information, and press F2 if you agree.

You'll see the following dialogue:

```
Reboot After Installation?

After Solaris software is installed, the system must be
rebooted. You can choose to have the system automatically
reboot, or you can choose to manually reboot the system if you
want to run scripts or do other customizations before the
reboot. You can manually reboot a system by using the
reboot(1M) command.

          [X] Auto Reboot
          [ ] Manual Reboot

F2_Begin Installation    F5_Cancel
```

**NOTE** Partition sizes and disk space requirements were discussed in Chapter 3. Review that chapter if you are unsure of the partitions and sizes that have been set up by the installation program.

*continues*

*continued*

**17.** Make your selection, and press F2 to begin the installation. This completes the interactive installation. You'll see the following dialogue as the software is being installed:

```
Preparing system for Solaris install

Configuring disk (c0t0d0)
        - Creating Solaris disk label (VTOC)

Creating and checking UFS file systems
        - Creating / (c0t0d0s0)
        - Creating /var (c0t0d0s1)
        - Creating /data (c0t0d0s4)
        - Creating /opt (c0t0d0s5)
        - Creating /usr (c0t0d0s6)
        - Creating /export/home (c0t0d0s7)

Beginning Solaris software installation

Solaris Initial Install
       MBytes Installed:      0.00
       MBytes Remaining:    711.51
```

A meter will appear at the bottom of the screen, showing the progress of the installation. When it reaches 100%, the system will prompt you for a password with the following message:

```
On this screen you can create a root password.

A root password can contain any number of characters, but only
the first eight characters in the password are significant.
(For example, if you create `a1b2c3d4e5f6' as your root
password, you can use `a1b2c3d4' to gain root access.)

You will be prompted to type the root password twice; for
security, the password will not be displayed on the screen as
you type it.

> If you do not want a root password, press Enter twice.

Root password:

Press Enter to continue.
```

**18.** Enter your root password.

You'll see another message displayed as follows:

```
System identification is completed.
==============================================================
This system is configured to conserve energy.
==============================================================
After 30 minutes of idle time on this system, your system
state will automatically be saved to disk, and the system will
power-off. Later, when you want to use the system again, and
you turn the power back on, your system will be restored to
its previous state, including all the programs that you were
running. Do you want this automatic power-saving shutdown?
(If this system is used as a server, answer n) [y,n,?]
```

**19.** Answer "n" to this question. You'll then be prompted with the following:

```
    Autoshutdown has been disabled.
Do you want the system to ask about this again, when you
next reboot? (This gives you the chance to try it before
deciding whether to keep it.) [y,n,?]
```

> **NOTE** See my comments on the Autoshutdown feature at the end of this section.

**20.** Answer "n" to this question. After pressing Enter, the following message will be displayed:

```
Please specify the media from which you will install
Solaris 8 (SPARC) Software.
Alternatively, choose the selection for "Skip" to skip
this CD and go on to the next one.

Media:
1.    CD
2.    Network File System
3.    Skip
```

In this example, I'll be installing from a CD, so I'll answer 1 and press Enter.

The CD currently in the CD-ROM drive will be ejected, and the following message will appear:

```
Please insert the CD for Solaris 8 (SPARC) Software.
After you insert the CD, please press Enter. Enter S to
skip this CD and go on to the next one. To select a
different media, enter B to go Back.  []
```

**21.** Insert the Solaris 8 Software CD number 1 of 2, and press the Enter key to continue. The installation will continue by extracting software from this CD. When the process of copying files is complete, the following message will be displayed:

```
Installation details:
     Product               Result     More Info
 1.  Solaris 8 Software 2  Installed  Available
 2.  Done

Enter the number corresponding to the desired selection
for more information, or enter 2 to continue [2]:

Press 2 followed by the Enter key to continue.  You'll
see the message:

End of Solaris 8 Software installation.
<Press Enter to continue>

Press Enter, and the system will reboot.
```

When the interactive installation is complete, you can install the Solstice Admin Pack and AdminSuite package, which are described in Chapter 19.

Two methods of power management are available on Sun Ultra systems: Device Power Management and Suspend-Resume. Both are design to reduce power consumption.

Device Power Management automatically reduces the amount of power used by individual devices when they are not in demand to perform some function. Disk drives, monitors, adapters, and even CPUs can provide this power-saving feature. The effect of device power management is transparent to the computer user. The overall system is still in operation and is able to respond to requests for service from devices. Those devices are able to power up for full service within seconds when needed. The exact nature of the power-saving mode your system goes into depends on your hardware and its compliance with the Energy Star specification.

Suspend-Resume is a time-saving feature that allows you to turn off the power to your system without losing the state of your current activities. When you use this feature, your workspace and files are preserved when the system is powered off and restored to the same state when the system is powered on.

The Suspend-Resume function can be set up during the installation process. If you recall, you were asked the following:

```
Do you want this automatic power-saving shutdown? (If this
system is used as a server, answer n) [y,n,?]
```

On a server, we always answer no. On a workstation, it's okay to use the Suspend-Resume function; on a server, it is not recommended. Users will be accessing these servers at any time during a 24-hour period. If the system is in a suspended mode, users will not be able to access the server without physically pressing the Power-On button on the server. If you accidentally answer "Yes" and configure the Power-Saving option, you can disable it by performing the following steps:

## STEP BY STEP

### 15.2 Disabling the Power-Management Feature in Solaris

1. The easiest way to disable power management is to use the Power Management tool, dtpower. Dtpower is a GUI tool available in the Common Desktop Environment. Get to the Power Manager tool by clicking on the Desktop Controls icon located in the front panel pop-up menu, as shown in Figure 15.1.

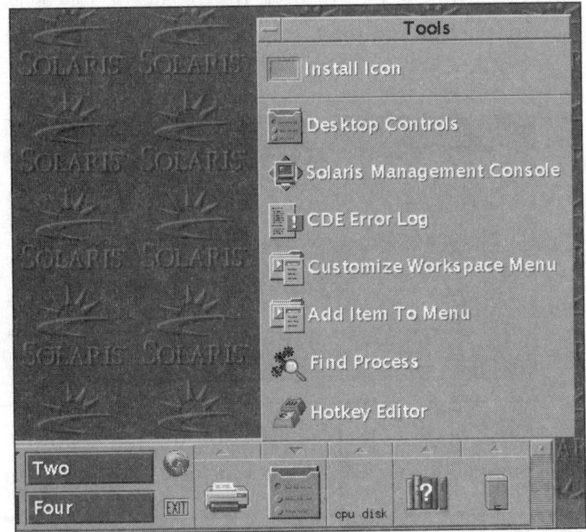


**FIGURE 15.1**
Front panel pop-up menu.

2. In the Application Manager window, click on the Power Manager icon, shown in Figure 15.2.

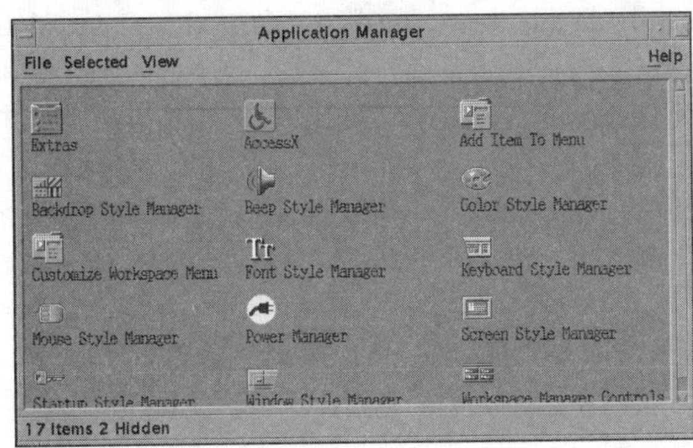


**FIGURE 15.2**
Power Manager icon.

*continues*

The Power Manager tool will appear, as shown in Figure 15.3.

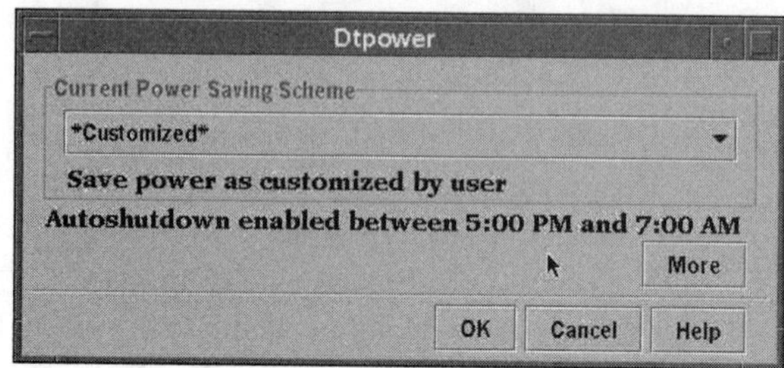


**FIGURE 15.3**
Power Manager tool.

3. Click on the Customized button in the Power Manager tool, and a pull-down menu will appear, as shown in Figure 15.4.

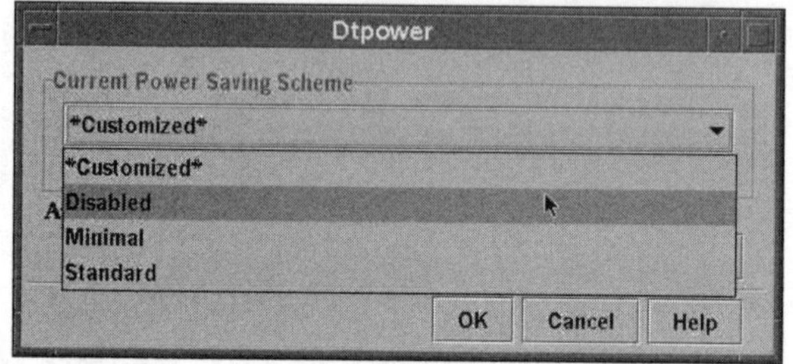


**FIGURE 15.4**
Power Management pull-down menu.

4. Click on the Disabled selection to disable power management. When finished, click on the OK button to exit.

---

The other method of disabling power management is from the command line, as follows:

Permanently disable the startup script from the /etc/rc2.d directory as follows:

```
mv /etc/rc2.d/S85power /etc/rc2.d/s85power
```

A third way to disable Power Management is by changing the /etc/power.conf file so that the Behavior field is changed from `shutdown` to `noshutdown`. Following is what the /etc/power.conf file looks like on a system that has power management configured:

```
more /etc/power.conf
#
# Copyright (c) 1996 - 1999 by Sun Microsystems, Inc.
# All rights reserved.
#
#pragma ident   "@(#)power.conf 1.14    99/10/18 SMI"
#
# Power Management Configuration File
#
# NOTE: The entry below is only used when no windowing \
environment
# is running.  When running windowing environment, monitor \
power
# management is controlled by the window system.
# Statefile     Path
statefile                /usr/.CPR
# Auto-Shutdown Idle(min)    Start/Finish(hh:mm)   Behavior \
autoshutdown    60              17:00 7:00         shutdown \
device-dependency /dev/fb /dev/kbd
device-dependency-property removable-media /dev/fb \
autopm      disable
```

In the previous example, power management is configured to auto-shutdown the system when it has been idle for 60 minutes anytime between the time of 5:00 p.m. and 7:00 a.m.

To disable auto-shutdown, change the following lines in the /etc/power.conf file as follows:

```
# Auto-Shutdown Idle(min)   Start/Finish(hh:mm)  Behavior \
autoshutdown    60              17:00 7:00       noshutdown
```

`shutdown` has been changed to `noshutdown`.

## CHAPTER SUMMARY

### KEY TERMS

- Client-server (know each type of server and client described in this chapter)
- nteractive installation
- Web Start
- Initial installation
- Upgrade
- Power management

This chapter described the various types of servers available in the Solaris 8 environment. When setting up a server, the system administrator must identify the type of server to be installed. All of the services that the server will be providing must be identified in advance so that the operating system can be properly set up to provide these services. Again, every server is different, so the requirements will vary from site to site.

This chapter discussed all of the prerequisites your system must meet before Solaris 8 can be installed. In addition, it discussed a list of information that must be gathered before you begin the installation.

Finally, I described the installation of the Solaris 8 operating environment onto a server using the interactive installation program. The interactive installation program provides a dialogue that allows the system administrator to select software packages and create file systems on the new server. Another method of installing the operating system using Web Start is covered later in Appendix A.

Many additional tasks take place after the operating system is installed, such as setting up the NIS and the network environment. These topics are covered in Chapter 13, "The Solaris Network Environment," and in Chapter 17, "The NFS Environment." Also, don't forget to back up your partitions (see Chapter 11, "Backup and Recovery") after you're finished setting up the server.

The next chapter describes device configuration and naming conventions. Now that you've installed the operating system, you'll see how the kernel communicates with the system's peripheral devices, such as disk and tape drives.

## APPLY YOUR KNOWLEDGE

## Exercises

### 15.1 Installing Solaris 8 Using the Interactive Installation Program

For this exercise, you'll use the interactive installation program to install the Solaris 8 operating environment onto your system.

**Estimated Time**: 1–2 hours depending on the speed of your system and CD-ROM

**Caution**: This exercise will destroy all data on your hard drive.

1. Insert the Solaris 8 Installation CD into the CD-ROM drive.
2. If the system is currently running, either log in as root and shut the system down, or abort the operating system by pressing Stop+A.
3. Boot the operating system from the CD as follows:

   ```
   boot cdrom <return>
   ```

4. The interactive installation program will begin. Refer to the section titled "Installing Software Using the Interactive Installation Program" and follow the steps outlined in that section for installing the operating system.

## Review Questions

1. Which of the following is a system that provides services to other systems in its networked environment?

   A. Server

   B. Client

   C. File Server

   D. AutoClientServer

2. Which of the following is a system that uses remote services from a server, has limited disk space, and requires a server to function?

   A. AutoClientServer

   B. File Server

   C. Client

   D. Stand-alone

3. Which type of installation preserves data?

   A. Initial

   B. Upgrade

   C. Preserve

   D. Web Start

4. What are the three phases of the installation process?

   A. System configuration, installation, and post installation

   B. Power on, boot from CD, execute the installation program

   C. Boot from CD, start installation program, post installation

   D. Boot from CD, system configuration, software installation

5. Which of the following is *not* a Software configuration cluster?

   A. Developer System Support

   B. End User System Support

   C. Basic System Support

   D. Entire Distribution Plus OEM System Support

## APPLY YOUR KNOWLEDGE

6. Which of the following is Sun's Java-based installation program?

   A. WebNFS

   B. JumpStart

   C. Interactive Installation

   D. Web Start

7. In the interactive software installation program, which of the following file systems are automatically set up for you?

   A. `/, swap, /usr, /opt, /var`

   B. `/, swap, /export/home`

   C. `/, swap, /usr, /export/home`

   D. `/, swap, /usr, /opt, /var, /export/home`

8. Which type of client is known as a "zero administration" client?

   A. The dataless client

   B. The JavaStation

   C. The diskless client

   D. The auto client

9. During installation, what is the default software cluster configuration?

   A. End user distribution

   B. Core distribution

   C. Developer distribution

   D. Entire distribution

10. What is the kernel architecture of an ultra 1?

    A. sun4m

    B. sun4c

    C. sun4u

    D. sun4

11. Which information is *not* required to install a server system?

    A. The server's Ethernet address

    B. The server's hostname

    C. The server's IP address

    D. The server's geographic region

## Answers to Review Questions

1. **A.** A server is a system that provides services or file systems, such as home directories or mail files, to other systems on the network.

2. **C.** A client is a system that uses remote services from a server. Some clients have limited disk storage capacity, or perhaps none at all; these clients must rely on remote file systems from a server to function.

3. **B.** The Upgrade option updates the Solaris software to the new release, preserving data and saving as many modifications to the previous version of Solaris software as possible.

4. **A.** The three phases of the installation process are system configuration, installation, and post installation.

5. **C.** Solaris 8 software configuration clusters include Entire Distribution plus OEM support (SPARC platform only), Entire Distribution, Developer System Support, User System Support, and Core System Support.

## APPLY YOUR KNOWLEDGE

6. **D**. Web Start is Sun's Java-based installation program.
7. **B**. In the interactive software installation program, `/,swap, and /export/home` file systems are set up by default.
8. **B**. The JavaStation is also known as a zero-administration client. This client has no local file system and its /home is accessed from a server across the network.
9. **A**. During the interactive installation, the End User System Support cluster is selected by default.
10. **C**. sun4u is the kernel architecture for all Sun Ultra systems.
11. **A**. The server's Ethernet address is not required to install a server system. During the installation, you will be prompted to enter the IP address, the hostname, and the geographic region.

## OBJECTIVES

The following test objectives are covered in this chapter:

**Understand device and driver naming conventions**

- The Solaris operating system accesses devices, such as disks and tape drives, through device path names. The system administrator must be familiar with the various path names that point to each piece of hardware connected to the system.

**Display device and driver configuration information**

- Solaris provides several methods for displaying information about device drivers. These commands and techniques will be described to help you identify which devices point to which peripherals, and which drivers are loaded in the kernel.

**Configure new devices**

- The system administrator is responsible for adding and configuring new hardware on the system. This chapter describes how new devices are configured into the Solaris operating environment.

CHAPTER 16

# Device Administration and Disk Management

## OUTLINE



## STUDY STRATEGIES

The following strategies will help you prepare for the test:

- Along with the chapter 13, "The Solaris Network Environment," this chapter introduces many new terms that you must know well enough to match to a description if it were to appear on the exam. Know the terms I've provided in the "Key Terms" section at the end of this chapter.
- Understand what a device driver is and the various device driver names. They are rather difficult to remember, but keep going over them until you can describe them from memory. Many questions on the exam refer to the various types of device names.
- Practice all the commands and step-by-steps until you can describe and perform them from memory. The best way to memorize them is to practice them repeatedly on a Solaris system.
- Finally, understand the concept of virtual volumes. You don't necessarily need to know how to create and configure them, but you need to know what they are, and their characteristics. Be prepared to list the advantages of a virtual volume and identify the characteristics and functions of Solstice DiskSuite and the StorEdge Volume Manager.

## INTRODUCTION

Device management in the Solaris 8 environment includes adding and removing peripheral devices, such as tape drives, disk drives, printers, and modems from a system. It might also involve adding a third-party device driver to support a device. System administrators need to know how to specify device names if using commands to manage disks, file systems, and other devices.

This chapter describes disk device management in detail. It also describes disk device naming conventions as well as adding, configuring and displaying information about disk devices that are attached to your system.

## DEVICE DRIVERS

A Sun computer typically uses a wide range of peripheral and mass-storage devices, such as a SCSI disk drive, a keyboard and a mouse, and some kind of magnetic backup medium. Other commonly used devices include CD-ROM drives, printers, and plotters. Solaris communicates with peripheral devices through files called device files or drivers. A *device driver* is a low-level program that allows the kernel to communicate with a specific piece of hardware. The driver serves as the operating system's "interpreter" for that piece of hardware. Before Solaris can communicate with a device, the device must have a device driver.

When a system is started for the first time, the kernel creates a device hierarchy to represent all the devices connected to the system. This is the auto-configuration process, which is described later in this chapter. If a driver is not loaded for a particular peripheral, that device is not functional. In Solaris, each disk device is described in three ways, using three distinct naming conventions:

- Physical device name. Represents the full device pathname in the device information hierarchy.
- Instance name. Represents the kernel's abbreviation name for every possible device on the system.
- Logical device name. Used by system administrators with most file system commands to refer to devices.

System administrators need to understand these device names when using commands to manage disks and file systems. We will discuss these device names throughout this chapter.

## Physical Device Name

Before the operating system (OS) is loaded, the system locates a particular device through the full device pathname. Full device pathnames are described in Chapter 2, "OpenBoot." However, after the kernel is loaded, a device is located by its physical device pathname. Physical device names represent the full device pathname for a device. Note that the two names have the same structure. For example, let's view the full device pathname for a SCSI disk at target 0 by typing `show-devs` at the OpenBoot prompt. The full device pathname is displayed as

```
/iommu@f,e0000000/sbus@f,e0001000/espdma@f,400000/esp@f, \
800000/sd
```

> **NOTE** This same information is also available in the /var/adm/messages file.

Now, let's look at the corresponding physical device name from the OS level. Use the `dmesg` command, described later in this section, to obtain information about devices connected to your system. By typing `dmesg` at the command prompt, you'll receive the following information about SCSI disk 0:

```
iommu0 at root: obio 0xe0000000
sbus0 at iommu0: obio 0xe0001000
espdma0 at sbus0: SBus slot f 0x400000
esp0:      esp-options=0x46
esp0 at espdma0: SBus slot f 0x800000 sparc ipl 4
sd0 at esp0: target 0 lun 0
sd0 is iommu@f,e0000000/sbus@f,e0001000/espdma@f,400000/
esp@f,800000/sd@0,0
    <SEAGATE-ST32550N-0014 cyl 3495 alt 2 hd 11 sec 109>
```

The physical device pathname for disk 0 is

```
/iommu@f,e0000000/sbus@f,e0001000/espdma@f,400000/
esp@f,800000/sd@0,0
```

As you can see, the physical device name and the full device name are the same. The difference is that the full device pathname is simply a path to a particular device. The physical device is the actual driver used by Solaris to access that device from the OS.

Physical device files are found in the /devices directory; therefore, the physical device file for SCSI disk 0 would be

```
/devices/iommu@f,e0000000/sbus@f,e0001000/espdma@f,400000/
esp@f,800000/sd@0,0:<#>
```

where `<#>` is a letter representing the disk slice.

The system commands used to provide information about physical devices are described in Table 16.1.

**TABLE 16.1**

**DEVICE INFORMATION COMMANDS**

| *Command* | *Description* |
|---|---|
| `prtconf` | Displays system configuration information, including the total amount of memory and the device configuration, as described by the system's hierarchy. This useful tool verifies whether a device has been seen by the system. |
| `sysdef` | Displays device configuration information, including system hardware, pseudo devices, loadable modules, and selected kernel parameters. |
| `dmesg` | Displays system diagnostic messages, as well as a list of devices attached to the system since the most recent restart. |

The following is an example of the output presented by the `prtconf` command:

```
#   prtconf
System Configuration:  Sun Microsystems  sun4u
Memory size: 128 Megabytes
System Peripherals (Software Nodes):

SUNW,Ultra-5_10
    packages (driver not attached)
        terminal-emulator (driver not attached)
        deblocker (driver not attached)
        obp-tftp (driver not attached)
        disk-label (driver not attached)
        SUNW,builtin-drivers (driver not attached)
        sun-keyboard (driver not attached)
        ufs-file-system (driver not attached)
    chosen (driver not attached)
    openprom (driver not attached)
```

```
            client-services (driver not attached)
        options, instance #0
        aliases (driver not attached)
        memory (driver not attached)
        virtual-memory (driver not attached)
        pci, instance #0
            pci, instance #0
                ebus, instance #0
                    auxio (driver not attached)
                    power, instance #0
                    SUNW,pll (driver not attached)
                    se, instance #0
    . . . . <output truncated>
```

Next is an example of the output displayed by the sysdef command:

```
# sysdef
*
* Hostid
*
  80a26382
*
* sun4u Configuration
*
*
* Devices
*
packages (driver not attached)
        terminal-emulator (driver not attached)
        deblocker (driver not attached)
        obp-tftp (driver not attached)
        disk-label (driver not attached)
        SUNW,builtin-drivers (driver not attached)
        sun-keyboard (driver not attached)
        ufs-file-system (driver not attached)
chosen (driver not attached)
openprom (driver not attached)
        client-services (driver not attached)
options, instance #0
aliases (driver not attached)
memory (driver not attached)
virtual-memory (driver not attached)
pci, instance #0
        pci, instance #0
                ebus, instance #0
                        auxio (driver not attached)
                        power, instance #0
                        SUNW,pll (driver not attached)
                        se, instance #0 . . . . <output has \
been truncated>
* System Configuration
*
```

```
  swap files
swapfile             dev  swaplo blocks   free
/dev/dsk/c0t0d0s1   136,1      16 1048928 1023008
*
* Tunable Parameters
*
 2482176   maximum memory allowed in buffer cache (bufhwm)
    1898   maximum number of processes (v.v_proc)
      99   maximum global priority in sys class \
(MAXCLSYSPRI)
    1893   maximum processes per user id (v.v_maxup)
      30   auto update time limit in seconds (NAUTOUP)
      25   page stealing low water mark (GPGSLO)
       5   fsflush run rate (FSFLUSHR)
      25   minimum resident memory for avoiding deadlock \
(MINARMEM)
      25        minimum swapable memory for avoiding \
deadlock (MINASMEM)
*
* Utsname Tunables
*
     5.8  release (REL)
 unknown  node name (NODE)
   SunOS  system name (SYS)
Generic_108528-07  version (VER)
*
* Process Resource Limit Tunables (Current:Maximum)
*
          Infinity:Infinity             cpu time
          Infinity:Infinity             file size
          Infinity:Infinity             heap size
0x0000000000800000:Infinity             stack size
          Infinity:Infinity             core file size
0x0000000000000100:0x0000000000000400   file descriptors
          Infinity:Infinity             mapped memory
*
* Streams Tunables
*
     9  maximum number of pushes allowed (NSTRPUSH)
 65536  maximum stream message size (STRMSGSZ)
  1024  max size of ctl part of message (STRCTLSZ)
*
* IPC Messages module is not loaded
*
*
* IPC Semaphores module is not loaded
*
*
* IPC Shared Memory
*
   1048576      max shared memory segment size (SHMMAX)
     1  min shared memory segment size (SHMMIN). . . \
<Output has been truncated>
```

Finally, here's an example of the device information for an Ultra system displayed using the `dmesg` command:

```
# dmesg
Aug  1 12:08:04 ultra5 genunix: [ID 540533 kern.notice] \
SunOS Release 5.8 Version Generic_108528-07 64-bit
Aug  1 12:08:04 ultra5 genunix: [ID 913631 kern.notice] \
Copyright 1983-2001 Sun Microsystems, Inc.  All rights reserved.
Aug  1 12:08:04 ultra5 genunix: [ID 678236 kern.info] \
Ethernet address = 8:0:20:a2:63:82
Aug  1 12:08:04 ultra5 unix: [ID 389951 kern.info] mem = 131072K (0x8000000)
Aug  1 12:08:04 ultra5 unix: [ID 930857 kern.info] avail mem = 122142720
Aug  1 12:08:04 ultra5 rootnex: [ID 466748 kern.info] root nexus = Sun Ultra 5/10 UPA/PCI \
(UltraSPARC-IIi 270MHz)
Aug  1 12:08:04 ultra5 rootnex: [ID 349649 kern.info] pcipsy0 at root: UPA 0x1f 0x0
Aug  1 12:08:04 ultra5 genunix: [ID 936769 kern.info] pcipsy0 is /pci@1f,0
Aug  1 12:08:04 ultra5 pcipsy: [ID 370704 kern.info] PCI-device: pci@1,1, simba0
Aug  1 12:08:04 ultra5 genunix: [ID 936769 kern.info] simba0 is /pci@1f,0/pci@1,1
Aug  1 12:08:04 ultra5 pcipsy: [ID 370704 kern.info] PCI-device: pci@1, simba1
Aug  1 12:08:04 ultra5 genunix: [ID 936769 kern.info] simba1 is /pci@1f,0/pci@1
Aug  1 12:08:20 ultra5 simba: [ID 370704 kern.info] PCI-device: ide@3, uata0
...... <the output has been truncated>
```

Use the output of the `prtconf` and `sysdef` commands to identify which disk, tape, and CD-ROM devices are connected to the system. As shown in the previous examples, some devices display the `driver not attached` message next to the device instance. This message does not always mean that a driver is unavailable for this device. It means that no driver is currently attached to the device instance because there is no device at this node, or the device is not in use. The OS automatically loads drivers when the device is accessed, and it unloads them when it is not in use.

The system determines what devices are attached to it at startup. This is why it is important to have all peripherals powered on at startup, even if they are not currently being used. During startup, the kernel configures itself dynamically, loading needed modules into memory. Device drivers are loaded when devices, such as disk and tape devices, are accessed for the first time. This process is called *auto-configuration*, because all kernel modules are loaded automatically if needed. As described in Chapter 2, the system administrator can customize the way in which kernel modules are loaded by modifying the /etc/system file.

# DEVICE AUTO-CONFIGURATION

Auto-configuration offers many advantages over the manual configuration method used in earlier versions of UNIX, in which device drivers were manually added to the kernel, the kernel was recompiled, and the system had to be restarted. Now, with auto-configuration, the administrator simply connects the new device to the system and performs a reconfiguration startup.

## STEP BY STEP

### 16.1 Performing a Reconfiguration Startup

1. Create the /reconfigure file with the following command:

   ```
   touch /reconfigure
   ```

   The /reconfigure file causes the Solaris software to check for the presence of any newly installed devices the next time you turn on or start up your system.

2. Shut down the system using the shutdown procedure described in Chapter 1, "System Startup and Shutdown."

   If you need to connect the device, turn off power to the system and all peripherals after Solaris has been properly shut down.

   After the new device is connected, restore power to the peripherals first and then to the system. Verify that the peripheral device has been added by attempting to access it.

**NOTE** The file named /reconfigure automatically gets removed during the boot-up process.

An optional method of performing a reconfiguration startup is to interrupt the start process and type `boot -r` at the OpenBoot prompt.

I prefer the first method described because the system administrator can instruct the system to perform the reconfiguration startup at any time by creating the /reconfigure file. Now, at the next restart, whether the administrator is there or not, the system performs the reconfiguration startup. This could happen at 3 a.m. if you like.

**NOTE** As root, you can also issue the `reboot -- -r` command from the UNIX shell. The `-- -r` passes the `-r` to the `boot` command.

During a reconfiguration restart, a device hierarchy is created in the /devices directory to represent the devices connected to the system. The kernel uses this to associate drivers with their appropriate devices. Also, any kernel parameter changes that were made to the /etc/system file are parsed by the kernel at this time.

Auto-configuration offers the following benefits:

- Main memory is used more efficiently because modules are loaded as needed.
- There is no need to reconfigure the kernel if new devices are added to the system. When you add devices such as disks or tape drives, however, the system needs to be shut down before you connect the hardware so that no damage is done to the electrical components.
- Drivers can be loaded and tested without having to rebuild the kernel and restart the system.

Occasionally, you might install a new device for which Solaris does not have a supporting device driver. Always check with the manufacturer to make sure that any device you plan to add to your system has a supported device driver. If a driver is not included with the standard Solaris release, the manufacturer should provide the software needed for the device to be properly installed, maintained, and administered.

Third-party device drivers are installed as software packages using the `pkgadd` command. At a minimum, this software includes a device driver and its associated configuration (.conf) file. The .conf files reside in the /kernel/drv directories. Table 16.2 describes the contents of the subdirectories located in the /kernel directory.

**TABLE 16.2**

**THE /KERNEL DIRECTORY**

| *Directory* | *Description* |
|---|---|
| drv | Contains loadable device drivers and pseudo-device drivers. |
| exec | Contains modules used to run different types of executable files or shell scripts. |
| fs | Contains file system modules, such as ufs, nfs, proc, and so on. |
| misc | Contains miscellaneous system-related modules, such as swap-generic and ipc. |
| sched | Contains OS schedulers. |
| strmod | Contains System V STREAMS loadable modules. |
| sys | Contains loadable system calls, such as system semaphore and system accounting operations. |

# INSTANCE NAME

The *instance name* represents the kernel's abbreviated name for every possible device on the system. For example, on an Ultra system, dad0 represents the instance name of the IDE disk drive, and hme0 is the instance name for the network interface. Instance names are mapped to a physical device name in the /etc/path_to_inst file. The following shows the contents of a path_to_inst file:

```
more /etc/path_to_inst
#
#       Caution! This file contains critical kernel state
"/pci@1f,0" 0 "pci"
"/pci@1f,0/pci@1,1" 0 "simba"
"/pci@1f,0/pci@1,1/ide@3" 0 "uata"
"/pci@1f,0/pci@1,1/ide@3/sd@2,0" 2 "sd"
"/pci@1f,0/pci@1,1/ide@3/dad@0,0" 0 "dad"
"/pci@1f,0/pci@1,1/ebus@1" 0 "ebus"
"/pci@1f,0/pci@1,1/ebus@1/fdthree@14,3023f0" 0 "fd"
"/pci@1f,0/pci@1,1/ebus@1/su@14,3062f8" 1 "su"
"/pci@1f,0/pci@1,1/ebus@1/se@14,400000" 0 "se"
"/pci@1f,0/pci@1,1/ebus@1/su@14,3083f8" 0 "su"
"/pci@1f,0/pci@1,1/ebus@1/ecpp@14,3043bc" 0 "ecpp"
"/pci@1f,0/pci@1,1/ebus@1/SUNW,CS4231@14,200000" 0 "audiocs"
"/pci@1f,0/pci@1,1/ebus@1/power@14,724000" 0 "power"
"/pci@1f,0/pci@1,1/network@1,1" 0 "hme"
"/pci@1f,0/pci@1,1/SUNW,m64B@2" 0 "m64"
```

```
"/pci@1f,0/pci@1" 1 "simba"
"/pci@1f,0/pci@1/pci@1" 0 "pci_pci"
"/pci@1f,0/pci@1/pci@1/SUNW,qfe@1,1" 1 "qfe"
"/pci@1f,0/pci@1/pci@1/SUNW,qfe@0,1" 0 "qfe"
"/pci@1f,0/pci@1/pci@1/SUNW,qfe@3,1" 3 "qfe"
"/pci@1f,0/pci@1/pci@1/SUNW,qfe@2,1" 2 "qfe"
"/options" 0 "options"
"/pseudo" 0 "pseudo"
#
```

Instance names can also be displayed by using the commands `dmesg`, `sysdef`, and `prtconf`, the only command that shows the mapping of the instance name to the physical device is the `dmesg` command, which displays the following information:

```
dad0 at pci1095,6460 target 0 lun 0
dad0 is /pci@1f,0/pci@1,1/ide@3/dad@0,0
```

If you have an older SPARCstation with an SBus and SCSI disk drives, here's similar output for a SCSI disk drive:

```
sd3 at esp0: target 3 lun 0
sd3 is/iommu@f,e0000000/sbus@f,e0001000,espdma@f,400000/
esp@f,800000/sd@3,0
```

In the first example, `dad0` is the instance name and `/pci@1f,0/pci@1,1/ide@3/dad@0,0` is the physical device name. After the instance name has been assigned to a device, it remains mapped to that device. To keep instance numbers consistent across restarts, the system records them in the /etc/path_to_inst file. This file is read only at startup, and it is updated by the `devfsadmd` daemon described later in this section.

**CAUTION**

Do not remove the path_to_inst file; the system cannot start up without it. The system relies on information found in this file to find the root, usr and swap devices. Make changes to this file only after careful consideration.

Devices already existing on a system are not rearranged when new devices are added, even if new devices are added to `sbus` slots that are numerically lower than those that are occupied by existing devices. In other words, the /etc/path_to_inst file is appended to, not rewritten, when new devices are added.

It is generally not necessary for the system administrator to change the path_to_inst file, because the system maintains it. The system administrator can, however, change the assignment of instance numbers by editing this file and doing a reconfiguration startup. However, any changes made in this file are lost if the `devfsadm` command is run before the system is restarted.

In Solaris 8, you can add new devices to a system without requiring a reboot. It's all handled by the `devfsadmd` daemon that transparently builds the necessary configuration entries. Before Solaris 7 release 11/99, you needed to run several devfs administration tools such as `drvconfig`, `disks`, `tapes`, `ports`, and `devlinks` to add in the new device and create the /dev and /devices entries necessary for the Solaris operating environment to access the new device. These tools are still available, but for compatibility purposes, `drvconfig` and the other link generators are symbolic links to the `devfsadm` utility. Furthermore, these older commands are not aware of hot-pluggable devices, nor are they flexible enough for devices with multiple instances. The `devfsadm` command should now be used in place of all these commands; however, because `devfsadmd`, the `devfsadm` daemon, automatically detects device configuration changes, so there should be no need to run this command interactively.

**NOTE** If you can't start up from the startup disk because of a problem with the /etc/path_to_inst file, you should start up from the CD-ROM (`boot -sw cdrom`) and copy the /etc/path_to_inst file contained on the CD-ROM to the /etc/path_to_inst on the startup disk. To do this, start up from the CD-ROM using `boot -sw cdrom` at the OpenBoot prompt. Then mount the startup disk on /a. Copy the /etc/path_to_inst file to /a/etc/path_to_inst. If you still can't start up, the problem is deeper than just with the /etc/path_to_inst file.

An example of when to use the `devfsadm` command would be if the system has been started, but the power to the CD-ROM or tape drive was not turned on. During startup, the system did not detect the device; therefore, its drivers were not installed. This can be verified by issuing the `sysdef` command and examining the output for sd6, the SCSI target ID normally used for the external CD-ROM:

```
sd, instance #6 (driver not attached)
```

To gain access to the CD-ROM, you could halt the system, turn on power to the CD-ROM, and start the system back up, or you could simply turn on power to the CD-ROM and issue the following command at the command prompt:

```
devfsadm
```

Now if you issue the `sysdef` command, you'll see the following output for the CD-ROM:

```
sd, instance #6
```

**NOTE** Two terms that are often interchanged (and confused) are hot-pluggable and hot-swappable. Hot-pluggable allows the connection and disconnection of peripherals or other components without rebooting the operating system. Dynamic reconfiguration, available on certain SPARC servers, allows a service provider to remove and replace hot-pluggable system I/O boards in a running system, eliminating the time lost in rebooting. Also, if a replacement board is not immediately available, the system administrator can use dynamic reconfiguration to shut down a failing board while allowing the system to continue operation. Hot-swappable allows the connection and disconnection of peripherals or other components without shutting down the hardware, but usually requires a system reboot.

# Major and Minor Device Numbers

Each device has a major and minor device number assigned. These numbers identify the proper device location and device driver to the kernel. This number is used by the operating system to key into the proper device driver whenever a physical device file corresponding to one of the devices it manages is opened. The major device number indicates the general device class, such as disk, tape, or serial line. The minor device number indicates the specific member within that class. All devices managed by a given device driver contain a unique minor number. Some drivers of pseudo-devices (software entities set up to look like devices) create new minor devices on demand. Together, the major and minor numbers uniquely define a device and its device driver.

Physical device files have a unique output when listed with the `ls -l` command, as shown in the following example:

```
cd /devices/iommu@f,e0000000/sbus@f,e0001000/espdma@f,400000/esp@f,800000
ls -l sd@0
```

The system responds with this:

```
brw-r-----   1 root   sys    32,  0 Jul 21 07:44 sd@0,0:a
crw-r-----   1 root   sys    32,  0 Jul 21 07:44 sd@0,0:a,raw
brw-r-----   1 root   sys    32,  1 Jul 21 07:44 sd@0,0:b
crw-r-----   1 root   sys    32,  1 Aug 16 06:15 sd@0,0:b,raw
brw-r-----   1 root   sys    32,  2 Jul 21 07:44 sd@0,0:c
crw-r-----   1 root   sys    32,  2 Jul 21 07:44 sd@0,0:c,raw
brw-r-----   1 root   sys    32,  3 Jul 21 07:44 sd@0,0:d
crw-r-----   1 root   sys    32,  3 Jul 21 07:44 sd@0,0:d,raw
brw-r-----   1 root   sys    32,  4 Jul 21 07:44 sd@0,0:e
crw-r-----   1 root   sys    32,  4 Jul 21 07:44 sd@0,0:e,raw
brw-r-----   1 root   sys    32,  5 Jul 21 07:44 sd@0,0:f
crw-r-----   1 root   sys    32,  5 Jul 21 07:44 sd@0,0:f,raw
brw-r-----   1 root   sys    32,  6 Jul 21 07:44 sd@0,0:g
crw-r-----   1 root   sys    32,  6 Aug 16 06:13 sd@0,0:g,raw
brw-r-----   1 root   sys    32,  7 Jul 21 07:44 sd@0,0:h
crw-r-----   1 root   sys    32,  7 Jul 21 07:44 sd@0,0:h,raw
```

This long listing includes columns showing major and minor numbers for each device. The sd driver manages all the devices listed in this example, which is major number 32 in this example. Minor numbers are listed after the comma.

During the process of building the /devices directory, the `devfsadmd` daemon assigns each device a major device number by using the name-to-number mappings held in the /etc/name_to_major file. This file is maintained by the system and is undocumented. The following is a sample of the /etc/name_to_major file:

```
more /etc/name_to_major
cn 0
rootnex 1
pseudo 2
ip 3
logindmux 4
icmp 5
fas 6
hme 7
p9000 8
p9100 9
sp 10
clone 11
sad 12
mm 13
iwscn 14
wc 15
conskbd 16
consms 17
ipdcm 18
dump 19
se 20
log 21
sy 22
ptm 23
pts 24
ptc 25
ptsl 26
bwtwo 27
audio 28
zs 29
cgthree 30
cgtwo 31
sd 32
st 33
...
...

envctrl 131
cvc 132
cvcredir 133
eide 134
hd 135
tadbat 136
ts102 137
simba 138
uata 139
dad 140
atapicd 141
```

To create the minor device entries, the `devfsadmd daemon` uses the information placed in the dev_info node by the device driver. Permissions and ownership information are kept in the /etc/minor_perm file.

## Logical Device Name

The final stage of the auto-configuration process involves the creation of the logical device name to reflect the new set of devices on the system. The logical device name is a link from the /dev directory to the physical device name located in the /devices directory. To see a list of logical device names for the disks connected to your system, execute a long listing on the /dev/dsk directory as follows:

```
ls -l /dev/dsk
total 48
lrwxrwxrwx   1 root     root          84 Jul 21 07:45 c0t0d0s0 -> \
../../devices/iommu@f,e0000000/sbus@f,e0001000/espdma@f,400000/esp@f, 800000/sd@0,0:a
lrwxrwxrwx   1 root     root          84 Jul 21 07:45 c0t0d0s1 -> \
../../devices/iommu@f,e0000000/sbus@f,e0001000/espdma@f,400000/esp@f, 800000/sd@0,0:b
lrwxrwxrwx   1 root     root          84 Jul 21 07:45 c0t0d0s2 -> \
../../devices/iommu@f,e0000000/sbus@f,e0001000/espdma@f,400000/esp@f, 800000/sd@0,0:c
lrwxrwxrwx   1 root     root          84 Jul 21 07:45 c0t0d0s3 -> \
../../devices/iommu@f,e0000000/sbus@f,e0001000/espdma@f,400000/esp@f, 800000/sd@0,0:d
lrwxrwxrwx   1 root     root          84 Jul 21 07:45 c0t0d0s4 -> \
../../devices/iommu@f,e0000000/sbus@f,e0001000/espdma@f,400000/esp@f, 800000/sd@0,0:e
lrwxrwxrwx   1 root     root          84 Jul 21 07:45 c0t0d0s5 -> \
../../devices/iommu@f,e0000000/sbus@f,e0001000/espdma@f,400000/esp@f, 800000/sd@0,0:f
...
...
```

On the second line of output from the `ls -l` command, notice that the logical device name c0t0d0s0 is linked to the physical device name:

```
../../devices/iommu@f,e0000000/sbus \
@f,e0001000/espdma@f,400000/esp@f,800000/sd@0,0:a
```

The logical device name is the name that the system administrator uses to refer to a particular device if running various Solaris file system commands. For example, if running the `mount` command, use the logical device name /dev/dsk/c0t0d0s7 to mount the file system /home:

```
mount /dev/dsk/c0t0d0s7 /home
```

Logical device files in the /dev directory are symbolically linked to physical device files in the /devices directory. Logical device names are used to access disk devices if you

- Add a new disk to the system.
- Move a disk from one system to another.
- Access (or mount) a file system residing on a local disk.
- Back up a local file system.
- Repair a file system.

Logical devices are organized in subdirectories under the /dev directory by their device types, as shown in Table 16.3.

**TABLE 16.3**

**DEVICE DIRECTORIES**

| *Directory* | *Description of Contents* |
|---|---|
| /dev/dsk | Block interface to disk devices |
| /dev/rdsk | Raw or character interface to disk devices |
| /dev/rmt | Tape devices |
| /dev/term | Serial line devices |
| /dev/cua | Dial-out modems |
| /dev/pts | Pseudo terminals |
| /dev/fbs | Frame buffers |
| /dev/sad | STREAMS administrative driver |

# Block and Raw Devices

Disk drives have an entry under both the /dev/dsk and the /dev/rdsk directories. The /dsk directory refers to the block or buffered device file, and the /rdsk directory refers to the character or raw device file. The "r" in rdsk stands for "raw." If you are not familiar with these devices, refer to Chapter 3, "Installing the Solaris 8 Software," in which block and character devices are described.

The /dev/dsk directory contains the disk entries for the block device nodes in /devices, as shown in the following command:

```
ls -l /dev/dsk
total 48
lrwxrwxrwx   1 root     root           84 Jul 21 07:45 c0t0d0s0 ->
/devices/iommu@f,e0000000/sbus@f,e0001000/espdma@f,400000/esp@f,800000/sd@0,0:a
lrwxrwxrwx   1 root     root           84 Jul 21 07:45 c0t0d0s1 ->
/devices/iommu@f,e0000000/sbus@f,e0001000/espdma@f,400000/esp@f,800000/sd@0,0:b
lrwxrwxrwx   1 root     root           84 Jul 21 07:45 c0t0d0s2 ->
/devices/iommu@f,e0000000/sbus@f,e0001000/espdma@f,400000/esp@f,800000/sd@0,0:c
...
...
```

The /dev/rdsk directory contains the disk entries for the character device nodes in /devices, as shown in the following command:

```
ls -l /dev/rdsk
lrwxrwxrwx   1 root     root           88 Jul 21 07:45 c0t0d0s0 ->
/devices/iommu@f,e0000000/sbus@f,e0001000/espdma@f,400000/esp@f, 800000/sd@0,0:a,raw
lrwxrwxrwx   1 root     root           88 Jul 21 07:45 c0t0d0s1 ->
/devices/iommu@f,e0000000/sbus@f,e0001000/espdma@f,400000/esp@f, 800000/sd@0,0:b,raw
lrwxrwxrwx   1 root     root           88 Jul 21 07:45 c0t0d0s2 ->
/devices/iommu@f,e0000000/sbus@f,e0001000/espdma@f,400000/esp@f, 800000/sd@0,0:c,raw
...
...
```

## VIRTUAL VOLUME MANAGEMENT

With standard disk devices, each disk slice has its own physical and logical device. Remember from Chapter 6, "Introduction to File Systems," that a file system cannot span more than one disk slice. In other words, the maximum size of a file system is limited to the size of a single disk. On a large server with many disk drives, standard methods of disk slicing are inadequate and inefficient. This has been a limitation in all UNIX systems until the introduction of virtual disks, also called virtual volumes. To eliminate the limitation of one slice per file system, there are virtual volume management packages that are able to create virtual volume structures in which a single file system can consist of nearly an unlimited number of disks or partitions. The key feature of these virtual volume management packages is that they transparently provide a virtual volume that can consist of many physical disk partitions. In other words, disk partitions are grouped across several disks to appear as one single volume to the operating system.

Each flavor of UNIX has its own methods of creating virtual volumes, and Sun has addressed virtual volume management with two software packages: Solstice DiskSuite and Sun StorEdge Volume Manager. DiskSuite is used primarily on smaller servers and workstations, and the StorEdge product is used on the larger Enterprise servers to manage Sun's StorEdge disk arrays.

## Solstice DiskSuite

Solstice DiskSuite comes bundled with the Solaris 8 operating system and uses virtual disks, called *metadevices*, to manage physical disks and their associated data. A metadevice is functionally identical to a physical disk in the view of an application. DiskSuite uses a special driver, called the metadisk driver, to coordinate I/O to and from physical devices and metadevices, enabling applications to treat a metadevice like a physical device. This type of driver is also called a logical, or pseudo, driver.

DiskSuite's metadevices are built from standard disk slices that have been created using the `format` utility. Using the DiskSuite command line utilities or the graphical user interface, DiskSuite Tool, the system administrator creates each device by dragging slices onto one of three types of metadevice objects: metadevices, state database replicas, and hot spare pools. These objects are described in Table 16.4.

**TABLE 16.4**

**DiskSuite Objects**

| *Object* | *Description* |
|---|---|
| Metadevice | A metadevice is a group of physical slices that appear to the system as a single, logical device. A metadevice is used to increase storage capacity and increase data availability. |
| Metadevice state database | A database that stores information about the state of the DiskSuite configuration. DiskSuite cannot operate until you have created the metadevice state database replicas. |
| Hot spare pool | A collection of slices (hot spares) reserved for automatic substitution in case of slice failure in either a submirror or RAID5 metadevice. Hot spares are used to increase data availability. |

The types of metadevices you can create are concatenations, stripes, concatenated stripes, mirrors, RAID5 metadevices, and trans metadevices, all described in Table 16.5.

**TABLE 16.5**

**TYPES OF METADEVICES**

| *Metadevice* | *Description* |
|---|---|
| Simple | Can be used directly, or as the basic building block for mirrors and trans devices. There are three types of simple metadevices: stripes, concatenations, and concatenated stripes. |
| Concatenation | Concatenations work much the way the UNIX `cat` command is used to concatenate two or more files to create one larger file. If partitions are concatenated, the addressing of the component blocks is done on the components sequentially. The file system can use the entire concatenation. |
| Stripe | A stripe is similar to concatenation, except that the addressing of the component blocks is interlaced on the slices rather than sequentially. Striping is used to gain performance. When data is striped across disks, multiple controllers can access data simultaneously. |
| Concatenated stripe | A concatenated stripe is a striped metadevice that has been expanded by concatenating additional striped slices. |
| Mirror | A mirror is composed of one or more simple metadevices called submirrors. A mirror replicates all writes to a single logical device (the mirror) and then to multiple devices (the submirrors) while distributing read operations. This provides redundancy of data in the event of a disk or hardware failure. |
| RAID5 | Stripes the data across multiple disks to achieve better performance (see striping). In addition to striping, RAID5 replicates data by using parity information. In the case of missing data, the data can be regenerated using available data and the parity information. A RAID5 metadevice is composed of multiple slices. Some space is allocated to parity information and is distributed across all slices in the RAID5 metadevice. The striped metadevice performance is better than the RAID5 metadevice, but it doesn't provide data protection (redundancy). |

| *Metadevice* | *Description* |
|---|---|
| Trans | Used to log a UFS file system. A trans metadevice is composed of a master device and a logging device. Both of these devices can be a slice, simple metadevice, mirror, or RAID5 metadevice. The master device contains the UFS file system. |

Metadevices can provide increased capacity, higher availability, and better performance. In addition, DiskSuite's hot spares can provide another level of data availability for mirrors and RAID5 metadevices. *A hot spare pool* is a collection of slices (hot spares) reserved by DiskSuite to be automatically substituted in case of a slice failure in either a submirror or RAID5 metadevice.

After you have set up your configuration, you can use DiskSuite Tool to report on its operation. You can also use DiskSuite's SNMP trap generating daemon to work with a network monitoring console to automatically receive DiskSuite error messages.

The metadevice driver is implemented as a set of loadable pseudo device drivers. It uses other physical device drivers to pass I/O requests to and from the underlying devices. The metadevice driver resides between the file system interface and the device driver interface, and it interprets information between the two. After passing through the metadevice driver, information is received in the expected form by both the file system and the device drivers. The metadevice is a loadable device driver, and it has all the same characteristics as any other disk device driver.

The standard metadevice name begins with "d," and is followed by a number. By default, there are 128 unique metadevices in the range 0 to 127. Additional metadevices can be added to the kernel by editing the /kernel/drv/md.conf file. The meta block device accesses the disk using the system's normal buffering mechanism. There is also a character (or raw) device that provides for direct transmission between the disk and the user's read or write buffer. The names of the block devices are found in the /dev/md/dsk directory, and the names of the raw devices are found in the /dev/md/rdsk directory. The following is an example of a block and raw logical device name for metadevice d0:

```
/dev/md/dsk/d0   - block metadevice d0
/dev/md/rdsk/d0  - raw metadevice d0
```

# STOREDGE VOLUME MANAGER

Sun StorEdge Volume Manager, also called the Veritas Volume Manager, is an unbundled software package, purchased separately from Sun, and does not come standard with Solaris 8. The StorEdge product is used for managing Sun's larger StorEdge disk arrays and is also known as the Veritas Volume Manager. Veritas Volume Manager is a third-party package licensed by Sun. It is widely used for performing Virtual Volume Management functions on large-scale systems such as Sun, Sequent, and HP. The Veritas Volume Manager is much more robust than the DiskSuite product, providing tools that identify and analyze storage access patterns so that I/O loads can be balanced across complex disk configurations. In addition, the Volume Manager package creates a Veritas file system, which is quickly becoming an industry standard on systems that utilize virtual volumes and creates a foundation for other value-added technologies such as Storage Area Network (SAN) environments, clustering and failover, automated management, backup, and remote browser-based management.

The StorEdge Volume Manager is a complex product that would take much more than this chapter to describe in detail. I will, however, introduce you to the StorEdge Volume Manager and some of the terms you may need to be aware of.

The Volume Manager builds virtual devices called *volumes* on top of physical disks. A *physical disk* is the underlying storage device (media), which may or may not be under Volume Manager control. A physical disk can be accessed using a device name such as /dev/rdsk/c#t#d. The physical disk, as explained in Chapter 3, "Installing the Solaris 8 Software," can be divided into one or more slices.

Volumes are accessed by the Solaris file system, a database, or other applications in the same way physical disk partitions would be accessed. Volumes and their virtual components are referred to as Volume Manager objects.

There are several Volume Manager objects that the Volume Manager uses to perform disk management tasks (see Table 16.6).

**TABLE 16.6**

**VOLUME MANAGER OBJECTS**

| *Object Name* | *Description* |
|---|---|
| VM Disk | A contiguous area of disk space from which the Volume Manager allocates storage. Each VM disk corresponds to at least one partition. A VM disk usually refers to a physical disk in the array. |
| Disk Group | A collection of VM disks that share a common configuration. The default disk group is rootdg (the root disk group). Additional disk groups can be created, as necessary. Volumes are created within a disk group; a given volume must be configured from disks belonging to the same disk group. Disk groups allow the administrator to group disks into logical collections for administrative convenience. |
| Subdisk | A set of contiguous disk blocks; subdisks are the basic units in which the Volume Manager allocates disk space. A VM disk can be divided into one or more subdisks. |
| Plex | Also referred to as a mirror, and consists of one or more subdisks located on one or more disks. |
| Volume | A virtual disk device that appears to applications, databases, and file systems. It is like a physical disk partition, but does not have the physical limitations of a physical disk partition. Volumes are created within a disk group; a given volume must be configured from disks belonging to the same disk group. |

**NOTE**

A number of plexes (usually 2) are associated with a volume to form a working mirror. Also, it is normally in the creation of the plex where stripes and concatenations are achieved.

Volume Manager objects can be manipulated in a variety of ways to optimize performance, provide redundancy of data, and perform backups or other administrative tasks on one or more physical disks without interrupting applications. As a result, data availability and disk subsystem throughput are improved.

StorEdge Volume Manager manages disk space by using contiguous sectors. The application formats the disks into only two slices: Slice 3 and Slice 4. Slice 3 is called a private area, and Slice 4 is the public area. Slice 3 maintains information about the virtual to physical device mappings, whereas Slice 4 provides space to build the virtual devices. The advantage to this approach is there is almost no limit to the number of subdisks you can create on a single drive. In a standard Solaris disk-partitioned environment, there is an eight-partition limit per disk.

The names of the block devices for virtual volumes created using the StorEdge Volume Manager are found in the /dev/vx/dsk/ *<disk_group>*/*<volume_name>* directory, and the names of the raw devices are found in the /dev/vx/rdsk/*<disk_group>*/*<volume_name>* directory. The following is an example of a block and raw logical device name:

```
/dev/vx/dsk/apps/vol01  - block device
/dev/vx/rdsk/apps/vol01  - raw device
```

## CHAPTER SUMMARY

**KEY TERMS**

- Device driver
- Device hierarchy
- Device Auto-configuration
- Reconfiguration startup
- Physical device
- Instance name
- Logical device
- Major device number
- Minor device number
- Block device
- Character device
- Virtual volume
- Metadevice (known all the types of metadevices)
- Metadisk
- Meta state database
- Hot spare pool
- Volume Manager object (know all the object types)
- Hot-pluggable
- Hot-swappable

This chapter discussed the various device drivers and device names that are used in Solaris 8. I described the Solaris commands and utilities used to obtain information about these devices and drivers. In addition to the devices that come standard with Solaris, this chapter also described virtual volume management and the added functionality it provides.

Device drivers are discussed in several chapters of this book because they are used in many aspects of the system administrator's job. Devices are referenced when we install and boot the OS (see Chapter 2, "OpenBoot" and Chapter 3, "Installing the Solaris 8 Software"), when creating and mounting file systems (see Chapter 6, "Introduction to File Systems"), when setting up printers (see Chapter 10, "LP Print Service"), and in general troubleshooting of system problems. It is very important that you have a good understanding of how device drivers are configured and named in the Solaris operating system.

The next chapter describes networked file systems (NFS). As I stated earlier, Solaris was designed to operate in a networked environment. Sun sums it up in its slogan "The network is the computer." Most administrators agree that Solaris without a network is like a fish out of water.

## APPLY YOUR KNOWLEDGE

# Exercises

### 16.1 Device Auto-Configuration

This exercise demonstrates three different methods that can be used to perform a reconfiguration boot so that the kernel recognizes new devices attached to the system.

**Estimated Time:** 15 minutes

1. From the OpenBoot prompt, type the following:

   ```
   boot -r
   ```

   The system performs a reconfiguration boot and a login prompt appears.

2. Log in as root, and create an empty file named /reconfigure as follows:

   ```
   touch /reconfigure
   ```

   Now reboot the system as follows:

   ```
   /usr/sbin/shutdown -y -g0 -i6
   ```

   The system performs a reconfiguration boot, and a login prompt appears.

3. Log in as root, and issue the following command:

   ```
   reboot -- -r
   ```

   The system performs a reconfiguration boot, and a login prompt appears.

### 16.2 Displaying Information About Devices

In this exercise, you'll use a few of the Solaris commands to display information about devices connected to your system.

**Estimated Time**: 5 minutes

1. Use the `dmesg` command to determine the mapping of an instance name to a physical device name. Type: `dmesg`

   In the output, identify the instance name assigned to each disk drive and peripheral attached to your system. On a system with IDE disks, you'll see entries similar to the following:

   ```
   sd0 is /pci@1f,0/pci@1,1/ide@3/sd@2,0
   ```

   Or on a system with SCSI disks, you'll see something like this:

   ```
   sd0 is /iommu@f,e0000000 \
   /sbus@f,e0001000/espdma@f,400000/ \
   esp@f,800000/sd@0,0
   ```

2. Use the `prtconf` command to see which drivers are attached to the instance names identified in the previous step.

   For example, you should see an entry something like this:

   ```
   sd, instance #0
   ```

### 16.3 Adding a New Device

In this exercise, you'll use the `devfsadm` command to add in a new device without rebooting the system.

**Estimated Time**: 15 minutes

1. Connect a tape drive, disk drive, or CD-ROM to the system and perform a reconfiguration reboot.

2. Log in, and issue the `dmesg` command to verify that the device has been installed. You should see an entry something like this if you're adding a SCSI disk drive:

   ```
   sd0 is /iommu@f,e0000000 \
   /sbus@f,e0001000/espdma@f,400000/esp@f,800000 \
   /sd@0,0
   ```

   Check to see that a driver is attached by issuing the `prtconf` command.

## APPLY YOUR KNOWLEDGE

3. Halt the system, turn off the new device, and boot the system back up using the `boot` command. Do not do a reconfiguration reboot.
4. Issue the `dmesg` command. The device should still be listed in the output.
5. Issue the `prtconf` command. It should display `(driver not attached)` next to the instance device name for that device.
6. Issue the `devfsadm` command.
7. Issue the `prtconf` command again. The message `(driver not attached)` next to the instance device name should be gone, and the device is now available for use.

## Review Questions

1. Which of the following represents the kernel's abbreviated name for every possible device on the system?

   A. Instance name

   B. Logical device

   C. Physical device name

   D. Pseudo device name

2. Physical device files are found in:

   A. /kernel/drv

   B. /dev

   C. /platform

   D. /devices

3. Which of the following displays device configuration information, including system hardware, pseudo devices, loadable modules and selected kernel parameters?

   A. `messages`

   B. `prtconf`

   C. `dmesg`

   D. `sysdef`

4. When you see the `driver not attached` message, it means:

   A. The device for this driver is not attached.

   B. A driver is unavailable for this device.

   C. No driver is currently attached to the device instance because there is no device at this node or the device is not in use.

   D. The kernel needs to be reconfigured to attach the device.

5. The conf files reside in:

   A. /kernel/drv

   B. /dev

   C. /devices

   D. /platform

6. Which of the following are mapped to a physical device name in the /etc/path_to_inst file?

   A. logical devices

   B. instance names

   C. physical devices

   D. pseudo device

## APPLY YOUR KNOWLEDGE

7. You can determine the mapping of an instance name to a physical device name by doing what? Choose all that apply.

   A. Looking at output from the `dmesg` command.

   B. Viewing the /var/adm/messages file.

   C. Looking at output from the `sysdef` command.

   D. Looking at output from the `prtconf` command.

8. The system relies on information found in which of the following files to find the root, usr, or swap device?

   A. /etc/vfstab

   B. path_to_inst

   C. kernel

   D. /kernel/drv/

   E. /etc/driver

9. Which of the following commands adds a new device driver to the system?

   A. `boot -r`

   B. `drvconfig`

   C. `devfsadm`

   D. devlinks

10. Which of the following commands is used to inform the system about newly installed device drivers?

    A. `devlinks`

    B. `drvconfig`

    C. `add_drv`

    D. devfsadm

11. Which of the following utilities is responsible for configuring the /devices directory to reflect the `dev_info` tree held in the kernel?

    A. `drvconfig`

    B. `add_drv`

    C. `devfsadm`

    D. devlinks

12. To gain access to the CD-ROM, you could halt the system, turn on power to the CD-ROM, and start the system back up, or you could issue which of the following commands at the command prompt?

    A. `drvconfig cdrom`

    B. `add_drv cdrom`

    C. `devfsadm`

    D. drvconfig –d

13. Which of the following indicates the general device class, such as disk, tape, or serial line, for a device driver?

    A. Minor device number

    B. Major device number

    C. Device tree

    D. Pseudo device

14. The minor device number:

    A. indicates the general device class, such as disk, tape, or serial line

    B. indicates the specific member within that class.

    C. uniquely defines a device and its device driver.

    D. identifies the proper device location and device driver to the kernel.

## Apply Your Knowledge

15. Logical device files in the /dev directory are symbolically linked to which of the following in the devices directory?

    A. Instance names

    B. Pseudo device files

    C. Full device path names

    D. Physical device files

16. Which of the following is a link from the /dev directory to the physical device name located in the /devices directory?

    A. Full device path name

    B. Pseudo device name

    C. Logical device name

    D. Instance name

17. /dev/dsk/c0t0d0s7 is what type of device?

    A. Logical device name

    B. Pseudo device name

    C. Full device path name

    D. Instance name

18. Which of the following commands creates entries in the /dev directory for disk drives attached to the system?

    A. `devfsadm`

    B. `add_drv`

    C. `drvconfig`

    D. boot –r

19. Which directory contains the disk entries to the block device nodes in /devices?

    A. /kernel/drv

    B. /dev/rdsk

    C. /dev

    D. /dev/dsk

20. Which of the following is a device that represents several disks or disk slices?

    A. Logical device

    B. Metadevice

    C. Pseudo device

    D. Instance

21. Which of the following provides redundancy of data in the event of a disk or hardware failure?

    A. Mirror

    B. Concatenated stripe

    C. Stripe

    D. Metadevice

22. Which of the following types of addressing interlaces component blocks across the slices?

    A. Metadevice

    B. Concatenated stripe

    C. Mirror

    D. Stripe

## APPLY YOUR KNOWLEDGE

23. Which of the following types of addressing is done sequentially across slices?

    A. Mirror

    B. Stripe

    C. Concatenation

    D. Metadevice

24. Which of the following devices was created using StorEdge Volume Manager?

    A. /dev/vx/dsk/apps/vol01

    B. /dev/md/dsk/d0

    C. /dev/dsk/vx/apps/vol01

    D. /dev/dsk/md/d0

25. In StorEdge Volume Manager, this is a group of physical slices that appear to the system as a single, logical device.

    A. Metadevice

    B. Volume

    C. Virtual disk

    D. Plex

26. A collection of slices reserved to be automatically substituted in case of slice failure in either a submirror or RAID5 metadevice.

    A. Hot spare pool

    B. Subdisks

    C. Plexes

    D. Disk group

27. A set of contiguous disk blocks; these are the basic units in which the Volume Manager allocates disk space.

    A. Disk group

    B. Plexes

    C. Subdisks

    D. Metadevice

28. Replicates data by using parity information. In the case of missing data, the missing data can be regenerated using available data and the parity information.

    A. Hot spare pool

    B. Mirroring

    C. Trans

    D. RAID5

29. This has an eight-partition limit per disk.

    A. DiskSuite

    B. StorEdge Volume Manager

    C. VM disk

    D. Standard Solaris disk

    E. Plex

## Answers to Review Questions

1. **A.** The instance name represents the kernel's abbreviation name for every possible device on the system.

2. **D.** Physical device files are found in the /devices directory.

## APPLY YOUR KNOWLEDGE

3. **D**. The `sysdef` command displays device configuration information, including system hardware, pseudo devices, loadable modules, and selected kernel parameters.

4. **C**. When you see the `driver not attached` message, it means no driver is currently attached to the device instance because there is no device at this node or the device is not in use.

5. **A**. The .conf files reside in the /kernel/drv directories.

6. **B**. Instance names are mapped to a physical device name in the /etc/path_to_inst file.

7. **A., B.** You can determine the mapping of an instance name to a physical device name by looking at the `dmesg` output and by viewing the /var/adm/messages file.

8. **B**. The system relies on information found in the /etc/path_to_list file to find the root, usr and swap devices .

9. **C**. The `devfsadm` command adds a new device driver to the system.

10. **D**. The `devfsadm` command is used to inform the system about newly installed device drivers.

11. **C**. The `devfsadm` utility is responsible for configuring the /devices directory to reflect the dev info tree held in the kernel. To create the minor device entries, the `devfsadmd` daemon uses the information placed in the dev_info node by the device driver.

12. **C**. An example of when to use the `devfsadm` command would be if the system has been started but the power to the CD-ROM or tape drive was not turned on. During startup, the system did not detect the device; therefore, its drivers were not installed. The `devfsadm` command will perform these tasks.

13. **B**. The major device number indicates the general device class, such as disk, tape, or serial line.

14. **B**. The minor device number indicates the specific member within that class.

15. **D**. The logical device name is a link from the /dev directory to the physical device name located in the /devices directory.

16. **C**. The logical device name is a link from the /dev directory to the physical device name located in the /devices directory.

17. **A**. The logical device name is a link from the /dev directory to the physical device name located in the /devices directory. The following is an example of a logical device name /dev/dsk/c0t0d0s7.

18. **A**. The `devfsadm` command can be used to create entries in the /dev directory for disk drives attached to the system.

19. **D**. The /dev/dsk directory contains the disk entries for the block device nodes in /devices.

20. **B**. A metadevice is a group of physical slices that appear to the system as a single logical device. A metadevice is used to increase storage capacity and increase data availability.

21. **A**. A mirror is composed of one or more simple metadevices called submirrors. A mirror replicates all writes to a single logical device (the mirror) and then to multiple devices (the submirrors) while distributing read operations. This provides redundancy of data in the event of a disk or hardware failure.

22. **D**. A stripe is similar to concatenation, except that the addressing of the component blocks is interlaced on the slices rather than sequentially.

## APPLY YOUR KNOWLEDGE

23. **C.** Concatenations work much the way the UNIX `cat` command is used to concatenate two or more files to create one larger file. If partitions are concatenated, the addressing of the component blocks is done on the components sequentially. The file system can use the entire concatenation.

24. **A.** The names of the block devices for virtual volumes created using the StorEdge Volume Manager are found in the /dev/vx/dsk/ <*disk_group*>/<*volume_name*> directory.

25. **B.** A volume is a virtual disk device that appears to applications, databases, and file systems like a physical logical device, but does not have the physical limitations of a physical disk partition.

26. **A.** Hot spare pool is a collection of slices (hot spares) reserved to be automatically substituted in case of slice failure in either a submirror or RAID5 metadevice.

27. **C.** A set of contiguous disk blocks; subdisks are the basic units in which the Volume Manager allocates disk space.

28. **D.** RAID5 replicates data by using parity information. In the case of missing data, the data can be regenerated using available data and the parity information.

29. **B.** In a standard Solaris disk partitioned environment, there is an eight-partition limit per disk.

## Objectives

The following test objectives are covered in this chapter:

**Understand Network File System (NFS) on Solaris and the relationship between NFS servers and NFS clients**

- Solaris 8 provides NFS to facilitate the sharing of data between systems. NFS servers share resources to be used by NFS clients. This chapter describes NFS and the tasks required to administer NFS servers and clients.

**Share and accessing remote resources**

- The Solaris operating environment allows sharing of directories and presents them to users as if they were local to their system. The system administrator however, must ensure that only authorized users have access to resources shared from a server. This chapter describes the process of sharing resources and accessing a server's resources across the network.

**Configure and using a CacheFS**

- CacheFS is used to improve the performance of networked file systems. When enabled, CacheFS enables data on the remote file system to be stored locally in a disk-based cache for quicker retrieval. This chapter describes how to setup and monitor the CacheFS file system.

**Configure and using AutoFS**

- AutoFS allows NFS directories to be mounted and unmounted automatically. It also provides for centralized administration of NFS resources. This chapter describes AutoFS and how to configure the various automount maps.

CHAPTER 17

# The NFS Environment

## OUTLINE



## STUDY STRATEGIES

The following strategies will help you prepare for the test:

- This is one of those topics that you learn best by practicing and gaining experience. You'll encounter several questions on the exam related to the topics I present in this chapter. Practice the step-by-steps and the commands I describe on a Solaris system until you can perform them from memory. Concentrate on the options that I use in the examples. These are the options most likely to appear on the exam. Again, you'll need two networked systems to practice these exercises effectively.
- Be sure you are clear on the concepts introduced in this chapter especially NFS servers versus NFS clients. Be sure that you know which NFS daemons must be running on each, for NFS to operate properly. Know how to make resources available for mounting using the /etc/dfs/dfstab file. Be prepared to state the functions of an NFS server and NFS client.
- Be sure you understand how to mount network resources and how to make an entry in the /etc/vfstab file, so that mount points are established automatically at system startup. Pay particular attention to the `mount`, `mountall`, `umountall`, `shareall`, and `unshareall` commands.
- Study the AutoFS section and get a firm understanding of the various AutoFS maps, how they are configured, and how they compare to each other. Be sure you can describe each type of AutoFS map. Know the benefits of using AutoFS and be familiar with how to setup the various maps.

## STUDY STRATEGIES

- Study the section on CacheFS thoroughly. Be prepared to explain how to configure and remove a CacheFS. Get acquainted with the commands used to setup and monitor a CacheFS.
- Finally, be sure that you know all the terms listed in the "Key Terms" section. On the exam, you might be asked to match these terms with their proper description, so be prepared.

# Introduction

The NFS service lets computers of different architectures, running different operating systems (OSs), share file systems across a network. Just as the `mount` command lets you mount a file system on a local disk, NFS lets you mount a file system that is located on another system anywhere on the network. Furthermore, NFS support has been implemented on many platforms, ranging from MS-DOS on personal computers to mainframe OSs, such as Multiple Virtual Storage (MVS). Each OS applies the NFS model to its file system semantics. For example, a Sun system can mount the file system from a Windows NT or Linux system located miles away. File system operations, such as reading and writing function as though they were accessing a local file. Response time might be slower because of network traffic, but the connection is transparent to the user regardless of the hardware or OS.

The NFS service provides the following benefits:

- Lets multiple computers use the same files so that everyone on the network can access the same data. This eliminates the need to have redundant data on several systems.
- Reduces storage costs by having computers share applications and data.
- Provides data consistency and reliability, because all users can read the same set of files.
- Makes mounting of file systems transparent to users.
- Makes accessing remote files transparent to users.
- Supports heterogeneous environments.
- Reduces system administration overhead.

The NFS service makes the physical location of the file system irrelevant to the user. You can use NFS to allow users to see all the data, regardless of location. Instead of placing copies of commonly used files on every system, NFS lets the system administrator place one copy on one computer's disk and have all other systems access it across the network. Under NFS operation, remote file systems are almost indistinguishable from local ones.

## SERVERS AND CLIENTS

With NFS, systems have a client-server relationship. The NFS server is where the file system resides. Any system with a local file system can be an NFS server. As described later in this chapter, the system administrator configures the NFS server to make file systems available to other systems and users. The system administrator has complete control over which file systems can be mounted and who can mount them.

An NFS client is a system that mounts a remote file system from an NFS server. I'll describe later in this chapter how the system administrator creates a local directory and mounts the file system. As you will see, a system can be both an NFS server and an NFS client.

## NFS ON SOLARIS

NFS was developed by Sun Microsystems, and it has been ported to most popular OSs. The implementation of NFS is large and varies from system to system. As the NFS service evolved, it went through a few different versions. Therefore, if you are using NFS to connect to another system, you need to be aware of the different versions of NFS.

NFS version 2 was the first version of the NFS protocol in wide use. It continues to be available on a large variety of platforms. SunOS releases prior to Solaris 2.5 support version 2 of the NFS protocol. It should be noted that NFS 2.0 suffers many shortcomings. For example, UNIX-based servers are now moving to faster 64-bit implementations, and the 8KB data packet size used by NFS version 2 is a bottleneck for transferring data. Sun, Digital, IBM, Hewlett-Packard, and Data General toiled with these and other problems. Together, they released NFS 3.0 in 1995 as RFC 1813. The only time you should have to deal with Version 2 is if you are dealing with an older version of an operating system such as Solaris 2.4 or HP-UX version 10.

NFS 3.0 was introduced with Solaris 2.5. Several changes have been made to improve interoperability and performance, including the following enhancements over version 2:

- Enables safe asynchronous writes onto the server, which improves performance by allowing the server to cache client write requests in memory. The client does not need to wait for the server to commit the changes to disk; therefore, the response time is faster.
- The server can batch requests, which improves the response time on the server.
- All NFS operations return the file attributes, which are stored in the local cache. Because the cache is updated more often, the need to do a separate operation to update this data arises less often. Therefore, the number of remote procedure calls to the server is reduced, improving performance.
- The process for verifying file access permissions has been improved. In particular, version 2 would generate a message reporting a "write error" or a "read error" if users tried to copy a remote file to which they did not have permission. In version 3, the permissions are checked before the file is opened, so the error is reported as an "open error."
- Version 3 removes the 8KB transfer size limit and lets the client and server negotiate a maximum transfer size.
- Access control list (ACL) support was added to the version 3 release. ACLs, described in Chapter 8, "System Security," provide a finer-grained mechanism to set file access permissions than is available through standard UNIX file permissions.
- The default transport protocol for the NFS protocol was changed from User Datagram Protocol (UDP) to Transport Control Protocol (TCP), which helps performance on slow networks and wide-area networks (WANs). UDP was preferred initially because it performed well on local-area networks (LANs) and was faster than TCP. Although UDP benefited from the high bandwidth and low latency typical of LANs, it performed poorly when subjected to the low bandwidth and high latency of WANs, such as the Internet. In recent years, improvements in hardware and TCP implementations have narrowed this advantage enough that TCP implementations

can now outperform UDP. A growing number of NFS implementations now support TCP. Unlike UDP, TCP provides congestion control and error recovery.

- Version 3 improved the network lock manager, which provides UNIX record locking and PC file sharing for NFS files. The locking mechanism is now more reliable for NFS files; therefore, commands such as `ksh` and `mail`, which use locking, are less likely to hang.

It should be noted that to take advantage of these improvements, the version 3 protocol must be running on both the NFS server and the NFS clients.

With Solaris 2.6, the NFS 3.0 protocol went through still more enhancements:

- Correct manipulation of files larger than 2GB, which was not formerly possible.
- Defaults to a 32KB transfer size. The effect of larger transfer sizes is to reduce the number of NFS requests required to move a given quantity of data, providing a better use of network bandwidth and I/O resources on clients and servers. If the server supports it, a client can issue a read request that downloads a file in a single operation.
- Supports dynamic failover of read-only file systems. This provides a high level of availability. With failover, multiple replicas are specified in case an NFS server goes down, and another mount point on an alternative server can be specified.
- Gives WebNFS the ability to make a file system on the Internet accessible through firewalls using an extension to the NFS protocol. WebNFS provides greater throughput, under a heavy load, than Hypertext Transfer Protocol (HTTP) access to a web server. In addition, it provides the ability to share files over the Internet without the administrative overhead of an anonymous File Transfer Protocol (FTP) site. WebNFS is described later in this chapter.
- Now under Solaris 8, NFS has added NFS server logging. NFS server logging allows an NFS server to provide a record of file operations performed on its file systems. This feature is particularly useful for sites that make anonymous FTP archives available to NFS and WebNFS clients.

NOTE

When using NFS, make sure that the systems you'll be connecting to are all at the same version of NFS. You might experience problems if your system is at NFS version 2 and the system to which you are trying to connect is at NFS 3.0.

## NFS Daemons

NFS uses a number of daemons to handle its services. These services are initialized at startup from the /etc/init.d/nfs.server and /etc/init.d/nfs.clients startup scripts. The most important NFS daemons are outlined in Table 17.1.

**TABLE 17.1**

**NFS DAEMONS**

| *Daemon* | *Description* |
|---|---|
| `nfsd` | An NFS server daemon that handles file system exporting and file access requests from remote systems. An NFS server runs multiple instances of this daemon. This daemon is usually invoked at run level 3 and is started by the /etc/init.d/nfs.server startup script. |
| `mountd` | An NFS server daemon that handles mount requests from NFS clients. This daemon also provides information about which file systems are mounted by which clients. Use the `showmount` command, described later in this chapter, to view this information. This daemon is usually invoked at run level 3 and is started by the /etc/init.d/nfs.server startup script. |
| `lockd` | This daemon runs on the NFS server and NFS client and provides file locking services in NFS. This daemon is started by the /etc/init.d/nfs.client script at run level 2. |
| `statd` | This daemon runs on the NFS server and NFS client and interacts with `lockd` to provide the crash and recovery functions for the locking services on NFS. This daemon is started by the /etc/init.d/nfs.client script at run level 2. |
| `rpcbind` | Facilitates the initial connection between the client and the server. |
| `nfslogd` | The `nfslogd` daemon provides operational logging to the Solaris NFS server. `nfslogd` is described later in this chapter. |

## Setting Up NFS

Servers let other systems access their file systems by sharing them over the NFS environment. A shared file system is referred to as a shared resource. You specify which file systems are to be shared by entering the information in a file called /etc/dfs/dfstab. Entries in this file are shared automatically whenever you start the NFS server operation. You should set up automatic sharing if you need to share the same set of file systems on a regular basis. Most file system sharing should be done automatically; the only time manual sharing should occur is during testing or troubleshooting.

The /etc/dfs/dfstab file lists all the file systems your NFS server shares with its NFS clients. It also controls which clients can mount a file system. If you want to modify /etc/dfs/dfstab to add or delete a file system or to modify the way sharing is done, edit the file with a text editor, such as vi or textedit. The next time the computer enters run level 3, the system reads the updated /etc/dfs/dfstab to determine which file systems should be shared automatically.

Each line in the dfstab file consists of a `share` command, as shown in the following example:

```
more /etc/dfs/dfstab
```

The system displays the contents of /etc/dfs/dfstab:

```
#       Place share(1M) commands here for automatic execution
#       on entering init state 3.
#
#       Issue the command '/etc/init.d/nfs.server start' to run the NFS
#       daemon processes and the share commands, after adding the very
#       first entry to this file.
#
#       share [-F fstype] [ -o options] [-d "<text>"] <pathname> [resource]
#       .e.g,
#       share  -F nfs  -o rw=engineering  -d "home dirs"  /export/home2
share -F nfs /export
share -F nfs /cdrom/solaris_srvr_intranet_ext_1_0
```

The `/usr/sbin/share` command exports a resource or makes a resource available for mounting. If invoked with no arguments, `share` displays all shared file systems. The `share` command, described in Table 17.2, can be run at the command line to achieve the same results as the /etc/dfs/dfstab file, but use this method only when testing.

The syntax for the `share` command is

```
share -F <FSType> -o <options> -d <description> <pathname>
```

where `<pathname>` is the name of the file system to be shared.

**TABLE 17.2**

### THE share COMMAND

| *Option* | *Description* | |
|---|---|---|
| -F <FSType> | Specify the file system type, such as NFS. If the -F option is omitted, the first file system type listed in /etc/dfs/fstypes is used as the default. | |
| -o <options> | Select from the following options: | |
| | rw | pathname is shared read/write to all clients. This is also the default behavior. |
| | rw=client[:client]... | pathname is shared read/write but only to the listed clients. No other systems can access pathname. |
| | ro | pathname is shared read-only to all clients. |
| | ro=client[:client]... | pathname is shared read-only, but only to the listed clients. No other systems can access pathname. |
| aclok | Allows the NFS server to do access control for NFS version 2 clients (running Solaris or earlier). When aclok is set on the server, maximum access is given to all clients. For example, with aclok set, if anyone has read permissions, everyone does. If aclok is not set, minimal access is given to all clients. | |
| anon=<uid> | Sets uid to be the effective user ID of unknown users. By default, unknown users are given the effective uid nobody. If uid is set to -1, access is denied. | |
| index=<file> | Loads a file rather than a listing of the directory containing this specific file when the directory is referenced by an NFS Uniform Resource Locator (URL). See the section "WebNFS" later in this chapter. | |
| nosub | Prevents clients from mounting subdirectories of shared directories. | |
| nosuid | The server file system silently ignores any attempt to enable the setuid or setgid mode bits. By default, clients can create files on the shared file system if the setuid or setgid mode is enabled. See Chapter 8 for a description of setuid and setgid. | |

| *Option* | *Description* |
|---|---|
| `public` | Enables NFS browsing of the file system by a WebNFS-enabled browser. Only one file system per server can use this option. The `-ro=list` and `-rw=list` options can be included with this option. |
| `root=host [: host]...` | Only root users from the specified hosts have root access. By default, no host has root access, so root users are mapped to an anonymous user ID (see the previous description of the `anon=<uid>` option). |
| `sec=<mode>` | Uses one or more of the security modes specified by `<mode>` to authenticate clients. The `<mode>` option establishes the security mode of NFS servers. If the NFS connection uses the NFS Version 3 protocol, the NFS clients must query the server for the appropriate `<mode>` to use. If the NFS connection uses the NFS Version 2 protocol, then the NFS client will use the default security mode, which is currently sys. NFS clients may force the use of a specific security mode by specifying the `sec=<mode>` option on the command line. However, if the file system on the server is not shared with that security mode, the client may be denied access. Valid modes are<br>`sys` Use AUTH_SYS authentication. The user's UNIX user-id and group-ids are passed in the clear on the network, unauthenticated by the NFS server.<br>`dh` Use a Diffie-Hellman public key system.<br>`krb4` Use the Kerberos Version 4 authentication.<br>`none` Use null authentication. |
| `log=`*`<tag>`* | Enables NFS server logging for the specified file system. The optional *`<tag>`* determines the location of the related log files. The tag is defined in etc/nfs/nfslog.conf. If no tag is specified, the default values associated with the `global` tag in etc/nfs/nfslog.conf should be used. NFS logging is described later in this chapter. |
| `-d <description>` | Provides a description of the resource being shared. |

To share a file system as read-only every time the system is started up, add this line to the /etc/dfs/dfstab file:

```
share -F nfs -o ro /data
```

NOTE

Even if you share a file system from the command line by typing the share command, mountd and nfsd still won't run until you make an entry into /etc/dfs/dfstab and run the nfs.server script.

After editing the /etc/dfs/dfstab file, restart the NFS server by either restarting it or by typing this:

```
/etc/init.d/nfs.server start
```

You only need to start the nfs.server script after you make the first entry in the /etc/dfs/dfstab file. This is because at startup, when the system enters run level 3, mountd and nfsd are not started if the /etc/dfs/dfstab file is empty. After you have made an initial entry and have executed the nfs.server script, you can modify /etc/dfs/dfstab without restarting the daemons. You simply execute the shareall command, and any new entries in the /etc/dfs/dfstab file are shared.

After you have at least one entry in the /etc/dfs/dfstab file and after both mountd and nfsd are running, you can share additional file systems by typing the share command directly from the command line. Be aware, however, that if you don't add the entry to the /etc/dfs/dfstab file, the file system is not automatically shared the next time the system is restarted.

The dfshares command displays information about the shared resources available to the host from an NFS server. Here is the syntax for dfshares:

```
dfshares <servername>
```

You can view the shared file systems on a remote NFS server by using the dfshares command as follows:

```
dfshares apollo
```

If no servername is specified, all resources currently being shared on the local host are displayed. Another place to find information on shared resources is in the server's /etc/dfs/sharetab file. This file contains a list of the resources currently being shared.

## NFS Security

With NFS, you need to be concerned about security. When you issue the share command, any system can access the file system through your network. It's a good idea to be more specific about who can mount the file system. The following examples illustrate how to set up a share with restrictions as to which hosts can mount the shared resource:

```
share -F nfs -o ro=apollo:neptune:zeus /data
```

The file system named /data is shared read-only to the listed clients only. No other systems can access /data. Another method is to share a file system read-only to some hosts and read-write to others. Use the following command to accomplish this:

```
share -F nfs -o ro=apollo rw=neptune:zeus /data
```

In this example, apollo has read-only access, and neptune and zeus have read-write access.

The next example specifies that root access be granted to the client named zeus. A root user coming from any other system is recognized only as nobody and has limited access rights:

```
share -F nfs -o root=zeus /data
```

To remove a shared file system, issue the `unshare` command on the server as follows:

```
unshare /data
```

The /data file system is no longer shared. You can verify this by issuing the `share` command with no options:

```
share
```

The system responds with this:

```
-           /home    ro,anon=0    ""
```

Only the file system named /home is returned as shared.

**CAUTION**

Root permissions should not be enabled on an NFS file system. Administrators might find this annoying if they're trying to modify a file through an NFS mount, but disastrous mistakes can be eliminated. For example, if a root user wants to purge a file system called /data on one host, an `rm -rf *` would be disastrous if there is an NFS mounted file system with root permission mounted under /data. If /data/thor is a mounted file system under /data, the files located on the NFS server would be wiped out.

**NOTE**

If `share` commands are invoked multiple times on the same file system, the last `share` invocation supersedes the previous ones. The options set by the last `share` command replace the old options.

# Mounting a Remote File System

Chapter 6, "Introduction to File Systems," described how to mount a local file system using the `mount` command. You'll use the same `mount` command to mount a shared file system on a remote host using NFS. Here is the syntax for mounting NFS file systems:

```
mount -F nfs <options> <-o specific_options > <-O> \
<server>:<filesystem> <mount_point>
```

In this example, `server` is the name of the NFS server in which the file system is located. `filesystem` is the name of the shared file system on the NFS server, and `mount_point` is the name of the local directory that serves as the mount point.

As you can see, this is similar to mounting a local file system. The options are described in Table 17.3.

**TABLE 17.3**

### NFS mount COMMAND

| *Option* | *Description* | |
|---|---|---|
| -F <Fstype> | Used to specify the FSType on which to operate. The FSType must be specified in /etc/vfstab, or by consulting /etc/default/fs or /etc/dfs/fstypes. | |
| -r | Mounts the specified file system as read-only. | |
| -m | Does not append an entry to the /etc/mnttab table of mounted file systems. | |
| -o <specific_options> | specific_options is any of the following options separated by a comma: | |
| | rw \| ro | The resource is mounted read-write or read-only. The default is rw. |
| | suid \| nosuid | setuid execution is enabled or disabled. The default is suid. |
| | remount | If a file system is mounted as read-only, this option remounts it as read-write. |
| | bg \| fg | If the first attempt to mount the remote file system fails, retry in the background (bg) or in the foreground (fg). The default is fg. |
| | quota | quota checks whether the user is over the quota on this file system. If the file system has quotas enabled on the server, quotas will still be checked for operations on this file system. |
| | noquota | Prevents quota from checking whether the user exceeded the quota on this file system. If the file system has quotas enabled on the server, quotas will still be checked for operations on this file system. |

| *Option* | *Description* |
|---|---|
| `retry=n` | The number of times to retry the mount operation. The default is 10000. |
| `vers=<NFS version number>` | By default, the version of NFS protocol used between the client and the server is the highest one available on both systems. If the NFS server does not support NFS 3.0 protocol, the NFS mount uses version 2. |
| `port=n` | The server IP port number. The default is NFS_PORT. |
| `rsize=<n>` | Sets the read buffer size to `<n>` bytes. The default value is 32768 if you're using version 3 of the NFS protocol. The default can be negotiated down if the server prefers a smaller transfer size. If you're using NFS version 2, the default value is 8192. |
| `wsize=<n>` | Sets the write buffer size to `<n>` bytes. The default value is 32768, if you're using version 3 of the NFS protocol. The default can be negotiated down if the server prefers a smaller transfer size. If you're using version 2, the default value is 8192. |
| `timeo=<n>` | Sets the NFS timeout to `<n>` tenths of a second. The default value is 11 tenths of a second for connectionless transports and 600 tenths of a second for connection-oriented transports. |
| `retrans=<n>` | Sets the number of NFS retransmissions to `<n>`; the default value is `5`. For connection-oriented transports, this option has no effect, because it is assumed that the transport will perform retransmissions on behalf of NFS. |

*continues*

**TABLE 17.3** *continued*

**NFS mount COMMAND**

<table>
<tr><th>Option</th><th>Description</th><th></th></tr>
<tr><td></td><td>soft | hard</td><td>Returns an error if the server does not respond (soft), or continues the retry request until the server responds (hard). If you're using hard, the system appears to hang until the NFS server responds. The default value is hard.</td></tr>
<tr><td></td><td>intr | nointr</td><td>Enables or does not enable keyboard interrupts to kill a process that hangs while waiting for a response on a hard-mounted file system. The default is intr, which makes it possible for clients to interrupt applications that might be waiting for an NFS server to respond.</td></tr>
<tr><td></td><td>-O</td><td>The overlay mount lets the file system be mounted over an existing mount point, making the underlying file system inaccessible. If a mount is attempted on a preexisting mount point without this flag's being set, the mount fails, producing the error "device busy."</td></tr>
</table>

Here's a note regarding foreground (fg) and background (bg) mounts: File systems mounted with the bg option indicate that mount is to retry in the background if the server's mount daemon (mountd) does not respond when, for example, the NFS server is restarted. From the NFS client, mount retries the request up to the count specified in the retry=<n> option. After the file system is mounted, each NFS request made in the kernel waits a specified number of seconds for a response (specified with the timeo=<n> option). If no response arrives, the timeout is multiplied by two, and the request is retransmitted. If the number of retransmissions has reached the number specified in the retrans=<n> option, a file system mounted with the soft option returns an error, and the file system mounted with the hard option prints a warning message and continues to retry the request. Sun recommends that file systems mounted as read-write, or containing executable files, should always be mounted with the `hard` option. If you use soft mounted file systems, unexpected I/O errors can occur. For example, consider a write request. If the NFS server goes down, the pending write request simply gives up, resulting in a corrupted file on the remote file system. A read-write file system should always be mounted with the specified `hard` and `intr` options. This lets users make their own decisions about killing hung processes. Use the following to mount a file system named /data located on a host named thor with the `hard` and `intr` options:

```
mount -F nfs -o hard,intr thor:/data /data
```

If a file system is mounted hard and the `intr` option is not specified, the process hangs until the remote file system reappears if the NFS server goes down. For a terminal process, this can be annoying. If `intr` is specified, sending an interrupt signal to the process kills it. For a terminal process, this can be done by pressing Ctrl+C. For a background process, sending an `INT` or `QUIT` signal as follows usually works:

```
kill -QUIT 3421
```

> **NOTE** Sending a `KILL` signal (`-9`) does not kill a hung NFS process.

To mount a file system called /data, which is located on an NFS server called thor, issue the following command, as root, from the NFS client:

```
mount -F nfs -o ro thor:/data /thor_data
```

In this case, the /data file system from the server thor is mounted read-only on /thor_data on the local system. Mounting from the command line enables temporary viewing of the file system. If the `umount` command is issued or the system is restarted, the mount is lost. If you would like this file system to be mounted automatically at every startup, add the following line to the /etc/vfstab file:

```
thor:/data - /thor_data nfs - yes ro
```

> **NOTE** The `mount` and `umount` commands require root access. The `umount` command and /etc/vfstab file are described in Chapter 6.

To view resources that can be mounted on the local or remote system, use the `dfmounts` command as follows:

```
dfmounts sparcserver
```

The system responds with a list of file systems currently mounted on sparcserver:

```
RESOURCE      SERVER PATHNAME             CLIENTS
   -          ultra5 /usr              192.168.1.201
              ultra5 /usr/dt           192.168.1.201
```

Sometimes you rely on NFS mount points for critical information. If the NFS server were to go down unexpectedly, you would lose the information contained at that mount point. You can address this issue by using client-side failover. With client-side failover, you specify an alternative file system to use in case the primary file system fails. These file systems should contain equivalent directory structures and identical files. This option is available only on read-only file systems. To set up client-side failover, use the following procedure.

On the NFS client, mount the file system using the `-ro` option. You can do this from the command line or by adding an entry to the /etc/vfstab file that looks like the following:

```
zeus,thor:/data  -  /remote_data  nfs  -  no  -o ro
```

If multiple file systems are named and the first server in the list is down, failover uses the next alternative server to access files. To mount a replicated set of NFS file systems, which might have different paths to the file system, use the following `mount` command:

```
mount -F nfs -o ro zeus:/usr/local/data,thor:/home/data \
/usr/local/data
```

Replication is discussed again in the section that describes AutoFS.

A new feature in Solaris 8 is NFS server logging. Logged file systems were discussed in Chapter 7, "Solaris File Systems: Advanced Topics." This extends that functionality to networked file systems. The daemon, `nfslogd`, provides NFS logging and is enabled using the `log=`*<tag>* option in the `share` command described later. When NFS logging is enabled, all NFS operations on the file system are recorded in a buffer by the kernel. The data recorded includes a timestamp, the client IP address, the UID of the requestor, the file handle of the resource that is being accessed, and the type of operation that occurred. The `nfslogd` daemon converts this information into ASCII records that are stored in ASCII log files.

## STEP BY STEP

### 17.1 Enabling NFS Server Logging

To enable nfs server logging, follow these steps:

1. As root, share the NFS file system using the following command:

```
share -F nfs -o ro,log=global <file system name>
```

Add this entry to your /etc/dfs/dfstab file if you want it to go into effect every time the server is booted.

2. If the nfslogd daemon is not already running, start it by typing:

```
/usr/lib/nfs/nfslogd
```

You can change the file configuration settings in the NFS server logging configuration file called /etc/nfs/nfslog.conf. This file defines path, filenames, and type of logging to be used by `nfslogd`. Each definition is associated with a tag. The `global` tag defines the default values, but you can create new tags and specify them for each file system you share. The NFS operations to be logged by nfslogd are defined in the /etc/default/nfslogd configuration file.

# WebNFS

WebNFS is a product from Sun Microsystems that extends its NFS to the Internet. Sun believes WebNFS offers considerable performance advantages over the current Internet protocols, HTTP and FTP. Netscape, Oracle, IBM, Apple, and Novell have announced support for WebNFS.

The World Wide Web has become the people's choice for information distribution and sharing across the Internet. The web's ease of use and widespread availability has helped it outshine similar technologies. Unfortunately, the protocol for the web and HTTP, leaves much to be desired in terms of performance. HTTP is a one-way protocol that transfers multiple data formats inefficiently. Entire pages and all their contents must be transferred at the same time to the requesting browser. On the other hand, NFS works with only portions of files at a time, usually only the sections that are in use. It is possible to update sections of a file with NFS, a task that is virtually impossible with HTTP. The following are the benefits of WebNFS over HTTP and FTP:

- **Connection management.** A WebNFS client can download multiple files over a single persistent TCP connection.

- **Concurrency.** WebNFS clients can issue multiple concurrent requests to an NFS server. The effect is a better use of server and network resources and better performance for the end user.
- **Fault tolerance.** WebNFS is well-known for its fault tolerance in the face of network and server failures. If interrupted, other FTPs require the download to be restarted from the beginning, causing users to retrace steps and waste time in duplicating efforts. However, if a WebNFS client faces an interruption, it can resume a download from where it left off.
- **Performance and scalability.** NFS servers currently handle over 21,000 operations per second. They are highly integrated with the OS, tuned for maximum system performance, and easy to administer.

WebNFS helps simplify remote file access. It can work with and through firewalls, meaning that system administrators can now specify which directories or files they want to export, or make available over the Internet. After these files are exported and an application requests them, WebNFS can automatically locate them, negotiate file access privileges, and transparently "mount" the files from anywhere on the Internet. Users can then access that data as if it were local to their machine.

Unlike current file access protocols, such as FTP and HTTP, WebNFS is a complete file system that supports in-place editing of a file, eliminating the need to download, edit, and upload the file. Instead, users can edit the original file right from their desktops. This saves time and preserves the integrity of shared files.

WebNFS can mount an entire file system at a time, or it can communicate with individual files on the server. This feature is known as multi-component lookup (MCL), and it lets the client look up a document based on a full given path to a file rather than having to look up individual components of that path until deriving the actual file location. For example, to look up a file such as /books/solaris/test.txt in NFS, you have to look up the individual components (books and solaris) before you can find test.txt. With WebNFS, you simply pass the entire path to the server itself and have the server return the file handle directly. This improves performance by saving several steps of data transfers.

WebNFS also follows the improvements in NFS 3.0 by including larger data transfers than the 8KB limit imposed in NFS 2.0, a 64-bit data word size for files, and file systems larger than 4GB.

To use WebNFS, your web browser needs a client, and the web or FTP server needs to have a WebNFS server. If you request a file with WebNFS, your URL would look something like one of the following:

```
nfs://computer.site.com/filedirectory/file
nfs://<server>:<port>/<path>
nfs://mymachine.javaworld.com:2049/home/rawn/webnfs.txt
nfs://mymachine.javaworld.com/pub/edit.doc
```

NFS replaces the HTTP or FTP schema and needs to be implemented directly into the browser. The default port number is 2049; if the port is omitted, it defaults to 2049. This is the NFS port for TCP connections. The directory structure just shown is actually a relative path from a base that the NFS server understands.

> **NOTE** Note that a pathname for an NFS URL should not begin with a slash. A path that begins with a slash is evaluated relative to the server's root rather than the public file handle directory.

## How to Enable WebNFS Access

Starting with Solaris 2.6, all file systems available for NFS mounting are automatically available for WebNFS access.

---

**STEP BY STEP**

### 17.2 Manually Configuring a File System for WebNFS

To manually configure a file system for WebNFS access, follow these steps:

1. Edit the /etc/dfs/dfstab file. Add one entry to the /etc/dfs/dfstab file for the file system you want shared automatically. The `index` tag is optional, but the `public` option enables NFS browsing of the file system by a WebNFS-enabled browser:

```
share -F nfs -o ro,public,index=index.html \
/export/ftp
```

*continues*

*continued*

2. Check that the NFS service is running on the server. If this is the first `share` command (or set of `share` commands) that you have initiated, it is likely that the NFS daemons are not running. The following commands kill and restart the daemons:

```
/etc/init.d/nfs.server stop
/etc/init.d/nfs.server start
```

3. Share the file system. After the entry is in /etc/dfs/dfstab, the file system can be shared either by restarting the system or by using the `shareall` command. If the NFS daemons were restarted in step 2, this command does not need to be run, because the init.d script runs the command.

```
shareall
```

4. Verify that the information is correct. Execute the `share` command to check that the correct options are listed:

```
share
```

The system should respond with output that looks something like this:

```
-    /export/share/man   ro   ""
-    /usr/src    rw=eng   ""
-    /export/ftp    ro,public,index=index.html   ""
```

## Using a Browser to Access an NFS URL

Browsers that can support WebNFS access should provide access using an NFS URL that looks something like this:

```
nfs://<server>:<port>/<path>
```

`server` is the name of the file server, `port` is the port number to use (the default value is 2049), and `path` is the path to the file or file system. The path can be either relative to the public file handle or relative to the root file system on the server.

You can enable WebNFS access for clients that are not part of the local subnet by configuring the firewall to enable a TCP connection on port 2049. Just allowing access for httpd does not allow NFS URLs to be used.

> **NOTE** Be sure your browser supports WebNFS. If it doesn't, you'll get an error similar to the following: "NFS URLs are not supported." Currently, Sun's HotJava browser supports WebNFS, and Netscape says that it will provide support in a future release. Microsoft's Internet Explorer does not support WebNFS.

## CacheFS

A fundamental factor in computer performance is file access time. In a networked environment using NFS, every file access request across the network affects performance. The Cache File System (CacheFS) can be used to improve performance of NFS mounted file systems or slow devices such as a CD-ROM. When a file system is cached, the data read from the remote file system or CD-ROM is stored in a cache on the local system's disk. First, let's introduce some terms:

- **Back file system.** The file system on the remote host, or CD-ROM, that is being cached. Typically this is an NFS or HSFS file system. Files in the back file system are called back files.
- **Front file system.** The file system that contains the cached data, typically a UFS file system. Files in the front file system are called front files.
- **Cached file system.** The file system that resides on the local disk. Files in it are cached files.
- **Cache directory**. The directory on the local disk where the data for the cached file system is stored.
- **Cold cache.** A cache that does not yet have any data in its front file system. To create a cache, requested data must be copied from the back file system to the front file system. This is referred to as populating the cache. An attempt to reference data that is not yet cached is referred to as a cache miss.
- **Warm cache.** A cache that contains the desired data in its front file system. Requested data is available to the user without requiring any action from the back file system. An attempt to reference data that is already cached is referred to as a cache hit.

## Creating the Cache

> **NOTE** Do not make the front file system read-only, and do not set quotas on it. A read-only front file system prevents caching, and file system quotas interfere with control mechanisms built into CacheFS.

A cache must exist before a CacheFS mount can be performed. No special disk partitioning is required for cache creation. A cache file system may be created in a subdirectory of an existing file system, or you can dedicate an entire file system to caching. The only requirement is that you create the cache in mounted local file systems. The `cfsadmin` command creates the local cache.

> **NOTE** After you have created the cache, do not perform any operations in the cache directory itself. This causes conflicts within the CacheFS software.

## STEP BY STEP

### 17.3 Setting up a Cached File System

There are two steps to setting up a cached file system:

1. Create the cache with the `cfsadmin` command. `cfsadmin` administers disk space used for caching file systems with CacheFS. The syntax for creating the cache with the `cfsadmin` command is

   ```
   cfsadmin -c <cache-directory>
   ```

   `<cache-directory>` indicates the name of the directory where the cache resides.

   The following example creates a cache:

   ```
   mkdir /local
   cfsadmin -c  /local/cache1
   ```

   The `cfsadmin` command creates a subdirectory called cache1 that contains the CacheFS data structures necessary to allow a CacheFS mount.

2. Mount the file system you want cached using the `-F cachefs` option to the `mount` command. Here is the syntax to mount a file system in a cache with the `mount` command:

   ```
   mount -F cachefs -o backfstype=<fstype>,cachedir= \
   <cache-directory>[, options] <back-filesystem \
   mount-point>
   ```

   `backfstype=<fstype>` indicates the file system type of the back file system. (`fstype` can be either `nfs` or `hsfs`.)

   `cachedir=<cache-directory>` indicates the name of the directory where the cache resides. This is the same name you specified when you created the cache in step 1.

`[options]` specifies other mount options that you can include when mounting a file system in a cache. These options, listed in Table 17-4, are preceded with `-o` and can be grouped in a comma-separated list with no spaces.

`<back-filesystem>` is the mount point of the back file system to cache. If the back file system is an NFS file system, you must specify the host name of the server from which you are mounting the file system and the name of the file system to cache (separated by a colon), such as `sparc21:/data`.

`<mount-point>` indicates the directory where the file system is mounted.

**TABLE 17.4**

**mount OPTIONS**

| *Option* | *Description* |
|---|---|
| `acdirmax=n` | Specifies that cached attributes are held for no more than n seconds after a directory update. After n seconds, all directory information is purged from the cache. The default value is 30 seconds. |
| `acdirmin=n` | Specifies that cached attributes are held for at least n seconds after directory update. After n seconds, CacheFS checks to see if the directory modification time on the back file system has changed. If it has, all information about the directory is purged from the cache, and new data is retrieved from the back file system. The default value is 30 seconds. |
| `acregmax=n` | Specifies that cached attributes are held for no more than n seconds after file modification. After n seconds, all file information is purged from the cache. The default value is 30 seconds. |
| `acregmin=n` | Specifies that cached attributes are held for at least n seconds after file modification. After n seconds, CacheFS checks to see if the file modification time on the back file system has changed. If it has, all information about the file is purged from the cache, and new data is retrieved from the back file system. The default value is 30 seconds. |
| `actimeo=n` | Sets `acregmin`, `acregmax`, `acdirmin`, and `acdirmax` to `n`. |

*continues*

**TABLE 17.4** *continued*

**mount Options**

| *Option* | *Description* |
|---|---|
| cacheid=<ID> | ID is a string specifying a particular instance of a cache. If you do not specify a cache ID, CacheFS constructs one. |
| demandconst | Verifies cache consistency only when explicitly requested, rather than the periodic checking that is done by default. You can request a consistency check by using the -s option of the cfsadmin command. This option is useful for back file systems that change infrequently, such as /usr/openwin. demandconst and noconst are mutually exclusive. |
| local-access | Causes the front file system to interpret the mode bits used for access checking instead of having the back file system verify access permissions. Do not use this argument with secure NFS. |
| noconst | Disables cache consistency checking. By default, periodic consistency checking is enabled. Specify noconst only when you know that the back file system will not be modified. Trying to perform a cache consistency check using cfsadmin -s results in an error. demandconst and noconst are mutually exclusive. |
| purge | Purges any cached information for the specified file system. |
| ro \| rw | Is read-only or read-write (the default). |
| suid \| nosuid | Allows (the default) or disallows setuid execution. |
| write-around \| non-shared | Write modes for CacheFS. The write-around mode (the default) handles writes the same as NFS does. In other words, writes are made to the back file system, and the affected file is purged from the cache. You can use non-shared mode when you are sure that no one else will be writing to the cached file system. In this mode, all writes are made to both the front and the back file system, and the file remains in the cache. |
| -O | Overlays mount. Allows the file system to be mounted over an existing mount point, making the underlying file system inaccessible. If you attempt a mount on a preexisting mount point without setting this flag, mount will fail with this error: mount -F cachefs: mount failed Device busy. |

The following example creates the mount point /sparc21data and mounts the NFS file system sparc21:/data as a cached file system named /sparc21data in the cache named /local/cache1:

```
mkdir /sparc21data
mount -F cachefs -o backfstype=nfs,cachedir=/local/cache1 sparc21:/data /sparc21data
```

Now the CacheFS mount point, /sparc21data, can be accessed just like any other mounted file system.

To make the mount point permanent, add the following line to your /etc/vfstab file as follows:

```
sparc21:/data  /local/cache1  /sparc21data  cachefs  3  yes  backfstype=nfs, cachedir=/local/cache1
```

Verify that the cache you created was actually mounted by using the `cachefsstat` command as follows:

```
cachefsstat /sparc21data
      /sparc21data
      cache hit rate:        0%    (0 hits, 8 misses)
      consistency checks:    7     (5 pass, 2 fail)
      modifies:              0
      garbage collection:    0
```

If the file system was not mounted in the cache, you will receive an error message similar to the following:

```
cachefsstat /sparc21data
cachefsstat: /sparc21data: not a cachefs mountpoint
```

There is some overhead when data is initially referenced from the CacheFS file system associated with the cache population, but subsequent references to the same data can be satisfied without access to the back file system. A warm cache provides performance close to that of a local file system, without the administration and overhead associated with local file systems. The performance of the CacheFS file system over traditional NFS mounts is much faster for clients accessing slow network links or heavily loaded servers.

You can also cache more than one file system in the same cache. There is no need to create a separate cache for each CacheFS mount. In other words, you should need to run `cfsadmin -c` only once to create a single cache for all your CacheFS mounts.

Many types of back file systems can potentially be cached. For example, there are performance benefits to caching slow media, such as a CD-ROM on a faster hard drive using CacheFS. However, local file systems (UFS) are usually not cached.

Any file system that is "read mostly" is a likely candidate for caching. An example of an excellent candidate for caching is /usr/share/man. File systems that are usually read one time only, such as /var/mail, are not good candidates for caching because data is typically read once and discarded. In this case, you pay the cost of cache population without gaining any of the benefits of subsequent cache accesses.

CacheFS provides no benefit for write operations. This is because CacheFS is strictly a "write-through" cache. CacheFS write performance will never be any better than that of the back file system.

CacheFS is not an NFS performance accelerator. It's possible that a single client will not see much of a performance boost from caching, particularly on a lightly loaded fast LAN where the server is a powerful machine with fast disks without much load. The benefits of caching show up on busy networks with heavily loaded servers.

## Monitoring the Cache

You can use CacheFS statistics to monitor the performance of your cache to determine the appropriate cache size. The three commands listed in Table 17.5 help you determine the trade-off between your cache size and the desired performance of the cache.

**TABLE 17.5**

**CACHEFS STATISTICS COMMANDS**

| *Command* | *Description* |
|---|---|
| `cachefslog` | Specifies the location of the log file. This command also displays where the statistics are currently being logged and lets you halt logging. |
| `cachefswssize` | Interprets the log file to give a recommended cache size. |
| `cachefsstat` | Displays statistical information about a specific file system or all cached file systems. The information provided in the output of this command is taken directly from the cache. |

The default values for the cache parameters used by `cfsadmin` are for a cache to use the entire front file system for caching. The parameter values should be changed if the cache is limited to only a portion of the front file system. The `cfsadmin` command allows you to specify the options listed in Table 17.6.

**TABLE 17.6**

**cfsadmin OPTIONS**

| *Options* | *Description* |
|---|---|
| maxblocks | Sets the maximum number of blocks that CacheFS is allowed to claim within the front file system. It does not guarantee that the resources are available for CacheFS. The default is 90%. Note: Performance decreases significantly if a UFS file system exceeds 90 percent capacity. |
| minblocks | Works together with threshblocks. It does not guarantee the availability of a minimum level of resources. The default is 0%. |
| threshblocks | Works together with minblocks. This value is ignored until the minblocks value is reached. CacheFS can claim more than minblocks only if the percentage of available blocks in the front file system is greater than threshblocks. This value applies to the entire front file system, not only the cached portion. The default is 85%. |
| maxfiles | Sets the maximum number of files (inodes) that CacheFS can claim. It does not guarantee that the resources are available for CacheFS. The default is 90%. |
| minfiles/threshfiles | Work together in the same fashion as minblocks and threshblocks. The minfiles default is 0% and the threshfiles default is 85%. |

You should not need to change any of these parameter values. They are set to default values to achieve optimal cache behavior. However, as shown in the next example, you might want to modify the maxblocks and maxfiles settings if you have some room in the front file system that is not used by the cache and you want to use it for some other file system. The following example creates a cache named /local/cache1 that can use up to 80 percent of the disk blocks in the front file system. It can grow to use 55 percent of the front file system blocks without restriction unless 60 percent (or more) of the front file system blocks are already used:

```
cfsadmin -c -o maxblocks=80,minblocks=55,threshblocks=60 \
/local/cache1
```

> **NOTE** The size of a cache, either by number of blocks or number of inodes, can only be increased. In the case of decreasing, the cache must be removed and recreated with a new value.

To modify a CacheFS parameter, first unmount the file system. The following example unmounts /local/cache1 and changes the `threshfiles` parameter to 65 percent:

```
umount /sparc21data
cfsadmin -u -o threshfiles=65 /local/cache1
mount /sparc21data
```

To display information about all file systems cached under the specified cache directory, type

```
cfsadmin -l <directory_name>
```

and press Enter.

The following example illustrates how to display cache information:

```
cfsadmin -l /local/cache1
```

The system responds with this:

```
cfsadmin: list cache FS information
    maxblocks     90%
    minblocks     0%
    threshblocks  85%
    maxfiles      90%
    minfiles      0%
    threshfiles   85%
    maxfilesize   3MB
  sparc21:_data:_mnt
  sparc21:_data:_sparc21data
```

The output displays statistics followed by the cacheID of all file systems stored in the cache. For example, the cacheID for the sparc21data file system is

```
sparc1: data: sparc21data
```

## Deleting a Cache

Before you delete a cached file system, you must unmount all the cached file systems for that cache directory.

To delete a file system in a cache, type the following:

```
cfsadmin -d <cache_id> <cache_directory>
```

and press Enter.

<cache_id> is part of the information returned by `cfsadmin -l`. In the previous example of the `cfsadmin -l` command, the cacheID was displayed as the last line of the output and is: `sparc1: data: sparc21data`

After one or more file systems are deleted, you must run the `fsck -F_cachefs` command to correct resource counts for the cache. The next example unmounts a cached file system, deletes it from the cache, and runs `fsck_-F cachefs`:

```
umount /sparc21data
cfsadmin -d sparc21:_data:_sparc21data  /local/cache1
fsck -F cachefs /local/cache1
```

You can delete all file systems in a particular cache by using `all` as an argument to the `-d` option, as shown in the following example. This example deletes all file systems cached under /local/cache1 and the specified cache directory:

```
cfsadmin -d all /local/cache1
```

## Checking Consistency

To ensure that the cached directories and files are up-to-date, CacheFS periodically checks the consistency of files stored in the cache with files on the back file system. To check consistency, CacheFS compares the current modification time to the previous modification time. If the modification times are different, all data and attributes for the directory or file are purged from the cache, and new data and attributes are retrieved from the back file system.

When a user requests an operation on a directory or file, CacheFS checks to see if it is time to verify consistency. If it is, CacheFS obtains the modification time from the back file system and performs the comparison.

By default, CacheFS always performs cache consistency checking. When the `noconst` keyword is specified with the `mount` command, consistency checking is disabled. In this mode, no attempt is made to see that the cache remains consistent with the back file system. In the case of a read-only back file system, consistency checking is completely unnecessary. Use the `noconst` keyword when the back file system is a read-only file system.

By specifying the demandconst option of the mount command, you can perform consistency checks only when you explicitly request them for file systems mounted with this option. After specifying the demandconst option, when you mount a file system in a cache, you use the cfsadmin command with the -s option to request a consistency check. By default, consistency checking is performed file by file as they are accessed. If no files are accessed, no checks are performed. Use of the demandconst option avoids a situation in which the network is flooded with consistency checks.

The following example uses the demandconst option to specify consistency checking on demand for the NFS cached file system /sparc21data, whose back file system is sparc21:/data:

```
mount -F cachefs -o backfstype=nfs,cachedir=/local/cache1,demandconst sparc21:/data /sparc21data
```

## AUTOFS

When a network contains even a moderate number of systems, all trying to mount file systems from each other, managing NFS can quickly become a nightmare. The Autofs facility, also called the automounter, is designed to handle such situations by providing a method in which remote directories are mounted only when they are being used.

When a user or application accesses an NFS mount point, the mount is established. When the file system is no longer needed, or it has not been accessed for a certain period, the file system is automatically unmounted. As a result, network overhead is lower, the system boots faster because NFS mounts are done later, and systems can be shut down with fewer ill effects and hung processes.

File systems shared through the NFS service can be mounted using Autofs. Autofs, a client-side service, is a file system structure that provides automatic mounting. The Autofs file system is initialized by automount, which is run automatically when a system is started. The automount daemon, named automountd, runs continuously, mounting and unmounting remote directories on an as-needed basis.

Mounting does not need to be done at system startup, and the user no longer needs to know the superuser password to mount a directory. With Autofs, users do not use the `mount` and `umount` commands. The Autofs service mounts file systems as the user accesses them and unmounts file systems when they are no longer required, without any intervention on the part of the user.

However, some file systems still need to be mounted using the `mount` command with root privileges. For example, a diskless computer must mount / (root), /usr, and /usr/kvm using the `mount` command and cannot take advantage of Autofs.

Two programs support the Autofs service: `automount` and `automountd`. Both are run when a system is started by the /etc/init.d/autofs script.

The `automount` service sets up the Autofs mount points and associates the information in the auto_master files with each mount point. The `automount` command, called at system startup time, reads the master map file named auto_master to create the initial set of Autofs mounts. These mounts are not automatically mounted at startup time. They are trigger points, also called trigger nodes, under which file systems are mounted in the future. The syntax for `automount` is

```
automount -t <duration> -v
```

`-t <duration>` sets the time, in seconds, that a file system is to remain mounted if it is not being used.

`-v` selects verbose mode. Running this command in verbose mode allows easier troubleshooting.

If not specifically set, the value for `duration` of an unused mount is set to 10 minutes. In most circumstances, this value is good; however, on systems that have many automounted file systems, you might need to increase the `duration` value. In particular, if a server has many users, active checking of the automounted file systems every five minutes can be inefficient. By unmounting the file systems every five minutes, it is possible that /etc/mnttab, which is checked by `df`, can get large. Checking the Autofs file systems every 1800 seconds (30 minutes) could be more optimal. Edit the /etc/init.d/
autofs script to change the default values.

If Autofs receives a request to access a file system that is not currently mounted, Autofs calls automountd, which actually mounts the requested file system under the trigger node.

The automountd daemon handles the mount and unmount requests from the Autofs service. The syntax of the command is

```
automountd  < -Tnv >  < -D name=value >
```

-T displays each Remote Procedure Call (RPC) to standard output. Use this option for troubleshooting.

-n disables browsing on all Autofs nodes.

-v logs all status messages to the console.

-D name=value substitutes value for the automount map variable indicated by name. The default value for the automount map is /etc/auto_master.

The automountd daemon is completely independent from the automount command. Because of this separation, it is possible to add, delete, or change map information without first having to stop and start the automountd daemon process.

To illustrate Autofs in action, here is what happens:

**NOTE** Mounts managed through the Autofs service should not be manually mounted or unmounted. Even if the operation is successful, the Autofs service does not check that the object has been unmounted, resulting in possible inconsistency. A restart clears all Autofs mount points.

automount and automountd initiate at startup time from the /etc/init.d/autofs script. If a request is made to access a file system at an Autofs mount point, the system goes through the following steps:

1. Autofs intercepts the request.
2. Autofs sends a message to the automountd daemon for the requested file system to be mounted.
3. automountd locates the file system information in a map and performs the mount.
4. Autofs allows the intercepted request to proceed.
5. Autofs unmounts the file system after a period of inactivity.

To see who might be using a particular NFS mount, use the showmount command, described in Table 17.7. The syntax for showmount is

```
showmount <options>
```

TABLE 17.7

**THE showmount COMMAND**

| *Option* | *Description* |
|---|---|
| -a | Prints all the remote mounts in the format hostname : directory. hostname is the name of the client, and directory is the root of the file system that has been mounted. |
| -d | Lists directories that have been remotely mounted by clients. |
| -e | Prints the list of shared file systems. |

The following example illustrates the use of showmount to display file systems currently mounted from remote systems. On the NFS server named neptune, type the following command:

```
showmount -a
```

The system displays the following information:

```
apollo:/export/home/neil
```

showmount tells you that the remote host, apollo, is currently mounting /export/home/neil on this server.

## Autofs Maps

The behavior of the automounter is governed by its configuration files, called maps. Autofs searches through these maps to navigate its way through the network. Map files contain information, such as the password entries of all users on a network or the names of all host computers on a network.

### Master Map

To start the navigation process, the automount command reads the master map at system startup. This map is what tells the automounter about map files and mount points. The _master map lists all direct and indirect maps and their associated directories.

The master map, which is in the /etc/auto_master file, associates a directory with a map. The master map is a list that specifies all the maps that Autofs should check. The following example shows what an auto_master file could contain:

```
# Master map for automounter
#
 +auto_master
 /net   -hosts     -nosuid,nobrowse
 /home  auto_home -nobrowse
 /xfn   -xfn
```

This example shows the default auto_master file. The lines beginning with # are comments. The line that contains `+auto_master` specifies the Autofs NIS table map, which is explained in Chapter 18, "Name Services." Each line thereafter in the master map, /etc/auto_master, has the following syntax:

```
<mount-point> <map-name> <mount-options>
```

Each field is described in Table 17.8.

**TABLE 17.8**

### /ETC/AUTO_MASTER FIELDS

| *Field* | *Description* |
|---|---|
| `mount-point` | This is the full (absolute) pathname of a directory that is used as the mount point. If the directory does not exist, Autofs creates it if possible. If the directory does exist and is not empty, mounting on it hides its contents. In this case, Autofs issues a warning. Using the notation /- as a mount point indicates that a direct map with no particular mount point is associated with the map. |
| `map-name` | This is the map that Autofs uses to find directions to locations or mount information. If the name is preceded by a slash (/), Autofs interprets the name as a local file. Otherwise, it searches for the mount information using the search specified in the name-service switch configuration file (/etc/nsswitch.conf). Name service switches are described in Chapter 18. |
| `mount-options` | This is an optional comma-separated list of options that applys to the mounting of the entries specified in map-name, unless the entries list other options. Options for each specific type of file system are listed in Table 17.3 under the `mount` command syntax. For NFS-specific mount points, the `bg` (background) and `fg` (foreground) options do not apply. |

Every Solaris installation comes with a master map, called /etc/auto_master, that has the default entries just shown. Without any changes to the generic system setup, clients should be able to access remote file systems through the /net mount point. The following entry in /etc/auto_master allows this to happen

```
/net    -hosts    -nosuid,nobrowse
```

**NOTE** A line beginning with a number sign (#) is a comment, and everything that follows it until the end of the line is ignored. To split long lines into shorter ones, put a backslash (\) at the end of the line. The maximum number of characters in an entry is 1024.

For example, say you have an NFS server named apollo that has the /export file system exported. Another system exists on the network named zeus. This system has the default /etc/auto_master file, and by default, it has a directory named /net. If you type

```
ls /net
```

the command comes back showing that the directory is empty—nothing is in it. Now type

```
ls /net/apollo
```

The system responds with this:

```
export
```

Why was it empty the first time I issued the `ls` command? When I issued `ls /net/apollo`, why did it find a subdirectory? This is the automounter in action. When I specified /net with a host name, `automountd` looked at the map file—in this case, /etc/hosts—and found apollo and its IP address. It then went to apollo, found the exported file system, and created a local mount point for /net/apollo/export. It also added this entry to the /etc/mnttab file:

```
-hosts  /net/apollo/export    autofs  nosuid,nobrowse,ignore,nest,dev=2b80005 941812769
```

This entry in the /etc/mnttab file is referred to as a trigger node.

If you type `mount`, you don't see anything mounted at this point:

```
mount
/ on /dev/dsk/c0t3d0s0 read/write/setuid/largefiles on Mon Nov  1 06:05:46 1999
/usr on /dev/dsk/c0t3d0s6 read/write/setuid/largefiles on Mon Nov  1 06:05:46 1999
/proc on /proc read/write/setuid on Mon Nov  1 06:05:46 1999
/dev/fd on fd read/write/setuid on Mon Nov  1 06:05:46 1999
/export on /dev/dsk/c0t3d0s3 setuid/read/write/largefiles on Mon Nov  1 06:05:49 1999
/export/swap on /dev/dsk/c0t3d0s4 setuid/read/write/largefiles on Mon Nov  1 06:5:49 _Â 1999
/tmp on swap read/write on Mon Nov  1 06:05:49 1999
```

Now type this:

```
ls /net/apollo/export
```

You'll notice a bit of a delay while automountd mounts the file system; the system then responds with this:

```
files   lost+found
```

The files listed are located on apollo in the /export directory. If you type mount, You'll see a file system mounted on apollo that wasn't listed before:

```
mount
/ on /dev/dsk/c0t3d0s0 read/write/setuid/largefiles on Mon Nov  1 06:05:46 1999
/usr on /dev/dsk/c0t3d0s6 read/write/setuid/largefiles on Mon Nov  1 06:05:46 1999
/proc on /proc read/write/setuid on Mon Nov  1 06:05:46 1999
/dev/fd on fd read/write/setuid on Mon Nov  1 06:05:46 1999
/export on /dev/dsk/c0t3d0s3 setuid/read/write/largefiles on Mon Nov  1 06:05:49 1999
/export/swap on /dev/dsk/c0t3d0s4 setuid/read/write/largefiles on Mon Nov  1 06:05:49 1999
/tmp on swap read/write on Mon Nov  1 06:05:49 1999
/net/apollo/export on apollo:/export nosuid/remote on Fri Nov  5 09:48:03 1999
```

The automounter automatically mounted the /export file system that was located on apollo. Now look at the /etc/mnttab file again, and you see additional entries:

```
more /etc/mnttab
/dev/dsk/c0t3d0s0       /       ufs     rw,suid,dev=800018,largefiles   941454346
/dev/dsk/c0t3d0s6       /usr    ufs     rw,suid,dev=80001e,largefiles   941454346
/proc   /proc   proc    rw,suid,dev=2940000     941454346
fd      /dev/fd fd      rw,suid,dev=2a00000     941454346
/dev/dsk/c0t3d0s3       /export ufs     suid,rw,largefiles,dev=80001b   941454349
/dev/dsk/c0t3d0s4       /export/swap    ufs     suid,rw,largefiles,dev=80001c
swap    /tmp    tmpfs   dev=1   941454349
-hosts  /net    autofs  ignore,indirect,nosuid,nobrowse,dev=2b80001     941454394
auto_home       /home   autofs  ignore,indirect,nobrowse,dev=2b80002    941454394
-xfn    /xfn    autofs  ignore,indirect,dev=2b80003     941454394
sparcserver:vold(pid246)        /vol    nfs     ignore,noquota,dev=2b40001 941454409
-hosts  /net/apollo/export      autofs  nosuid,nobrowse,ignore,nest,dev=2b80005
apollo:/export /net/apollo/export       nfs     nosuid,dev=2b40003 941813283
```

If the /net/apollo/export directory is accessed, the Autofs service completes the process with these steps:

1. It pings the server's mount service to see if it's alive.
2. It mounts the requested file system under /net/apollo/export. Now /etc/mnttab file contains the following entries:

```
-hosts   /net/apollo/export     autofs  nosuid,nobrowse,ignore,nest,dev=2b80005 941812769
apollo:/export /net/apollo/export     nfs     nosuid,dev=2b40003 941813283
```

Because the automounter lets all users mount file systems, root access is not required. It also provides for automatic unmounting of file systems, so there is no need to unmount them when you are done.

## Direct Map

A direct map lists a set of unrelated mount points, which might be spread out across the file system. A complete path (that is, /usr/local/bin or /usr/man) is listed in the map as a mount point. The best example of where to use a direct mount point is for /usr/man. The /usr directory contains many other directories, such as /usr/bin and /usr/local; therefore, it cannot be an indirect mount point. If you were to use an indirect map for /usr/man, the local /usr file system would be the mount point, and you would cover up the local /usr/bin and /usr/etc directories when you established the mount. A direct map lets automounter complete mounts on a single directory entry such as /usr/man, appearing as a link with the name of the direct mount point.

A direct map is specified in a configuration file called /etc/auto_direct. With a direct map, there is a direct association between a mount point on the client and a directory on the server. Direct maps have a full pathname and indicate the relationship explicitly. This is a typical /etc/auto_direct map:

```
/usr/local     -ro
/bin   ivy:/export/local/sun4
/share ivy:/export/local/share
/src   ivy:/export/local/src
/usr/man     -ro       oak:/usr/man \
     rose:/usr/man \
```

> **NOTE** A backslash at the end of a line splits it into two shorter lines. The operating system sees it as one line.

```
     willow:/usr/man
/usr/game     -ro        peach:/usr/games
/usr/spool/news     -ro        pine:/usr/spool/news \
     willow:/var/spool/news
```

Lines in direct maps have the following syntax:

```
<key> <mount-options> <location>
```

The fields are described in Table 17.9.

**TABLE 17.9**

**DIRECT MAP FIELDS**

| *Field* | *Description* |
|---|---|
| `key` | This field indicates the pathname of the mount point in a direct map. This pathname specifies the local directory on which to mount the NFS file system. |
| `mount-options` | This field indicates the options you want to apply to this particular mount. They are required only if they differ from the map default options specified in the /etc/auto_master file. Options are listed in Table 17.3 under the `mount` command syntax. There is no concatenation of options between the automounter maps. Any options added to an automounter map override all the options listed in previously searched maps. For instance, options included in the auto_master map would be overwritten by corresponding entries in any other map. |
| `location` | This field indicates the remote location of the file system specified as server:pathname. More than one location can be specified. The pathname should not include an automounted mount point; it should be the actual absolute path to the file system. For instance, the location of a home directory should be listed as server:/export/home/username, not as server:/home/username. |

In the previous example of the /etc/auto_direct map file, the mount points, /usr/man and /usr/spool/news, list more than one location:

```
/usr/man        -ro    apollo:/usr/man \
                zeus:/usr/man \
                neptune:/usr/man
/usr/spool/news        -ro    jupiter:/usr/spool/news \
                saturn:/var/spool/news
```

Multiple locations, such as those shown here, are used for replication, or failover. For the purposes of failover, a file system can be called a replica if each file is the same size and is the same type of file system. Permissions, creation dates, and other file attributes are not a consideration. If the file size or the file system types are different, the remap fails, and the process hangs until the old server becomes available.

Replication makes sense only if you mount a file system that is read-only, because you must have some control over the locations of files you write or modify. You don't want to modify one server's files on one occasion and, minutes later, modify the same file on another server. The benefit of replication is that the best available server is used automatically without any effort required by the user.

If the file systems are configured as replicas, the clients have the advantage of using failover. Not only is the best server automatically determined, but, if that server becomes unavailable, the client automatically uses the next-best server.

An example of a good file system to configure as a replica is the manual (man) pages. In a large network, more than one server can export the current set of manual pages. Which server you mount them from doesn't matter, as long as the server is running and exporting its file systems. In the previous example, multiple mount locations are expressed as a list of mount locations in the map entry. With multiple mount locations specified, you can mount the man pages from the apollo, zeus, or neptune servers. The best server depends on a number of factors, including the number of servers supporting a particular NFS protocol level, the proximity of the server, and weighting. The process of selecting a server goes like this:

- During the sorting process, a count of the number of servers supporting the NFS version 2 and 3.0 protocols is made. The protocol supported on the most servers is the protocol supported by default. This provides the client with the maximum number of servers to depend on. If version 3 servers are more abundant, the sorting process becomes more complex. Normally servers on the local subnet are given preference over servers on a remote subnet. A version 2 server can complicate matters, because it could be closer than the nearest version 3 server. If there is a version 2 server on the local subnet and the closest version 3 server is on a remote subnet, the version 2 server is given preference. This is checked only if there are more version 3 servers than version 2 servers. If there are more version 2 servers, only a version 2 server is selected.

- After the largest subset of servers that have the same protocol version is found, that server list is sorted by proximity. Servers on the local subnet are given preference over servers on a remote subnet. The closest server is given preference, which reduces latency and network traffic. If several servers are supporting the same protocol on the local subnet, the time to connect to each server is determined, and the fastest is used.
- You can also influence the selection of servers at the same proximity level by adding a numeric weighting value in parentheses after the server name in the Autofs map. For example:

  ```
  /usr/man -ro apollo,zeus(1),neptune(2):/usr/man
  ```

  Servers without a weighting have a value of 0, which makes it the most likely server to be selected. The higher the weighting value, the less chance the server has of being selected. All other server selection factors are more important than weighting. Weighting is considered only when selecting between servers with the same network proximity.

With failover, the sorting is checked once at mount time, to select one server from which to mount, and again if the mounted server becomes unavailable. Failover is particularly useful in a large network with many subnets. Autofs chooses the nearest server and therefore confines NFS network traffic to a local network segment. In servers with multiple network interfaces, Autofs lists the host name associated with each network interface as if it were a separate server. It then selects the nearest interface to the client.

In this example, I set up a direct map for /usr/local on zeus. Currently, zeus has a directory called /usr/local with the following directories:

```
ls /usr/local
```

The following local directories are displayed:

```
bin   etc   files   programs
```

If you set up the automount direct map, you'll see how the /usr/local directory is overwritten by the NFS mount.

First, I need to add the following entry in the master map file called /etc/auto_master:

```
/-    /etc/auto_direct
```

Next, create the direct map file called /etc/auto_direct with the following entry:

```
/usr/local   zeus:/usr/local
```

Because I'm modifying a direct map, I need to stop and restart automount as follows:

```
/etc/init.d/autofs stop
/etc/init.d/autofs start
```

Now, if you have access to the /usr/local directory, the NFS mount point is established using the direct map you have set up. The contents of /usr/local have changed because the direct map has covered up the local copy of /usr/local:

**NOTE** The local contents of /usr/local have not been overwritten. After the NFS mount point is unmounted, the original contents of /usr/local are redisplayed.

```
ls /usr/local
```

You'll see the following directories listed:

```
fasttrack   answerbook
```

By typing the `mount` command, you see that /usr/local is now mounted remotely from zeus:

```
mount
/ on /dev/dsk/c0t3d0s0 read/write/setuid/largefiles on Mon Nov 1 06:05:46 1999
/usr on /dev/dsk/c0t3d0s6 read/write/setuid/largefiles on Mon Nov 1 06:05:46 1999
/proc on /proc read/write/setuid on Mon Nov 1 06:05:46 1999
/dev/fd on fd read/write/setuid on Mon Nov 1 06:05:46 1999
/export on /dev/dsk/c0t3d0s3 setuid/read/write/largefiles on Mon Nov 1 06:05:49 1999
/export/swap on /dev/dsk/c0t3d0s4 setuid/read/write/largefiles on Mon Nov 1 06:05:49 1999
/tmp on swap read/write on Mon Nov 1 06:05:49 1999
/usr/local on zeus:/usr/local read/write/remote on Sat Nov 6 08:06:40 1999
```

## Indirect Map

Indirect maps are the simplest and most useful automounter conventions. An indirect map uses a key's substitution value to establish the association between a mount point on the client and a directory on the server. Indirect maps are useful for accessing specific file systems, such as home directories, from anywhere on the network.

The following entry in the /etc/auto_master file is an example of an indirect map:

```
/share      /etc/auto_share
```

With this entry in the /etc/auto_master file, /etc/auto_share is the name of the indirect map file for the mount point /share. For this entry, you also need to create an indirect map file named /etc/auto_share, which would look like this:

```
# share directory map for automounter
 #
 ws          neptune:/export/share/ws
```

If the /share directory is accessed, the Autofs service creates a trigger node for /share/ws, and the following entry is made in the /etc/mnttab file:

```
-hosts  /share/ws     autofs \
nosuid,nobrowse,ignore,nest,dev=###
```

If the /share/ws directory is accessed, the Autofs service completes the process with these steps:

1. It pings the server's mount service to see if it's alive.
2. It mounts the requested file system under /share. Now /etc/mnttab file contains the following entries:

   ```
   -hosts  /share/ws     autofs \
   nosuid,nobrowse,ignore,nest,dev=###
   neptune:/export/share/ws /share/ws   nfs \
   nosuid,dev=####    #####
   ```

Lines in indirect maps have the following general syntax:

```
<key>  <mount-options>  <location>
```

The fields in this line are described in Table 17.10.

**TABLE 17.10**

**INDIRECT MAP FIELDS**

| *Field* | *Description* |
|---|---|
| `key` | `key` is a simple name (no slashes) in an indirect map. |
| `mount-options` | The `mount-options` are the options you want to apply to this particular mount. They are described in Table 18-4. They are required only if they differ from the map default options specified in the /etc/auto_master file. |
| `location` | `location` is the remote location of the file system specified as server:pathname. More than one location can be specified. The pathname should not include an automounted mount point; it should be the actual absolute path to the file system. For instance, the location of a directory should be listed as server:/usr/local, not as server:/net/server/usr/local. |

An example of an indirect map would be for user home directories. As users log into several different systems, their home directory is not always local to the system. It's convenient to use automounter to access their home directory regardless of the system to which they log in. To accomplish this, the default /etc/auto_master map file needs to contain the following entry:

```
/home       /etc/auto_home          -nobrowse
```

/etc/auto_home is the name of the indirect map file that contains the entries to be mounted under /home. A typical /etc/auto_home map file might look like this:

```
more /etc/auto_home
 dean                       willow:/export/home/dean
 william                    cypress:/export/home/william
 nicole                     poplar:/export/home/nicole
 glenda                     pine:/export/home/glenda
 steve                      apple:/export/home/steve
 burk                       ivy:/export/home/burk
 neil     -rw,nosuid         peach:/export/home/neil
```

Now let's assume that the /etc/auto_home map is on the host oak. If user neil has an entry in the password database specifying his home directory as /home/neil, whenever he logs in to computer oak, Autofs mounts the directory /export/home/neil residing on the computer peach. His home directory is mounted read-write, nosuid. Anyone, including Neil, has access to this path from any computer set up with the master map referring to the /etc/auto_home map in this example.

Under these conditions, user neil can run `login`, or `rlogin`, on any computer that has the /etc/auto_home map setup, and his home directory is mounted in place for him.

Another example of when to use an indirect map is if you want to make all project-related files available under a directory called /data. This directory is to be common across all workstations at the site.

# STEP BY STEP

## 17.4 Setting Up an Indirect Map

Follow these steps to set up the indirect map:

1. Add an entry for the /data directory to the /etc/auto_master map file:

```
/data      /etc/auto_data     -nosuid
```

The auto_data map file, named /etc/auto_data, determines the contents of the /data directory.

2. Add the `-nosuid` option as a precaution.

The `-nosuid` option prevents users from creating files with the `setuid` or `setgid` bit set. Refer to Chapter 8, if you're unfamiliar with `setuid/setgid`.

3. Create the /etc/auto_data file and add entries to the auto_data map.

The auto_data map is organized so that each entry describes a subproject. Edit /etc/auto_data to create a map that looks like the following:

```
compiler    apollo:/export/data/&
window      apollo:/export/data/&
files       zeus:/export/data/&
drivers     apollo:/export/data/&
man         zeus:/export/data/&
tools       zeus:/export/data/&
```

**NOTE** The ampersand (&) at the end of each entry is an abbreviation for the entry key. For instance, the first entry is equivalent to `compiler apollo:/export/data/compiler`

Because the servers apollo and zeus view similar Autofs maps locally, any users who logs in to these computers finds the /data file system as expected. These users are provided direct access to local files through loopback mounts instead of NFS mounts.

4. Because you changed the /etc/auto_master map, the final step is to stop Autofs and restart it as follows:

```
/etc/init.d/autofs stop
/etc/init.d/autofs start
```

Now, if a user changes to the /data/compiler directory, the mount point to apollo:/export/data/compiler is created:

```
cd /data/compiler
```

5. Type `mount` to see the mount point that was established:

```
mount
```

The system shows that /data/compiler is mapped to apollo:/export/data/compiler as follows:

```
/data/compiler on apollo:/export/data/compiler read/write/remote on Fri Nov  5 17:17:02 1999
```

If the user changes to /data/tools, the mount point to zeus:/export/data/tools is created under the mount point /data/tools.

The system administrator can modify, delete, or add entries to maps to meet the needs of the environment. As applications (and other file systems that users require) change their location, the maps must reflect those changes. You can modify Autofs maps at any time. However, changes do not take place until the file system is unmounted and remounted. If a change is made to the auto_master map, or to a direct map, those changes do not take place until the automounter is restarted as follows:

```
/etc/init.d/autofs stop
/etc/init.d/autofs start
```

**NOTE** There is no need to create the directory /data/compiler to be used as the mount point. Automounter creates all the necessary directories before establishing the mount.

Another method is to force auto_master and direct map changes to be recognized immediately by running `automount` from the command line as follows:

```
automount -v
```

# When to Use Automount

The most common and most advantageous use of automount is for mounting infrequently used file systems on an NFS client, such as online reference manual pages. Another common use is accessing user home directories anywhere on the network. This use works well for users who do not have a dedicated system and who tend to log in from different locations. In the past, to permit access, the system administrator had to create home directories on every system into which the user logged in. Data had to be duplicated everywhere, and it was always out of sync. You certainly don't want to create permanent NFS mounts for all user home directories on each system, so this is an excellent use for automount.

Automount is also used if a read-only file system exists on more than one server. By using automount instead of conventional NFS mounting, you can configure the NFS client to query all the servers on which the file system exists and mount from the server that responds first.

Avoid using automount to mount frequently used file systems, such as those containing user commands or frequently-used applications; conventional NFS mounting is more efficient in this situation. It is quite practical and typical to combine the use of automount with conventional NFS mounting on the same NFS client.

## CHAPTER SUMMARY

By now you should have a good understanding of what NFS is and how to share resources on an NFS server. You should understand the security issues associated with using NFS and know how to share NFS resources so that only authorized users can access them. There are many options available when sharing resources on an NFS server. The system administrator needs to understand each of them and make informed decisions when sharing resources, so that system security is not compromised.

Accessing resources on the NFS client from a server were discussed. I described AutoFS and the many options available when mounting NFS resources so that user downtime is minimized by unplanned system outages and unavailable resources.

Finally, I described how to maximize efficiency and system performance on NFS mounted resources using AutoFS and CacheFS.

When managing NFS, and especially automounter, a system administrator can quickly become overwhelmed with all the configuration files that must be kept consistent across the many different systems. For example, the /etc/auto_master and the related direct and indirect map files must be updated whenever the name of a host or file system changes. This can be nearly impossible on a large network. Chapter 18, describes how Network Information Services (NIS) can be used to help manage all these configuration files, including/etc/passwd and /etc/hosts, from a single location.

### KEY TERMS

- NFS
- NFS server
- NFS client
- Dynamic failover (as it relates to NFS)
- WebNFS
- NFS daemons
- Shared resource
- `Hard` mount
- `Soft` mount
- Replication
- NFS logging
- WebNFS
- Back file system
- Front file system
- Cached file system
- Cache directory
- Cold cache
- Warm cache
- Consistency checking
- AutoFS Maps (know each of them)
- Trigger point

## APPLY YOUR KNOWLEDGE

# Exercises

The following exercises require a minimum of two networked Solaris systems. Determine in advance, which system will serve as the NFS server and which system will be the NFS client. The NFS server must have manual pages installed in the /usr/share/man directory.

### 17.1 NFS Server setup

In this exercise, you'll set up an NFS server to share the contents of the /usr/share/man directory for read-only access.

**Estimated Time**: 30 minutes

1. Make the following entry in the /etc/dfs/dfstab file:

```
share -F nfs -o ro /usr/share/man
```

2. Restart the /etc/init.d/nfs.server script to start the `nfsd` and `mountd` daemons:

```
/etc/init.d/nfs.server start
```

3. Verify that the two daemons are running by typing:

```
ps -ef|grep nfs
```

4. Verify that the resource is shared by typing the following:

```
share
```

The system should display:

```
-     /usr/share/man   ro   ""
```

5. On the NFS client, rename the /usr/share/man directory so that man pages are no longer accessible by typing:

```
cd /usr/share
mv man man.bkup
```

6. Verify that the manual pages are no longer accessible by typing the following:

```
man tar
```

7. Create a new man directory to be used as a mount point as follows:

```
mkdir man
```

8. Verify that you are able to see the shared resource on the NFS server by typing the following:

```
dfshares <nfs server name>
```

The system should display a message similar to the following:

```
RESOURCE                     SERVER ACCESS TRANSPORT
192.168.0.4:/usr/share/man  192.168.0.4    -
```

9. Mount the /usr/share/man directory located on the NFS server to the directory you created in the previous step as follows:

```
mount <nfs server name>:/usr/share/man \
/usr/share/man
```

10. Now see if the man pages are accessible by typing the following:

```
man tar
```

11. Verify the list of mounts that the server is providing by typing:

```
dfmounts <nfs server name>
```

The system displays something like this:

```
RESOURCE      SERVER PATHNAME \
CLIENTS
 -           192.168.0.4 /usr/share/man \
192.168.0.21
```

12. Unmount the directory on the NFS client as follows:

```
umountall -r
```

Note that the `-r` option specifies that only remote file system types are to be unmounted.

## APPLY YOUR KNOWLEDGE

13. Verify that the file system is no longer mounted by typing:

```
dfmounts <nfs server name>
```

14. On the NFS server, unshare the /usr/share/man directory by typing the following:

```
unshare /usr/share/man
```

15. On the NFS client, try to mount the /usr/share/man directory from the NFS server as follows:

```
mount <nfs server name>:/usr/share/man \
/usr/share/man
```

It should not allow you to mount it.

16. Check the shared resources on the NFS server by typing the following:

```
dfshares <nfs server name>
```

The file system can no longer be mounted because it is no longer shared.

### 17.2 Using AutoFS

The following exercise demonstrates the use of AutoFS.

**Estimated Time**: 30 minutes

1. The NFS server should already have an entry in the /etc/dfs/dfstab file from the previous exercise. It looks like this:

```
share -F nfs -o ro /usr/share/man
```

The `nfsd` and `mountd` daemons should also be running on this server.

2. On the NFS client, verify that the man pages are not working by typing the following:

```
man tar
```

3. On the NFS client, remove the directory you created in the previous exercise:

```
rmdir /usr/share/man
```

4. On the NFS client, edit the /etc/auto_master file to add the following line for a direct map:

```
/-     auto_direct
```

5. On the NFS client, use vi to create a new file named /etc/auto_direct and add the following line in the file:

```
/usr/share/man   <nfs server name>:/usr/share/man
```

6. Run the `automount` command to update the list of directories managed by AutoFS:

```
automount -v
```

7. Now see if man pages are working on the NFS client by typing the following:

```
man tar
```

8. On the NFS client, check to see that AutoFS automatically mounted the remote directory on the NFS server:

```
mount
```

9. On the NFS server, unshare the shared directory by typing the following:

```
unshareall
```

10. On the NFS server, shutdown the NFS server daemons as follows:

```
/etc/init.d/nfs.server stop
```

11. On the NFS client, edit the /etc/auto_master file and remove the line that reads:

```
/-   auto_direct
```

12. On the NFS client, remove the file named /etc/auto_direct:

```
rm /etc/auto_direct
```

## APPLY YOUR KNOWLEDGE

13. On the NFS client, run the automount command to update the list of directories managed by AutoFS as follows:

```
automount -v
```

14. On the NFS client, return /usr/share/man to its original state as follows:

```
cd /usr/share
rmdir man
mv man.bkup man
```

## Review Questions

1. Which of the following conditions does not need to be met to share files in the NFS environment?

   A. The server must be running NFS version 3.

   B. The system must be at run level 3.

   C. The system must be on a network and be accessible by other systems.

   D. The resources must be made available using the share command.

2. If resources are added to the following files, can you then make it available and unavailable using the shareall and unshareall commands.

   A. /etc/dfs/dfstab

   B. /etc/dfs/sharetab

   C. /etc/vfstab

   D. /etc/mnttab

3. By default, all file systems shared via NFS are available for WebNFS access.

   A. True

   B. False

4. In WebNFS, to make URLs relative to the resource as opposed to the servers root directory, include which of the following options in /etc/dfs/dfstab?

   A. `nosub`

   B. `index`

   C. `secure`

   D. `public`

5. To stop and restart NFS to enable a new share, type:

   A. `/etc/init.d/autofs stop; /etc/init.d/autofs start`

   B. `/etc/init.d/nfs.client stop; /etc/init.d/nfs.client start`

   C. `/etc/init.d/nfs.server stop; /etc/init.d/nfs.server start`

   D. `automount -v`

6. Which of the following eliminates the need of having remote file systems (NFS mounts) listed in /etc/vfstab, which allows faster booting and shutdown?

   A. /etc/dfs/dfstab

   B. `automount`

   C. /etc/mnttab

   D. `vold`

7. In AutoFS, which of the following associates a directory with a map?

   A. indirect

   B. direct

   C. `auto_master`

   D. `automountd`

## APPLY YOUR KNOWLEDGE

8. Which of the following maps has a full path name and indicates the relationship explicitly?

   A. NIS

   B. auto_master

   C. indirect

   D. direct

9. Which of the following maps is useful for accessing specific file systems such as home directories?

   A. auto_master

   B. indirect

   C. direct

   D. NIS

10. Modifications to existing entries in a direct map or any changes to an indirect map do not require restarting automount.

    A. True

    B. False

11. Which of the following enables computers of different architectures running different operating systems to share files and applications across a network?

    A. FTP

    B. NIS

    C. TCP/IP

    D. NFS

12. NFS daemons are started at bootup from which of the following files?

    A. /etc/init.d/nfs.server

    B. /etc/init.d/nfs.client

    C. /etc/init.d/autofs

    D. /etc/inittab

13. NFS client daemons are started at which run level?

    A. 1

    B. 2

    C. 3

    D. 4

14. Which of the following is *not* an NFS daemon?

    A. `rpcd`

    B. `mountd`

    C. `lockd`

    D. `statd`

15. Which NFS daemons are only found on the NFS server?

    A. `nfsd`

    B. `lockd`

    C. `mountd`

    D. `nfslogd`

16. You specify which file systems are to be shared by entering the information in which of the following files?

    A. /etc/dfs/sharetab

    B. /etc/dfs/dfstab

    C. /etc/vfstab

    D. /etc/mnttab

## APPLY YOUR KNOWLEDGE

17. Which of the following command(s) makes a resource available for mounting?

    A. `export`

    B. `share`

    C. `exportfs`

    D. All of the above

18. Which of the following commands displays information about shared resources available to the host from an NFS server?

    A. `shareall`

    B. `share`

    C. `dfshares`

    D. `dfinfo`

19. File systems mounted with which of the following options indicate that mount is to retry in the background if the server's `mount` daemon (`mountd`) does not respond?

    A. `intr`

    B. `fg`

    C. `bg`

    D. `soft`

20. Which of the following options to the `mount` command specifies how long (seconds) each NFS request made in the kernel should wait for a response?

    A. `retrans`

    B. `timeo`

    C. `retry`

    D. `remount`

21. File systems that are mounted read-write or that contain executable files should always be mounted with which of the following options?

    A. `hard`

    B. `intr`

    C. `soft`

    D. `nointr`

22. From the NFS client, this option makes `mount` retry the request up to a specified number of times when the NFS server becomes unavailable:

    A. `retry`

    B. `retrans`

    C. `remount`

    D. `timeo`

23. When an NFS server goes down, which of the following options to the `mount` command allows you to send a kill signal to a hung NFS process?

    A. `bg`

    B. `nointr`

    C. `intr`

    D. `timeo`

24. Which of the following extends the NFS to the Internet?

    A. TCP/IP

    B. AutoFS

    C. Webstart

    D. WebNFS

## APPLY YOUR KNOWLEDGE

25. Which of the following programs support the AutoFS service?

    A. `automount`

    B. `automountd`

    C. `mount`

    D. `share`

26. automountd starts from which of the following files?

    A. /etc/init.d/volmgt

    B. /etc/init.d/autofs

    C. /etc/init.d/nfs.server

    D. /etc/init.d/nfs.client

27. Which of the following commands do you use to see who might be using a particular NFS mount?

    A. `fuser`

    B. `dfshares`

    C. `showmount`

    D. `ps`

28. Which of the following files lists all direct and indirect maps for AutoFS?

    A. /etc/auto_master

    B. /etc/auto_direct

    C. /etc/auto_share

    D. /etc/init.d/autofs

29. Every Solaris installation comes with a default master map with default entries. Without any changes to the generic system setup, clients should be able to access remote file systems through which of the following mount points?

    A. /tmp_mnt

    B. /net

    C. /export

    D. /export/home

30. Which of the following is the simplest and most useful automounter convention?

    A. Direct map

    B. Indirect map

    C. Master map

    D. All are equal

31. The following entry in the /etc/auto_master file, /share /etc/auto_share, is an example of what type of map?

    A. NIS

    B. Direct

    C. Master

    D. Indirect

## APPLY YOUR KNOWLEDGE

32. To force auto_master and direct map changes to get recognized immediately, which of the following commands should you run?

    A. `automount -v`

    B. `automount -f`

    C. `automount -r`

    D. `umount` and `remount` the file system

33. Which of the following daemons is found in a NFS client?

    A. `mountd`

    B. `nfsd`

    C. `statd`

    D. `rpc.nisd`

34. What is the default time for the automountd to unmount a file system if not in use?

    A. 300 seconds

    B. 60 seconds

    C. 120 seconds

    D. 180 seconds

35. What types of maps are available in automounter?

    A. Direct and indirect

    B. Master, direct and indirect

    C. Master and direct

    D. Master and indirect

36. Which of the following commands is used to specify a disk resource to be made available to other systems via through NFS?

    A. `mount`

    B. `share`

    C. `export`

    D. `dfshares`

37. Which script starts up the NFS log daemon:

    A. `/usr/lib/nfs/nfslogd`

    B. `/etc/nfs/nfslog.conf`

    C. `/etc/dfs/dfstab`

    D. `/etc/init.d/nfs.server`

38. This daemon provides NFS logging:

    A. `syslogd`

    B. `nfsd`

    C. `statd`

    D. `nfslogd`

## Answers to Review Questions

1. **A.** It's not necessary for all systems to run NFS version 3. Systems using NFS can be using various versions of NFS.

2. **A.** Execute the `shareall` command, and any new entries in the /etc/dfs/dfstab file are shared. Execute the `unshareall` command and any entries in the /etc/dfs/dfstab file are unshared.

## APPLY YOUR KNOWLEDGE

3. **A.** True, all file systems shared through NFS are available for WebNFS access.

4. **D.** In WebNFS, to make URLs relative to the resource as opposed to the servers root directory, include the `public` option in the /etc/dfs/dfstab file entry.

5. **C.** To stop and restart NFS to enable a new share, type: `/etc/init.d/nfs.server stop; /etc/init.d/nfs.server start.`

6. **B.** `Automount` eliminates the need of having remote file systems (NFS mounts) listed in /etc/vfstab and allows faster booting and shutdown.

7. **C.** The `automount` command, called at system startup time, reads the master map file named `auto_master` to create the initial set of Autofs mounts.

8. **D.** With a direct map, there is a direct association between a mount point on the client and a directory on the server. Direct maps have a full pathname and indicate the relationship explicitly.

9. **B.** Indirect maps are useful for accessing specific file systems, such as home directories, from anywhere on the network.

10. **A.** Modifications to existing entries in a direct map or any changes to an indirect map do not require restarting automount.

11. **D.** The NFS service lets computers of different architectures, running different OSs, share file systems across a network.

12. **A., B.** NFS uses a number of daemons to handle its services. These services are initialized at startup from the `/etc/init.d/nfs.server` and `/etc/init.d/nfs.client startup scripts.`

13. **B.** NFS client daemons are started by the `/etc/init.d/nfs.client` script at run level 2.

14. **A.** `mountd`, `lockd`, and `statd` are all NFS daemons. `rpcd` is not an NFS daemon.

15. **A., C., D.** The NFS daemons found only on the NFS server are: `nfsd`, `mountd`, and `nfslogd`.

16. **B.** A shared file system is referred to as a shared resource. You specify which file systems are to be shared by entering the information in a file called /etc/dfs/dfstab.

17. **B.** The `share` command exports a resource and makes a resource available for mounting.

18. **C.** The `dfshares` command displays information about the shared resources available to the host from an NFS server.

19. **C.** File systems mounted with the `bg` option indicate that `mount` is to retry in the background if the server's mount daemon (`mountd`) does not respond when, for example, the NFS server is restarted.

20. **B.** After the file system is mounted, each NFS request made in the kernel waits a specified number of seconds for a response (specified with the `timeo=<n>` option).

21. **A.** Sun recommends that file systems mounted as read-write, or containing executable files, should always be mounted with the `hard` option.

22. **A.** From the NFS client, mount retries the request up to the count specified in the `retry=<n>` option. After the file system is mounted, each NFS request made in the kernel waits a specified number of seconds for a response.

## APPLY YOUR KNOWLEDGE

23. **C.** If a file system is mounted hard and the `intr` option is not specified, the process hangs until the remote file system reappears if the NFS server goes down. If `intr` is specified, sending an interrupt signal to the process kills it.

24. **D.** WebNFS provides the ability to make a file system on the Internet accessible through firewalls using an extension to the NFS protocol.

25. **A., B.** File systems shared through the NFS service can be mounted using Autofs. Autofs, which is a client-side service, also is a file system structure that provides automatic mounting. The Autofs file system is initialized by `automount`, which is run automatically when a system is started. The `automount` daemon, named `automountd`, runs continuously, mounting and unmounting remote directories on an as-needed basis.

26. **B.** Two programs support the Autofs service: `automount` and `automountd`. Both are run when a system is started by the `/etc/init.d/autofs` script.

27. **C.** To see who might be using a particular NFS mount, use the `showmount` command.

28. **A.** The master map, which is in the /etc/auto_master file, associates a directory with a map. The master map is a list that specifies all the maps that Autofs should check.

29. **B.** Without any changes to the generic system setup, clients should be able to access remote file systems through the `/net` mount point.

30. **B.** `Indirect` maps are the simplest and most useful automounter conventions. Indirect maps are useful for accessing specific file systems, such as home directories, from anywhere on the network.

31. **D.** The following entry in the /etc/auto_master file: `/etc/auto_share` is the name of the indirect map.

32. **A.** To force auto_master and direct map changes to be recognized immediately, execute the following command: `automount -v`

33. **C.** The `statd` daemon runs on the NFS server and NFS client and interacts with `lockd` to provide the crash and recovery functions for the locking services on NFS.

34. **A.** The `-t` option to the `automount` command sets the time, in seconds, that a file system is to remain mounted if it is not being used. The default is 300 seconds.

35. **B.** The three types of AutoFS maps are master, direct, and indirect maps.

36. **B.** The `share` command is used to specify a disk resource to be made available to other systems through NFS. share exports a resource or makes a resource available for mounting.

37. **A.** The `/usr/lib/nfs/nfslogd` script starts up the NFS log daemon (`nfslogd`).

38. **D.** The `nfslogd` daemon provides NFS logging and is enabled using the `log=`*<tag>* option in the `share` command. When NFS logging is enabled, all NFS operations on the file system are recorded

## OBJECTIVES

The following test objectives are covered in this chapter:

**Understand the Solaris naming services**

- The name services in Solaris help to centralize the shared information on your network. This chapter describes the name services available in Solaris 8 so that you can identify the appropriate name service to use for your network.

**Configure and Manage Network Information Service (NIS)**

- NIS provides centralized control of a system's network information. NIS helps the system administrator manage information about system hosts, users, and various other network resources. This chapter describes how to configure and manage NIS.

CHAPTER 18

# Name Services

## Outline



## Study Strategies

The following strategies will help you prepare for the test:

- As you study this chapter, be prepared to state the purpose of a name service and the information it is used to manage. You'll need at least two networked Solaris systems to practice the examples and step-by-step exercises. I highly recommend that you practice the tasks until you can perform them from memory.
- I cover NIS in-depth, but only provide a brief description of the other name services. That is because the exam will focus on NIS with only a few questions on the other name services. Be sure that you understand everything on how to configure NIS master servers, slave servers, and clients. You'll need to understand entries in the NIS name service switch file. Also, you'll need to know how to add a new NIS map.
- For all the name services, be prepared to describe the characteristics of each of them, compare their functionality, and identify the associated name service switch file.
- Finally, study the terms provided at the end of this chapter in the "Key Terms" section. Also, be sure you can describe each command I've described in this chapter, specifically the ones I've used as examples. On the exam, you will be asked to match a command or term with the appropriate description.

## INTRODUCTION

This chapter explains how to configure and administer the servers and clients in a NIS (Network Information Service) domain. NIS is a huge topic that could potentially span several volumes. The purpose of this chapter is to prepare you for questions regarding NIS that might appear on the exam. I also want to provide an overview of NIS, complete enough so that you are equipped to set up a basic NIS network and understand its use.

## NAME SERVICES OVERVIEW

Name services store information in a central location that users, systems, and applications must have to communicate across the network. Information is stored in files, maps, or database tables. Without a central name service, each system would have to maintain its own copy of this information. Therefore, centrally locating this data makes it easier to administer large networks. The information handled by a name service includes

- System (host) names and addresses
- User names
- Passwords
- Access permissions

The Solaris 8 release provides the name services listed in Table 18.1.

**TABLE 18.1**

**NAME SERVICES**

| *Name Service* | *Description* |
|---|---|
| /etc files | The original UNIX naming system |
| NIS | The Network Information Service |
| NIS+ | The Network Information Service Plus (NIS+ is described in greater detail later in this chapter) |
| DNS | The Domain Name System (DNS is described in greater detail later in this chapter) |
| LDAP | Lightweight Directory Access Protocol (LDAP is described in greater detail later in this chapter) |

A name service enables centralized management of host files so that systems can be identified by common names instead of by numerical addresses. This simplifies communication because users do not have to remember and try to enter cumbersome numerical addresses such as 129.44.3.1.

Addresses are not the only network information that systems need to store. They also need to store security information, email addresses, information about their Ethernet interfaces, network services, groups of users allowed to use the network, services offered on the network, and so on. As networks offer more services, the list grows. As a result, each system might need to keep an entire set of files similar to /etc/hosts.

As this information changes, without a name service, administrators must keep it current on every system in the network. In a small network, this is simply tedious, but on a medium or large network, the job becomes not only time-consuming, but also nearly unmanageable.

A name service solves this problem. It stores network information on servers and provides the information to any workstation that asks for it.

## /ETC FILES

/etc files are the traditional UNIX way of maintaining information about hosts, users, passwords, groups, and automount maps, to name just a few. These files are text files located on each individual system that can be edited using the vi editor or Solstice AdminSuite. They are described in Chapters 5, 8, 13, and 17.

Each file needs to be individually maintained, and on a large network, this can be a difficult task. As IP addresses change, and user's accounts are added and deleted, it can become difficult to maintain all these files and keep them in sync between each system. On a large changing network, the traditional approach to maintaining this information had to change, therefore, the following name services were introduced.

# NIS

> **NOTE** As stated, the NIS was formerly known as the Sun Yellow Pages (YP). The functionality of the two remains the same; only the name has changed. The name "Yellow Pages" is a registered trademark in the United Kingdom of British Telecommunications PLC, and it may not be used without permission.

The NIS, formerly called the Yellow Pages (YP), is a distributed database system that lets the system administrator administer the configuration of many hosts from a central location. Common configuration information, which would have to be maintained separately on each host in a network without NIS, can be stored and maintained in a central location and then propagated to all the nodes in the network. NIS stores information about workstation names and addresses, users, the network itself, and network services. This collection of network information is referred to as the NIS namespace.

Before I begin a discussion of the structure of NIS, you need to be aware that the NIS administration databases are called maps. A domain is a collection of systems that share a common set of NIS maps.

## Structure of the NIS Network

The systems within a NIS network are configured in the following ways:

- Master server
- Slave servers
- Clients of NIS servers

The center of the NIS network is the NIS master server. The system designated as master server contains the set of maps that you, the NIS administrator, create and update as necessary. After the NIS network is set up, any changes to the maps must be made on the master server. Each NIS domain must have one, and only one, master server. The master server should be a system that can propagate NIS updates with minimal performance degradation.

In addition to the master server, you can create backup servers, called NIS slave servers, to take some of the load off the master server and to substitute for the master server if it goes down. If you create a NIS slave server, the maps on the master server are transferred to the slave server. A slave server has a complete copy of the master set of

NIS maps. If a change is made to a map on the master server, the updates are propagated among the slave servers. The existence of slave servers lets the system administrator evenly distribute the load that results from answering NIS requests. It also minimizes the impact of a server becoming unavailable.

Typically, all the hosts in the network, including the master and slave servers, are NIS clients. If a process on a NIS client requests configuration information, it calls NIS instead of looking in its local configuration files. For group and password information and mail aliases, the /etc/files might be consulted first, and then NIS might be consulted if the requested information is not found in the /etc/files.

Any system can be a NIS client, but only systems with disks should be NIS servers, whether master or slave. Servers are also clients of themselves.

As mentioned earlier, the set of maps shared by the servers and clients is called the NIS domain. The master copies of the maps are located on the NIS master server, in the directory /var/yp/*<domainname>*, in which *<domainname>* is the chosen name for your own domain. Under the *<domainname>* directory, each map is stored as two files: mapname.dir and mapname.pag. Each slave server has an identical directory containing the same set of maps.

When a client starts up, it broadcasts a request for a server that serves its domain. Any server that has the set of maps for the client's domain, whether it's a master or a slave server, can answer the request. The client "binds" to the first server that answers its request, and that server then answers all its NIS queries.

A host cannot be the master server for more than one NIS domain. However, a master server for one domain might be a slave server for another domain. A host can be a slave server for multiple domains. A client belongs to only one domain.

## Determining How Many NIS Servers You Need

The following guidelines can be used to determine how many NIS servers you need in your domain:

- You should put a server on each subnetwork in your domain. When a client starts up, it broadcasts a message to find the nearest server. Solaris 8 does not require the server to be on the same subnet; however, earlier implementations of NIS historically required that a server exist on every subnet using NIS.
- In general, a server can serve about 30 NIS clients if the clients and servers run at the same speed. If the clients are faster than the servers, you need more servers. If the clients are slower than the servers, each server can serve 50 or more clients.

## Determining Which Hosts Will Be NIS Servers

Determine which systems on your network will be NIS servers, as follows:

- Choose servers that are reliable and highly available.
- Choose fast servers that are not used for CPU-intensive applications. Do not use gateways or terminal servers as NIS servers.
- Although it isn't a requirement, it's a good idea to distribute servers appropriately among client networks. In other words, each subnet should have enough servers to accommodate the clients on that subnet.

## Information Managed by NIS

As discussed, NIS stores information in a set of files called maps. Maps were designed to replace UNIX /etc files, as well as other configuration files.

NIS maps are multicolumn tables. One column is the key, and the other column is the information value related to the key. NIS finds information for a client by searching through the keys. Some information is stored in several maps because each map uses a different key. For example, the names and addresses of systems are stored in two maps: hosts.byname and hosts.byaddr. If a server has a system's name and needs to find its address, it looks in the hosts.byname map. If it has the address and needs to find the name, it looks in the hosts.byaddr map.

Maps for a domain are located in each server's /var/yp/<*domainname*> directory. For example, the maps that belong to the domain pyramid.com are located in each server's /var/yp/pyramid.com directory.

NOTE: Never `make` the maps on a slave server. Always run the `make` command on the master server.

A NIS makefile is stored in the /var/yp directory of the NIS server at installation time. If you run the `/usr/ccs/bin/make` command in that directory, `makedbm` creates or modifies the default NIS maps from the input files. For example, an input file might be /etc/hosts. By now, you should be familiar with the content of this file. Issue the following commands to create the NIS map files:

```
cd /var/yp
/usr/ccs/bin/make
```

Creating NIS maps is described in more detail in the later section "Configuring a NIS Master Server."

Solaris provides a default set of NIS maps. They are described in Table 18.2. You might want to use all or only some of these maps. NIS can also use whatever maps you create or add if you install other software products.

**TABLE 18.2**

**DEFAULT NIS MAPS**

| *Map Name* | *Corresponding NIS Admin File* | *Description* |
|---|---|---|
| `bootparams` | bootparams | This map contains the pathnames that clients need during startup: root, swap, and possibly others. |
| `ethers.byaddr` | ethers | This map contains system names and Ethernet addresses. The Ethernet address is the key in the map. |
| `ethers.byname` | ethers | This map contains system names and Ethernet addresses. The system name is the key. |
| `group.bygid` | group | This map contains group security information. The GID (group ID) is the key. |
| `group.byname` | group | This map contains group security information. The group name is the key. |
| `hosts.byaddr` | hosts | This map contains the system name and IP address. The IP address is the key. |
| `hosts.byname` | hosts | This map contains the system name and IP address. The system (host) name is the key. |
| `mail.aliases` | aliases | This map contains aliases and mail addresses. The alias is the key. |
| `mail.byaddr` | aliases | This map contains mail addresses and aliases. The mail address is the key. |
| `netgroup` | netgroup | This map contains the group name, user name, and system name. The group name is the key. |
| `netgroup.byhost` | netgroup | This map contains the group name, user name, and system name. The system name is the key. |
| `netgroup.byuser` | netgroup | This map contains the group name, user name, and system name. The user name is the key. |
| `netid.byname` | passwd | This map is used for UNIX-style hosts and group authentication. It contains the system name and mail address (including domain name). If a netid file is available, it is consulted, in addition to the data available through the other files. |

*continues*

**TABLE 18.2** *continued*

**DEFAULT NIS MAPS**

| *Map Name* | *Corresponding NIS Admin File* | *Description* |
|---|---|---|
| `netmasks.byaddr` | netmasks | This map contains the network masks to be used with IP subnetting. The address is the key. |
| `networks.byaddr` | networks | This map contains names of networks known to your system and their IP addresses. The address is the key. |
| `networks.byname` | networks | This map contains names of networks known to your system and their IP addresses. The name of the network is the key. |
| `passwd.adjunct.byname` | passwd and shadow | This map contains auditing shadow information and the hidden password information for C2 clients. |
| `passwd.byname` | passwd and shadow | This map contains password and shadow information. The user name is the key. |
| `passwd.byuid` | passwd and shadow | This map contains password and shadow information. The user ID is the key. |
| `protocols.byname` | protocols | This map contains the network protocols known to your network. The protocol is the key. |
| `protocols.bynumber` | protocols | This map contains the network protocols known to your network. The protocol number is the key. |
| `rpc.bynumber` | rpc | This map contains the program number and the name of Remote Procedure Calls (RPCs) known to your system. The program number is the key. |
| `services.byname` | services | This map lists Internet services known to your network. The key port or protocol is the key. |
| `services.byservice` | services | This map lists Internet services known to your network. The service name is the key. |
| ypservers | N/A | This map lists the NIS servers known to your network. It's a single column table with the system name as the key. |

The information in these files is put into NIS databases automatically when you create a NIS master server. Other system files can also be managed by NIS if you want to customize your configuration.

NIS makes updating network databases much simpler than with the /etc file system. You no longer have to change the administrative /etc files on every system each time you modify the network environment. For example, if you add a new system to a network running NIS, you only have to update the input file in the master server and run `/usr/ccs/bin/make`. This process automatically updates the hosts.byname and hosts.byaddr maps. These maps are then transferred to any slave servers and made available to all the domain's client systems and their programs.

Just as you use the `cat` command to display the contents of a text file, you can use the `ypcat` command to display the values in a map. Here is the basic `ypcat` syntax:

```
ypcat [-k] <mapname>
```

If a map is composed only of keys, as in the case of ypservers, use `ypcat -k` otherwise, `ypcat` prints blank lines.

In this case, `mapname` is the name of the map you want to examine.

You can use the `ypwhich` command to determine which server is the master of a particular map:

```
ypwhich -m <mapname>
```

In this case, `mapname` is the name of the map whose master you want to find. `ypwhich` responds by displaying the name of the master server.

These and other NIS commands are covered in the following sections.

# Planning Your NIS Domain

Before you configure systems as NIS servers or clients, you must plan the NIS domain. Each domain has a domain name, and each system sharing the common set of maps belongs to that domain.

## STEP BY STEP

### 18.1 Planning Your NIS Domain

Follow these steps to plan your domain:

1. Decide which systems will be in your NIS domain.
2. Choose a NIS domain name. An NIS domain name can be up to 256 characters long, although much shorter names are more practical. A good practice is to limit domain names to no more than 32 characters. Domain names are case-sensitive. For convenience, you can use your Internet domain name as the basis for your NIS domain name. For example, if your Internet domain name is pdesigninc.com, you can name your NIS domain `pdesigninc.com`.
3. Before a system can use NIS services, the correct NIS domain name, and system name must be set. This must be done on the NIS servers as well as the clients. A system's name is set by the system's /etc/nodename file, and the system's domain name is set by the system's /etc/defaultdomain file. These files are read at startup, and the contents are used by the `uname -s` and `domainname` commands, respectively. A sample /etc/nodename file would look like this:

   ```
   more /etc/nodename
   ```

   The system responds with this:

   ```
   sparcserver
   ```

   A sample /etc/defaultdomain file would look like this:

   ```
   more /etc/defaultdomain
   ```

   The system responds with this:

   ```
   pdesigninc.com
   ```

   You are now ready to configure your NIS master server.

## Configuring a NIS Master Server

Before configuring a NIS master server, be sure the NIS package is installed. The package names are SUNWypu and SUNWypr. Use the `pkginfo` command to check for these packages. Both packages are part of the standard Solaris 8 release. The daemons that support the NIS service are described in Table 18.3.

**TABLE 18.3**

**NIS DAEMONS**

| *Daemon* | *Function* |
|---|---|
| `ypserv` | This daemon is the NIS database lookup server. The `ypserv` daemon's primary function is to look up information in its local database of NIS maps. If the /var/yp/ypserv.log file exists when `ypserv` starts up, log information is written to it if error conditions arise. At least one `ypserv` daemon must be present on the network for the NIS service to function. |
| `ypbind` | This daemon is the NIS binding process that runs on all client systems that are set up to use NIS. The function of `ypbind` is to remember information that lets all NIS client processes on a node communicate with some NIS server process. |
| `ypxfr` | This daemon is the high-speed map transfer. `ypxfr` moves a NIS map in the default domain to the local host. It creates a temporary map in the directory /var/yp/ypdomain. |
| `rpc.yppasswdd` | This daemon handles password change requests from the `yppasswd` command. It changes a password entry in the passwd, shadow, and security/passwd.adjunct files. |
| `rpc.ypupdated` | This daemon updates NIS information. ypupdated consults the updaters file in the /var/yp directory to determine which NIS maps should be updated and how to change them. |

The commands that you use to manage the NIS service are shown in Table 18.4. I'll describe some of these commands in more detail later as I show examples of setting up NIS.

**TABLE 18.4**

## NIS Commands

| *Utility* | *Function* |
|---|---|
| make | This command updates NIS maps by reading the makefile (if run in the /var/yp directory). You can use make to update all maps based on the input files or to update individual maps. |
| makedbm | This command creates a dbm file for a NIS map. The `makedbm` command takes the infile and converts it to a pair of files in ndbm format. When you run `make` in the /var/yp directory, `makedbm` creates or modifies the default NIS maps from the input files. |
| ypcat | This command lists data in a NIS map. |
| ypinit | This command builds and installs a NIS database and initializes the NIS client's (and server's) ypservers list. `ypinit` is used to set up a NIS client system. You must be the superuser to run this command. |
| yppoll | This command gets a map order number from a server. The `yppoll` command asks a ypserv process what the order number is, and which host is the master NIS server for the named map. |
| yppush | This command propagates a new version of a NIS map from the NIS master server to NIS slave servers. |
| ypset | This command sets binding to a particular server. `ypset` is useful for binding a client node that is on a different broadcast network. |
| ypstart | This command is used to start NIS. After the host has been configured using the `ypinit` command, `ypstart` automatically determines the machine's NIS status and starts the appropriate daemons. |
| ypstop | This command is used to stop the NIS. |
| ypwhich | This command returns the name of the NIS server that supplies the NIS name services to a NIS client, or it returns the name of the master for a map. |

A NIS master server holds the source files for all the NIS maps in the domain. Any changes to the NIS maps must be made on the NIS master server. The NIS master server delivers information to NIS clients and supplies the NIS slave servers with up-to-date maps. Before the NIS master server is started, some of the NIS source files need to be created.

One of the primary uses of NIS is to manage user logins and host files in a large networked environment. In a large network of systems, with several hundred users, imagine trying to keep the /etc/hosts, /etc/passwd, and /etc/group files up-to-date. Without NIS, every time a new system is added or removed, the /etc/hosts file must be updated. It's important to keep your /etc/hosts files in sync on every system on the network. Furthermore, without NIS, if a user changes a password, that user must notify the system administrator that his or her password has changed. The system administrator must then be sure that all the /etc/shadow files are updated across the network. If they aren't, the user can't log in to another system using the new password.

The system administrator can manage the system configuration files, such as /etc/hosts and /etc/passwd, using NIS. With NIS, the system administrator sets up the /etc/hosts, /etc/passwd, and /etc/group files on one server. Rather than keeping a copy of the configuration file on each system, all systems look to this server for configuration information.

## Creating the Master passwd File

The first task in setting up a NIS master server is to prepare the source file for the passwd map. However, be careful with this source file. The source files can be located either in the /etc directory on the master server or in some other directory. Locating the source files in /etc is undesirable because the contents of the maps are then the same as the contents of the local files on the master server. This is a special problem for passwd and shadow files, because all users would have access to the master server maps and because the root password would be passed to all YP clients through the passwd map.

Sun recommends that for security reasons, and to prevent unauthorized root access, the files used to build the NIS password maps should not contain an entry for root. Therefore, the password maps should not be built from the files located in the master server's /etc directory. The password files used to build the passwd maps should have the root entry removed from them, and they should be located in a directory that can be protected from unauthorized access.

For this exercise, copy all the source files from the /etc directory into the /var/yp directory. Because the source files are located in a directory other than /etc, modify the makefile in /var/yp by changing the `DIR=/etc` line to `DIR=/var/yp`. Also, modify the PWDIR password macro in the makefile to refer to the directory in which the passwd and shadow files reside by changing the line `PWDIR=/etc` to `PWDIR=/var/yp`.

Now, to create the passwd source file, use a copy of the /etc/passwd file on the system that becomes the master NIS server. Create a passwd file that has all the logins in it. This file is used to create the NIS map.

**NOTE** NIS does not require that the passwd file be sorted in any particular way. Sorting the passwd file simply makes it easier to find duplicate entries.

## STEP BY STEP

### 18.2 Creating the Password Source File

1. Copy the /etc/passwd file from each host in your network to the /var/yp directory on the host that will be the master server. Name each copy /var/yp/passwd.<*hostname*>, in which <*hostname*> is the name of the host it came from.

2. Concatenate all the passwd files into a temporary passwd file, as follows:

```
cd /var/yp
cat passwd passwd.hostname1 passwd.hostname2 ... > \
passwd.temp
```

3. Issue the `sort` command to sort the temporary passwd file by user name, and then pipe it to the `uniq` command to remove duplicate entries:

```
sort -t : -k 1,1 /var/yp/passwd.temp | uniq > \
/var/yp/passwd.temp
```

4. Examine /var/yp/passwd.temp for duplicate user names that were not caught by the previous `uniq` command. This could happen if a user login occurs twice, but the lines are not exactly the same. If you find multiple entries for the same user, edit the file to remove redundant ones. Be sure each user in your network has a unique user name and UID (user ID).

5. Issue the following command to sort the temporary passwd file by UID:

```
sort -o /var/yp/passwd.temp -t: -k 3n,3 \
/var/yp/passwd.temp
```

6. Examine /var/yp/passwd.temp for duplicate UIDs once more. If you find multiple entries with the same UID, edit the file to change the UIDs so that no two users have the same UID.

7. Remove the root login from the /var/yp/passwd.temp file. If you notice that the root login occurs more than once, remove all entries.

8. After you have a complete passwd file with no duplicates, move /var/yp/passwd.temp (the sorted, edited file) to /var/yp/passwd. This file is used to generate the passwd map for your NIS domain. Remove all the /var/yp/passwd.*<hostname>* files from the master server.

## Creating the Master Group File

Just like creating a master /var/yp/passwd file, the next task is to prepare one master /var/yp/group file to be used to create a NIS map.

## STEP BY STEP

### 18.3 Creating the Master Group File

1. Copy the /etc/group file from each host in your NIS domain to the /var/yp directory on the host that will be the master server. Name each copy /var/yp/group.*<hostname>*, in which *<hostname>* is the name of the host it came from.

2. Concatenate all the group files, including the master server's group file, into a temporary group file:

```
cd /var/yp
cat group group.hostname1 group.hostname2 ... > \
group.temp
```

*continues*

*continued*

3. Issue the following command to sort the temporary group file by group name:

```
sort -o /var/yp/group.temp -t: -k1,1 \
/var/yp/group.temp
```

   NIS does not require that the group file be sorted in any particular way. Sorting the group file simply makes it easier to find duplicate entries.

4. Examine /var/yp/group.temp for duplicate group names. If a group name appears more than once, merge the groups that have the same name into one group, and remove the duplicate entries.

5. Issue the following command to sort the temporary group file by GID:

```
sort -o /var/yp/group.temp -t: -k 3n,3 \
/var/yp/group.temp
```

6. Examine /var/yp/group.temp for duplicate GIDs. If you find multiple entries with the same GID, edit the file to change the GIDs so that no two groups have the same GID.

7. Move /var/yp/group.temp (the sorted, edited file) to /var/yp/group. This file is used to generate the group map for your NIS domain.

8. Remove the /var/yp/group.<*hostname*> files from the master server.

## Creating the Master hosts File

Now create the master /etc/hosts file the same way you created the master /var/yp/passwd and /var/yp/group files.

# STEP BY STEP

## 18.4 Creating the Master Hosts File

1. Copy the /etc/hosts file from each host in your NIS domain to the /var/yp directory on the host that will be the master server. Name each copy /var/yp/hosts.<*hostname*>, in which <*hostname*> is the name of the host from which it came.

2. Concatenate all the host files, including the master server's host file, into a temporary hosts file, as follows:

```
cd /var/yp
cat hosts hosts.hostname1 hosts.hostname2 ... > \
hosts.temp
```

3. Issue the following command to sort the temporary hosts file so that duplicate IP addresses are on adjacent lines:

```
sort -o /var/yp/hosts.temp /var/yp/hosts.temp
```

4. Examine /var/yp/hosts.temp for duplicate IP addresses. If you need to map an IP address to multiple host names, include them as aliases in a single entry.

5. Issue the following command to sort the temporary hosts file by host name:

```
sort -o /var/yp/hosts.temp -b -k 2,2 \
/var/yp/hosts.temp
```

6. Examine /var/yp/hosts.temp for duplicate host names. A host name can be mapped to multiple IP addresses only if the IP addresses belong to different LAN cards on the same host. If a host name appears in multiple entries that are mapped to IP addresses on different hosts, remove all the entries but one.

7. Examine the /var/yp/hosts.temp file for duplicate aliases. No alias should appear in more than one entry.

8. Move /var/yp/hosts.temp (the sorted, edited file) to /var/yp/hosts. This file is used to generate the host's map for your NIS domain.

9. Remove the /var/yp/hosts.<*hostname*> files from the master server.

## Other Source Files

The following files can also be copied to the /var/yp directory to be used as source files for NIS maps, but first be sure that they reflect an up-to-date picture of your system environment:

- auto.home or auto_home
- auto.master or auto_master
- bootparams
- ethers
- netgroup
- netmasks
- networks
- protocols
- rpc
- services
- shadow

Unlike other source files, the /etc/mail/aliases file cannot be moved to another directory. This file must reside in the /etc/mail directory. Be sure that the /etc/mail/aliases source file is complete by verifying that it contains all the mail aliases that you want to have available throughout the domain.

## Preparing the Makefile

After checking the source files and copying them into the source file directory, you need to convert those source files into the ndbm format maps that the NIS service uses. This is done automatically for you by ypinit. I describe how to set up ypinit in the next section.

The ypinit script calls the program `make`, which uses the Makefile located in the /var/yp directory. A default Makefile is provided for you in this directory. It contains the commands needed to transform the source files into the desired ndbm format maps.

The function of the Makefile is to create the appropriate NIS maps for each of the databases listed under "all." After passing through `makedbm`, the data is collected in two files, mapname.dir and mapname.pag. Both files are located in the /var/yp/<domainname> directory on the master server.

The Makefile builds passwd maps from the /PWDIR/passwd, /PWDIR/shadow, and /PWDIR/security/passwd.adjunct files, as appropriate.

## Setting Up the Master Server with ypinit

The /usr/sbin/ypinit shell script sets up master and slave servers and clients to use NIS. It also initially runs `make` to create the maps on the master server.

---

## STEP BY STEP

### 18.5 Using ypinit to Set Up the Master Server

To use ypinit to build a fresh set of NIS maps on the master server, follow these steps:

1. Become root on the master server, and ensure that the name service receives its information from the /etc files, not from NIS, by typing the following:
   `cp /etc/nsswitch.files /etc/nsswitch.conf`
2. Edit the /etc/hosts file to add the name and IP address of each of the NIS servers.
3. To build new maps on the master server, type
   `/usr/sbin/ypinit -m`

   ypinit prompts you for a list of other systems to become NIS slave servers. Type the name of the server you are working on, along with the names of your NIS slave servers. Enter the server name and then press Enter. Do this for each server. Enter each server on a separate line. Press Ctrl+D when you're finished.
4. ypinit asks whether you want the procedure to terminate at the first nonfatal error or to continue despite nonfatal errors. Type `y`.

*continues*

*continued*

> **NOTE**
> A nonfatal error might be displayed if some of the map files are not present. These errors do not affect the functionality of NIS.

If you typed `y`, ypinit exits upon encountering the first problem; you can then fix the problem and restart ypinit. This procedure is recommended if you are running ypinit for the first time. If you prefer to continue, you can manually try to fix all the problems that might occur and then restart ypinit.

5. ypinit asks whether the existing files in the /var/yp/<*domainname*> directory can be destroyed.

   This message is displayed only if NIS was previously installed. You must answer `yes` to install the new version of NIS.

6. After ypinit has constructed the list of servers, it invokes `make`.

   The `make` command uses the instructions contained in the makefile located in /var/yp. It cleans any remaining comment lines from the files you designated and then runs `makedbm` on them, creating the appropriate maps and establishing the name of the master server for each map.

7. To enable NIS as the naming service, type
   `cp /etc/nsswitch.nis /etc/nsswitch.conf`

   This command replaces the current switch file with the default NIS-oriented one. You can edit this file as necessary. See the section "Name Service Switch" for information on the contents of this file.

Now that the master maps are created, you can start the NIS daemons on the master server.

## Starting and Stopping NIS on the Master Server

To start up the NIS service on the master server, you need to start `ypserv` on the server and run `ypbind`. The daemon `ypserv` answers information requests from clients after looking them up in the NIS maps. You can start up the NIS service on the server by running the

/usr/lib/netsvc/yp/ypstart script from the command line. After you configure the NIS master server by running ypinit, `ypstart` is automatically invoked to start up `ypserv` whenever the system is started up.

To stop the NIS service, run the `ypstop` command on the server as follows:

```
/usr/lib/netsvc/yp/ypstop
```

## Name Service Switch

The next step in setting up the NIS service is to set up the name service switch, which involves editing the /etc/nsswitch.conf file. The name service switch controls how a client workstation or application obtains network information. The name service switch is often simply referred to as "the switch." The switch determines which naming services an application uses to obtain naming information, and in what order. It is a file called nsswitch.conf, which is stored in each system's /etc directory.

Each workstation has a name service switch file in its /etc directory named nsswitch.conf. Also in every system's /etc directory, you'll find templates that can be used as the nsswitch.conf file which are described in Table 18.5. Whatever name service you choose, select the appropriate name service switch template, customize it, and rename it `nsswitch.conf`.

**TABLE 18.5**

**NAME SERVICE SWITCH TEMPLATE FILES**

| *Name* | *Description* |
|---|---|
| nsswitch.files | Use this template when local files in the /etc directory are to be used and no name service exists. |
| nsswitch.nis | Uses the NIS database as the primary source of all information except the passwd, group, automount, and aliases maps. These are directed to use the local /etc files first and then the NIS databases. |
| nsswitch.nisplus | Uses the NIS+ database as the primary source of all information except the passwd, group, automount, and aliases tables. These are directed to use the local /etc files first and then the NIS+ databases. |

*continues*

**TABLE 18.5** *continued*

**NAME SERVICE SWITCH TEMPLATE FILES**

| *Name* | *Description* |
|---|---|
| nsswitch.dns | Sets up the name service to search the local /etc files for all entries except the hosts entry. The hosts entry is directed to use DNS for lookup. |
| nsswitch.ldap | Uses LDAP as the primary source of all information except the passwd, group, automount, and aliases tables. These are directed to use the local /etc files first and then the LDAP databases. |

Look for a template file called /etc/nsswitch.nis that was installed when you loaded Solaris 8. This template file contains the default switch configurations used by the NIS service and local files. When the Solaris 8 release software is first installed, if you designate NIS as the default name service, the template file is copied to /etc/nsswitch.conf. If during software installation you select "files" as the default name service, /etc/nsswitch.conf is created from nsswitch.files, which looks like this:

```
#
# /etc/nsswitch.files:
#
# An example file that could be copied over to \
/etc/nsswitch.conf; it
# does not use any naming service.
#
# "hosts:" and "services:" in this file are used only if \
the
# /etc/netconfig file has a "-" for nametoaddr_libs of \
"inet" transports.

passwd:   files
group:    files
hosts:    files
networks:  files
protocols: files
rpc:     files
ethers:   files
netmasks:  files
bootparams: files
publickey: files
# At present there isn't a 'files' backend for netgroup; \
the system will
#  figure it out pretty quickly, and won't use netgroups at \
all.
netgroup:  files
automount: files
aliases:  files
services:  files
sendmailvars:  files
```

If you did not select NIS as your name service during software installation, you can move this file into place manually as follows:

```
cp /etc/nsswitch.nis /etc/nsswitch.conf
```

The default /etc/nsswitch.nis file looks like this:

```
#
# /etc/nsswitch.nis:
#
# An example file that could be copied over to /etc/nsswitch.conf; it
# uses NIS (YP) in conjunction with files.
#
# "hosts:" and "services:" in this file are used only if the
# /etc/netconfig file has a "-" for nametoaddr_libs of "inet" transports.

# the following two lines obviate the "+" entry in /etc/passwd and /etc/group.
passwd:   files nis
group:   files nis

# consult /etc "files" only if nis is down.
hosts:   xfn nis [NOTFOUND=return] files
networks:  nis [NOTFOUND=return] files
protocols: nis [NOTFOUND=return] files
rpc:    nis [NOTFOUND=return] files
ethers:   nis [NOTFOUND=return] files
netmasks:  nis [NOTFOUND=return] files
bootparams: nis [NOTFOUND=return] files
publickey: nis [NOTFOUND=return] files

netgroup:  nis

automount: files nis
aliases:  files nis

# for efficient getservbyname() avoid nis
services:  files nis
sendmailvars:  files
```

Each line of the /etc/nsswitch.nis file identifies a particular type of network information, such as host, password, and group; followed by one or more sources, such as NIS+ tables, NIS maps, the DNS hosts table, or the local /etc. The source is where the client looks for the network information. For example, the system should first look for the passwd information in the /etc/passwd file. Then, if it does not find the login name there, it needs to query the NIS server.

The name service switch file lists many types of network information, called databases, with their name service sources for resolution, and the order in which the sources are to be searched. Table 18.6 lists valid sources that can be specified in this file.

**TABLE 18.6**

**DATABASE SOURCES**

| *Source* | *Description* |
|---|---|
| files | Refers to the client's local /etc files |
| nisplus | Refers to an NIS+ table |
| nis | Refers to an NIS table |
| User | Applies to the printers entry |
| dns | Applies only to the hosts entry |
| ldap | Refers to a dictionary information tree (DIT) |
| compat | Supports an old style "+" syntax that used to be used in the passwd and group information. |

As shown in the previous nsswitch.nis template file, the name service switch file can contain action values for several of the entries. When the naming service searches a specified source, such as local files or NIS, the source returns a status code. These status codes are described in Table 18.7.

**TABLE 18.7**

**NAME SERVICE SEARCH STATUS CODES**

| *Source* | *Description* |
|---|---|
| SUCCESS | Requested entry was found |
| UNAVAIL | Source was unavailable |
| NOTFOUND | Source contains no such entry |
| TRYAGAIN | Source returned "I am busy, try later" message |

For each status code, two actions are possible:

- Continue Try the next source
- Return Stop looking for an entry

Therefore, the default actions are

SUCCESS = return

UNAVAIL = continue

NOTFOUND = continue

TRYAGAIN = continue

For example, the following entry in the nsswitch.nis template:

```
hosts: nis [NOTFOUND=return] files
```

states that only the NIS hosts table in the NIS map is searched. If the NIS map has no entry for the host lookup, the system would not reference the local /etc/hosts file. Remove the `[NOTFOUND=return]` entry if you want to search the NIS hosts table and the local /etc/hosts file.

## Setting Up NIS Clients

As root, you must perform four tasks to set up a system as a NIS client:

- Remove user account information from the /etc/passwd and /etc/group files on the client.
- Set the domain name on the client.
- Set up the nsswitch.conf file on the client as described in the preceding section.
- Configure the client to use NIS, as explained next.

The first step is to remove from the /etc/passwd file all the user entries that are managed by the NIS server. Don't forget to update the /etc/shadow file. Also, remove entries from /etc/group, the /etc/hosts file, and any other network files that are now managed by NIS.

After setting up the nsswitch.conf file and setting your domain name as described in the section titled "Planning your NIS Domain" you configure each client system to use NIS by logging in as root and running the `ypinit` command as follows:

```
ypinit -c
```

You will be asked to identify the NIS servers from which the client can obtain name service information. Enter each server name, followed by a carriage return. You can list one master and as many slave servers as you want. The servers that you list can be located anywhere in the domain. It is a good practice to first list the servers closest (in network terms) to the system, followed by the more distant servers on the net because the client will attempt to bind to the first server on the list.

Test the NIS client by logging out and logging back in using a login name that is no longer in the /etc/passwd file and is managed by NIS. Test the host's map by pinging a system that is not identified in the local /etc/hosts file.

## Setting Up NIS Slave Servers

Before setting up the NIS slave server, you must first set it up as a NIS client. After you've verified that the NIS master server is functioning properly by testing the NIS service on this system, you can set up the system as a slave server. Your network can have one or more slave servers. Having slave servers ensures the continuity of NIS services if the master server is unavailable. Before actually running `ypinit` to create the slave servers, you should run the `domainname` command on each NIS slave to be sure the domain name is consistent with the master server. Remember, the domain name is set by adding the domain name to the /etc/defaultdomain file.

**STEP BY STEP**

### 18.6 Setting Up the NIS Slave Server

1. As root, edit the /etc/hosts file on the slave server to add the name and IP addresses of all the other NIS servers. This step is optional and for convenience only. At this point, I'm assuming you're not using DNS to manage hostnames (as will be explained later in this chapter). Step 3 prompts you for the hostname of the NIS server. You need an entry for this hostname in the local /etc/hosts file; otherwise, you need to specify the IP address of the NIS server.

2. Change directories to /var/yp on the slave server.

3. To initialize the slave server as a client, type the following:

   ```
   /usr/sbin/ypinit -c
   ```

   The `ypinit` command prompts you for a list of NIS servers. Enter the name of the local slave you are working on first, then the master server, followed by the other NIS slave servers in your domain, in order, from the physically closest to the furthest (in network terms).

4. Next, you need to determine if `ypbind` is already running. If it is running, you need to stop and restart it. Check to see if `ypbind` is running by typing:

   ```
   ps -ef | grep ypbind
   ```

   If a listing is displayed, `ypbind` is running. If `ypbind` is running, stop it by typing:

   ```
   /usr/lib/netsvc/yp/ypstop
   ```

5. Type the following to restart `ypbind`:

   ```
   /usr/lib/netsvc/yp/ypstart
   ```

6. To initialize this system as a slave, type the following:

   ```
   /usr/sbin/ypinit -s master
   ```

   In this example, *`master`* is the system name of the existing NIS master server.

   Repeat the procedures described in these steps for each system you want configured as a NIS slave server.

7. Now you can start daemons on the slave server and begin the NIS service. First, you must stop all existing yp processes by typing:

   ```
   /usr/lib/netsvc/yp/ypstop
   ```

   To start `ypserv` on the slave server and run `ypbind`, you can either restart the server or type the following:

   ```
   /usr/lib/netsvc/yp/ypstart
   ```

# NIS+

> **NOTE** NIS+ is not covered in depth on the System Administrator Certification exam, Part II. You are asked a few general overview questions regarding NIS+ that are covered in this book, but a working knowledge of NIS+ is not required until you take the S examination.

NIS+ is similar to NIS, but with more features. NIS+ is not an extension of NIS, but a new software program. It was designed to replace NIS.

NIS addresses the administrative requirements of small-to-medium client/server computing networks—those with fewer than a few hundred clients. Some sites with thousands of users find NIS adequate as well. NIS+ is designed for the now-prevalent larger networks, in which systems are spread across remote sites in various time zones, and in which clients number in the thousands. In addition, the information stored in networks today changes much more frequently, and NIS had to be updated to handle this environment. Last, systems today require a high level of security, and NIS+ addresses many security issues that NIS did not.

## Hierarchical Namespace

NIS+ lets you store information about workstation addresses, security, mail, Ethernet interfaces, and network services in central locations where all workstations on a network can access it. This configuration of network information is referred to as the NIS+ namespace.

The NIS+ namespace is the arrangement of information stored by NIS+. The namespace can be arranged in a variety of ways to fit an organization's needs. NIS+ can be arranged to manage large networks with more than one domain. Although the arrangement of a NIS+ namespace can vary from site to site, all sites use the same structural components: directories, tables, and groups. These components are called objects, and they can be arranged into a hierarchy that resembles a UNIX file system.

Directory objects form the skeleton of the namespace. When arranged in a treelike structure, they divide the namespace into separate parts, much like UNIX directories and subdirectories. The topmost directory in a namespace is the root directory. If a namespace is flat, it has only one directory—the root directory. The directory objects beneath the root directory are called directories.

A namespace can have several levels of directories. When identifying the relation of one directory to another, the directory beneath is called the child directory, and the directory above is the parent.

Although UNIX directories are designed to hold UNIX files, NIS+ directories are designed to hold NIS+ objects: other directories, tables, and groups. Any NIS+ directory that stores NIS+ groups is named groups_dir, and any directory that stores NIS+ system tables is named org_dir.

## NIS+ Tables

In a NIS+ environment, most namespace information is stored in NIS+ tables; think of them as being similar to NIS maps, which were described earlier. All NIS+ tables are stored in the domain's org_dir NIS+ directory object except the admin and groups tables, which are stored in the groups_dir directory object. The tables that come as default with the standard distribution of NIS+ are described in Table 18.8. Users and application developers frequently create NIS+-compatible tables for their own purposes.

**TABLE 18.8**

**STANDARD NIS+ TABLES**

| *NIS+ Table* | *Description* |
|---|---|
| auto_home | This table is an indirect automounter map that allows a NIS+ client to mount the home directory of any user in the domain. |
| auto_master | This table lists all the automounter maps in a domain. For direct maps, the auto_master table provides a map name. For indirect maps, it provides both a map name and the top directory of its mount point. |
| bootparams | This table stores configuration information about every diskless workstation in a domain. A diskless workstation is a workstation that is connected to a network but has no hard disk. |
| client_info | This optional internal NIS+ table is used to store server preferences for the domain in which it resides. |
| cred | This table stores credential information about NIS+ principals. Each domain has one cred table, which stores the credential information of client workstations that belong to that domain and the client users who can log into them. |

*continues*

**TABLE 18.8** *continued*

**STANDARD NIS+ TABLES**

| *NIS+ Table* | *Description* |
|---|---|
| ethers | This table stores information about the 48-bit Ethernet addresses of workstations in the domain. |
| group | This table stores information about UNIX user groups. |
| hosts | This table associates the names of all the workstations in a domain with their IP addresses. The workstations are usually NIS+ clients, but they don't have to be. |
| mail_aliases | This table lists the domain's mail aliases recognized by sendmail. |
| netgroup | This table defines network-wide groups used to check permissions for remote mounts, logins, and shells. The members of net groups used for remote mounts are workstations; for remote logins and shells, the members are users. |
| netmasks | This table contains the network masks used to implement standard internetwork subnetting. |
| networks | This table lists the networks of the Internet. It is normally created from the official network table maintained at the Network Information Control Center (NIC), although you might need to add your local networks to it. |
| passwd | This table contains information about the accounts of users in a domain. These users generally are NIS+ principals, but they don't have to be. However, remember that if they are NIS+ principals, their credentials are not stored here but in the domain's cred table. The passwd table usually grants read permission to the world (or to nobody). This table contains all logins except root, which is stored in the local /etc/passwd file. |
| protocols | This table lists the protocols used by the internetwork. |
| rpc | This table lists the names of RPC programs. |
| services | This table stores information about the services available on the internetwork. |
| timezone | This table lists the default time zone of every workstation in the domain. |

NIS+ tables can be manipulated with AdminTool. The NIS+ master server updates its objects immediately; however, it tries to batch several updates before it propagates them to its replicas (slaves).

## NIS+ Security

NIS+ security is enhanced in two ways. First, it can authenticate access to the service, so it can discriminate between access that is enabled to members of the community and other network entities. Second, it includes an authorization model that allows specific rights to be granted or denied based on this authentication.

## Authentication

Authentication is used to identify NIS+ principals. A NIS+ principal might be someone who is logged in to a client system as a regular user, someone who is logged in as superuser, or any process that runs with superuser permission on a NIS+ client system. Thus, a NIS+ principal can be a client user or a client workstation. Every time a principal (user or system) tries to access a NIS+ object, the user's identity and secure RPC password are confirmed and validated.

## Authorization

Authorization is used to specify access rights. Every time NIS+ principals try to access NIS+ objects, they are placed in one of four authorization classes, or categories:

- Owner: A single NIS+ principal
- Group: A collection of NIS+ principals
- World: All principals authenticated by NIS+
- Nobody: Unauthenticated principals

The NIS+ server finds out what access rights are assigned to that principal by that particular object. If the access rights match, the server answers the request. If they do not match, the server denies the request and returns an error message.

NIS+ authorization is the process of granting NIS+ principals access rights to a NIS+ object. Access rights are similar to file permissions. There are four types of access rights:

- Read: The principal can read the contents of the object.
- Modify: The principal can modify the contents of the object.

- Create: The principal can create new objects in a table or directory.
- Destroy: The principal can destroy objects in a table or directory.

Access rights are displayed as 16 characters. They can be displayed with the command `nisls -l` and changed with the command `nischmod`.

The NIS+ security system lets NIS+ administrators specify different read, modify, create, and destroy rights to NIS+ objects for each class. For example, a given class could be permitted to modify a particular column in the passwd table but not read that column, or a different class could be allowed to read some entries of a table but not others.

The implementation of the authorization scheme I just described is determined by the domain's level of security. A NIS+ server can operate at one of three security levels. They are summarized in Table 18.9.

**TABLE 18.9**

**NIS+ SECURITY LEVELS**

| *Security Level* | *Description* |
|---|---|
| 0 | Security level 0 is designed for testing and setting up the initial NIS+ namespace. A NIS+ server running at security level 0 grants any NIS+ principal full access rights to all NIS+ objects in the domain. Level 0 is for setup purposes only, and administrators should use it only for that purpose. Regular users should not use level 0 on networks in normal operation. |
| 1 | Security level 1 uses AUTH_SYS security. This level is not supported by NIS+, and it should not be used. |
| 2 | Security level 2 is the default. It is the highest level of security currently provided by NIS+, and is the default level assigned to a NIS server. It authenticates only requests that use Data Encryption Standard (DES) credentials (DES is described in the next section). Requests with no credentials are assigned to the nobody class, and have whatever access rights have been granted to that class. Requests that use invalid DES credentials are retried. After repeated failures to obtain a valid DES credential, requests with invalid credentials fail with an |

| *Security Level* | *Description* |
|---|---|
| | authentication error. (A credential might be invalid for a variety of reasons, such as the principal making the request is not keylogged in on that system, the clocks are out of sync, there is a key mismatch, and so forth.) |

# DES Authentication

DES (Data Encryption Standard) authentication uses the DES and public key cryptography to authenticate both users and systems in the network. DES is a standard encryption mechanism; public key cryptography is a cipher system that involves two keys: one public and one private.

The security of DES authentication is based on a sender's ability to encrypt the current time, which the receiver can then decrypt and check against its own clock. The timestamp is encrypted with DES. Two things are necessary for this scheme to work: The two agents must agree on the current time, and the sender and receiver must be using the same encryption key.

If a network runs a time synchronization program, the time on the client and the server is synchronized automatically. If a time synchronization program is not available, timestamps can be computed using the server's time instead of the network time. The client asks the server for the time before starting the RPC session, and then it computes the time difference between its own clock and the server's. This difference is used to offset the client's clock when computing timestamps. If the client and server clocks become out of sync to the point where the server begins to reject the client's requests, the DES authentication system resynchronizes with the server.

The client and server arrive at the same encryption key by generating a random conversation key and then using public key cryptography (an encryption scheme involving public and secret keys) to deduce a common key. The common key is a key that only the client and server are capable of deducing. The conversation key is used to encrypt and decrypt the client's timestamp; the common key is used to encrypt and decrypt the conversation key.

# DNS

DNS is the name service provided by the Internet for Transmission Control Protocol/Internet Protocol (TCP/IP) networks. It was developed so that workstations on the network could be identified by common names instead of Internet addresses. DNS is a program that converts domain names to their IP addresses. Without it, users would have to remember numbers instead of words to get around the Internet. The process of finding a computer's IP address by using its host name as an index is referred to as name-to-address resolution, or mapping.

The collection of networked systems that use DNS are referred to as the DNS namespace. The DNS namespace can be divided into a hierarchy of domains. A DNS domain is simply a group of systems. Two or more name servers support each domain: the primary, secondary, or cache-only server. Each domain must have one primary server and should have at least one secondary server to provide backup.

Each server implements DNS by running a daemon called `in.named`. On the client side, DNS is implemented through the resolver. The resolver's function is to resolve users' queries. The resolver is neither a daemon nor a single program; rather, it is a set of dynamic library routines used by applications that need to know system names. After the resolver is configured, a system can request DNS service from a name server. If a system's /etc/nsswitch.conf file specifies `hosts: dns`, the resolver libraries are automatically used. If the nsswitch.conf file specifies some other name service before DNS, such as NIS, that name service is consulted first for host information. Only if that name service does not find the host in question are the resolver libraries used.

For example, if the hosts line in the nsswitch.conf file specifies `hosts: nis dns`, the NIS name service is first searched for host information. If the information is not found in NIS, the DNS resolver is used. Because name services, such as NIS and NIS+, contain only information about hosts in their own network, the effect of a `hosts:nis dns` line in a switch file is to specify the use of NIS for local host information and DNS for information on remote hosts on the Internet. If the resolver queries a name server, the server returns either the requested information or a referral to another server.

Name-to-address mapping occurs if a program running on your local system needs to contact a remote computer. The program most likely knows the host name of the remote computer, but might not know how to locate it, particularly if the remote system is in another company, miles from your site. To obtain the remote system's address, the program requests assistance from the DNS software running on your local system, which is considered a DNS client.

Your system sends a request to a DNS name server, which maintains the distributed DNS database. The files in the DNS database bear little resemblance to the NIS+ host table or even to the local /etc/hosts file, although they maintain similar information: the host names, IP addresses, and other information about a particular group of computers. The name server uses the host name your system sent as part of its request to find or "resolve" the IP address of the remote system. It then returns this IP address to your local system if the host name is in its DNS database.

If the host name is not in that name server's DNS database, this indicates that the system is outside its authority, or, to use DNS terminology, outside the local administrative domain.

Because maintaining a central list of domain name/IP address correspondences would be impractical, the lists of domain names and IP addresses are distributed throughout the Internet in a hierarchy of authority. A DNS server that maps the domain names in your Internet requests or forwards them to other servers in the Internet. It is probably within close geographic proximity to your Internet access provider.

**NOTE** DNS is not covered in depth on the System Administrator Certification Exam, Part II. You need to know the definition of DNS, but a working knowledge of it is not required until you take the Sun Certified Network Administrator examination.

# Lightweight Directory Access Protocol (LDAP)

LDAP is the latest name lookup service to be added to Solaris. Specifically, LDAP is a directory service. A directory service is like a database, but contains more descriptive, attribute-based information. The information in a directory is generally read, not written.

LDAP is used as a resource locator, but is practical only in read-intensive environments where you do not need frequent updates. LDAP can be used to store the same information that is stored in NIS or NIS+. Use LDAP as a resource locator for an on-line phone directory to eliminate the need for a printed phone directory. This application is mainly read-intensive but authorized users will be able to update the contents to maintain its accuracy.

> **NOTE**
> LDAP is a protocol that email programs can use to look up contact information from a server. For instance, every email program has a personal address book, but how do you look up an address for someone who's never sent you email? Client programs can ask LDAP servers to look up entries in a variety of ways. The LDAP search operation allows some portion of the directory to be searched for entries that match some criteria specified by a search filter.

LDAP provides a hierarchical structure that more closely resembles the internal structure of an organization and can access multiple domains, similar to DNS or NIS+. NIS only provides a flat structure and is accessible by only one domain. In LDAP, directory entries are arranged in a hierarchical tree-like structure that reflects political, geographic, and/or organizational boundaries. Entries representing countries appear at the top of the tree. Below them are entries representing states or national organizations. Below them might be entries representing people, organizational units, printers, documents, or just about anything else you can think of.

LDAP has provisions for adding and deleting an entry from the directory, changing an existing entry, and changing the name of an entry. Most of the time, though, LDAP is used to search for information in the directory.

LDAP servers index all the data in their entries, and "filters" may be used to select just the person or group you want, and return just the information you want to see. Information can be requested from each entry that matches the criteria. For example, here's an LDAP search translated into plain English: "Search people located in Hudsonville whose name contains "Bill" that have an email address. Return their full name and email address."

Perhaps you want to search the entire directory subtree below the University of Michigan for people with the name Bill Calkins, retrieving the email address of each entry found. LDAP lets you do this easily. Or you might want to search the entries directly below the U.S. entry for organizations with the string "Pyramid" in their names, and that have a fax number. LDAP lets you do this.

Some directory services provide no protection, allowing anyone to see the information. LDAP provides a method for a client to authenticate, or prove its identity to a directory server, paving the way for rich access control to protect the information the server contains.

LDAP was designed at the University of Michigan to adapt a complex enterprise directory system, called X.500, to the modern Internet. A directory server runs on a host computer on the Internet, and various client programs that understand the protocol can log into the server and look up entries. X.500 is too complex to support on desktops and over the Internet, so LDAP was created to provide this service to general users.

## CHAPTER SUMMARY

This chapter covered all the name service topics that appear on the Certified Solaris Administrator examination for Solaris 8, Part II, which includes the local files in the /etc directory, NIS, NIS+, DNS, and LDAP.

This chapter described how to configure the master server, slave servers, and clients for the most commonly used name service, NIS. It also described the name service switch file used by the operating system for any network information lookups.

Of course, better understanding of the topics will come as you use the products described and become experienced over time. Many large networks that use a name service are heterogeneous, meaning that they have more than just Solaris systems connected to the network. You need to refer to the vendor's documentation for each particular system type to understand how each different operating system implements name services. You will see that most are similar in their implementation, with only subtle differences. As you gain experience and complete the Solaris Administrator Certification exams, your next goal should be to become certified as a Sun Network Administrator for Solaris. Certification in both fields is valuable for any UNIX system administrator.

The next chapter describes the Solstice AdminSuite product and how it can help you manage your network.

### KEY TERMS

- Name service
- NIS
- NIS+
- DNS
- LDAP
- Master NIS server
- Slave NIS server
- NIS client
- NIS map
- NIS source file
- Makefile
- Name service switch
- Hierarchical Namespace
- NIS+ objects
- NIS+ tables
- NIS+ Authentication
- NIS+ Authorization (know the 4 classes and the four types of access rights)
- NIS+ Security levels (know the 3 levels)
- DNS resolver

## APPLY YOUR KNOWLEDGE

# Exercises

For these exercises, you'll need two Solaris systems attached to a network. One system will be configured as the NIS master server, and the other will be the NIS client.

### 18.1 Setting Up the NIS Master Server

In this exercise, you'll go through the steps to set up your NIS Master server.

**Estimated Time**: 20 minutes

1. Log in as root.
2. Set your domain name if it is not already set:

   ```
   domainname <yourname>.com
   ```

   Populate the /etc/defaultdomain file with your domain name:

   ```
   domainname > /etc/defaultdomain
   ```

3. On the system that will become your master NIS server, create the master /etc/passwd, /etc/group, and /etc/hosts files. Follow the instructions described in this chapter to create these files.
4. Change entries for /etc to /var/yp in /var/yp/Makefile as follows:

   ```
   DIR = /etc
   PWDIR = /etc
   ```

   Change to:

   ```
   DIR = /var/yp
   PWDIR = /var/yp
   ```

5. Create the name service switch file by copying the NIS template file as follows:

   ```
   cp /etc/nsswitch.nis /etc/nsswitch.conf
   ```

6. Run the `ypinit` command as follows to set up this system as the NIS master:

   ```
   ypinit -m
   ```

   When asked for the next host to add as a NIS slave server, enter CTRL+D. For this exercise, we will not be adding an NIS slave server.

   Indicate you do not want `ypinit` to quit on non-fatal errors by typing `N` when asked.

   You'll know the process was successful when you get the message indicating that the current system was set up as a Master server without any errors.

7. Start up the NIS service on the master server by running:

   ```
   /usr/lib/netsvc/yp/ypstart
   ```

8. Verify that the NIS master server is up by typing:

   ```
   ypwhich -m
   ```

### 18.2 Setting Up the NIS Client

In this exercise, you'll go through the steps to set up your NIS client.

**Estimated time**: 10 minutes

1. Log in as root.
2. Set your domain name if it is not already set:

   ```
   domainname <yourname>.com
   ```

   Populate the /etc/defaultdomain file with your domain name:

   ```
   domainname > /etc/defaultdomain
   ```

3. Create the name service switch file by copying the NIS template file as follows:

   ```
   cp /etc/nsswitch.nis /etc/nsswitch.conf
   ```

4. Configure the client system to use NIS by running the `ypinit` command as follows:

   ```
   ypinit -c
   ```

## APPLY YOUR KNOWLEDGE

You will be asked to identify the NIS server from which the client can obtain name service information. Type the NIS master server name, followed by a carriage return.

When asked for the next host to add, press Ctrl+D.

5. Start the NIS daemons by executing the following script:

```
/usr/lib/netsvc/yp/ypstart
```

6. Verify that the NIS client is bound to the NIS master by typing:

```
ypwhich
```

The master server name should be displayed.

7. Test the NIS client by logging out and logging back in using a login name that is no longer in the local /etc/passwd file and is managed by NIS.

## Review Questions

1. Which of the following services stores information that users, systems, and applications must have to communicate across the network, in a central location?

   A. NIS service

   B. NFS service

   C. Automount

   D. AutoFS

2. Which of the following is **not** a Solaris name service?

   A. `DES`

   B. `/etc`

   C. `NIS+`

   D. `DNS`

3. Which of the following is the traditional UNIX way of maintaining information about hosts, users, passwords, groups, and automount maps?

   A. `DNS`

   B. `NIS`

   C. `NIS+`

   D. `/etc`

4. The NIS administration databases are called:

   A. Files

   B. Tables

   C. Maps

   D. Objects

5. The set of maps shared by the servers and clients is called:

   A. A table

   B. An object

   C. The NIS domain

   D. None of the above

6. When you add a new system to a network running NIS, you have to update the input file in the master server and run:

   A. `makedbm`

   B. `make`

   C. `yppush`

   D. `ypinit`

## APPLY YOUR KNOWLEDGE

7. Which of the following commands is used to display the values in a NIS map?

   A. `ypcat`

   B. `ypwhich`

   C. `ypserv`

   D. `ypbind`

8. Which of the following commands can be used to determine which server is the master of a particular map?

   A. `ypbind`

   B. `ypcat`

   C. `ypserv`

   D. `ypwhich`

9. Which of the following propagates a new version of a NIS map from the NIS master server to NIS slave servers?

   A. `ypinit`

   B. `yppush`

   C. `make`

   D. `yppoll`

10. Which of the following sets up master and slave servers and clients to use NIS?

    A. `makedbm`

    B. `make`

    C. `ypinit`

    D. `yppush`

11. Which of the following is the configuration file for the name service switch?

    A. nsswitch.conf

    B. resolve.conf

    C. /etc/netconfig

    D. nsswitch.nis

12. Each line of which of the following files identifies a particular type of network information, such as host, password, and group; followed by one or more sources, such as NIS+ tables, NIS maps, the DNS hosts table, or local /etc?

    A. resolve.conf

    B. nsswitch.conf

    C. /etc/netconfig

    D. nsswitch.nis

13. In the name service switch file, what does the following entry mean?

    `hosts: nis [NOTFOUND=return] files`

    A. Search the NIS map and then the local /etc/hosts file.

    B. Search only the NIS hosts table in the NIS map.

    C. Search only the local files, not the NIS files.

    D. Do not search the NIS hosts table or the local /etc/hosts file.

14. Which name service switch template files are found in Solaris 8?

    A. nsswitch.files

    B. nsswitch.nis+

## APPLY YOUR KNOWLEDGE

C. nsswitch.nisplus

D. nsswitch.fns

15. The components of a NIS+ namespace are called:

A. Tables

B. Objects

C. Maps

D. Directories

16. Which of the following is **not** one of the four authorization classes of NIS+?

A. All

B. Owner

C. Group

D. Nobody

17. What are the four types of NIS+ access rights?

A. `read, write, create, modify`

B. `read, write, execute, no access`

C. `read, write, delete, modify`

D. `read, modify, create, destroy`

18. How many security levels are there in NIS+?

A. 2

B. 1

C. 3

D. 4

19. Which security level is the default in NIS+?

A. 3

B. 0

C. 1

D. 2

20. Which of the following is the name service provided by the Internet for TCP/IP networks?

A. DNS

B. NIS

C. NIS+

D. None of the above

21. Each server implements DNS by running a daemon called

A. `named`

B. `in.named`

C. `nfsd`

D. `dnsd`

22. The primary task of DNS is to provide

A. security service

B. name-to-address resolution

C. name service

D. namespace services

23. Which of the following describes the difference between NIS authentication and authorization?

A. Authentication is checking if the information requester is a valid user on the network, and authorization determines whether the particular user is allowed to have or modify the information.

B. Authorization is checking if the information requester is a valid user on the network, and authentication determines whether the particular user is allowed to have or modify the information.

## APPLY YOUR KNOWLEDGE

24. Entries in which of the following files determine how a particular type of information is obtained (that is, which naming services (NIS, NIS+, DNS, etc.) can be used to obtain which types of information (host, password, group) and in which order the naming services should be queried)?

    A. /etc/nsswitch.conf

    B. /etc/resolve.conf

    C. /etc/nsswitch.nis

    D. /etc/nsswitch.nisplus

25. How many name services does Solaris 8 support?

    A. 3

    B. 4

    C. 5

    D. 6

26. Which of the following is the name service used by the Internet?

    A. DNS

    B. NIS

    C. NIS+

    D. DES

27. Which of the following commands is used to set up a NIS master server?

    A. `ypserver -m`

    B. `nisinit -m`

    C. `nisserver -m`

    D. `ypinit -m`

## Answers to Review Questions

1. **A.** `NIS` stores information about workstation names and addresses, users, the network itself, and network services.
2. **A.** `DES` is not a Solaris name service.
3. **D.** `/etc` files are the traditional UNIX way of maintaining information about hosts, users, passwords, groups, and automount maps.
4. **C.** The NIS administration databases are called maps.
5. **C.** The set of maps shared by the servers and clients is called the NIS domain.
6. **B.** To update the input file in the master server with a new system name, you'll execute the `/usr/ccs/bin/make` command.
7. **A.** Just as you use the `cat` command to display the contents of a text file, you can use the `ypcat` command to display the values in a map.
8. **D.** You can use the `ypwhich` command to determine which server is the master of a particular map.
9. **B.** The command `yppush` propagates a new version of a NIS map from the NIS master server to NIS slave servers.
10. **C.** The `ypinit` command builds and installs a NIS database and initializes the NIS client's (and server's) ypservers list.
11. **A.** In setting up the NIS service, set up the name service switch, which involves editing the /etc/`nsswitch.conf` file.

## APPLY YOUR KNOWLEDGE

12. **B**. Each line of the /etc/nsswitch.nis file identifies a particular type of network information, such as host, password, and group; followed by one or more sources, such as NIS+ tables, NIS maps, the DNS hosts table, or the local /etc.

13. **B**. The following entry in the nsswitch.nis template:

    hosts: nis [NOTFOUND=return] files

    states that `only the NIS hosts table in the NIS map` is searched.

14. **A., C.** The following template files are available: nsswitch.files, nsswitch.`nisplus`, nsswitch.nis, nsswitch.dns, and nsswitch.ldap

15. **B**. The arrangement of a NIS+ namespace can vary from site to site; all sites use the same structural components: directories, tables, and groups. These components are called objects, and they can be arranged into a hierarchy that resembles a UNIX file system.

16. **A**. The four authorization classes of NIS+ are Owner, Group, World, and Nobody.

17. **D**. Access rights are similar to file permissions. There are four types of access rights: `read`, `modify`, `create`, and `destroy`.

18. **C**. There are `three` security levels: 0, 1, and 2.

19. **D**. Security level 2 is the default. It is the highest level of security currently provided by NIS+.

20. **A**. DNS is the name service provided by the Internet for Transmission Control Protocol/Internet Protocol (TCP/IP) networks.

21. **B**. Each server implements DNS by running a daemon called `in.named`.

22. **B**. The process of finding a computer's IP address by using its host name as an index is referred to as name-to-address resolution, or mapping. The primary task of DNS is to provide name-to-address resolution.

23. **A**. Authentication is used to identify NIS+ principals. A NIS+ principal can be a client user or a client workstation. Every time a principal (user or system) tries to access a NIS+ object, the user's identity and secure RPC password are confirmed and validated. Authorization is used to specify access rights.

24. **A**. The /etc/nsswitch.conf file determines how a particular type of information is obtained and in which order the naming services should be queried.

25. **C**. There are five name services that Solaris 8 supports: /etc files, NIS, NIS+, DNS, and LDAP.

26. **A**. DNS is the name service used by the Internet.

27. **D**. To build new maps on the master server, type: `/usr/sbin/ypinit -m`.

## OBJECTIVES

The following test objectives are covered in this chapter:

**Understand the Solaris Management Console (SMC)**

- SMC is a Java tool to assist system administrators in the administration of their servers. It provides a centralized tool for important applications and services.

**Understand Solaris AdminSuite**

- Similar to the Admintool and SMC, Solaris AdminSuite provides GUI tools to assist the system administrator in setting up user accounts, host administration, file system administration, and configuring serial ports in a local or name service environment.

CHAPTER 19

# Solaris Management Console and Solaris AdminSuite

## Outline



## Study Strategies

The following strategies help you prepare for the exam:

- The best way for you to learn about SMC and AdminSuite is to use the products. On a Solaris system, make sure both products are installed. You might need to download and install AdminSuite as described in this chapter. Practice every step-by-step in this chapter. The examples walk you through every major feature.

- Be prepared to list and describe the major features of the SMC and AdminSuite.

## INTRODUCTION

Solaris Management Console (SMC) is a collection of GUI tools to make administering your servers easier. Based on Java technology, SMC allows you to manage administrative and network services on your servers from a remote location. For example, using SMC, the administrator can manage system processes, schedule and manage jobs, and manage disk partitions both locally and on remote systems. One of the main advantages of SMC is the concept of Role-Based Access Control (RBAC), which enables administrators to delegate specific administrative rights to users within a secure system.

Solaris AdminSuite is another collection of GUI tools and commands used to perform administrative tasks, such as managing users, groups, hosts, file systems, NFS resources, terminals, and modems. AdminSuite is similar to Admintool in that it helps the system administrator with tasks such as setting up serial ports, file systems, and user accounts. The main difference from Admintool is that Solaris AdminSuite allows you to perform these tasks either locally or over the network from one system. It also differs from SMC in that it does not use RBAC and does not provide tools for managing disks, scheduling jobs, or managing processes.

## SOLARIS MANAGEMENT CONSOLE

Solaris Management Console (SMC) uses GUI tools to make your servers easier to administer. Based on Java technology, Solaris Management Console 2.0 software simplifies the task of administering both local and remote Solaris servers by providing the following:

- An easy-to-navigate GUI-based console and a context-sensitive help panel that integrates online documentation
- Administration of multiple Solaris systems by a single console and a single login
- Role-Based Access Control that enables administrators to delegate specific administrative rights to users within a secure system

- An open and extensible environment that integrates Java applications, X.11 legacy applications, wizards, and HTML through the Solaris Management Console 2.0 Software Development Kit (SDK)

SMC enables administrators to run applications remotely and view the activity locally on all their servers. Central and remote management of all servers can be handled from any server on the network.

SMC has three components:

- The SMC Client, called SMC or Console
- The SMC Server
- The SMC Toolbox Editor

The SMC Console is a window that contains three panes, four bars, and two tabs.

The SMC Console relies on SMC Servers running on one or more computers to perform modifications and report data. Each of these Servers is a repository for code, which the Console can retrieve after the server has authenticated the user of the console.

The SMC uses the concept of a Toolbox to provide a view of various system administration tools or applications. The Toolbox is a hierarchical collection of folders, tools, legacy applications, and links to other toolboxes. The SMC comes complete with a default Toolbox, the "root" Toolbox called "Management Tools," which contains GUI tools to handle the following tasks:

- Manage processes. Suspend, resume, monitor, and control processes.
- Manage users. Set up and maintain user accounts, user templates, groups, mailing lists, administrative roles, and rights. Grant or deny rights to users and to administrative roles to control the specific applications each can work with and tasks each user can perform.
- Schedule jobs. Schedule, start, and manage jobs.
- Manage file system mounts and shares. View and manage mounts, shares, and usage information.
- Manage disks. Create and view disk partitions.

- Manage serial ports. Configure and manage existing serial ports.
- Manage Log Viewer. View application and command-line messages and manage log files.

The console can retrieve toolboxes from the server. These toolboxes are descriptions of organized collections of tools available on a server. After one of these toolboxes is loaded, the console displays it and the tools referenced in it.

The Solaris Management Console can also run in a terminal (non-graphical mode) for use over remote connections or non-interactively from a script.

## Using SMC

The Solaris Management Console is installed when you install the Solaris 8 operating environment version 1/01 or later, and is started at bootup by the /etc/init.d/init.wbem script. At any time, you can check the status of the SMC server by typing the following:

```
/etc/init.d/init.wbem status
```

If SMC is running, you get the following message:

```
SMC server version 2.0.0 running on port 898.
```

## STEP BY STEP

### 19.1 Using SMC

1. Start the Solaris Management Console by typing the following:

```
/usr/sbin/smc &
```

On a bitmapped display, you see SMC initializing with the screen shown in Figure 19.1.

*continues*

*continued*

**FIGURE 19.1**
Solaris Management Console splash screen.

After it is initialized, the Solaris Management Console window appears, as shown in Figure 19.2. You can start SMC as a non-root user, but some tools and applications might not load unless you log in as root or assume a role. This is described later in this section.

> **NOTE** The first time you start SMC, it might take several minutes to start up.

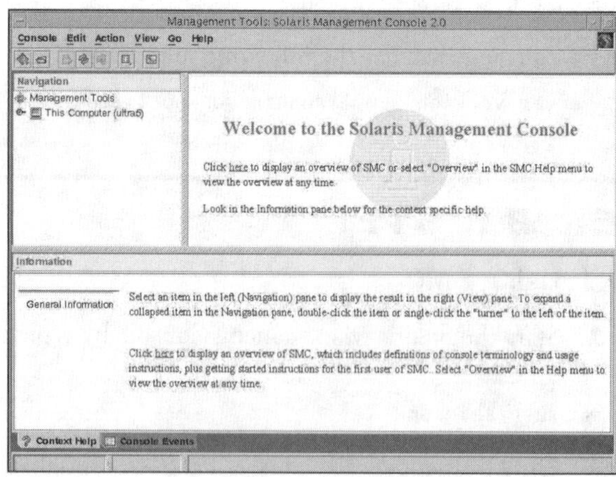


**FIGURE 19.2**
SMC window.

2. On the left side of the window is a navigation pane. When you expand an item in the navigation pane, details of that item are displayed in the right pane. For example, when I click This Computer (ultra5), the window panes change, as shown in Figure 19.3.

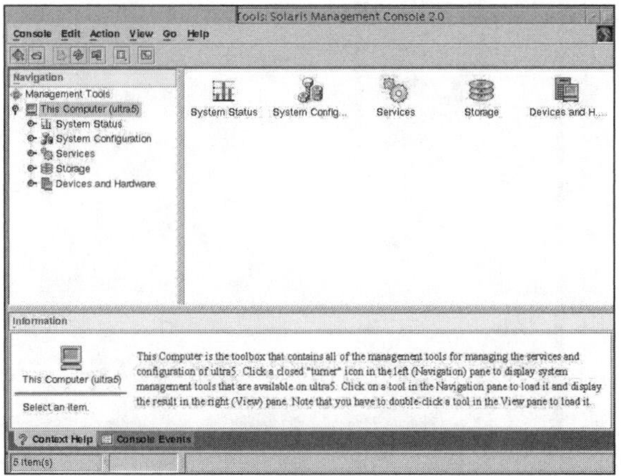


**FIGURE 19.3**
The Navigation pane display.

Items displayed in the navigation pane are applications that the SMC can manage. These applications have been registered as SMC applications for the current host.

The first time you log in as root and start up the SMC, you have the responsibility for setting up at least one account with the right of primary administrator, and for providing rights for other users. For instance, you can give another non-root user privileges to manage user accounts on the system. To set up a primary administrator account, you must assign roles to user account. This is referred to as Role-Based Access Control and is described in Chapter 20, "Role-Based Access Control." Roles are special accounts used to grant rights to administrators. To set up the primary user account, click Action in the toolbar located at the top of the SMC window when the pull-down menu appears, as shown in Figure 19.4. Then, click Add Administrative Role. The Add Administrative Role window appears, as shown in Figure 19.5.

*continues*

*continued*

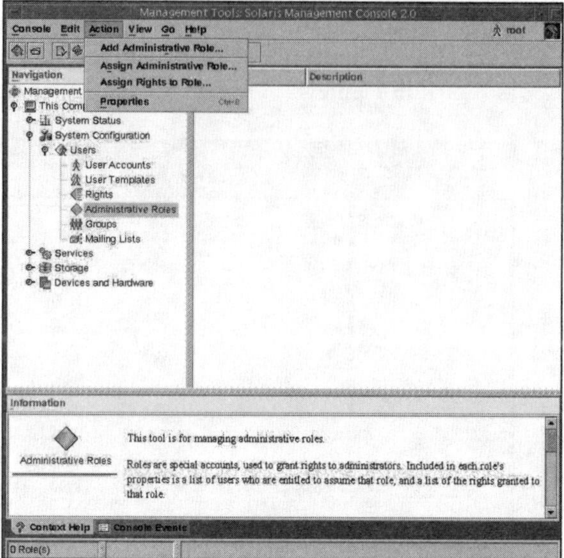


**FIGURE 19.4**
Action pull-down menu.

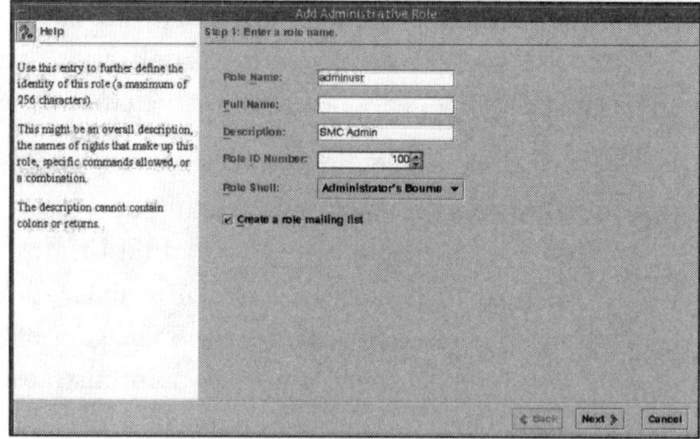


**FIGURE 19.5**
Add Administrative Role window.

**3.** Fill in the appropriate fields, as described in Table 19.1, and click the Next button when you are finished.

**TABLE 19.1**

**ADD ADMINISTRATIVE ROLE FIELDS**

| *Field* | *Description* |
|---|---|
| Role Name | The name the user uses to log into a specific role. This name must be unique, contain 2–32 letters and numbers, begin with a letter, have at least one lowercase letter, and be unique within a domain. |
| Full Name | A full descriptive name for this role. |
| Description | A description of the role, using a maximum of 256 characters. |
| Role ID Number | The identification number assigned to this role. It must be a whole number from 10–2147483647, and must be unique within a domain. |

4. You are asked to enter a password for the role, as shown in Figure 19.6.

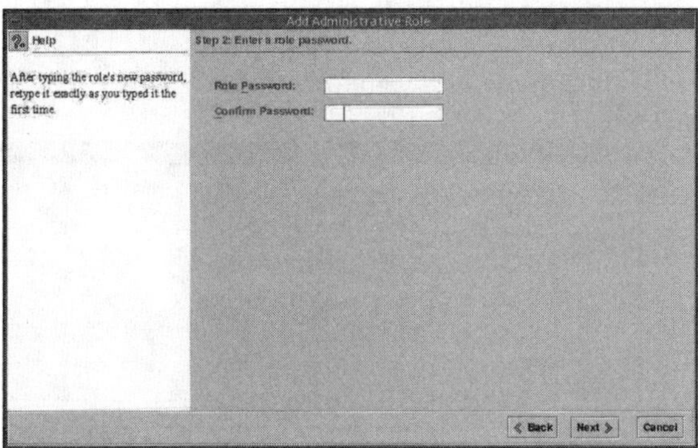


**FIGURE 19.6**
SMC Password window.

The password must consist of from 6–15 case-sensitive letters, numbers, and special characters. Only the first eight are actually used, but some users like longer passwords because they are easier to remember. Within the first six characters, at least two must be alphabetic, and at least one must be a number or special character. Click the Next button and the Select Role Rights window appears, as shown in Figure 19.7.

*continues*

*continued*

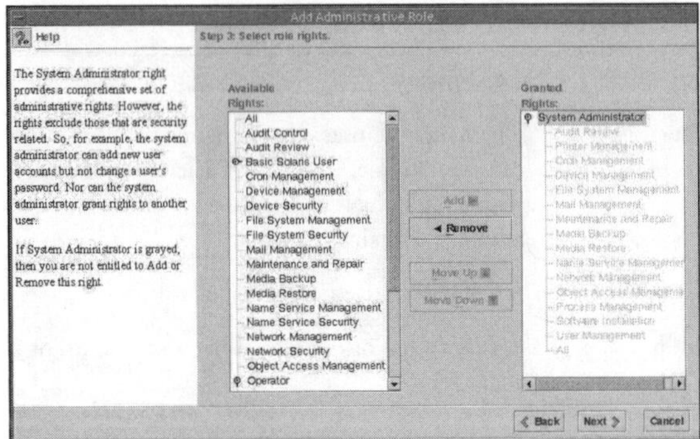


**FIGURE 19.7**
Select Role Rights window.

5. In the middle windowpane is a list of rights that can be assigned to the user. As you click each item, a description of that right appears in the Help pane. In the example shown in Figure 19.7, I added System Administrator rights, which automatically grant a list of rights such as User and Printer Management. Click the Next button when you are finished assigning rights. The Select a Home Directory window appears, as shown in Figure 19.8.

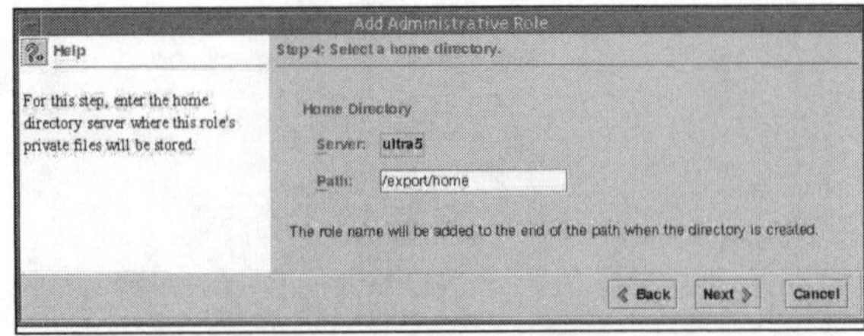


**FIGURE 19.8**
Select a Home Directory window.

6. Enter a home directory where this role's private files should be stored. In the example, I selected the default directory of /export/home. After you click the Next button, you are asked to assign the list of users to be permitted to assume this role. In the example shown in Figure 19.9, I entered a user named `bcalkins` and clicked the Add button.

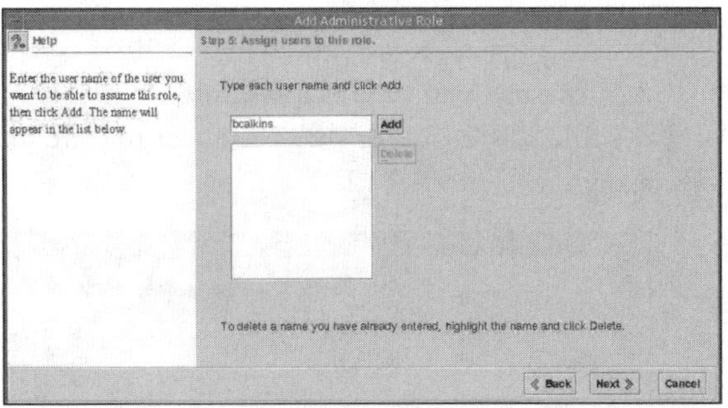


**FIGURE 19.9**
Assign Users to This Role window.

7. Click the Next button, and the summary window shown in Figure 19.10 appears.

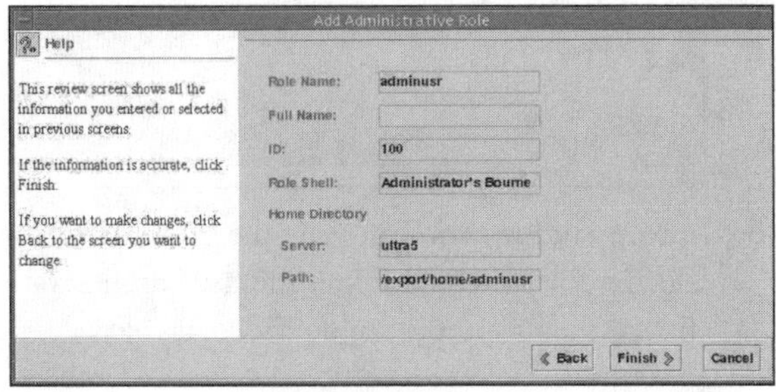


**FIGURE 19.10**
Add Administrative Role summary window.

8. Click the Finish button to return to the Solaris Management Console window. The new role is displayed, as shown in Figure 19.11.

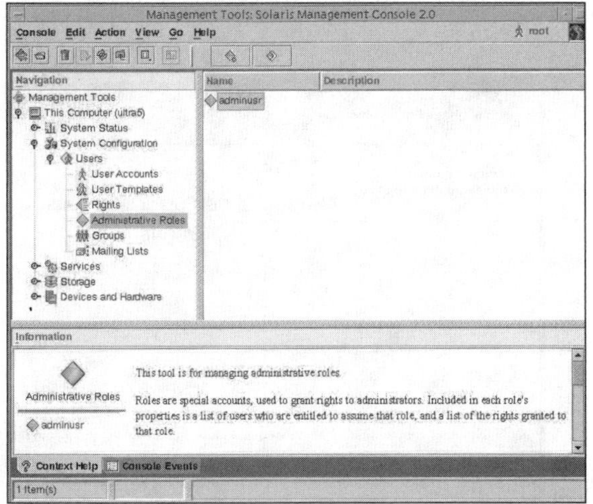


**FIGURE 19.11**
The New Role in the Solaris Management Console window.

*continues*

*continued*

At any time, you can click the role, such as adminusr, and the role properties for that particular role are displayed, as shown in Figure 19.12.

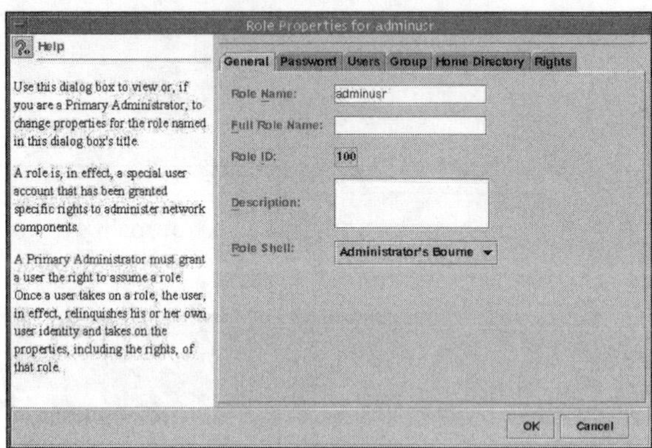


**FIGURE 19.12**
Role Properties window.

9. In this window, you can view the properties for the selected role. If you are the primary administrator, you can change the properties for a particular role.

   Now that a role has been defined, and users have been associated with that role, those users can start up SMC, assume their role, and use the functions that have been assigned to that role. For example, when bcalkins starts up SMC, the SMC window console window is displayed, as shown in Figure 19.13.

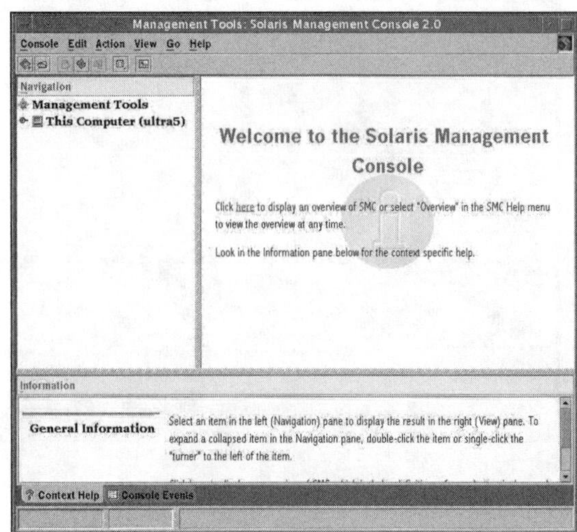


**FIGURE 19.13**
Solaris Management Console window.

10. When the user clicks on the This Computer icon in the navigation pane, and then under the System Configuration icon, The Users icon appears, as shown in Figure 19.14.

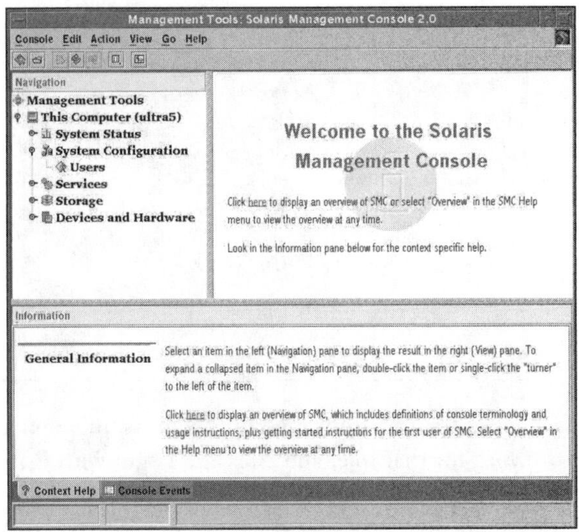


**FIGURE 19.14**
The Users icon in the Solaris Management Console window.

11. When bcalkins clicks on the Users icon, the Log In window shown in Figure 19.15 opens, prompting for a password.

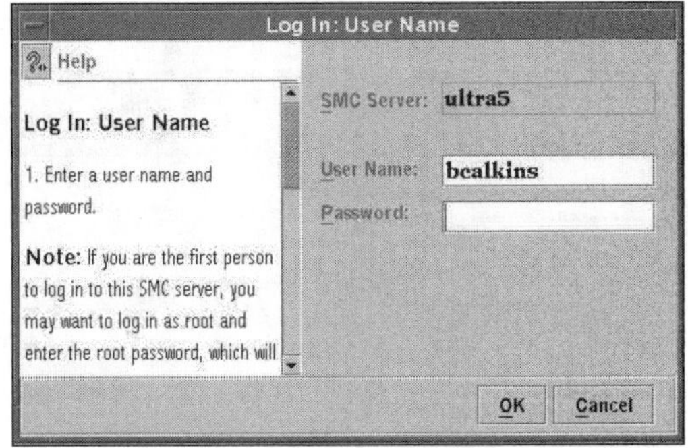


**FIGURE 19.15**
SMC Log In window.

*continues*

*continued*

**12.** bcalkins enters his password, clicks the OK button, and the Role Name selection window shown in Figure 19.16 appears.

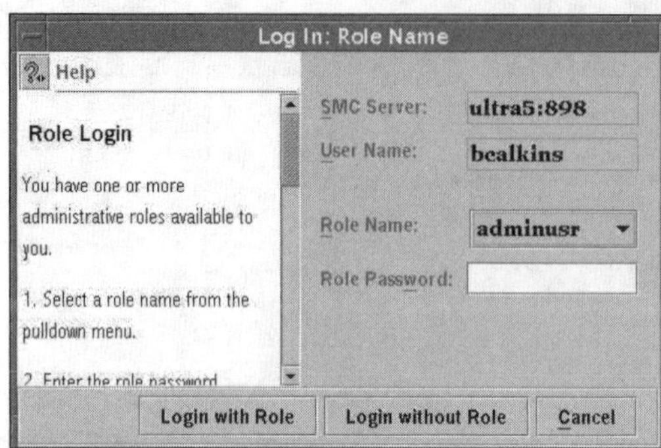


**FIGURE 19.16**
Role Name Selection window.

**13.** Select the role from the pull-down menu, enter the password for that role, and click the Login with Role button.

Note that you should use the password that the primary administrator entered when the role was created, not the user login password.

The Solaris Management Console window now displays icons for the functions to which you have been granted rights, as shown in Figure 19.17.

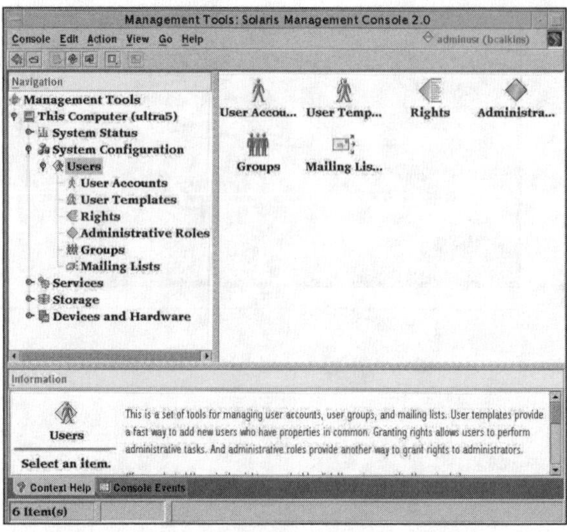


**FIGURE 19.17**
Icons Representing User Functions in the SMC Window.

For a more in-depth description of Role-Based Access Control (RBAC), see Chapter 20.

## Solaris AdminSuite

By now, you should be familiar with Admintool. I have described it several times as an easy-to-use graphical interface for user, printer, and serial device administration. Solaris AdminSuite is similar to Admintool in that it provides an easy-to-use GUI to facilitate routine server administration tasks. AdminSuite 3.0 provides an integrated suite of tools for administering your Solaris systems. Wizards and dialog boxes provide assistance and direction for managing user accounts, groups, mailing lists, computers/networks, file system mounts/shares, serial ports, log files, and name service domains. Each of these is described in detail later in this section.

Admintool is used to manage a stand-alone system, whereas AdminSuite addresses your needs for reducing the cost and complexity of managing distributed systems. AdminSuite can assist you in administering your network in the following ways:

- It offers local administration of Solaris workgroups by using network services, such as Network Information Service (NIS). This centralizes desktop administration and makes remote management painless.
- It automates routine administrative tasks, such as host setup, printer setup, and user setup.
- It provides easy-to-use system administration tools consisting of an extensive GUI to facilitate centralized setup and maintenance of the network environment. Administration is done without requiring root privileges, making centralized administration a reality.

As of this writing, AdminSuite 3.0.1 was not available with the Solaris 8 Operating Environment software, but it can be downloaded free of charge from `www.sun.com/bigadmin/content/adminPack`.

## Using Solaris AdminSuite

Before AdminSuite can be started, you must first make sure that the AdminSuite server daemon is running. Do this by typing the following:

```
ps -ef |grep admin.server
```

If it's running, the system displays a message similar to the following:

```
root 2497   1  0 13:46:28 ? 0:05 \
/usr/java1.1/bin/sparc/native_threads/java \
-mx32m -Dadmin.server.properties=/et
```

The server daemon reads the management server properties file that was created when AdminSuite was installed to obtain its configuration information. The server daemon also initializes the security provider and creates instances of the common services, such as the logging service. After it is configured and initialized, the management server receives requests from AdminSuite 3.0 management clients. Each installed version of the AdminSuite server application has a single instance of the AdminSuite management server daemon process.

The AdminSuite 3.0 management server daemon process is automatically started when the server system boots up through /etc/init.d/admsvr3_0. This script is installed when the AdminSuite product is installed.

To start up AdminSuite, type the following:

```
/opt/SUNWseam/3_0/bin/admapp &
```

As AdminSuite initializes, you see the splash, as shown in Figure 19.18.

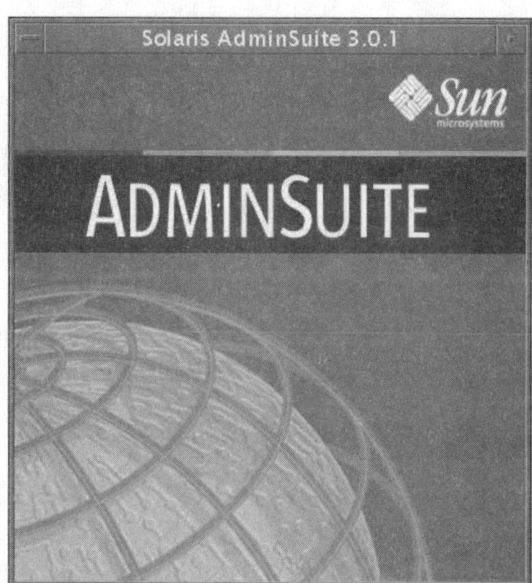


**FIGURE 19.18**
AdminSuite initialization screen.

When the AdminSuite Log On screen appears, as shown in Figure 19.19, enter the AdminSuite Primary Administrator login and password.

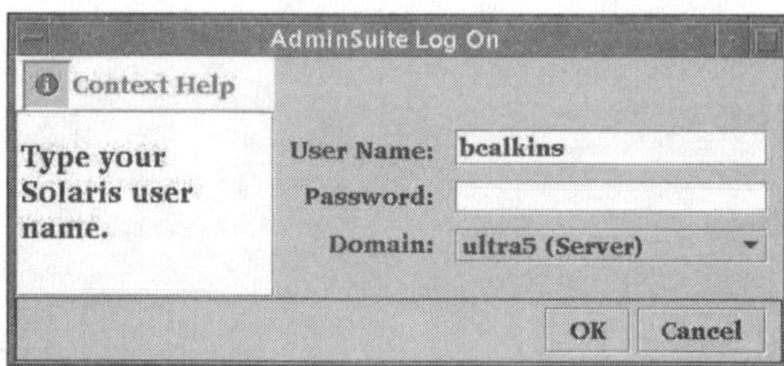


**FIGURE 19.19**
AdminSuite Log On window.

> **NOTE** The system administrator specified a Primary Administrator login when the AdminSuite software was installed.

In the example, *bcalkins* is the primary administrator. I entered the login and password and clicked the OK button to continue. After a few seconds, the Solaris AdminSuite Main window appears, as shown in Figure 19.20.

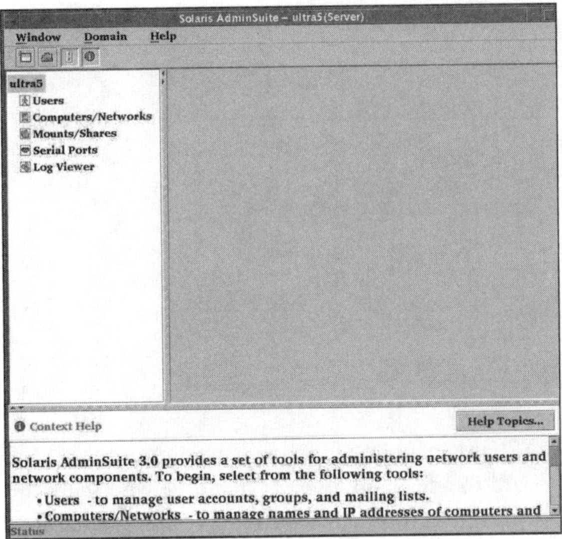


**FIGURE 19.20**
AdminSuite main window.

The AdminSuite Main window displays GUI tools that can be used to perform various administrative tasks, which include the following:

- Users
- Computers/Networks
- Mounts/Shares
- Serial Ports
- Log Viewer

Each of these is discussed in the following sections.

## Users

Click the Users icon to manage user accounts, groups, and mailing lists. Select one of two wizards for adding user accounts, as shown in Figure 19.21.

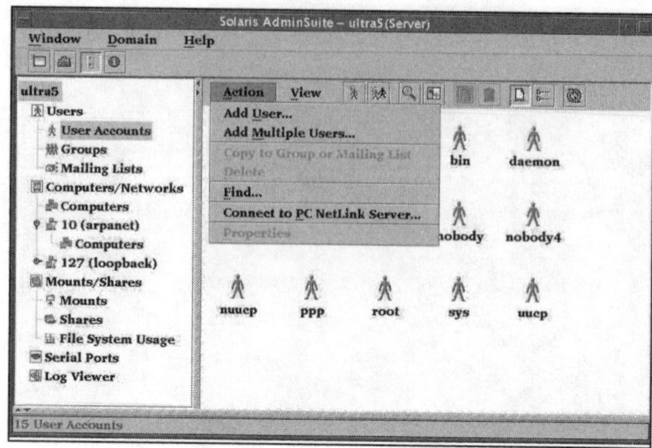

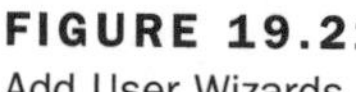
**FIGURE 19.21**
Add User Wizards.

Use the Add User Wizard to add one user at a time, or use the Add Multiple Users Wizard to add many users at one time who share the same properties. In addition, tools are available for managing groups and mailing lists.

Following are the files to be modified by the User Management tool:

- passwd. User account information file.
- shadow. Password information file.
- aliases. Email address information file.
- group. Group information file.
- auto_home. AutoFS map file (see Chapter 18, "Name Services").
- user_attr. User rights file that is associated with user roles (see RBAC in Chapter 21, "Jumpstart").

## Computers/Networks

The Computers/Networks tool lets you view, define, modify, delete, find, sort, and filter computers, networks, and subnetworks. Click the Computers' Network tool, and the window shown in Figure 19.22 is displayed.

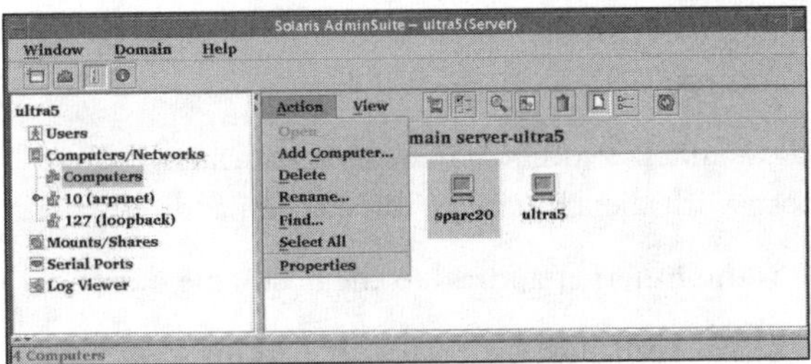


**FIGURE 19.22**
Computers/Networks window.

As shown in the pop-up menu on Figure 19.22, you can add a computer to the network.

Double-click the Computers icon, and all of the computers in your domain are displayed, as shown in Figure 19.23.

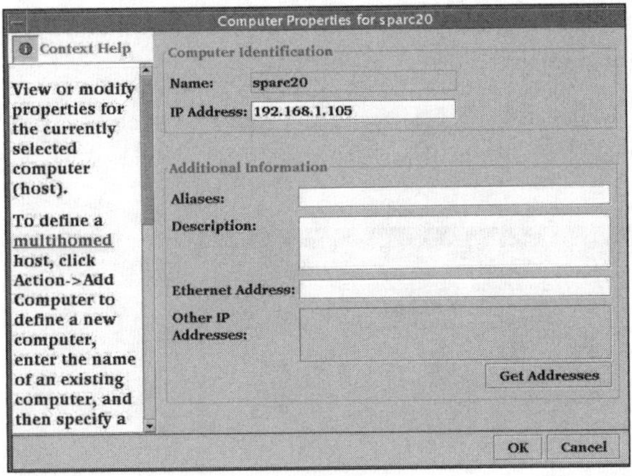


**FIGURE 19.23**
Computers in your domain.

Double-click the specific computer's icon, and the Computers Properties window appears, as shown in Figure 19.24.

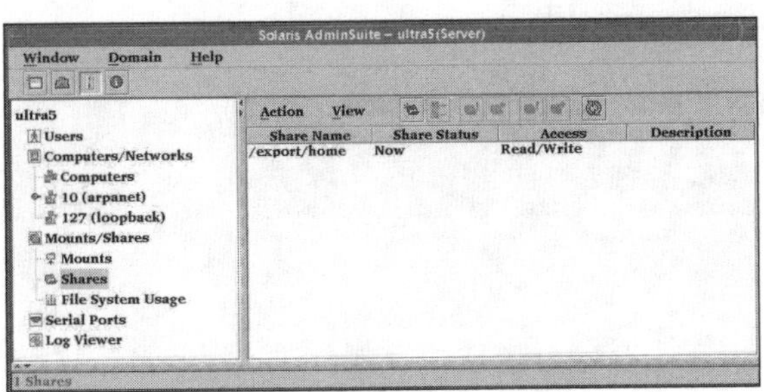


**FIGURE 19.24**
Computers Properties window.

**NOTE** Mount/Shares works only with single servers because it is not possible to define a share or a mount for an entire name service domain. You can create a share or a mount on a specific server.

Following are the files that can be modified by the Computers/Networks tool:

- hosts. The hosts file is a local database that associates the names of hosts with their Internet Protocol (IP) addresses.
- ethers. This is the Ethernet address to the hostname database.
- networks. The networks file is a local source of information regarding the networks that comprise the Internet.
- netmasks. The netmasks file contains network masks used to implement IP subnetting.

## Mount/Shares

Use this tool to view and manage file system mounts and shares within the current domain.

In Figure 19.25, I clicked on the Shares tool, and the system displayed all the local shares on this system.

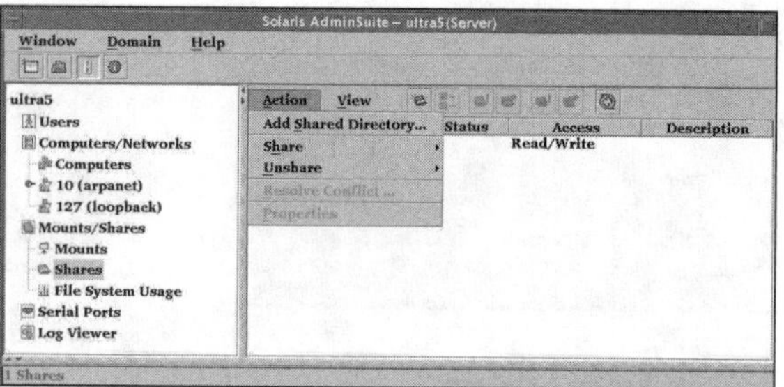


**FIGURE 19.25**
Mounts/Shares window.

By clicking the Action button, as shown in Figure 19.26, I can share or unshare additional directories.

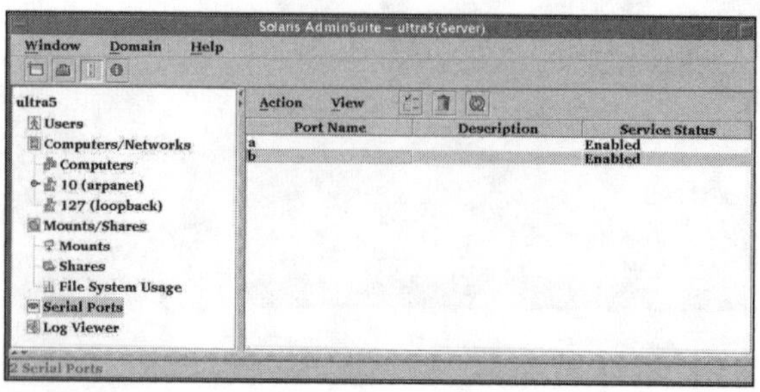


**FIGURE 19.26**
Mount/Shares Actions menu.

Following are the files to be modified by the Mount/Shares tool:

- /etc/mnttab. Mount information generated by the `mount` command.
- /etc/dfs/sharetab. Share information generated by the `share` command, which contains a table of local shared resources.
- /etc/nfssec.conf. Lists the authorization parameters defined on an NFS client computer.
- /etc/nsswitch.conf. Configuration file for the name service switch (see Chapter 18).
- /etc/vfstab. This file, which is read at boot time, describes defaults for each file system to be mounted.
- /etc/dfs/dfstab. This file is read at boot time and contains commands for sharing resources across a network.

## Serial Port Management

The Serial Ports tool is used to add and maintain port services for terminals and modems. Using Serial Port Manager to configure serial ports allows you to set up terminals and modems without having to create and edit the necessary files manually. It can display serial port information and facilitate port setup, modification, or deletion. It also provides templates for common terminal and modem configurations. The Serial Ports management tool is shown in Figure 19.27.

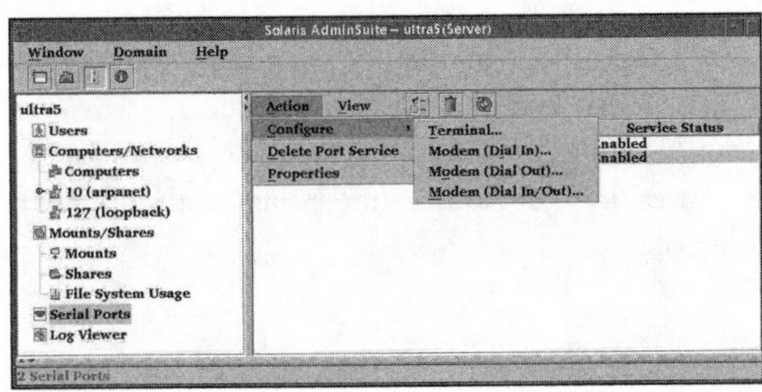


**FIGURE 19.27**
Serial Ports window.

By highlighting a serial port and clicking on the Action button located in the top toolbar, as shown in Figure 19.28, a pop-up menu appears with selections for configuring, deleting, or viewing the properties on a particular serial port.

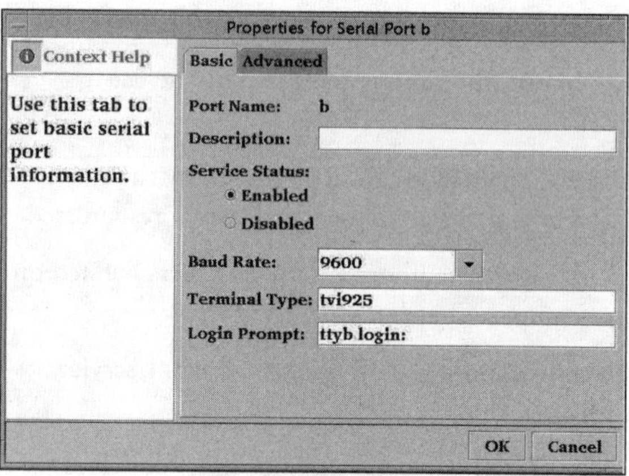


**FIGURE 19.28**
Serial Port Actions menu.

For example, I can highlight port B, click the Action button in the top toolbar, and select Properties from the pop-up menu. The Properties menu appears, and allows me to view or modify the properties for serial port B.

You can use Serial Port Manager to manage serial port information on the local system or on a remote system if you have the appropriate access privileges.

Following are the files to be modified by the Serial Port tool:

- /etc/saf/_sactab. Serial port monitor information.
- /etc/saf/zsmon/_pmtag. Serial port configuration information.

## Log Viewer

The Log Viewer tool lets you view and manage log files for AdminSuite tools and events. Log files are stored in the /var/opt/SUNWseam/3_0/log directory by default. Log viewer records and views entries only for AdminSuite events, and does not display all system log files.

## Chapter Summary

### KEY TERMS

- SMC
- AdminSuite
- SMC components
- SMC console
- SMC server
- Primary administrator
- AdminSuite management server

The Solaris Management Console provides a collection of tools to facilitate server administration. SMC provides the system administrator with easy-to-use, Java-based GUI tools for managing processes, users, local and NFS file systems, disk partitions, serial ports, and processes from anywhere. In addition, SMC provides the capability to delegate administrative tasks to other users without giving them access to the superuser account.

Solaris AdminSuite provides many of the same tools as SMC, but it does not provide the capability to delegate administrative tasks using RBAC. It also does not provide tools for job scheduling or disk and process management. The tools provided in AdminSuite do, however, provide an easy-to-use graphical interface for managing your systems from anywhere on the network. Using the tools and commands in the GUI is much faster than using numerous Solaris commands to perform the same tasks.

Spend some time becoming familiar with the tools available in SMC and AdminSuite. Whenever you are in the GUI, you can click the Help button to obtain more information.

I introduced Role-Based Access Control when I described SMC. The next chapter describes this topic in greater detail.

## APPLY YOUR KNOWLEDGE

# Exercises

### 19.1 Using AdminSuite

In this exercise, you use AdminSuite to add a new user account.

**Estimated Time**: 10 minutes

1. Log in as root, and start up AdminSuite as follows:

   ```
   /opt/SUNWseam/3_0/bin/admapp &
   ```

2. When the AdminSuite Log On screen appears, select the local system and fill in the empty fields:

   User Name: `root`

   Password: *`<root password>`*

3. From the AdminSuite main window, click the Users icon.
4. Click the User Accounts Icon in the right pane.
5. With the User Accounts icon still highlighted, click the Action button located in the toolbar in the right pane.
6. From the pull-down menu, click Add User.

   A wizard for setting up the new user account appears.

7. In the first window that appears, fill in the fields as follows:

   User Name: `admin1`

   Full Name: `Administrative Assistant`

8. Click the right arrow located at the bottom of the window to continue.
9. In the next window, accept the default User ID number that is assigned, and click the right arrow to continue.
10. In this window, click the radio button next to User Must Use This Password At First Login. Then, assign a password in the Password fields, and click the right arrow to continue.
11. In the next two windows, you are prompted for a Primary group and home directory for the new user account. Accept the defaults that are presented.
12. A summary window follows. Click Finish on the summary window, and the new user account is set up.

### 19.2 Using the Solaris Management Console

In this exercise, you add an administrative role in the Solaris Management Console and delegate administrative tasks to a non-root user.

**Estimated Time**: 15 minutes

1. For this exercise, you need an account for a non-root user named *admin1*. Create a new account for *admin1* with a group ID of 10.
2. As root, start up the Solaris Management Console as follows:

   ```
   smc &
   ```

3. Click This Computer in the navigation pane of the Console window. Then click the System Configuration tool and the Users tool. When the Log In window appears, enter `root` as the username, and enter the root password. Click the OK button to continue.

## APPLY YOUR KNOWLEDGE

4. A list of User Management tools appears in the right panel. Click the Administrative Roles tool.

5. Click Action in the toolbar located at the top of the SMC window. From the pull-down menu, click Add Administrative Role. The Add Administrative Role window appears. Fill in the fields with the following information:

   Role Name: `adminusr`

   Full Name: `Administrative Assistant`

   Description: `Admin assistant for performing general administrative tasks`

   Role ID number: *`<accept the default>`*

   Role Shell: `Administrator's Bourne`

6. The next screen asks you to enter a role password. Enter a password that is 6–15 characters long. Click the Next button to proceed.

7. The next window is where you assign the rights. In the middle pane, select System Administrator and click the Add button. Under the Granted Rights pane, it should display `System Administrator`. Click the Next button to continue.

8. Select a home directory, and click the Next button.

9. In the next window, titled Assign Users to This Role, enter `admin1` in the first field, and click the Add button. Click the Next button to continue.

10. When the summary window appears, click the Finish button. The process of assigning a role to a user is complete.

11. Log out and log back in as `admin1`. Start up SMC, and test the new user role. You should have general system administration privileges such as adding new users, scheduling jobs, and sharing file systems.

## Review Questions

1. Which three statements about Solaris Management Console are true?

   A. It provides a graphical means to manage meta devices.

   B. It simplifies administration by bringing the system administration tools together in one location.

   C. It allows management of all Solaris Management Console servers in one location.

   D. It allows a system administrator to delegate administrative tasks to non-root users without giving out the root password.

2. AdminSuite 3.0 is used to accomplish which of these tasks? Choose all that apply.

   A. Manage user accounts

   B. Manage shared resources

   C. Manage disks

   D. Manage processes

   E. Schedule processes

   F. Manage serial ports

   G. Set up AutoClients

## APPLY YOUR KNOWLEDGE

3. SMC is used to accomplish which of the following tasks? Choose all that apply.

   A. Manage user accounts

   B. Manage shared resources

   C. Manage disks

   D. Manage processes

   E. Schedule processes

   F. Manage serial ports

   G. Set up AutoClients

4. What are the three components of SMC?

   A. GUI tools

   B. SMC Client

   C. SMC Server

   D. Toolbox Editor

   E. RBAC

5. Which command is used to start up AdminSuite?

   A. It must be started from the Solaris Management Console.

   B. `admapp`.

   C. `solstice`.

   D. `adminsuite`.

   E. `smc`.

   F. `admsvr`.

6. What are the main differences, if any, between SMC and AdminSuite 3.0? Choose all that apply.

   A. Only SMC supports Role-Based Access Control.

   B. Only AdminSuite can manage user accounts.

   C. Only SMC can manage disks.

   D. Only AdminSuite can manage printers.

   E. SMC requires SMC Server to be running; AdminSuite does not require a server daemon.

## Answers to Review Questions

1. **B.**, **C.**, **D**. SMC simplifies administration by bringing the system administration tools together in one location. It also allows management of all Solaris Management Console servers in one location. Finally, it allows a system administrator to delegate administrative tasks to non-root users without giving out the root password.

2. **A.**, **B.**, **F**. AdminSuite 3.0 provides an integrated suite of tools for administering your Solaris systems. Wizards and dialog boxes provide assistance and direction for managing user accounts, groups, mailing lists, computers/networks, file system mounts/shares, serial ports, log files, and name service domains.

## APPLY YOUR KNOWLEDGE

3. **A.**, **B.**, **C.**, **D.**, **E.**, **F.** SMC allows you to manage administrative and network services on your servers from a remote location. Using SMC, the administrator can manage system processes, network resources, user accounts, serial ports, and disk partitions both locally and on remote systems.

4. **B.**, **C.**, **D.** SMC has three components:

    - The SMC Client, called SMC or Console
    - The SMC Server
    - The SMC Toolbox Editor

5. **B.** To start up AdminSuite, type the following:

    `/opt/SUNWseam/3_0/bin/admapp.`

6. **A.**, **C.** The main differences between SMC and AdminSuite 3.0 are that only SMC supports Role-Based Access Control, and only SMC can manage disks.

## OBJECTIVES

The following test objectives are covered in this chapter:

**Understand Role-Based Access Control**

- Traditional superuser-based systems grant full superuser powers to anyone who can become superuser. With Role-Based Access Control (RBAC) in the Solaris 8 operating environment, administrators can assign limited administrative capabilities to non-root users. This chapter describes RBAC with regard to Solaris security.

**Understand RBAC Support Databases**

- RBAC relies on four databases to provide users with access to privileged operations. This chapter describes the RBAC databases and configuration commands.

CHAPTER 20

# Role-Based Access Control (RBAC)

## Outline



## Study Strategies

The following strategies help you prepare for the exam:

- Know the terms that I've provided in the Key Terms section located at the end of this chapter. Be prepared to state the purpose of RBAC with regard to Solaris security. Also be prepared to select the statements that describe RBAC database features.
- Practice using RBAC to become familiar with its features. On a Solaris system, go through the step-by-step examples that are provided in this chapter.

# INTRODUCTION

Granting superuser access to non-root users has always been an issue in UNIX systems. In the past, you had to rely on a third-party package, sudo, to provide this functionality. The problem was that sudo was an unsupported piece of freeware that had to be downloaded from the Internet and installed onto your system. In extreme cases, the system administrator had to set the UID permission bit on the file so that a user could execute the command as root.

**CAUTION**

Most often, you will probably use RBAC to provide superuser access to administrative tasks within the system. Be careful to exercise caution to avoid creating security lapses by providing access to administrative functions by unauthorized users.

With Role-Based Access Control (RBAC) in the Solaris 8 operating environment, administrators can assign limited administrative capabilities to non-root users. This is achieved through three new features:

- Authorizations. User rights that grant access to a restricted function.
- Execution profiles. Bundling mechanisms for grouping authorizations and commands with special attributes; for example, user and group IDs or superuser ID.
- Roles. Special types of user accounts intended for performing a set of administrative tasks.

# USING RBAC

To better describe RBAC, it's easier to first describe how a system administrator would utilize RBAC to delegate an administrative task to a non-root user in a fictional setting at Acme Corp.

At a fictional company called Acme Corp., the system administrator is overwhelmed with tasks. He is going to delegate some of his responsibility to Neil, a user from the engineering department who helps out sometimes with system administration tasks.

The system administrator first needs to define which tasks he wants Neil to help out with. He has identified three tasks:

- Change user passwords, but not add or remove accounts
- Mount and share file systems
- Shut down the system

In RBAC, when we speak of delegating administrative tasks, it is referred to as a role account. A *role account* is a special type of user account that is intended for performing a set of administrative tasks. It is like a normal user account in most respects, except that users can gain access to it only through the `su` command after they have logged into the system with their normal login account. A role account is not accessible for normal logins, for example, through the CDE login window. From a role account, a user can access commands with special attributes, typically the root user IDs, which are not available to users in normal accounts.

At Acme Corp., the system administrator needs to define a role username for the tasks he wants to delegate. Let's use the role username "adminusr". After Neil logs in with his normal login name of `ncalkins`, he then needs to issue the `su` command and switch to adminusr whenever he wants to perform administrative tasks.

The easiest way to define a role account is by using the Solaris Management Console, as described in the previous chapter. Chapter 19, "Solaris Management Console and Solstice AdminSuite," provides all of the information you need to define this administrative role for a user. In this chapter, however, I'll describe how to create a role via the command line.

So far, we have determined that we want to name the role account adminusr. The system administrator creates the role account using the `roleadd` command. The `roleadd` command adds a role account to the /etc/passwd, etc/shadow, and /etc/user_attr files. The syntax for the `roleadd` command is as follows:

```
roleadd [-c comment] [-d dir] [-e expire] [-f inactive] \
[-g group] [-G group] [-m] [-k skel_dir] [-u uid] \
[-s shell] [-A authorization] <role username>
```

You'll notice that `roleadd` looks a great deal like the `useradd` command described in Chapter 5, "Setting Up User Accounts." Table 20.1 describes the options for the `roleadd` command.

**TABLE 20.1**

**roleadd OPTIONS**

| *Option* | *Description* |
|---|---|
| -c <*comment*> | Any text string to provide a brief description of the role. |
| -d <*dir*> | The home directory of the new role account. |
| -m | Creates the new role's home directory if it does not already exist. |
| -s <*shell*> | Specifies the user's shell on login. The default is /bin/sh. |
| -A <authorization> | Both of these options respectively assign authorizations and profiles to the role. |
| -P <profile> | Authorizations and profiles are described later in this section. |

The other options are the same options that were described for the `useradd` command, outlined in Chapter 5, "Setting Up Use Accounts."

When creating a role account with the `roleadd` command, you need to specify an authorization and profile to the role. An authorization is a user right that grants access to a restricted function. It is a unique string that identifies what is being authorized as well as who created the authorization.

Certain privileged programs check the authorizations to determine whether users can execute restricted functionality. Following are the predefined authorizations from the /etc/security/auth_attr file that apply to the tasks to be delegated:

```
solaris.admin.usermgr.pswd:::Change User Passwords::help=UserMgrPswd.html
solaris.system.shutdown:::Shutdown the System::help=SysShutdown.html
solaris.admin.fsmgr.write:::Mount/Share File Systems::help=FsMgrWrite.html
```

All authorizations are stored in the auth_attr database, so the system administrator needs to use one or more of the authorizations that are stored in that file. For the Acme Corp. example, the system administrator needs to specify the authorizations named, as shown here:

```
solaris.admin.usermgr.pswd
solaris.system.shutdown
solaris.admin.fsmgr.write
```

Therefore, the system administrator would issue the `roleadd` command as follows:

```
roleadd -m -d /export/home/adminusr -c "Admin Assistant" \
-A solaris.admin.usermgr.pswd,solaris.system.shutdown, \
solaris.admin.fsmgr.write adminusr
```

A role account named adminusr with the required directory structures has been created. The next step is to set the password for the adminusr role account by typing the following:

```
passwd adminusr
<enter the new password twice>
```

Now we need to set up Neil's account so he can access the new role account named adminusr. With the `usermod` command, we assign the role to the user account using the `-R` option as follows:

```
usermod -R adminusr neil
```

To access the administrative functions, Neil needs to first log in using his regular user account named `neil`. Neil can check which roles he has been granted by typing the following:

```
roles
```

The system responds with the roles that have been granted to the user account `neil` as follows:

```
adminusr
```

Neil then needs to `su` to the adminusr account by typing the following:

```
su adminusr
<enter the password for adminusr>
```

Now, Neil can modify user passwords, shut down the system, and mount and share file systems. Any other user trying to `su` to the adminusr account gets this message:

```
$ su adminusr
Password:
Roles can only be assumed by authorized users
su: Sorry
$
```

If later on, the system administrator wants to assign additional authorizations to the role account named adminusr, he would do so using the `rolemod` command. The `rolemod` command modifies a role's login information on the system. The syntax for the `rolemod` command is as follows:

```
rolemod [-u uid] [-o] [-g group] [-G group] [-d dir] [-m] \
[-s shell] [-c comment] [-l new_name] [-f inactive] \
[-e expire] [-A Authorization] [-P profile] <role account>
```

Options to the `rolemod` command are described in Table 20.2.

**TABLE 20.2**

**rolemod OPTIONS**

| *Option* | *Description* |
|---|---|
| `-A <authorization>` | One or more comma-separated authorizations as defined in the auth_attr database. This replaces any existing authorization setting. |
| `-c <comment>` | Specifies a comment string. *<comment>* can be any text string. It is generally a short description of the login, and is currently used as the field for the user's full name. This information is stored in the user's /etc/passwd entry. |
| `-d <dir>` | Specifies the new home directory of the role. It defaults to *<base_dir>*/login, in which *<base_dir>* is the base directory for new login home directories, and login is the new login. |
| `-e <expire>` | Specifies the expiration date for a role. After this date, no user can access this role. The *<expire>* option argument is a date entered using one of the date formats included in the template file /etc/datemsk. |
| | For example, you can enter 12/30/01 or December 30, 2001. A value of " " defeats the status of the expired date. |
| `-f <inactive>` | Specifies the maximum number of days allowed between uses of a login ID before that login ID is declared invalid. Normal values are positive integers. |
| `-g <group>` | Specifies an existing group's integer ID or character-string name. It redefines the role's primary group membership. |
| `-G <group>` | Specifies an existing group's integer "ID" "," or character string name. It redefines the role's supplementary group membership. Duplicates between groups with the `-g` and `-G` options are ignored. |

*continues*

**TABLE 20.2** *continued*

**rolemod Options**

| *Option* | *Description* |
|---|---|
| `-l <new_logname>` | Specifies the new login name for the role. The <*new_logname*> argument is a string no more than eight bytes long, consisting of characters from the set of alphabetic characters, numeric characters, period (.), underline (_), and hyphen (-). The first character should be alphabetic, and the field should contain at least one lowercase alphabetic character. A warning message is written if these restrictions are not met. A future Solaris release might refuse to accept login fields that do not meet these requirements. The <*new_logname*> argument must contain at least one character and must not contain a colon (:) or NEWLINE (\n). |
| `-m` | Moves the role's home directory to the new directory specified with the `-d` option. If the directory already exists, it must have permissions read/write/execute by group, in which group is the role's primary group. |
| `-o` | Allows the specified UID to be duplicated (non-unique). |
| `-P <profile>` | Replaces any existing profile setting. One or more comma-separated execution profiles are defined in the auth_attr database. |
| `-s <shell>` | Specifies the full pathname of the program that is used as the role's shell on login. The value of shell must be a valid executable file. |
| `-u <uid>` | Specifies a new UID for the role. It must be a non-negative decimal integer. The UID associated with the role's home directory is not modified with this option; a role does not have access to its home directory until the UID is manually reassigned using the `chown` command. |

To add the ability to purge log files, you need to add solaris.admin.logsvc.purge to the list of authorizations for adminusr. To do this, issue the `rolemod` command as follows:

```
rolemod -A \
solaris.admin.usermgr.pswd,solaris.system.shutdown, \
solaris.admin.fsmgr.write,solaris.admin.logsvc.purge \
adminusr
```

If you want to remove a role account, use the roledel command as follows:

```
roledel [-r] <role account name>
```

The -r option removes the role's home directory from the system. For example, to remove the adminusr role account, issue the following command:

```
roledel -r adminusr
```

The next section discusses each of the RBAC databases in detail, describing the entries made when I executed the roleadd and usermod commands.

> **NOTE** The rolemod command does not add to the existing authorizations; it replaces any existing authorization setting.

# RBAC Components

RBAC relies on the following four databases to provide users access to privileged operations:

- user_attr (extended user attributes database). Associates users and roles with authorizations and profiles.
- auth_attr (authorization attributes database). Defines authorizations and their attributes and identifies the associated help file.
- prof_attr (rights profile attributes database). Defines profiles, lists the profile's assigned authorizations, and identifies the associated help file.
- exec_attr (profile attributes database). Defines the privileged operations assigned to a profile.

These four databases interact with each other.

## Extended User Attributes (user_attr) Database

The /etc/user_attr database supplements the passwd and shadow databases. It contains extended user attributes, such as authorizations and profiles. It also allows roles to be assigned to a user. Following is a copy of the /etc/user_attr database:

```
more /etc/user_attr
# Copyright (c) 1999 by Sun Microsystems, Inc. All rights reserved.::::
#::::
# /etc/user_attr::::
#::::
# user attributes. see user_attr(4)::::
#::::
#pragma ident   "@(#)user_attr  1.2     99/07/14 SMI"::::
#::::
root::::type=normal;auths=solaris.*,solaris.grant;profiles=All
adminusr::::type=role;auths=solaris.admin.usermgr.pswd,/
solaris.system.shutdown,solaris.admin.fsmgr.write;profiles=All
neil::::type=normal;roles=adminusr
```

The following fields in the user_attr database are separated by colons:

```
user:qualifier:res1:res2:attr
```

Each field is described in Table 20.3.

**TABLE 20.3**

**USER_ATTR FIELDS**

| *Field Name* | *Description* |
|---|---|
| user | Describes the name of the user as specified in the passwd database. |
| qualifier | Reserved for future use. |
| res1 | Reserved for future use. |
| res2 | Reserved for future use. |
| attr | Contains an optional list of semicolon-separated (;) key-value pairs that describe the security attributes to be applied when the user runs commands. Four valid keys exist: auths, profiles, roles, and type. |

| *Field Name* | *Description* |
|---|---|
| auths | Specifies a comma-separated list of authorization names chosen from names defined in the auth_attr database. Authorization names can include the asterisk (*) character as a wildcard. For example, solaris.device.* means all of the Solaris device authorizations. |
| profiles | Contains an ordered, comma-separated list of profile names chosen from prof_attr. A profile determines which commands a user can execute and with which command attributes. At minimum, each user in user_attr should have the All profile, which makes all commands available but without attributes. The order of profiles is important; it works similarly to UNIX search paths. The first profile in the list that contains the command to be executed defines which (if any) attributes are to be applied to the command. I'll describe profiles further in the section titled "Authorizations (auth_attr) Database." |
| roles | Can be assigned to the user using a comma-separated list of role names. Note that roles are defined in the same user_attr database. They are indicated by setting the *type* value to role. Roles cannot be assigned to other roles. |
| type | Can be set to normal, if this account is for a normal user, or to role, if this account is for a role. A normal user assumes a role after he has logged in. |

In the previous section, I issued the following `roleadd` command to add a role named adminusr:

```
roleadd -m -d /export/home/adminusr -c "Admin Assistant" \
-A \ solaris.admin.usermgr.pswd,solaris.system.shutdown, \
solaris.admin.fsmgr.write adminusr
```

The `roleadd` command made the following entry in the user_attr database:

```
adminusr::::type=role;auths=solaris.admin.usermgr.pswd, \
solaris.system.shutdown, solaris.admin.fsmgr.write;profiles=All
```

I then issued the following `usermod` command to assign the new role to the user neil:

```
usermod -R useradmin neil
```

and I made the following entry to the user_attr database:

```
neil::::type=normal;roles=adminusr
```

## Authorizations (auth_attr) Database

An authorization is a user right that grants access to a restricted function. In the previous section, the system administrator wanted to delegate some of the system administrative tasks to Neil. Assigning authorizations to the role named adminusr did this. An *authorization* is a unique string that identifies what is being authorized as well as who created the authorization. Remember that we used the following authorizations to give Neil the ability to modify the user password, shut down the system, and mount and share file systems:

```
solaris.admin.usermgr.pswd
solaris.system.shutdown
solaris.admin.fsmgr.write
```

Certain privileged programs check the authorizations to determine whether users can execute restricted functionality. For example, the solaris.jobs.admin authorization is required for one user to edit another user's crontab file.

All authorizations are stored in the auth_attr database. If no name service is used, the database is located in a file named /etc/security/auth_attr. Authorizations can be assigned directly to users (or roles), in which case they are entered in the user_attr database. Authorizations can also be assigned to profiles, which in turn are assigned to users. They are described in the "Rights Profiles (prof_attr) Database" section.

The fields in the auth_attr database are separated by colons, as shown here:

```
authname:res1:res2:short_desc:long_desc:attr
```

Each field is described in Table 20.4.

**TABLE 20.4**

**AUTH_ATTR FIELDS**

| *Field Name* | *Description* |
|---|---|
| authname | A unique character string used to identify the authorization in the format *prefix.[suffix]*. Authorizations for the Solaris operating environment use solaris as a prefix. All other authorizations should use a prefix that begins with the reverse-order Internet domain name of the organization that creates the authorization (for example, com.xyzcompany). The suffix indicates what is being authorized, typically the functional area and operation.<br><br>When no suffix exists (that is, the authname consists of a prefix and functional area and ends with a period), the authname serves as a heading for use by applications in their GUIs rather than as an authorization. The authname solaris.printmgr. is an example of a heading.<br><br>When authname ends with the word *grant*, the authname serves as a grant authorization, and allows the user to delegate related authorizations (that is, authorizations with the same prefix and functional area) to other users. The authname solaris.printmgr.grant is an example of a grant authorization; it gives the user the right to delegate such authorizations as solaris.printmgr.admin and solaris.printmgr.nobanner to other users. |
| res1 | Reserved for future use. |
| res1 | Reserved for future use. |
| short_desc | A shortened name for the authorization suitable for displaying in user interfaces, such as in a scrolling list in a GUI. |
| long_desc | A long description. This field identifies the purpose of the authorization, the applications in which it is used, and the type of user interested in using it. The long description can be displayed in the help text of an application. |
| attr | An optional list of semicolon-separated (;) key-value pairs that describes the attributes of an authorization. Zero or more keys can be specified.<br><br>The keyword *help* identifies a help file in HTML. Help files can be accessed from the index.html file in the /usr/lib/help/auths/locale/Cdirectory. |

The following are some typical values found in the default auth_attr database:

```
solaris.admin.usermgr.pswd:::Change User Passwords::help=UserMgrPswd.html
solaris.system.shutdown:::Shutdown the System::help=SysShutdown.html
solaris.admin.fsmgr.write:::Mount/Share File Systems::help=FsMgrWrite.html
```

Look at the relationship between the auth_attr and the user_attr databases for the adminusr role we added earlier:

```
adminusr::::type=role;auths=solaris.admin.usermgr.pswd, \
solaris.system.shutdown, solaris.admin.fsmgr.write;profiles=All
```

Notice the authorization entries that are **bold**. These authorization entries came out of the auth_attr database, which are shown above. The `solaris.system.shutdown` authorization, which is defined in the auth_attr database, gives the role the right to shut down the system.

> **NOTE** Depending on the version of Solaris 8 you have installed, some of the profiles described in this section might not appear in the prof_attr file. For example, the 10/00 version does not include the Operator or Media Backup profile. If the profile doesn't appear, you might want to consider loading a more recent version of Solaris 8.

## Rights Profiles (prof_attr) Database

I've referred to rights profiles, or simply profiles, earlier in this chapter. Up to now, we assigned authorization rights to the role account. Defining a role account that has several authorizations can be tedious. In this case, it's better to define a profile, which is several authorizations bundled together under one name, called a *profile name*. The definition of the profile is stored in the prof_attr database. Following is an example of a profile named Operator, which is in the default prof_attr database. Again, if you are not using a name service, the prof_attr file is located in the /etc/security directory.

```
Operator:::Can perform simple administrative tasks:profiles=Printer Management,Media \
Backup,All;help=RtOperator.html
```

Several other profiles are defined in the prof_attr database. Colons separate the fields in the prof_attr database, as follows:

```
profname:res1:res2:desc:attr
```

The fields are defined in Table 20.5.

**TABLE 20.5**

**prof_attr FIELDS**

| *Field Name* | *Description* |
|---|---|
| profname | The name of the profile. Profile names are case sensitive. |
| res1 | A field reserved for future use. |
| res1 | A field reserved for future use. |
| desc | A long description. This field should explain the purpose of the profile, including what type of user would be interested in using it. The long description should be suitable for displaying in the help text of an application. |
| attr | An optional list of key-value pairs separated by semicolons (;) that describe the security attributes to apply to the object upon execution. Zero or more keys can be specified. The two valid keys are *help* and *auths*.<br>The keyword *help* identifies a help file in HTML. Help files can be accessed from the index.html file in the /usr/lib/help/auths/locale/C directory.<br>*auths* specifies a comma-separated list of authorization names chosen from those names defined in the auth_attr database. Authorization names can be specified using the asterisk (*) character as a wildcard. |

Perhaps the system administrator wants to create a new role account and delegate the task of printer management and backups. He could look through the user_attr file for each authorization and assign each one to the new role account using the `roleadd` command, or he could use the Operator profile currently defined in the prof_attr database, which looks like this:

```
Operator:::Can perform simple administrative tasks:profiles=Printer Management,Media \
Backup,All;help=RtOperator.html
```

The Operator profile consists of three other profiles:

- Printer Management
- Media Backup
- All

Let's look at each of these profiles as defined in the prof_attr database:

```
Printer Management:::Manage printers, daemons, spooling:help=RtPrntAdmin.html; \
auths=solaris.admin.printer.read,solaris.admin.printer modify,solaris.admin. printer.delete
Media Backup:::Backup files and file systems:help=RtMediaBkup.html
All:::Execute any command as the user or role:help=RtAll.html
```

Printer Management has the following authorizations assigned to it:

- solaris.admin.printer.read
- solaris.admin.printer.modify
- solaris.admin.printer.delete

When I look at these three authorizations in the auth_attr database, I see the following entries:

```
solaris.admin.printer.read:::View Printer Information::help=AuthPrinterRead.html
solaris.admin.printer.modify:::Update Printer Information::help=AuthPrinterModify.html
solaris.admin.printer.delete:::Delete Printer Information::help=AuthPrinterDelete.html
```

I now see that assigning the Printer Management profile is the same as assigning the three authorizations for viewing, updating, and deleting printer information.

The Media Backup profile provides authorization for backing up data, but not restoring data. The Media Backup profile does not have authorizations associated with it like the Print Management profile has. I'll describe how this profile is defined in the next section when I describe Execution Attributes.

The All profile grants the right for a role account to use any command when working in an administrator's shell. These shells can only execute commands that have been explicitly assigned to a role account through granted rights. We'll explore this concept further when I describe execution attributes in the next section.

To create a new role account named admin2 specifying the Operator profile, use the `roleadd` command with the `-P` option, as follows:

```
roleadd -m -d /export/home/admin2 -c "Admin Assistant" -P \
Operator admin2
```

The following entry is added to the user_attr database:

```
admin2::::type=role;profiles=Operator
```

At any time, users can check which profiles have been granted to them with the `profiles` command, as follows:

```
profiles
```

The system lists the profiles that have been granted to that particular user account.

## Execution Attributes (exec_attr) Database

An execution attribute associated with a profile is a command (with any special security attributes) that can be run by those users or roles to which the profile is assigned. For example, in the previous section, we looked at the profile named Media Backup in the prof_attr database. Although no authorizations were assigned to this profile, the Media Backup profile was defined in the exec_attr database as follows:

```
Media Backup:suser:cmd:::/usr/bin/mt:euid=0
Media Backup:suser:cmd:::/usr/sbin/tar:euid=0
Media Restore:suser:cmd:::/usr/sbin/tar:euid=0
Media Backup:suser:cmd:::/usr/lib/fs/ufs/ufsdump:euid=0;gid=sys
Media Restore:suser:cmd:::/usr/bin/cpio:euid=0
Media Restore:suser:cmd:::/usr/bin/mt:euid=0
Media Restore:suser:cmd:::/usr/lib/fs/ufs/ufsrestore:euid=0
```

The fields in the exec_attr database are as follows and are separated by colons:

```
name:policy:type:res1:res2:id:attr
```

The fields are defined in Table 20.5.

**TABLE 20.5**

**EXEC_ATTR FIELDS**

| *Field Name* | *Description* |
|---|---|
| Name | The name of the profile. Profile names are case-sensitive. |
| policy | The security policy associated with this entry. Currently, suser (the superuser policy model) is the only valid policy entry. |
| type | The type of entity whose attributes are specified. Currently, the only valid type is cmd (command). |
| res1 | This field is reserved for future use. |
| res2 | This field is reserved for future use. |
| id | A string identifying the entity; the asterisk wildcard can be used. Commands should have the full path or a path with a wildcard. To specify arguments, write a script with the arguments, and point the id to the script. |
| attr | An optional list of semicolon (;) separated key-value pairs that describe the security attributes to apply to the entity upon execution. Zero or more keys can be specified. The list of valid keywords depends on the policy being enforced. Four valid keys exist: euid, uid, egid, and gid.<br><br>euid and uid contain a single username or numeric user ID. Commands designated with euid run with the effective UID indicated, which is similar to setting the setuid bit on an executable file. Commands designated with uid run with both the real and effective UIDs.<br><br>egid and gid contain a single group name or numeric group ID. Commands designated with egid run with the effective GID indicated, which is similar to setting the setgid bit on an executable file. Commands designated with gid run with both the real and effective GIDs. |

Looking back to the Media Backup profile as defined in the exec_attr database, we see that the following commands have an effective UID of 0 (superuser):

```
/usr/bin/mt
/usr/sbin/tar
/usr/lib/fs/ufs/ufsdump
/usr/bin/cpio
/usr/lib/fs/ufs/ufsrestore
```

Therefore, any user that has been granted the Media Backup profile can execute the previous backup commands with an effective userID of 0 (superuser).

In the prof_attr database, we also saw that the Operator profile consisted of a profile named All. Again, All did not have authorizations associated with it. When we look at the exec_attr database for a definition of the All profile, we get this entry:

```
All:suser:cmd:::*:
```

Examining each field, we see that All is the profile name, the security policy is suser, and the type of entity is cmd. The attribute field has an *.

It's common to grant all users the All profile. The * is a wildcard entry that matches every command. In other words, the user has access to any command while working in the shell. Without the All profile, a user would have access to the privileged commands, but no access to normal commands such as `ls` and `cd`. Notice that no special process attributes are associated with the wildcard, so the effect is that all commands matching the wildcard run with the UID and GID of the current user (or role). Always assign the All profile last in the list of profiles. If it is listed first, no other rights are consulted when you look up command attributes.

## Chapter Summary

This chapter has taken a look at Role-Based Access Control for delegating limited administrative capabilities to non-root users. It described the features that are inherent with RBAC, which include the following:

- Roles. Special user accounts intended for performing a set of administrative tasks.
- Authorizations. Sometimes referred to as "rights" that grant access to an otherwise restricted function.
- Execution profiles. Bundling mechanisms for grouping authorizations and commands with special attributes. Execution profiles are similar to the concept of setting the UID and GID permission bits on executable files.

**KEY TERMS**

- RBAC
- Role account
- Authorization
- RBAC databases (know the specifics of all four)
- Rights profile

This chapter also described the four databases that interact with each other to provide users with access to privileged operations:

- user_attr. Associates users and roles with authorizations and execution profiles.
- auth_attr. Defines authorizations and their attributes, and identifies the associated help file.
- prof_attr. Defines profiles, lists the profile's assigned authorizations, and identifies the associated help file.
- exec_attr. Defines the privileged operations assigned to a profile.

Now that you know more about RBAC, I recommend that you go back to Chapter 20 to review the Solaris Management Console, which provides an easy-to-use GUI for creating and assigning roles and assigning rights to the roles. You will find it much easier to use than the command-line equivalents.

The next chapter examines setting up a server to support stand-alone installations using the JumpStart utility. Using JumpStart, clients on the network look to the server for the installation of their operating system. JumpStart can be used to automate the entire software installation process.

## APPLY YOUR KNOWLEDGE

## Exercises

### 20.1 Creating a User and a Role

**Estimated Time**: 20 minutes

To create a user and a role, perform the following steps:

1. Create the role named admin1, as shown here:

```
roleadd -u 2000 -g 10 -d /export/home/
admin1 -m admin1
passwd admin1
<assign a password to the role account>
```

2. Create a profile to allow the user to shut down a system.

   Edit the /etc/security/prof_attr file and enter the following line:

```
Shutdown:::Permit system shutdown:
```

   Save and exit the file.

3. Add the Shutdown and All profiles to the role as follows:

```
rolemod -P Shutdown,All admin1
```

4. Verify that the changes have been made to the user_attr database:

```
more /etc/user_attr
```

5. Create the user account and assign it access to the admin1 role:

```
useradd -u 3000 -g 10 -d /export/home/
trng1 -m -s /bin/ksh -R admin1 trng1
```

6. Assign a password to the new user account as follows:

```
passwd trng1
<assign a password>
```

7. Verify that the entry has been made to the passwd, shadow, and user_attr files as follows:

```
more /etc/passwd
more /etc/shadow
more /etc/user_attr
```

8. Assign commands to the Shutdown profile:

   Edit the /etc/security/exec_attr file and add the following line:

```
Shutdown:suser:cmd:::/usr/sbin/shutdown:uid=0
```

   Save and exit the file.

9. Test the new role and user account as follows:

   a. Log in as trng1.

   b. List the profiles that are granted to you by typing the following:

```
roles
```

   c. Use the su command to assume the role admin1:

```
su admin1
<enter the password for admin1>
```

   d. List the profiles that are granted to you by typing the following:

```
profiles
```

   e. Shut down the system:

```
/usr/sbin/shutdown -i 0 -g 0
```

## APPLY YOUR KNOWLEDGE

## Review Questions

1. Which two statements about the `roleadd` command are true?

   A. `roleadd` looks similar to the `useradd` command.

   B. `roleadd` uses the same default shell as the `useradd` command.

   C. The `-A` option associates an account with a profile.

   D. An account created with `roleadd` is the same as a normal login account.

2. Which component of RBAC associates users and roles with authorizations and profiles?

   A. `user_attr`

   B. `prof_attr`

   C. `auth_attr`

   D. `exec_attr`

3. Which component of RBAC defines the privileged operations assigned to a profile?

   A. `user_attr`

   B. `prof_attr`

   C. `auth_attr`

   D. `exec_attr`

4. In the execution attributes database, which of the following is not a valid value for the attr field?

   A. euid

   B. uid

   C. egid

   D. suid

5. After creating an RBAC role, you find that the only commands that can be executed within the role are the privileged commands that you have set up. Ordinary non-privileged commands are not available. The RBAC setup has a problem. What is the cause of this problem?

   A. The role is not associated with a correct profile.

   B. The access mechanism to the role is not initializing properly.

   C. The role's profile is not associated with the correct commands.

   D. The file identifying the privileged commands has missing entries.

   E. The role's profile is not associated with the correct authorizations.

6. Which three files does RBAC use?

   A. /etc/usr_attr

   B. /etc/user_attr

   C. /etc/security/exec_attr

   D. /etc/security/prof_attr

7. You want to enable a user to administer all user `cron` tables. This includes amending entries in any user's `crontab`. Given due care to system security, what should you do to enable the user to carry out this duty?

   A. Give the user the root password.

   B. Set the suid on the `crontab` command.

   C. Use RBAC to authorize the user to administer `cron` tables.

   D. Use RBAC to give the user an ID of root when executing the `crontab` command.

## APPLY YOUR KNOWLEDGE

E. Use the ACL mechanism to give the user RW access to each `crontab` table.

8. Which command(s) grants a user access to a role account?

   A. `roleadd`

   B. `rolemod`

   C. `useradd`

   D. `usermod`

9. Which option to the `rolemod` command appends an authorization to an exiting list of authorizations?

   A. `-A`

   B. `-P`

   C. `-a`

   D. `-o`

   E. None

10. In which files are profiles defined?

   A. `prof_attr`

   B. `user_attr`

   C. `exec_attr`

   D. `auth_attr`

11. What statements are true regarding the following line:

```
Media Restore:suser:cmd:::/usr/lib/fs/ufs/
ufsrestore:euid=0
```

   A. It represents a profile in the `exec_attr` database.

   B. Any role that has Media Restore as a profile is able to execute the `ufsrestore` command with an effective UID of root.

   C. It represents a profile in the `prof_attr` database.

   D. It represents a role definition in the `user_attr` database.

12. In RBAC, which of the following is a bundling mechanism for grouping authorizations and commands with special attributes?

   A. Profile

   B. Role

   C. Authorization

   D. Group

## Answers to Review Questions

1. **A.**, **B.** The `roleadd` command looks very similar to the `useradd` command, and it uses the same default shell as the `useradd` command.

2. **A.** `user_attr` (extended user attributes database) associates users and roles with authorizations and profiles.

3. **D.** `exec_attr` (profile attributes database) defines the privileged operations assigned to a profile.

4. **D.** Four valid keys exist: euid, uid, egid, and gid.

5. **A.** If a role is not associated with a correct profile, the only commands that can be executed within the role are the privileged commands that you have set up. Ordinary non-privileged commands are unavailable.

6. **B.**, **C.**, **D.** The three files that RBAC uses are /etc/user_attr, /etc/security/exec_attr, and /etc/security/prof_attr.

## APPLY YOUR KNOWLEDGE

7. **C.** To enable a user to administer all user `cron` tables, configure RBAC to authorize the user to administer `cron` tables.

8. **C.**, **D.** Use the `roleadd` command to create a role account. Then, with the `usermod` command, assign the role to the user account using the `-R` option.

9. **E.** The `rolemod` command does not add to the existing authorizations; it replaces any existing authorization setting.

10. **A.**, **C.** `prof_attr` (rights profile attributes database) defines profiles, lists the profile's assigned authorizations, and identifies the associated help file. `exec_attr` (profile attributes database) defines the privileged operations assigned to a profile.

11. **A.**, **B.** The following entry in the `exec_attr` database

    ```
    Media Restore:suser:cmd:::/usr/lib/fs/ufs/
    ufsrestore:euid=0
    ```

    represents a profile named Media Restore. Any role that has Media Restore as a profile can execute the `ufsrestore` command with an effective UID of root.

12. **A.** Execution profiles are bundling mechanisms for grouping authorizations and commands with special attributes.

## OBJECTIVES

The following test objective is covered in this chapter:

**Understand a JumpStart installation**

- This chapter will help you to understand all the components of a JumpStart network installation. You'll learn about setting up servers and clients to support a JumpStart installation including JumpStart-related commands, configuration files, and services.

CHAPTER 21

# JumpStart

## OUTLINE

## Study Strategies

The following strategies will help you prepare for the test:

- Practice the step-by-step examples that I provide in this chapter on a Solaris system. Be sure that you understand every step and can describe the process of setting up a boot server, an install server, and a configuration server. You should also be able to identify the events that occur during the JumpStart client boot sequence.
- Understand each of the commands I've described. Get familiar with all the options, especially those that I used in the examples. You'll see questions related to the add_install_client, add_to_install_server, and modify_install_server scripts.
- State the purpose of the sysidcfg file, the class file, and the rules file. Given the appropriate software source, be prepared to explain how to create a configuration server with a customized rules file and class files.
- State the purpose of the JumpStart server, and identify the main components of each type of server. Learn the terms I've listed in the "Key Terms" section of this chapter. Be prepared to provide a description of each term.

NOTE

You'll see the class file referred to as the profile in many Sun documents, scripts, and programs that relate to JumpStart. In the Sun System Administration training classes, however, it is referred to as class file. That's how I'll refer to it throughout this chapter. On the exams, it will also be referred to as a class file. The same is true for the configuration server. Sometimes Sun will refer to this server as a profile server.

# INTRODUCTION

There are four ways to install the Solaris software on a system: interactive installation (described in Chapter 3, "Installing the Solaris 8 Software"), custom JumpStart (described in this chapter), Web Start (described in Appendix A, "Web Start"), and installation over the network (also described in Chapter 3). To install the operating system (OS) on a server, you'll use the interactive method described in Chapter 15, "Installing a Server." This chapter describes how to install the Solaris OS on clients using the custom JumpStart method.

# OVERVIEW

There are two versions of JumpStart: JumpStart and custom JumpStart. JumpStart lets you automatically install the Solaris software on a SPARC-based system just by inserting the Solaris CD and powering on the system. You do not need to specify the `boot` command at the `ok` prompt. The software that is installed is specified by a default class file that is chosen based on the system's model and the size of its disks; you can't choose the software that is installed. For new SPARC systems shipped from Sun, this is the default method of installing the OS when you first power on the system.

The custom JumpStart method of installing the OS provides a way to install groups of similar systems automatically and identically. If you use the interactive method to install the OS, you must carry on a dialogue with the installation program by answering various questions. At a large site with several systems that are to be configured exactly the same, this task can be monotonous and time-consuming. In addition, there is no guarantee that each system will be set up the same. Custom JumpStart solves this problem by providing a method to create sets of configuration files beforehand so that the installation process can use them to configure each system.

Custom JumpStart requires up-front work, creating custom configuration files before the systems can be installed, but it's the most efficient way to centralize and automate the OS installation at large enterprise sites. Custom JumpStart can be set up to be completely "hands off."

The custom configuration files that need to be created for JumpStart are the rules and class files. Both of these files consist of several keywords and values, and are described in this chapter.

Table 21.1 lists the various commands that are introduced in this chapter.

**TABLE 21.1**

**JUMPSTART COMMANDS**

| *Command* | *Description* |
|---|---|
| `setup_install_server` | Sets up an install server to provide the OS to the client during a JumpStart installation. |
| `add_to_install_server` | A script that copies additional packages within a product tree on the Solaris 8 Software and Solaris 8 Languages CDs to the local disk on an existing install server. |
| `modify_install_server` | A script that adds the Solaris Web Start user interface software to the Solaris 8 Software and Solaris 8 Languages CD images on an existing install server, thus enabling users to use Solaris Web Start to boot a system and install the Solaris 8 software over a network. |
| `add_install_client` | A command that adds network installation information about a system to an install or boot server's /etc files so the system can install over the network. |
| `rm_install_client` | Removes JumpStart clients that were previously set up for network installation. |
| `check` | Validates the information in the rules file. |
| `pfinstall` | Performs a "dry run" installation to test the class file. |
| `patchadd -C` | A command to add patches to the files located in the miniroot (that is, Solaris_8/Tools/Boot) on an image of an installation CD image created by `setup_install_server`. This facility enables you to patch Solaris installation commands and other miniroot-specific commands. |

> **NOTE**
> At times, I describe the boot server, the install server, and the configuration server as if they are three separate systems. The reality, however, is that most companies have one system that performs all three functions. I'll describe this in more detail in the "Install Server" section later in this chapter.

There are three main components to JumpStart:

- Boot and Client Identification Services. These services are provided by a networked boot server, and provide the information that a JumpStart client needs to boot using the network.
- Installation Services. These are provided by a networked install server, which provides an image of the Solaris Operating Environment the JumpStart client uses as its source of data to install.
- Configuration Services. These are provided by a networked configuration server, and provides information that a JumpStart client uses to partition disks and create file systems, add or remove Solaris packages, and perform other configuration tasks.

Each of these components is described in this chapter. If any of these three components is improperly configured, the JumpStart clients can:

- Fail to boot.
- Fail to find a Solaris Operating Environment to load.
- Ask questions interactively for configuration.
- Fail to partition disks, create file systems, and load the operating environment.

## Preparing for a Custom JumpStart Installation

The first step in preparing a custom JumpStart installation is to decide how you want the systems at your site to be installed. Here are some questions that need to be answered before you begin:

- Will the installation be an initial installation or an upgrade?
- What applications will the system support?
- Who will use the system?
- How much swap space is required?

These questions will help you group the systems when you create the class file and rules files later in this chapter.

Additional concerns to be addressed include what software packages need to be installed and what size to make the disk partitions. After you answer these questions, group systems according to their configuration (as shown in the example of a custom JumpStart near the end of this chapter).

The next step in preparing a custom JumpStart installation is to create the configuration files that will be used during the installation: the rules.ok file (a validated rules file) and a class file for each group of systems. The rules.ok file is a file that should contain a rule for each group of systems you want to install. Each rule distinguishes a group of systems based on one or more system attributes. The rule links each group to a class file, which is a text file that defines how the Solaris software is to be installed on each system in the group. Both the rules.ok file and the class files must be located in a JumpStart directory that you define.

The custom JumpStart configuration files that you need to set up can be located on either a diskette (called a configuration diskette) or a server (called a configuration server). Use a configuration diskette when you want to perform custom JumpStart installations on non-networked, stand-alone systems. Use a configuration server when you want to perform custom JumpStart installations on networked systems that have access to the server. This chapter covers both procedures.

# What Happens During a Custom JumpStart Installation?

This section provides a quick overview of what takes place during a custom JumpStart installation. Each step is described in detail in this chapter.

To prepare for the installation, you create a set of JumpStart configuration files, the rules and class files, on a server that is located on the same network as the client you are installing. Next, you set up the server to provide a startup kernel that is passed to the client across the network. This is called the `boot server` (sometimes, it is referred to as the `startup server`).

After the client starts up, the boot server directs the client to the JumpStart directory, which is usually located on the boot server. The configuration files in the JumpStart directory direct and automate the entire Solaris installation on the client.

To be able to start up and install the OS on a client, you need to set up three servers: a boot server, an install server, and a configuration server. These can be three separate servers; however, in most cases, one server provides all these services.

## Boot Server

The boot server, also called the startup server, is where the client systems access the startup files. This server must be on the local subnet (not across routers). Though it is possible to install systems over the network that are not on the same subnet as the install server, there must be a boot server that resides on the same subnet as the client.

> **NOTE** As I described in Chapter 13, "The Solaris Network Environment," rarpd is a network service that is not always running. The `inetd` daemon is the network listener that starts rarpd automatically whenever a request is made.

When a client is first turned on, it does not have an OS installed or an IP address assigned; therefore, when the client is first started, the boot server provides this information. The boot server running the RARP (Reverse Address Resolution Protocol) daemon, `in.rarpd`, looks up the ethernet address in the /etc/ethers file, checks for a corresponding name in its /etc/hosts file, and passes the Internet address back to the client.

RARP is a method by which a client is assigned an IP address based on a lookup of its ethernet address. After supplying an IP address, the server searches for a symbolic link named for the client's IP address expressed in hexadecimal format. This link points to a boot program for a particular Solaris release and client architecture. For SPARC systems, the file name is *<hex-IP address.architecture>*, for example:

```
C009C864.SUN4U -> inetboot.sun4u.Solaris_8-1
```

The boot server uses the `in.tftpd` daemon to transmit the boot program to the client via trivial file transfer program (tftp). The client runs this boot program to start up.

The boot program tries to mount the root file system. To do so, it issues the `whoami` request to discover the client's hostname. The boot server running the boot parameter daemon, `rpc.bootparamd`, looks up the hostname and responds to the client. The boot program then issues a `getfile` request to obtain the location of the client's root and swap space. The boot server responds with the information obtained from the /etc/bootparams file.

Once the client has its boot parameters, the boot program on the client mounts the / (root) file system from the boot server. The client loads its kernel and starts the `init` program. When the boot server is finished bootstrapping the client, it redirects the client to the configuration server.

The client searches for the configuration server using the bootparams information. The client mounts the configuration directory, and runs `sysidtool`. The client then uses the bootparams information to locate and mount the installation directory where the Solaris image resides. The client then runs the `suninstall` program and installs the operating system.

For boot operations to proceed, these files and directories must be properly configured on the boot server: /etc/ethers, /etc/hosts,/etc/bootparams,/etc/dfs/dfstab, and /tftpboot. The following sections describe each file.

## /etc/ethers

When the JumpStart client boots, it has no IP address, so it broadcasts to the network using RARP and its ethernet address. The boot server receives this request and attempts to match the client's ethernet address with an entry in the local /etc/ethers file.

If a match is found, the client name is matched to an entry in the /etc/hosts file. In response to the RARP request from the client, the boot server sends the IP address from the /etc/hosts file back to the client. The client continues the boot process using the assigned IP address.

An entry for the JumpStart client must be created by editing the /etc/ethers file or using the add_install_client script described later in this chapter in the section titled "Setting up Clients."

## /etc/hosts

The /etc/hosts file was described in Chapter 13, "The Solaris Network Environment." The /etc/hosts file is the local file that associates the names of hosts with their IP addresses. The boot server references this file when trying to match an entry from the local /etc/ethers file in response to a RARP request from a client. In a name service environment, this file would be controlled by NIS. See Chapter 18, "Name Services," for more information on how this file can be managed by NIS.

## /tftpboot

/tftpboot is a directory that contains the inetboot.SUN4x.Solaris_8-1 file that is created for each JumpStart client when the add_install_client script is run.

The client's IP address is expressed in hexadecimal format. This link points to a boot program for a particular Solaris release and client architecture.

When booting over the network, the JumpStart client's boot PROM makes a RARP request, and when it receives a reply, the PROM broadcasts a TFTP request to fetch the inetboot file from any server that responds and executes it. See how this directory is configured in the section titled "Setting Up Clients."

## /etc/dfs/dfstab

The /etc/dfs/dfstab file lists local file systems to be shared to the network. This file is described in detail in Chapter 17, "The NFS Environment."

## /etc/bootparams

The /etc/bootparams file contains entries that network clients use for booting. JumpStart clients retrieve the information from this file by issuing requests to a server running the `rpc.bootparamd` program. See the section titled "Setting Up Clients" later in this chapter for more information on how this file is configured.

## Setting Up the Boot Server

The boot server is set up to answer RARP requests from clients using the `add_install_client` command. Before a client can start up from a boot server, the `setup_install_server` command is used to set up the boot server. If the same server is going to be used as a boot server and an install server, proceed to the next section titled "The Install Server."

> **NOTE**
>
> Normally, the install server also provides the boot program for booting clients. However, the Solaris network booting architecture requires you to set up a separate boot server when the install client is on a different subnet than the install server. Here's the reason: SPARC install clients require a boot server when they exist on different subnets because the network booting architecture uses the reverse address resolution protocol (RARP). When a client boots, it issues a RARP request to obtain its IP address. RARP, however does not acquire the netmask number, which is required to distribute information across a router on a network. If the boot server exists across a router, the boot will fail because the network traffic cannot be routed correctly without a netmask number.

## STEP BY STEP

### 21.1 Setting Up the Boot Server

Follow these steps to set up the server as a boot server only:

1. On the system that is the boot server, log in as root. Ensure the system has an empty directory with approximately 250MB of available disk space.

2. Insert the Solaris 8 OS Installation CD into the CD-ROM drive, allowing `vold` to automatically mount the CD. Change the directory to the mounted CD. Here's an example:

```
cd /cdrom/cdrom0/s0/Solaris_8/Tools
```

3. Use the setup_install_server command to set up the boot server. The -b option copies just the startup software from the Solaris CD to the local disk. Enter this command:

```
./setup_install_server -b <boot_dir_path>
```

where `-b` specifies that the system is set up as a boot server and *<boot_dir_path>* specifies the directory where the CD image is to be copied. You can substitute any directory path, as long as that path is shared across the network.

For example, the following command copies the kernel architecture information into the /export/jumpstart directory:

```
./setup_install_server -b /export/jumpstart
```

*continues*

NOTE

The following error indicates that there is not enough room in the directory to install the necessary files:

```
ERROR: Insufficient space to
copy Install Boot image
152691 necessary -
69372 available.
```

You'll need to either clean up files in that file system to make more room or choose a different file system.

You'll see the following error if the target directory is not empty:

```
The target directory
/export/jumpstart is not
empty. Please choose an
empty directory or remove
all files from the specified
directory and run this
program again.
```

*continued*

The system responds with this:

```
Verifying target directory...
Calculating space required for the installation boot image
Copying Solaris_8 Tools hierarchy...
Install Server setup complete
```

If no errors are displayed, the boot server is now set up. This boot server will handle all boot requests on this subnet. A client can only boot to a boot server located on its subnet. If you have JumpStart clients on other subnets, you'll need to create a boot server on each subnet. The installation program will create a subdirectory named Solaris_8 in the *<boot_dir_path>* directory.

## Install Server

As explained in the previous section, the boot server and the install server are typically the same system. The exception is when the client on which Solaris 8 is to be installed is located on a different subnet than the install server, a boot server is required on that subnet.

The install server is a networked system that provides Solaris 8 CD images from which you can install Solaris 8 on another system on the network. You can create an install server by copying the images on the Solaris installation media onto the server's hard disk.

By copying these CD images to the server's hard disk, you enable a single install server to provide Solaris 8 CD images for multiple releases, including Solaris 8 CD images for different platforms. For example, a SPARC install server could provide the following:

- Solaris 8 Software 1 of 2 SPARC Platform Edition CD image
- Solaris 8 Software 2 of 2 SPARC Platform Edition CD image
- Solaris 8 Languages SPARC Platform Edition CD image

as well as the following:

- Solaris 8 Software 1 of 2 Intel Platform Edition CD image
- Solaris 8 Software 2 of 2 Intel Platform Edition CD image
- Solaris 8 Languages Intel Platform Edition CD image

# STEP BY STEP

## 21.2 Setting Up a Server as a Boot and Install Server

In this section, I'm going to assume that all systems are on the same subnet and the boot and install server are to be on the same system.

1. The first step is to copy the Solaris 8 Installation CD image to the server by performing the following steps:

   Insert the CD labeled Solaris 8 OS Installation into the CD-ROM, and allow `vold` to automatically mount the CD. Change to the Tools directory on the CD as follows:

   ```
   cd /cdrom/cdrom0/s0/Solaris_8/Tools
   ```

2. Use the `setup_install_server` command to install the software onto the hard drive. The syntax for the `setup_install_server` command is

   ```
   ./setup_install_server <install_dir_path>
   ```

   *<install_dir_path>* is the path to which the CD images will be copied. This directory must be empty, and must be shared so that the JumpStart client can access it across the network during the JumpStart installation. Many system administrators like to put the CD images for the boot server and install server into /export/install. It's a personal preference; just be sure that the target directory is empty, shared, and has approximately 1GB of space available.

   To install the operating environment software into the /export/jumpstart directory, issue the following command:

   ```
   ./setup_install_server /export/jumpstart
   ```

   The system responds with:

   ```
   Verifying target directory…
   Calculating space required for the installation \
   boot image
   Copying Solaris_2.8 Tools hierarchy…
   Install Server setup complete
   ```

*continues*

*continued*

3. Eject the CD, and insert the CD labeled Solaris 8 Software 1 of 2 into the CD-ROM, allowing `vold` to automatically mount the CD.

   Change to the Tools directory on the mounted CD as follows:

   ```
   cd /cdrom/cdrom0/Solaris_8/Tools
   ```

4. Run the add_to_install_server script to install the additional software into the installation directory on the install server into the <*install_dir_path*> as follows:

   ```
   ./add_to_install_server <install_dir_path>
   ```

   For example, to copy the software into the /export/jumpstart directory, I issue the following command:

   ```
   ./add_to_install_server /export/jumpstart
   ```

   The system will respond with the following messages:

   ```
   The following Products will be copied to
   /export/jumpstart/install/Solaris_8/Product:

   Solaris_1_of_2

   If only a subset of products is needed enter
   Control-C and invoke ./add_to_install_server with
   the -s option.

   Checking required disk space...
   Copying the Early Access products...
   202847 blocks
   Processing completed successfully.
   ```

   After checking for the required disk space, the image is copied from CD to disk. When it's finished installing, repeat the process with the Solaris 8 Software 2 of 2 CD and then the Solaris 8 Languages CDs.

   After copying the Solaris CDs, you can use the `patchadd -c` command to patch the Solaris CD image on the install server's hard disk so that every client does not need to be patched after the installation.

## Configuration Server

If you are setting up custom JumpStart installations for systems on the network, you have to create a directory on a server called a configuration directory. This directory contains all the essential custom JumpStart configuration files, such as the rules file, the rules.ok file, the class file, the check script, and the optional begin and finish scripts.

The server that contains a JumpStart configuration directory is called a *configuration server*. It is usually the same system as the install and boot server, although it can be a completely different server. The configuration directory on the configuration server should be owned by root, and should have permissions set to 755.

## Setting up the Configuration Server

**STEP BY STEP**

### 21.3 Setting Up a Configuration Server

To set up a configuration server, follow these steps:

1. Choose the system that acts as the server, and log in as root.
2. Create the configuration directory anywhere on the server (such as `/jumpstart`).
3. To be certain that this directory is shared across the network, edit the /etc/dfs/dfstab file, and add the following entry:

   ```
   share -F nfs -o ro,anon=0 /jumpstart
   ```
4. Execute the `/etc/init.d/nfs.server start` command. If the system is already an NFS server, you need to only type `shareall` and press Enter.
5. Place the JumpStart files (that is, rules, rules.ok, and class files) in the /jumpstart directory. The rules, rules.ok, and class files are covered later in this section.

You can also use the add_install_client script to make an entry into the /etc/dfs/dfstab file for you. The add_install_client script is described in the section titled "Setting up Clients."

## Setting up a Configuration Disk

An alternative to setting up a configuration server is to create a configuration diskette (provided that the system to be installed has a diskette drive). If you use a diskette for custom JumpStart installations, the essential custom JumpStart files (the rules file, the rules.ok file, and the class files) must reside in the root directory on the diskette. The diskette that contains JumpStart files is called a configuration diskette. The custom JumpStart files on the diskette should be owned by root, and should have permissions equal to 755.

### STEP BY STEP

#### 21.4 Setting Up a Configuration Disk

Here are the steps to create a configuration disk:

1. Format the disk by typing
   ```
   fdformat -U
   ```
2. Create a UFS file system on the disk. If your system uses Volume Manager, insert the disk, and it will be mounted automatically.
3. Create a file system on the disk by issuing the `newfs` command:
   ```
   newfs /vol/dev/aliases/floppy0
   ```
   (The `newfs` command is covered in Chapter 4, "Introduction to File Systems.")
4. Eject the disk by typing
   ```
   eject floppy
   ```
5. Insert the formatted disk into the disk drive.

You have completed the creation of a disk that can be used as a configuration disk. Now you can create the rules file and create class files on the configuration disk to perform custom JumpStart installations.

# The Rules File

The *rules file* is a text file that should contain a rule for each group of systems you want to install automatically. Each rule distinguishes a group of systems based on one or more system attributes, and links each group to a class file, which is a text file that defines how the Solaris software is installed on each system in the group.

After deciding how you want each group of systems at your site to be installed, you need to create a rules file for each specific group of systems to be installed. The rules.ok file is a validated version of the rules file that the Solaris installation program uses to perform a custom JumpStart installation.

After you create the rules file, validate it with the `check` script by changing to the /jumpstart directory and issuing the `check` command. If the `check` script runs successfully, it creates the rules.ok file. During a custom JumpStart installation, the Solaris installation program reads the rules.ok file and tries to find the first rule that has a system attribute matching the system being installed. If a match occurs, the installation program uses the class file specified in the rule to install the system.

A sample rules file for a Sun Ultra is shown next. You'll find a sample rules file on the install server located in the *<install_dir_path>*/Solaris_8/Misc/jumpstart_sample directory. Where *<install_dir_path>* is the directory that was specified using the setup_install_server script when the install server was setup.

Notice that all the lines in the file are commented out. These are simply instructions and sample entries to help the system administrator make the correct entry. The last uncommented line is the rule I added for the example. I'll describe the syntax later. Each line in the code table has a rule keyword and a valid value for that keyword. The Solaris installation program scans the rules file from top to bottom. If the program matches an uncommented rule keyword and value with a known system, it installs the Solaris software specified by the class file listed in the class file field.

```
#
#       @(#)rules 1.12 94/07/27 SMI
#
# The rules file is a text file used to create the rules.ok file for
# a custom JumpStart installation. The rules file is a lookup table
# consisting of one or more rules that define matches between system
# attributes and profiles.
#
# This example rules file contains:
#   o syntax of a rule used in the rules file
#   o rule_keyword and rule_value descriptions
#   o rule examples
#
# See the installation manual for a complete description of the rules file.
#
#
##############################################################################
#
# RULE SYNTAX:
#
# [!]rule_keyword rule_value [&& [!]rule_keyword rule_value]... begin profile finish
#
#    "[ ]"  indicates an optional expression or field
#    "..."  indicates the preceding expression may be repeated
#     "&&"  used to "logically AND" rule_keyword and rule_value pairs together
#      "!"  indicates negation of the following rule_keyword
#
#  rule_keyword       a predefined keyword that describes a general system
#                     attribute. It is used with the rule_value to match a
#                     system with the same attribute to a profile.
#
#  rule_value  a value that provides the specific system attribute
#                     for the corresponding rule_keyword. A rule_value can
#                     be text or a range of values (NN-MM).
#                     To match a range of values, a system's value must be
#                     greater than or equal to NN and less than or equal to MM.
#
#  begin       a file name of an optional Bourne shell script
#              that will be executed before the installation begins.
#              If no begin script exists, you must enter a minus sign(-)
#              in this field.
#
#  profile     a file name of a text file used as a template by the
#              custom JumpStart installation software that defines how
#              to install Solaris on a system.
#
#  finish      a file name of an optional Bourne shell script
#              that will be executed after the installation completes.
#              If no finish script exists, you must enter a minus sign (-)
#              in this field.
#
```

```
# Notes:
# 1.        You can add comments after the pound sign (#) anywhere on a line.
# 2.        Rules are matched in descending order: first rule through the last rule.
# 3.        Rules can be continued to a new line by using the backslash (\) before
#           the carriage return.
# 4.        Don't use the "*" character or other shell wildcards, because the rules
#           file is interpreted by a Bourne shell script.
#
#
###############################################################################
#
# RULE_KEYWORD AND RULE_VALUE DESCRIPTIONS
#
#
#       rule_keyword   rule_value Type     rule_value Description
# ------        --------.       -----------
#       any   minus sign (-) always matches
#       arch   text   system's architecture type
#       domainname    text   system's domain name
#       disksize      text range    system's disk size
#                     disk device name (text)
#                     disk size (MBytes range)
#       hostname      text   system's host name
#       installed     text text     system's installed version of Solaris
#                     disk device name (text)
#                     OS release (text)
#       karch text    system's kernel architecture
#       memsize       range  system's memory size (MBytes range)
#       model text    system's model number
#       network       text   system's IP address
#       totaldisk     range  system's total disk size (MBytes range)
#
#
###############################################################################
#
# RULE EXAMPLES
#
# The following rule matches only one system:
#

#hostname sample_host    -       host_class      set_root_pw

# The following rule matches any system that is on the 924.222.43.0 network
# and has the sun4u kernel architecture:
#    Note: The backslash (\) is used to continue the rule to a new line.

#network 924.222.43.0 && \
#        karch sun4c    -       net924_sun4u     -

# The following rule matches any sparc system with a c0t3d0 disk that is
# between 400 to 600 MBytes and has Solaris 2.1 installed on it:

#arch sparc && \
#               disksize c0t3d0 400-600 && \
#               installed c0t3d0s0 solaris_2.1 - upgrade  -
```

```
#
# The following rule matches all x86 systems:

#arch i386    x86-begin    x86-class    -

#
# The following rule matches any system:

#any -    -    any_machine    -
#
# END RULE EXAMPLES
#
#
karch sun4u    -        basic_prof        -
```

Table 21.2 describes the syntax that the rules file must follow.

**TABLE 21.2**

**RULE SYNTAX**

| *Field* | *Description* |
|---|---|
| ! | Use this before a rule keyword to indicate negation. |
| [ ] | Use this to indicate an optional expression or field. |
| ... | Use this to indicate that the preceding expression might be repeated. |
| rule_keyword | A predefined keyword that describes a general system attribute, such as a hostname (hostname) or the memory size (memsize). It is used with rule_value to match a system with the same attribute to a profile. The complete list of rule_keywords is described in Table 21.3. |
| rule_value | Provides the specific system attribute value for the corresponding rule_keyword. See Table 21.3 for the list of rule_values. |
| && | Use this to join rule keyword and rule value pairs in the same rule (a logical AND). During a custom JumpStart installation, a system must match every pair in the rule before the rule matches. |
| <begin> | A name of an optional Bourne shell script that can be executed before the installation begins. If no begin script exists, you must enter a minus sign (-) in this field. All begin scripts must reside in the JumpStart directory. See the section "Begin and Finish Scripts" for more information. |

| *Field* | *Description* |
|---|---|
| `<profile>` | The name of the class file, a text file that defines how the Solaris software is installed on the system if a system matches the rule. The information in a class file consists of class file keywords and their corresponding class file values. All class files must reside in the JumpStart directory. Class files are described in the section "Creating Class Files." |
| `<finish>` | The name of an optional Bourne shell script that can be executed after the installation completes. If no finish script exists, you must enter a minus sign (-) in this field. All finish scripts must reside in the JumpStart directory. See the section "Begin and Finish Scripts" for more information. |

The rules file must have the following:

- At least one rule
- The name "rules"
- At least a rule keyword, a rule value, and a corresponding profile
- A minus sign (-) in the `begin` and `finish` fields if there is no entry

The rules file should be saved in the JumpStart directory, should be owned by root, and should have permissions equal to 644.

The rules file allows the following:

- A comment after the pound sign (#) anywhere on a line. If a line begins with a #, the entire line is a comment. If a # is specified in the middle of a line, everything after the # is considered a comment.
- Blank lines.
- Rules to span multiple lines. You can let a rule wrap to a new line, or you can continue a rule on a new line by using a backslash (\) before Enter gets pressed.

Table 21.3 describes the various `rule_keywords` and `rule_values` that were introduced earlier.

**TABLE 21.3**

**RULE KEYWORD AND RULE VALUE DESCRIPTIONS**

| *Rule Keyword* | *Rule Value* | *Description* |
|---|---|---|
| `any` | Minus sign (-) | The match always succeeds. |
| `Arch` | `processor_type` | The following table lists the valid values for `processor_type`: |
| `Platform` SPARC x86 | `processor_type sparc i386` | Matches a system's processor type. The `uname -p` command reports the system's processor type. |
| `domainname` | `domain_name` | Matches a system's domain name, which controls how a name service determines information. If you have a system already installed, the `domainname` command reports the system's domain name. |
| disksize | <disk_name> <size_range> <disk_name> A disk name in the Form c?t?d?, such as c0t3d0, or the special word rootdisk. If rootdisk is used, the disk to be matched is determined in the following order: 1. The disk that contains the preinstalled boot image (a new SPARC-based system with factory JumpStart installed) 2. The c0t3d0s 0 disk, if it exists. 3. The first available disk (searched in kernel probe order). 4. `<size_range>` The size of disk, which must be specified as a range of MB (xx-xx). | Matches a system's disk (in MB). Example: disksize c0t3d0 1000-2000. This example tries to match a system with a c0t3d0 disk that is between 250 and 300MB. Note: When calculating `size_range`, remember that a megabyte equals 1,048,576 bytes. A disk might be advertised as a "535MB" disk, but it might have only 510 million bytes of disk space. The Solaris installation program views the "535MB" disk as a 510MB disk because 535,000,000 / 1,048,576 = 510. Therefore, a "535MB" disk would not match a `size_range` equal to 530 to 550MB. |
| `hostaddress` | `<IP_address>` | Matches a system's IP address. |
| `hostname` | `<host_name>` | Matches a system's host name. If you have a system already installed, the `uname -n` command reports the system's host name. |
| `installed` | `<slice> <version><slice>` A disk slice name in the form c?t?d?s?, such as c0t3d0s5, or the special words `any` or `rootdisk`. If `any` is used, all the system's disks will try to be matched (in kernel probe order). If `rootdisk` is used, the disk to be matched is determined in the following order: 1. The disk that contains the preinstalled boot image (a new SPARC- based system with factory JumpStart installed). 2. The c0t3d0s0 if it exists. 3. The first available disk (searched in kernel probe order). 4. `<version>` A version name, Solaris_2.x, or the special words `any` or `upgrade`. If `any` is used, any Solaris or SunOS release is matched. If `upgrade` is used, any upgradeable Solaris 2.1 or greater release is matched. | Matches a disk that has a root file system corresponding to a particular version of Solaris software. Example: `installed c0t3d0s1 Solaris_2.7`. This example tries to match a system that has a Solaris 2.5 root file system on 0t3d0s1. |

| *Rule Keyword* | *Rule Value* | *Description* |
|---|---|---|
| `karch` | `<platform_group>` Valid values are `sun4d`, `sun4c`, `sun4m`, `sun4u`, `i86pc`, and `prep`. | Matches a system's platform group. If you have a system already installed, the `arch -k` command or the `uname -m` command reports the system's platform group. |
| `memsize` | `<physical_mem>` The value must be a range of MB (xx-xx) or a single MB value. | Matches a system's physical memory size (in MB). Example: `memsize 64-128` The example tries to match a system with a physical memory size between 64 and 128MB. If you have a system already installed, the output of the `prtconf` command (line 2) reports the system's physical memory size. |
| `model` | `<platform_name>` | Matches a system's platform name. Any valid platform name will work. To find the platform name of an installed system, use the `uname -i` command or the output of the `prtconf` command (line 5). Note: If the `<platform_name>` contains spaces, you must enclose it in single quotes (`'`). Example: `'SUNW,Ultra-5_10'` |
| `network` | `<network_num>` | Matches a system's network number, which the Solaris installation program determines by performing a logical AND between the system's IP address and the subnet mask. Example: `network 193.144.2.1`. This example tries to match a system with a 193.144.2.0 IP address (if the subnet mask were 255.255.255.0). |
| `osname` | `<Solaris_2.x>` | Matches a version of Solaris software already installed on a system. Example: `osname Solaris_2.7`. This example tries to match a system with Solaris 2.7 already installed. |
| `totaldisk` | `<size_range>` The value must be specified as a range of MB (xx-xx). | Matches the total disk space on a system (in MB). The total disk space includes all the operational disks attached to a system. Example: `totaldisk 1000-2000`. This example tries to match a system with a total disk space between 1G and 2GB. |

During a custom JumpStart installation, the Solaris installation program attempts to match the system being installed to the rules in the rules.ok file in order—the first rule through the last rule. A rule match occurs when the system being installed matches all the system attributes defined in the rule. As soon as a system matches a rule, the Solaris installation program stops reading the rules.ok file and begins installing the software based on the matched rule's class file.

Here are a few example rules:

```
karch sun4u  -  basic_prof  -
```

Specifies that the Solaris installation program should automatically install any system with the sun4u platform group based on the information in the basic_prof class file. There is no begin or finish script.

```
hostname pyramid2   -   ultra_class   -
```

The rule matches a system on the network called pyramid2. The class file to be used is named ultra_class. No begin or finish script is specified.

```
network 192.168.0.0 && ! model 'SUNW,Ultra-5_10' - \
net_class set_root_passwd
```

The third rule matches any system on the network that is not an Ultra 5 or Ultra 10. The class file to be used is named net_class, the finish script to be run is named set_root_passwd.

```
any - - generic_class -
```

The last example matches any system. The class file to be used is named generic_class and there is no begin or finish script.

## Validating the Rules File

Before the rules file can be used, you must run the check script to validate that this file is set up correctly. If all the rules are valid, the rules.ok file is created.

To validate the rules file, use the check script provided in the *<install_dir_path>*/Solaris_8/Misc/jumpstart_sample directory on the install server.

Change the directory to the JumpStart directory, and run the check script to validate the rules file:

```
<install_dir_path>/Solaris_8/Misc/jumpstart_sample/check \
[-p path] [-r file_name]
```

```
<install_dir_path> is the directory that was specified \
using the setup_install_server script when the install \
server was setup.
```

The check script options are described in Table 21.4.

**TABLE 21.4**

**CHECK SCRIPT OPTIONS**

| *Option* | *Description* |
|---|---|
| -p <path> | Validates the rules file by using the check script from a specified Solaris 8 CD image, instead of the check script from the system you are using. <path> is the pathname to a Solaris installation image on a local disk or a mounted Solaris CD. Use this option to run the most recent version to see if your system is running a previous version of Solaris. |
| -r <file_name> | Specifies a rules file other than a file named "rules." Using this option, you can test the validity of a rule before integrating it into the rules file. With this option, a rules.ok file is not created. |

When you use check to validate a rules file, the following things happen:

1. The rules file is checked for syntax. `check` makes sure that the rule keywords are legitimate, and the `<begin>`, `<class>`, and `<finish>` fields are specified for each rule.
2. If no errors are found in the rules file, each class file specified in the rules file is checked for syntax.
3. If no errors are found, `check` creates the rules.ok file from the rules file, removing all comments and blank lines, retaining all the rules, and adding the following comment line to the end:

   `version=2 checksum=<num>`

   As the check script runs, it reports that it is checking the validity of the rules file and the validity of each class file. If no errors are encountered, it reports the following:

   `The custom JumpStart configuration is ok.`

The following is a sample session that uses `check` to validate a rules and class file. I named the rules file "rulestest" temporarily, the class file is named "basic_prof," and I am using the `-r` option. With `-r`, the rules.ok file is not created, and only the rulestest file is checked.

```
#/export/jumpstart/install/Solaris_8/Misc/jumpstart_sample/ \
check -r /tmp/rulestest
Validating /tmp/rulestest...
Validating profile basic_prof...
```

NOTE

Notice in the error message, the use of the term "profile." Again, on the Sun exams, this term will be referred to as a class file.

```
Error in file "/tmp/rulestest", line 113
                any - - any_maine -
ERROR: Profile missing: any_maine
```

In this example, the check script found a bad option. I misspelled "any_machine" as "any_maine." The check script reported this error.

In the next example, I fixed the error, copied the file from "rulestest" to "rules," and re-ran the check script:

```
#cp rulestest rules
#/export/jumpstart/install/Solaris_8/Misc/jumpstart_sample/ \
check
Validating /tmp/rules...
Validating profile basic_prof...
Validating profile any_machine...
The custom JumpStart configuration is ok.
```

As the check script runs, it reports that it is checking the validity of the rules file and the validity of each class file. If no errors are encountered, it reports `The custom JumpStart configuration is ok.` The rules file is now validated.

After the rules.ok file is created, verify that it is owned by `root` and that it has permissions equal to 644.

CAUTION

Be careful not to specify something in the script that would prevent the mounting of file systems to /a during an initial or upgrade installation. If the Solaris installation program cannot mount the file systems to /a, an error occurs, and the installation fails.

## Begin and Finish Scripts

A *begin script* is a user-defined Bourne shell script, located in the JumpStart configuration directory on the configuration server, specified within the rules file, that performs tasks before the Solaris software is installed on the system. You can set up begin scripts to perform the following tasks:

- Backing up a file system before upgrading
- Saving files to a safe location
- Loading other applications

Output from the begin script goes to /var/sadm/begin.log.

Begin scripts should be owned by root, and should have permissions equal to 744.

In addition to begin scripts, you can also have finish scripts. A *finish script* is a user-defined Bourne shell script, specified within the rules file, that performs tasks after the Solaris software is installed on the system, but before the system restarts. Finish scripts can be used only with custom JumpStart installations. You can set up finish scripts to perform the following tasks:

- Move saved files back into place
- Add packages or patches
- Set the system's root password

Output from the finish script goes to /var/sadm/finish.log.

When used to add patches and software packages, begin and finish scripts can ensure that the installation is consistent between all systems.

## Creating Class Files

A *class file* is a text file that defines how to install the Solaris software on a system. Every rule in the rules file specifies a class file that defines how a system is installed when the rule is matched. You usually create a different class file for every rule; however, the same class file can be used in more than one rule.

A class file consists of one or more class file keywords (they are described in the following sections). Each class file keyword is a command that controls one aspect of how the Solaris installation program installs the Solaris software on a system. Use the vi editor (or any other text editor) to create a class file in the JumpStart configuration directory on the configuration server. You can create a new class file or edit one of the sample profiles located in /cdrom/cdrom0/s0/Solaris_2.8/Misc/jumpstart_sample on the Solaris CD. The class file can be named anything, but it should reflect the way in which it installs the Solaris software on a system. Sample names are basic_install, eng_profile, and accntg_profile.

A class file must have the following:

- The `install_type` keyword as the first entry
- Only one keyword on a line

- The root_device keyword if the systems being upgraded by the class file have more than one root file system that can be upgraded

A class file allows the following:

- A comment after the pound sign (#) anywhere on a line. If a line begins with a #, the entire line is a comment. If a # is specified in the middle of a line, everything after the # is considered a comment.
- Blank lines

The class file is made up of keywords and their values. They are described in the following sections.

## backup_media

backup_media defines the medium that is used to back up file systems if they need to be reallocated during an upgrade because of space problems. If multiple tapes or disks are required for the backup, you are prompted to insert these during the upgrade. Here is the backup_media syntax:

```
backup_media <type> <path>
```

type can be one of the keywords listed in Table 21.5.

**TABLE 21.5**

**BACKUP_MEDIA KEYWORDS**

| *Keyword* | *Description* |
|---|---|
| local_tape | Specifies a local tape drive on the system being upgraded. The <path> must be the character (raw) device path for the tape drive, such as /dev/rmt/0. |
| local_diskette | Specifies a local diskette drive on the system being upgraded. The <path> is the local diskette, such as /dev/rdiskette0. The diskette must be formatted. |
| local_filesystem | Specifies a local file system on the system being upgraded. The <path> can be a block device path for a disk slice or the absolute <path> to a file system mounted by the /etc/vfstab file. Examples of <path> are /dev/dsk/c0t0d0s7 and /home. |

| *Keyword* | *Description* |
|---|---|
| remote_filesystem | Specifies an NFS file system on a remote system. The <path> must include the name or IP address of the remote system (host) and the absolute <path> to the NFS file system. The NFS file system must have read/write access. A sample <path> is sparc1:/home. |
| remote_system | Specifies a directory on a remote system that can be reached by a remote shell (rsh). The system being upgraded must have access to the remote system through the remote system's .rhosts file. The <path> must include the name of the remote system and the absolute path to the directory. If a user login is not specified, the login is tried as root. A sample <path> is bcalkins@sparc1:/home. |

Here are some examples:

```
backup_media local_tape /dev/rmt/0
backup_media local_diskette /dev/rdiskette0
backup_media local_filesystem /dev/dsk/c0t3d0s7
backup_media local_filesystem /export
backup_media remote_filesystem sparc1:/export/temp
backup_media remote_system bcalkins@sparc1:/export/temp
```

backup_media must be used with the upgrade option only when disk space reallocation is necessary.

## boot_device

boot_device designates the device where the installation program installs the root file system and consequently what the system's startup device is. The EEPROM value also lets you update the system's EEPROM if you change its current startup device so that the system can automatically start up from the new startup device.

Here's the boot_device syntax:

```
boot_device <device> <eeprom>
```

The device and eeprom values are described in Table 21.6.

**TABLE 21.6**

**BOOT_DEVICE KEYWORDS**

| *Keyword* | *Description* |
|---|---|
| `<device>` | Specifies the startup device by specifying a disk slice, such as c0t1d0s0. It can be the keyword `existing`, which places the root file system on the existing startup device, or the keyword `any`, which lets the installation program choose where to put the root file system. |
| `<eeprom>` | Specifies whether you want to update the system's EEPROM to the specified startup device. `<eeprom>` specifies the value update, which tells the installation program to update the system's EEPROM to the specified startup device, or preserve, which leaves the startup device value in the system's EEPROM unchanged. An example is boot_device c0t1d0s0 update. |

The installation program installs the root file system on c0t1d0s0 and updates the EEPROM to start up automatically from the new startup device.

## client_arch

`client_arch` indicates that the OS server supports a platform group other than its own. If you do not specify `client_arch`, any diskless client or Solstice AutoClient system that uses the OS server must have the same platform group as the server. `client_arch` can be used only when `system_type` is specified as the server. You must specify each platform group that you want the OS server to support.

Here's the `client_arch` syntax:

```
client_arch karch_value [karch_value...]
```

Values for `karch_value` include `sun4d`, `sun4c`, `sun4m`, `sun4u`, and `i86pc`.

Here's an example:

```
client_arch sun4m
```

## client_root

`client_root` defines the amount of root space, in MB, to allocate for each client. If you do not specify `client_root` in a server's profile, the installation software automatically allocates 15MB of root space per client. The size of the client root area is used in combination with the `num_clients` keyword to determine how much space to reserve for the /export/root file system.

Here's the syntax:

```
client_root <root_size>
```

`root_size` is specified in MB.

Here's an example:

```
client_root 20
```

**NOTE** When allocating root space, 20MB is an adequate size. 15MB is the minimum size required. Any more than 20MB is just wasting disk space.

## client_swap

`client_swap` defines the amount of swap space, in MB, to allocate for each diskless client. If you do not specify `client_swap`, 32MB of swap space is allocated. Physical memory plus swap space must be a minimum of 32MB. If a class file does not explicitly specify the size of swap, the Solaris installation program determines the maximum size that the swap file can be, based on the system's physical memory. The Solaris installation program makes the size of swap no more than 20 percent of the disk where it resides, unless there is free space left on the disk after the other file systems are laid out.

Here's the syntax:

```
client_swap <swap_size>
```

`swap_size` is specified in MB.

Here's an example:

```
client_swap 64
```

This example specifies that each diskless client has a swap space of 64MB.

## cluster

`cluster` designates which software group to add to the system. The software groups are listed in Table 21.7.

**TABLE 21.7**

**SOFTWARE GROUPS**

| *Software Group* | *group_name* |
|---|---|
| Core | XSUNWCreq |
| End-user system support | SUNWCuser |
| Developer system support | SUNWCprog |
| Entire distribution | SUNWCall |
| Entire distribution plus OEM support | SUNWCXall (SPARC-based systems only) |

You can specify only one software group in a profile, and it must be specified before other cluster and package entries. If you do not specify a software group with `cluster`, the end-user software group, SUNWCuser, is installed on the system by default.

Here is `cluster`'s syntax:

```
cluster <group_name>
```

Here's an example:

```
cluster SUNWCall
```

This example specifies that the Entire distribution group should be installed.

The `cluster` keyword can also be used to designate whether a cluster should be added to or deleted from the software group that was installed on the system. `add` and `delete` indicate whether the cluster should be added or deleted. If you do not specify `add` or `delete`, `add` is set by default.

Here's the syntax:

```
cluster <cluster_name> [add | delete]
```

`<cluster_name>` must be in the form SUNWCname. To view detailed information about `clusters` and their names, start AdminTool on an installed system and choose Browse, Software.

## dontuse

`dontuse` designates one or more disks that you don't want the Solaris installation program to use. By default, the installation program uses all the operational disks on the system. `<disk_name>` must be specified in the form c?t?d? or c?d?, such as c0t0d0.

Here's the syntax:

```
dontuse disk_name [disk_name...]
```

Here's an example:

```
dontuse c0t0d0 c0t1d0
```

> **NOTE** You cannot specify the `usedisk` keyword and the `dontuse` keyword in the same class file.

## filesys

`filesys` sets up the installed system to mount remote file systems automatically when it starts up. You can specify `filesys` more than once. The following syntax describes using `filesys` to set up mounts to remote systems:

```
filesys <server>:<path> <server_address> <mount_pt_name> \
[mount_options]
```

The `filesys` keywords are described in Table 21.8.

**TABLE 21.8**

**FILESYS KEYWORDS**

| *Keyword* | *Description* |
|---|---|
| `<server>:` | The name of the server where the remote file system resides. Don't forget to include the colon (:). |
| `<path>` | The remote file system's mount point name. |
| `<server_address>` | The IP address of the server specified in `<server>:<path>`. If you don't have a name service running on the network, this value can be used to populate the /etc/hosts file with the server's IP address, but you must specify a minus sign (-). |

*continues*

**TABLE 21.8**

**FILESYS KEYWORDS**

| *Keyword* | *Description* |
|---|---|
| *<mount_pt_name>* | The name of the mount point where the remote file system will be mounted on. |
| [mount_options] | One or more mount options that are added to the /etc/vfstab entry for the specified *<mount_pt_name>*. If you need to specify more than one mount option, the mount options must be separated by commas and no spaces. An example is ro,quota. |

Here's an example:

```
filesys zeus:/export/home/user1 192.9.200.1 /home ro,bg,intr
```

filesys also can be used to create local file systems during the installation by using this syntax:

```
filesys <slice> <size> [file_system] [optional_parameters]
```

The values listed in Table 21.9 can be used for *<slice>*.

**TABLE 21.9**

**<SLICE> VALUES**

| *Value* | *Description* |
|---|---|
| any | This variable tells the installation program to place the file system on any disk. |
| c?t?d?s? or c?d??z | The disk slice where the Solaris installation program places the file system, such as c0t0d0s0. |
| rootdisk.sn | The variable that contains the value for the system's root disk, which is determined by the Solaris installation program. The sn suffix indicates a specific slice on the disk. |

The values listed in Table 21.10 can be used for *<size>*.

**TABLE 21.10**

**<SIZE> VALUES**

| *Value* | *Description* |
|---|---|
| `num` | The size of the file system in MB. |
| `existing` | The current size of the existing file system. |
| `auto` | The size of the file system is determined automatically, depending on the selected software. |
| `all` | The specified slice uses the entire disk for the file system. When you specify this value, no other file systems can reside on the specified disk. |
| `free` | The remaining unused space on the disk is used for the file system. |
| `<start>:<size>` | The file system is explicitly partitioned. `<start>` is the cylinder where the slice begins, and `<size>` is the number of cylinders for the slice. |

`file_system` is an optional field when `slice` is specified as `any` or `c?t?d?s?`. If `file_system` is not specified, `unnamed` is set by default, but you can't specify the `optional_parameters` value.

The values listed in Table 21.11 can be used for `file_system`.

**TABLE 21.11**

**FILE_SYSTEM VALUES**

| *Value* | *Description* |
|---|---|
| `<mount_pt_name>` | The file system's mount point name, such as /opt. |
| `<swap>` | The specified slice is used as swap. |
| `<overlap>` | The specified slice is defined as a representation of the whole disk. `overlap` can be specified only when `<size>` is `existing`, `all`, or `start:size`. |
| `<unnamed>` | The specified slice is defined as a raw slice, so the slice does not have a mount point name. If `file_system` is not specified, `unnamed` is set by default. |
| `<ignore>` | The specified slice is not used or recognized by the Solaris installation program. This can be used to ignore a file system on a disk during an installation so that the Solaris installation program can create a new file system on the same disk with the same name. `ignore` can be used only when existing partitioning is specified. |

In the following example, the size of swap is set to 64MB, and it is installed on c0t3d0s1:

```
filesys                    c0t3d0s1 64 swap
```

In the next example, /usr is based on the selected software, and the installation program determines what disk to put it on when you specify the `any` value:

```
filesys                    any auto /usr
```

The `optional_parameters` field can be one of the options listed in Table 21.12.

**TABLE 21.12**

**OPTIONAL_PARAMETERS OPTIONS**

| *Option* | *Description* |
|---|---|
| `preserve` | The file system on the specified slice is preserved. `preserve` can be specified only when size is existing and slice is c?t?d?s?. |
| `mount_options` | One or more mount options that are added to the /etc/vfstab entry for the specified mount_pt_name. |

## install_type

`install_type` specifies whether to perform the initial installation option or the upgrade option on the system. `install_type` must be the first class file keyword in every profile.

Here's the syntax:

```
install_type [initial_install | upgrade]
```

Select either `initial_install` or `upgrade`.

Here's an example:

```
install_type initial_install
```

## geo

The `geo` keyword followed by a *`locale`* designates the regional locale or locales you want to install on a system (or to add when upgrading a system). The syntax is

```
geo <locale>
```

Values you can specify for `locale` are listed in Table 21.13.

**TABLE 21.13**

**locale VALUES**

| *Value* | *Description* |
|---|---|
| N_Africa | Northern Africa, including Egypt |
| C_America | Central America, including Costa Rica, El Salvador, Guatemala, Mexico, Nicaragua, Panama |
| N_America | North America, including Canada, United States |
| S_America | South America, including Argentina, Bolivia, Brazil, Chile, Colombia, Ecuador, Paraguay, Peru, Uruguay, Venezuela |
| Asia | Asia, including Japan, Republic of Korea, Republic of China, Taiwan, Thailand |
| Ausi | Australasia, including Australia, New Zealand |
| C_Europe | Central Europe, including Austria, Czech Republic, Germany, Hungary, Poland, Slovakia, Switzerland |
| E_Europe | Eastern Europe, including Albania, Bosnia, Bulgaria, Croatia, Estonia, Latvia, Lithuania, Macedonia, Romania, Russia, Serbia, Slovenia, Turkey |
| N_Europe | Northern Europe, including Denmark, Finland, Iceland, Norway, Sweden |
| S_Europe | Southern Europe, including Greece, Italy, Portugal, Spain |
| W_Europe | Western Europe, including Belgium, France, Great Britain, Ireland, Netherlands |
| M_East | Middle East, including Israel |

Refer to the Solaris 8 Advanced Installation Guide for a complete listing of locale values.

Here's an example where the locale specified is `S_America`:

```
geo S_America
```

## isa_bits

The `isa_bits` keyword specifies whether 64-bit or 32-bit Solaris 8 packages are to be installed. The syntax is

```
isa_bits <bit_switch>
```

`<bit_switch>` represents the option `64` or `32`, which you use to indicate whether 64-bit or 32-bit Solaris 8 packages are to be installed. If you do not set this keyword in the class file, JumpStart installs:

```
64-bit packages on UltraSPARC(TM) systems
32-bit packages on all other systems
```

For example, to specify that only 32-bit Solaris 8 packages are to be loaded, use the following entry in the class file:

```
isa_bits 32
```

## layout_constraint

`layout_constraint` designates the constraint that auto-layout has on a file system if it needs to be reallocated during an upgrade because of space problems. `layout_constraint` can be used only for the `upgrade` option when disk space reallocation is required.

With `layout_constraint`, you specify the file system and the constraint you want to put on it.

Here's the syntax:

```
layout_constraint <slice> <constraint> [minimum_size]
```

The `<slice>` field specifies the file system disk slice on which to specify the constraint. It must be specified in the form `c?t?d?s?` or `c?d?s?`.

Table 21.14 describes the options for `layout_constraint`.

**TABLE 21.14**

**LAYOUT_CONSTRAINT OPTIONS**

| *Option* | *Description* |
|---|---|
| changeable | Auto-layout can move the file system to another location and can change its size.<br><br>You can change the file system's size by specifying the minimum_size value. When you mark a file system as changeable and minimum_size is not specified, the file system's minimum size is set to 10 percent greater than the minimum size required. For example, if the minimum size for a file system is 100MB, the changed size would be 110MB. If minimum_size is specified, any free space left over (the original size minus the minimum size) is used for other file systems. |
| movable | Auto-layout can move the file system to another slice on the same disk or on a different disk, and its size stays the same. |
| available | Auto-layout can use all the space on the file system to reallocate space. All the data in the file system is then lost. This constraint can be specified only on file systems that are not mounted by the /etc/vfstab file. |
| collapse | Auto-layout moves (collapses) the specified file system into its parent file system.<br><br>You can use this option to reduce the number of file systems on a system as part of the upgrade. For example, if the system has the /usr and /usr/openwin file systems, collapsing the /usr/openwin file system would move it into /usr (its parent). |
| minimum_size | This value lets you change the size of a file system by specifying the size you want it to be after auto-layout reallocates. The size of the file system might end up being more if unallocated space is added to it, but the size is never less than the value you specify. You can use this optional value only if you have marked a file system as changeable. The minimum size cannot be less than the file system needs for its existing contents. |

The following are some examples:

```
layout_constraint c0t3d0s1 changeable 200
```

The file system c0t3d0s1 can be moved to another location, and its size can be changed to more than 200MB, but no less than 200MB.

```
layout_constraint c0t0d0s4 movable
```

The file system on slice c0t0d0s4 can move to another disk slice, but its size stays the same.

```
layout_constraint c0t2d0s1 collapse
```

c0t2d0s1 is moved into its parent directory to reduce the number of file systems.

## locale

`locale` designates which language or locale packages should be installed for the specified `locale_name`. A locale determines how online information is displayed for a specific language or region, such as date, time, spelling, and monetary value. Therefore, if you want English as your language, but you also want to use the monetary values for Australia, you would choose the Australia locale value (`en_AU`) instead of the English language value (`C`).

The English language packages are installed by default. You can specify a `locale` keyword for each language or locale you need to add to a system.

Here's the `locale` syntax:

```
locale locale_name
```

Here's an example:

```
locale es
```

This example specifies Spanish as the language package you want installed.

## num_clients

When a server is installed, space is allocated for each diskless client's root (/) and swap file systems. `num_clients` defines the number of diskless clients that a server supports. If you do not specify `num_clients`, five diskless clients are allocated.

Here's the syntax:

```
num_clients client_num
```

Here's an example:

```
num_clients 10
```

In this example, space is allocated for 10 diskless clients.

## package

`package` designates whether a package should be added to or deleted from the software group that is installed on the system. `add` or `delete` indicates the action required. If you do not specify `add` or `delete`, `add` is set by default.

Here's the syntax:

```
package package_name [add | delete]
```

package_name must be in the form `SUNW`*`name`*.

Here's an example:

```
package SUNWxwman delete
```

In this example, `SUNWxwman` (X Window online man pages) is not installed on the system.

## partitioning

`partitioning` defines how the disks are divided into slices for file systems during the installation. If you do not specify partitioning, the default is set.

Here's the syntax:

```
partitioning default |existing |explicit
```

The partitioning options are described in Table 21.15.

**TABLE 21.15**

**PARTITIONING OPTIONS**

| *Option* | *Description* |
|---|---|
| `default` | The Solaris installation program selects the disks and creates the file systems where the specified software is installed. Except for any file systems specified by the `filesys` keyword, rootdisk is selected first. Additional disks are used if the specified software does not fit on rootdisk. |
| `existing` | The Solaris installation program uses the existing file systems on the system's disks. All file systems except /, /usr, /usr/openwin, /opt, and /var are preserved. The installation program uses the last mount point field from the file system superblock to determine which file system mount point the slice represents. When you specify the `filesys` class file keyword with `partitioning, existing` must be specified. |
| `explicit` | The Solaris installation program uses the disks and creates the file systems specified by the filesys keywords. If you specify only the root (/) file system with the `filesys` keyword, all the Solaris software is installed in the root file system. When you use the explicit class file value, you must use the `filesys` class file keyword to specify which disks to use and what file systems to create. |

## root_device

`root_device` designates the system's root disk.

Here's the syntax:

```
root_device slice
```

Here's an example:

```
root_device c0t3d0s2
```

## system_type

`system_type` defines the type of system being installed. If you do not specify `system_type` in a class file, `standalone` is set by default.

Here's the syntax:

```
system_type [standalone | server]
```

Here's an example:

```
system_type server
```

## usedisk

`usedisk` designates one or more disks that you want the Solaris installation program to use when the `partitioning` default is specified. By default, the installation program uses all the operational disks on the system. `disk_name` must be specified in the form `c?t?d?` or `c?d?`, such as `c0t0d0`. If you specify the `usedisk` class file keyword in a class file, the Solaris installation program uses only the disks that you specify.

Here's the syntax:

```
usedisk disk_name [disk_name]
```

Here's an example:

```
usedisk c0t0d0 c0t1d0
```

> **NOTE** You cannot specify the `usedisk` keyword and the `dontuse` keyword in the same class file.

# TESTING CLASS FILES

After you create a class file, you can use the `pfinstall` command to test it. Testing a class file is sometimes called a "dry run" installation. By looking at the installation output generated by `pfinstall`, you can quickly determine whether a class file will do what you expect. For example, you can determine if a system has enough disk space to upgrade to a new release of Solaris before you actually perform the upgrade.

To test a class file for a particular Solaris release, you must test it within the Solaris environment of the same release. For example, if you want to test a class file for Solaris 8, you have to run the `pfinstall` command on a system running Solaris 8.

To test the class file, change to the JumpStart directory that contains the class file and type

```
/usr/sbin/install.d/pfinstall -d
```

or

```
/usr/sbin/install.d/pfinstall -D
```

> **CAUTION**
> Without the -d or -D option, pfinstall actually installs the Solaris software on the system by using the specified class file, and the data on the system is overwritten.

Here is the syntax for pfinstall:

```
/usr/sbin/install.d/pfinstall [-D | -d] disk_config \
[-c path] profile
```

The pfinstall options are described in Table 21.16.

**TABLE 21.16**

**PFINSTALL OPTIONS**

| *Option* | *Description* |
|---|---|
| -D | Tells pfinstall to use the current system's disk configuration to test the class file against. |
| -d *<disk_config>* | Tells pfinstall to use a disk configuration file, *<disk_config>*, to test the class file against. If the *<disk_config>* file is not in the directory where pfinstall is run, you must specify the path. This option cannot be used with an upgrade class file (an install-type upgrade). You must always test an upgrade class file against a system's disk configuration using the -D option. A disk configuration file represents a disk's structure. It describes a disk's bytes per sector, flags, and slices.<br><br>See the example following this table of how to create the *<disk_config>* file. |
| -c path | Specifies the path to the Solaris CD image. This is required if the Solaris CD is not mounted on /cdrom. For example, use this option if the system is using Volume Manager to mount the Solaris CD. |
| profile | Specifies the name of the class file to test. If class file is not in the directory where pfinstall is being run, you must specify the path. |

> **NOTE**
> c?t?d?s2 designates a specific target for a SCSI disk, and c?d?s2 designates a non-SCSI disk.

You can create a *<disk_config>* file by issuing the following command:

```
prtvtoc /dev/rdsk/<device_name> <disk_config>
```

/dev/rdsk/*<device_name>* is the device name of the system's disk. *<device_name>* must be in the form c?t?d?s2 or c?d?s2. *<disk_config>* is the name of the disk configuration file.

Here's an example:

```
prtvtoc /dev/rdsk/c0t3d0s2 >test
```

The file named "test" created by this example would be your <*disk_config*> file, and it would look like this:

```
* /dev/rdsk/c0t3d0s2 partition map
*
* Dimensions:
*     512 bytes/sector
*     126 sectors/track
*       4 tracks/cylinder
*     504 sectors/cylinder
*    4106 cylinders
*    4104 accessible cylinders
*
* Flags:
*    1: unmountable
*   10: read-only
*
*                        First   Sector Last
* Partition     Tag      Flags   Sector Count   Sector   Mount Directory
      0          2       00      0      268632  268631   /
      1          3       01      268632 193032  461663
      2          5       00      0      2068416 2068415
      3          0       00      461664 152712  614375   export
      4          0       00      614376 141624  755999   export/swap    /
      6          4       00      756000 1312416 2068415  /usr
```

> **NOTE** If you want to test installing Solaris software on multiple disks, concatenate single disk configuration files and save the output to a new file.

The following example tests the ultra_class class file against the disk configuration on a Solaris 8 system on which `pfinstall` is being run. The ultra_class class file is located in the /jumpstart directory, and the path to the Solaris CD image is specified because Volume Management is being used.

In addition, if you want to test the class file for a system with a specific system memory size, set `SYS_MEMSIZE` to the specific memory size in MB as follows:

```
SYS_MEMSIZE=memory_size
export SYS_MEMSIZE
cd /jumpstart/usr/sbin/install.d/pfinstall -D -c /cdrom/cdrom0/ s0 ultra_class
```

The system tests the class file and displays several pages of results. Look for the following message, which indicates that the test was successful:

```
Installation complete
Test run complete. Exit status 0.
```

## sysidcfg FILE

When a JumpStart client boots for the first time, the booting software first tries to obtain system identification information (such as the system's hostname, IP address, locale, timezone, and root password) from a file named sysidcfg, and then from the name service database. If you're not using a name service, you'll use this file to answer system identification questions during the initial part of the installation. If you're using a name service, you'll want to look over the next section titled, "Setting up JumpStart in a Name Service Environment."

You'll use the sysidcfg file to answer system identification questions during the initial part of the installation. If the JumpStart server provides this information, the client bypasses the initial system identification portion of the Solaris 8 installation process. Without the sysidcfg file, the client displays the appropriate interactive dialogue to request system identification information. You must create a unique sysidcfg file for every system that requires different configuration information.

The sysidcfg file can reside on a shared NFS directory or the root (/) directory on a UFS file system. It can also reside on a PCFS file system located on a diskette. Only one sysidcfg file can reside in a directory or on a diskette. The location of the sysidcfg file is specified by the `-p` argument to the `add_install_client` script used to create a JumpStart client information file.

Creating a sysidcfg file requires the system administrator to specify a set of keywords in the sysidcfg file to preconfigure a system. There are two types of keywords you use in the sysidcfg file: independent and dependent. Here's an example illustrating independent and dependent keywords:

```
name_service=NIS {domain_name=pyramid.com \
name_server=server(192.168.0.1)}
```

**NOTE** Enclose all dependent keywords in curly braces {} to tie them to their associated independent keyword. Values can optionally be enclosed in single ` or double quotes ".

In this example, `name_service` is the independent keyword, whereas `domain_name` and `name_server` are the dependent keywords.

To help explain sysidcfg keywords, I'll group them in categories and describe each of them in detail.

# NAME SERVICE, DOMAIN NAME, AND NAME SERVER KEYWORDS

The following keywords are related to the name service you will be using.

```
name_service=<value>
```

This keyword is assigned one of five values that specify the name service to be used: NIS, NIS+, LDAP, DNS, NONE. For example, if your are using NIS, specify:

```
name_service=NIS
```

For the NIS and NIS+ values, additional keywords are specified, which are:

```
domain_name=<value>
```

Where the *<value>* is the domain name such as pyramid.com.

```
name_server=<value>
```

Where the *<value>* is the hostname or IP address for the name server. For the name_server *<value>*, you can specify up to three IP addresses for the name_server. For example,

```
name_server=192.168.0.1,192.168.0.2,192.168.0.3
```

If the DNS keyword is specified for the name_service *<value>*, as follows: name_service=DNS

Then you'll need to specify the following additional dependent keywords:

```
domain_name=<value>
```

Enter the domain name for the domain_name *<value>*. For example, if the domain name is pyramid.com, specify it as follows: domain_name=pyramid.com

```
name_server=<value>
```

For the name_server *<value>*, you can specify up to three IP addresses for the name_server. For example,

```
name_server=192.168.0.1,192.168.0.2,192.168.0.3
```

```
search=<value>
```

where *<value>* is the search entry, which cannot exceed 250 characters. Here's an example DNS search entry:

```
search=pyramid.com,east.pyramid.com,west.pyramid.com
```

If the LDAP keyword is specified for the name_service *<value>* as follows: name_service=LDAP

Then you'll need to specify the following additional dependent keywords:

```
domain_name=<value>
```

Enter the domain name for the domain_name *<value>*. For example, if the domain name is pyramid.com, specify it as follows: domain_name=pyramid.com

```
profile=<value>
```

where *<value>* is the profile name.

```
profile_server=<value>
```

where *<value>* is the IP address of the profile server.

Here's an example LDAP entry with its dependent keywords:

```
name_service_LDAP
{domain_name=west.pyramid.com
profile=default
profile_server=192.168.0.100}
```

## Network-Related Keywords

```
network_interface=<value>
```

Specify a <value> of NONE or PRIMARY as follows:

```
network_interface=primary
```

The following dependent keywords apply as follows:

If you are not using DHCP, the dependent keywords for PRIMARY are:

```
hostname=<hostname>
ip_address=<ip_address>
netmask=<netmask value>
protocol_ipv6=<yes or no>
```

For example, if your primary network interface is named le0, here's a sample sysidcfg file:

```
network_interface=le0
{hostname=client1
ip_address=192.168.0.10
netmask=255.255.255.0
protocol_ipv6=no}
```

If you are using DHCP, the only keywords available will be:

```
dhcp;protocol_ipv6=<yes or no>
```

For example, here's a sample entry:

```
network_interface=primary
{dhcp protocol_ipv6=no}
```

Whether using DHCP or not, the protocol_ipv6 keyword is optional.

## Setting the Root Password

The root password keyword is:

```
root_password=<encrypted passwd>
```

The value for *<encrypted passwd>* is taken from the /etc/shadow file. For example, an entry might look like this:

```
root_password=XbcjeAgl8jLeI
```

The following is the security related keyword:

```
Security_policy=<value>
```

Where *<value>* is either KERBEROS or NONE.

When specifying the KERBEROS value, you'll need to also specify the following dependent keywords:

```
default_realm=<fully qualified domain name>

admin_server=<fully qualified domain name>

kdc=<value>
```

Where *<value>* can list a maximum of three key distribution centers (KDCs) for a security_policy keyword. At least one is required. Here's an example using the security_policy keyword:

```
security_policy=kerberos
{default_realm=pyramid.com
admin_server=krbadmin.pyramid.com
kdc=kdc1.pyramid.com,kdc2.pyramid.com}
```

## Setting the System Locale, Terminal, Timezone, and Time Server

The keyword to set the system locale is:

```
system_locale=<value>
```

Where *<value>* is an entry from the /usr/lib/locale directory. The following example sets the value to English:

```
system_locale=en_US
```

The keyword to set the terminal type is:

```
terminal=<terminal_type>
```

Where *<terminal_type>* is an entry from the /usr/share/lib/erminfo database. The following example sets the terminal type to vt100:

```
terminal=vt100
```

The keyword to set the timezone is:

```
timezone=<timezone>
```

Where *<timezone>* is an entry from the /usr/share/lib/zoneinfo directory. The following entry sets the timezone to Eastern Standard Time:

```
timezone=EST
```

The keyword to set the time server is

```
timeserver=<value>
```

Where *<value>* can be LOCALHOST, HOSTNAME, or IP_ADDRESS. The following example sets the time server to be the localhost:

```
timeserver=localhost
```

The following rules apply to keywords in the sysidcfg file:

- Keywords can be in any order.
- Keywords are not case-sensitive.
- Keyword values can be optionally enclosed in single quotes (').
- Only the first instance of a keyword is valid; if you specify the same keyword more than once, the first keyword specified will be used.

The following is a sample sysidcfg file, located in the configuration directory named /jumpstart:

```
system_locale=en_US
timezone=EST
timeserver=localhost
terminal=vt100
name_service=NONE
security_policy=none
root_password=XbcjeAgl8jLeI
network_interface=primary {protocol_ipv6=no netmask=255.255.255.0}
```

## Setting Up JumpStart in a Name Service Environment

As stated in the previous section, you can use the sysidcfg file to answer system identification questions during the initial part of installation, regardless of whether a name service is used. When the sysidcfg file is used with the NIS naming service, identification parameters, such as locale and timezone, can be provided from the name service. The sysidcfg file necessary for installing a JumpStart client on a network running the NIS name service is typically much shorter, and a separate sysidcfg file for each client is unnecessary.

You'll use the /etc/locale, /etc/timezone, /etc/hosts/, /etc/ethers, and /etc/netmasks files as the source for creating NIS databases to support JumpStart client installations. See Chapter 18, "Name Services," for more information on NIS and how to create NIS maps.

## Setting Up Clients

Now you need to set up the clients to install over the network. After setting up the /jumpstart directory and the appropriate files, use the `add_install_client` command on the install server to set up remote workstations to install Solaris from the install server. The command syntax for the add_install_client command is as follows:

```
add_install_client -e <ethernet_addr> -i <ip_addr> -s <install_svr:/dist> -c <config_svr:/config_dir> \
-p <sysidcfg_svr/sysid_config_dir> <client_name> <client_arch>
```

The `add_install_client` options are described in Table 21.17.

**TABLE 21.17**

**ADD_INSTALL_CLIENT OPTIONS**

| *Option* | *Description* |
|---|---|
| -e *<ethernet_addr>* | Specifies the ethernet address of the install client, and is necessary if the client is not defined in the name service. |
| -i *<ip_addr>* | Specifies the IP address of the install client and is necessary if the client is not defined in the name service. |
| -d | Specifies the client as a DHCP client. |
| -s *<install_svr:/dist>* | Specifies the name of the install server (*install_svr*) and the path to the Solaris 8 operating environment distribution (*/dist*). This option is necessary if the client is being added to a boot server. |
| -p < *sysidcfg_svr/sysid_config_dir>* | Specifies the configuration server (*sysidcfg_svr*) and the path to the sysidcfg file (*sysid_config_dir*). This option is available on Solaris 8 OS and later distributions. |
| `<client_name>` | The hostname for the install client. |
| `-c <config_svr:/config_dir>` | Specifies the configuration server (config_svr) and path (*/config_dir*) to the configuration directory. |
| *<client_arch>* | Specifies the platform group of the systems that use *<servername>* as an install server. |

For additional options to the `add_install_client` command, see the Solaris online manual pages.

In the following steps, I'll be creating a JumpStart client that will boot from a system that is configured as both the boot and install server. In addition, the entire Solaris 8 media has been copied to the local disk.

# STEP BY STEP

## 21.5 Creating a JumpStart Client

Perform the following steps to setup the JumpStart client:

1. On the install server, change to the directory that contains the installed Solaris 8 Operating Environment image as follows:

```
cd /export/jumpstart/Solaris_8/Tools
```

2. Create the JumpStart client using the `add_install_client` script found in the local directory as follows:

```
./add_install_client -s ultra5:/export/jumpstart/install \
-c ultra5:/jumpstart -p ultra5:/jumpstart -e 8:0:20:21:49:25 \
-i 192.168.1.106 client1 sun4u
```

The system responds with:

```
Adding Ethernet number for client1 to /etc/ethers
Adding "share -F nfs -o ro,anon=0 /export/jumpstart/install" to /etc/dfs/dfstab
making /tftpboot
enabling tftp in /etc/inetd.conf
updating /etc/bootparams
copying inetboot to /tftpboot
```

The add_install_client script automatically made entries into the following files and directory:

/etc/ethers

```
8:0:20:21:49:25  client1
```

/etc/dfs/dfstab

```
share -F nfs -o ro,anon=0 /export/jumpstart
```

/etc/bootparams

```
client1  root=ultra5:/export/jumpstart/Solaris_8/Tools/Boot install=ultra5:/export/jumpstart boottype= \
:in sysid_config=ultra5:/jumpstart install_config=ultra5:/jumpstart rootopts=:rsize=32768
```

/tftpboot directory

```
lrwxrwxrwx   1 root    other       26 Jun 19 16:11 \ C0A8016A -> inetboot.SUN4U.Solaris_8-1
lrwxrwxrwx   1 root    other       26 Jun 19 16:11 \ C0A8016A.SUN4U -> inetboot.SUN4U.Solaris_8-1
-rwxr-xr-x   1 root    other   158592 Jun 19 16:11 \ inetboot.SUN4U.Solaris_8-1
-rw-r—r—     1 root    other      317 Jun 19 16:11 rm.192.168.1.106
lrwxrwxrwx   1 root    other        1 Jun 19 16:11  tftpboot -> .
```

*continues*

**NOTE**

In the following steps, the following associations have been made in the examples:

| | |
|---|---|
| Install Server name | –server |
| Distribution directory \ –/export/jumpstart/install | |
| Configuration Server name | –server |
| Configuration directory \ –/export/jumpstart/config | |
| Boot server name | –server |
| Install client | –client1 |
| Client architecture | –sun4m |

3. Use the rm_install_client command to remove a JumpStart client's entries and configuration information from the boot server as follows:

```
./rm_install_client client1
```

The system responds with:

```
removing client1 from bootparams
removing /etc/bootparams, since it is empty
removing /tftpboot/inetboot.SUN4U.Solaris_8-1
removing /tftpboot
disabling tftp in /etc/inetd.conf
```

# A Sample JumpStart Installation

The following example shows how you would set up a custom JumpStart installation for a fictitious site. The network consists of an Enterprise 3000 server and five Sparc10 workstations.

## Setting Up the Install Server

The first step is to set up the install server. You'll choose the enterprise server. This is where the contents of the Solaris CD are located. The contents of the CD can be made available by either loading the CD in the CD-ROM drive or copying the CD to the server's local hard drive. For this example, you will copy the files to the local hard drive. Use the `setup_install_server` command to copy the contents of the Solaris CD to the server's local disk. Files are copied to the /export/install directory.

**STEP BY STEP**

**21.6 Setting Up the Install Server**

Follow these steps to create the install server:

1. Insert the Solaris Installation CD into the server's CD-ROM drive.

2. Type the following:

```
cd /cdrom/cdrom0/s0/Solaris_8/Tools
./setup_install_server /export/install
```

The system responds with this:

```
Verifying target directory...
Calculating space required for the installation boot image
Copying Solaris_8 Tools hierarchy...
Install Server setup complete
```

3. Eject the Solaris 8 Installation CD, and put in the Solaris 8 Software 1 of 2 CD. Let `vold` automatically mount the CD.

4. Change to the Tools directory on the CD as follows:
```
cd /cdrom/cdrom0/Solaris_8/Tools
```

5. Execute the add_to_install_server script as follows to copy the images from the CD to the /export/install directory:
```
./add_to_install_server /export/install
```

6. Repeat the procedure with the CD labeled Solaris 8 Software 2 of 2.

## Creating the JumpStart Directory

After you install the install server, you need to set up a JumpStart configuration directory on the server. This directory holds the files necessary for a custom JumpStart installation of the Solaris software. You set up this directory by copying the sample directory from one of the Solaris CD images that has been put in /export/install. Do this by typing the following:

```
mkdir /jumpstart
cp -r /export/install/Solaris_8/Misc/jumpstart_sample /jumpstart
```

Any directory name can be used. You'll use /jumpstart for this example.

## Setting Up a Configuration Server

### STEP BY STEP

#### 21.7 Setting up a Configuration Server

The next step is to set up a configuration server. Follow these steps:

> **NOTE** It may be necessary to run the /etc/init.d/nfs.server startup script if the NFS server daemons are not running. See Chapter 17, "The NFS Environment," for more information.

1. Log in as root on the server where you want the JumpStart configuration directory to reside.
2. Edit the /etc/dfs/dfstab file. Add the following entry:
   `share -F nfs -o ro,anon=0 /jumpstart`
3. Type `shareall` and press Enter. This makes the contents of the /jumpstart directory accessible to systems on the network.
4. Working with the sample class file and rules files that were copied into the JumpStart directory earlier, use them to create configuration files that represent your network. For this example, I create a class file named engrg_prof. It looks like this:

```
#Specifies that the installation will be treated as an initial
#installation, as opposed to an upgrade.
install_type initial_install
#Specifies that the engineering systems are standalone systems.
system_type standalone
#Specifies that the JumpStart software uses default disk
#partitioning for installing Solaris software on the engineering
#systems.
partitioning default
#Specifies that the developer's software group will be
#installed.
Cluster    SUNWCprog
#Specifies that each system in the engineering group will have 50
#Mbytes of swap space.
filesys any 50 swap
```

The rules file contains the following rule:

```
network 192.9.200.0 - engrg_prof -
```

This rules file states that systems on the 192.9.200.0 network are installed using the engrg_prof class file.

5. Validate the rules and class files as follows:

```
cd /jumpstart
./check /usr/sbin/install.d/pfinstall -c /export/install engrg_prof
```

If `check` doesn't find any errors, it creates the rules.ok file. Look for the following message, which indicates that the `pfinstall` test was successful:

```
Installation complete
Test run complete. Exit status 0.
```

You are finished creating the configuration server.

## Setting Up Clients

Now, on the install server, set up each client as follows:

```
cd /export/install/Solaris_8/Tools
./add_install_client -s sparcserver:/export/install \
-c sparcserver:/jumpstart -p sparcserver:/jumpstart \
-e 8:0:20:21:49:25 -i 192.9.200.106 sun1 sun4u.

./add_install_client -s sparcserver:/export/install \
-c sparcserver:/jumpstart -p sparcserver:/jumpstart \
-e 8:0:20:21:49:24 -i 192.9.200.107 sun2 sun4u
```

This example sets up two engineering workstations, sun1 and sun2, so that they can be installed over the network from the install server named sparcserver.

## Starting Up the Clients

After the setup is complete, you can start up the engineering systems by using the following startup command at the `ok` (PROM) prompt of each system:

```
boot net - install
```

You'll see the following displayed on the screen:

```
Rebooting with command: net - install
Boot device: /iommu/sbus/ledma@f,400010/le@f,c00000  File and args: - install
20800
SunOS Release 5.8 Version Generic_108528-05 32-bit
Copyright 1983-2000 Sun Microsystems, Inc.  All rights reserved.
whoami: no domain name
Configuring /dev and /devices
Using RPC Bootparams for network configuration information.
Configured interface le0
Using sysid configuration file 192.9.200.101:/jumpstart/sysidcfg
The system is coming up.  Please wait.
Starting remote procedure call (RPC) services: sysidns done.
Starting Solaris installation program...
Searching for JumpStart directory...
Using rules.ok from 192.9.200.101:/jumpstart.
Checking rules.ok file...
Using profile: engrg_prof
Executing JumpStart preinstall phase...
Searching for SolStart directory...
Checking rules.ok file...
Using begin script: install_begin
Using finish script: patch_finish
Executing SolStart preinstall phase...
Executing begin script "install_begin"...
Begin script install_begin execution completed.
Processing default locales
        - Specifying default locale (en_US)
Processing profile
        - Selecting cluster (SUNWCprog)

WARNING: Unknown cluster ignored (SUNWCxgl)
        - Selecting package (SUNWaudmo)
        - Selecting locale (en_US)

Installing 32 Bit Solaris Packages
- Selecting all disks
- Configuring boot device
- Configuring swap (any)
- Configuring /opt (any)
- Automatically configuring disks for Solaris operating environment

Verifying disk configuration
Verifying space allocation
        - Total software size:  401.60 Mbytes
Preparing system for Solaris install
Configuring disk (c0t3d0)
        - Creating Solaris disk label (VTOC)

Creating and checking UFS file systems
- Creating / (c0t3d0s0)
- Creating /opt (c0t3d0s5)

Beginning Solaris software installation
```

```
Starting software installation
SUNWxwrtl...done.  401.55 Mbytes remaining.
SUNWulcf....done.  397.28 Mbytes remaining.
SUNWuium....done.  397.25 Mbytes remaining.
SUNWuiu8....done.  390.46 Mbytes remaining.
  <output truncated>
Completed software installation
Solaris 8 software installation succeeded
Customizing system files
        - Mount points table (/etc/vfstab)
        - Network host addresses (/etc/hosts)
Customizing system devices
        - Physical devices (/devices)
        - Logical devices (/dev)
Installing boot information
        - Installing boot blocks (c0t3d0s0)
Installation log location
        - /a/var/sadm/system/logs/install_log (before \
reboot)
        - /var/sadm/system/logs/install_log (after reboot)
Installation complete
Executing SolStart postinstall phase...
Executing finish script "patch_finish"...
Finish script patch_finish execution completed.
Executing JumpStart postinstall phase...
The begin script log 'begin.log'
is located in /var/sadm/system/logs after reboot.
The finish script log 'finish.log'
is located in /var/sadm/system/logs after reboot.
syncing file systems... done
rebooting...
```

The client reads the sysidcfg file, then the class file, and then the rules.ok files on the server. If any system identification information is missing in the sysidcfg file, the client will display the appropriate dialogue, requesting identification information. The system then automatically installs the Solaris operating environment.

This completes the JumpStart configuration.

## CHAPTER SUMMARY

**KEY TERMS**

- JumpStart server
- JumpStart client
- Class file
- Rules files
- Custom JumpStart
- Boot server
- Install server
- Configuration server
- RARP
- Profile
- Check script

It's been my experience that JumpStart is not widely used, mainly because of its complexity. Many system administrators would rather go through an interactive installation for each system than automate the process. Many of the popular UNIX systems have installation programs similar to JumpStart, and most are underutilized. System administrators could save a great deal of time if they would only learn more about this type of installation.

I've described the entire process of installing a networked system via JumpStart. I described how to set up the boot server, the install server, and the configuration files located on the configuration server. I also described the necessary procedures that need to be performed for each client that you plan to install.

This concludes the study material for the second exam. I encourage you to use the test exams on the enclosed CD-ROM to test your knowledge of the chapters you've read. If you fully understand all the material covered in this book, you will have no problem passing both exams. If you don't score well on the enclosed CD-ROM, go back and review the chapters you are weak in.

Before taking the exam however, visit my web site, `www.pdesigninc.com`, and read up-to-date information about the exams, comments from others that have taken the exams, test-taking tips, and links to additional study materials to be sure you are adequately prepared before spending $150 for the exam.

When you're confident that you understand all the material covered in this section, you are ready to take the real exam. Good luck!

APPLY YOUR KNOWLEDGE

## Exercises

### 21.1 Creating JumpStart Servers

In this exercise, you'll create a JumpStart boot server, install server, configuration server, and configuration files; and configure a JumpStart client to automatically install the Solaris 8 Operating environment across the network.

For this exercise, you'll need two systems connected on a network. One system will serve as the boot/install/configuration server, so it needs at least 1GB of free disk space. The second system will be the client, and will have the entire disk destroyed and the operating system reloaded.

> **CAUTION**
> This procedure destroys data on the disk. Be sure you have proper backups if you want to save any data on these systems.

**Estimated Time:** 1 hour

1. On the system that will be used as the boot and install server, log in as root.
2. Edit the /etc/hosts file, and make an entry for the JumpStart client.
3. Create the boot server as follows:

   a) Insert the CD labeled Solaris 8 Installation CD, and let `vold` automatically mount the CD.

   b) Change to the Tools directory on the CD as follows:

   ```
   cd /cdrom/cdrom0/s0/Solaris_8/Tools
   ```

   c) Run the setup_install_server script and specify the location for the CD image. Be sure you have at least 1GB of free space and the target directory is empty. In the following example, I'm using /export/install as the install directory:

   ```
   ./setup_install_server /export/install
   ```

4. Add the additional software as follows:

   a) Eject the Solaris 8 Installation CD, and put in the Solaris 8 Software 1 of 2 CD. Let `vold` automatically mount the CD.

   b) Change to the Tools directory on the CD as follows:

   ```
   cd /cdrom/cdrom0/Solaris_8/Tools
   ```

   c) Execute the add_to_install_server script as follows to copy the images from the CD to the /export/install directory:

   ```
   ./add_to_install_server /export/install
   ```

   d) Repeat the procedure with the CD labeled Solaris 8 Software 2 of 2.

5. Now create the JumpStart configuration directory as follows:

   ```
   mkdir /jumpstart
   ```

6. Add the following entry in the /etc/dfs/dfstab file for this directory to share it across the network:

   ```
   share -F nfs -o ro,anon=0 /jumpstart
   ```

7. Start the NFS server as follows if the `nfsd` daemon is not running:

   ```
   /etc/init.d/nfs.server start
   ```

8. In the /jumpstart directory, use the vi editor to create a class file named basic_class with the following entries:

## APPLY YOUR KNOWLEDGE

```
#Specifies that the installation will be
treated as an initial
#installation, as opposed to an upgrade.
install_type initial_install
#Specifies that the engineering systems are
standalone systems.
system_type standalone
#Specifies that the JumpStart software uses
default disk
#partitioning for installing Solaris software
on the engineering
#systems.
partitioning default
#Specifies that the developer's software
group will be
#installed
cluster SUNWCprog
#Specifies that each system in the
engineering group will have 50
#Mbytes of swap space.
filesys any 50 swap
```

9. In the /jumpstart directory, use the vi editor to create a rules file named "rules" with the following entry:

   ```
   hostname sun1 - basic_class -
   ```

10. Validate the class and rules files with the `check` and `pfinstall` commands as follows:

    ```
    cd /jumpstart

    /export/install/Solaris_8/Misc/jumpstart \
    _sample/check

    /usr/sbin/install.d/pfinstall -c \
    /export/install basic_class
    ```

11. Now set up the JumpStart client as follows:

    ```
    cd /export/install/Solaris_8/Tools
    ./add_install_client -s \
    <SERVERNAME>:/export/install \
    -c <SERVERNAME>:/jumpstart -p \
    <SERVERNAME>:/jumpstart \
    -e <MAC ADDRESS> -i <IP ADDRESS> \
    <CLIENTNAME> <PLATFORM>
    ```

    Where SERVERNAME is the hostname of your boot/install server

    MAC ADDRESS is your client's Ethernet address

    IP ADDRESS is your client's IP address.

    CLIENTNAME is your client's hostname

    PLATFORM is your clients architecture (ie.\ Sun4m, sun4u)

    For example:

    ```
    ./add_install_client -s \
    sparcserver:/export/install \
    -c sparcserver:/jumpstart -p \
    sparcserver:/jumpstart \
    -e 8:0:20:21:49:24 -i 192.168.1.107 sun1 \
    sun4u
    ```

12. Go to the client, turn on the power, and at the boot PROM, issue the following command:

    ```
    boot net - install
    ```

The jumpstart installation executes.

## Review Questions

1. Which of the following is a method to automatically install Solaris on a new SPARC system by inserting the Solaris Operating System CD-ROM in the drive and powering on the system?

   A. JumpStart

   B. WebStart

   C. Interactive installation

   D. Custom JumpStart

2. Which of the following is a method to automatically install groups of identical systems?

   A. Custom JumpStart

   B. JumpStart

   C. WebStart

   D. Interactive installation

## APPLY YOUR KNOWLEDGE

3. Which of the following sets up an install server to provide the operating system to the client during a JumpStart installation?

   A. `add_install_client`

   B. `add_install_server`

   C. `pfinstall`

   D. `setup_install_server`

4. For a JumpStart installation, which of the following files should contain a rule for each group of systems that you want to install?

   A. rules

   B. rules.ok

   C. profile

   D. check

5. For a JumpStart installation, which of the following servers is set up to answer RARP requests from clients?

   A. Boot server

   B. Install server

   C. Configuration server

   D. JumpStart server

6. Which of the following is used as an alternate to setting up a configuration directory?

   A. Boot server

   B. Install server

   C. Configuration disk

   D. rules.ok file

7. For a JumpStart installation, which of the following files contains the name of a finish script?

   A. check

   B. profile

   C. rules.ok

   D. profile diskette

8. Which of the following is a user-defined Bourne shell script, specified within the rules file?

   A. add_install_client script

   B. class file

   C. check script

   D. begin script

9. In JumpStart, which of the following files defines how to install the Solaris software on a system?

   A. class file

   B. rules

   C. rules.ok

   D. install.log

10. Which of the following is used to test a JumpStart class file?

    A. `check`

    B. `pfinstall`

    C. `rules`

    D. `add_install_client`

## APPLY YOUR KNOWLEDGE

11. When working with JumpStart, which of the following files is *not* used to provide information about clients?

    A. rules

    B. sysidcfg

    C. check

    D. class

12. Which of the following is not a valid entry in the first field in the rules file?

    A. `karch`

    B. `any`

    C. `hostname`

    D. `ip_address`

13. Which of the following files is the JumpStart file that can use any name and still work properly?

    A. class

    B. rules

    C. sysidcfg

    D. profile

14. Which of the following scripts will update or create the rules.ok file?

    A. `pfinstall` script

    B. `check` script

    C. `setup_install_server` script

    D. `install_type` script

15. Which of the following supplies the OS during a JumpStart installation.

    A. Setup Server

    B. Install server

    C. Profile server

    D. /jumpstart directory

16. Which of the following contains the JumpStart directory and configuration files such as the class file and the rules file?

    A. Profile diskette

    B. Setup server

    C. Install Server

    D. Configuration server

17. Which of the following commands is issued on the install server to set up remote workstations to install Solaris from the install server?

    A. `add_install_client`

    B. `add_install_server`

    C. `setup_install_client`

    D. `setup_client`

18. Which of the following commands sets up a system as a boot server only?

    A. `setup_install_server`

    B. `add_install_server -b`

    C. `setup_install_server -b`

    D. `setup_boot_server`

## APPLY YOUR KNOWLEDGE

19. Which of the following commands is used on a JumpStart client to start the installation?

    A. `boot net — install`

    B. `boot net`

    C. `boot — jumpstart`

    D. `boot net — jumpstart`

20. Which script copies additional packages within a product tree to the local disk on an existing install server?

    A. `add_install_server -a`

    B. `add_to_install_server`

    C. `setup_install_server`

    D. `_server -a`

## Answer to Review Questions

1. **A.** JumpStart lets you automatically install the Solaris software on a SPARC-based system just by inserting the Solaris CD and powering on the system. You do not need to specify the `boot` command at the `ok` prompt.

2. **A.** The custom JumpStart method of installing the OS provides a way to install groups of similar systems automatically and identically.

3. **D.** `The setup_install_server` script sets up an install server to provide the OS to the client during a JumpStart installation.

4. **B.** The rules.ok file is a file that should contain a rule for each group of systems you want to install.

5. **A.** The boot server is set up to answer RARP requests from a JumpStart client.

6. **C.** A configuration disk is used as an alternate to setting up a configuration directory.

7. **C.** The rules.ok file contains the name of a finish script.

8. **D.** A begin script is a user-defined Bourne shell script, located in the JumpStart configuration directory on the configuration server, specified within the rules file, that performs tasks before the Solaris software is installed on the system.

9. **A.** A class file is a text file that defines how to install the Solaris software on a system.

10. **B.** After you create a class file, you can use the `pfinstall` command to test it.

11. **C.** The sysidcfg, rules, and class files all provide information about the JumpStart client. The check script is used to validate the rules file.

12. **D.** `any`, `hostname`, and `karch` are all valid keywords that can be used in the rules file.

13. **A.** The class file can be named anything, but it should reflect the way in which it installs the Solaris software on a system.

14. **B.** The `check` script will update or create the rules.ok file.

15. **B.** The install server supplies the OS during a JumpStart installation.

16. **D.** The configuration server contains all the essential custom JumpStart configuration files, such as the rules file, the rules.ok file, the class file, the check script, and the optional begin and finish scripts.

## APPLY YOUR KNOWLEDGE

17. **A.** Use the `add_install_client` command on the install server to set up remote workstations to install Solaris from the install server.

18. **C.** `setup_install_server -b` sets up a system as a boot server only.

19. **A.** `boot net — install` is used on a JumpStart client to start the installation.

20. **B.** The `add_install_server -a` script copies additional packages within a product tree to the local disk on an existing install server.

SECTION

# Final Review

- Fast Facts
- Study & Exam Prep Tips
- Practice Exam

# Fast Facts

## Solaris 8 System Administrator Certification

The chapters of this book covered in detail the subjects you need to know for the Solaris System Administrator exam. Now that it's time for the test, you'll need to brush up on the major areas and refresh your memory. What are the most important areas to study?

The following section is a condensed version of the rest of the book. It covers the more crucial concepts, presenting information you'll need concisely. Remember: It is important to understand these concepts, not just memorize them, and you'll be on your way to passing the exam.

## System Startup

You can supply several options to the boot command at the `ok` prompt. Summary Table 1 describes each of these.

**SUMMARY TABLE 1**
**Boot Command Options**

| *Option* | *Description* |
|---|---|
| `-a` | An interactive boot |
| `-r` | A reconfiguration boot |
| `-s` | A single-user boot |
| `-v` | A verbose-mode boot |

The following list describes the steps for booting interactively:

1. At the `ok` prompt, type `boot -a`, and press Enter. The boot program prompts you interactively.
2. Press Enter to use the default kernel (/kernel/unix) as prompted, or type the name of the kernel to use for booting and press Enter.

3. Press Enter to use the default modules directory path as prompted, or type the path for the modules directory and press Enter.

4. Press Enter to use the default /etc/system file as prompted, or type the name of the system file and press Enter.

5. Press Enter to use the default root file system type as prompted (ufs for local disk booting, or nfs for diskless clients).

6. Press Enter to use the default physical name of the root device as prompted, or type the device name.

Solaris has eight system-run states, 0–6 and s (see Summary Table 2). The run level is initially set by the kernel during the boot process, or it can be set by booting to single user mode (boot –s) or with the `init` command after boot.

### SUMMARY TABLE 2
### THE EIGHT SYSTEM RUN STATES

| *Run State* | *Description* |
|---|---|
| 0 | Stops system services and daemons. Terminates all running processes. Unmounts all file systems. |
| S,s | Single-user (system administrator) state. Only root is allowed to log in at the console, and any users logged in are logged out when entering this run level. All file systems previously mounted remain mounted and accessible. All services except the most basic operating system services are shut down in an orderly manner. |
| 1 | Single-user (system administrator) state. All file systems are still available, and any logged-in users can remain logged in. All services except the most basic operating system services are shut down in an orderly manner. |
| 2 | Normal multiuser operation without NFS file systems shared. Sets the timezone variable. Mounts the /usr file system. Cleans up the /tmp and /var/tmp directories. Loads the network interfaces and starts processes. Starts the `cron` daemon. Cleans up the uucp tmp files. Starts the lp system. Starts the `sendmail` daemon. |
| 3 | Normal multiuser operation of a file server with NFS systems shared. Completes all the tasks in run level 2. Starts the NFS system daemons. |
| 4 | Alternative multiuser state (currently not used). |
| 5 | Power-down state. Shuts down the system so that it is safe to turn off power to the system. If possible, automatically turns off system power on systems that support this feature. |
| 6 | Reboots. |

## COMMANDS TO SHUT DOWN THE SYSTEM

When preparing to shut down a system, you need to determine which of the following commands is appropriate for the system and the task at hand:

`/usr/sbin/shutdown`

`/sbin/init`

`/usr/sbin/halt`

`/usr/sbin/reboot`

`/usr/sbin/poweroff`

Stop+A or L1+A (to be used as a last resort)

# OpenBoot

A full device pathname is a series of node names separated by slashes (/). The root of the tree is the machine node, which is not named explicitly but is indicated by a leading slash (/). The components of the device pathname are described in Summary Table 3.

### Summary Table 3
### Device Pathname Parameters

| *Parameter* | *Description* |
|---|---|
| `driver-name` | A human-readable string consisting of 1–31 letters, digits, and the following punctuation characters: , . _ + -<br><br>Uppercase and lowercase characters are distinct. In some cases, the driver name includes the name of the device's manufacturer and the device's model name, separated by a comma. Typically, the manufacturer's uppercase, publicly listed stock symbol is used as the manufacturer's name (that is, SUNW,hme0). For built-in devices, the manufacturer's name is usually omitted (that is, sbus or pci).<br><br>@ must precede the address parameter and serves as a separator between the driver name and unit address. |
| `unit-address` | A text string representing the physical address of the device in its parent's address space. The exact meaning of a particular address depends on the bus to which the device is attached. In this example:<br><br>`/sbus@1f,0/esp@0,40000/sd@3,0:a`<br><br>`1f,0` represents an address on the main system bus; the SBus is directly attached to the main system bus in this example.<br><br>`0,40000` is an SBus slot number. The example shows that the device is in SBus slot 0 and the offset is `40000`.<br><br>`3,0` is a SCSI target and logical unit number. In the example, the disk device is attached to a SCSI bus at target 3, logical unit 0.<br><br>See Appendix D, "Overview of SCSI Devices," for more information on SCSI host adapters, targets, and logical units. |
| `device-arguments` | A text string whose format depends on the particular device. It can be used to pass additional information to the device's software. In this example:<br><br>`/sbus@1f,0/scsi@2,1/sd@3,0:a`<br><br>the argument for the disk device is "a." The software driver for this device interprets its argument as a disk partition, so the device pathname refers to partition "a" on that disk. |

Summary Table 4 describes the `devalias` command, which is used to examine, create, and change OpenBoot aliases.

### Summary Table 4
### devalias

| *Command* | *Description* |
|---|---|
| `devalias` | Displays all current device aliases. |
| `devalias_alias` | Displays the device pathname corresponding to `alias`. |
| `devalias_alias device-path` | Defines an `alias` representing `device-path`. |

# Installing the Solaris 8 Software

The computer must meet the following requirements before you can install Solaris 8 using the interactive installation method:

- The system must have a minimum of 64MB of RAM. Sufficient memory requirements are determined by several factors, including the number of active users and applications you plan to run.
- The media is distributed on CD-ROM only, so a CD-ROM is required either locally or on the network.
- The system must have a minimum of 2.3GB of disk space. See the next section for disk space requirements for the specific Solaris software that you plan to install. Also, add more disk space to support your environment's swap space requirements.
- The system must be a SPARC-based or an INTEL-based system.

Summary Table 5 gives a brief overview of each system configuration. It outlines which file systems are local and which are accessed over the network.

Solaris allocates disk space into separate file systems. The following is a typical partitioning scheme for a system with a single disk drive:

- root (/) and /usr. Solaris normally creates two partitions for itself: root (/) and /usr. The installation program determines how much space you need. Most of the files in these two partitions are static. If the root (/) file system fills up, the system will not operate properly.
- swap. This area on the disk doesn't have files in it. In UNIX, you're allowed to have more programs than will fit into memory. The pieces that aren't currently needed in memory are transferred into swap to free up physical memory for other active processes.
- /home. On a single-disk system, everything not in root (/), /usr, or swap should go into a separate partition. /home is where you would put user-created files.

### SUMMARY TABLE 5
### SYSTEM CONFIGURATIONS

| *System Type* | *Local File Systems* | *Local Swap* | *Remote File Systems* |
|---|---|---|---|
| Server | root (/), /usr, /opt/ | Yes | Optional export /home,/export/home |
| JavaStation | None | No | /home |
| Diskless client | None | No | root (/), swap, /usr, /home |
| AutoClient | cached root (/), cached /usr | Yes | /var |
| Stand-alone | root (/), /usr | Yes | Optional /usr, /export/home |

- /var (optional). Solaris uses this area for system log files, print spoolers, and email.
- /opt (optional). By default, the Solaris installation program loads optional software packages here. Also, third-party applications are usually loaded into /opt.

Use the output of the `prtconf` and `sysdef` commands to identify which disk, tape, and CD-ROM devices are connected to the system. The output of these commands displays the `driver not attached` message next to the device instances. Because some system process is always monitoring these devices, the `driver not attached` message is usually a good indication that there is physically no device at that device instance.

Logical devices are organized into subdirectories under the /dev directory by their device types, as shown in Summary Table 6.

#### SUMMARY TABLE 6
#### DEVICE LOCATIONS

| *Directory* | *Device Type* |
|---|---|
| /dev/dsk | Block interface to disk devices |
| /dev/rdsk | Raw or character interface to disk devices |
| /dev/rmt | Tape devices |
| /dev/term | Serial-line devices |
| /dev/cua | Dial-out modems |
| /dev/pts | Pseudo terminals |
| /dev/fbs | Frame buffers |
| /dev/sad | STREAMS administrative driver |

The fields of the logical device name are described in Summary Table 7.

#### SUMMARY TABLE 7
#### DISK DRIVE LOGICAL DEVICE NAME

| *Field* | *Description* |
|---|---|
| `cx` | Refers to the SCSI controller number |
| `tx` | Refers to the SCSI bus target number |
| `dx` | Refers to the disk number (always 0, except on storage arrays) |
| `sx` | Refers to the slice or partition number |

## SOFTWARE PACKAGE ADMINISTRATION

Solaris provides tools for adding and removing software from a system. Those tools are described in Summary Table 8.

#### SUMMARY TABLE 8
#### TOOLS FOR MANAGING SOFTWARE

| *Command* | *Description* |
|---|---|
| ***Managing Software from the Command Line*** | |
| `pkgadd` | Adds software packages to the system. |
| `pkgrm` | Removes software packages from the system. |
| `pkgchk` | Checks the accuracy of a software package installation. |
| `pkginfo` | Displays software package information. |
| `pkgask` | Stores answers in a response file so that they can be supplied automatically during an installation. |
| `pkgparam` | Displays package parameter values. |
| ***Managing Software from the Graphical User Interface*** | |
| `admintool` | Invokes a GUI from within CDE or OpenWindows. |

You might want to know more about patches that have previously been installed. Summary Table 9 shows commands that provide useful information about patches already installed on a system.

### SUMMARY TABLE 9
### HELPFUL COMMANDS FOR PATCH ADMINISTRATION

| *Command* | *Function* |
|---|---|
| `showrev -p` | Shows all patches applied to a system. |
| `pkgparam pkgid PATCHLIST` | Shows all patches applied to the package identified by `pkgid`. |
| `pkgparam pkgid PATCH_` | Shows the installation date and name of the host from which the patch was applied. |
| `patchadd -R client_root_` | Shows all patches applied to a client from the server's console. |
| `patchadd -p` | Shows all patches applied to a system. |
| `patchrm patchname` | Removes a specified patch. |

## SETTING UP USER ACCOUNTS

When adding a new user in Admintool, you must fill in a number of fields. Summary Table 10 describes each of these.

### SUMMARY TABLE 10
### ADD USER FIELDS IN ADMINTOOL

| *Item* | *Description* |
|---|---|
| User Name | Enter a unique login name that will be entered at the Solaris login prompt. Choose a name unique to your organization. The name can contain 2–8 uppercase characters (A–Z), lowercase characters (a–z), or digits (0–9), but no underscores or spaces. The first character must be a letter, and at least one character must be a lowercase letter. |
| User ID | Enter the unique user ID (discussed in Chapter 8, "System Security"). Admintool automatically assigns the next available UID; however, in a networked environment, make sure that another user on another system does not duplicate this number. All UIDs must be consistent across the network. The UID is typically a number from 100–60002, but it can go as high as 2147483647. See the note in the description for "Primary Group" regarding UIDs over 60000. |
| Primary Group | Enter the primary group name or GID (group ID) number for the group to which the user will belong. This is the group that the operating system will assign to files the user creates. Group 10 (staff) is a predefined group that is usually sufficient for most users. GIDs can range from 0–60002, but they can go as high as 2147483647. |
| Secondary Groups | (Optional) Enter the names or GIDs, separated by spaces, of any additional groups to which the user belongs. A user can belong to as many as 16 secondary groups. |
| Comment | (Optional) Enter any comments, such as the full username or phone number. |
| Login Shell | Click this button to select the shell the user will use, such as /bin/csh. If nothing is selected, the default shell is the Bourne shell (/bin/sh). |

| | | |
|---|---|---|
| Password | Click this button to specify the password status. Selectable options are as follows: | |
| | Cleared until first login. | This is the default. The account does not have a password assigned. The user is prompted for a password on first login, unless `passreq=no` is set in /etc/default/login. |
| | Account is locked. | The account is disabled with an invalid password and can be unlocked by assigning a new password. This type of account allows a user to own files but not to log in. |
| | No password; `setuid` only. | The account cannot be logged into directly. This allows programs such as `lp` and `uucp` to run under an account without allowing a user to log in. |
| | Normal password. | The account will have a password that you set in the pop-up window that appears. |
| | Min Change. | (Optional). Enter the minimum number of days allowed between password changes. This is intended to prevent a user from changing the password and then changing it back a few seconds later, which would defeat the concept of password aging. The default is 0. |
| | Max Change. | (Optional) Enter the maximum number of days the password is valid before it must be changed; otherwise, the account is locked. Leaving the field blank means the password never has to be changed. |
| | Max Inactive. | (Optional) Enter the maximum number of days an account can go without being accessed before it is automatically locked. A blank field means the account remains active no matter how long it goes unused. |
| | Expiration Date. | (Optional) Enter the date when the user account expires. `None` means no expiration. |
| | Warning. | (Optional) Enter the number of days to begin warning the user before the password expires. A blank means no warning is given. |
| | Create Home Dir. | Check this box to have the user's home directory automatically created. |
| | Path. | Use the Path field to point to an existing directory or to specify a new directory to create. |

Another way to manage user accounts is from the command line. Although using the command line is more complex than using the Admintool GUI interface, the command line provides a little more flexibility. Solaris supplies the user administration commands described in Summary Table 11 for setting up and managing user accounts.

## SUMMARY TABLE 11
## ACCOUNT ADMINISTRATION COMMANDS

| *Command* | *Description* |
|---|---|
| `useradd` | Adds a new user account |
| `userdel` | Deletes a user account |
| `usermod` | Modifies a user account |
| `groupadd` | Adds a new group |
| `groupmod` | Modifies a group (for example, changes the group ID or name) |
| `groupdel` | Deletes a group |

The most common customizations to shell startup scripts are environment variables. Summary Table 12 describes environment and shell variables you might want to customize in a user initialization file.

### SUMMARY TABLE 12
### SHELL AND ENVIRONMENT VARIABLE DESCRIPTIONS

| *Variable* | *Description* |
|---|---|
| `history` | Sets the history for the C shell. |
| `HOME` | Sets the path to the user's home directory. |
| `LPDEST` | Sets the user's default printer. |
| `PATH` (or `path` in the C shell) | Lists, in order, the directories that the shell searches to find the program to run when the user types a command. If the directory is not in the search path, the user must type the complete pathname of a command. |
| `prompt` | Defines the shell prompt for the C shell. |
| `TERM` (or `term` in the C shell) | Defines the terminal. This variable should be reset in /etc/profile or /etc/.login. |
| `MAIL` | Sets the path to the user's mailbox. |
| `MANPATH` | Sets the search path for system manual pages. |
| `umask` | Sets the default user mask. |

## INTRODUCTION TO FILE SYSTEMS

A file system is a structure of directories used to organize and store files on disk in a standard UNIX file system format. All disk-based computer systems have a file system. In UNIX, file systems have two basic components: files and directories. A *file* is the actual information as it is stored on the disk, and a *directory* is a listing of the filenames. In addition to keeping track of filenames, the file system must also keep track of files' access dates and ownership.

A *hard disk* consists of several separate disk platters mounted on a common spindle. Data stored on each platter surface is written and read by disk heads. The circular path a disk head traces over a spinning disk platter is called a *track*.

Each track is made up of a number of sectors laid end to end. A *sector* consists of a header, a trailer, and 512 bytes of data. The header and trailer contain error-checking information to help ensure the accuracy of the data. Taken together, the set of tracks traced across all of the individual disk platter surfaces for a single position of the heads is called a cylinder.

Following are the four types of disk-based file systems used by Solaris 8:

- UFS. The UNIX file system, which is based on the BSD FAT Fast file system (the traditional UNIX file system). The UFS file system is the default disk-based file system used in Solaris.
- HSFS. The High Sierra and ISO 9660 file system. The HSFS file system is used on CD-ROMs, and is a read-only file system.
- PCFS. The PC file system, which allows read/write access to data and programs on DOS-formatted disks written for DOS-based personal computers.
- UDFS. New in Solaris 8 is the UDF (Universal Disk Format) file system. UDF is the new industry -standard format for storing information on the optical media technology called *DVD* (Digital Versatile Disc or Digital Video Disc).

The *Network File System (NFS)* or remote file systems are file systems made available from remote systems. NFS is the only available network-based file system. (NFS is discussed in detail in Chapter 17, "The NFS Environment," and is covered on the second exam.)

When you create a UFS file system, the disk slice is divided into cylinder groups. The slice is then divided into blocks to control and organize the structure of the files within the cylinder group. A UFS file system has the following four types of blocks. Each performs a specific function in the file system:

- Boot block. Stores information used when booting the system.
- Superblock. Stores much of the information about the file system.
- Inode. Stores all information about a file except its name.
- Storage or data block. Stores data for each file.

File systems can be mounted from the command line by using the `mount` command. The commands in Summary Table 13 are used from the command line to mount and unmount file systems.

### SUMMARY TABLE 13
### FILE SYSTEM COMMANDS

| *Command* | *Description* |
|---|---|
| `mount` | Mounts specified file systems and remote resources |
| `mountall` | Mounts all file systems specified in a file system table (vfstab) |
| `umount` | Unmounts specified file systems and remote resources |
| `umountall` | Unmounts all file systems specified in a file system table |

## Displaying a File System's Disk Space Usage

Use the `df` command and it's options to see the capacity of each file system mounted on a system, the amount of space available, and the percentage of space already in use. Use the `du` (directory usage) command to report the number of free disk blocks and files.

# SOLARIS FILE SYSTEMS: ADVANCED TOPICS

`mkfs` constructs a file system on the character (or raw) device found in the /dev/rdsk directory. Again, it is highly recommended that you do not run the `mkfs` command directly, but instead use the friendlier `newfs` command, which automatically determines all the necessary parameters required by `mkfs` to construct the file system. In the following example, the `-v` option to the `newfs` command will output all the parameters passed to the `mkfs` utility.

The `tunefs` command options are described in Summary Table 14.

### SUMMARY TABLE 14
### THE *TUNEFS* COMMAND

| *Option* | *Description* |
|---|---|
| `-a <maxcontig>` | Specifies the maximum number of contiguous blocks that are laid out before forcing a rotational delay (see the `-d` option). The default value is 1 because most device drivers require an interrupt per disk transfer. For device drivers that can chain several buffers together in a single transfer, set this to the maximum chain length. |
| `-d <rotdelay>` | Specifies the expected time (in milliseconds) to service a transfer completion interrupt and to initiate a new transfer on the same disk. It is used to decide how much rotational spacing to place between successive blocks in a file. |
| `-e <maxbpg>` | Sets the maximum number of blocks that any single file can allocate from a cylinder group before it is forced to begin allocating blocks from another cylinder group. |
| `-m <minfree>` | Specifies the percentage of space held back from normal users (the minimum free space threshold). The default value is 10 percent. |
| `-o <value>` | Changes the optimization strategy for the file system. The `value` is either `space` or `time`. Use `space` to conserve space; use `time` to attempt to organize file layout to minimize access time. Generally, optimize a file system for time unless it is more than 90% full. |
| `<special>/<filesystem>` | Enter either the special device name (such as /dev/rdsk/c0t0d0s6) or the file system name (such as /home). |

Several other commands help you administer the volume manager on your system. They are described in Summary Table 15.

### SUMMARY TABLE 15
### VOLUME MANAGER COMMANDS

| *Command* | *Description* |
|---|---|
| `rmmount` | Removable media mounter. Used by `vold` to automatically mount /cdrom and /floppy if a CD or floppy disk is installed. |
| `volcancel` | Cancels a user's request to access a particular CD-ROM or floppy file system. This command, issued by the system administrator, is useful if the removable medium containing the file system is not currently in the drive. |
| `volcheck` | The system administrator issues this command to check the drive for installed media. By default, it checks the drive pointed to by /dev/diskette. |
| `volmissing` | This action, which is specified in vold.conf, notifies the user if an attempt is made to access a CD or floppy disk that is no longer in the drive. |
| `vold` | The volume manager daemon, controlled by /etc/vold.conf. |

## SYSTEM SECURITY

Protecting your system against intruders begins with the following:

- Physical security. Limiting physical access to the computer equipment.
- Controlling system access. Limiting user access via passwords and permissions.

- Controlling file access. Limiting access to data by assigning file access permissions.
- Auditing users. Monitoring user activities to detect a threat before damage occurs.
- Network security. Protecting against access through phone lines, serial lines, or the network.
- Securing superuser access. Reserving superuser access for system administration use only.

File access permissions are shown by the `ls -la` command. The first column returned describes the type of file and its access permissions for the user, group, and others using letters. The `r`, `w`, and `x` are described in Summary Table 16.

### SUMMARY TABLE 16
### FILE ACCESS PERMISSIONS

| *Symbol* | *Permission* | *Means That Designated Users...* |
|---|---|---|
| `r` | Read | Can open and read the contents of a file. |
| `w` | Write | Can write to the file (modify its contents), add to it, or delete it. |
| `x` | Execute | Can execute the file (if it is a program or shell script). |
| - | Denied | Cannot read, write to, or execute the file. |

When listing the permissions on a directory, all columns of information are the same as for a file, with one exception. The `r`, `w`, and `x` found in the first column are treated slightly differently than for a file. These are described in Summary Table 17.

### SUMMARY TABLE 17
### DIRECTORY ACCESS PERMISSIONS

| *Symbol* | *Permission* | *Means That Designated Users...* |
|---|---|---|
| `r` | Read | Can list files in the directory. |
| `w` | Write | Can add or remove files or links in the directory. |
| `x` | Execute | Can open or execute files in the directory. Also can make the directory and the directories beneath it current. |
| - | Denied | Do not have read, write, or execute privileges. |

Use the commands listed in Summary Table 18 to modify file access permissions and ownership, but remember that only the owner of the file or root can assign or modify these values.

### SUMMARY TABLE 18
### FILE ACCESS COMMANDS

| *Command* | *Description* |
|---|---|
| `chmod` | Changes access permissions on a file. You can use either symbolic mode (letters and symbols) or absolute mode (octal numbers) to change permissions on a file. |
| `chown` | Changes the ownership of a file. |
| `chgrp` | Changes the group ownership of a file. |

It is critical to turn off all unneeded network services because many of the services run by `inetd`, such as `rexd`, pose serious security threats. `rexd` is the daemon responsible for remote program execution. On a system connected to the rest of the world via the Internet, this could create a potential entry point for a hacker. TFTP should absolutely be disabled if you don't have diskless clients taking advantage of it. Many sites will also disable finger so that external users can't figure out the usernames of your internal users. Everything else depends on the needs of your site.

Solaris 8's File Transfer Protocol (FTP) is a common tool for transferring files across the network. Although most sites leave FTP enabled, you need to limit who can use it. Solaris 8 contains a file named /etc/ftpusers that is used to restrict access via FTP. The /etc/ftpusers file contains a list of login names that are prohibited from running an FTP login on the system.

The following are the advantages of using SUDO for root access:

- You don't have to give out the root password to everyone. It's a handy way to give users controlled access for commands they need to get their work done.
- SUDO is a good tool to get beginning system administrators started without giving them full access.
- The audit logs are quite handy to track root activities. If something changes, you can go to the log to see when it happened and who did it.
- It works well and is a simple but effective point solution.

The Solaris 8 system software includes the Automated Security Enhancement Tool (ASET), which helps you monitor and control system security by automatically performing tasks you would otherwise do manually. ASET performs the following seven tasks, each making specific checks and adjustments to system files and permissions to ensure system security:

- Verifies appropriate system file permissions
- Verifies system file contents
- Checks the consistency and integrity of /etc/passwd and /etc/group entries
- Checks on the contents of system configuration files
- Checks environment files (.profile, .login, .cshrc)
- Verifies appropriate `eeprom` settings
- Builds a firewall on a router

A system administrator can have the best system security measures in place, but without the users' cooperation, system security will be compromised. The system administrator must teach common-sense rules regarding system security, such as the following:

- Use proper passwords. Countless sites use passwords such as "admin" or "supervisor" for their root accounts.
- Don't give your password to anyone, no matter who he says he is. One of the best system crackers of our time said that he would simply pose as a system support person, ask a user for his password, and get free reign to the system.
- If you walk away from the system, log out or lock the screen. Think of the damage if someone walked up to your station and sent a scathing email to the president of your company—with your name attached!
- Don't connect modems to your system without approval from the system administrator.

## Process Control

A process is distinct from a job or command, which can be composed of many processes working together to perform a specific task. Each process has a process ID associated with it and is referred to as a pid. You can monitor processes that are currently executing by using one of the commands listed in Summary Table 19.

### SUMMARY TABLE 19
### COMMANDS TO DISPLAY PROCESSES

| *Command* | *Description* |
|---|---|
| `ps` | Executed from the command line to display information about active processes. |
| `pgrep` | Executed from the command line to find processes by a specific name or attribute. |
| `prstat` | Executed from the command line to display information about active processes on the system. |
| CDE Process Manager | A GUI used to display and control processes on a system. This utility requires a terminal capable of displaying graphics. |

A process has certain attributes that directly affect execution. These are listed in Summary Table 20.

### SUMMARY TABLE 20
### PROCESS ATTRIBUTES

| *Attribute* | *Description* |
|---|---|
| `PID` | The process identification (a unique number that defines the process within the kernel). |
| `PPID` | The parent `PID` (the creator of the process). |
| `UID` | The user ID number of the user who owns the process. |
| `EUID` | The effective user ID of the process. |
| `GID` | The group ID of the user who owns the process. |
| `EGID` | The effective group ID that owns the process. |
| `Priority` | The priority at which the process runs. |

## Using the *kill* Command

The `kill` command sends a terminate signal (signal 15) to the process, and the process is terminated. Signal 15, which is the default when no options are used with the `kill` command, is a gentle kill that allows a process to perform cleanup work before terminating. Signal 9, on the other hand, is called a sure, unconditional kill because it cannot be caught or ignored by a process. If the process is still around after a `kill -9`, it is either hung up in the UNIX kernel, waiting for an event such as disk I/O to complete, or you are not the owner of the process.

Often, a long-running job should have its priority lowered to lessen its impact on the system, letting shorter or more urgent jobs have more system resources. In these cases, use the `nice` command as described in Summary Table 21 when submitting a program or command.

### SUMMARY TABLE 21
### SETTING PRIORITIES WITH `nice`

| *Command* | *Description* |
|---|---|
| ***Lowering the Priority of a Process*** | |
| `nice <command_name>` | Increases the nice number by four units (the default). |
| `nice +4 <command_name>` | Increases the nice number by four units. |
| `nice +10 <command_name>` | Increases the nice number by 10 units. |
| ***Increasing the Priority of a Process*** | |
| `nice -10 <command_name>` | Raises the priority of the command by lowering the nice number. |
| `nice - -10 <command_name>` | Raises the priority of the command by lowering the nice number. The two minus signs are required. The first is the option sign, and the second indicates a negative number. |

Summary Table 22 describes the fields in the `crontab` file for scheduling jobs to run on a regular basis.

### SUMMARY TABLE 22
### THE `crontab` FILE

| *Field* | *Description* | *Values* |
|---|---|---|
| 1 | Minute | 0–59. An * in this field means every minute. |
| 2 | Hour | 0–23. An * in this field means every hour. |
| 3 | Day of month | 1–31. An * in this field means every day of the month. |
| 4 | Month | 1–12. An * in this field means every month. |
| 5 | Day of week | 0–6 (0 = Sunday). An * in this field means every day of the week. |
| 6 | Command | Enter the command to be run. |

## SCHEDULING A SINGLE SYSTEM EVENT (at)

The `at` command is used to schedule jobs for execution at a later time. Unlike `crontab`, which schedules a job to happen at regular intervals, a job submitted with `at` executes once, at the designated time.

## THE LP PRINT SERVICE

Many methods can be used to define a printer on a Solaris system. Summary Table 23 describes the tools Solaris provides for adding printers.

### SUMMARY TABLE 23
### SOLARIS PRINTER UTILITIES

| *Utility* | *Description* |
|---|---|
| SunSoft Print Client Software | An interface that was previously available only with the Solstice AdminSuite set of administration tools. It is now available as part of the standard Solaris distribution software and is used to set up print clients. |
| Admintool | A graphical user interface used to create, modify, and delete printers on a local system. This is the recommended way for novice users to add printers. |
| Solstice Print Manager | A graphical user Print Manager interface used to manage printers in a name service environment. Available only with the Solaris 8 server software distribution. |
| LP Print Service Commands | The command-line utilities used to set up and manage printers. These commands provide complete functionality; Admintool and the AdminSuite packages are somewhat limited for advanced tasks. |

Summary Table 24 lists the `lp` commands, which are the command line means for controlling printers and print queues.

#### SUMMARY TABLE 24
#### SOLARIS *LP* COMMANDS

| *Command* | *Description* |
|---|---|
| `accept/reject` | Enables or disables any further requests for a printer or class entering the spooling area. |
| `cancel` | Lets the user stop the printing of information. |
| `enable/disable` | Enables or disables any more output from the spooler to the printer. |
| `lp` | The user's print command. Places information to be printed into the spooler. |
| `lpadmin` | Allows the configuration of the print service. |
| `lpmove` | Moves print requests between destinations. |
| `lpsched` | Starts the print service. |
| `lpshut` | Stops the print service. |
| `lpstat` | Displays the status of the print service. |

## BACKUP AND RECOVERY

Solaris provides the utilities listed in Summary Table 25. They can be used to copy data from disk to removable media and restore it.

#### SUMMARY TABLE 25
#### BACKUP UTILITIES

| *Utility* | *Description* |
|---|---|
| `tar` | Archives data to another directory, system, or medium. |
| `dd` | Copies data quickly. |
| `cpio` | Copies data from one location to another. |
| `pax` | Copies files and directory subtrees to a single tape. This command provides better portability than `tar` or `cpio`, so it can be used to transport files to other types of UNIX systems. |
| `ufsdump` | Backs up all files in a file system. |
| `ufsrestore` | Restores some or all of the files archived with the `ufsdump` command. |

## WRITING SHELL SCRIPTS AND PROGRAMS

The Solaris 8 operating environment offers three commonly used shells:

- The Bourne shell (/sbin/sh). The default shell. It is a command programming language that executes commands read from a terminal or a file.
- The C shell (/bin/csh). A command interpreter with a C-like syntax. The C-shell provides a number of convenient features for interactive use that are not available with the Bourne shell, including filename completion, command aliasing, and history substitution.
- The Korn shell (/bin/ksh). A command programming language that executes commands read from a terminal or a file.

The login shell is the command interpreter that runs when you log in. The Solaris 8 operating environment offers the three most commonly used shells, as described in Summary Table 26.

### SUMMARY TABLE 26
### BASIC FEATURES OF THE BOURNE, C, AND KORN SHELLS

| *Feature* | *Bourne* | *C* | *Korn* |
|---|---|---|---|
| Syntax compatible with sh | Yes | No | Yes |
| Job control | Yes | Yes | Yes |
| History list | No | Yes | Yes |
| Command-line editing | No | Yes | Yes |
| Aliases | No | Yes | Yes |
| Single-character abbreviation | No | Yes | Yes |
| Protect files from overwriting | No | Yes | Yes (noclobber) |
| Ignore Ctrl+D (ignoreeof) | No | Yes | Yes |
| Enhanced cd | No | Yes | Yes |
| Initialization file separate | No | Yes | Yes |
| Logout file | No | Yes | No |

## The Solaris Network Environment

In the ISO/OSI model, individual services that are required for communication are arranged in seven layers that build on one another. Think of the layers as steps that must be completed before you can move on to the next step and ultimately, communicate between systems. Summary Table 27 describes the function of each individual layer.

### SUMMARY TABLE 27
### NETWORK LAYERS

| *ISO/OSI Layer* | *Function* |
|---|---|
| Physical | Layer 1 describes the network hardware, including electrical and mechanical connections to the network. |
| Data Link | Layer 2 splits data into frames for sending on the physical layer and receives acknowledgement frames. It performs error checking and retransmits frames not received correctly. |
| Network | Layer 3 manages the delivery of data via the Data Link layer and is used by the Transport layer. The most common network layer protocol is IP. |
| Transport | Layer 4 determines how to use the Network layer to provide a virtual error-free, point-to-point connection so that host A can send messages to host B, and they will arrive uncorrupted and in the correct order. |
| Session | Layer 5 uses the Transport layer to establish a connection between processes on different hosts. It handles security and creation of the session. |
| Presentation | Layer 6 performs functions such as text compression and code or format conversion to try to smooth out differences between hosts. Allows incompatible processes in the application layer to communicate via the Session layer. |
| Application | Layer 7 is concerned with the user's view of the network (that is, formatting electronic mail messages). The Presentation layer provides the Application layer with a familiar local representation of data independent of the format used on the network. |

## Network Definitions

Following are network definitions:

- Packet. A packet is the basic unit of information to be transferred over the network.
- Ethernet. Ethernet is a standard that defines the physical components a machine uses to access the network and the speed at which the network runs. It includes specifications for cabling, connectors, and computer interface components.

- FDDI. Fiber Distributed Data Interface (FDDI) is a standard for data transmission on fiber-optic lines in a LAN that can extend up to 200km (124 miles). The FDDI protocol is based on the token-ring protocol.

## Network Hardware

The network hardware is the physical part of the network you can actually see. The physical components connect the systems and include the NIC, host, cabling, connectors, hubs, and routers. Following are definitions of these components:

- NIC. The computer hardware that lets you connect it to a network is known as a *Network Interface Card* (NIC) or network adapter.
- Hosts. If you are an experienced Solaris user, you are no doubt familiar with the term *host*, often used as a synonym for "computer" or "machine." From a TCP/IP perspective, only two types of entities exist on a network: routers and hosts.
- Hubs and cabling. Ethernet cabling is run to each system from a hub. The hub does nothing more than connect all the Ethernet cables so that the computers can connect to one another. It does not boost the signal or route packets from one network to another.
- Routers. A router is a machine that forwards Ethernet packets from one network to another. In other words, the router connects LANs, and the hub connects computers.

## TCP/IP Commands

Following are TCP/IP commands:

- `telnet`. `telnet` is used to log into another system on the network.
- `rlogin`. `rlogin` is also a command for logging into another system on the network. Unlike `telnet`, `rlogin` has a mechanism whereby you don't have to enter a login name and password if the /.rhosts and /etc/hosts.equiv files are in place.
- `ftp`. The File Transfer Protocol (FTP) is used to transfer one or more files between two systems on the network.
- `rcp`. You can also use the `rcp` (remote copy) command to transfer one or more files between two hosts on a network. The other system must trust your ID on the current host.
- `rsh`. You use the `rsh` (remote shell) command to execute a shell on another system on the network. The other system must trust your ID on the current system.
- `rexec`. The `rexec` command is also used to execute a shell on a remote system. This command differs from `rsh` in that you must enter a password. At many sites, `rsh` is disabled for security reasons and `rexec` is used as a replacement.
- `finger`. The `finger` command displays information about users logged on to the local system or other systems.
- `rup`. The `rup` command shows the host status of remote systems, similar to the `uptime` command.
- `ping`. Use the `ping` command to test network connectivity to a particular host.

# CLASS NETWORKS

There are five classes of IP addresses: A, B, C, D, and E. The following is a brief description of each class.

## Class A Networks

Class A networks are used for large networks with millions of hosts, such as the Internet. A class A network number uses the first 8 bits of the IP address as its network ID. The remaining 24 bits comprise the host part of the IP address. The values assigned to the first byte of class A network numbers fall within the range 0–127. For example, consider the IP address 75.4.10.4. The value 75 in the first byte indicates that the host is on a class A network. The remaining bytes, 4.10.4, establish the host address. The InterNIC assigns only the first byte of a class A number. Use of the remaining 3 bytes is left to the discretion of the owner of the network number. Only 127 class A networks can exist; each of these networks can accommodate up to 16,777,214 hosts.

## Class B Networks

Class B networks are medium-sized networks, such as universities and large businesses with many hosts. A class B network number uses 16 bits for the network number and 16 bits for host numbers. The first byte of a class B network number is in the range 128–191. In the number 129.144.50.56, the first two bytes, 129.144, are assigned by the InterNIC and comprise the network address. The last two bytes, 50.56, make up the host address and are assigned at the discretion of the network's owner. A class B network can accommodate a maximum of 65,534 hosts.

## Class C Networks

Class C networks are used for small networks containing fewer than 254 hosts. Class C network numbers use 24 bits for the network number and 8 bits for host numbers. A class C network number occupies the first three bytes of an IP address; only the fourth byte is assigned at the discretion of the network's owner. The first byte of a class C network number covers the range 192–223. The second and third bytes each cover the range 1–255. A typical class C address might be 192.5.2.5, with the first three bytes, 192.5.2, forming the network number. The final byte in this example, 5, is the host number. A class C network can accommodate a maximum of 254 hosts.

## Class D and E Networks

Class D addresses cover the range 224–239 and are used for IP multicasting as defined in RFC 988. Class E addresses cover the range 240–255 and are reserved for experimental use.

# SOLARIS PSEUDO FILE SYSTEMS AND SWAP SPACE

Sometimes referred to as ram-based or virtual file systems, the distinguishing feature is that a pseudo file system does not reside on hard physical media. Pseudo file systems reside only in physical memory while the operating system is running. The pseudo file systems supported in the Solaris 8 operating environment are listed in Summary Table 28.

**SUMMARY TABLE 28**
**SOLARIS PSEUDO FILE SYSTEMS**

| *File System* | *Description* |
|---|---|
| procfs | The Process file system contains a list of active processes, named according to process number, in the /proc directory. Images of active processes are stored here by their process ID number. Process tools are available in the /usr/proc/bin directory that displays highly detailed information about the processes listed in the /proc directory. |
| tmpfs | This is a temporary file system for file storage in memory without the overhead of writing to a disk-based file system. Data in this file system is destroyed every time the file system is unmounted or the system is rebooted. |
| fdfs | The File Descriptor file system provides explicit names for opening files using file descriptors. |
| swapfs | The Swap file system is used by the kernel to manage swap space on disks. |

# INSTALLING A SERVER

The server must meet a few minimum requirements before Solaris 8 can be installed:

- The Solaris 8 release supports all sun4c, sun4d, sun4u, and sun4m platforms. Some sun4c systems might not be supported in future releases of Solaris 8 beyond the 11/99 release. Check with your hardware vendor if you have a sun4c system to make sure it is supported before proceeding.
- To run a graphical user interface (GUI) installation, the system must have a minimum of 32MB of RAM. As a server, however, it is typical to have 256MB of RAM or more.
- The disk needs to be large enough to hold the Solaris operating system, swap space, and the additional software, such as Solstice AdminSuite and AutoClient. You'll also need to allocate additional disk space on an operating system server in the /export file system for diskless clients or Solstice AutoClient systems. Plan on a minimum of 1GB of disk space, but realistically you should have 2GB or more.

Summary Table 29 lists some commands that will help gather information about your server.

**SUMMARY TABLE 29**
**SYSTEM IDENTIFICATION INFORMATION**

| *Information Required* | *Command(s) Used to Gather the Information* |
|---|---|
| System name | /usr/bin/uname -u |
| Primary network interface | `ifconfig -a` |
| IP address | `ypmatch <system_name> <host>` |
| | `nismatch <system_name>` |
| | `more /etc/inet/hosts` |
| Domain name | `/usr/bin/domainname` |
| Whether part of a subnet | `more /etc/netmasks` |
| What name service is used | `more /etc/nsswitch.conf` |

# DEVICE ADMINISTRATION AND DISK MANAGEMENT

In Solaris, each disk device is described in three ways, using three distinct naming conventions:

- Physical device name. Represents the full device pathname in the device information hierarchy.
- Instance name. Represents the kernel's abbrevia-

tion name for every possible device on the system.

- Logical device name. Used by system administrators with most file system commands to refer to devices.

The system commands used to provide information about physical devices are described in Summary Table 30.

### SUMMARY TABLE 30 DEVICE INFORMATION COMMANDS

| *Command* | *Description* |
|---|---|
| `prtconf` | Displays system configuration information, including the total amount of memory and the device configuration, as described by the system's hierarchy. This useful tool verifies whether the system has seen a device. |
| `sysdef` | Displays device configuration information, including system hardware, pseudo devices, loadable modules, and selected kernel parameters. |
| `dmesg` | Displays system diagnostic messages, as well as a list of devices attached to the system since the most recent restart. |

Logical devices are organized in subdirectories under the /dev directory by their device types, as shown in Summary Table 31.

### SUMMARY TABLE 31 DEVICE DIRECTORIES

| *Directory* | *Description of Contents* |
|---|---|
| /dev/dsk | Block interface to disk devices |
| /dev/rdsk | Raw or character interface to disk devices |
| /dev/rmt | Tape devices |
| /dev/term | Serial line devices |
| /dev/cua | Dial-out modems |
| /dev/pts | Pseudo terminals |
| /dev/fbs | Frame buffers |
| /dev/sad | STREAMS administrative driver |

Using the DiskSuite command-line utilities or the graphical user interface, DiskSuite Tool, the system administrator creates each device by dragging slices onto one of three types of metadevice objects: metadevices, state database replicas, and hot spare pools, which are described in Summary Table 32.

### SUMMARY TABLE 32 DISKSUITE OBJECTS

| *Object* | *Description* |
|---|---|
| Metadevice | A metadevice is a group of physical slices that appear to the system as a single, logical device. A metadevice is used to increase storage capacity and increase data availability. |
| Metadevice state database | A database that stores information about the state of the DiskSuite configuration. DiskSuite cannot operate until you have created the metadevice state database replicas. |
| Hot Spare Pool | A collection of slices (hot spares) reserved to be automatically substituted in case of slice failure in either a submirror or RAID5 metadevice. Hot spares are used to increase data availability. |

# THE NFS ENVIRONMENT

The NFS service allows computers of different architectures, running different operating systems (OSs), to share file systems across a network. Just as the `mount` command lets you mount a file system on a local disk, NFS lets you mount a file system that is located on another system anywhere on the network. The NFS service provides the following benefits:

- Lets multiple computers use the same files so that everyone on the network can access the same data. This eliminates the need to have redundant data on several systems.
- Reduces storage costs by having computers share applications and data.
- Provides data consistency and reliability because all users can read the same set of files.
- Makes mounting of file systems transparent to users.
- Makes accessing remote files transparent to users.
- Supports heterogeneous environments.
- Reduces system administration overhead.

NFS uses a number of daemons to handle its services. These services are initialized at startup from the /etc/init.d/nfs.server and /etc/init.d/nfs.clients startup scripts. The most important NFS daemons are outlined in Summary Table 33.

## SUMMARY TABLE 33
## NFS DAEMONS

| *Daemon* | *Description* |
|---|---|
| `nfsd` | This daemon handles file system exporting and file access requests from remote systems. An NFS server runs multiple instances of this daemon. This daemon is usually invoked at run level 3, and is started by the /etc/init.d/nfs.server startup script. |
| `mountd` | This daemon handles mount requests from NFS clients. This daemon also provides information about which file systems are mounted by which clients. Use the `showmount` command, described later in this chapter, to view this information. This daemon is usually invoked at run level 3, and is started by the /etc/init.d/nfs.server startup script. |
| `lockd` | This daemon runs on the NFS server and NFS client, and provides file-locking services in NFS. This daemon is started by the /etc/init.d/nfs.client script at run level 2. |
| `statd` | This daemon runs on the NFS server and NFS client, and interacts with `lockd` to provide the crash and recovery functions for the locking services on NFS. This daemon is started by the /etc/init.d/nfs.client script at run level 2. |
| `rpcbind` | This daemon facilitates the initial connection between the client and the server. |
| `nfslogd` | This daemon provides operational logging to the Solaris NFS server. `nfslogd` is described later in this chapter. |

## WebNFS

WebNFS is a product and proposed standard protocol from Sun Microsystems that extends its NFS to the Internet. Sun believes WebNFS offers considerable performance advantages over the current Internet protocols, HTTP and FTP.

## CacheFS

A fundamental factor in computer performance is file access time. In a networked environment using NFS, every file access request across the network affects performance. The Cache File System (CacheFS) can be used to improve performance of NFS mounted file systems or slow devices, such as a CD-ROM. When a file system is cached, the data read from the remote file system or CD-ROM is stored in a cache on the local system's disk.

## Autofs

When a network contains even a moderate number of systems, all trying to mount file systems from each other, managing NFS can quickly become a nightmare. The Autofs facility, also called the automounter, is designed to handle such situations by providing a method in which remote directories are mounted only when they are being used.

# Name Services

The information handled by a name service includes the following:

- System (host) names and addresses
- Usernames
- Passwords
- Access permissions

Summary Table 34 describes the name services available in Solaris 8.

**SUMMARY TABLE 34**
**NAME SERVICES**

| *Name Service* | *Description* |
|---|---|
| /etc files | The original UNIX naming system. |
| NIS | The Network Information Service. |
| NIS+ | The Network Information Service Plus. (NIS+ is described in greater detail later in this chapter.) |
| DNS | The Domain Name System. (DNS is described in greater detail later in this chapter.) |
| LDAP | Lightweight Directory Access Protocol. (LDAP is described in greater detail later in this chapter.) |

## NIS

The NIS, formerly called the Yellow Pages (YP), is a distributed database system that allows the system administrator to administer the configuration of many hosts from a central location. Common configuration information, which would have to be maintained separately on each host in a network without NIS, can be stored and maintained in a central location and then propagated to all the nodes in the network. NIS stores information about workstation names and addresses, users, the network itself, and network services.

The systems within a NIS network are configured in the following ways:

- Master server
- Slave servers
- Clients of NIS servers

The name service switch controls how a client workstation or application obtains network information. Each workstation has a name service switch file in its /etc directory. In every system's /etc directory, you'll find templates for the nsswitch.conf file. These templates are described in Summary Table 35.

#### SUMMARY TABLE 35
#### NAME SERVICE SWITCH TEMPLATE FILES

| *Name* | *Description* |
|---|---|
| nsswitch.files | This template file is used when local files in the /etc directory are to be used and no name service exists. |
| nsswitch.nis | This template file uses the NIS database as the primary source of all information except the passwd, group, automount, and aliases maps. These are directed to use the local /etc files first and then the NIS databases. |
| nsswitch.nisplus | This template file uses the NIS+ database as the primary source of all information except the passwd, group, automount, and aliases tables. These are directed to use the local /etc files first and then the NIS+ databases. |
| nsswitch.dns | This template file searches the local /etc files for all entries except the hosts entry. The hosts entry is directed to use DNS for lookup. |
| nsswitch.ldap | This template file uses LDAP as the primary source of all information except the passwd, group, automount, and aliases tables. These are directed to use the local /etc files first and then the LDAP databases. |

The name service switch file contains a list of more than 19 types of network information, called databases, with their name service sources for resolution, and the order in which the sources are to be searched. Summary Table 36 lists valid sources that can be specified in this file.

#### SUMMARY TABLE 36
#### DATABASE SOURCES FOR SERVICES IN /ETC/NSSWITCH.CONF

| *Source* | *Description* |
|---|---|
| files | Refers to the client's local /etc files |
| nisplus | Refers to an NIS+ table |
| nis | Refers to an NIS table |
| User | Applies to the printers entry |
| dns | Applies only to the hosts entry |
| ldap | Refers to a dictionary information tree (DIT) |
| compat | Supports an old-style + syntax that was used in the passwd and group information |

## NIS+

NIS+ is similar to NIS, but with more features. NIS+ is not an extension of NIS, but a new software program. It was designed to replace NIS.

NIS addresses the administrative requirements of small-to-medium client/server computing networks—those with fewer than a few hundred clients. Some sites with thousands of users find NIS adequate as well. NIS+ is designed for the now-prevalent larger networks in which systems are spread across remote sites in various time zones and in which clients number in the thousands. In addition, the information stored in networks today changes much more frequently, and NIS had to be updated to handle this environment. Last, systems today require a high level of security, and NIS+ addresses many security issues that NIS did not.

## DES Authentication

DES (Data Encryption Standard) authentication uses the DES and public key cryptography to authenticate both users and systems in the network. DES is a standard encryption mechanism; public key cryptography is a cipher system that involves two keys: one public and one private.

## DNS

DNS is the name service provided by the Internet for Transmission Control Protocol/Internet Protocol (TCP/IP) networks. It was developed so that workstations on the network could be identified by common names instead of Internet addresses. DNS is a program that converts domain names to their IP addresses. Without it, users have to remember numbers instead of words to get around the Internet. The process of finding a computer's IP address by using its hostname as an index is referred to as name-to-address resolution, or mapping.

## Lightweight Directory Access Protocol (LDAP)

LDAP is the latest name-lookup service to be added to Solaris 8. Specifically, LDAP is a directory service. A directory service is like a database, but tends to contain more descriptive, attribute-based information. The information in a directory is generally read, not written.

## Solaris Management Console

Solaris Management Console (SMC) uses GUI tools to make your servers easier to administer. Based on Java technology, Solaris Management Console 2.0 software simplifies the task of administering both local and remote Solaris servers by providing the following:

- An easy-to-navigate GUI-based console and a context-sensitive help panel that integrates online documentation
- Administration of multiple Solaris systems by a single console and single login
- Role-Based Access Control that enables administrators to delegate specific administrative rights to users within a secure system
- An Open and Extensible Environment which Integrates Java applications, X.11 legacy applications, wizards, and HTML through the Solaris Management Console 2.0 Software Development Kit (SDK)

SMC enables administrators to run applications remotely and view the activity locally on all their servers. Central and remote management of all servers can be handled from any one server on the network.

## Solaris AdminSuite

Solaris AdminSuite is similar to Admintool in that it provides an easy-to-use GUI to facilitate routine server administration tasks. AdminSuite 3.0 provides an integrated suite of tools for administering your Solaris systems. Wizards and dialog boxes provided assistance and direction for managing user accounts, groups, mailing lists, computers/networks, file system mounts/shares, serial ports, log files, and name service domains.

Admintool is used to manage a stand-alone system, whereas AdminSuite addresses your needs for reducing the cost and complexity of managing distributed systems.

## ROLE-BASED ACCESS CONTROL (RBAC)

With role-based access control (RBAC) in the Solaris 8 operating environment, administrators can assign limited administrative capabilities to non-root users. This is achieved through three new features:

- Authorizations. User rights that grant access to a restricted function
- Execution profiles. Bundling mechanisms for grouping authorizations and commands with special attributes; for example, user and group IDs or superuser ID
- Roles. Special types of user accounts intended for performing a set of administrative tasks

RBAC relies on the following four databases to provide users access to privileged operations:

- user_attr (extended user attributes database). Associates users and roles with authorizations and profiles
- auth_attr (authorization attributes database). Defines authorizations and their attributes and identifies the associated help file
- prof_attr (rights profile attributes database). Defines profiles, lists the profile's assigned authorizations, and identifies the associated help file
- exec_attr (profile attributes database). Defines the privileged operations assigned to a profile

## JUMPSTART

JumpStart has three main components:

- Boot and Client Identification Services. Provided by a networked boot server, these services list the information that a JumpStart client needs to boot using the network.
- Installation Services. Provided by a networked install server, Installation Services provide an image of the Solaris Operating Environment that JumpStart client uses as its source of data to install.
- Configuration Services. Provided by a networked configuration server, these services provide information that a JumpStart client uses to partition disks and create file systems, add or remove Solaris packages, and perform other configuration tasks.

Summary Table 37 lists and describes some JumpStart commands.

**SUMMARY TABLE 37**
**JUMPSTART COMMANDS**

| *Command* | *Description* |
|---|---|
| `setup_install_server` | Sets up an install server to provide the operating system to the client during a JumpStart installation. |
| `add_to_install_server` | Copies additional packages within a product tree on the Solaris 8 Software and Solaris 8 Languages CDs to the local disk on an existing install server. |
| `modify_install_server` | Adds the Solaris Web Start user interface software to the Solaris 8 Software and Solaris 8 Languages CD images on an existing install server, thus enabling users to use Solaris Web Start to boot a system and install the Solaris 8 software over a network. |

*continues*

## SUMMARY TABLE 37 *continued*
## JUMPSTART COMMANDS

| *Command* | *Description* |
|---|---|
| `add_install_client` | Adds network installation information about a system to an install or boot server's /etc files so the system can install over the network. |
| `rm_install_client` | Removes JumpStart clients that were previously set up for network installation. |
| `check` | Validates the information in the rules file. |
| `pfinstall` | Performs a "dry run" installation to test the profile. |
| `patchadd -C` | Adds patches to the files located in the miniroot (that is, Solaris_8/Tools/Boot) on an image of an installation CD image created by `setup_install_server`. This facility enables you to patch Solaris installation commands and other miniroot-specific commands. |

# Study and Exam Prep Tips

These "Study and Exam Prep Tips" provide you with some general guidelines to help prepare for the Sun Certified System Administrator exam. The information is organized into two sections. The first section addresses your pre-exam preparation activities, and covers general study tips. The second section offers some tips and hints for the actual test-taking situation. Before tackling those areas, however, think a little bit about how you learn.

## Learning as a Process

To better understand the nature of preparation for the exams, it is important to understand learning as a process. You probably are aware of how you best learn new material. You might find that outlining works best for you, or you might need to "see" things as a visual learner. Whatever your learning style, test preparation takes place over time. Obviously, you cannot start studying for this exam the night before you take it; it is important to understand that learning is a developmental process; and as part of that process, you need to focus on what you know and what you have yet to learn.

Learning takes place when we match new information to old. You have some previous experience with computers, and now you are preparing for this certification exam. Using this book, software, and supplementary materials will not just add incrementally to what you know; as you study, you will actually change the organization of your knowledge as you integrate this new information into your existing knowledge base. This will lead you to a more comprehensive understanding of the tasks and concepts outlined in the objectives and of computing in general. Again, this happens as a repetitive process rather than a singular event. Keep this model of learning in mind as you prepare for the exam, and you will make better decisions concerning what to study and how much more studying you need to do.

# STUDY TIPS

There are many ways to approach studying, just as there are many different types of material to study. The following tips, however, should work well for the type of material covered on the certification exam.

## Study Strategies

Although individuals vary in the ways they learn, some basic principles apply to everyone. You should adopt some study strategies that take advantage of these principles. One of these principles is that learning can be broken into various depths. Recognition (of terms, for example) exemplifies a more surface level of learning in which you rely on a prompt of some sort to elicit recall. Comprehension or understanding (of the concepts behind the terms, for example) represents a deeper level of learning. The ability to analyze a concept and apply your understanding of it in a new way represents an even deeper level of learning.

Your learning strategy should enable you to know the material at a level or two deeper than mere recognition. This will help you do well on the exam. You will know the material so thoroughly that you can easily handle the recognition-level types of questions used in multiple-choice testing. You also will be able to apply your knowledge to solve new problems.

### Macro and Micro Study Strategies

One strategy that can lead to this deeper learning includes preparing an outline that covers all the objectives for the exam. You should delve a bit further into the material, and include a level or two of detail beyond the stated objectives for the exam. Then expand the outline by coming up with a statement of definition or a summary for each point in the outline.

An outline provides two approaches to studying. First, you can study the outline by focusing on the organization of the material. Work your way through the points and subpoints of your outline with the goal of learning how they relate to one another. Be certain, for example, that you understand how each of the objective areas is similar to and different from the others. Next, you can work through the outline, focusing on learning the details. Memorize and understand terms and their definitions, facts, rules and strategies, advantages and disadvantages, and so on. In this pass through the outline, attempt to learn detail rather than the big picture (the organizational information that you worked on in the first pass through the outline).

Research has shown that attempting to assimilate both types of information at the same time seems to interfere with the overall learning process. To better perform on the exam, separate your studying into these two approaches.

### Active Study Strategies

Develop and exercise an active study strategy. Write down and define objectives, terms, facts, and definitions. In human information-processing terms, writing forces you to engage in more active encoding of the information. Just reading over it exemplifies more passive processing.

Next, determine whether you can apply the information you have learned by attempting to create examples and scenarios on your own. Think about how or where you could apply the concepts you are learning. Again, write down this information to process the facts and concepts in a more active fashion.

### Commonsense Strategies

Finally, you also should follow commonsense practices when studying. Study when you are alert, reduce or eliminate distractions, take breaks when you become fatigued, and so on.

## Pre-Testing Yourself

Pre-testing enables you to assess how well you are learning. One of the most important aspects of learning is what has been called meta-learning. Meta-learning has to do with realizing when you know something well or when you need to study some more. In other words, you recognize how well or how poorly you have learned the material you are studying.

For most people, this can be difficult to assess objectively on their own. Practice tests are useful in that they reveal more objectively what you have learned and what you have not learned. You should use this information to guide review and further study. Developmental learning takes place as you cycle through studying, assessing how well you have learned, reviewing, and assessing again until you think you are ready to take the exam.

You may have noticed the practice exam included in this book. Use it as part of the learning process. The ExamGear software on the CD-ROM also provides a variety of ways to test yourself before you take the actual exam. By using the practice exam, you can take an entire timed, practice test quite similar in nature to that of the actual Solaris exam. The ExamGear Adaptive Exam option can be used to take the same test in an adaptive testing environment. This mode monitors your progress as you are taking the test to offer you more difficult questions as you succeed. By using the Study Mode option, you can set your own time limit, focus only on a particular domain (for instance, System Security), and also receive instant feedback on your answers.

Set a goal for your pre-testing. A reasonable goal would be to score consistently in the 90% range.

See Appendix F, "Using the ExamGear, Training Guide Edition Software," for a more detailed explanation of the test engine.

# Exam Prep Tips

The Solaris certification exam reflects the knowledge domains established by Sun. The exam is based on a fixed set of exam questions. The individual questions are presented in random order during a test session. If you take the same exam more than once, you will see the same number of questions, but you won't necessarily see the same questions.

Solaris exams are identical in terms of content coverage, number of questions, and allotted time, but the questions differ. You might notice, however, that some of the same questions appear on, or rather are shared among, different final forms. When questions are shared among multiple final forms of an exam, the percentage of sharing is generally small.

Solaris exams also have a fixed time limit in which you must complete the exam. The ExamGear test engine on the CD-ROM that accompanies this book provides fixed-form exams.

Finally, the score you achieve on a fixed-form exam is based on the number of questions you answer correctly. The exam's passing score is the same for all final forms of a given fixed-form exam.

Table 1 shows the format for the exam.

**TABLE 1**

**TIME, NUMBER OF QUESTIONS, AND PASSING SCORE FOR EXAM**

| *Exam* | *Time Limit in Minutes* | *Number of Questions* | *Passing %* |
|---|---|---|---|
| Solaris 8 Certified System Administrator for the Solaris 8 Operating environment: Part 1 | 90 | 57 | 66 |
| Solaris 8 Certified System Administrator for the Solaris 8 Operating environment: Part 2 | 90 | 61 | 70 |

Question types on both exams are multiple choice, fill in the blank, and matching.

Remember that you do not want to dwell on any one question for too long. Your 120 minutes of exam time can be consumed very quickly.

## Putting It All Together

Given all these different pieces of information, the task now is to assemble a set of tips that will help you successfully tackle the Solaris certification exam.

### More Pre-Exam Prep Tips

Generic exam-preparation advice is always useful. Tips include the following:

- Become familiar with general terminology, commands, and equipment. Hands-on experience is one of the keys to success; it will be difficult, but not impossible, to pass the exam without that experience. Review the chapter-specific study tips at the beginning of each chapter for instructions on how to best prepare for the exam.
- Review the current exam-preparation guide on the Sun web site. Visit my web site, `www.unixed.com`, for late-breaking changes and up-to-date study tips from other administrators who have taken the exam.
- Memorize foundational technical detail, but remember that you need to be able to think your way through questions as well.
- Take any of the available practice tests. I recommend the ones included in this book and the ones you can create using the ExamGear software on the CD-ROM. The test engine on this CD is designed to complement the material in this book and help you prepare for the real exam. For more sample test questions, you can visit my web site, `www.unixed.com`. I'll try to keep the questions up-to-date and relevant. In addition, you can share your experiences with other Solaris administrators who are preparing for the exam, just like you. In addition, this web site will provide up-to-date links to the official Sun certification web sites.

### During the Exam Session

The following generic exam-taking advice that you have heard for years applies when taking this exam:

- Take a deep breath, and try to relax when you first sit down for your exam session. It is important to control the pressure you might (naturally) feel when taking exams.
- You will be provided with scratch paper. Take a moment to write down any factual information and technical detail that you committed to short-term memory.

- Carefully read all information and instruction screens. These displays have been put together to give you information relevant to the exam you are taking.
- Read the exam questions carefully. Reread each question to identify all relevant details.
- Tackle the questions in the order they are presented. Skipping around will not build your confidence; the clock is always counting down.
- Do not rush, but also do not linger on difficult questions. The questions vary in degree of difficulty. Don't let yourself be flustered by a particularly difficult or verbose question.
- Note the time allotted and the number of questions appearing on the exam you are taking. Make a rough calculation of how many minutes you can spend on each question, and use this to pace yourself through the exam.
- Take advantage of the fact that you can return to and review skipped or previously answered questions. Record the questions you cannot answer confidently, noting the relative difficulty of each question, on the scratch paper provided. After you have made it to the end of the exam, return to the more difficult questions.
- If session time remains after you have completed all questions (and if you aren't too fatigued!), review your answers. Pay particular attention to questions that seem to have a lot of detail or that involve graphics.
- As for changing your answers, the general rule of thumb here is *don't*! If you read the question carefully and completely the first time and felt like you knew the right answer, you probably did. Do not second-guess yourself. If as you check your answers, one clearly stands out as incorrectly marked, then change it. If you are at all unsure, however, go with your first instinct.

If you have done your studying and follow the preceding suggestions, you should do well. Good luck!

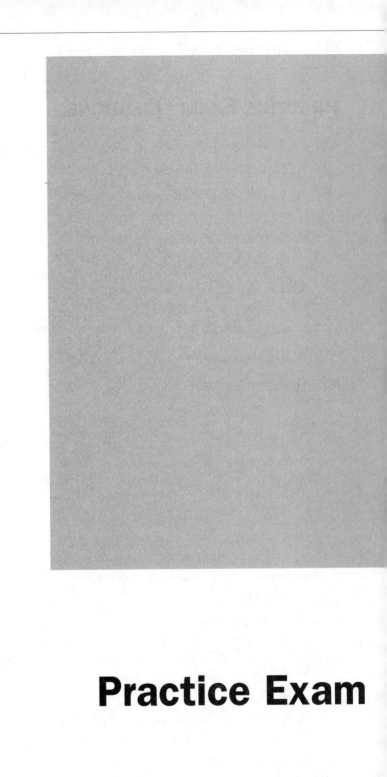

# Practice Exam

## PRACTICE EXAM QUESTIONS

1. The kernel consists of which of the following?

   A. The shell and environment variables

   B. A small static core and many dynamically loadable modules

   C. Boot PROM and the operating system

   D. System run states 0, 1, and s

2. What are the characteristics of changing to run level s? Choose all that apply.

   A. Single-user mode.

   B. Shutdown state.

   C. All users are logged out.

   D. File systems remain mounted.

3. Which command is used to change run levels?

   A. `sudo`

   B. `kill`

   C. `init`

   D. `run`

4. Which of the following restricts the set of operations that users are allowed to perform at the OpenBoot prompt?

   A. security-password

   B. set-security

   C. set-secure

   D. security-mode

5. The bootstrap procedure consists of which of the following basic phases? Choose all that apply.

   A. Load the kernel.

   B. autoboot (if autoboot? is set).

   C. Hardware power-up.

   D. Execute Power-on self-test (POST).

6. What is the best command to find your hardware platform and current operating system release?

   A. `init -q`

   B. `sysdef`

   C. `uname -a`

   D. `arch`

7. What information will you need during the installation process? Choose all that apply.

   A. IP address

   B. Product code

   C. Timezone

   D. Root password

8. Which of the following conditions will not prevent a patch from being installed? Choose all that apply.

   A. The patch being installed requires another patch that is not installed.

   B. The patch is incompatible with another, already installed patch.

   C. The patch was removed.

   D. The patch version is not the most up-to-date version.

9. What does the `pkgchk` command do?

   A. Displays software package information

   B. Stores answers in a response file so that they can be supplied automatically during an installation

   C. Determines the accuracy of a software package installation

   D. Displays package parameter values

10. In Admintool, what is the field that corresponds to the maximum number of days an account can go without being accessed before it is automatically locked?

    A. Max Change

    B. Max Inactive

    C. Expiration Date

    D. Max Days

11. Respectively, what are the user initialization files for the Bourne, Korn, and C shell?

    A. .bshrc, .kshrc, .cshrc.

    B. .exrc, .profile, .login.

    C. .profile, .profile, .login.

    D. .profile works for all shells.

12. Which of the following file systems can reside on a local physical disk? Choose all that apply.

    A. HSFS

    B. TMPFS

    C. UFS

    D. NFS

13. Which file system block contains information about the file system?

    A. Boot block

    B. Superblock

    C. Inode

    D. Data block

14. To view the capacity of all file systems mounted on a system, which command should you use?

    A. `du -a`

    B. `ls`

    C. `df`

    D. `mountall`

15. Which command is a friendlier way to create a file system?

    A. `mkfs`

    B. `newfs`

    C. `fsck`

    D. `mknod`

16. Which of the following commands cannot be used to copy file systems?

    A. `dd`

    B. `ufsdump`

    C. `fsck`

    D. `volcopy`

17. Which command might you use to see which process is preventing a file system from being unmounted?

    A. `ps`

    B. `mountall`

    C. `fsck`

    D. `fuser`

18. Which of the following is an easily guessed password?

    A. Britney

    B. TnK0Tb!

    C. Dietcoke

    D. ZunSp0ts

19. What would a default umask of 023 set as default permissions on new files?

    A. Owner no rights; Group write only; World write and execute only

    B. Owner read, write, execute; Group read only; World execute only

    C. Owner read, write, execute; Group read and execute only; World read only

    D. Owner no rights; Group read and execute only; World read only

20. What is true of the `sudo` command? Choose all that apply.

    A. It comes standard with Solaris 8.

    B. It can be used to grant selective superuser access.

    C. It prevents the need for giving out the root password.

    D. It tracks superuser commands in an audit log.

21. What would you use the `prstat` command to do? Choose all that apply.

    A. Get information on all the processes for a particular user.

    B. Determine disk usage.

    C. Determine which processes are consuming the most CPU cycles.

    D. Change system run levels.

22. Which of the following signals stops a process unconditionally?

    A. SIGHUP

    B. SIGKILL

    C. SIGTERM

    D. SIGQUIT

23. What does the `at` command do?

    A. Stands for "all terminate""; kills all non-root processes.

    B. Runs a batch job once at a specific time in the future.

    C. Sets a repeating batch job to run at a specific time of day.

    D. Displays the time of last login for a user.

24. Which of the following printer tasks cannot be performed from Admintool?

    A. Add a local print queue.

    B. Add a network printer.

    C. Select a default printer.

    D. Change a printer type.

25. Which command(s) could tell you if a print queue is down? Choose all that apply.

    A. `lpadmin`

    B. `lpstat`

    C. `admintool`

    D. `HP jetadmin`

26. Which shell has all of the following options: command-line editing, syntax compatibility with Bourne shell, and a history list?

    A. csh

    B. ksh

    C. sh

    D. None of the above

27. What does the command `tar xvf /tmp/backup.tar` do? Choose all that apply.

    A. Extracts the archives in /tmp/backup.tar to the current directly

    B. Prints a verbose listing of the files and directories in /tmp/backup.tar

    C. Compresses /tmp/backup.tar

    D. Archives the current directory and its contents to /tmp/backup.tar

28. Which of the following statements about the `dd` command is false?

    A. It quickly converts and copies files with different data formats.

    B. It can be used to copy an entire file system or partition to tape.

    C. It can compress files quickly and efficiently.

    D. It can be used to read standard input from another program to write to tape.

29. What does a file need to make it a Bourne shell script? Choose all that apply.

    A. The first line should be `#!/bin/sh`.

    B. The last line should be `done`.

    C. A `main` function should exist.

    D. The file needs to have an execute bit set with `chmod`.

30. How can you send a text file named testfile.txt to `user@devnull.org` through email from the command line? Choose all that apply.

    A. mail user@devnull.org > testfile.txt

    B. cat testfile.txt | mail user@devnull.org

    C. mail user@devnull.org < testfile.txt

    D. mail testfile.txt > user@devnull.org

31. In the ISO/OSI network reference model, what is the Session layer described as?

    A. It manages the delivery of data via the Data Link layer, and is used by the Transport layer. The most common network layer protocol is IP.

    B. It determines how to use the Network layer to provide a virtual error-free, point-to-point connection so that host A can send messages to host B and they will arrive uncorrupted and in the correct order.

    C. It uses the Transport layer to establish a connection between processes on different hosts. It handles security and creation of the session.

    D. It performs functions such as text compression and code or format conversion to try to smooth out differences between hosts.

32. Which of the following usually spans more than one network?

    A. Hub

    B. Router

    C. NIC

    D. Host

33. How many IP addresses are available to be assigned within a Class C network?

    A. 254

    B. 24

    C. 65,534

    D. none

34. Which pseudo file system resides on a physical disk?

    A. procfs

    B. swapfs

    C. tmpfs

    D. Fdfs

35. To what do the directories in /proc correspond?

    A. File systems

    B. Physical and virtual devices attached to the system

    C. Active process IDs

    D. Active UIDs

36. For what does an AutoClient system rely on the server? Choose all that apply.

    A. Remote disk space for /usr and root (/) file systems

    B. Software to set up its /usr and root (/) file systems

    C. Remote swap space

    D. Nothing after the initial install

37. Which of the following cannot have Solaris 8 software installed on it?

    A. Diskless client

    B. Java station

    C. AutoClient

    D. AutoClient server

38. In Solaris, each disk device is described by which naming conventions? Choose all that apply.

    A. Instance name

    B. Physical device name

    C. Virtual name

    D. Logical device name

39. Which of the following is *not* based on NFS?

    A. WebNFS

    B. AutoFS

    C. CacheFS

    D. UFS

40. File systems that are mounted read-write or that contain executable files should always be mounted with which of the following options? Choose all that apply.

    A. hard

    B. intr

    C. soft

    D. nointr

41. What does the `statd` do?

    A. It handles file system exporting and file access requests from remote systems.

    B. It handles mount requests from NFS clients.

    C. It runs on the NFS server and NFS client and provides file locking.

    D. It runs on the NFS server and NFS client and interacts with `lockd` to provide the crash and recovery functions for the locking services on NFS.

42. Which of the following provides a means for selective access to administrative capabilities? Choose all that apply.

    A. Giving a user the root password

    B. Use of the `sudo` command

    C. RBAC

    D. usermod

43. Information handled by a name service includes which of the following? Choose all that apply.

    A. System hostnames and addresses

    B. Usernames

    C. Access permissions

    D. Assigning IP addresses dynamically

44. How would you determine the NIS server used by a given machine?

    A. Use `ypwhich`

    B. Use `ypcat`.

    C. Look in the /etc/nsswitch.conf directory.

    D. Look in the /var/yp directory.

45. What file would you edit to make the local /etc/hosts file take precedence over DNS or NIS host lookups?

    A. /etc/inetd.conf

    B. /etc/resolv.conf

    C. /etc/defaultrouter

    D. /etc/nsswitch.conf

46. Which statements about Solaris Management Console are false?

    A. It provides single console, single login administration of multiple Solaris systems.

    B. It provides an easy-to-navigate GUI console.

    C. It has a command-line interface in addition to the GUI controls.

    D. It uses Role-Based Access Control.

47. What can the SMC Toolbox Editor do? Choose all that apply.

    A. Suspend, resume, monitor, and control processes.

    B. Install software packages and patches.

    C. Schedule, start, and manage jobs.

    D. View and manage mounts, shares, and usage information.

48. Solaris AdminSuite does everything SMC does except for what? Choose all that apply.

    A. Use RBAC to delegate administrative tasks.

    B. Provide tools for job scheduling.

    C. Administer user accounts.

    D. Manage local and NFS file systems.

49. Which of the following is a method to automatically install groups of identical systems?

    A. Web Start

    B. Custom JumpStart

    C. Interactive Installation

    D. Network Install

50. What command would you use to do a "dry run" installation to test a JumpStart profile?

    A. `check`

    B. `patchadd -C`

    C. `fsck`

    D. `pfinstall`

# PRACTICE EXAM ANSWERS

1. **B.** The kernel consists of a small static core and many dynamically loadable kernel modules. Many kernel modules are loaded automatically at boot time, but for efficiency, others—such as device drivers—are loaded from the disk as needed by the kernel.

2. **A., C., D.** Run level s is the single-user (system administrator) state. Only root is allowed to log in at the console, and any users logged in are logged out when entering this run level. All file systems previously mounted remain mounted and accessible. All services except the most basic OS services are shut down in an orderly manner.

3. **C.** The `init` command is used to change run levels, also called `init` states.

4. **D.** Security-mode restricts the set of operations that users are allowed to perform at the OpenBoot prompt.

5. **B., C., D.** On most SPARC-based systems, the bootstrap procedure consists of some basic phases. First, the system hardware is powered on or the system firmware (PROM) executes a power-on self-test (POST). After the tests have been completed successfully, the firmware attempts to autoboot if the appropriate OpenBoot configuration variable (auto-boot?) has been set.

6. **C.** The `uname` command, with the `-a` flag set, displays basic information currently available from the system, including hardware platform and current operating system release.

7. **A., C., D.** The Solaris Installation program prompts you for the following: hostname, IP address, Subnet mask, whether to install Ipv6, name service, whether to install Kerberos security, timezone, root password, and language.

8. **C., D.** A patch might not be installed if it requires another patch that is not installed or if the patch is incompatible with another, already installed patch.

9. **C.** The `pkgchk` command checks the accuracy of a software package installation.

10. **B.** Max Inactive. This field contains the maximum number of days an account can go without being accessed before it is automatically locked. A blank field means the account remains active no matter how long it goes unused.

11. **C.** Bourne and Korn shells initialize with a .profile, whereas the C shell uses .login and .cshrc.

12. **A., C.** The High Sierra (HSFS) file system is a read-only file system used on CD-ROMs, and the UNIX file system (UFS) is the default disk-based file system used by Solaris. TMPFS resides in memory. Data in this type of file system is destroyed upon reboot. NFS is the Network File System, which is remotely mounted over the network.

13. **B.** The superblock stores much of the information about the file system. The boot block stores information used when booting the system. An inode stores all information about a file except its name. A storage or data block stores data for each file.

14. **C.** The `df` command and its options can be used to see the capacity of each file system mounted on a system, the amount of space available, and the percentage of space already in use.

15. **B.** The `newfs` command automatically determines all the necessary parameters to pass to mkfs to construct new file systems. `newfs` was added in Solaris to make the creation of new file systems easier.

16. The `fsck` command checks and repairs file systems. Any of the others could be used to copy one file system to another.

17. **D.** The `fuser` command can be used to display which processes are using a particular file system. The following example uses the fuser command to find out why /cdrom is busy:

```
fuser -u /cdrom
```

18. **A., C.** Although it is debatable what a "good" password might be, a proper name (Britney) is easy for a password guesser to guess. A password should contain a combination of letters, numbers, and symbols (such as space, comma, period, and so on). Varying case and mixing words can also help expand the number of possibilities that must be covered by a password-guessing program.

19. **C.** A umask of 023 makes a mask, automatically unsetting those permission bits from otherwise full permissions. Because each digit represents an octal number corresponding respectively to Owner, Group, and World, the permissions displayed by the `ls` command would be displayed as `rwxr-xr—`. The first three permission bits are `rwx` (read, write, execute) for Owner, followed by `r-x` (read, execute) for Group, and finally `r` (read only) for World.

20. **B., C., D.** Although `sudo` does not come as a standard part of Solaris 8, it is an excellent tool for restricting superuser access and keeping a log of superuser activity without having to give out the root password.

21. **A., D.** The `prstat` command is used from the command line to monitor system processes. Like the `ps` command, it provides information on active processes. The difference is that you can specify whether you want information on specific processes, UIDs, CPU IDs, or processor sets. By default, `prstat` displays information about all processes sorted by CPU usage.

22. **B.** The SIGKILL signal can be sent to a process with `kill -9` or `kill -SIGHUP`. Signal 9 is called a sure, unconditional kill because it cannot be caught or ignored by a process. If the process is still around after a `kill -9`, it is either hung up in the UNIX kernel, waiting for an event such as disk I/O to complete, or you are not the owner of the process.

23. **B.** The `at` command is used to schedule jobs for execution at a later time. Unlike `crontab`, which schedules a job to happen at regular intervals, a job submitted with `at` executes once, at the designated time.

24. **C.** If the user doesn't specify a printer name or class in a valid style, the command checks the user's PRINTER or LPDEST environment variable for a default printer name. If neither environment variable for the default printer is defined, the command checks the .printers file in the user's home directory for the default printer alias. If the command does not find a default printer alias in the .printers file, it then checks the print client's /etc/printers.conf file for configuration information. If the printer is not found in the /etc/printers.conf file, the command checks the name service (NIS or NIS+), if any.

25. **B., D.** The `lpstat -p <printer>` command will tell you whether a printer is active or idle, when it was enabled or disabled, and whether it is accepting print requests. HP's Jetadmin tool is a menu-driven way to administer and monitor print queues.

26. **B.** The Korn shell (ksh) has all three features. The Bourne shell (sh) has only syntax compatibility with itself. The C shell (csh) isn't syntax compatible with the Bourne shell.

27. **A., B.** This command uses the flags *x* (extract archive), *v* (verbose, lists all files and directories extracted) and *f* (archive is in the file following this argument).

28. **C.** The `dd` command quickly converts and copies files with different data formats, such as differences in block size or record length. `dd` can be used to copy an entire file system or partition to tape, and can take input from other programs through standard input. It cannot, however, compress files as it copies because it is a byte-by-byte image copy.

29. **A., D.** Any shell script needs, as its first line, `#!` followed by the full path to the interpreter; in this case, `/bin/sh` for Bourne shell. Also, the script file needs to have execute bits set so that Solaris will consider it to be a program, rather than a data file.

30. **B., C.** Answer A would overwrite the testfile.txt because output of the mail program is redirected to that file with the > character. Answer D would create a file called user@devnull.org with the output of the `mail` command.

31. **C.** Answer A is the Network layer, Answer B is the Transport layer, and Answer D is the Presentation layer.

32. **B.** A router is a machine that forwards Ethernet packets from one network to another. In other words, the router connects LANs, and the hub connects computers. A host *can* be a router, but this is not usually the case. A NIC (Network Interface Card) is the hardware in a host that allows it to connect to a network.

33. **A.** Class C network numbers use 24 bits for the network number and 8 bits for host numbers. A class C network number occupies the first three bytes of an IP address; only the fourth byte is assigned at the discretion of the network's owner. A class C network can accommodate a maximum of 254 hosts.

34. **B.** The swapfs pseudo file system is either a swap partition on a disk, or a swap file residing in another filesystem on a disk. The procfs, tmpfs, and fdfs all reside in memory.

35. **C.** Each entry in the /proc directory is a decimal number corresponding to a process ID. Each directory in /proc has files that contain more detailed information about that process.

36. **A., B.** For AutoClient systems, an operating system server provides all system software required to set up the individual root (/) and /usr file systems required for local swapping and caching. System types are defined by how they access the root (/) and /usr file systems, including the swap area. Stand-alone and server systems mount these file systems from a local disk, whereas diskless and AutoClient clients mount the file systems remotely, relying on servers to provide these services.

37. **B.** A JavaStation is a client that has no local file system and whose /home is accessed from a server across the network. The JavaStation runs only applications that are 100% pure Java. All data, applications, and configuration information reside on a centralized server that is running Netra J software, a Solaris operating environment. Java applications are downloaded on demand and are executed locally.

38. **A., B., D.** In Solaris, each disk device is described in three ways, using three distinct naming conventions:

    - Physical device name. Represents the full device pathname in the device information hierarchy.
    - Instance name. Represents the kernel's abbreviation name for every possible device on the system.
    - Logical device name. Used by system administrators with most file system commands to refer to devices.

39. **D.** UFS is the UNIX File System. WebNFS is a product and proposed standard protocol from Sun Microsystems that extends its NFS to the Internet. The Cache File System (CacheFS) can be used to improve performance of NFS-mounted file systems or slow devices such as a CD-

ROM. The Autofs facility, also called the automounter, makes NFS mounting simpler by providing a method in which remote directories are mounted only when they are being used.

40. **A., B.** Sun recommends that file systems mounted as read-write, or containing executable files, should always be mounted with the hard option. If you use soft-mounted file systems, unexpected I/O errors can occur. For example, consider a write request. If the NFS server goes down, the pending write request simply gives up, resulting in a corrupted file on the remote file system. A read-write file system should always be mounted with the specified hard and intr options. This lets users make their own decisions about killing hung processes.

41. **D.** Answer A describes `nfsd`, B describes `mountd`, and C describes `lockd`.

42. **B., C.** Both `sudo` and role-based access control (RBAC) allow the system administrator to assign limited administrative capabilities to non-root users. Giving out the root password allows a user full access to all the restricted powers of root, making for very poor security.

43. **A., B., C.** Name services also provide password information. Name services available in Solaris 8 include NIS, NIS+, DNS, LDAP, and /etc files.

44. **A.** With no arguments, the `ypwhich` command displays the current NIS master server.

45. **D.** The name service switch, /etc/nsswitch.conf, controls how a client workstation or application obtains network information. In this case, you would edit the /etc/nsswitch.conf file, and change the hosts line to read hosts: files dns nis.

46. **C.** No command-line interface exists for the Solaris Management Console.

47. **A., C., D.** The SMC Toolbox Editor manages processes, users, file system mounts and shares, disks, serial ports, schedules jobs, and has a log viewer.

48. **A., B.** Solaris AdminSuite provides many of the same tools as SMC, but does not provide the capability of delegating administrative tasks using RBAC. It also does not provide tools for job scheduling or disk and process management. The tools provided in AdminSuite do, however, provide an easy-to-use graphical interface for managing your systems from anywhere on the network. The tools and commands in the GUI are much faster than using numerous Solaris commands to perform the same tasks.

49. **B.** The Custom JumpStart method of installing the operating system provides a way to install groups of similar systems automatically and identically. If you use an interactive method to install the operating system, you must carry on a dialogue with the installation program by answering various questions.

50. **D.** After you create a profile, you can use the `pfinstall` command to test it. Testing a class file is sometimes called a "dry run" installation. By looking at the installation output generated by `pfinstall`, you can quickly determine whether a class file will do what you expect.

SECTION

# APPENDIXES

A Web Start

B Administration and Configuration of the CDE

C The History of Solaris

D Overview of Certification Process

E What's on the CD-ROM

F Using the ExamGear, Training Guide Edition Software

APPENDIX A

# Web Start

Web Start 3.0 is Sun's Java-based installation program that simplifies and accelerates the installation of Solaris Software. Web Start uses technology from InstallShield, which is widely recognized as the provider of de facto installation technology for Microsoft Windows applications. This tool allows network administrators to use a familiar web browser that uses a point-and-click interface to install all the software bundled with Solaris. Through Solaris Web Start, you select and install all the software your machine requires, including the Solaris software group and Solstice utilities. In addition, Web Start is the only installation utility that also installs the other software provided on the additional CDs. It's much like the Solaris interactive installation program described in Chapter 15, "Installing a Server," but with a much more user-friendly interface. Solaris Web Start uses the JumpStart utility to read the configuration profile automatically, thus installing the Solaris software and other selected products with minimal intervention. Following are a few highlights regarding Web Start:

- With Solaris Web Start software and the Solaris Web Start Wizards Technology, the Solaris Operating Environment and other applications can be installed interactively with a browser-based interface.
- Web Start Flash technology enables administrators to take a complete system image of the Solaris Operating Environment and system configuration, and replicate that image onto multiple servers over the network. This feature is available starting with the 04/01 release of Solaris 8.
- Web Start takes advantage of the Solaris JumpStart technology, and can provide automated installation and setup of Solaris systems.
- Solaris Live Upgrade technology reduces the usual service outage typically associated with an operating system upgrade.

If you're setting up a machine that includes a frame buffer, keyboard, and monitor, you can run Web Start directly from that machine. If you only have a character-based terminal connected via the serial port, you can still use Web Start's command-line interface (CLI).

## Minimum System Requirements for Solaris Web Start

If you want to run Solaris Web Start, your computer must have the following:

- At least 64MB of RAM.
- A 1.05GB startup disk just to run Solaris Web Start, after which the program determines whether your system has enough disk space to install the products you selected. 2GB of disk space is recommended for installing server software.

# Installing Solaris Using Web Start

Solaris Web Start lets you take advantage of the ease and convenience of a GUI installation. However, you can use Web Start in either of two ways:

- Graphical-User Interface (GUI). Requires a local or remote CD-ROM drive or network connection, frame buffer, keyboard, and bitmapped monitor.
- Command-Line Interface (CLI). Requires a local or remote CD-ROM drive or network connection, keyboard, and monitor.

To start a Web Start installation, boot up the system from the Solaris 8 Installation CD as follows:

```
ok boot cdrom - browser
```

If during bootup, Web Start detects a frame buffer for the system, it uses the GUI; if Web Start does not detect a frame buffer, it uses CLI. The content and sequence of instructions in both are the same.

After the system boots from CD-ROM, Web Start starts the appropriate user interface, and asks for some general system identification information. You are asked for the same information that the interactive installation asked for in Chapter 15, except the system uses a different GUI with a slightly different look and feel. The first window to appear is the Network Connectivity window, as shown in Figure A.1.

Select whether your system will be connected to a network and then click the Next button. The DHCP window appears, as shown in Figure A.2.

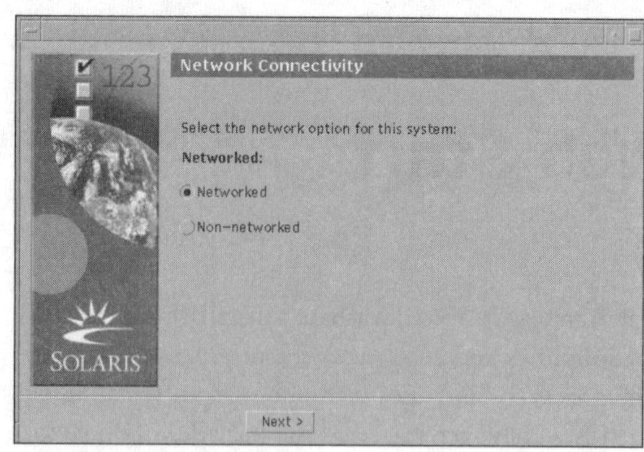


**FIGURE A.1**
Network Connectivity window.

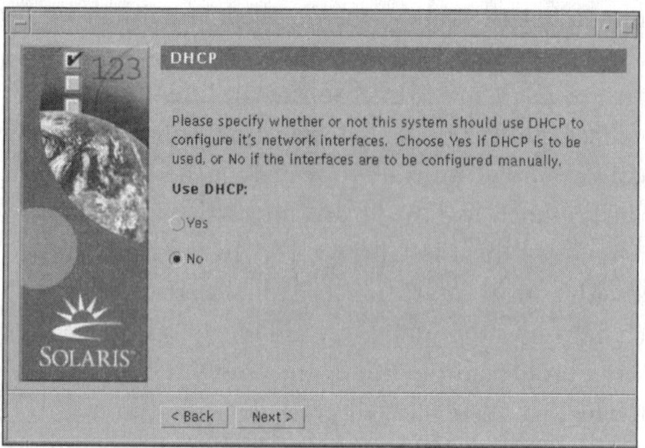


**FIGURE A.2**
DHCP window.

This window asks whether you will use DHCP to configure the network interface, or if the interface will be configured manually. After selecting whether to use DHCP to configure the system's network interface, click the Next button. In the example, I indicated that DHCP would *not* be used to configure the network interface card, so I will now be prompted for the information to be used to configure the primary network interface. If I indicated that DHCP *would be* used, I would not be prompted for this information, and the DHCP server would supply the network interface information automatically at bootup. When I click the Next button, the Host Name window appears, as shown in Figure A.3.

Enter the hostname for this system. The hostname can have 2–255 characters. After entering the hostname, click Next to continue. The IP Address window appears, as shown in Figure A.4.

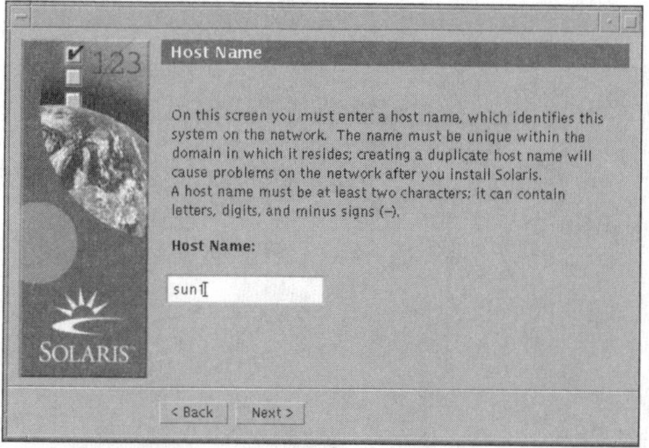


**FIGURE A.3**
Host Name window.

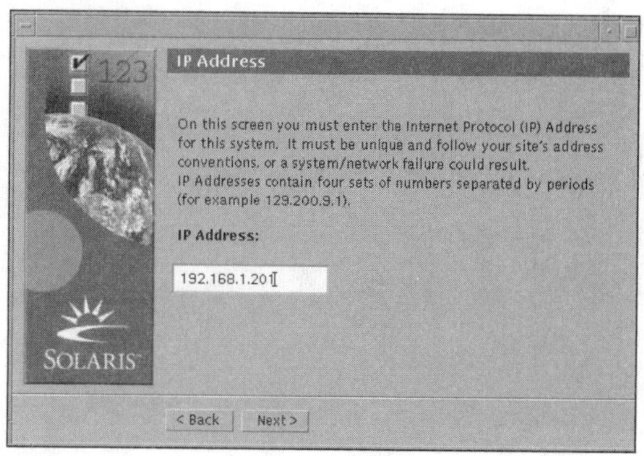


**FIGURE A.4**
IP Address window.

Enter the IP address for this system, click Next, and the Netmask window appears, as shown in Figure A.5.

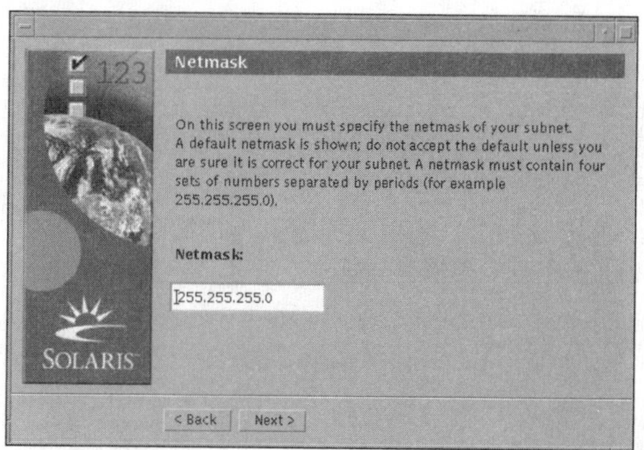


**FIGURE A.5**
Netmask window.

Specify the netmask value for your subnet, click the Next button to continue, and the Ipv6 window appears, as shown in Figure A.6.

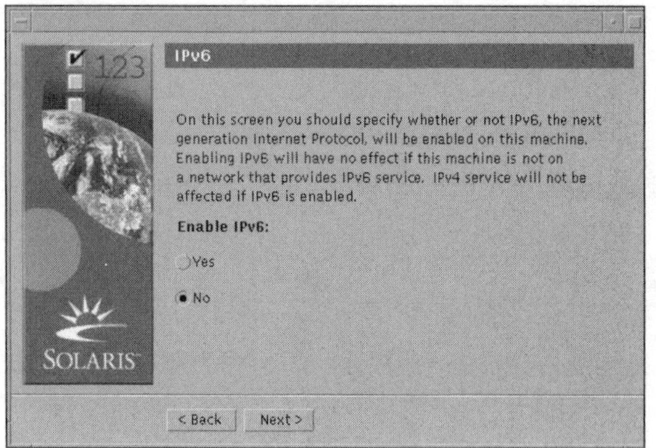


**FIGURE A.6**
Ipv6 window.

Specify whether Ipv6, the new Internet protocol, will be enabled for this system. Click the Next button to continue, and the Name Service window appears, as shown in Figure A.7.

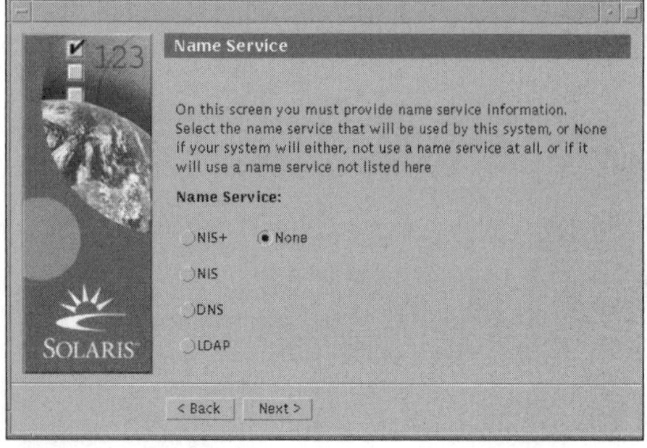


**FIGURE A.7**
Name Service window.

Specify whether the system will be using a name service, and click the Next button to continue. The Default Router window appears, as shown in Figure A.8.

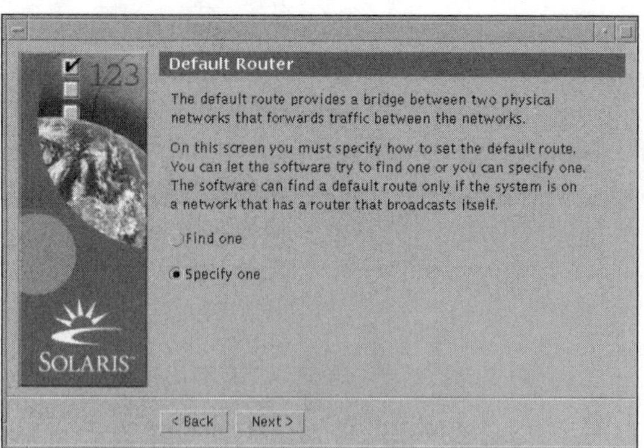


**FIGURE A.8**
Default Router window.

If you want to specify a default router, do so here. After you make your selection, click the Next button. In the example, I indicated that I wanted to specify a default router, so the next window asks for the router address, as shown in Figure A.9.

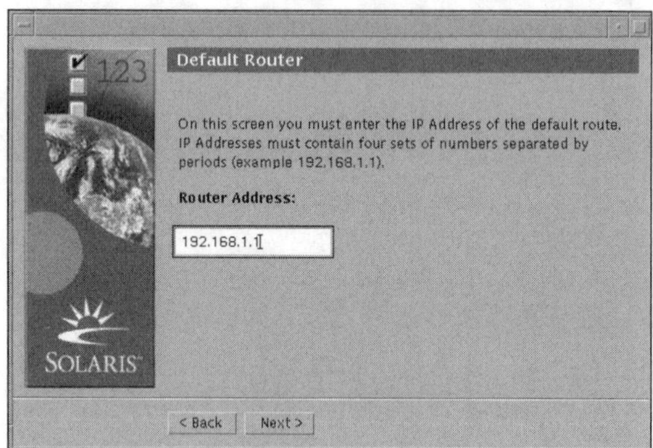


**FIGURE A.9**
Default router.

Specify the IP address for the default router, and click the Next button. The Time Zone window is displayed, as shown in Figure A.10.

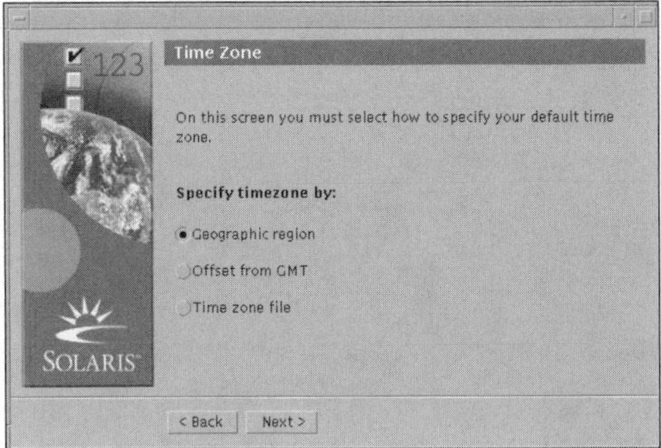


**FIGURE A.10**
Time Zone window.

In the Time Zone window, specify the appropriate option to set the default time zone:

- Geographic Region
- Offset from GMT
- Time Zone File

After selecting the appropriate option, click the Next button to continue. In the example, I selected Geographic Region, so the next window, shown in Figure A.11, asks me to enter my geographic region.

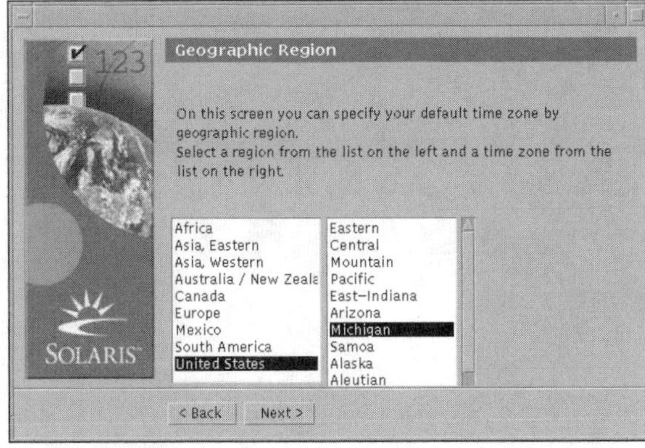


**FIGURE A.11**
Geographic Region window.

Select your geographic region, and click the Next button to continue. The Date and Time window appear, as shown in Figure A.12.

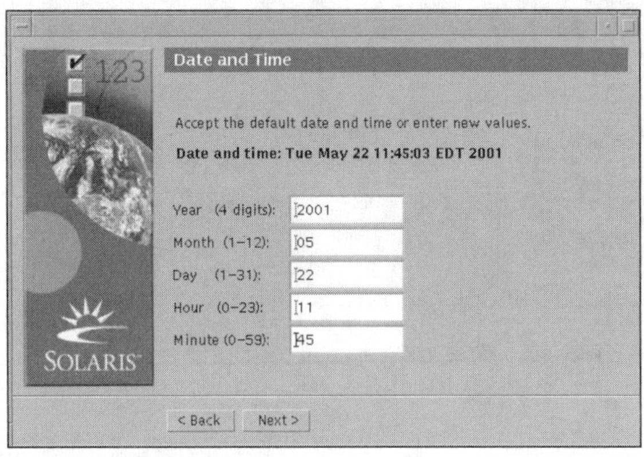


**FIGURE A.12**
Date and Time window.

In the Date and Time window, accept the default time shown or enter a new value, then click the Next button to continue. The next window, shown in Figure A.13, asks you to enter the root password.

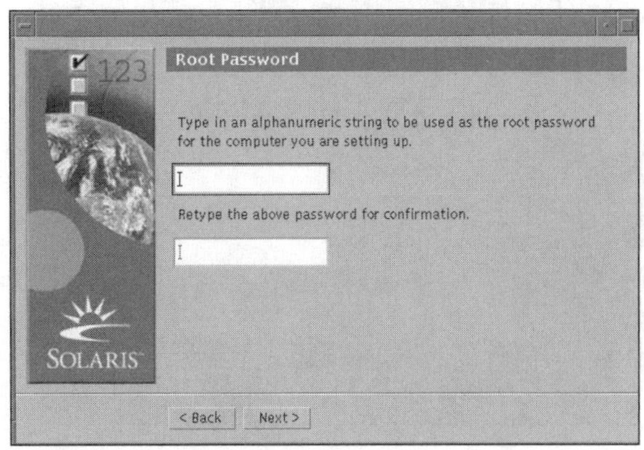


**FIGURE A.13**
Root Password window.

Enter the root password for this system, enter it again for confirmation, and click the Next button to continue. The Proxy Server Configuration window appears, as shown in Figure A.14.

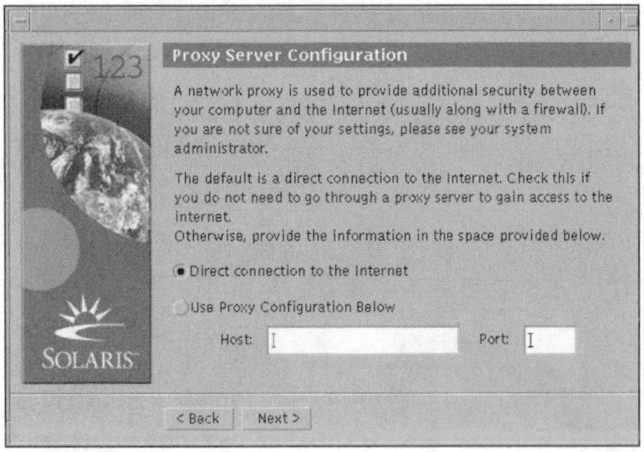

**FIGURE A.14**
Proxy Server Configuration window.

A proxy server acts as an intermediary between a host and the Internet to ensure security, administrative control, and a caching service. If you do not use a proxy server, accept the default for a direct connection to the Internet. After making your selection, click the Next button to continue. A Confirmation Information window appears, as shown in Figure A.15.

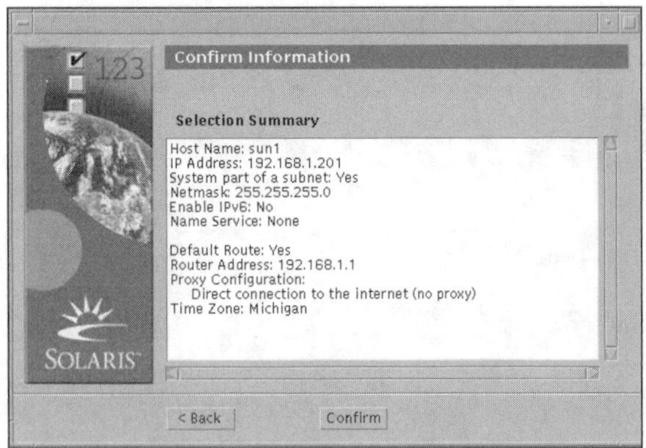


**FIGURE A.15**
Confirm Information window.

Verify that all the information shown is correct; then click the Confirm button to continue. The system identification portion of Web Start is complete, and the system will be configured using the settings you provided. After a few minutes, the Welcome window is displayed, as shown in Figure A.16.

**FIGURE A.16**
Web Start Welcome window.

Click the Next button to proceed. The next window asks you to specify the installation media, as shown in Figure A.17.

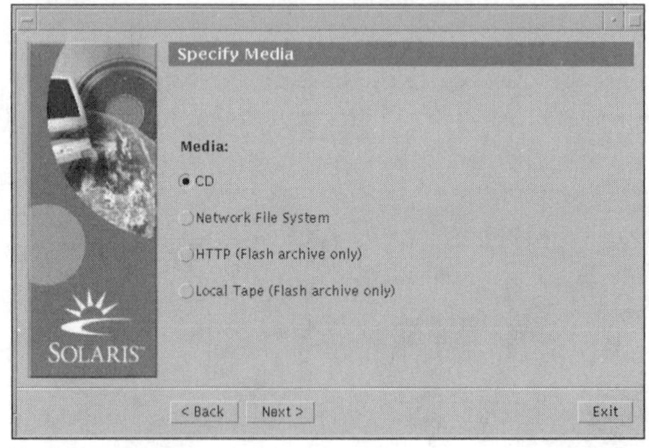


**FIGURE A.17**
Specify Media window.

After making your selection, click the Next button. In the example, I selected CD, so the next window asks me to insert the first CD, as shown in Figure A.18.

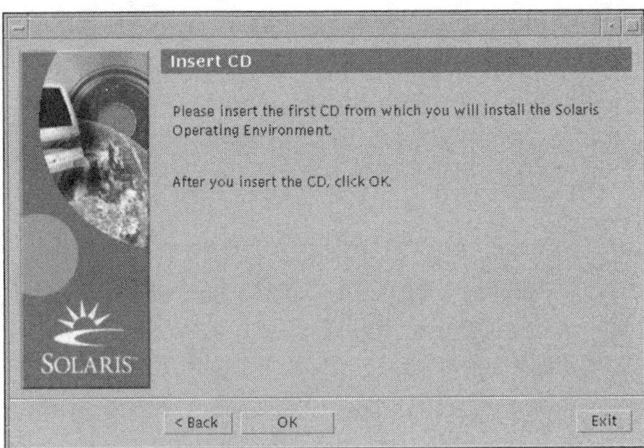


**FIGURE A.18**
Insert CD window.

I insert the CD labeled Solaris 8 OS Installation, and click the OK button to continue. A window indicating that the system is being initialized is displayed, as shown in Figure A.19.

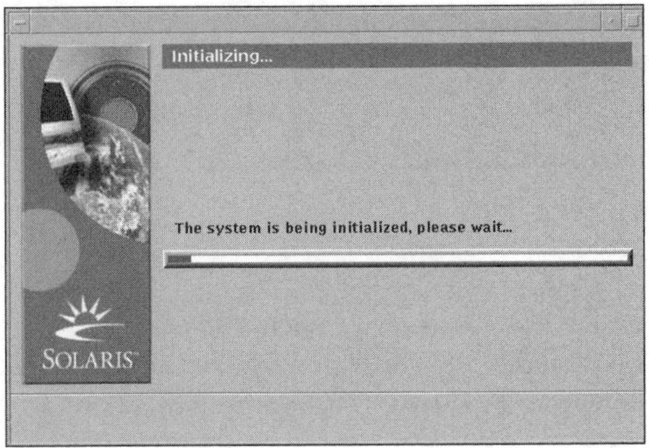


**FIGURE A.19**
Initializing window.

The next window, shown in Figure A.20, asks you to specify the type of installation: Default or Custom.

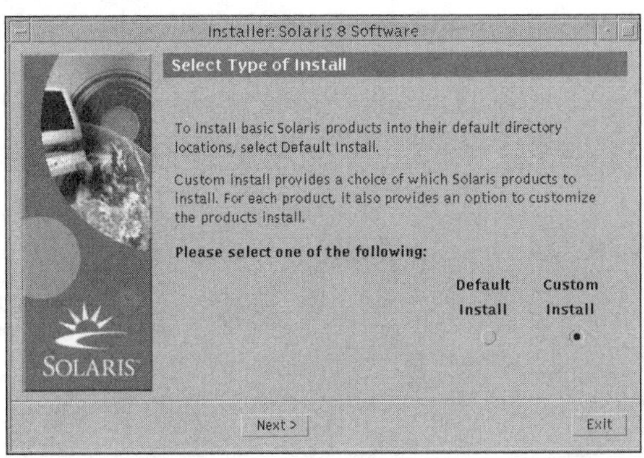


**FIGURE A.20**
Select Type of Install window.

The Default installation leads you through a generic installation process, providing default answers to all the configuration options. If you have special requirements, select Custom installation.

The Custom installation requires more in-depth knowledge of the installation process. You are prompted to make decisions such as selecting the installation disk and a partition scheme for the disk. In the example, I chose Custom Install and clicked the Next button to continue. The next window asks you to select your software localization, as shown in Figure A.21.

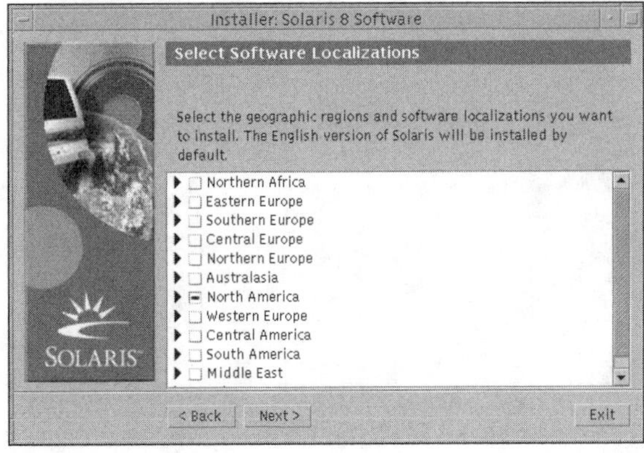


**FIGURE A.21**
Select Software Localizations window.

The English version is installed by default. Select any additional geographic regions, and click the Next button to continue. The next window displays the initial system locale, as shown in Figure A.22.

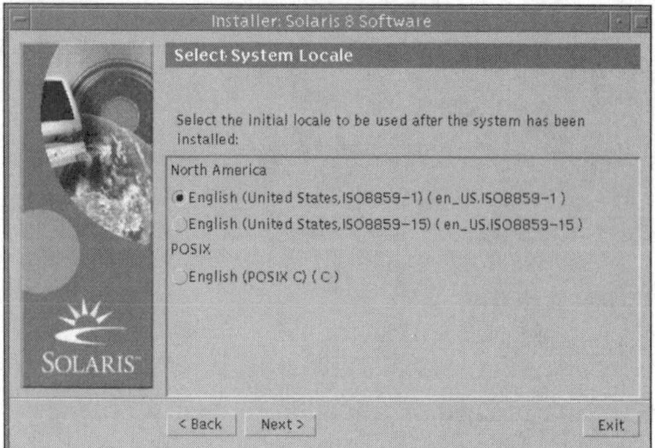


**FIGURE A.22**
Select System Locale.

This window allows you to select a more definitive language localization, relative to any languages that were selected in the previous window. Select the locale, click the Next button to continue, and the Select Products window is displayed, as shown in Figure A.23.

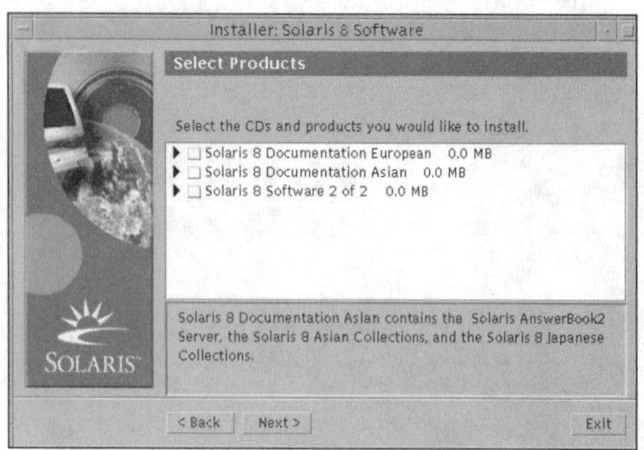


**FIGURE A.23**
Select Products window.

Additional software products are listed and can be marked for installation. After your selections are complete, click the Next button to continue. You are then asked if you want to scan for additional products that are Web Start-ready, as shown in Figure A.24.

**NOTE**

As of this writing, The Solaris software 2 of 2 CD contains DiskSuite 4.2.1, Live Upgrade 1.0, and Sunscreen 3.1 Lite.

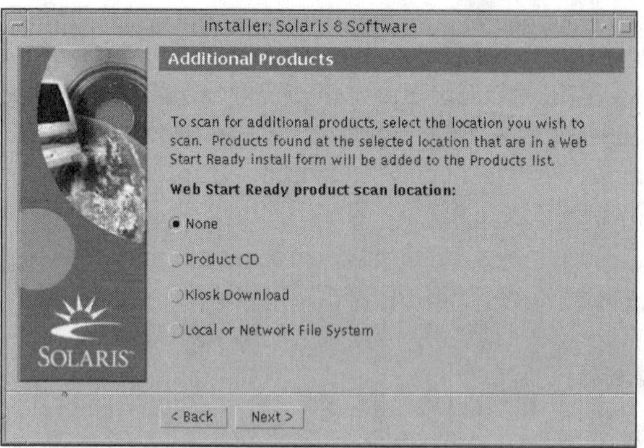


**FIGURE A.24**
Additional Products window.

Select the location of any additional products you might have that are Web Start-ready, and click the Next button to continue. The next window, shown in Figure A.25, asks if you want 64-bit or 32-bit support enabled.

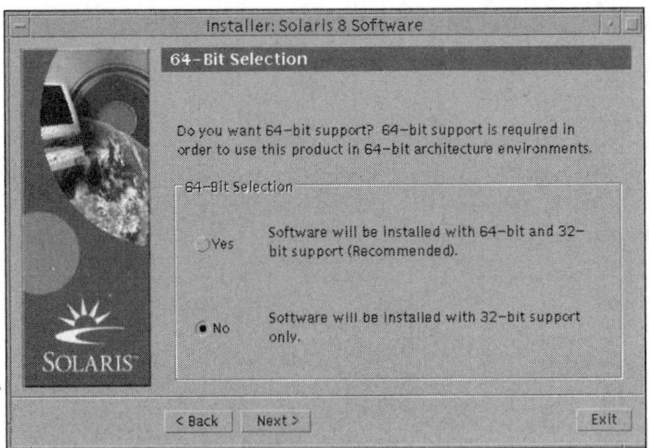


**FIGURE A.25**
64-Bit Selection window.

If your system supports the 64-bit architecture, click Yes. When your selection is complete, click the Next button to continue. The next window, shown in Figure A.26, allows you to select the software group to install.

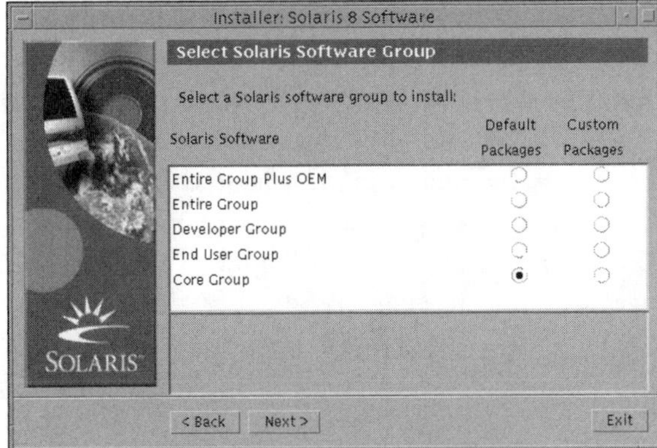


**FIGURE A.26**
Installer window.

Each of these software groups was described in Chapter 3, "Installing the Solaris 8 Software," and Chapter 4, "Software Package Administration." Select your software group, and click the Next button to continue. The Disk Selection window appears, as shown in Figure A.27.

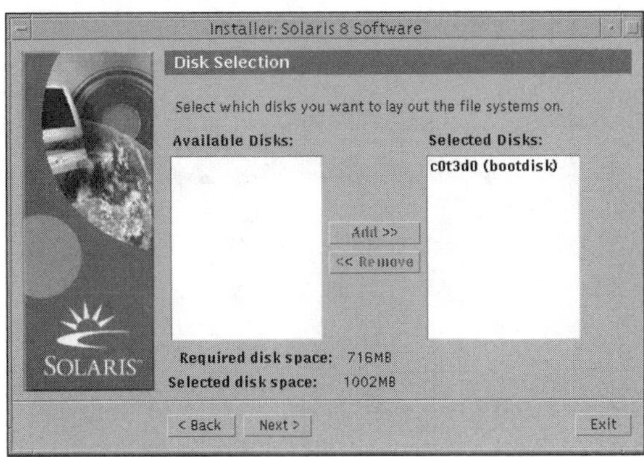


**FIGURE A.27**
Disk Selection window.

Select the disk(s) that you want to install the software onto, and click the Next button to continue. A window indicating that the installation program is gathering disk space requirements is displayed, as shown in Figure A.28.

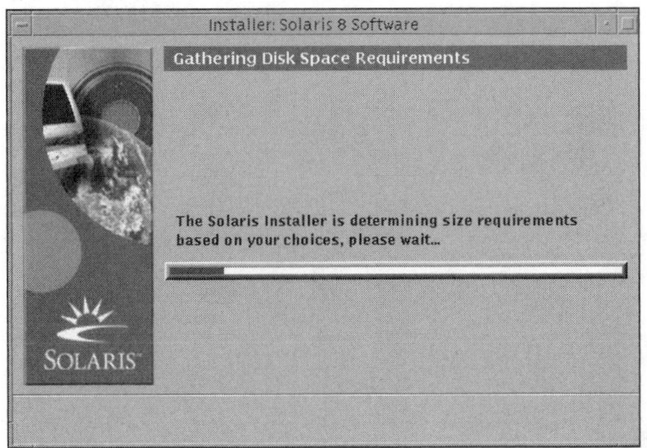


**FIGURE A.28**
Gathering Disk Space Requirements window.

After it has been verified that you have enough disk space to hold the selected software, the Lay Out File Systems window is displayed, as shown in Figure A.29.

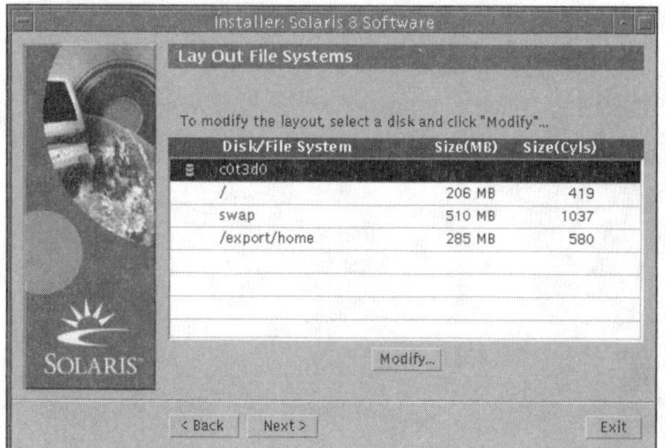


**FIGURE A.29**
Lay Out File Systems window.

If you're satisfied with the disk partition scheme displayed, click the Next button. In the example, I want to modify the partition scheme, so I highlight the disk (c0t3d0) and then click the Modify button. The Disk Modification window is displayed, as shown in Figure A.30.

Disk c0t3d0

Disk c0t3d0 - 1,002 MB

| Slice | File System | Size | Min. Size |
|---|---|---|---|
| 0 | / | 206 | 206 MB |
| 1 | swap | 510 | |
| 3 | | | |
| 4 | | | |
| 5 | | | |
| 6 | | | |
| 7 | /export/home | 285 | |

Capacity: 1002 MB
Allocated: 1002 MB
Free: 0 MB
Rounding Error: 1 MB

MB | Cyl

OK | Apply | Reset | Cancel

**FIGURE A.30**
Disk Modification window.

I revised the values and added separate partitions for the /var, /opt, and /usr file systems, as shown in Figure A.31.

Disk c0t3d0

Disk c0t3d0 - 1,002 MB

| Slice | File System | Size | Min. Size |
|---|---|---|---|
| 0 | / | 55 | 45 MB |
| 1 | swap | 510 | |
| 3 | /var | 50 | 16 MB |
| 4 | /opt | 50 | 14 MB |
| 5 | /usr | 261 | 132 MB |
| 6 | | | |
| 7 | /export/home | 75 | |

Capacity: 1002 MB
Allocated: 1002 MB
Free: 0 MB
Rounding Error: 1 MB

MB | Cyl

OK | Apply | Reset | Cancel

**FIGURE A.31**
Modifications in the Disk Modification window.

After making the modifications, click the OK button to apply the changes. You see the Lay Out File Systems window displayed again, which should display the changes, as shown in Figure A.32.

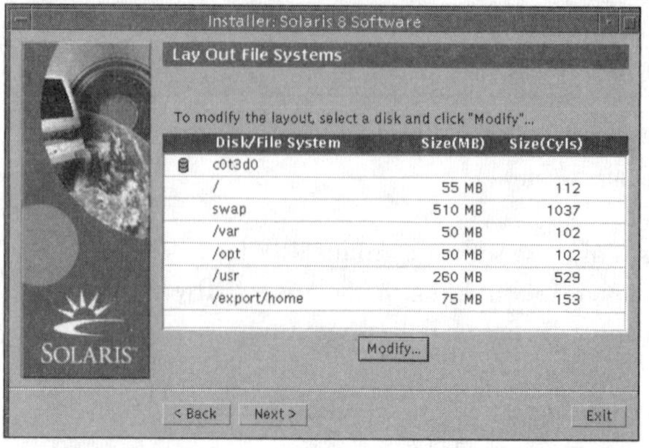


**FIGURE A.32**
Displayed changes in the Lay Out File Systems window.

Verify the changes and click the Next button to continue. The Ready to Install window, as shown in Figure A.33, is displayed to summarize your selections.

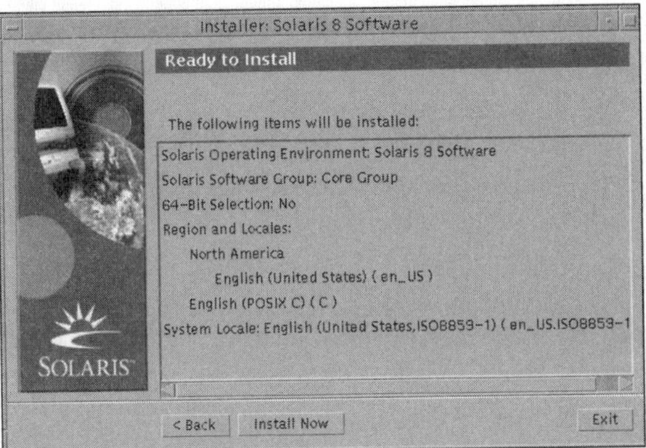


**FIGURE A.33**
Ready to Install window.

If everything looks ok, click the Install Now button, and the Installing window appears, as shown in Figure A.34.

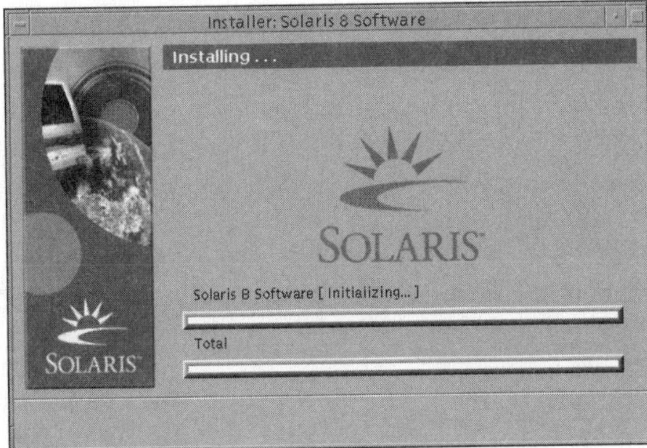


**FIGURE A.34**
Installing window.

Status messages and the name of each package being installed are displayed above the progress bars. The duration of the install depends on the software groups selected and the speed of the installation media.

As additional CDs are required, such as the Solaris 8 Software 1 of 2 and Software 2 of 2 CDs, you are prompted to remove a CD and install the required CD. You see a window indicating the progress of the installation for each CD. When the installation is complete, the CD ejects, and an installation summary window is displayed. Each product that was installed is listed along with a status message indicating whether the installation was successful.

## SUMMARY

As you have seen in this section, Web Start provides a friendly user interface for installing the Solaris 8 operating system. It also aids in installing additional web Start-ready software that the interactive installation method does not. You can use Web Start in either of two ways:

- Graphical-User Interface (GUI). This requires a local or remote CD-ROM drive or network connection, frame buffer, keyboard, and bitmapped monitor.
- Command-Line Interface (CLI). This requires a local or remote CD-ROM drive or network connection, keyboard, and monitor.

This concludes the discussion of Web Start. For more information on Web Start Flash and Web Start Wizards, consult the online documentation at `http://docs.sun.com`.

APPENDIX B

# Administration and Configuration of the CDE

The Solaris Common Desktop Environment (CDE) is an easy-to-use graphical interface that provides a consistent look and feel across UNIX environments and even some non-UNIX environments, such as OpenVMS. SunSoft, Inc., Hewlett-Packard, IBM, and Novell, Inc. Each contributed "best-of-breed" technologies to establish the new standard for user and application interfaces based on the X Window System and MOTIF. While maintaining compliance with the CDE standards, Solaris CDE offers additional benefits to its users and developers. For example, you can use an image viewer to display, rotate, zoom, and convert images and PostScript files.

If you have used Sun's older windowing environment, OpenWindows, you have seen the familiar backdrops, color palettes, and pop-up Workspace menu. In CDE, a user can also run OpenWindows applications without modification. For instance, CDE supports drag-and-drop interaction between OpenWindows applications and CDE applications.

The key features available to you within CDE are the environment and the desktop tools. This chapter discusses customization and administration of the CDE environment, which consists of the following:

- Login Manager. A graphical login window that comes up after the system is booted.
- Session Manager. A service that starts users' applications on the desktop at login and "remembers" the desktop state the next time the users log in.
- Front Panel. The set of pop-ups and icons that appear at the bottom of the CDE screen and set the CDE back to its default environment.
- Actions and data types. Associate commands with icons.
- Application Manager. The desktop container that displays applications available to the user.
- `dtksh` shell. `kshell` scripting within the desktop.

## The Login Manager

The Login Manager is a server responsible for displaying a login screen, authenticating users, and starting a user's session. Displays managed by the login server can be directly attached to the login server or to an X terminal or workstation on the network.

The login screen, displayed by the login server, is an attractive alternative to the traditional character-mode login screen. It provides capabilities beyond those provided by a character-mode login. As with a character-mode login, the user enters a username, followed by a password. If the user is authenticated, the login server starts a desktop session for the user. When the user exits the desktop session, the login server displays a new login screen, and the process begins again.

You can customize the login screen in the following ways:

- Change the login screen appearance.
- Configure X server authority.
- Change the default language.
- Issue commands prior to displaying the login screen.
- Change the contents of the login screen Language menu.
- Specify the command to start the user's session.
- Issue commands prior to the start of the user's desktop session.
- Issue commands after the user's session ends.

Each of these customizations can be done for all displays or on a per-display basis. Because these customizations are not on the exam, I do not cover them in this chapter. If you're interested in learning more about customizing CDE, I recommend that you refer to the Solaris CDE Advanced User's and System Administrator's Guide.

## Starting the Login Server

The Login Server, also called the Login Manager, usually starts up the CDE environment when the system is booted via the /etc/rc2.d/S99dtlogin script. It can also be started from the command line. For example, to start the login server from the command line, type the following:

```
/etc/init.d/dtlogin start
```

or

```
/usr/dt/bin/dtlogin -daemon; exit
```

To stop the Login Server, type the following:

```
/etc/init.d/dtlogin stop
```

> **NOTE** Although you can start the Login Server from the command line for temporary configuration testing, you normally set it up to start when the system is booted.

To set the Login Server to start CDE the next time the system is booted, type the following:

```
/usr/dt/bin/dtconfig -e
```

The Login Server then starts automatically after the user reboots the system.

## Stopping the Login Server

To disable the Login Server CDE startup the next time the system is booted, type the following:

```
/usr/dt/bin/dtconfig -d
```

This command tells the system not to start the Login Server on the next reboot.

You can stop the Login Server immediately by killing its process ID. Type the following:

```
/usr/dt/bin/dtconfig -kill
```

This issues the `kill` command *<login_server_process_ID>*.

> **CAUTION** If the user is logged in to the desktop at the time you kill the login server, the desktop session immediately terminates.

## Displaying a Login Screen on a Local Display

On startup, the Login Server checks the Xservers file to determine whether an Xserver needs to be started and to determine whether and how login screens should be displayed on local or network displays. Following is the format of a line in the Xservers file:

```
<display_name> <display_class> <display_type> \
<X_server_command>
```

Each field in the Xservers file is described in Table B.1.

**TABLE B.1**

**FIELDS IN THE XSERVERS FILE**

| *Field* | *Description* |
|---|---|
| display_name | Tells the Login Server what name to use when connecting to the Xserver (:0 in the following example). A value of * (asterisk) is expanded to hostname:0. The number specified must match the number specified in the X_server_command connection number. |
| display_class | Identifies resources specific to this display (Local in the following example). |
| display_type | Tells the Login Server whether the display is local or network and how to manage the Command Line Login option on the login screen (local@console in the following example). |
| X_server_command | Identifies the command line, connection number, and other options that the Login Server uses to start the Xserver (/usr/bin/X11/X:0 in the following example). The connection number specified must match the number specified in the display_name field. |

The default line in the Xservers file is similar to this:

```
:0 Local local@console /usr/bin/X11/X:0
```

To modify the Xservers file, copy it from /usr/dt/config to /etc/dt/config. The /etc/dt directory contains customized workstation-specific configuration files. If /etc/dt does not exist, you need to create it. The system administrator can modify the system default resources by creating the /etc/dt/config/ directory. In this directory, you can create configuration files to override default resources or to specify additional resources for all desktop users. This file is merged into the desktop default resources during session startup. Resources specified in this file take precedence over those specified in the desktop default resource file. After modifying /etc/dt/config/Xservers, tell the Login Server to reread Xservers by typing this:

```
/usr/dt/bin/dtconfig -reset
```

`dtconfig -reset` issues the command `kill -HUP login_server_process_ID`.

If your Login Server system has a character display instead of a bitmap display, you need to set `display_terminal_device` to `none` in the Xservers file to disable the login screen and enable the character-mode login screen.

# The Session Manager

A *session* is the collection of applications, settings, and resources present on the user's desktop. Session management is a set of conventions and protocols that let the Session Manager save and restore a user's session. When users log in to the desktop for the first time, a default initial session is loaded. Afterward, users can log in to the system and see the same set of running applications, settings, and resources that were present when they last logged out.

Session Manager is responsible for starting the desktop, and automatically saving and restoring running applications, colors, fonts, mouse behavior, audio volume, and keyboard clicks. Using Session Manager, you can do the following:

- Customize the initial session for all desktop users.
- Customize the environment and resources for all desktop users.
- Change the session startup message.
- Change parameters for session startup tools and daemons.
- Customize desktop color usage for all users.

Session Manager is started through /usr/dt/bin/Xsession. When the user logs in using Login Manager, Xsession is started by default. When Session Manager is started, it goes through the following steps to start the user's session:

1. Sources the `.dtprofile` script.
2. Sources the Xsession.d scripts.
3. Displays a welcome message.
4. Sets up desktop search paths.
5. Gathers available applications.
6. Optionally sources $HOME/.profile or $HOME/.login.
7. Starts the ToolTalk messaging daemon.
8. Loads session resources.
9. Starts the color server.
10. Starts the Workspace Manager.
11. Starts the session applications.

## Sourcing the `$HOME/.dtprofile` Script

At session startup, the Xsession script sources the user's `$HOME/.dtprofile` script—a /bin/sh or /bin/ksh script that lets users set up environment variables for their sessions. .dtprofile accepts only sh or ksh syntax. The desktop default is /usr/dt/config/sys.dtprofile. If the `$HOME/.dtprofile` script does not exist (for example, when a user is logging in for the first time), Xsession copies the desktop default sys.dtprofile to `$HOME/.dtprofile`.

You can customize the `sys.dtprofile` script by copying it from /usr/dt/config to /etc/dt/config and editing the new file. You can also set up personal environment variables in `$HOME/.dtprofile`. For example, `export MYVARIABLE="value"` sets the variable `MYVARIABLE` in the user's environment at the next login.

To set system-wide environment variables, create a file in the /etc/dt/config/Xsession.d directory that sets and exports the variable. For example, if you create an executable `ksh` script, /etc/dt/config/Xsession.d/sitevars, that contains `export SITEVARIABLE="value"`, the variable `SITEVARIABLE` is set in each user's environment at the next login.

> **NOTE** Although Session Manager does not automatically read the .profile or .login files, it can be configured to use these files. To tell `Xsession` to source the `.profile` or `.login` scripts, set the variable `DTSOURCEPROFILE` to `true` in $HOME/.dtprofile.

## Sourcing the Xsession.d Scripts

After sourcing the `$HOME/.dtprofile` script, the `Xsession` script sources the `Xsession.d` scripts. These scripts set up additional environment variables and start optional daemons for the user's session.

> **CAUTION**
> Errors in any of the session startup files could prevent a user from logging in. To troubleshoot session startup problems, check the file $HOME/.dt/startlog. Session Manager logs each user's session startup progress in this file.

## Customizing the Welcome Message

After sourcing /etc/dt/config/sys.dtprofile (if it exists), $HOME/.dtprofile, and the `Xsession.d` scripts, `Xsession` displays a welcome message that covers the screen. You can customize the welcome message or turn it off entirely.

The `dthello` client is used to display the welcome message. To alter the message text, change the `dthello` options by modifying the `dtstart_hello[0]` variable. To change `dtstart_hello[0]`, create a `/usr/dt/config/Xsession.d` script that sets the new value. For example, to display the message of the day for all users, create an executable `sh` or `ksh` script called `usr/dt/config/Xsession.d/myvars`, and set `dtstart_hello[0]` as follows:

```
dtstart_hello[0]="/usr/dt/bin/dthello -file \
/etc/motd &"
```

Users can also change the welcome message for their sessions by setting `dtstart_hello[0]` in $HOME/.dtprofile.

To turn off the welcome message, set `dtstart_hello[0]=" "`.

## Setting Desktop Search Paths

The desktop uses search paths, created at login, to locate applications and their associated desktop files. The desktop provides four search paths, described in Table B.2.

**TABLE B.2**

**DESKTOP SEARCH PATHS**

| *Search Path* | *Description* |
|---|---|
| Applications | Used to locate applications. Application Manager uses the Applications search path to dynamically populate its top level when a user logs in. |
| Database | Used to specify additional locations for action- and data-type definition files (*.dt files) and Front Panel files (*.fp files). |
| Icons | Used to specify additional locations for icons. |
| Help data | Used to specify additional locations for desktop help data. |

### Modifying a Search Path

**STEP BY STEP**

**B.1 Modifying a Search Path**

To modify the search path for a particular user, follow these steps:

1. Open $HOME/.dtprofile for editing.
2. Add or edit a line that defines and exports the personal input variable.

For example, the following line adds a location to the user's personal application search path:

```
export DTSPUSERAPPHOSTS=/projects1/editors
```

3. To make the change take effect, log out and then log back in.

## Gathering Available Applications

After you set up the desktop search paths, the next step is to gather available applications by using `dtappgather`. These are the applications to be displayed in the Application Manager window. The `dtappgather` utility gathers application files for presentation by the Application Manager and is responsible for creating and refreshing the user's Application Manager subdirectory.

To alter `dtappgather`'s command-line options, modify the `dtstart_appgather` variable either in the /etc/dt/config/Xsession.d/sitevars file for all users or in $HOME/.dtprofile for individual users. Set `dtstart_appgather` as follows:

```
dtstart_appgather="/usr/dt/bin/dtappgather &"
```

## Sourcing a User .profile or .login File

`Xsession` can source a user's traditional `$HOME/.profile` or `$HOME/.login` scripts, but by default this capability is disabled. To instruct `Xsession` to source the `.profile` or `.login` script, set `DTSOURCEPROFILE` to `true` in $HOME/.dtprofile as follows:

```
DTSOURCEPROFILE=true
```

## Starting the ToolTalk Messaging Daemon

The next task for `Xsession` is to start the ToolTalk messaging daemon. The ToolTalk service allows independent applications to communicate without having direct knowledge of each other. Applications create and send ToolTalk messages to communicate with each other. The ToolTalk service receives these messages, determines the recipients, and then delivers the messages to the appropriate applications. Users can change the `ttsession` options for their own sessions by setting the `dtstart_ttsession` variable in $HOME/.dtprofile as follows:

```
dtstart_ttsession="/usr/dt/bin/ttsession -s"
```

## Loading Session Resources

Resources are used by applications to set certain aspects of appearance and behavior. For example, Style Manager (`dtstyle`) provides resources that allow you to specify where the system looks for files containing information about color palettes by entering the following line of information in the sys.resources file located in the /etc/dt/config/<language> directory:

```
dtstyle*paletteDirectories: /usr/dt/palettes/C \
/$HOME/.dt/palettes
```

**NOTE** If the sys.resources file does not exist, it might need to be created using the instructions in the next paragraph.

Session Manager loads resources at session startup. The desktop default resources can be found in /usr/dt/config/*<language>*/sys.resources. These resources are made available to each user's session via the `RESOURCE_MANAGER` property. This file should not be edited because it is overwritten on subsequent desktop installations. The system administrator can modify the system default resources by creating /etc/dt/config/*<language>*/ sys.resources. In this file, you can override default resources or specify additional resources for all desktop users. To set personal resources, make the entries in the $HOME/.Xdefaults file.

Users can modify the desktop default and system-wide resources through their $HOME/.Xdefaults file. Resources specified in this file take precedence over those specified in the desktop default or system administrator resource files.

## Starting the Color Server

You can choose a wide range of colors for your display, either by using the Style Manager (as shown in Figure B.1) or by customizing color resources used by Style Manager to control desktop color usage.

**FIGURE B.1**
The Style Manager.

Set color server resources for all users by creating /etc/dt/config/*<language>*/sys.resources and specifying the color server resources in that file. Users can similarly set these for their own sessions by specifying them in $HOME/.Xdefaults.

## Starting the Workspace Manager

The Session Manager is responsible for starting the Workspace Manager. By default, /usr/dt/bin/dtwm is started. The Workspace Manager is the window manager provided by the desktop. It controls the following:

- The appearance of window frame components
- The behavior of windows, including their stacking order and focus behavior
- Key bindings and button bindings
- The appearance of minimized windows
- Workspace and window menus

In addition, the Workspace Manager controls the desktop components outlined in Table B.3.

**TABLE B.3**

**DESKTOP COMPONENTS**

| *Component* | *Description* |
|---|---|
| Workspaces | The Workspace Manager controls the number of workspaces and keeps track of which windows are open in each workspace. |
| Workspace backdrops | The user can change the backdrop image by using Style Manager. Backdrop management, however, is a function of the Workspace Manager. |
| Front Panel | Although the Front Panel uses its own configuration files, it is created and managed by the Workspace Manager. |

Additional modifications that can be made to the Workspace Manager include changing the number of workspaces and providing system-wide workspace names.

### Changing the Number of Workspaces on a System-Wide Basis

The default desktop configuration provides four workspaces. The user can add, delete, and rename workspaces by using the pop-up menu associated with the workspace switch.

In the /usr/dt/app-defaults/C/Dtwm file, the `workspaceCount` resource is set to the following default number of workspaces:

```
Dtwm*0*workspaceCount: 4
Dtwm*workspaceCount:   1
```

Multiple workspaces are specified on screen 0; a single workspace is specified on any other screen. You can create the /etc/dt/config/C/sys.resources file (or modify it if it exists) to change the default number of workspaces for all new users on a workstation.

Use the `0*workspaceCount` resource to set the system-wide default on the primary screen:

```
Dtwm*0*workspaceCount: number
```

For example, the following resource sets the number of workspaces system-wide on the primary screen to 6:

```
Dtwm*0*workspaceCount: 6
```

### Providing System-Wide Workspace Names

Internally, the workspaces are numbered by the numbering convention ws<*n*>, in which *n* is 0, 1, 2, and so on. For example, the default four workspaces are numbered internally ws0 through ws3.

Use the `title` resource to change the name of a specified workspace in the sys.resources file described earlier:

```
Dtwm*wsn*title: name
```

For example, the following resources set the default four workspaces to the specified names:

```
Dtwm*ws0*title:  Glenda
Dtwm*ws1*title:  Neil
Dtwm*ws2*title:  Nicole
Dtwm*ws3*title:  William
```

### Starting the Session Applications

At session startup, Session Manager restarts any applications saved in the previous session. The system default set of applications to be restored as part of the user's initial session can be found in /usr/dt/config/<*language*>/sys.session. Do not edit this file.

A system administrator can replace the set of applications started as part of the user's initial session by copying /usr/dt/config/<*language*>/sys.session to /etc/dt/config/<*language*>/sys.session and modifying the latter file. Unlike the resource files, this file is used as a complete replacement for the desktop default file.

## THE FRONT PANEL

The Front Panel contains a set of icons and pop-up menus (more like roll-up menus) that appear at the bottom of the screen. The two main elements of the Front Panel are the Main Panel and the subpanels. The Main Panel includes the workspace switch, shown in Figure B.2, which contains the buttons you use to change from one workspace to the next.

**FIGURE B.2**
The Front Panel workspace switch.

If a control in the Main Panel has an arrow on top of it, that control has a subpanel, as shown in Figure B.3.

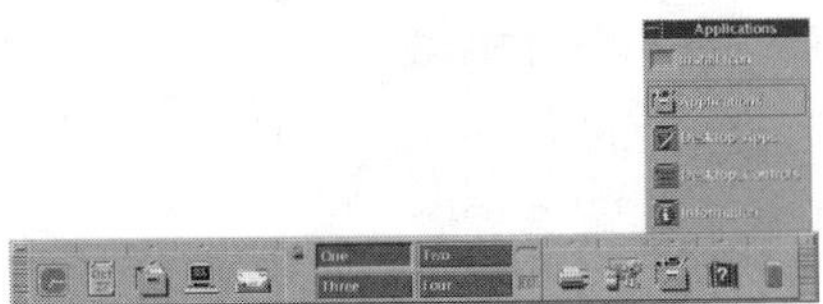

**FIGURE B.3**
A subpanel.

Users can drag and drop icons from the File Manager or Application Manager to add them to the subpanels. Up to 12 additional workspaces can be configured, each with different backgrounds and colors. Each workspace can have any number of applications running in it, and an application can be set to appear in one, more than one, or all workspaces simultaneously. In some instances, the system administrator might find it necessary to lock the Front Panel so that users can't change it.

Using the desktop's interface, the Front Panel can easily be modified in the following ways:

- Customizing a workspace
- Adding and deleting a workspace
- Renaming a workspace
- Adding and deleting controls to subpanels

The System Administrator can also do more advanced customization outside the CDE environment by editing CDE configuration files directly from the UNIX command line. However, advanced customization is not covered on the exam. Therefore, for more information on advanced Front Panel customization, see the CDE Advanced User's and System Administrator's Guide.

## Customizing Workspaces

Users can use the Front Panel workspace switch to rename or change the number of workspaces. Click on the workspace buttons to change workspaces. When the cursor is positioned on a workspace button, clicking the third mouse button displays its pop-up menu, as shown in Figure B.4.

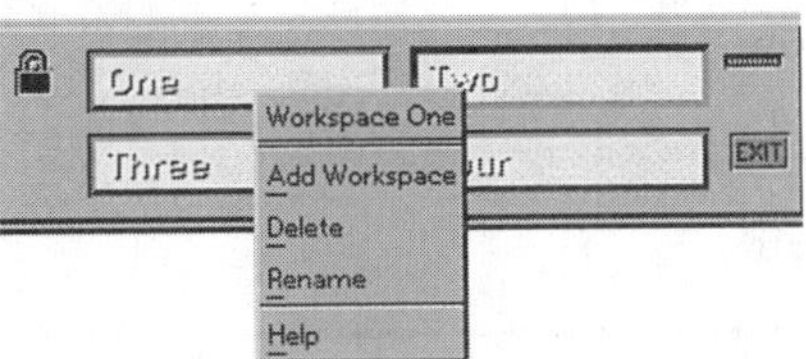


**FIGURE B.4**
The workspace button pop-up menu.

The workspace button pop-up menu includes the items described in Table B.4.

**TABLE B.4**

**POP-UP MENU OPTIONS**

| *Option* | *Description* |
|---|---|
| Add Workspace | Adds a workspace to the list of workspaces |
| Delete | Deletes the workspace |
| Rename | Changes the button into a text field for editing the name |
| Help | Displays help for the workspace switch |

## STEP BY STEP

### B.2 Renaming a Workspace

Use the pop-up menu to modify workspace button parameters. For example, to rename a workspace, follow these steps:

1. Point to the button of the workspace you want to rename.

*continues*

*continued*

2. Choose Rename from the button's pop-up menu (displayed when you click the third mouse button). The workspace button turns into a text field.
3. Edit the text field.
4. Press Enter.

**STEP BY STEP**

### B.3 Adding a Workspace

To add a workspace, follow these steps:

1. Point to any area in the workspace switch, and click the third mouse button to display the pop-up menu.
2. Choose Add Workspace from the pop-up menu. The new workspace, named New, is placed at the end of the set of workspaces. (If more than one new workspace is created, the workspaces are named New_1, New_2, and so on.)
3. Rename the workspace as described earlier.

**STEP BY STEP**

### B.4 Removing a Workspace

To remove a workspace, follow these steps:

1. Point to the workspace button of the workspace you want to remove.
2. Choose Delete from the button's pop-up menu (displayed when you press the third mouse button).

## Customizing Workspace Controls

Customizing the controls in the workspace switch is an advanced task that requires the system administrator to create a Front Panel configuration file. This section describes some easy customizations that can be performed from the desktop. Advanced customization is covered in the CDE Advanced User's and System Administrator's Guide.

## Customizing the Front Panel Switch Area

The switch area shown in Figure B.5 is the portion of the workspace switch that is not occupied by other controls or workspace buttons.

**FIGURE B.5**
The switch area.

The switch area has a pop-up menu containing these items:

| | |
|---|---|
| Add Workspace | Adds a workspace, and creates a workspace button in the workspace switch |
| Help | Displays help for the workspace switch |

## Adding an Application or Other Icon to a Subpanel

The user can add any type of File Manager or Application Manager icon to the Front Panel. The most convenient use of this feature is to add application icons.

**STEP BY STEP**

### B.5 Adding an Application Icon to a Subpanel

To add an application icon to a subpanel, follow these steps:

1. Display the object's icon in File Manager or Application Manager.
2. Display the subpanel to which the object is to be added.
3. Drag the object to the Install Icon control, by using the first mouse button, and drop it on the control.

The behavior of controls added to the Front Panel by using the Install Icon control depends on the type of icon dropped. Table B.5 describes the control behavior for each type of icon.

**TABLE B.5**

**ICON CONTROL BEHAVIOR**

| *Type of Icon* | *Behavior* |
|---|---|
| File | Displays the contents of the file, ready to be edited, when the user clicks the File icon. The same behavior as the file's icon in File Manager. |
| Folder | Opens a File Manager view of the folder. |
| Application group | Opens an Application Manager view of the application group. |
| Application icon | Automatically launches the application when the user clicks the icon. The same behavior as an application's icon in File Manager or Application Manager. |

## Resetting All User Customizations

**STEP BY STEP**

### B.6 Resetting the Front Panel

To reset the Front Panel and remove all user customizations, follow these steps:

1. Open Application Manager, and double-click the Desktop_Tools application group icon.
2. Double-click Restore Front Panel.

The screen goes blank for several seconds while the Workspace Manager is restarted. The Restore Front Panel action removes all customizations made by using the Install Icon control or the Front Panel's pop-up menus.

**NOTE** This procedure does not affect advanced customizations made by manually editing Front Panel configuration files.

# Actions and Data Types

*Actions* are instructions that automate desktop tasks such as running applications and opening data files. Actions work much the same as application macros or programming functions. They can be assigned to icons so that associated commands are invoked when an icon is clicked.

## STEP BY STEP

### B.7 Creating an Action

You can create an action by using the Create Action menu, as described in the following steps:

1. Bring up the Applications pop-up menu, shown in Figure B.6.

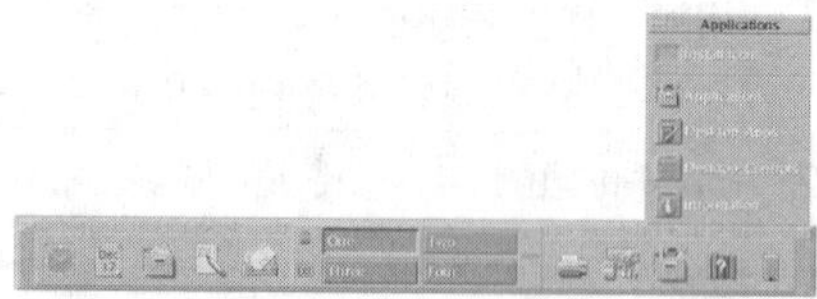

**FIGURE B.6**
The Applications pop-up menu.

2. Select Desktop_Apps from the pop-up menu. The Desktop_Apps window appears, as shown in Figure B.7.

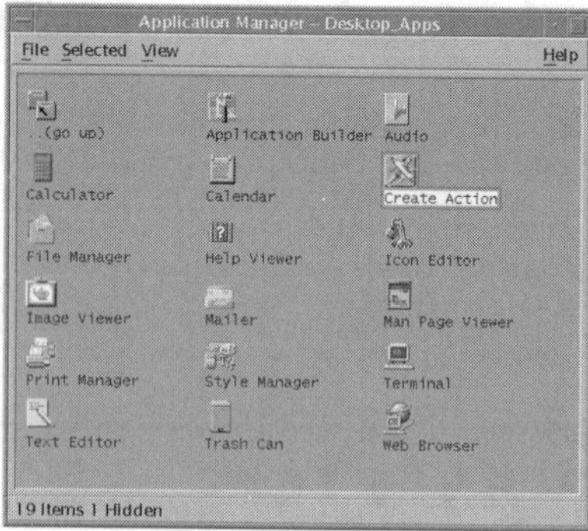


**FIGURE B.7**
The Desktop_Apps window.

3. In the Desktop_Apps window, click the Create Action icon. The Create Action window appears, as shown in Figure B.8.

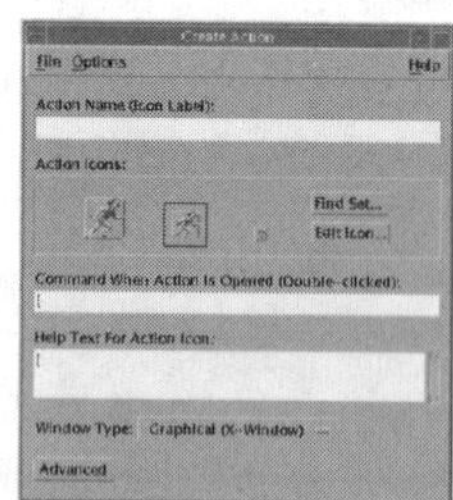


**FIGURE B.8**
The Create Action window.

**NOTE**

For information on filling in the appropriate fields and creating an action, click Help, located at the top of the Create Action window.

After you define an action, you can use that action in the desktop user interface to simplify tasks. The desktop provides the ability to attach user interface components such as icons, Front Panel controls, and menu items to actions. Each of these icons performs an action when the icon is double-clicked.

Another common use of actions is in menus. Data files usually have actions in their selected menu in File Manager. For example, XWD files (files with names ending in .xwd or .wd) have an Open action that displays the screen image when you run the Xwd action.

Actions and data types are powerful components for integrating applications into the desktop. They provide a way to create a user interface for starting applications and manipulating data files. For more information on creating actions, see the Solaris CDE Advanced User's and System Administrator's Guide.

## The Application Manager

Application Manager is the desktop container displaying applications available to users. It is selected from the Applications pop-up menu located on the Front Panel, shown earlier in Figure B.6.

When initially opened, the Application Manager window displays the top-level directory of the Application Manager. User interaction with the Application Manager is similar to the use of the File Manager, except that the Application Manager contains executable modules. The user launches the Application Manager from an icon on the Front Panel, opening the window shown in Figure B.9.

**FIGURE B.9**
The Application Manager window.

Programs and icons can be installed in the Application Manager by the system administrator, and can be pushed out to other workstations as part of the installation process. By default, the Application Manager comes preconfigured to include several utilities and programs (see Figure B.9). Each of these utilities is located in a directory, which—with its contents—is called an application group. Application groups provided with the default desktop are described in Table B.6.

**TABLE B.6**

**APPLICATION GROUPS**

| *Group* | *Description* |
|---|---|
| Desktop_Apps | Desktop applications such as File Manager, Style Manager, and Calculator. |
| Desktop_Tools | Desktop administration and operating system tools such as User Registration, Reload Application, vi text editor, and Check Spelling. |
| Information | Icons representing frequently used help topics. |
| System_Admin | Tools used by system administrators. |
| Desktop Controls | Tools to set your CDE environment, such as mouse behavior, desktop fonts, screen saver, and window behavior. |
| OpenWindows | Group that contains several OpenWindows-style actions, such as the mail tool and File Manager. |

The top-level directory for the Application Manager is the directory /var/dt/appconfig/appmanager/login-host-name-display, created dynamically each time the user logs in. For example, if user bcalkins logs in from display sparc1:0, the following Application Manager directory is created:

```
/var/dt/appconfig/appmanager/bcalkins-sparc1:0
```

The Application Manager is built by gathering application groups from directories located along the application search path. The default path consists of the locations listed in Table B.7.

**TABLE B.7**

**DEFAULT APPLICATION SEARCH PATH LOCATIONS**

| *Scope* | *Location* |
|---|---|
| Built-in | /usr/dt/appconfig/appmanager/<*language*> |
| System-wide | /etc/dt/appconfig/appmanager/<*language*> |
| Personal | $HOME/.dt/appmanager |

To create the top-level directory of the Application Manager, links are created at login time from the application group directories to the Application Manager directory, which is /var/dt/appconfig/appmanager/<*login-hostname-display*>. The gathering operation is done by the desktop utility `dtappgather`, which is automatically run by Login Manager after the user has successfully logged in.

For example, the desktop provides the built-in application group /usr/dt/appconfig/appmanager/<*language*>/Desktop_Tools. At login time, a symbolic link is created to /var/dt/appconfig/appmanager/<*login-hostname-display*>/Desktop_Tools.

Applications can be added to the Application Manager by copying icons from other application groups to the personal application group.

## STEP BY STEP

### B.8 Creating Personal Application Groups

To create a personal application group, follow these steps:

1. From your home folder, change to the .dt/appmanager subfolder.
2. Create a new folder. The folder name becomes the name of the new application group.
3. Double-click Reload Applications in the Desktop_Apps application group.
4. Your new application group becomes registered at the top level of Application Manager.

A personal application group is an application group that users can alter because they have write permission to it. For example, users can copy (by pressing the Ctrl key and dragging) the Calculator icon from the Desktop_Tools application group to a new personal application group. Another method is to create an action for an application and then place an application (action) icon in the personal application group.

## THE *DTKSH* SHELL

Available in CDE is the Desktop KornShell (`dtksh`), which gives `kshell` scripting the ability to easily access most of the existing Xt and MOTIF functions. The Desktop KornShell is based on `ksh-93`, which provides a powerful set of tools and commands for the shell programmer, and supports the standard set of `kshell` programming commands. Developers and programmers use `dtksh` to create MOTIF applications for the CDE environment.

## SUMMARY

This question always arises: Should users be allowed to customize the CDE environment themselves? Most large institutions frown on letting users customize their own environments. Usually, the system administrator provides a default setup that is applied to all users. This default setup promotes consistency and prevents the "self-inflicted" problems that can occur when users incorrectly modify system files. The answer also depends on how much pain you're willing to endure for the good of your user community. Users love an administrator who gives them the flexibility to arrange their own desktops. However, you can quickly have plenty of problems if users are not properly trained in the use of customization utilities.

The graphical user interface available in CDE is a welcome enhancement to UNIX. With CDE, users no longer need to be exposed to the cryptic UNIX shell. Most of the routine tasks performed by users can now be done by using the menus and icons provided through CDE. As a system administrator, your job is to customize and manage CDE, using the tools provided, to facilitate tasks and maintain productivity in your specific environment.

Customizing the CDE environment is a weighty topic. Although this section introduced you to some basic customization topics, additional information can be found in publications focusing on the subject.

APPENDIX C

# The History of Solaris

UNIX is plural. It is not one operating system, but many implementations of an idea that originated in 1965. As a system administrator, you need to understand the history of the UNIX operating system—where it came from, how it was built, and where it is now. Understanding the various versions of UNIX and its origins makes it clear why UNIX became known as a somewhat hostile operating system. For example, UNIX was not developed by a single company with a large marketing organization driving the user interface. (In other words, it did not follow the development path of, say, Microsoft Windows.) On the other hand, UNIX was not invented by hackers who were fooling around; it grew out of strong academic roots. The primary contributors to UNIX were highly educated mathematicians and computer scientists employed by what many people feel is the world's premier industrial research center, Bell Laboratories. Although knowledgeable and experienced in their own right, these developers maintained professional contacts with researchers in academia, leading to an exchange of ideas that proved beneficial for both sides. Understanding the symbiotic relationship between UNIX and the academic community means understanding the background of the system's inventors and the history of interactions between universities and Bell Laboratories.

## How It All Began

It all began at Bell Labs, the research lab of AT&T, one of the largest and most powerful companies of our time. Ironically, AT&T was not interested in developing and selling computers or operating systems. In fact, the U.S. Department of Justice did not allow AT&T to sell software. However, AT&T's existing systems, made up of people and paper, were in danger of being overwhelmed in the boom of the 1960s. By the 1970s, the phone business was in jeopardy. Out of desperation and need, Ken Thompson of AT&T set out to develop what no computer company was ready to provide—a multiuser, multiprocessing operating system to be used in-house for its own information processing department. Specifically, the goal was an operating system to support several programmers simultaneously in a more hospitable environment.

What follows is an account of major dates and events in the development cycle of the UNIX operating system.

# 1965–1969

In 1965, Bell Labs joined with MIT and General Electric in a cooperative development of Multics, a multiuser interactive operating system running on a GE 645 mainframe computer. However, unhappy with the progress in the development of a system that was experiencing many delays and high costs, Bell Labs dropped out of the development of Multics in 1969.

In 1969, Ken Thompson, exposed to Multics at Bell Labs, met up with Dennis Ritchie, who provided a Digital Equipment Corporation PDP-7 minicomputer to continue the development of an operating system capable of supporting a team of programmers in a research environment. After they created a prototype, Thompson returned to Bell Labs to propose the use of this new operating system as a document preparation tool in the Bell Labs patent department. The new operating system was named UNIX to distinguish it from the complexity of Multics. Efforts to develop UNIX continued, and UNIX became operational at Bell Labs in 1971.

The first version of UNIX was written in assembly language on a PDP-11/20. It included the file system, `fork`, `roff`, and `ed`. It was used as a text-processing tool for the preparation of patents.

# 1970–1972

During the early 1970s, UNIX began to gain popularity throughout Bell Labs, and as word of the new operating system spread, universities embraced it. However, although UNIX was viewed favorably by the academic and high-tech sectors, it was with skepticism by the business community. In a move to heighten the popularity of UNIX, AT&T began to license the UNIX source code to universities at a minimal cost. AT&T gave many licensees the software code and manuals, but didn't provide technical support. By the late 1970s, 70% of all colleges and universities had UNIX. Computer science graduates were using it, even modifying the code to make it more robust. UNIX was written in assembly language and ran primarily on DEC hardware—first on the PDP-7, and then the PDP-11/40, the 11/45, and finally the 11/70, on which it gained wide popularity.

# 1973–1979

This period became the most significant in the development of UNIX. Ritchie and Thompson had developed the C programming language between 1969 and 1973, and now rewrote the UNIX kernel in the high-level C language. The operating system could be compiled to run on different computers. Within months, UNIX could be ported to new hardware. Modifications to the operating system were easy. Again, Thompson resonated with members of the academic community who were already using UNIX in many of their system design courses. UNIX, written in a general-purpose language featuring modern commands, began to take off in the areas of word processing and programming.

By this point, UNIX was at version 6. This was the first release of UNIX to be picked up by a commercial firm, Whitesmiths, Inc., which created a commercial copy of version 6 called Idris.

In 1975, Thompson visited Berkeley while on sabbatical, and installed version 6 on a PDP-11/70. It was at this time that two graduate students, Bill Joy and Chuck Haley, got involved with version 6 and later played an important role in the development of the UNIX system at Berkeley. The first project they worked on was the development of the UNIX ex editor.

Joy and Haley began to take interest in the internal operations of UNIX—specifically, the kernel. Joy put together a distribution of UNIX called the Berkeley Software Distribution (BSD). He included enhancements such as the C shell (a C-like interface to UNIX) and the vi editor. 1BSd was released in 1975. By the second release of BSD in 1978, Joy had added virtual memory support, which allowed programs to run even if they required more physical memory than was available at the time. This second edition of BSD had a strong influence on the release of Bell Labs' version 7 of UNIX, which was released in 1979 and was the last of the "clean" versions of UNIX (produced solely by Bell Labs). Version 7 gave rise to a number of UNIX ports to other platforms, and for the first time, both industry and academia supplied enhancements, which were incorporated into future releases.

In the late 1970s, the United States Department of Defense's Advanced Research Projects Agency (DARPA) decided to base its universal computing environment on Berkeley's version of UNIX. In the 4.1 release of BSD, DARPA provided some important performance tune-ups. The `fast` file system, which provided a way to improve the file system's performance and prevent file fragmentation, was added in release 4.2.

# 1982–1983

AT&T formally released a beta version of UNIX to the commercial sector in 1982. In 1983, AT&T released the first true production version of UNIX, naming it System III (Systems I and II never existed). Although it was based on version 7 of UNIX, and thus included some BSD utilities, the release of System III did not include the vi editor or the C shell. Instead, AT&T included the programmer's workbench.

With the release of System III, AT&T saw a future in UNIX, and soon released System V. (System IV was never seen outside of AT&T.) System V included the editor, `curses` (the screen-oriented software libraries), and the `init` program, which was used to start up processes at UNIX boot-up.

In the early 1980s, Joy left Berkeley with a master's degree in electrical engineering, and became cofounder of Sun Microsystems (Sun stands for Stanford University Network). Sun's implementation of BSD was called SunOS. Sun extended the networking tools of the operating system to include the Networked File System (NFS), which was to become an industry standard. Sun also did some of the early work in developing windowing software for UNIX. SunOS was first released in 1983.

With workstation products now offered by Sun, UNIX began to gain acceptance in the high-tech arena, especially in computer-aided design and computer-aided engineering (CAD/CAE) environments. The early 1980s saw CAD/CAE become popular. Additional workstation vendors, such as HP and Apollo, began to exploit CAD/CAE capabilities and performance gains over the popular personal computers of the time. These UNIX workstations could outperform PCs and, with UNIX as an operating system, could provide a multiuser environment.

In other business computing environments, however, UNIX was still considered a hostile environment, and did not pose a threat to the mainframes of the time. UNIX had yet to define itself as a user-friendly, tried-and-tested operating system. However, it was gaining ground in the areas of multitasking and networking. More important, UNIX was being touted as the operating system that provided portability between different hardware architectures, and as a consequence, software developers were getting excited about UNIX. In theory, a program written in C for UNIX would be portable to any hardware platform running the UNIX operating system.

## 1984–1987

In 1984, AT&T released System V, release 2, and in 1987, release 3. Release 2 introduced the terminal capability database `termcap` file, named `terminfo`, which provided support for various CRT terminals connected to the UNIX system. Other changes included the addition of `Streams` and Remote File Systems.

## 1988–1992

In 1988, AT&T shocked the UNIX community by purchasing a percentage of Sun Microsystems, already a leader in the industry. Other hardware vendors saw this as an unfair advantage for Sun, so they quickly formed a consortium group called the Open Software Foundation (OSF). Together, they raised millions of dollars to develop a new UNIX standard to compete against Sun's.

In a counterstrike, AT&T, Sun, Data General, and Unisys joined forces to start their own organization to fight OSF. This consortium of companies, called UNIX International (UI), was formed to oversee the development of System V standards. OSF and UI turned out to be the two major competing commercial standards for UNIX.

By the late 1980s, AT&T concluded that UNIX was a distraction from the company's focus on producing hardware. As a result, AT&T formed the UNIX Software LAB (USL), ultimately purchased by Novell in 1992.

In 1992, at the summer UseNIX conference, Berkeley announced it would conclude its development activities at version 4.4 of BSD. Several people who were involved with BSD formed smaller companies to try to continue the development of BSD, but without Berkeley and ARPA, it was not the same.

In the 1990s, BSD and System V dominated the industry, with several vendors providing their versions of one of the two operating systems. Soon UNIX, an operating system meant to provide portability of applications between multiple hardware platforms, was getting out of control. Applications were not portable between UNIX System V, release 3, and BSD. To create even more confusion, hardware vendors were enhancing their versions of BSD and System V.

## 1993

Sun announced that SunOS, release 4.1.4, would be its last release of an operating system based on BSD. Sun saw the writing on the wall and moved to System V, release 4, which they named Solaris. System V, release 4 (SRV4) was a merger of System V and BSD, incorporating the important features found in SunOS.

As more hardware vendors, such as Sun, began to enter the picture, a proliferation of UNIX versions emerged. Although these hardware vendors had to purchase the source code from AT&T and port UNIX to their hardware platforms, AT&T's policy toward licensing the UNIX brand name allowed nearly any hardware vendor willing to pay for a license to pick up UNIX. Because UNIX was a trademark, hardware vendors had to give their operating systems a unique name. Here are a few of the more popular versions of UNIX that have survived over the years:

- SCO UNIX. SCO Open Desktop and SCO Open Server from the Santa Cruz Operation for the Intel platform. Based on System V.

- SunOS. Sun's early operating system and the best-known BSD operating system.
- Solaris. Sun's SRV4 implementation, also referred to as SunOS 5.x.
- HP-UX. Hewlett-Packard's version of UNIX. HP-UX 9.x was System V, release 3, and HP-UX 11i is based on the System V, release 4 OS.
- Digital UNIX. Digital Equipment's version of OSF/1.
- IRIX. The Silicon Graphics version of UNIX. Early versions were BSD-based; version 6 was System V, release 4.
- AIX. IBM's System V-based UNIX.
- Linux. A free UNIX operating system for the INTEL platform; it was quickly gaining a hold in the UNIX community. Versions of Linux became available on Sun, HP, and IBM systems.

With the uncontrolled proliferation of UNIX versions, standards became a major issue. In 1993, Sun announced that it was moving to System V in an effort to promote standards in the UNIX community. With two major flavors of UNIX, standards could not become a reality. Without standards, UNIX would never be taken seriously as a business computing system. Thus, Sun developed BSD, but provided its users with System V, release 4, shrink-wrapped directly from AT&T. In addition, any applications developed by Sun to be added onto UNIX were to be SRV4-compliant. Sun challenged its competitors to provide true portability for the user community.

The Graphical User Interface (GUI) was the next wave in the development of the UNIX operating system. As each hardware vendor tried to outdo the others, ease of use became an issue. Again, in this area especially, standards were important. Applications that were to be portable needed a GUI standard. Therefore, Sun and AT&T started promoting OPEN LOOK, which they jointly developed. Their goal was to create a consistent look and feel for all flavors of UNIX; unfortunately, OSF had its own GUI called OSF/MOTIF. Thus, round two of the fight for standards began, with MOTIF beating out OPEN LOOK.

MOTIF was based on a GUI developed at MIT named the X Window System, which allowed a user sitting at one machine to run programs on a remote machine while still interacting with the program locally. X was, in effect, one way for different systems to interface with each other. X allowed a program run on one computer to display its output on another computer, even when the other computer was of a different operating system and hardware architecture. The program displayed its output on the local machine, and accepted keyboard and mouse input from the local machine, but it executed on the CPU of the remote machine.

The local machine was typically a workstation or terminal called a dedicated X terminal, and was built specifically to run the X Window System. The remote machine might be a minicomputer or server, a mainframe, or even a supercomputer. In some cases, the local machine and the remote machine might, in fact, be the same. In summary, X was a distributed, intelligent, device-independent, operating-system-independent windowing system.

As stated earlier, MOTIF beat OPEN LOOK in the standards war. Sun conceded, and started to provide a package that contained both OPEN LOOK and MOTIF—called the Common Desktop Environment (CDE)—as standard equipment beginning with Solaris 2.5.1.

## 2001 and Beyond

Today, many hardware vendors have buried the hatchet and, for the sake of users, are moving their implementations of UNIX to be SRV4-compliant. SVR4 will clearly be the dominant flavor of UNIX across most major platforms. As all vendors begin to implement SVR4 along with the CDE or GNOME interface, users will begin to see a more consistent implementation of UNIX. In addition, software providers can be assured that applications written to be SVR4-compliant will be portable across many hardware platforms.

Look for the GNOME desktop around mid-2002 with the release of Solaris 9. This new desktop will eventually replace CDE, and will be much better than CDE in terms of usability, visual design, and core features. Most major UNIX vendors will be moving toward GNOME.

Linux will still be a major player. Now that most of the major UNIX vendors—including Sun, HP, and IBM—have embraced it, Linux will not go away.

### Solaris

No other flavor of UNIX is more popular or has enjoyed a wider user base and cultural following than Sun Microsystems' Solaris. Since it was founded in 1982, Sun Microsystems' focus has been on UNIX, and it appears to have no intention of moving away from the UNIX operating system. Sun's user base has strong loyalty to the company, as well as to the operating system. Sun's most recent version is Solaris 8, based on System V, release 4. The Solaris operating system is available for the SPARC architecture, Sun's own processor, and the Intel platform.

## Milestones in the Development of Solaris

1965 Bell Laboratories joins with MIT and General Electric to develop Multics.

1970 Ken Thompson and Dennis Ritchie develop UNIX.

1971 The B-language version of the operating system runs on a PDP-11.

1973 UNIX is rewritten in the C language.

1974 Thompson and Ritchie publish a paper and generate enthusiasm in the academic community. Berkeley starts the BSD program.

1975 The first licensed version of BSD UNIX is released.

1979 Bill Joy introduces "Berkeley Enhancements" as BSD 4.1.

1982 AT&T first markets UNIX. Sun Microsystems is founded.

1983 Sun Microsystems introduces SunOS.

1984 About 100,000 UNIX sites exist worldwide.

1988 AT&T and Sun start work on SVR4, a unified version of UNIX.

1988 OSF and UI are formed.

1989 AT&T releases System V, release 4.

1990 OSF releases OSF/1.

1992 Sun introduces Solaris, which is based on System V, release 4. SunOS, which is based on BSDF UNIX, will be phased out.

1993 Novell buys UNIX from AT&T.

1994 Solaris 2.4 is available.

1995 Santa Cruz Operation buys UNIXware from Novell. SCO and HP announce a relationship to develop a 64-bit version of UNIX. Solaris 2.5 is available.

1997 Solaris 2.6 is available.

1998 Solaris 7 is available.

2000 Solaris 8 is available.

2001 Solaris 9 in Beta testing Q3.

APPENDIX D

# Overview of the Certification Process

## Description of the Path to Certification

Sun provides a number of different types and levels of professional certification for Java developers and Solaris administrators. The certifications directly related to the content of this *Training Guide* are those having to do with the Solaris 8 operating system: the Sun Certified System Administrator and the Sun Certified Network Administrator.

## About the Solaris 8 Certification Program

The Sun Certified Solaris 8 certifications are industry-recognized certifications designed to reflect the competencies exhibited by those knowledgeable in the areas of Solaris 8 system and network administration. Each of the certifications and its requirements is discussed in the next two sections.

### Sun Certified System Administrator for Solaris 8

Sun, like many of the other product vendors who have turned to a certification program, has responded to the need in the industry for standardized credentials indicative of a certain level of expertise with the Solaris operating system. In the case of the Sun Certified System Administrator certification, it is meant to reflect a demonstrated level of knowledge and skills with the operating system in many areas—including printing, security, disk management, backup, and recovery.

The successful Sun Certified System Administrator for Solaris 8 candidate must pass two examinations. The two exams, 310-011 and 310-012, are referred to as Part I and Part II. Part I is, in essence, a prerequisite for Part II; you must pass the 310-011 exam before attempting the 310-012 exam. The Part I exam requires you to pass 66% of 57 questions (38 correct). You will be presented with multiple-choice, free-response, and drag-and-drop questions. You will have 90 minutes to complete the exam. The Part II exam requires you to have passed the Part I exam and then to pass 70% of 61 questions (43 correct). This exam also is based on multiple-choice, free-response, and drag- and drop-questions. It also allows you 90 minutes to complete the exam.

Sun has suggested that scenario questions might appear on the Solaris 8 exams. Scenario questions are simply multiple-choice questions with longer "stems" that present you with an information technology situation. You are typically asked what action you would take in that situation to resolve a problem or bring about a desired state. Scenario questions are used in an attempt to evaluate analysis and problem-solving skills rather than just recall factual information. The intent behind these questions is to measure more "real-world" ability to apply skills rather than simple "book" knowledge.

## Sun Certified Network Administrator for Solaris 8

With the Network Administrator certification, Sun has again responded to the need in the industry for a standardized credential. In this case, it is indicative of a more advanced level of expertise with the Solaris 8 operating system. This certification is meant to reflect a demonstrated superior level of expertise that encompasses the system administrator skills and the ability to implement more complex local area networks in a client-server environment, including TCP/IP and associated protocols.

To become certified as a Sun Certified Network Administrator for Solaris 8, you must first be certified as a Sun Certified System Administrator for the Solaris Operating Environment version 2.5, 2.6, 7, or 8. Then, you must pass the Sun Certified Network Administrator (310-043) exam. That exam requires you to pass 67% of 58 questions (39 correct). You are given 120 minutes to complete the exam. Question formats are similar to those for the System Administrator exams: multiple-choice, fill-in, drag-and-drop, and scenario questions.

## How to Schedule an Exam

To schedule an exam, call Prometric at 1-800-795-EXAM, or visit its web site at `www.2test.com`. Sun recommends that the price of the exam be $150, but the cost might vary by country. You can find out how you did on the exam by going to `http://www.galton.com/~sun/`. Test results are received there after four business days have elapsed. We are confident that after working through the material in this *Training Guide*, you will not have to retake an exam. However, if this need should arise, be aware that Sun policy requires that you wait a minimum of two weeks before taking the exam again.

APPENDIX **E**

# What's on the CD-ROM

This appendix is a brief rundown of what you will find on the CD-ROM that accompanies this book. For a more detailed description of the ExamGear test engine, see Appendix F, "Using the ExamGear, Training Guide Edition Software."

## ExamGear

ExamGear is a test engine developed exclusively for New Riders Publishing. It is, we believe, the best test engine available because it closely emulates the look and feel of the Prometric test engine and the Solaris 8 exams. The CD contains 181 questions that reflect the content of the exam objectives and the style of the questions on the actual exam. Each time you run ExamGear, it randomly selects a set of questions from the question database, so you never take the same exam twice.

In addition to providing a way to evaluate your knowledge of the exam material, ExamGear features several innovations that help you improve your mastery of the subject matter.

The practice tests enable you to check your score by exam area or category, for example, to determine which topics you need to study further. Other test preparation modes provide immediate feedback on your responses, and explanations of correct answers. Again, for a complete description of the benefits of ExamGear, see Appendix F.

## Exclusive Electronic Version of Text

The CD-ROM also contains the electronic version of this book in Portable Document Format (PDF). You can use this version to help search for terms you need to study or for other book elements. The electronic version comes complete with all figures as they appear in the book.

## Copyright Information and Disclaimer

APPENDIX F

# Using the ExamGear, Training Guide Edition Software

This *Training Guide* includes a special version of ExamGear—a revolutionary new test engine designed to give you the best in certification exam preparation. ExamGear offers sample and practice exams for many of today's most in-demand technical certifications. This special Training Guide Edition is included with this book as a tool to utilize in assessing your knowledge of the *Training Guide* material while also providing you with the experience of taking an electronic exam. The focus of the exam questions is on the material covered in the *Training Guide*.

This appendix describes in detail what ExamGear, Training Guide Edition is, how it works, and what it can do to help you prepare for the exam.

## EXAM SIMULATION

One of the main functions of ExamGear, Training Guide Edition is exam simulation. To prepare you to take the actual vendor certification exam, the Training Guide Edition of this test engine is designed to offer the most effective exam simulation available.

### Question Quality

The questions provided in the ExamGear, Training Guide Edition simulations are written to high standards of technical accuracy. The questions tap the content of the *Training Guide* chapters and help you assess and review your knowledge before you take the actual exam.

### Interface Design

The ExamGear, Training Guide Edition exam simulation interface provides you with the experience of taking an electronic exam. This enables you to effectively prepare for taking the actual exam by making the test experience a familiar one. Using this test simulation can help eliminate the sense of surprise or anxiety that you might experience in the testing center because you will already be acquainted with computerized testing.

## STUDY TOOLS

ExamGear provides you with several learning tools to help prepare you for the actual certification exam.

## Effective Learning Environment

The ExamGear, Training Guide Edition interface provides a learning environment that not only tests you through the computer, but also teaches the material you need to know to pass the certification exam. Each question comes with a detailed explanation of the correct answer and provides reasons why the other options were incorrect. This information helps to reinforce the knowledge you have already and also provides practical information you can use on the job.

## Automatic Progress Tracking

ExamGear, Training Guide Edition automatically tracks your progress as you work through the test questions. From the Item Review tab (discussed in detail later in this Appendix), you can see at a glance how well you are scoring by objective, by chapter, or on a question-by-question basis (see Figure F.1). You also can configure ExamGear to drill you on the skills you need to work on most.

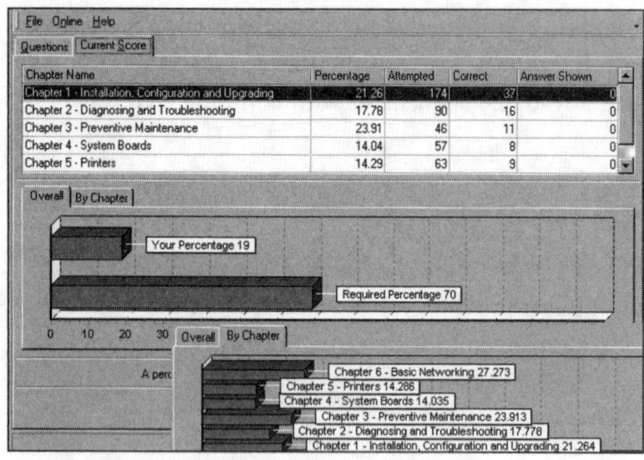


**FIGURE F.1**
Item review.

# How ExamGear, Training Guide Edition Works

ExamGear comprises two main elements: the interface and the database. The interface is the part of the program that you use to study and to run practice tests. The database stores all the question-and-answer data.

## Interface

The ExamGear, Training Guide Edition interface is designed to be easy to use, and provides the most effective study method available. The interface enables you to select from the following modes:

- **Study mode.** In this mode, you can select the number of questions you want to see and the time you want to allow for the test. You can select questions from all the chapters or from specific chapters. This enables you to reinforce your knowledge in a specific area or strengthen your knowledge in areas pertaining to a specific objective. During the exam, you can display the correct answer to each question along with an explanation of why it is correct.

- **Practice exam mode.** In this mode, you take an exam designed to simulate the actual certification exam. Questions are selected from all test-objective groups. The number of questions selected and the time allowed are set to match those parameters of the actual certification exam.

## Database

The ExamGear, Training Guide Edition database stores a group of approximately 180 test questions and answers. The questions are organized by chapters. You can purchase 600 additional questions at UnixEd.com.

# Installing and Registering ExamGear, Training Guide Edition

This section provides instructions for ExamGear, Training Guide Edition installation, and describes the process and benefits of registering your Training Guide Edition product.

## Requirements

ExamGear requires a computer with the following:

- Microsoft Windows 95, Windows 98, Windows NT 4.0, Windows 2000, or Windows ME.

  A Pentium or later processor is recommended.

- 20–30MB free disk space.

- A minimum of 32MB of RAM.

  As with any Windows application, the more memory, the better your performance.

- A connection to the Internet.

  An Internet connection is not required for the software to work, but it is required for online registration and for downloading product updates.

- A web browser.

  A web browser is not required for the software to work, but it is invoked from the Online, web sites menu option.

## Installing ExamGear, Training Guide Edition

Install ExamGear, Training Guide Edition by running the setup program on the ExamGear, Training Guide Edition CD. Follow these instructions to install the Training Guide Edition on your computer:

1. Insert the CD into your CD-ROM drive. The AutoRun feature of Windows launches the software. If you have AutoRun disabled, click Start and choose Run. Go to the root directory of the CD and choose START.EXE. Click Open and then click OK.

2. Click the button in the circle. A Welcome screen appears. From here, you can install ExamGear. Click the ExamGear button to begin installation.

3. The Installation Wizard appears onscreen and prompts you with instructions to complete the installation. Select a directory on which to install ExamGear, Training Guide Edition.

4. The Installation Wizard copies the ExamGear, Training Guide Edition files to your hard drive, adds ExamGear, Training Guide Edition to your

Program menu, adds values to your Registry, and installs the test engine's DLLs to the appropriate system folders. To ensure that the process was successful, the setup program finishes by running ExamGear, Training Guide Edition.

5. The Installation Wizard logs the installation process, and stores this information in a file named INSTALL.LOG. This log file is used by the uninstall process in the event that you choose to remove ExamGear, Training Guide Edition from your computer. Because the ExamGear installation adds Registry keys and DLL files to your computer, it is important to uninstall the program appropriately (see the section "Removing ExamGear, Training Guide Edition from Your Computer").

## Registering ExamGear, Training Guide Edition

The Product Registration Wizard appears when you start ExamGear, Training Guide Edition for the first time. ExamGear checks at startup to see whether you are registered. If you are not registered, the main menu is hidden, and a Product Registration Wizard appears. Remember that your computer must have an Internet connection to complete the Product Registration Wizard.

The first page of the Product Registration Wizard details the benefits of registration; however, you can always elect not to register. The Show This Message at Startup Until I Register option enables you to decide whether the registration screen should appear every time ExamGear, Training Guide Edition is started. If you click the Cancel button, you return to the main menu. You can register at any time by selecting Online, Registration from the main menu.

The registration process is composed of a simple form for entering your personal information, including your name and address. You are asked for your level of experience with the product on which you are testing. In addition, you are asked whether you purchased ExamGear, Training Guide Edition from a retail store or over the Internet. The information will be used by our software designers and marketing department to provide us with feedback about the usability and usefulness of this product. It takes only a few seconds to fill out and transmit the registration data. A confirmation dialog box appears when registration is complete.

After you have registered and transmitted this information to New Riders, the registration option is removed from the pull-down menus.

### Registration Benefits

Registering enables New Riders to notify you of product updates and new releases.

## Removing ExamGear, Training Guide Edition from Your Computer

In the event that you elect to remove the ExamGear, Training Guide Edition product from your computer, you can use ExamGear's uninstall process to ensure that the software is removed from your system safely and completely. Follow these instructions to remove ExamGear from your computer:

1. Click Start, Settings, Control Panel.
2. Double-click the Add/Remove Programs icon.
3. You are presented with a list of software that is installed on your computer. Select ExamGear, Training Guide Edition from the list, and click

the Add/Remove button. The ExamGear, Training Guide Edition software is then removed from your computer.

It is important that the INSTALL.LOG file be present in the directory where you have installed ExamGear, Training Guide Edition should you ever choose to uninstall the product. Do not delete this file. The uninstall process uses the INSTALL.LOG file to safely remove the files and Registry settings that were added to your computer by the installation process.

# USING EXAMGEAR, TRAINING GUIDE EDITION

ExamGear is designed to be user-friendly and intuitive, eliminating the need for you to learn a confusing piece of software just to practice answering questions. Because the software has a smooth learning curve, your time is maximized because you start practicing almost immediately.

## General Description of How the Software Works

ExamGear has two modes of operation: study mode and practice exam mode. (See Figure F.2). Both sections have the same easy-to-use interface. Using study mode, you can hone your knowledge as well as your test-taking abilities through the use of the Show Answers option. While you are taking the test, you can expose the answers along with a brief description of why the given answers are right or wrong. This gives you the ability to better understand the material presented.

The practice exam section has many of the same options as study mode, but you cannot reveal the answers. This way, you have a more traditional testing environment with which to practice.

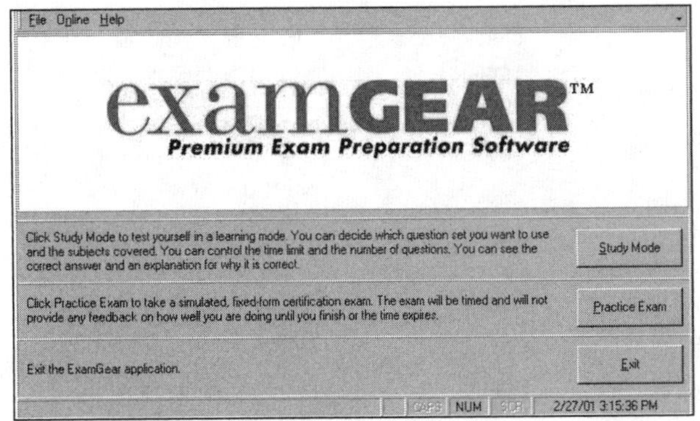


**FIGURE F.2**
The opening screen offers three testing modes.

## Menu Options

The ExamGear, Training Guide Edition interface has an easy-to-use menu that provides the following options:

| *Menu* | *Command* | *Description* |
|---|---|---|
| File | `Print` | Prints the current screen. |
| | `Print Setup` | Enables you to select the printer. |
| | `Exit ExamGear` | Exits the program. |
| Online | `Registration` | Starts the Registration Wizard, and enables you to register online. This menu option is removed after you have successfully registered the product. |
| | `Check for Product Updates` | Opens the ExamGear web site with available updates. |
| | `web sites` | Opens the web browser with either the New Riders Publishing or ExamGear home pages. |
| Help | `Contents` | Opens ExamGear, Training Guide Edition's Help file. |
| | `About` | Displays information about ExamGear, Training Guide Edition, including serial number, registered owner, and so on. |

### File

The File menu enables you to exit the program and configure print options.

### Online

In the Online menu, you can register ExamGear, Training Guide Edition, check for product updates (update the ExamGear executable as well as check for free, updated question sets), and surf applicable web sites. The Online menu is always available, except when you are taking a test.

#### Registration

Registration is free, and enables you to access updates. Registration is the first task that ExamGear, Training Guide Edition asks you to perform. You will not have access to the free product updates if you do not register.

#### Check for Product Updates

This option takes you to the ExamGear, Training Guide Edition's web site, where you can update the software. You must be connected to the Internet to use this option. The ExamGear web site lists the options that have been made available since your version of ExamGear was installed on your computer.

#### web sites

This option provides a convenient way to start your web browser, and connect to either the New Riders or ExamGear home page.

### Help

As it suggests, this menu option gives you access to ExamGear's Help system. It also provides important information, such as your serial number, software version, and so on.

## Starting a Study-Mode Session

Study mode enables you to control the test in ways that actual certification exams do not allow:

- You can set your own time limits.
- You can concentrate on selected skill areas (chapters).
- You can reveal answers or have each response graded immediately with feedback.
- You can restrict the questions you see again to those missed or those answered correctly a given number of times.

- You can control the order in which questions are presented—random order or in order by skill area (chapter).

To begin testing in study mode, click the Study Mode button from the main Interface screen. You are presented with the Study Mode configuration page (see Figure F.3).

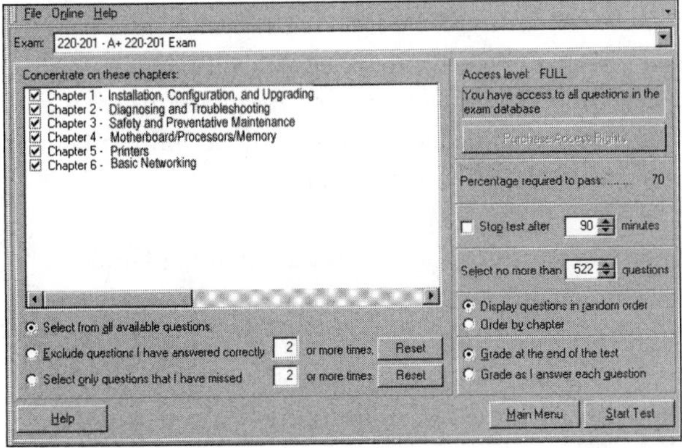


**FIGURE F.3**
The Study Mode configuration page.

At the top of the Study Mode configuration screen, you see the Exam drop-down list. This list shows the activated exam that you have purchased with your ExamGear, Training Guide Edition product, as well as any other exams you might have downloaded or any Preview exams that were shipped with your version of ExamGear. Select the exam with which you want to practice from the drop-down list.

Below the Exam drop-down list, you see the questions that are available for the selected exam. Each exam has at least one question set. You can select the individual question set or any combination of the question sets if more than one is available for the selected exam.

Below the question set list is a list of skill areas or chapters on which you can concentrate. These skill areas or chapters reflect the units of exam objectives defined by Sun for the exam. Within each skill area, you will find several exam objectives. You can select a single skill area or chapter on which to focus, or you can select any combination of the available skill areas/chapters to customize the exam to your individual needs.

In addition to specifying which question sets and skill areas on which you want to test yourself, you also can define which questions are included in the test based on your previous progress working with the test. ExamGear, Training Guide Edition automatically tracks your progress with the available questions. When configuring the study-mode options, you can opt to view all the questions available within the question sets and skill areas you have selected, or you can limit the questions presented. Choose from the following options:

- Select from All Available Questions. This option causes ExamGear, Training Guide Edition to present all available questions from the selected question sets and skill areas.
- Exclude Questions I Have Answered Correctly *X* or More Times. ExamGear offers you the option to exclude questions that you have previously answered correctly. You can specify how many times you want to answer a question correctly before ExamGear considers you to have mastered it (the default is two times).
- Select Only Questions That I Have Missed *X* or More Times. This option configures ExamGear, Training Guide Edition to drill you only on questions that you have missed repeatedly. You can specify how many times you must miss a question before ExamGear determines that you have not mastered it (the default is two times).

At any time, you can reset ExamGear, Training Guide Edition's tracking information by clicking the Reset button for the feature you want to clear.

At the top-right side of the Study Mode configuration sheet, you can see your access level to the question sets for the selected exam. Access levels are either Full or Preview. For a detailed explanation of each of these access levels, see the section "Obtaining Updates" in this Appendix.

Under your access level, you see the score required to pass the selected exam. Below the required score, you can select whether the test will be timed and how much time will be allowed to complete the exam. Select the Stop Test After 90 Minutes check box to set a time limit for the exam. Enter the number of minutes you want to allow for the test. (The default is 90 minutes.) Deselecting this check box enables you to take an exam with no time limit.

You also can configure the number of questions included in the exam. The default number of questions changes with the specific exam you have selected. Enter the number of questions you want to include in the exam in the Select No More Than *X* Questions option.

You can configure the order in which ExamGear, Training Guide Edition presents the exam questions. Select from the following options:

- **Display Questions in Random Order.** This option is the default option. When selected, it causes ExamGear, Training Guide Edition to present the questions in random order throughout the exam.
- **Order by Skill Area.** This option causes ExamGear to group the questions presented in the exam by skill area. All questions for each selected skill area are presented in succession. The test progresses from one selected skill area to the next, until all the questions from each selected skill area have been presented.

ExamGear offers two options for scoring your exams. Select one of the following options:

- **Grade at the End of the Test.** This option configures ExamGear, Training Guide Edition to score your test after you have been presented with all the selected exam questions. You can reveal correct answers to a question, but if you do, that question is not scored.
- **Grade as I Answer Each Question.** This option configures ExamGear to grade each question as you answer it, providing you with instant feedback as you take the test. All questions are scored unless you click the Show Answer button before completing the question.

You can return to the ExamGear, Training Guide Edition main startup screen from the Study Mode configuration screen by clicking the Main Menu button. If you need assistance configuring the study-mode exam options, click the Help button for configuration instructions.

After you have finished configuring all the exam options, click the Start Test button to begin the exam.

## Starting the Practice Exam

This section describes the practice exam, defines the exam options and the study-mode option, and provides instructions for starting it.

### Differences Between the Practice Exam and Study Mode

Question screens in the practice exam is identical to those found in study mode, except that the Show Answer, Grade Answer, and Item Review buttons are not available while you are in the process of taking a practice exam. The practice exam provides you with a report screen at the end of the exam.

When taking a practice exam, the Item Review screen is not available until you have answered all the questions. This is consistent with the behavior of most vendors' current certification exams. In study mode, Item Review is available at any time.

When the exam timer expires, or when you click the End Exam button, the Examination Score Report screen appears.

## Starting an Exam

From the ExamGear, Training Guide Edition menu screen, click the Practice Exam button to begin the exam.

# Question Types and How to Answer Them

Because certification exams from different vendors vary, you will face many types of questions on any given exam. ExamGear, Training Guide Edition presents you with different question types to enable you to become familiar with the various ways an actual exam will test your knowledge. This section describes each of the question types presented by ExamGear and provides instructions for answering each type.

## Multiple Choice

Most of the questions you see on a certification exam are multiple choice (see Figure F.4). This question type asks you to select an answer from the list provided. Sometimes you must select only one answer, often indicated by answers preceded by option buttons (round selection buttons). At other times, multiple correct answers are possible, indicated by check boxes preceding the possible answer combinations.

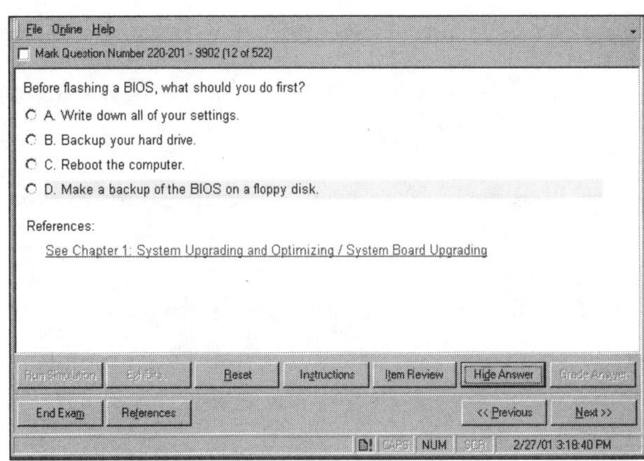


**FIGURE F.4**
A typical multiple-choice question.

You can use three methods to select an answer:

- Click the option button or check box next to the answer. If more than one correct answer to a question is possible, the answers will have check boxes next to them. If only one correct answer to a question is possible, each answer will have an option button next to it. ExamGear, Training Guide Edition prompts you with the number of answers you must select.
- Click the text of the answer.
- Press the alphabetic key that corresponds to the answer.

You can use any one of three methods to clear an option button:

- Click another option button.
- Click the text of another answer.
- Press the alphabetic key that corresponds to another answer.

You can use any one of three methods to clear a check box:

- Click the check box next to the selected answer.
- Click the text of the selected answer.
- Press the alphabetic key that corresponds to the selected answer.

To clear all answers, click the Reset button.

Remember that some of the questions have multiple answers that are correct. Do not let this throw you off. The multiple-correct questions do not have one answer that is more correct than another. In the single-correct format, only one answer is correct. ExamGear, Training Guide Edition prompts you with the number of answers you must select.

## Standard ExamGear, Training Guide Edition Options

Regardless of question type, a consistent set of clickable buttons enables you to navigate and interact with questions. The following list describes the function of each of the buttons you might see. Depending on the question type, some of the buttons will be grayed-out and will be inaccessible. Buttons that are appropriate to the question type are active.

- **Run Simulation.** This button is enabled if the question supports a simulation. (It is disabled for this book.) Clicking this button begins the simulation process.
- **Exhibits.** This button is enabled if exhibits are provided to support the question. An exhibit is an image, video, sound, or text file that provides supplemental information needed to answer the question. If a question has more than one exhibit, a dialog box appears, listing exhibits by name. If only one exhibit exists, the file is opened immediately when you click the Exhibits button.
- **Reset.** This button clears any selections you have made and returns the question window to the state in which it appeared when it was first displayed.
- **Instructions.** This button displays instructions for interacting with the current question type.
- **Item Review.** This button leaves the question window and opens the Item Review screen. For a detailed explanation of the Item Review screen, see the "Item Review" section later in this Appendix.
- **Show Answer.** This option displays the correct answer with an explanation of why it is correct. If you choose this option, the current question will not be scored.
- **Grade Answer.** If Grade at the End of the Test is selected as a configuration option, this button is disabled. It is enabled when Grade as I Answer Each Question is selected as a configuration option. Clicking this button grades the current question immediately. An explanation of the correct answer is provided, just as if the Show Answer button were pressed. The question is graded, however.
- **End Exam.** This button ends the exam and displays the Examination Score Report screen.
- **Previous.** This button displays the previous question on the exam.
- **Next.** This button displays the next question on the exam.
- **Previous Marked.** This button displays if you have opted to review questions that you have marked using the Item Review screen. This button displays the previous marked question. Marking questions is discussed in more detail later in this Appendix.

- **Previous Incomplete.** This button displays if you have opted to review questions that you have not answered using the Item Review screen. This button displays the previous unanswered question.
- **Next Marked.** This button displays if you have opted to review questions that you have marked using the Item Review screen. This button displays the next marked question. Marking questions is discussed in more detail later in this Appendix.
- **Next Incomplete.** This button displays if you have opted to review questions, using the Item Review screen, that you have not answered. This button displays the next unanswered question.

## Mark Question and Time Remaining

ExamGear provides you with two methods to aid in dealing with the time limit of the testing process. If you find that you need to skip a question or if you want to check the time remaining to complete the test, use one of the options discussed in the following sections.

### Mark Question

Check this box to mark a question so that you can return to it later using the Item Review feature. The adaptive exam does not allow questions to be marked because it does not support item review.

### Time Remaining

If the test is timed, the Time Remaining indicator is enabled. It counts down minutes remaining to complete the test. The adaptive exam does not offer this feature because it is not timed.

## Item Review

The Item Review screen enables you to jump to any question. ExamGear, Training Guide Edition considers an incomplete question to be any unanswered question or any multiple-choice question for which the total number of required responses has not been selected. If the question prompts for three answers and you selected only A and C, for example, ExamGear considers the question to be incomplete.

The Item Review screen enables you to review the exam questions in different ways. You can enter one of two browse sequences (series of similar records): Browse Marked Questions or Browse Incomplete Questions. You also can create a custom grouping of the exam questions for review based on a number of criteria.

When using Item Review, if Show Answer was selected for a question while you were taking the exam, the question is grayed out in item review. The question can be answered again if you use the Reset button to reset the question status.

The Item Review screen contains two tabs. The Questions tab lists questions and question information in columns. The Current Score tab provides your exam score information, presented as a percentage for each chapter and as a bar graph for your overall score.

## The Item Review Questions Tab

The Questions tab on the Item Review screen (see Figure F.5) presents the exam questions and question information in a table. You can select any row you want by clicking in the grid. The Go To button is enabled whenever a row is selected. Clicking the Go To button displays the question on the selected row. You also can display a question by double-clicking that row.

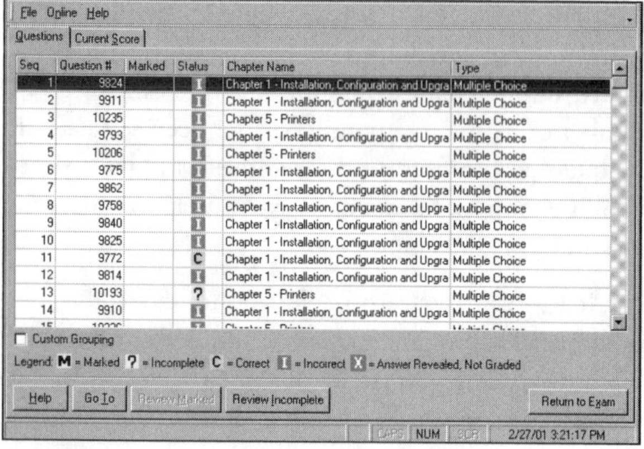


**FIGURE F.5**
The Questions tab on the Item Review screen.

### Columns

The Questions tab contains the following six columns of information:

- **Seq.** Indicates the sequence number of the question as it was displayed in the exam.
- **Question Number.** Displays the question's identification number for easy reference.
- **Marked.** Indicates a question that you have marked using the Mark Question check box.
- **Status.** The status can be M for Marked, ? for Incomplete, C for Correct, I for Incorrect, or X for Answer Shown.
- **Chapter Name.** The chapter associated with each question.
- **Type.** The question type, which can be Multiple Choice or Hot Spot.

To resize a column, place the mouse pointer over the vertical line between column headings. When the mouse pointer changes to a set of right and left arrows, you can drag the column border to the left or right to make the column more or less wide. Just click with the left mouse button, and hold that button down while you move the column border in the desired direction.

The Item Review screen enables you to sort the questions on any of the column headings. Initially, the list of questions is sorted in descending order on the sequence number column. To sort on a different column heading, click that heading. You will see an arrow appear on the column heading indicating the direction of the sort (ascending or descending). To change the direction of the sort, click the column heading again.

The Item Review screen also enables you to create a custom grouping. This feature enables you to sort the questions based on any combination of criteria you prefer. For instance, you might want to review the question items sorted first by whether they were marked, then by the chapter name, and then by sequence number. The Custom Grouping feature enables you to do this. Start by checking the Custom Grouping check box (see Figure F.6). When you do so, the entire questions table shifts down a bit onscreen, and a message appears at the top of the table that reads `Drag a Column Header Here to Group by That Column`.

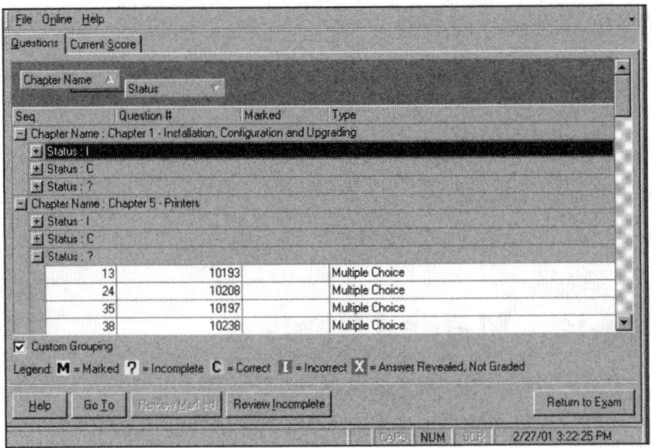

**FIGURE F.6**
The Custom Grouping check box enables you to create your own question sort order.

Just click the column heading you want with the left mouse button, hold that button down, and move the mouse into the area directly above the Questions table (the custom grouping area). Release the left mouse button to drop the column heading into the custom grouping area. To accomplish the custom grouping previously described, first check the Custom Grouping check box. Then drag the Marked column heading into the custom grouping area above the Questions table. Next, drag the Chapter Name column heading into the custom grouping area. You will see the two column headings joined together by a line that indicates the order of the custom grouping. Finally, drag the Seq column heading into the custom grouping area. This heading will be joined to the Chapter Name heading by another line indicating the direction of the custom grouping.

Notice that each column heading in the custom grouping area has an arrow indicating the direction in which items are sorted under that column heading. You can reverse the direction of the sort on an individual column-heading basis using these arrows. Click the column heading in the custom grouping area to change the direction of the sort for that column heading only. For example, using the custom grouping created previously, you can display the question list sorted first in descending order by whether the question was marked, in descending order by chapter name, and then in ascending order by sequence number.

The custom grouping feature of the Item Review screen gives you enormous flexibility in how you choose to review the exam questions. To remove a custom grouping and return the Item Review display to its default setting (sorted in descending order by sequence number), just uncheck the Custom Grouping check box.

## The Current Score Tab

The Current Score tab of the Item Review screen (see Figure F7) provides a real-time snapshot of your score. The top half of the screen is an expandable grid. When the grid is collapsed, scores are displayed for each chapter. Chapters can be expanded to show percentage scores for objectives and subobjectives. Information about your exam progress is presented in the following columns:

- **Chapter Name.** This column shows the chapter name for each objective group.
- **Percentage.** This column shows the percentage of questions for each objective group that you answered correctly.
- **Attempted.** This column lists the number of questions you answered either completely or partially for each objective group.
- **Correct.** This column lists the actual number of questions you answered correctly for each objective group.

- **Answer Shown.** This column lists the number of questions for each objective group for which you chose to display the answer using the Show Answer button.

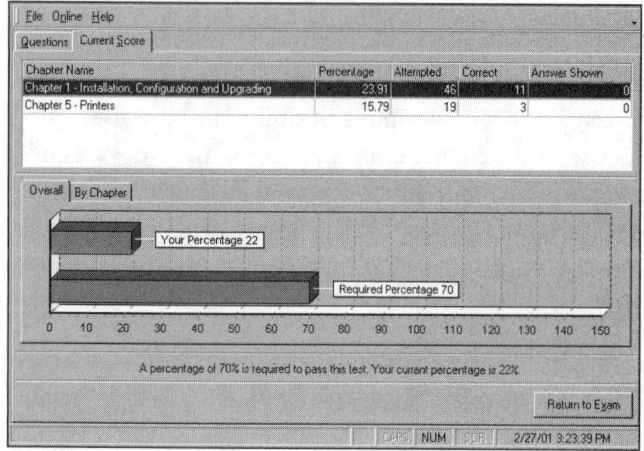


**FIGURE F.7**
The Current Score tab on the item review screen.

The columns in the scoring table are resized and sorted in the same way as those in the questions table on the Item Review Questions tab. Refer to the earlier section "The Item Review Questions Tab" for more details.

A graphical overview of the score is presented below the grid. The graph depicts two red bars: The top bar represents your current exam score; the bottom bar represents the required passing score. To the right of the bars in the graph is a legend that lists the required score and your score. Below the bar graph is a statement that describes the required passing score and your current score.

In addition, the information can be presented on an overall basis or by exam chapter. The Overall tab shows the overall score. The By Chapter tab shows the score by chapter.

Clicking the End Exam button terminates the exam and passes control to the Examination Score Report screen.

The Return to Exam button returns to the exam at the question from which the Item Review button was clicked.

## Review Marked Items

The Item Review screen enables you to enter a browse sequence for marked questions. When you click the Review Marked button, questions that you have previously marked using the Mark Question check box are presented for your review. While browsing the marked questions, you will see the following changes to the buttons available:

- The caption of the Next button becomes Next Marked.
- The caption of the Previous button becomes Previous Marked.

## Review Incomplete

The Item Review screen enables you to enter a browse sequence for incomplete questions. When you click the Review Incomplete button, the questions you did not answer or did not completely answer display for your review. While browsing the incomplete questions, you will see the following changes to the buttons:

- The caption of the Next button becomes Next Incomplete.
- The caption of the Previous button becomes Previous Incomplete.

## Examination Score Report Screen

The Examination Score Report screen (see Figure F.8) appears when the study mode, practice exam, or adaptive exam ends—as the result of timer expiration, completion of all questions, or your decision to terminate early.

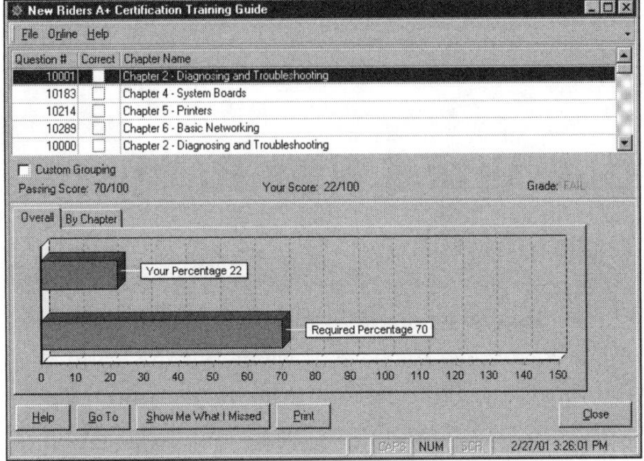


**FIGURE F.8**
The Examination Score Report screen.

This screen provides you with a graphical display of your test score, along with a tabular breakdown of scores by chapter. The graphical display at the top of the screen compares your overall score with the score required to pass the exam. Buttons below the graphical display allow you to open the Show Me What I Missed browse sequence, print the screen, or return to the main menu.

### Show Me What I Missed Browse Sequence

The Show Me What I Missed browse sequence is invoked by clicking the Show Me What I Missed button from the Examination Score Report or from the configuration screen of an adaptive exam.

Note that the window caption is modified to indicate that you are in the Show Me What I Missed browse sequence mode. Question IDs and position within the browse sequence appear at the top of the screen, in place of the Mark Question and Time Remaining indicators. Main window contents vary, depending on the question type. The following list describes the buttons available within the Show Me What I Missed browse sequence and the functions they perform:

- **Return to Score Report.** Returns control to the Examination Score Report screen. In the case of an adaptive exam, this button's caption is Exit, and control returns to the adaptive exam configuration screen.
- **Run Simulation.** Opens a simulation in Grade mode, causing the simulation to open displaying your response and the correct answer. If the current question does not offer a simulation, this button is disabled.
- **Exhibits.** Opens the Exhibits window. This button is enabled if one or more exhibits are available for the question.
- **Instructions.** Shows how to answer the current question type.
- **Print.** Prints the current screen.
- **Previous or Next.** Displays missed questions.

## CHECKING THE WEB SITE

To check the New Riders home page or the ExamGear, Training Guide Edition home page for updates or other product information, choose the desired web site from the web sites option of the Online menu. You must be connected to the Internet to reach these web sites.

### Frequently Asked Questions

ExamGear FAQ can be found at `http://www.newriders.com/examgear/support/faq.cfm`.

## Obtaining Updates

The procedures for obtaining updates are outlined in this section.

### The Catalog web site for Updates

Selecting the Check for Product Updates option from the Online menu shows you the full range of products you can either download free or purchase from your web browser. You must be connected to the Internet to reach these web sites.

### Types of Updates

Several types of updates might be available for download, including various free updates and additional items available for purchase.

#### Free Program Updates

Free program updates include changes to the ExamGear, Training Guide Edition executables and runtime libraries (DLLs). When any of these items are downloaded, ExamGear automatically installs the upgrades. ExamGear, Training Guide Edition will be reopened after the installation is complete.

#### Free Database Updates

Free database updates include updates to the exam or exams that you have registered. Exam updates are contained in compressed, encrypted files and include exam databases and exhibits. ExamGear, Training Guide Edition automatically decompresses these files to their proper location and updates the ExamGear software to record version changes and import new question sets. You can purchase an additional database of questions from UnixEd.com.

## Contacting New Riders Publishing

At New Riders, we strive to meet and exceed the needs of our customers. We have developed ExamGear, Training Guide Edition to surpass the demands and expectations of network professionals seeking technical certifications, and we think it shows. What do you think?

If you need to contact New Riders regarding any aspect of the ExamGear, Training Guide Edition product line, feel free to do so. We look forward to hearing from you. Contact us at the following address or phone number:

New Riders Publishing<br>
201 West 103 Street<br>
Indianapolis, IN 46290<br>
800-545-5914

You can also reach us on the web:

`http://www.newriders.com`

## Technical Support

Technical support is available at the following phone number during the hours specified:

Telephone: 317-581-3833, Monday through Friday, 10 a.m–3 p.m. Central Standard Time.

You can also reach us by email at examgear@newriders.com.

Finally, you can visit the online support web site at www.newriders.com/support and submit a support request over the Internet.

## Customer Service

If you have a damaged product and need a replacement or refund, please call the following phone number:

800-858-7674

## Product Updates

You can obtain product updates by choosing ExamGear, Training Guide Edition's Online pull-down menu and selecting Check for Product Updates. You will be taken to a web site with full details.

## Product Suggestions and Comments

We value your input! Please email your suggestions and comments to the following address:

nrfeedback@newriders.com

# LICENSE AGREEMENT

YOU SHOULD CAREFULLY READ THE FOLLOWING TERMS AND CONDITIONS BEFORE BREAKING THE SEAL ON THE PACKAGE. AMONG OTHER THINGS, THIS AGREEMENT LICENSES THE ENCLOSED SOFTWARE TO YOU AND CONTAINS WARRANTY AND LIABILITY DISCLAIMERS. BY BREAKING THE SEAL ON THE PACKAGE, YOU ARE ACCEPTING AND AGREEING TO THE TERMS AND CONDITIONS OF THIS AGREEMENT. IF YOU DO NOT AGREE TO THE TERMS OF THIS AGREEMENT, DO NOT BREAK THE SEAL. YOU SHOULD PROMPTLY RETURN THE PACKAGE UNOPENED.

# LICENSE

Subject to the provisions contained herein, New Riders Publishing (NRP) hereby grants to you a nonexclusive, nontransferable license to use the object-code version of the computer software product (Software) contained in the package on a single computer of the type identified on the package.

# SOFTWARE AND DOCUMENTATION

NRP shall furnish the Software to you on media in machine-readable object-code form and may also provide the standard documentation (Documentation) containing instructions for operation and use of the Software.

## LICENSE TERM AND CHARGES

The term of this license commences upon delivery of the Software to you and is perpetual unless earlier terminated upon default or as otherwise set forth herein.

## TITLE

Title, ownership right, and intellectual property rights in and to the Software and Documentation shall remain in NRP and/or in suppliers to NRP of programs contained in the Software. The Software is provided for your own internal use under this license. This license does not include the right to sublicense and is personal to you and therefore may not be assigned (by operation of law or otherwise) or transferred without the prior written consent of NRP. You acknowledge that the Software in source code form remains a confidential trade secret of NRP and/or its suppliers and therefore you agree not to attempt to decipher or decompile, modify, disassemble, reverse engineer, or prepare derivative works of the Software or develop source code for the Software or knowingly allow others to do so. Further, you may not copy the Documentation or other written materials accompanying the Software.

## UPDATES

This license does not grant you any right, license, or interest in and to any improvements, modifications, enhancements, or updates to the Software and Documentation. Updates, if available, may be obtained by you at NRP's then-current standard pricing, terms, and conditions.

## LIMITED WARRANTY AND DISCLAIMER

NRP warrants that the media containing the Software, if provided by NRP, is free from defects in material and workmanship under normal use for a period of sixty (60) days from the date you purchased a license to it.

THIS IS A LIMITED WARRANTY AND IT IS THE ONLY WARRANTY MADE BY NRP. THE SOFTWARE IS PROVIDED "AS IS" AND NRP SPECIFICALLY DISCLAIMS ALL WARRANTIES OF ANY KIND, EITHER EXPRESS OR IMPLIED, INCLUDING, BUT NOT LIMITED TO, THE IMPLIED WARRANTY OF MERCHANTABILITY AND FITNESS FOR A PARTICULAR PURPOSE. FURTHER, COMPANY DOES NOT WARRANT, GUARANTEE, OR MAKE ANY REPRESENTATIONS REGARDING THE USE, OR THE RESULTS OF THE USE, OF THE SOFTWARE IN TERMS OR CORRECTNESS, ACCURACY, RELIABILITY, CURRENTNESS, OR OTHERWISE AND DOES NOT WARRANT THAT THE OPERATION OF ANY SOFTWARE WILL BE UNINTERRUPTED OR ERROR FREE. NRP EXPRESSLY DISCLAIMS ANY WARRANTIES NOT STATED HEREIN. NO ORAL OR WRITTEN INFORMATION OR ADVICE GIVEN BY NRP, OR ANY NRP DEALER, AGENT, EMPLOYEE, OR OTHERS SHALL CREATE, MODIFY, OR EXTEND A WARRANTY OR IN ANY WAY INCREASE THE SCOPE OF THE FOREGOING WARRANTY, AND NEITHER SUBLICENSEE OR PURCHASER MAY RELY ON ANY SUCH INFORMATION OR ADVICE. If the media is subjected to accident, abuse, or improper use, or if you violate the terms of this Agreement, then this warranty shall immediately be terminated. This warranty shall not apply if the

Software is used on or in conjunction with hardware or programs other than the unmodified version of hardware and programs with which the Software was designed to be used as described in the Documentation.

## LIMITATION OF LIABILITY

Your sole and exclusive remedies for any damage or loss in any way connected with the Software are set forth below.

UNDER NO CIRCUMSTANCES AND UNDER NO LEGAL THEORY, TORT, CONTRACT, OR OTHERWISE, SHALL NRP BE LIABLE TO YOU OR ANY OTHER PERSON FOR ANY INDIRECT, SPECIAL, INCIDENTAL, OR CONSEQUENTIAL DAMAGES OF ANY CHARACTER INCLUDING, WITHOUT LIMITATION, DAMAGES FOR LOSS OF GOODWILL, LOSS OF PROFIT, WORK STOPPAGE, COMPUTER FAILURE OR MALFUNCTION, OR ANY AND ALL OTHER COMMERCIAL DAMAGES OR LOSSES, OR FOR ANY OTHER DAMAGES EVEN IF NRP SHALL HAVE BEEN INFORMED OF THE POSSIBILITY OF SUCH DAMAGES, OR FOR ANY CLAIM BY ANOTHER PARTY. NRP'S THIRD-PARTY PROGRAM SUPPLIERS MAKE NO WARRANTY, AND HAVE NO LIABILITY WHATSOEVER, TO YOU. NRP's sole and exclusive obligation and liability and your exclusive remedy shall be: upon NRP's election, (i) the replacement of our defective media; or (ii) the repair or correction of your defective media if NRP is able, so that it will conform to the above warranty; or (iii) if NRP is unable to replace or repair, you may terminate this license by returning the Software. Only if you inform NRP of your problem during the applicable warranty period will NRP be obligated to honor this warranty. SOME STATES OR JURISDICTIONS DO NOT ALLOW THE EXCLUSION OF IMPLIED WARRANTIES OR LIMITATION OR EXCLUSION OF CONSEQUENTIAL DAMAGES, SO THE ABOVE LIMITATIONS OR EXCLUSIONS MAY NOT APPLY TO YOU. THIS WARRANTY GIVES YOU SPECIFIC LEGAL RIGHTS AND YOU MAY ALSO HAVE OTHER RIGHTS WHICH VARY BY STATE OR JURISDICTION.

## MISCELLANEOUS

If any provision of the Agreement is held to be ineffective, unenforceable, or illegal under certain circumstances for any reason, such decision shall not affect the validity or enforceability (i) of such provision under other circumstances or (ii) of the remaining provisions hereof under all circumstances, and such provision shall be reformed to and only to the extent necessary to make it effective, enforceable, and legal under such circumstances. All headings are solely for convenience and shall not be considered in interpreting this Agreement. This Agreement shall be governed by and construed under New York law as such law applies to agreements between New York residents entered into and to be performed entirely within New York, except as required by U.S. Government rules and regulations to be governed by Federal law.

YOU ACKNOWLEDGE THAT YOU HAVE READ THIS AGREEMENT, UNDERSTAND IT, AND AGREE TO BE BOUND BY ITS TERMS AND CONDITIONS. YOU FURTHER AGREE THAT IT IS THE COMPLETE AND EXCLUSIVE STATEMENT OF THE AGREEMENT BETWEEN US THAT SUPERSEDES ANY PROPOSAL OR PRIOR AGREEMENT, ORAL OR WRITTEN, AND ANY OTHER COMMUNICATIONS BETWEEN US RELATING TO THE SUBJECT MATTER OF THIS AGREEMENT.

## U.S. Government Restricted Rights

# Index

## Symbols



## A

# B

# C

## D

# E

# F

## G



## H



## I

# J

## K



## L

# M

# N

# O

# Q

# R

# T

## U

## X-Y-Z

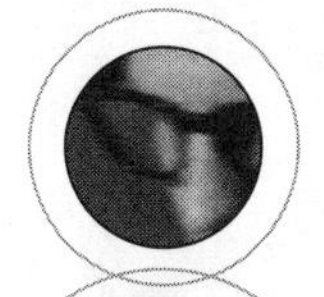

# HOW TO CONTACT US

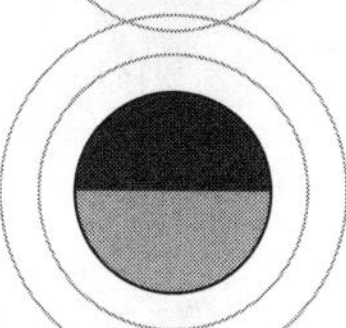

## VISIT OUR WEB SITE

WWW.NEWRIDERS.COM

On our web site, you'll find information about our other books, authors, tables of contents, and book errata. You will also find information about book registration and how to purchase our books, both domestically and internationally.

## EMAIL US

Contact us at: **nrfeedback@newriders.com**

- If you have comments or questions about this book
- To report errors that you have found in this book
- If you have a book proposal to submit or are interested in writing for New Riders
- If you are an expert in a computer topic or technology and are interested in being a technical editor who reviews manuscripts for technical accuracy

Contact us at: **nreducation@newriders.com**

- If you are an instructor from an educational institution who wants to preview New Riders books for classroom use. Email should include your name, title, school, department, address, phone number, office days/hours, text in use, and enrollment, along with your request for desk/examination copies and/or additional information.

Contact us at: **nrmedia@newriders.com**

- If you are a member of the media who is interested in reviewing copies of New Riders books. Send your name, mailing address, and email address, along with the name of the publication or web site you work for.

## BULK PURCHASES/CORPORATE SALES

If you are interested in buying 10 or more copies of a title or want to set up an account for your company to purchase directly from the publisher at a substantial discount, contact us at 800-382-3419 or email your contact information to `corpsales@pearsontechgroup.com`. A sales representative will contact you with more information.

## WRITE TO US

New Riders Publishing
201 W. 103rd St.
Indianapolis, IN 46290-1097

## CALL/FAX US

Toll-free (800) 571-5840
If outside U.S. (317) 581-3500
Ask for New Riders
FAX: (317) 581-4663

VOICES THAT MATTER

WWW.NEWRIDERS.COM